Rethinking
the
Western
Tradition

*The volumes in this series
seek to address the present debate
over the Western tradition
by reprinting key works of
that tradition along with essays
that evaluate each text from
different perspectives.*

Selected Writings

JEREMY BENTHAM

Edited and with an Introduction by
Stephen G. Engelmann
with essays by
Philip Schofield
David Lieberman
Jennifer Pitts
Mark Canuel

Yale
UNIVERSITY
PRESS

New Haven and London

Published with assistance from the foundation established in memory of
Philip Hamilton McMillan of the Class of 1894, Yale College.

Yale University Press books may be purchased in quantity for educational,
business, or promotional use. For information, please e-mail sales.press@yale.edu
(U.S. office) or sales@yaleup.co.uk (U.K. office).

Set in Times Roman type by Keystone Typesetting, Inc.

Printed in the United States of America.

Library of Congress Cataloging-in-Publication Data
Bentham, Jeremy, 1748–1832.
[Selections. 2011]
Selected writings / Jeremy Bentham ; edited and with an introduction by
Stephen G. Engelmann ; with essays by Philip Schofield . . . [et al.].
p. cm. — (Rethinking the Western tradition)
Includes index.
ISBN 978-0-300-11237-5 (pbk. : alk. paper)
1. Philosophy. I. Engelmann, Stephen G., 1961– II. Schofield, Philip, 1958– III. Title.
B1574.B31E54   2011
192 — dc22
2010017111

A catalogue record for this book is available from the British Library.

10 9 8 7 6 5 4 3 2 1

Contributors

Mark Canuel is Professor of English at the University of Illinois, Chicago.

David Lieberman is Jefferson E. Peyser Professor of Law, Jurisprudence and Social Policy Program, University of California, Berkeley.

Jennifer Pitts is Associate Professor of Political Science at the University of Chicago.

Philip Schofield is Professor of the History of Legal and Political Thought, Director of the Bentham Project, and General Editor of the Collected Works of Jeremy Bentham, University College London.

For Philip Schofield

and his colleagues at the

Bentham Project

Contents

Preface

It is difficult to do justice to the scope of Jeremy Bentham's work in one volume. He simply wrote too much, and on too many things. What I have attempted here is to give a sense of the range of his thought and a sample of new critical commentary. A few of the texts I prepared for inclusion were subsequently dropped, to keep the size and cost of the book manageable. Readers who want to read more should consult *The Collected Works of Jeremy Bentham* (London and Oxford, 1968–) as well as the less reliable but still indispensable *Works of Jeremy Bentham* (Edinburgh, 1838–43). Bentham wrote so many millions of words that some of his work remains virtually undiscovered or has been discovered and lost again; readers who crave still more can visit depositories of manuscripts, by far the biggest of which is the roughly sixty thousand sheets in University College London's Bentham Collection at 140 Hampstead Road.

The editorial collective behind the new *Collected Works* is the Bentham Project of UCL's Faculty of Laws. Philip Schofield is the project director and general editor of the *Collected Works*. Because of his generous assistance, this book includes new Bentham: the opening treatise on sex has never been published, except for short excerpts as an appendix to C. K. Ogden's edition of *Theory of Legislation* (1931). Also, "Place and Time" has never appeared before now as reconstructed exclusively from Bentham manuscript (and fully annotated). Although definitive versions of these works will eventually appear in the *Collected Works,* Professor Schofield has used Bentham Project methods to produce faithful editions for this volume. We thank University College London Library for permission to publish from the Bentham Collection.

Most of the remaining material in this selection consists of texts either published in English under Bentham's name during his lifetime or reproduced with permission from the new *Collected Works* (for exceptions to this rule, see the textual notes to "Pannomial Fragments," "Of Publicity," and the excerpt from "Manual of Political Economy," respectively, pp. 240, 291–92, and 308 below). Space constraints have been challenging, but I have tried not to rely too much on bits. And I have worked hard to avoid taking the path of other editors of Bentham readers, who make extensive use of John Bowring's *Works*. Nineteenth-century editorial conventions were different from our own: Bowring's Bentham is marred by scattered bowdlerizations and emendations; some of these come from simply retranslating into English the French texts of Bentham's contemporary Étienne Dumont, who was himself quite free with Bentham's manuscripts. (Dumont's recensions, beginning with the *Traités de Législation* of 1802, were very successful and really made Bentham's reputation, but they did so without much involvement from Bentham himself. In a characteristic letter to Dumont dated June 20, 1800, Bentham writes, "I leave out for you seven packets of MSS. God knows what they contain.") I am grateful for the early permission of the Bentham Committee of University College London to make extensive use of the new *Collected Works*. But after struggling with Oxford University Press over licensing fees, I can see why so much that is published today under Bentham's name consists of reprints of Bowring, however inadequate these might be. The monopoly privileges conferred by copyright were once granted according to a broadly republican and utilitarian rationale: a temporary period of private appropriation provided the incentive to produce more for a commonwealth of public use. Now, it seems, intellectual property has become ratified as a near natural right of publishers and other proprietors. I am thankful to Ben Kennedy of OUP for working to bring down the fees and to my university as well as Yale University Press for meeting them.

This project has had a huge amount of support from other sources as well, support without which I never could have completed it. An early sabbatical leave from the University of Illinois at Chicago and a summer stipend from the National Endowment for the Humanities were both essential. I also benefited from an award and a supplementary stipend from UIC's Office of the Vice Chancellor for Research as well as additional travel support from my own household, for which I thank Sophia Mihic and Mia Engelmann, and from that of my parents, for which I am grateful to Mary Engelmann and to my late father, Fred. Dean Dwight McBride and the College of Liberal Arts and Sciences at UIC provided crucial late-stage research funding. The Special Collections library staff of University College London have been cheerful and helpful through several visits; thanks also to the British Library in London and UIC's Daley Library in Chicago. I am particularly grateful for the hospitality of the Bentham Project and for consultations with several of its members. These individuals have given invaluable advice and encouragement, as have other denizens of a worldwide community of Bentham scholars from the United Kingdom, Canada,

France, Germany, Italy, and Japan. The Department of Political Science at UIC was generous with research assistantships, and I am thankful to Clifford Deaton, John French, Vanessa Guridy, Wael Haboub, Nawojka Lesinski, Cosmina Menghes, Jason Stodolka, and Nora Willi for all their help — special thanks to Wael and John for pulling extra duty. Tommy Barnett, William Lee, Amanda Martin, and Dana Williams provided enthusiastic and capable undergraduate support (mostly through UIC's Honors College), as did Mark Fisher, who volunteered while on break from his studies abroad. My colleague Allan Kershaw provided invaluable advice on Latin translation, and Sunil Agnani gave great annotation research advice. John Casey and Wendy Doniger responded cheerfully to last-minute queries. All remaining mistakes in this volume — and no doubt there are some — are of course my responsibility alone.

Larisa Heimert, formerly of Yale University Press, was instrumental in launching this project; Jack Borrebach, William Frucht, Larry Kenney, and three anonymous reviewers for YUP saw it through to completion. Many thanks to them, and to Cynthia Crippen for the index. Sophia and Mia have been unfailingly patient and loving about the drawn-out "Bentham book," although Mia doesn't want it to ruin another summer vacation. I am especially thankful for the sacrifices, guidance, and patience of my brilliant and steadfast contributors: Mark Canuel, David Lieberman, Jennifer Pitts, and Philip Schofield. It is to Philip above all that this book owes its existence, and so I dedicate it to him and to the members of the Bentham Project.

Introduction

STEPHEN G. ENGELMANN

Knowing Bentham

Jeremy Bentham (1748–1832) is famous, but there was a time when he was much more famous than he is now. He became famous — or notorious — in the early nineteenth century and remained so well into the twentieth: the acknowledged leader, in a rapidly modernizing Britain, of a transnational sect of thinkers known as utilitarians and Radicals.[1] Much of what Bentham thought has since been absorbed into our common sense. But the form in which he thought it and some of the conclusions to which he came still have the capacity to shock.

Today, Bentham is more known of than known. He is known, for instance, for trying to build an innovative prison. Bits of his Panopticon plan — popularized by the French philosopher and historian Michel Foucault as a kind of synecdoche for modern disciplinary power — have enshrined Bentham across scholarly fields as a master theorist of discipline and in particular of surveillance and self-surveillance. (For reasons of space I too have included only a small excerpt; see Panopticon Letters, pp. 283–90 below.) Bentham's fuller reputation in Anglophone letters remains that of a great classical utilitarian and legal positivist, and so chapters from *An Introduction to the Principles of Morals and Legislation* (*IPML*) are often assigned to introduce students to these schools (see excerpt pp. 103–51 below). Philosophical utilitarianism and legal positivism today represent fairly well defined yet controversial perspectives. Utilitarianism holds that what counts in determining the goodness of actions is only their consequences for happiness; positivism holds that legal obligations are completely conventional and do not have any necessary connection with morality. Although these perspectives, especially philosophical utilitarianism, indeed owe much to Bentham, we miss his importance if we think of his positivism and utilitarianism in these terms (for a thorough historical and analytical introduction to these issues, see Schofield, below pp. 425–59). Consider, instead, what is not so controversial. Law is now universally seen as an instrument of policy, and policy is understood in cost/benefit terms. Yet before Bentham these, like pervasive mutual surveillance, were revolutionary ideas. Their sources and success involve much more than the work of one man or even one generation. But because he was so consistent and insistent in his instrumental and calculating worldview, we can reasonably characterize our instrumental, calculating, and thoroughly disciplined world as, for better and worse, Benthamic.

Calculation and discipline make us think of a character like Charles Dickens's Gradgrind, the schoolmaster from *Hard Times*.[2] But Gradgrind's limiting and humorless passion for fact over fancy has little or nothing to do with Bentham. Consider another fairly well known fact about Bentham: he directed that his body be dissected, then preserved and displayed, and it can still be viewed in its case at University College London. Less well known is his whimsical *Auto-Icon; or, Farther Uses of the Dead to the Living,* in which it is clear that this direction is about having fun with making good use of otherwise useless and unenjoyable corpses.[3] Even in an age of widespread organ donation and ubiquitous comedy-horror entertainments, this remains a provocative because profoundly profaning extension of utilitarian reasoning (and the care of the dead is, for most of us, no laughing matter). How much do we really know about this Bentham, who is apparently just as serious about promoting illicit pleasure as he is about discipline? Too often, only small bits of Bentham are actually read. The purpose of this volume is to go beyond the usual bits and to break with the labels that have constrained and still constrain Bentham's reception.

Even those who read a lot of Bentham will tend to read him primarily as a normative theorist of politics and ethics and as a foundational theorist of law. Bentham did indeed care deeply about the principle of utility or greatest happiness principle — the principle that grounds good in pleasure and evil in pain — and its implications for public and private life. But he didn't dwell at length on controversies about its definition. (Sketches of the history of utility tend to rely only on the first few chapters of *IPML;* for other formulations and the shift to the language of happiness see "Pannomial Fragments" and "On Retrenchment" below, especially pp. 266–79 and 395–405, and see also Schofield, pp. 427–44 below.) And Bentham was indeed a powerful critic of natural and common law doctrines — seeing law instead as a matter of statutes issuing from authorities with the power to punish — but he cared much more about law as a tool for securing expectations and reducing their disappointment than he did about law as a foundation of order (see Lieberman, pp. 460–77 below, for a comprehensive account of Bentham's codification efforts). Bentham was not really a moral or political or legal philosopher in our sense; he was a moral philosopher in the sense of his contemporaries: not a natural philosopher but a philosopher of human affairs.[4] And his approach to human affairs was that of a relentlessly critical reformer. He saw everywhere around him misgovernment contributing to misery; he aimed for better government contributing to felicity.

In order to promote the end of greater happiness Bentham developed a comprehensively *economic* approach. To understand this approach we need to recognize that utilitarianism has evolved considerably since Bentham's time, developing separate strains of normative and descriptive philosophical and social-scientific work that have changed the very meanings of words like "economy" and "utility." Bentham's own approach to utilitarian economy entailed the study of institutions and their interactions with a view to maximize aggregate pleasure and minimize aggregate pain ("maximize" and "minimize" are two of Bentham's several lasting contributions to the English language).[5] The scope of his concerns extended to all men and women and beyond; thus Bentham is also known for his feminism and his attention to animal welfare. Having said that, it remains unclear what this expansive critical and impartial calculus means for him. It does mean, as we might expect, that his were some of the earliest writings calling for female suffrage,[6] and that well before Marx and Darwin he broke with nationalism and humanism in his vision of a continuum of sensitive beings. It also means, however, that in one text — published here complete for the first time — we can find condemnation of masturbation, toleration of bestiality, and approval of infanticide as a means of women's self-defense.[7] (Various constraints prevent me from publishing a differently provocative text that combines a vigorous defense of free markets with a proposal to tattoo the entire British population for identification purposes.)[8] Rather than react to Bentham's conclusions with approval or disapproval, it might serve us better to know more of his thought. Bentham simply didn't share some fundamental and familiar assumptions about freedom, intervention, and the special dignity of the human subject. But aren't there many researchers in our universities who tell us that fairness is irrational, or that all goods are commensurable, or that a comprehensive science of human/animal behavior is not only possible but has arrived? And haven't many of us today come to equate freedom with extensive choice under conditions of mutual surveillance, and don't we often look to experts for the latest strategies of pleasure seeking and self-management, while other experts — sometimes the same ones — assure us that there is really no self to manage? Perhaps despite, or rather because of, his distance from us, we can use Bentham's sometimes troubling consistencies to reflect on what is missing, latent, contradictory, or disturbing in contemporary theory and practice.

Life and Work

Bentham was born in London on February 15, 1748. His father was a wealthy attorney; his mother died when he was not quite eleven. Bentham's only surviving full sibling was his younger brother Samuel, with whom he remained close. His memories of his mother were fond ones, but he seems to have had a difficult time with his father, who had high expectations for this precocious child but lacked understanding of his rather pronounced sensitivity.[9] Bentham's father dreamed that he would one day be a great lawyer; perhaps the single most important biographical fact about Bentham is his thorough rejection of his father's profession. Not only did he not become a lawyer, he wrote the following at the age of eighty to the Duke of Wellington about the "army of lawyers": "About sixty years ago I deserted from it, and have been carrying on against them a guerilla war ever since."[10] The war began with Bentham's first monograph, *A Fragment on Government* (1776), a scathing attack on the great William Blackstone, whose lectures he had heard at Oxford.[11] In *A Fragment* Bentham introduced many themes and approaches that would reappear throughout his writing life. He followed David Hume in taking a critical approach to institutions as creatures of habit and interest, not justified by the fictions of nature and original contract.[12] And he demanded a systematic account that would separate law as it is from law as it might or should be and that would break down specialized legal discourse and connect it with pain, pleasure, and everyday life. Utility could then become a kind of common language that would ground only those productive fictions that are involved whenever we need to do complex things with words, so that we would disagree rationally rather than irrationally in the assessment and reform of our practices.[13]

Bentham's war on lawyers concluded decades later with an impressive, if unsuccessful, coalition-building effort for law reform, of which the communications with the Tory Wellington were a part. He was careful to separate this more mainstream push for legal reform from his other causes and from broader British political reform in particular, which he came to think was necessary by 1809.[14] By 1818 it was clear to Bentham that utility required expansion of the suffrage, representation by population through annual elections, disestablishment of the Church, and the abolition of monarchy and aristocracy — and that fundamental constitutional change was a necessary precondition for political reform.[15] At the same time he was involved in political agitation Bentham was writing new notes into the final year of his life for the introduction to a "pannomion," or comprehensive legal code, that might effectively replace existing legal structures (see "Pannomial Fragments," pp. 240–80 and Lieberman, pp. 460–61 below). He died at the age of eighty-four on June 6, 1832, one day before the great Reform Act became law: a crucial, if partial, step toward the representative democracy for which he fought in the last years of his life.

Because Bentham's analysis of fictions and his attack on fallacies showed a keen awareness of the centrality of language and rhetoric, and because he attended more to propositions than to words, he has been seen to anticipate in certain respects the linguistic turn of twentieth-century philosophy.[16] Although his critique of Blackstone was mostly an attack on conservative cant, he had no patience for the related fallacies of American and French revolutionaries (see "Nonsense Upon Stilts," pp. 318–94 below). All of common law, natural law, and natural rights came in for criticism. Bentham's sustained attack on discourses of custom and nature was always combined with a constructive attempt to build, through codification, a legal system of plain and clear imperatives. Thus he is rightly associated with support for the growth of modern bureaucracy against both traditionalism and radical state-phobia.[17] Yet he is also rightly associated with the most enduring critiques of the bureaucratic state: from the laissez-faire critique of state knowledge and other attacks on governmental inefficiency (see "Manual of Political Economy," pp. 314–16, and "On Retrenchment," pp. 409–17 below) to the critique of insufficient neutrality (see sinister interest discussion in "Constitutional Code Rationale," pp. 231–38 below) as well as insufficient transparency and accountability (see "Publicity" below, pp. 291–307, "Constitutional Code Rationale," p. 236, and Lieberman, pp. 470–73).[18]

Bentham began to read at an early age, and as a child he read whatever he could lay hands on; he was trained in ancient Greek and Latin as well as in French. François Fénelon's *Telemachus* was a big influence, as were works of Voltaire (he read *Telemachus* when he was seven and still spoke of it in his old age, and his first published book was a translation of Voltaire's *Le Taureau Blanc*).[19] Although he was widely read in classical literature and appreciative of John Locke, Hume, and other English and Scottish writers, Bentham's encounters with the Marchese di Beccaria and especially Claude Adrien Helvétius as a young adult confirm the importance of the Continental Enlightenment to his lifework. He became convinced of the importance of the expectation and apprehension of pleasure and pain in determining individual conduct: of the basics of the theory of motivation that would be outlined in full in *A Table of the Springs of Action* (1815, 1817).[20] And he was already persuaded that all institutions of public and private life should be grounded in the principle of utility: they should serve to enhance happiness, or pleasure, and diminish unhappiness, or pain.

Bentham acquired very disciplined habits of writing early in his life; he wrote voluminously on a variety of subjects, often with some reference to the law as he expansively understood it. He was notorious for starting work but not finishing it, returning to projects and adding new material to them over the years. His efforts can be roughly divided into three periods: penal law and general jurisprudence early on (some under the generous sponsorship of Lord Shelburne, an Enlightenment patron);[21] civil law, political economy, and what we would call public policy in the middle phase — here his only extended and distant trip abroad, to live with his brother in Russia, was key;[22] and ontology, religion, political reform, and constitutional law late in life. But his interests ranged beyond these subjects, and all of them received beginnings, additions, and new treatments throughout his writing life.[23] Bentham wrote an enormous amount — ten to twenty manuscript pages a day, of which some twenty million words survive — and was fully able to support this writing life after his father's death in 1792. He needed an editor and popularizer to make his name, though, and one came along in the form of the Genevan Étienne Dumont, who published the first of his recensions, *Traités de Législation civile et pénale,* in 1802. At the same time that his failure to build Panopticon confirmed, in his view, his marginal status at home, Dumont's books were building his reputation abroad. He lived his last decades as a beacon to and correspondent with reforming statesmen and dissident thinkers at home and abroad, rarely venturing far from his home at Queen's Square Place in London.[24]

For us today, *IPML* (see short excerpt, pp. 103–51 below) is Bentham's most famous work, and it exhibits many of the marks of his work as a whole. It was printed in 1780 but not published until 1789, by which time its "flaws" produced "disgust" in their author.[25] Bentham's view in 1789 is that *IPML* is radically incomplete; he envisions the Pannomion that continued to capture his attention in his final years.[26] In the first printing of the book, chapter 16, on the division of offences, had exploded in size to a third of the volume, and various writing projects of the 1780s were initially drafted as chapters that would follow chapter 17 (these chapters are not included in the excerpt below); "Place and Time" is one of these projects, and it has been restored here entirely from manuscript for the first time (pp. 152–219 below).[27] Still, *IPML* does provide a useful introduction to Bentham's thought: to the principle of utility and, perhaps more important, to the theory of sanctions (or "sources of pain and pleasure") that informs his whole approach to government.

Legacies and Rethinking

What emerges from a reading of Bentham as theorist of sanctions is that he is not so much a normative philosopher as he is a student of the art and science of government. He doesn't construct, in the manner of more recent political theory, a theory of the good life, in order to criticize a reality that doesn't live up to it. Instead he studies what governs human conduct, in order to figure out how to induce people to govern themselves and one another more harmoniously. It is through the eyes of Bentham's greatest disciple, John Stuart Mill (1806–73), that we tend to see the master as limited man and limited theorist. Bentham the individual gets caricatured as a man-child, and Bentham the theorist as primitive.[28] Of course Mill's own view was more nuanced;[29] and Mill himself was not a normative philosopher in our sense so much as a theorist of government. Readings of Mill and Bentham as political or moral or legal philosophers are not so much anachronistic as they are proleptic (and teleological, as is evident from their classification as "classical utilitarians").[30] But even if we read Bentham more correctly, as a moral scientist and legal reformer concerned above all with the art and science of government, we are in danger if we do so mostly through Mill's influential accounts.[31]

What does it mean for Bentham to have largely been read through Mill? It means that we see Bentham primarily as a classical utilitarian. Again, this perspective is not so much wrong as it is skewed and highly limited. On this view, Bentham is usually the relatively crude precursor to Mill's more refined view of utilitarianism's greatest happiness principle. If Bentham is the rationalist calculator of pleasures, Mill leavens this rationalism with Romanticism and empiricism. If Bentham is insufficiently attuned to the differences among pleasures calculated, Mill opposes this with an aesthetic sensibility and critical judgment. If Bentham is relatively unconcerned with the interior of the self, Mill makes up for this lack with a theory of character. If Bentham is willing to sacrifice liberty to a utilitarian calculus, Mill provides a robust utilitarian defense of liberty. The picture that emerges is one of Bentham as bold but flawed visionary, inspiring a superior follower who can better serve as a philosophical hero. The tendency to read Bentham through Mill and to celebrate Mill accordingly is reinforced by the relative inaccessibility of Bentham's texts. We rely on bits of Bentham, or secondhand Bentham, and accept thumbnail sketches and characterizations. And we're not encouraged to go further because of another tradition — that of excoriating Bentham the stylist, from William Hazlitt to Karl Marx and beyond. (Hazlitt joked that Bentham's work should be "translated into English," and Marx called him "that insipid, pedantic, leather-tongued oracle of the ordinary bourgeois intelligence of the 19th century.")[32]

We can usefully divide Bentham's legacy into several stages. First, we have the old Radical: the "hermit of Queen's Square Place," living with his amanuenses and several longtime and daily visitors, receiving dinner guests one at a time, and corresponding with republicans worldwide. This Bentham was convinced that dramatic reform of English institutions was necessary, and he was known for his involvement in several liberal causes of the day (the word "liberal" in its political sense dates from this time, and so Bentham was among the first generation of English liberals). His analyses showed that lawyers, Church, aristocracy, and monarchy formed so many "sinister interests": that they composed a "ruling few" who used their positions to their own benefit and to the detriment of the "subject many." The aged Bentham became increasingly bold in his rhetoric — for example, calling the king the "great baby"[33] — and he served as inspiration shortly after his death for a range of nineteenth-century reform movements covering the spectrum from socialist Chartism to Manchester free trade-ism.[34] It is not true, as widely reported, that he either founded or left his estate to University College London (then London University). But this first English secular institution of higher education was established by what he called " 'an association of liberals,' " several of whom were friends or disciples of his, and it was established largely in accordance with his principles.[35]

If political radicalism and anticlericalism were his immediate legacy, then these were somewhat blunted by his followers and first apologists. John Bowring, his executor, was not comfortable with the content of much of Bentham's heterodoxy, and his writings on religion are conspicuously absent from the voluminous *Works*. James Mill, the father of John Stuart and Bentham's most prominent associate, came to be seen as more political than Bentham and even as being responsible for Bentham's supposed conversion to radicalism. This meant, ironically, that Bentham himself was made more palatable for rising Victorian misogyny, racism, and imperial apologetics.[36] Bentham became the philosopher, supposedly less involved and concerned than his followers with practical affairs, yet the inspiration for their modern outlook and all their projects of improvement. This picture was shared by friends and foes alike as moderate utilitarianism, dissenting religion, free trade, and political reform increasingly became the ideological common sense for a new ruling class and its allies in the emerging professions.

We can see this legacy continuing into the early years of the twentieth century. What changed was the formation of a strong intellectual reaction against so-called Benthamite utilitarianism. This is a complicated story, but, to radically simplify, Bentham became associated with philosophical reductionism and illiberal political rationalism. We see the former in the development of nineteenth-century intra-utilitarian debates that substituted refinements for the core doctrine and in G. E. Moore's critique in 1903 of the "naturalistic fallacy," suggesting that Benthamic hedonism is not only crude but confused.[37] We see the potential for the latter already in Élie Halévy's monumental *La Formation du Radicalisme Philosophique* (1901–04), which argues that Bentham combines a "natural identity of interests" in economics with an "artificial identification of interests" in politics.[38] What follows after World War II is a more sinister portrait in Friedrich Hayek's references to Bentham as a bad rather than good liberal, as a "rational constructivist," substituting for the spontaneous order of Adam Smith and the Scottish Enlightenment a bureaucratic doctrine that anticipates and justifies the planned societies of the twentieth century.[39] A steadily declining literary reputation exacerbated legacies of unsophistication in philosophy and unfreedom in politics. (Although the supposed contrast between Bentham and Romanticism goes back at least as far as J. S. Mill's essays on Bentham and Coleridge and his popularization of Bentham's comparison between the pleasures of push-pin — a children's game — and poetry, this opposition became canonical in the mid-twentieth century; for a stark reappraisal of Bentham and Romanticism, see the Canuel essay below, pp. 500–19).[40] The specters of crude philosophy and tyrannical planning are merged and reinforced in the influential portrayal by John Rawls in 1971 of classical utilitarianism as a theory that fails to adequately distinguish among persons and that is willing to sacrifice their rights to a conception of the good.[41] And the American reception especially of Foucault's analyses in the 1970s of the disciplinary power of Bentham's Panopticon has largely only contributed to this despotic legacy.[42]

The new Collected Works project began to bear fruit in the late 1960s, and it provoked a significant wave of revisionist studies of Bentham.[43] These studies produced a rethinking of the caricature that culminated in the reception of Rawls's and Foucault's treatments. The new wave produced several fine works. They were, however, sometimes marred by a tendency to take their cues from the images and assumptions of the day and a tendency to concern themselves with defending Bentham's reputation. The most prominent strain along these lines would defend Bentham's liberalism, often understood in contemporary terms.[44] It is true that the caricature of Bentham as illiberal had gone so far as to suggest that he was opposed to rights, whereas rights have a fundamental place in his jurisprudence. He is a powerful critic of *natural* rights (see "Nonsense Upon Stilts" below, pp. 322–35); rights are understood as products of law but are essential to good government (see "Pannomial Fragments," pp. 256, 260 below).

No doubt my introduction and the essays at the end of the volume are influenced by Bentham revisionism and can justifiably be seen as part of this continuing trend. The hope is, however, that we have entered an era of postrevisionism in Bentham studies. What this entails and will continue to entail is a combination of studies that aim at either faithful contextual readings or painstaking textual reconstructions — or some combination thereof — to produce results that are relatively unconstrained by reigning assumptions. There has certainly always been some of this kind of work but much remains to be done: instead of shaping Bentham to our tastes, we can show how careful study of his thought on its own terms might call into question elements of received wisdom. Perhaps questioning of this sort can emerge from an account of Bentham's work that understands him as a theorist of the art and science of government.

What do I mean by this? Briefly, we tend now to take for granted that the reason to study human affairs is to figure out how they work so that we can intervene and improve them, or so that we can highlight their self-regulating qualities to warn that intervention will make them worse. But this is not at all obvious. And it is even less obvious that we should think of politics and government as such a matter of intervention or nonintervention for the good or ill of society. Bentham's work presents a turning point in the history of the Western art and science of government. He writes in the age of enlightenment and revolution, but still for the most part prior to the development of the many disciplines that we associate with social improvement and its limits — with the whole technopolitical establishment of the policy sciences. His project is to improve, but to do so with a kind of science of arrangement: a science that assesses people as they are and considers how they could be more harmoniously self-governing and mutually governing. Any revolutionary impulses on Bentham's part are constrained by the outlook of general economy, which includes the importantly conservative disappointment-prevention principle (see "On Retrenchment," below pp. 395–97): once someone comes to expect something, however absurd (like the expectations of aristocratic privilege or inherited wealth), it is painful to them if those expectations are dashed. Bentham's great innovation is that he has a basic framework for understanding the structural relations among the elements of what we would call a social system, and these are what he calls the sanctions.

The Four Sanctions

Think of the sanctions as an early theory of incentives. Incentives and disincentives are everywhere in our market-oriented — what critical theorists call our neoliberal — societies. We have even recently invented an ugly verb — "incentivize" — to describe the management of others' incentives. When we talk about incentives and disincentives, we work with an implicit theory of what motivates people to do what they do. For Bentham, this is all about pleasure and pain; we seek pleasures (our economists call these preferences), and we avoid pains. Bentham tends to focus on the disincentives rather than the incentives; more classically liberal than today's economists and psychologists, he thinks that pleasure seeking will largely take care of itself and that what for the most part needs managing is pain. Pains can be grouped into sanctions. Obviously, just as with (dis)incentives, we identify as sanctions things that are, within limits, subject to manipulation. Government becomes a practical science, like medicine; we study the social body, just as we study the physical body, to identify those elements and relationships that can effectively be changed for the better.

In *IPML* the sanctions are four in number:[45] "There are four distinguishable sources from which pleasure and pain are in use to flow: considered separately, they may be termed the *physical,* the *political,* the *moral,* and the *religious*: and inasmuch as the pleasures and pains belonging to each of them are capable of giving a binding force to any law or rule of conduct, they may all of them be termed *sanctions*."[46] What these sanctions do in any given time and place is form a kind of landscape that arranges the conduct of the individuals that inhabit it. I see as best I can the prospects of pleasure and pain to be had from a range of actions and their consequences, and I choose that which will produce the most good.[47] The physical sanction is that which is engaged whenever I feel and satisfy hunger or hit my head on a piece of furniture. But it is also the "ground-work" of all the other sanctions; they are, in the final analysis, understood to have a physical basis. Bentham was very interested throughout his life in the physical sciences, particularly chemistry, and in physical arts from medicine to architecture. His attention to the details of the physical sanction is evident in his voluminous Panopticon and Poor Law writings. From the late 1780s through the first years of the nineteenth century, Bentham sank a great deal of money, time and energy into plans for Panopticon, a proposal for a new prison that, despite his best efforts, was never built. Panopticon made use of the Inspection-House principle: an architectural innovation that promised dramatic reform in the government of all sorts of institutions: prisons, asylums, workhouses, hospitals, schools, etc. (see pp. 284–85 below). This principle was a new "engine of management"[48] that would deploy the omnipresent possibility of surveillance by others to induce continuous self-surveillance and attendant good behavior. In these and other architectural designs we see the extent of Bentham's attention to physical detail (in the interest of space I deleted a long footnote on plumbing design from the second Panopticon letter, pp. 285–87 below). We also see that the physical sanction is most often routed through the medium of the individual imagination; here and elsewhere it is the *prospect* of punishment or reward that serves as a source of motivation.[49]

We can usefully view Bentham's work — especially in this middle period, but really his work as a whole — as being preoccupied with the better arrangement of complex assemblages of persons and things, understanding the physical sanction as a primary way that persons relate to one another and to things. Political economy — the art and science concerned with wealth and population — is, for Bentham as for Smith, primarily aimed at figuring out how to implement what Smith, in *The Wealth of Nations,* called the "system of natural liberty" (see "Manual of Political Economy" excerpt, pp. 308–17 below).[50] Just as optimal management policy will deploy individuals to govern themselves within institutions, optimal economic policy will deploy individuals to govern themselves and one another in the provision and distribution of society's goods and services. The prospect of not eating induces me to find work with an employer, and the prospect of losing his business to competitors induces my employer to make his goods and services as cheap as possible (and so to use my labor, among other inputs, as efficiently as possible). The sanction — most directly in the case of the worker — is one of imagined or even of experienced physical privation. And so for Bentham free markets in labor and goods are a form of "indirect legislation":[51] the law of property and contract and attendant punishments issue directly from the political apparatus, but the self-policing and mutual policing produced by competition issues only indirectly from it. Both Bentham's civil law and his political economy aim at four fundamental ends: security, subsistence, abundance, and equality (see "Pannomial Fragments," pp. 241–45 below, and "Manual," p. 312 and n. below). The market in money must also be encouraged rather than discouraged, to allow the imagined rewards of "projectors" (a term covering both our celebrated entrepreneurs and our disparaged speculators) to induce them to proliferate their schemes.[52]

The political sanction involves any pleasure or pain that issues from political authorities. And so the penalties for theft and fraud in the criminal law and the liabilities for breach of contract in the civil law, for example, are all political sanctions, the prospect of which governs the conduct of individuals. (Bentham's perspective entails a weakening or even jettisoning of the distinction between civil and criminal law. The line between these becomes somewhat arbitrary — see *IPML*, Preface p. 108 below — and he preferred "penal" to "criminal," even though the mapping of these onto one another is inexact.)[53] In his jurisprudence, the abiding concern is a kind of calibration of punishments to offences.[54] Bentham is always taking care that penalties be neither too high nor too low. Too high is a waste; all punishment is pain and is an evil, and so more punishment is more evil. Too low is also a kind of waste because it doesn't effectively deter crime; all laws and their attendant penalties present prospects to be factored into the potential criminal's calculation of his or her interest. In fact, this prospect is all that obligation really is for Bentham; the radicalism of Bentham's theory is such that for a range of traditional perspectives — from Christian natural law to Thomas Hobbes and Immanuel Kant — he has arguably done away with duty altogether (by undermining its absolutism, by turning it into an interest among other interests).[55] From Bentham's own point of view duty remains fundamental and is defined according to utility; the challenge is always to reconcile duty with interest, through what he would in later years call the "junction-of-interests-prescribing principle" ("Constitutional Code Rationale," pp. 231–32 below).

The sanctions of the penal law make it in my interest to avoid doing various types of grievous harm to others. Not only does such harm take away directly from another's happiness (and probably to a greater degree than it contributes to mine); the prospect of such harm creates a condition of "alarm" throughout the population, which always outweighs any benefit to perpetrators of criminal acts. So if I don't do harm to others, what is it that I do? The sanctions of the civil law and of policies of political economy ideally make it in my interest to direct my activities such that they contribute to aggregate utility. Here, as we have seen, the political sanction creates a framework spurring innovative activity and self-policing and mutual policing. And the policy of taxation should raise public revenue in conformity with subjects' interests by avoiding tyranny — which Bentham equates with the disappointment of expectations — as much as possible.[56] The sanctions of constitutional law are geared to join the duties of offices with the interests of their occupants as far as possible. (This is the junction-of-interests-prescribing principle.) Bentham is concerned here about everything from, again, the physical details of architecture to the specification of functions; here political sanctions are organized to mobilize as far as possible the moral or popular sanction (see "Of Publicity," pp. 292–93, and "Constitutional Code Rationale," pp. 236–37 below). The political sanctions in all branches of law are so many "instruments of security"[57] that together ground and direct conduct in an ideally harmonious manner. But in the Constitutional Code and other forms of direct and indirect legislation there is no set hierarchy of sanctions; the sanctions instead form a kind of dynamic complex that is present in all human societies and is ever amenable to utilitarian study and improvement. The moral sanction from public opinion is, for example, crucial to negotiating the difficult but all-too-necessary project of governing governors and would be institutionalized in the imaginary yet highly effective assembly of the "Public Opinion Tribunal."[58] The complex of sanctions has to be compatible, for Bentham, with legislative supremacy; the separation of powers is repeatedly and explicitly rejected in favor of a kind of continuous policing of governmental practice through the mobilization of information and publicity.[59]

What is the moral sanction, then? If the political sanction is the pain or pleasure issuing from political authorities, the moral sanction is the pain or pleasure issuing from anyone at all, in response to one's actions: it is a matter of accountability to others and to the public. This is why the moral sanction is also known as the popular, and why publicity is itself such an important instrument of security and device of government. The popular sanction, though, raises a real difficulty for Bentham. If most of the public are not partisans of the principle of utility but are instead partisans, like so many moralists and legislators, of the "principle of sympathy and antipathy," why should one give free rein to their flawed judgments (which they, unlike good utilitarians, are unable to separate from their preferences)? The problem with the principle of sympathy and antipathy, or with what Bentham would also call "ipsedixitism," is that I make my own likes and dislikes into a rule for everyone. Thus I give no thought to the important fact of plurality: to the fact that, for example, others have different pleasures from my own and to the principle that those pleasures should, if their satisfaction is harmless, be indulged. This problem, however, doesn't loom so large for publicity's narrower purpose, which is to make the victims of the machinations of rulers aware of those machinations, so that they can put a stop to them. Individuals know their own interests best and can be counted on to defend them under threat. Concerned though he is about the presence of systematically generated prejudice, Bentham's lifelong advocacy of freedom of the press seems to share the broader Enlightenment faith that publicity ultimately circulates truth and that the circulation of truth tends to educate publics.[60] And this education can presumably help to curb those manifestations of the moral sanction that involve the suppression of minority pleasures. That Bentham is very concerned to defend such pleasures is clear from his writings on sex and religion.

Much of Bentham's writing on religion is hostile and is aimed at religion as establishment. He was clearly troubled by his forced subscription to the English Church's Thirty-nine Articles at Oxford. And it seems that what bothered him in his family's Anglicanism was not so much piety, which to his mind was even lacking, as it was the apparently blind insistence upon the manners and rituals prescribed by the Church. The history of Bentham's opinions on religion has a direct relationship to the history of his opinions on politics, a reminder that, in the context of eighteenth-century Britain and perhaps well beyond, religion and politics are inseparable. To his young critical sensibility, the problem with religious leaders is their preaching of asceticism: religion, then, is an enemy insofar as it identifies earthly pain as a good and earthly pleasure as a bad, reversing the principle of utility (see *IPML*, pp. 117–21, and material on Islam and Christianity in "Place and Time" pp. 152–219 below). The problem with political leaders is their proneness to a different error: they govern according to their own tastes — according to the nonprinciple of sympathy and antipathy — and not in accordance with utility. Even lawyers, those sowers of unnecessary confusion and vexation, were often thought to be deluded rather than deliberate. Bentham quite early on advocates many positions that anticipate his late radicalism: in his revolutionary-era writings on France (which include "Of Publicity" and "Nonsense Upon Stilts" from this volume) we can read calls for universal suffrage (including at one point all literate men and women) and the gradual expropriation of Church property.[61] But these calls are for this time and place; they are not necessarily seen as transferable to England — especially not following the French Terror — and they are certainly not seen as any kind of condition of utilitarian government. It is only following the discovery and analysis of "sinister interest" in the early nineteenth century — first traced in the legal establishment but then extended to all of Church and State and probably shaped by the frustrations of the experience with Panopticon — that Bentham develops what we might call a social theory; the mistakes of lawyers, priests, and government officials are no longer possibly innocent but are tied to the maintenance of the class advantages derived from their misrule.[62]

Hostility to religion as establishment, however, is perfectly consistent with a friendliness to religion not only as system of belief, but also as an aid to government, understood broadly as the arrangement of conduct. The fourth sanction from *IPML* — the religious sanction — understands that religion can play a positive as well as a negative role in the utilitarian reform of government. The Eighth Commandment, for example, is a useful supplement to the political and moral sanctions against theft, especially in cases where detection might be highly unlikely. The religious sanction involves mainly the apprehension of punishment in this or in a future life by an unseen Deity. As Bentham became more suspicious of the functions of false doctrines, however, he became more critical of extant theology: his more famous utilitarian contemporary, the Reverend William Paley, drew special opprobrium from him for his use of Christian theology to justify, in Bentham's view, the patently unutilitarian character of many contemporary institutions.[63] Bentham's writings on sexual nonconformity, a subject he explored as early as the 1770s, became entwined in the nineteenth century with his development of a Christian countertheology: in a fascinating genealogy of morals, he accuses the Apostle Paul of hijacking the pleasure-positive perspectives of Jesus for a doctrine of asceticism (see "Sex" below, especially pp. 43–47, 68). Thus Bentham the advocate of the moral or popular sanction — so important as a democratic check to misrule — was no apologist for popular morality. On the contrary, he hoped at one point to be able to appeal directly to the public for full liberty and broad toleration in sexual and other tastes, after demolishing the flawed reading of scripture upon which Christian asceticism, to his mind, relied.[64] Turning away from an intolerant Paul and toward a tolerant Jesus would restrain, rather than encourage, majorities' pernicious tendencies to make their desires and disgusts into the rule of action for all.[65]

Reading Bentham

The reading of Bentham as a theorist of sanctions opens up a perspective on government that might help to illuminate modern times. We can no longer afford to pretend that government is a matter of a state that intervenes or doesn't intervene in a distinct civil society or economy, that markets are distinct from the regulatory and other nonmarket regimes that infuse them, or that individuals' properties and other interests are somehow prior to a system that arranges and values them. The Bentham texts presented here offer a different set of assumptions, assumptions that approach human affairs as a complex assemblage of persons and things. Whether Bentham's instrumental and calculating approach to this assemblage and his particular strategies and tactics of improvement are in any way adequate is a different matter from the importance of this change in perspective. His texts offer a kind of rationalism that is useful as a reorientation, even if that reorientation serves, in several of its particulars, as a kind of warning about its own limits. If it's fair to think of him as helping to inaugurate the rule of experts, then at least we can appreciate that his experts were to be much more carefully watched than ours apparently have been. Consider what Bentham might have to tell us about the globally destructive U.S. political and economic crises of the early twenty-first century. If the problem is in large part a problem of what he calls sinister interest, it is not a problem of virtue, however broadly understood: of immoral or incompetent politicians, generals, bankers, CEOs, lawyers, academics, or media and other watchdogs. Sinister interest is primarily a political, not a moral or technical, phenomenon. It is the stuff of certain establishments, their incentives, and their relations — the stuff of hostile class formations — and not the stuff of the characters and capabilities of the people who make them up.[66]

Four essays follow the Bentham texts in this volume. In the first, Philip Schofield investigates the meaning of the principle of utility and the question of its implications for the tradition of legal positivism. In the second, David Lieberman gives an account of Bentham's lifelong project of codification. In the third, Jennifer Pitts examines the relationship between Bentham's utilitarianism and British imperialism. And in the fourth, Mark Canuel investigates the links between Bentham's work and the English Romanticism with which it is often contrasted. These essays — three of which are original to this volume — serve both as valuable introductions to whole areas of Bentham's thought in context and as accessible samples of current critical trends from leading scholars in their fields.

Finally, a word about the first text: Bentham's "Sex." Why begin with this selection? First, there is the profound interest of the work itself, published here complete for the first time. Louis Crompton mentions this manuscript from 1814–16 in his *Journal of Homosexuality* (1978) introduction to Bentham's c. 1785 "Paederasty" (a term which in Bentham's usage referred broadly to male same-sex erotic relations). Whereas Crompton labeled the piece he published reformist in its plea for decriminalization of sexual nonconformity, he called this later essay revolutionary for its advocacy of "irregular" practices.[67] "Sex" is written in the shadow of Malthus's famous *Population*. Here sex is treated as part of a new natural/social matrix; and that matrix, in Bentham's hands, demands not moral restraint or birth control so much as the privileging and promotion of nonreproductive sex. The text can virtually be summarized by the following pithy, if androcentric, note: "Love of women frequently and notoriously a cause of public mischief: paederasty, never."[68]

Besides its importance as queer writing, "Sex" serves as an introduction to Bentham: it shows his basic principles and methods at work. Sex is a source of pleasure and can be highly consequential, so it is worthy of utilitarian appraisal. Sex also, like anything else, can be opened to systematic analysis: Bentham does this in his usual manner, which makes the piece in places quite dry and technical. He attempts the impartial classification and cost/benefit assessment of a range of practices, with an eye to both expository and censorial jurisprudence (regulation as it is, and regulation as it should be). No aspersions are cast on any makeup of desires; although he writes of "sexual irregularity," as opposed to "sexual nonconformity," the regular is by no means prescriptive. Bentham's argument: an all-comprehensive liberty in consensual sex is warranted, as it would add significantly to the sum of society's happiness. In the course of making this argument he comes to some startling conclusions. Among these are the superiority of same-sex over regular modes (because they do not lead to pregnancy), sex among children as a virtuous substitute for masturbation (which is too available and enervating), and the absurdity of laws against infanticide (which sacrifice the genuine happiness of the aware to the only imputed feelings of the unaware).[69] However disturbed we might be at one or more of these conclusions, or about any imputation of association between them, Bentham's provocations spur us to revisit our own assumptions. And his treatment both illustrates his bracing egalitarianism and introduces us to his place in a rich tradition of subversive reflections on sexual-political order. Sex for Bentham is democratic, even anarchic: "These are precisely the only pleasures of sense which are as fully and effectually within the reach of the most indigent . . . as within the most affluent classes of mankind: they are equally within the reach of the subject many as of the ruling few" ("Additions to Happiness," below p. 92).

NOTES

1. "Utilitarianism" and "Radicalism" were newly coined philosophical and political labels in Bentham's time, both of which were proudly worn by him

(although the latter not until the last decades of his life). The *Oxford English Dictionary* cites Bentham for first use of "utilitarian" [1781] and "radicalism" [1817], although "radical" was used by others in a political sense as early as the 1780s. For Bentham's own understandings of utilitarianism and radicalism, see the "Article on Utilitarianism" (1829) — of which there are two versions — in Jeremy Bentham, *Deontology, Together with A Table of the Springs of Action and Article on Utilitarianism*, ed. Amnon Goldworth (Oxford: Clarendon Press, 1983), 283–328, and "Radicalism Not Dangerous" (1819–20), in John Bowring, ed., *The Works of Jeremy Bentham*, 11 vols. (Edinburgh: William Tait, 1838–43), iii. 599–622 (hereafter Bowring). John Stuart Mill (1806–73) probably did more than anyone else to popularize the use of these labels, so that in nineteenth-century England, at least, utilitarian Radicals were institutionalized as a middle-class sect disappointed in the slow pace of political reform. Both terms have since proliferated and been projected well back in time, especially "radical" as a political label, which now has no particular doctrinal location — although it does, when not capitalized, usually suggest an openness to sweeping reform of some sort. For recent discussions of the history and historiography of English radicalism, see Glenn Burgess and Matthew Festenstein, eds., *English Radicalism, 1550–1850* (Cambridge: Cambridge University Press, 2007), which includes an article on Bentham (F. Rosen, "Jeremy Bentham's Radicalism," 217–40).

2. Charles Dickens, *Hard Times: A Norton Critical Edition* (New York: W. W. Norton, 2000 [1854]).

3. "Auto-Icon" was posthumously printed c. 1842, and there is very little surviving manuscript. For a recent edition, see James E. Crimmins, ed., *Jeremy Bentham's Auto-Icon and Related Writings* (Bristol: Thoemmes Continuum, 2002).

4. Ross Harrison nicely captures the gulf between Bentham's understanding of utilitarian moral philosophy and our own: "His thought . . . was centrally concerned with the organisation of social, or public, institutions"; and "much of the concern with utilitarianism this century has been with it as a system of personal ethics," which "Bentham regarded as a relatively peripheral part of his work" (Harrison, *Bentham* [London: Routledge and Kegan Paul, 1983], 4).

5. He again (see note 1) earns first citation in the *Oxford English Dictionary* for these words; perhaps his most prominent contribution to the language is "international."

6. He called in 1789 for the enfranchisement of all literate and sane women and men in one of his proposed constitutional codes for revolutionary France; see P. Schofield, C. Pease-Watkin, and C. Blamires, eds., *Rights, Representation, and Reform: Nonsense upon Stilts and Other Writings on the French Revolution* (Oxford: Clarendon Press, 2002), 231.

7. See for examples pp. 54, 58, and 83 below. The most disturbing infanticide

passage is on p. 52 ("Of a hundred thousand new-born infants . . ."). Note that Bentham's position on infanticide is far more extreme than any similar contemporary argument, but it is also completely universal; it is not at all selective, and so there is no eugenic intent. Note also that Bentham's bestiality passages are compromised by a certain inconsistency, as they don't say anything about beasts' pleasures, pains, or consent.

8. I mean here the fascinating essay "Indirect Legislation," written c. 1782. The manuscript is mostly in University College London Bentham Collection boxes 87 and 62 (hereafter UC). The published version is quite limited; it is a retranslation of Étienne Dumont's recension in Bowring, i. 533–80 (the market is mentioned in the Introduction and tattooing in chap. 12). For a discussion and interpretation of this essay, see Stephen G. Engelmann, " 'Indirect Legislation': Bentham's Liberal Government," *Polity* 35:3 (spring 2003).

9. See Bowring, x. 4–5, 26.

10. Ibid., xi. 9.

11. J. H. Burns and H. L. A. Hart, eds., *A Comment on the Commentaries and A Fragment on Government* (London: Athlone Press, 1977); Bentham, *A Fragment on Government* (Cambridge: Cambridge University Press, 1988).

12. David Hume, "Of the Original Contract" (1748), in Knud Haakonssen, ed., *Hume: Political Essays* (Cambridge: Cambridge University Press, 1994), 186–201.

13. Bentham, *A Fragment on Government*, 104–05 and passim.

14. For a comprehensive account of the development of Bentham's political thought see Philip Schofield, *Utility and Democracy: The Political Thought of Jeremy Bentham* (Oxford: Oxford University Press, 2006). Schofield revises the received story of an early flirtation with and later transition to political radicalism; see, for example, J. R. Dinwiddy, "Bentham's Transition to Political Radicalism, 1809–10," *Journal of the History of Ideas* 36:4 (1975), 683–700.

15. See Schofield, *Utility and Democracy*, 221 and passim. Schofield shows both the relative consistency of Bentham's orientation throughout his working life, and what a political difference it made when Bentham discovered in the first decade of the nineteenth century that bad government was not an accident but a product of the "sinister interest" of ruling classes; he also usefully distinguishes Bentham's advocacy of democratization from his later insistence on a republican constitution as a prerequisite for broader reform.

Note that Bentham's advocacy of democracy is about utility, and never about the implementation of an authoritative principle of sovereignty — a principle that anyone, including "the people," is simply entitled to rule. Instead, sovereignty itself is quite diffuse in his mature thought; for a provocative interpretation of Bentham on sovereignty and utility see Oren Ben-Dor, *Constitutional Limits and the Public Sphere* (Oxford: Hart Publishing, 2000).

16. See C. K. Ogden's introduction to Ogden, ed., *Bentham's Theory of Fictions* (London: Routledge and Kegan Paul, 1932); see also W. V. Quine, *Theories and Things* (Cambridge: Harvard University Press, 1986), 68–70. For a dissent from this appropriation that situates Bentham on language firmly in the Enlightenment context see Emmanuelle de Champs, "The Place of Jeremy Bentham's Theory of Fictions in Eighteenth-Century Linguistic Thought," *Journal of Bentham Studies* 2 (1999).

17. See L. J. Hume, *Bentham and Bureaucracy* (Cambridge: Cambridge University Press, 1981).

18. Bentham's concern with language — and in particular his criticism of the specialized, nontransparent language of lawyers — anticipates today's plain-language movement's attempts to abolish officialese; ironically, it was probably his own search for linguistic transparency-through-innovation that led him, late in life, to write increasingly opaque prose.

19. *The White Bull:* see Bowring, x. 82–83; on *Telemachus* see ibid., 10–11.

20. See *Deontology, Together with A Table of the Springs of Action and Article on Utilitarianism,* 1–115. This edition is quite comprehensive but the table itself is broken up (79–86), which spoils the tabular effect. I had hoped to include the table in this volume, but it would have made the cost prohibitive. A good image of the table is now available on the World Wide Web at http://www.ucl.ac.uk/Bentham-Project/info/table.htm.

21. Shelburne was for a short time (1782–83) prime minister, during which he negotiated the peace with the new United States that would be ratified after his term. He was named first marquis of Landsdowne in 1784. On the relationship between Bentham and Shelburne/Landsdowne, see Élie Halévy's *The Growth of Philosophical Radicalism,* trans. Mary Morris (Clifton, N.J.: A. M. Kelley, 1972 [1901–04]), which remains quite useful as a comprehensive introduction to Bentham's life and thought.

22. See Ian R. Christie, *The Benthams in Russia* (Oxford: Berg Publishers, 1993).

23. Even constitutional law and political reform, which seem like staples of the old Radical, receive much in the way of anticipation already in the 1780s and early 1790s. The final chapter of the essay on indirect legislation (see note 8 above and note 60 below) is a treatment of "expedients against misrule" that lays out some of the basic principles and mechanisms that would inform Bentham's constitutional work some forty years later. The writings for revolutionary France (see note 6 above) contain much that would inform his nineteenth-century reform work (see especially "Of Publicity," pp. 291–307 below).

24. For an idea of the scope and extent of his activities and contacts, there is no better source than the *Correspondence* volumes of the new *Collected Works;* see

especially volumes ix–xii. Among others throughout the world Bentham corresponded with James Madison, John Quincy Adams, Simón Bolívar, and Bernardino Rivadavia in the Americas.

25. Bentham, *An Introduction to the Principles of Morals and Legislation*, ed. J. H. Burns and H. L. A. Hart (London: Athlone Press, 1970) [hereafter *IPML*], author's preface; see pp. 103–4 below.

26. Ibid., pp. 107–8 below; see also "Pannomial Fragments," pp. 241–45 below, and Lieberman, pp. 461–63 below.

27. "Indirect Legislation" (see note 8 above) is another part of this projected work, as is the entire *Of the Limits of the Penal Branch of Jurisprudence*, ed. Philip Schofield (Oxford: Oxford University Press, 2010). "Of the Limits of the Penal Branch of Jurisprudence" is the title of chapter 17 of *IPML* (not included in this volume); this book-length expansion of that chapter, reconstructed anew from manuscript, replaces *Of Laws in General*, H. L. A. Hart, ed. (London: Athlone Press, 1970).

28. The man-child caricature dates at least from William Hazlitt (*Spirit of the Age* [London: Henry Colburn, 1825], 5) and is probably only reinforced by Philip Lucas's and Anne Sheeran's retrospective diagnosis in "Asperger's Syndrome and the Eccentricity and Genius of Jeremy Bentham" (*Journal of Bentham Studies* 8 [2006]). The primitive theorist has recently been resurrected in Martha Nussbaum's "Mill Between Aristotle and Bentham" (*Daedalus* 133:2 [March 2004], 60–68).

29. For J. S. Mill on Bentham see "Remarks on Bentham's Philosophy" (1833) and "Bentham" (1838) in J. M. Robson, ed., *Essays on Ethics, Religion and Society* (Toronto: University of Toronto Press, 1969), 1–18, 75–115 (Robson, ed., *Collected Works of John Stuart Mill*, vol. x). References to Bentham are scattered throughout Mill's works, from *A System of Logic* (1843) through the *Autobiography* (1873).

30. Prolepsis involves projecting later meanings (uses) of words onto earlier uses of the same word (in prolepsis the word itself is not anachronistic). See the discussion of prolepsis, teleology, and other problems in treating some keywords of Anglophone political thought in J. C. D. Clark, *English Society, 1660–1832*, rev. ed. (Cambridge: Cambridge University Press, 2000), 1–13.

31. See Stephen G. Engelmann, "Mill, Bentham, and the Art and Science of Government," *Revue d'études benthamiennes* 4 (February 2008).

32. Hazlitt, *The Spirit of the Age*, 23; Karl Marx, *Capital* (New York: International Publishers, 1967 [1867]), i. 570–71. M. P. Mack includes additional insults from Ralph Waldo Emerson and Friedrich Nietzsche, among others, in the dismissal of these caricatures that begins her absorbing *Jeremy Bentham: An Odyssey of Ideas* (New York: Columbia University Press, 1963).

33. Jeremy Bentham, *First Principles Preparatory to Constitutional Code*, ed. Philip Schofield (Oxford: Clarendon Press, 1989), 211. Although this phrase wasn't published during Bentham's lifetime, it doesn't seem he would have minded if it had been. Bentham frequently mocked "matchless Constitution" (the English constitution); see for example "On Retrenchment," pp. 413 and 416 below.

34. A list of long-term and regular visitors (on top of the correspondents mentioned above in note 24) gives some idea of the range of his associations. The list would include, among others, Sarah Austin, Henry Brougham, Harriet Grote, John Neal, Daniel O'Connell, Francis Place, William Thompson, Anna Wheeler, and Frances Wright.

35. Negley Harte, "The Owner of Share No. 633: Jeremy Bentham and University College London," in *The Old Radical: Representations of Jeremy Bentham*, ed. Catherine Fuller (London: University College London, 1998), 5–8. Bentham's main educational treatise is *Chrestomathia* (Oxford: Clarendon Press, 1984 [1815–17]).

36. For pertinent contrasts on imperialism between Bentham on the one hand and James Mill and the utilitarian legacy on the other see Jennifer Pitts, *A Turn to Empire: The Rise of Imperial Liberalism in Britain and France* (Princeton: Princeton University Press, 2005), 101–62. Bentham's writings, including those in this volume, certainly express many of the prejudices that would be systematized in Victorian letters; but they contain surprisingly little of the accounts of civilizational development and hierarchy that would inform and sustain these systems.

37. The naturalistic fallacy seems to be involved for Moore whenever goodness is reduced to a natural object like pleasure. See G. E. Moore, *Principia Ethica* (Cambridge: Cambridge University Press, 1993 [1903]), esp. chap. 1 (but note Moore's self-criticism regarding his use of the phrase in an unpublished preface from 1922 included in this edition). See also the discussion in the Schofield essay below, pp. 425–27.

38. Halévy, *The Growth of Philosophical Radicalism*, 17 and passim.

39. F. A. Hayek, "The Principles of a Liberal Social Order," in *Studies in Philosophy, Politics, and Economics* (Chicago: University of Chicago Press, 1967), 160–63. Interestingly, Hayek was a founder of the first Bentham Committee at University College London (Stephen Kresge and Leif Wenar, eds., *Hayek on Hayek: An Autobiographical Dialogue* [New York: Routledge, 1994], 124), and one of Hayek's important contributions to economic thought — his emphasis on information, on the vast superiority of the knowledge of dispersed economic agents to that of any central authority — is straight out of Bentham (see the excerpt from *Manual of Political Economy*, pp. 314–16, and compare Hayek's "The Use of Knowledge in Society," *American Economic Review* 35 [September 1945], 519–30. For a comparison of Bentham and Hayek that demonstrates just how Benthamic

Hayek's work remained see Allison Dube, *The Theme of Acquisitiveness in Bentham's Political Thought* (New York: Garland, 1991), 198–313.

40. On push-pin and poetry see J. S. Mill, *Essays on Ethics, Religion and Society*, 113. The Bentham passage — Mill's quotation is a loose one — can be found in *The Rationale of Reward* (1825), Bowring, ii. 253: "Prejudice apart, the game of push-pin is of equal value with the arts and sciences of music and poetry. If the game of push-pin furnish more pleasure, it is more valuable than either. Everybody can play at push-pin: poetry and music are relished only by a few." Compare the passage in "Sex," below, p. 92 (push-pin has been used as a euphemism for sexual intercourse, although there is no reason to suspect innuendo here on Bentham's part). The literary-critical opposition between Bentham and Romanticism maps onto a broader contrast between mechanism and organicism; see, for example, Meyer Abrams's influential study *The Mirror and the Lamp* (Oxford: Oxford University Press, 1971), 300–303.

41. See John Rawls, *A Theory of Justice* (Cambridge: Harvard University Press, 1971), esp. 22–33. Although Rawls sees himself as presenting "an alternative to utilitarian thought generally" (22), his work is marked throughout by its utilitarian roots and affiliations; on these see S. M. Amadae, *Rationalizing Capitalist Democracy* (Chicago: University of Chicago Press, 2003).

42. See the discussion of "panopticism" in Michel Foucault, *Discipline and Punish*, trans. Alan Sheridan (New York: Pantheon, 1977 [1975]), 195–228, and "L'Oeil du Pouvoir" (The Eye of Power), the preface to a French edition of Bentham's panopticon writings (1977), in Foucault, *Power/Knowledge* (New York: Pantheon, 1980), 146–65. The work of Frances Ferguson represents an important exception to the rule that American post-Foucaultian or disciplinary readings of Bentham tend to reinforce the Rawlsian portrait; see for example her appreciation of Bentham in the fascinating *Pornography, the Theory: What Utilitarianism Did to Action* (Chicago: University of Chicago Press, 2004). Foucault's own immersion in Bentham goes well beyond panopticism and becomes increasingly evident in his late lectures; see Anne Brunon-Ernst, "Foucault Revisited," *Journal of Bentham Studies* 9 (2007).

43. The first article of the inaugural issue of the University College London Bentham Project's *The Bentham Newsletter* (1978) is titled "Revisionism in Bentham Studies"; two landmark revisionist studies are Frederick Rosen's *Jeremy Bentham and Representative Democracy* (Oxford: Oxford University Press, 1983), and Gerald Postema's *Bentham and the Common Law Tradition* (Oxford: Oxford University Press, 1986).

44. For example, P. J. Kelly's influential *Utilitarianism and Distributive Justice* (Oxford: Oxford University Press, 1990) responds directly to the Rawlsian critique.

45. Bentham would later revise this number upward to include, for example, an internal "sympathetic sanction," the contemplated force of which might restrain us from causing pain in others (assuming, for example, that we have no ties of antipathy with those others, in which case there is a strong counteracting pleasure to be experienced from their pain). See Bentham, *Deontology*, 201–05, and for the pleasures, interest, and motives of antipathy see http://www.ucl.ac.uk/Bentham-Project/info/table.htm or *Deontology*, 85 ("Table," no. 11).

46. *IPML*, chap. 3, pp. 132–33 below.

47. Note that because of ties and motives of sympathy and antipathy this is a hedonistic, but not an egoistic, theory of action. See David Lyons, *In the Interest of the Governed* (Oxford: Oxford University Press, 1991 [1973]).

48. Jeremy Bentham, *Writings on the Poor Laws, Volume I*, ed. Michael Quinn (Oxford: Clarendon Press, 2001), i, 202, 204.

49. Stephen G. Engelmann, "Imagining Interest," *Utilitas* 13:3 (2001), 289–322.

50. Bentham's version of laissez-faire is, however, different from Smith's; there are some respects in which it anticipates the "active laissez-faire" of today's neoliberalism (which is not the revival of classical liberalism it often purports to be). "The problem of neo-liberalism [is] not how to cut out or contrive a free space of the market within an already given political society, as in the liberalism of Adam Smith and the eighteenth century." It is "rather how the overall exercise of political power can be modeled on the principles of a market economy" (Michel Foucault, *The Birth of Biopolitics*, trans. Graham Burchell [New York: Palgrave Macmillan, 2008], 131 [lecture of 14 February 1979]). See Stephen G. Engelmann, *Imagining Interest in Political Thought*, 1–16, 141–49, and Engelmann, "Posner, Bentham and the Rule of Economy," *Economy and Society* 34:1 (2005), 32–50.

51. Bowring, i. 534; Bentham Papers, University College London Library MSS lxxxvii.168.

52. Jeremy Bentham, *Defence of Usury* (1787), in W. Stark, ed., *Jeremy Bentham's Economic Writings* (London: George Allen and Unwin, 1952), i. 123–207.

53. On the distinction between civil and criminal law see section 19 of *Of the Limits of the Penal Branch of Jurisprudence* (corresponding to chap. 17 of *Of Laws in General*).

54. On punishment, calibration, and the imagination in the Romantic era see Mark Canuel, *The Shadow of Death* (Princeton: Princeton University Press, 2007).

55. Even the legal positivist H. L. A. Hart is disturbed by the absence of an "authoritative legal reason" in Bentham; see the discussion in Hart, *Essays on Bentham* (Oxford: Oxford University Press, 1982), 253–55.

56. On tyranny as pain of disappointment, see Bowring, i. 325 ("Principles of the Civil Code"). Some caution must be exercised with regard to this text, which is

a retranslation of Dumont; there is no modern edition. But see also *Supply Without Burthen or Escheat Vice Taxation*, which was published by Bentham in 1795, in *Jeremy Bentham's Economic Writings*, i. 279–367, "Pannomial Fragments," p. 271, and "On Retrenchment," pp. 405–07 below.

57. Frederick Rosen, *Bentham, Byron, and Greece* (Oxford: Oxford University Press, 1992), 34.

58. Jeremy Bentham, *Constitutional Code*, vol. i, ed. F. Rosen and J. H. Burns (Oxford: Clarendon Press, 1983), 35–39 and passim. See the reference to this "fictitious tribunal" in "Constitutional Code Rationale," p. 236 below.

59. For a succinct reconstruction of this constitutional vision that explains how it relates to but is much more than a political economy, see David Lieberman, "Economy and Polity in Bentham's Science of Legislation," in Stefan Collini, Richard Whatmore, and Brian Young, eds., *Economy, Polity, and Society: British Intellectual History 1750–1950* (Cambridge: Cambridge University Press, 2000), 107–34.

60. For a discussion of "interest-begotten" and "authority-begotten" prejudice that contains elements of a sophisticated theory of ideology and self-deception see *The Book of Fallacies: From Unfinished Papers of Jeremy Bentham* (London: John and H. L. Hunt, 1824), 372–78. (Note, however, that the editor [Peregrine Bingham] acknowledges on p. iv that Bentham had nothing to do with overseeing the production of this work.) On press freedom see for example Jeremy Bentham, *On the Liberty of the Press, and Public Discussion* (London: William Hone, 1821); a new edition of this work is in production for a *Collected Works* volume, *Writings for Spain and Portugal*, ed. Catherine Pease-Watkin (Oxford: Clarendon Press, forthcoming). Publication of state proceedings and liberty of the press were already identified by Bentham as "expedients against misrule" in his early work on indirect legislation (*Works* i. 554–55, 570–78, and UC lxxxvii. 102–27). As technologies of publicity (see "Of Publicity" below, pp. 302–3) they would be fundamental in his late work to the establishment and maintenance of the Public Opinion Tribunal.

61. See Jeremy Bentham, *Rights, Representation, and Reform: Nonsense Upon Stilts and Other Writings on the French Revolution*, ed. Philip Schofield, Catherine Pease-Watkin, and Cyprian Blamires (Oxford: Clarendon Press, 2002), 231, 202–03, 214–17.

62. See the discussion in Schofield, *Utility and Democracy*, chap. 5 (109–36). See also Bentham's 1822 addition to *IPML*, chap. 1 note h, pp. 115–16 below and Lieberman, p. 471 below. Finally, see the reference to "hostile" interest in the *Rationale of Judicial Evidence* excerpt below, p. 224). We don't know just when this earlier material was composed; William Twining dates the relevant transi-

tional writing to the period 1803–12; see Twining, *Theories of Evidence: Bentham and Wigmore* (Palo Alto: Stanford University Press, 1986), 2.

63. See James E. Crimmins, "Religion, Utility and Politics: Bentham versus Paley," in Crimmins, ed., *Religion, Secularization and Political Thought: Thomas Hobbes to J. S. Mill* (London: Routledge, 1990), 130–52, and Crimmins, *Secular Utilitarianism* (Oxford: Oxford University Press, 1990).

64. See UC clxi. 15–19 ("Not Paul but Jesus — Plan").

65. For Bentham, the pleasures of what we call homophobia are like the pleasures of any cruelty or antipathy (see end of Bentham's long note l to *IPML* chap. 2, p. 129 below) Not condemnable in themselves — no pleasures are, but see p. 79 below — they are pleasures that should be frustrated or redirected rather than satisfied because of their harmful consequences. Throughout his work, Bentham consistently refuses a focus on character and its education or cure.

66. Not coincidentally, perhaps, the apogee of flawed thinking on these matters, from a Benthamic point of view, is found in statements by George W. Bush and Alan Greenspan. Bush rode to office on, among other things, a campaign about character (see, for example, the Republican Party nomination acceptance speech of 3 August 2000); Greenspan at one point diagnosed the financial crisis as a problem of reduced concern for reputation among individuals ("Markets and the Judiciary," Sandra Day O'Connor Project Conference, 2 October 2008).

67. Louis Crompton, "Jeremy Bentham's Essay on 'Paederasty': An Introduction," reprinted in Bhikhu Parekh ed., *Jeremy Bentham: Critical Assessments, vol. IV* (London: Routledge, 1993), 260.

68. UC lxxiv. 165. Note how opposite this is to Malthus's own similarly androcentric call for "moral restraint" in the 1803 and subsequent editions of his *Population*, and how different in sensibility it is from the tutelary prudence of much of the emerging neo-Malthusian birth control movement associated with Bentham's followers.

69. Pp. 50, 87, and 51–52.

Texts

I

Pleasure and Liberty

Sex
Edited by Philip Schofield

This is a preliminary text based on two sequences of manuscripts — the first written in 1814 for a penal code, and the second written in 1816 for a wide-ranging work on religion — which Bentham collected together with the view of integrating them; they are deposited in University College London Library, box 74, folios 35–222. Although there is some repetition and some lacuna, the text is reasonably complete and coherent.

The text has been established in line with the conventions adopted in the new authoritative edition of *The Collected Works of Jeremy Bentham*. Some of the more salient references have been lightly annotated — with thanks to Catherine Pease-Watkin, Michael Quinn, Catherine Fuller, George Letsas, and Allan Kershaw for help in this respect.

The following symbols are used: | | gap in manuscript; [. . . ?] illegible word(s); thus[?] doubtful reading; [thus] editorial insertion.

CHAPTER I.
Cause — Occasion — Apologetica[1]

[074–037]

If, then, by St Paul, the species of acts in question having indisputably been taken for the subjects of condemnation,[2] if by Jesus they have not been spoken of, nor, from what appears, considered, in that same light, then so it is that, taking the discourses of Paul for the standard of right and wrong — or at any rate for the standard of reference — here — on the part of Jesus — has been an omission. Thereupon comes the question — Jesus, in respect of this omission, has he done wrong: his scheme of instruction — ought it on that account to be regarded as imperfect? Such was the question and, after an examination — the closeness and laboriousness of which seems little in danger of being found disputable — the answer, it has been found, could not be given any otherwise than the *negative*.

Under these circumstances an option seemed to be called for — called for as matter of inevitable necessity, between Paul and Jesus: in so much that, if Jesus be to be justified, Paul can not but be condemned.
[074–038]

§ 2. Apology for this work — dangers attendant on it

In the present has been found one of those unhappy occasions — on which, in his endeavours to render service to his fellow creatures, a man must expose himself to their reproach: and assuredly, of all the occasions which it is possible for reflection — or so much as for imagination — to embrace, not one can be found on which, whether it be considered in respect of intensity or of extent, the load to which it is necessary he should expose himself is by many degrees equally great and appalling.

Never, surely, except such as expose the author to punishment at the hands of the law on the score of treason or other such offence against the existing government — never did work appear from which, in the way of personal advantage and mischief — those words being taken in their ordinary sense — never one from which, in the way of reputation — never one from which at the hands of public opinion — a man found so much to fear, so little to hope.
[074–039]

Not only in their result, and in their particulars as they lead to that result, are the considerations which the work is composed of thus formidable and repulsive, but at the very outset and even at and from the very first word. The veil which the law of delicacy throws over the subject in question must from the very first entrance upon it be compleatly drawn aside.

True it is that so far as concerns the law of delicacy, were this all, the indulgence given to the writer on medical subjects on all occasions and in all his forms might, in the character of an excuse or even of a justification, and as such for a compleat protection, be relied on without difficulty. But here, not so much in that cause of disgust which is produced by the mere violation of those rigid laws, as from the results that will be found deduced by it, will the danger and difficulty be seen to have its root.

Of the present enquiry the sole objects are general utility — or the maximum of human happiness — and in so far as conducive to that object, the truth of things or, in one word, useful truth. But in the whole assemblage of thinking and talking beings, in comparison of those in whose regard the law of delicacy as applied to this subject occupies a much higher place, the number of those in whose regard the maximum of happiness occupies the highest place, is small indeed.

[074–040]

Under these circumstances, a warning which, for the sake of the reader as well as for the sake of the writer, it is absolutely necessary to give is — that, unless the regard for human happiness has such an influence over his mind as, in pursuit of that object, to enable and force it to endure from beginning to end the extremity of disgust — disgust in its most repulsive form — he would do well to close the book at this very place, and not suffer his eyes to behold another syllable.

CHAPTER 2.

Physical division of the subject

[074–042]

In some sorts of instances the act is regularly exercised, in others irregularly: in this distinction may be seen the source of the first division which there will be need to make.

By *regularly* is meant in a manner conformable to rule: viz. the rule prescribed by public opinion in the community to which the party belongs: by irregularity in a manner unconformable to that same rule. This rule, then, what is it? it can be no other than that which has been derived from the observation of the mode of thinking which, on the part of members in general, has most extensively had place.

Among the sorts of instances in which it is regularly exercised, in some it is exercised in such a manner as to be capable of being prolific, in others in such a manner as *not* to be capable of being productive of that effect. Say — *mode potentially prolific* — mode *not potentially prolific,* or say essentially unprolific.

Cases in which it is not potentially prolific are the case in which the female is already impregnated, and the case in which, by reason of relative bodily infirmity, whether produced by old age or by any other less extensively operating cause, she is unsusceptible of being impregnated. As to the case in which she is rendered unsusceptible of that condition by immaturity of age, this belongs to the other branch of this first division — viz. the case of irregular exercise.

Say 1. impregnation already performed — 2. impregnation impossible.

[074–043]

In both instances the operation has for its *effect* the preservation of the species. But in both has it for its object — for its end in view — the production of that effect? No: nor yet in either. The operation by which the matter of nourishment is taken in is among the first operations which, as in the case of other animals, so in the case of the human animal, is performed: months and even years before the time at which any such conception as that of the cessation of life considered as the effect of a deficiency in the necessary quantity of nourishment can find entrance into the juvenile mind.

So again as to that operation, which under certain circumstances has for its effect the making an addition to the number of individuals of the species in question at that time in existence, and thence giving continuance to the species — for its object has it essentially or even generally any such object? By no means. On the part of the inferior animals, it never has any such object: if, on the part of the human animal, it is directed to any such object, it is only in a highly cultivated state of the species, and in that state only in a comparatively small number of instances, and as it were by accident. The titled aristocrat of Europe, yes: — but the savage of Asia, of Africa, of America, what cares he about the continuance of his race? If in the least opulent classes of the community, which are always the most numerous, the only case in which it has place is the sentimental and comparatively rare case where, by the strength of the affection between the two individuals thus united, a desire is produced of seeing a token of their mutual felicity and a security for the continuance of it produced in the person of a third being who partakes of both. But this object would not be thus sentimental as it is if it were not correspondently rare.

[074–044]

Thus close is the analogy between the one of these modes of action and the other. The doctrine of final causes — of a universal creator, directed in his actions by the view of a general result and the desire of effecting it — is this notion to be admitted? — then are they both of them means directed to the same end.

On every question of moral propriety, considerable, it is evident, can not but be the light reflected on the subject from this source. True it is, analogy is not itself utility: upon the effect of this or that mode of action upon human happiness it exerts not any direct influence. True: but mighty is the influence which it is wont to exercise upon the judgements formed and the affections entertained by men in relation to it.

[074–045]

So many distinguishable senses, so many sources of present pleasure or of exemption from present pain.

In some of these instances, the present pleasure or exemption has for its ulterior, and more or less remote result, a good of a more important nature: in others not.

Those which present themselves as being in the former case are the following: | |

Those which present themselves as being in the latter case are the following: | |

The circumstance of its being attended with an ulterior effect good or bad, as it may happen, with reference not only to the individual in question, but to the whole species to which he belongs, and in respect of which it is impossible to foreknow whether it will be in the one case or in the other — does it in any instance, and if in any, in what, and for what cause, afford a conclusive reason for abstaining from that good which, by being immediate, is certain, and of which the value can not be misconceived?

[074–046]

Now as to cases in which the exercise is regarded as irregular.

Now comes the task of the moral or ethical anatomist: now comes the case in which disgust awaits the reader, and through that disgust, reproach the author. Now comes the trial of the patience of the one, and thence of the fortitude of the other.

Case 1. The operation solitary, or say single-seated — no second person concerned in it.

2. Persons two — one of each sex — but the two not united in the artificial and pneumatic bonds of the matrimonial contract.

3. Persons two as before: but one or both bound by the matrimonial contract with another person.

4. Sexes — the two corresponding and opposite both concerned as before — but on one part or the other or both, the age below the age susceptible of impregnation, active or passive. Between the two persons no matrimonial contract can in this case have had place: the sanction of law not being obtainable for it.[a]

5. Sexes, both concerned as before; but on the one side or the other the part of the body employed not susceptible of being contributory to impregnation, and thence regarded as improper.

5. Number of persons concerned plural, but the sexes not the cor-

---

a. Where, be the age of the male what it may, the age of the female is below ten, the act is, in the instance of the male, by English law placed in the list of offences, and the punishment attached to it is death. In the instance of the male, let the age of the male be ever so immature, the act has no place in the list of offences. See further Ch. | |.[3]

respondent and opposite, but the same: in the first place say both males, impregnation consequently impossible.

6. Sexes the same; — but both female: consequently impregnation equally impossible.[b]

[074–047]

[7.] Number of the parties whose bodies are the seats of the operation, plural: but one of them, though a living animal, an animal not belonging to the category of *persons:* an animal of a species different from the human.

This case exhibits two sub-cases: 1. the agent human, the patient not human: 2. the agent not human, the patient human.[c]

[074–048]

[8.] One of the bodies concerned not belonging to the class of animated beings. This will naturally be considered as coinciding with the case of solitary gratification.[d]

[074–062]

b. Under the English law, between male and male, this species of irregular intercourse is punished with death: between female and female, it is left altogether exempt from punishment. See further Ch. ⌐ ⌐.

c. In both these cases, under English law, the operation constitutes an offence punished with death.

Suppose the species the same on both sides: sexes correspondent and opposite: but on one side life extinct. English lawyers, what would they do with it? in this case, as in so many others, they would do with it as they pleased. An humane and unprejudiced Judge would regard it as coming under Case 1: and thence as standing exempt from all punishment: a prejudiced and misery-manufacturing or misery-manufacture-loving Judge might perhaps make a separate case of it and, after thus separating it from the rest, then by analogy applying it to some one of the others and thence fitting it up in the character of a punishable offence.[4]

Other circumstances remaining as before, sexes now suppose the same: the patient no longer endued with life. The humane Judge would probably refer this case as well as the other to Case 1: the tiger Judge to Case 5. To this case at any rate he would refer it in theory: but in practice the law of evidence would stand in his way: for to make a perfect case — to give compleatness to the demand for punishment — those rules require emission: and in this case as in others, a dead man tells no tales. — Well, but suppose the place of the dead man supplied by an anatomist? Ah! how dear would this anatomist be to certain Judges?

d. This case seems beyond danger of dispute referable to Case 1. No room for the claw of the tiger here.

CHAPTER 3.

Moral division of the subject

Thus much as to that division of the subject which in the first instance is taken from a *physical* source.

Now for a division drawn from an ethical source. Under the principle of utility there can be but one such source, viz. the effect of the operation on the sum of happiness — the operation is preponderantly noxious or it is *not*.

Note here that unless and until effects not only noxious, but noxious in a preponderant degree, can be shewn to flow from it, the operation can not but be acknowledged to be not simply innoxious but positively beneficial: for, unless attended with pleasure, it never is performed: and if pleasure be not an ingredient in the composition of happiness — a species and the only positive species of which happiness is made — exemption from pain being the only other species, and that but a negative one — then nothing is.

[074–063]

By a rational system of classification, grounded on the principle of utility, the labour of the enquirer may on this occasion be rendered an easy task. In the works of Mr Bentham, this rational system has been found.[e]

1. Noxiousness to the operator himself, and him alone, on the score of health. In the case in question, whether the operation be of that quality or not is a question that belongs, if the operator be in an adult state, to the cognizance of the medical adviser — if in an unadult state, to that of the parent or his substitute, the guardian: at any rate, if the party concerned be but one — in other words the operation solitary — it will not belong to the cognizance of the Judge.

The demand which this case presents is a demand for prudential care on the part of the individual himself, or those under whose guardianship his condition in life has placed him, but not for any interference on the part of the legislator. By error in respect of frequency or even in respect of time, consequences destructive to health and even to life may have place even in the bonds of the purest wedlock: and neither has human tyranny nor human folly ever swollen to any such pitch as to take the promotion of error in this shape for a subject of direct legislation, much or still less to assign to the error itself a place in the list of punishable crimes.

[074–064]

2. Noxiousness to the operator himself and him alone, on the score of

e. See Bentham, *Introd.* or Bentham par Dumont, *Legisl. civ. et pen.*[5]

reputation: to the operator, if no more than one: to the operators or concurrers, if more than one.

To this case, with little variation, the same observations apply as to the case last mentioned. Upon each man's own reputation it belongs, according to his condition in life as above, according as it is under his own care or under that of some other agent that he acts, — to set a value: it is for him to pronounce of which of the two articles the value is the greatest — the good consisting of the present pleasure, or the evil consisting of the future contingent loss in the article of reputation.

[074–065]

3. Noxiousness to one of the two or more parties, the party or parties being either actually repugnant, or at least not consenting, or being so circumstanced in respect of infirmity of mind, by reason of immaturity or otherwise, that in their instance consent is not considered as possessing that exculpative virtue which it is considered as possessing in some other instances.[6]

[074–066]

4. Noxiousness with reference to a third person — a determinate individual.

[074–067]

5. Noxiousness with reference to third persons at large: i.e. to individuals indeterminate in respect of identity and number.

[074–071r1]

CHAPTER 4.

State of the public mind in England in relation to the irregularities of the sexual appetite

Of the state of the public mind in England in relation to this subject, it will not be possible, if taking the subject in its full amplitude, to express in a very small compass any such representation as shall approach in any degree to the truth.

Of such varieties as the nature of the case seemed to admitt of, a methodized list has been given above.[7] Among the articles which compose it, some there are of which, so rarely do they come under notice, the public mind can hardly be said to take under its cognizance: on others it pours forth the full vial of its wrath.

Of so vast a difference in a case in which the nature of the case considered in itself presents so little, if the cause be asked for, the answer will probably be found in a great measure in the state of the law. In this way whatsoever may have place in practice, decency, according to the prevailing notions attached to that word, will in general keep it excluded out of the field of conversation: the cases and almost the only cases in which it makes its appearance in that field are those in which they are dragged into notice by the hand of the law.

[074–071r2]

On comparing one with another the two aggregates, towards the noxious class it is comparatively indulgent: for the innoxious it reserves the hottest of its fire. Not that even in this case, as between the members of this division, there is any thing like approach to consistency in the aspect shewn to them. In the case where the intercourse is between two persons of the same sex are included two *sub-cases:* one where it is between male and male, the other where it is between female and female. In the latter of these two so exactly corresponding cases, scarcely does the public mind appear to bestow any portion of its notice: but in this way whatever is deficient in this one is amply made up by what is bestowed upon the other. Partly on account of the probable comparative unfrequency, partly on account of the difficulty attached to the extraction of evidence, even on the supposition of the existence of the practice, that which has place between female and female has been left unnoticed by the law: and in this last-mentioned circumstance may be seen another cause of the apathy which, in relation to this one of the two sub-cases, has place in the public mind. But for its repose in this sub-case, it makes ample amends by its activity in the other.

[074–072]

Of the several cases in which the quality of noxiousness may be and has been shewn to belong to the act, *adultery*[f] and *rape,* especially when in the latter case a female in the state of virginity is the subject of it, present the clearest and strongest marks of that guilty character: *adultery* on account of the magnitude to which the mischief is *capable* of rising in the case of the individual injured by the violation of this most important of all contracts;

f. On this occasion adultery is considered rather in respect of that degree up to which it is capable of rising in the scale of injury, than in respect of its average height: for though in some instances the mischief of it is capable perhaps of surmounting that of any other injury, yet in other cases — and those perhaps the most frequently recurring — it stands at zero: for such, as between instance and instance, to the party who, if there be injury, is the object of it, may be the difference between value and value of the possession which, by this breach of the contract, is lost. The adulteress is (suppose) a common prostitute: the possession having thus compleatly lost its value, injury to the husband of the adulteress has no place.

rape, on account of the extent over which the public alarm, produced by the sort of war thus waged against one half of the species, will on such an occasion be apt to spread. But compared even with that produced by a case of sexual intercourse, even though on both sides voluntary, between male and male, the anger excited by a case of rape — though, except in the case of an anterior and voluntary intercourse between the same parties, the mischief admitts not of any considerable palliative — is very inconsiderable.

Of the place occupied on this occasion in the scale of intensity by the dissocial passion, the consideration of the causes belongs to another head:[8] on the present occasion the sole subject of consideration is the effect itself. [074–073]

In Scotland the degree of general exasperation may be stated as standing at much the same pitch as in England. In Ireland, as rising if possible still higher: and so in the Anglo-American States.

Italy may be stated as the country in which the degree of exasperation produced, if any, stands at the opposite point of the scale. In Italy, in some parts at least of that country, for a demand of this nature, a supply may, or at least not long ago might, be obtained from the one sex with little less facility than from the other. In France, to the public mind, it has always been an object of indifference: and to the laws, though in their tenor still more severe than in Britain — burning alive being the punishment, yet in the execution, for more than the last half century, an object of connivance.

In Germany, the example of Frederic the great[9] of itself, not to speak of a Landgrave of Hesse and other sovereigns, would have sufficed to procure for this propensity, at the hands of the public mind, if not favour, a pretty extensively prevalent indifference.

In Holland, the example, howsoever studiously concealed, of the King which that country gave to England,[10] added to the recent example of a not long since departed Prince, must, notwithstanding the rigorous execution of the laws upon such transgressors as were not above their power, have in a degree more or less considerable been productive of the like effect.

Further to the North, the propensity, though being but now and then manifested, seems to have been little noticed. [074–074]

In all these countries, the law in this part of the field having been copied from the Mosaic, the aspect of it towards the transgression has been in nearly equal degrees severe: in the degree of steadiness and consistency given to the execution — in this has been the difference. In all these countries, the official establishment furnishes a public prosecutor, without whose active concurrence, generally speaking, punishment can in no case be inflicted. In him, therefore, resides not indeed exactly the power of pardoning, but a power still more efficient. For of the power of pardoning, even though it be antecedently to conviction, the exercise involves in it a certain degree of publicity: of publicity whereby the attention of the public is to a certain extent attracted to the subject, and the public mind set to work: and it is obvious how much more perfect [is] that degree of impunity which is the work of causes purely negative, such as inaction and silence.

Accordingly, to all those countries, Britons, whose misfortune it is to have become notorious in respect of this propensity, fly for refuge from the flame by which, in their own country, they would be consumed. But on this part of the subject, more in another place.[11]

[074–075]

CHAPTER 5.

Origin of the horror with which certain of these irregularities, and thence those who practiced them, have been regarded

Asceticism and physical antipathy — in the conjunct influence of these two principles of action in the character of causes may the origin of the horror in question be found.

Asceticism, as is known to every body by whom the import of the word is known, has its origin in religion. It consists in sacrifice. To draw his picture of the Almighty, man looks in his own glass, and with a little heightening pourtrays his own image. In the case of visible pictures, this is true in the literal sense: in the case of invisible ones, it has all that sort of truth of which that species of representation is susceptible.

To those who humble themselves before him, man is not always unwilling to shew marks of favour. But for this favour, in some shape or other he expects something in the way of return. If nothing else be obtainable or thought fit to be obtained, humiliation, in the character of a pledge of general obsequiousness, is not altogether without its value.

[074–076]

Thus it is with man: thus it is with the God man makes to himself. The return which this God of his making expects is called *sacrifice*.

The more ardent the fears and the hopes of which his God is the object and of the realization of which the favour or the wrath of that same God is the looked for source, the more strenuous his wishes to make sure of that favour and save himself from that wrath — the more strenuous those wishes, the greater the sacrifices he is disposed to make.

To this temper of the mind, whatsoever was in the eyes of the votary most pretious and at the same time in his power was taken for the subject of this sacrifice. The priest, being the interpreter of the will of the deity whom he announced, presented an irresistible claim to his portion of this sacrifice.

The Gods were subtle aërial beings. When butchers' meat was the subject of the sacrifice, the gasseous matter was best or alone suited to their refined tastes. The solid residuum was best suited to the physical faculties, and satisfied the wishes of their holy interpreters.

In the wine countries, butchers' meat and wine constituted those articles which, for ordinary use, [were][12] most valuable. In honour of the God, the meat was, as the word is rendered, burnt: as it might and ought to be rendered, roasted. Of this roast meat, the priest[s] obtained the part best suited to their demand: the Gods what best suited theirs. Of the wine, a portion was poured out on the ground or it would not, along with the exhalation of the meat, have found its way to the nostrils of the deity. But in this shape likewise, so [he was][13] first served, a small portion of the sacrifice satisfied the refined taste of the God: the rest was left by him to reward the zeal and fidelity of the holy men, his chosen servants.

[074–077]

The God of Moses, though at times greedy enough, was at other times sick of these vulgar sacrifices. As men's tastes grew more refined, so did the tastes of their Gods, so did the sacrifices allotted for the gratification of those tastes.

Meat and wine were the exterior instruments of certain pleasures. These for a time sufficed the appetites and suited the taste of their Gods. But those were among the things which every man had not to offer.

The pleasures, these were things which every man had to offer: these were things which by every man might be sacrificed.

Of all pleasures, the most exquisite were the pleasures of the sexual appetite. Of all objects of sacrifice, these were best adapted to the nature of a God of the most refined class — of a God taken at the highest pitch of refinement and civilization. The pleasure would indeed have been sensual: but the sacrifice of it was the reverse of sensual: it was a sort of negative sacrifice: nothing imaginable could be more refined.

The pleasures could not be reaped in perfection without more or less of impurity — physical impurity. But the sacrifice of this pleasure was the very reverse of impurity: it was purity itself.[g]

[074–078]

Next came the matter of nutrition: food and drink.

g. See Ch. | l. Purity and Impurity.[14]

By sacrifices made in this shape — sacrifices regularly and periodically repeated — titles to exemption from everlasting torment accompanied with the possession of everlasting felicity continue to be made under the Church of Rome. Piety is manifested by devouring the inhabitants of the waters instead of the inhabitants of the land: piety is manifested by eating in the egg the inhabitants of the air, instead of waiting till they become chickens.

By the Church of England, the same commodities are purchased upon cheaper terms: the time of dinner is retarded: the appetite sharpened: the pleasure of eating encreased: and this called a fast. Victories are the article in the purchase of which this sacrifice, such as it is, seems chiefly to be employed. To the commission of murder in the wholesale way upon neighbours under the name of enemies, sin is, it seems, the great obstacle: by dining an hour or two later on some one day, eating or not eating on that same day a quantity of fish with or without butchers' meat, the sin is removed, and victory takes its place in the room of it.

[074–079]

When once it is become a settled matter that heaven and licence of absence from hell are to be purchased upon these terms — purchased by giving up what a man likes, or in the vulgar phrase quarrelling with his bread and butter, reasons for sacrifice can never be wanting. Some articles are sacrificed because their value is so great: for the greater the value given to God, the greater the value of what will be to be received from him in return. On this principle it is that all enjoyment derivable from intercourse with the correspondent and opposite sex has found such multitudes to sacrifice it. Other articles are sacrificed because the value of them is so small: little as it costs to give them up to God, there is no saying to how great an amount value may be given for them in return.

Consistency is not to be found in man. In the Greek Church fasts are observed with a degree of rigour not to be matched in any other. But intoxication affords a pleasure for which, in the estimation of the Russian priest or congregation, neither among the pleasures of heaven nor among the pains of hell, i.e. among the exemptions corresponding to those pains, any equivalent is to be found. To perform a religious ceremony is to sacrifice to the God the time and labour expended in the performance. In the Russian Church, brandy is too dear to be sacrificed: but when expended in ceremonies, time and labour are not grudged. For in these ceremonies, the principal if not sole actor is the priest: and of this time and labour, prostration of understanding and will[15] on the part of the congregation, seeers and hearers, is the fruit.

[074–080]

Readily indeed is the sacrifice made of a pleasure for which a man has no relish: and if he have not only no relish for it, but an aversion to it, the stronger the aversion, the more glad the sacrifice. In this state of things the principle of antipathy — physical antipathy — joins in the sacrifice: thus combined the two principles operate with united force in passing condemnation on the act. From the act to the agent, the agent not being a man's self, the transition in such a case is easy: applied to the act, the antipathy is of the physical cast: applied to the agent, it assumes a moral cast. Of this morality, a congenial sort of logic is the fruit: this man does what I should not like to do: therefore, he deserves punishment at my hands. The more vehemently I should dislike to do what he does, the greater the punishment he deserves.

Here, then, is a species of sacrifice in the making of which an incomparably better bargain is made than by any other: in the ordinary case, the pleasure sacrificed is a man's own pleasure: in this case, it is another man's pleasure. Giving meat of one's own to be roasted for a dinner to God and Priest would cost money: taking a man and roasting him costs nothing: and moreover it makes a spectacle. On these considerations, about the middle of the last century a French Abbé — the Abbé Des Fontaines — was roasted alive at Paris.[16]

[074–081]

Of the effects of this combination of asceticism and antipathy, more ardent than all the genuine ones put together, Paul the pseudo-Apostle exhibited the first known example.

On this subject Jesus had been altogether silent. He had called for no such sacrifice: by him no such antipathy had been expressed.

Among the multitudes to whom in such a multitude of places Paul addressed himself, it would be strange indeed if the practices in question, eccentric as they were, did not find many by whom the preference given to pleasure in these irregular forms to the same pleasure in the more regular form was but slight, many who had no relish for them, still more to whom they were objects of physical abhorrence: to the two last of these, the abstinence would be no sacrifice: and to those to whom it was in some degree a sacrifice, the pleasure of sitting in judgment and passing judgment on their neighbours — the pleasure of the triumph which the praying Pharisee enjoyed over the praying Publican[17] — would afford an equivalent for the pleasure lost by the sacrifice.

Without hope from heaven or fear from hell — without equivalent in any shape other than the gratification afforded in that same way to the passion of pride — a set of heathen philosophers — the Stoics — gave up or professed at least to give up these in the lump with a whole multitude of other pleasures:

pleasures in the choice of which not more consistency was manifested than in so many other sacrifices. While yet remaining in the bosom of a flower, the essential oil of a rose might be applied to the organ of smell without reproach: but where separated from the flower and collected in drops, it became a profane and then (ask *Seneca*[18] else) no expression of abhorrence could be strong enough for the wretch who had thus contaminated himself with it.

[074–082]

For calling for the sacrifice of these pleasures at the hands of all those in whom he could expect to find obedience, Paul, in the vocation he had embraced, wanted not for other motives. What has at all times been visible to all leaders of sects was sufficiently visible to Paul, viz. the more sedulously men were occupied by other pursuits of all sorts — whether pursuits of business or pursuits of pleasure — the less sedulously would they be occupied with the pursuits in which it was his design and endeavour to engage them: the pursuits in which he led and they followed: the pursuits by which they were made sources of the good things of this wicked world — distinction, power, and money — to himself: the pursuits by means of which they became instruments in his hands. Such was his sensibility to these considerations — so far was he led in his race for power — that ever and anon not content with calling for the sacrifice of the irregularities of the appetite by which alone the species is continued, he was for calling for the sacrifice of it in its most regular forms — not only pæderasty, but fornication — not only fornication, but marriage — was to him an object of condemnation. If in any one instance, say reason and consistency, then why not in all? But he saw enough to be assured that the call for such a sacrifice would not be obeyed by any number of persons considerable enough to effect by their abstinence any formidable reduction in the population of his votaries — of the subjects to his celestial throne.

[074–083]

By Jesus himself no call having been made for any such sacrifices — for the sacrifice of any of these pleasures — no wonder that among the earliest embracers of his religion traces should still remain of the existence of associations by whom no such sacrifices were professed to be made. But of this mention may come to be made in another place.[19]

[074–084]

In one of Lucian's dialogues,[20] a lover of the opposite sex and a lover of his own sex carry on a debate on the question which of the two tastes is the best. By reasoning it is not very common for a man to be made to change his opinion: still less common for him to be made to change his taste. To every man that which is his own taste is the best taste: to say that it is, is tautology: to say that it is not, is self-contradiction. In the case of the fine arts, when the object is of a complex nature, by being made to observe this or that circumstance which he had not observed before — this or that feature of defect or excellence which till now had passed unobserved — a man may now and then be made to change his taste. But in the field of appetite — of physical appetite — so simple is the object, no place can be found for any such discovery. The man to whom habit has rendered the use of tobacco a source of gratification, whether in the way of snuffing, smoking or mastication, by nothing that any one can say to him will he be convinced that that taste of his is a bad taste. Let him see that by taking it he inflicts annoyance on those in whose presence he is taking it, you may make him abstain from it, but never can you make him in his own mind acknowledge it to be a bad taste. [074–085]

In Lucian, to prove that his own taste is the best, the lover of the opposite sex tells a story: it is of a statue of Venus, with which a young man was so enamoured, that, without waiting for its undergoing the metamorphosis experienced by that of Pygmalion,[21] he stole into the temple in which it stood, and contrived to be locked up all night with the representation of the Goddess that he might pursue his amour with leisure. Thus much the lover of his own sex admitted to be true, but on the strength of a circumstance which, though true, he said had not been mentioned by his antagonist, he claimed the victory. The part to which the lover had paid his addresses was not any part which is peculiar to the female sex, but a part which is common to that sex and the male: and of the truth of this part of the case, marks were found, he said, which left no doubt: and of the two, sure enough these are the only parts of which any visible likeness could be exhibited by the sculptor's art.

[074–086]

Among the Athenians, pæderasty — the gratification of this appetite by a male by means of a male — was a capital crime: in England, it could not be a higher one. But what the crime consisted in was — not the identity of sex, but the condition in life, joined to the age, of that one of the two actors by whom the part of the patient was performed: if it were that of a slave, it was all lawful and right: and among the Athenians, at least when they were in their glory, for one freeman, there were ten slaves.

Not that by this law any proof was afforded of the real state of public opinion. Never was law more compleatly a dead letter.

The wonder is how a law, and that so highly penal an one, to which no man had ever paid any regard had ever come to be made.

Not but that when two men were at enmity with one another, the two Orators Aeschines and Demosthenes for example, each of them, when upon the look out for matter of vituperation to throw in the teeth of his enemy, would object to him this practice.[22] Yes: but on what score? not on the score of the mode of gratification, but on the score of the excess with which it was supposed to be accompanied, just as in England an whoremaster will be levelled by another with the multitude of his amours: the being to such a degree devoted to sensuality, to the pleasures of sense, not the particular form which happened to be the object of his choice.

[074–087]

So among the Romans. Without giving the smallest offence, a man avowedly for this purpose would buy in open market any number of slaves he chose.

CHAPTER 6.

Causes of the proscription to which these propensities are subjected — viz. Well-principled and ostensible causes — viz. considerations deduced from the principle of utility

[074–129]

I. Injury to population. Of all the alleged effects which in this case have been brought to view in the character of grounds for legal punishment, this is by far the most plausible. But the more closely and thoroughly it is examined into, the more plainly it will be perceived to be unsubstantial and ineffective.

1. It is incapable of having any effect on population.

2. In regard to population, its effect, if it had any, would be rather favourable than unfavourable.

3. If it had any effect unfavourable to population, punishment applied to such practices would not be a proper course for filling up the supposed deficiency.[23]

[074–130]

1. It is not capable of producing any effect on population.

The apprehension, real or pretended, of seeing the quantity of population in any country suffer diminution from any such cause, is upon the face of it so palpably absurd that it is not easy to speak of it with that seriousness which the importance of the subject demands. Not more absurd would be the apprehension of the effect of a famine as about to be produced by the taste for chewing tobacco. For keeping up the quantity of population up to the level at which it is found existing in any given country at any given point of time, less than an hundredth or a two-hundredth part of the capacity of procreation would, if reduced to act, suffice: if reduced to that regular mode of which parturition is the result.

[074–131]

2. If [by] the irregularity in question population were capable of being affected in any way, the way in which it would be affected would rather be favourable than unfavourable.

From excess of population comes no small part of the unhappiness with which, and in a degree proportionable to that of its civilization, the civilized part of the population of the globe, and in particular that of the British empire, is afflicted. By any circumstance, if any circumstance there were other than human suffering, by which a check could be applied to the effect of this tendency, the balance on the side of happiness would be encreased.

Urged by desire, the opposite and corresponding sexes contract this union. But setting aside the instances to the contrary produced by casual imprudence, the female will not join in it unless her partner of the other sex will, in and by the matrimonial contract, bind himself, amongst other per-formances, to continue with her during their joint lives in the bonds of the same engagement, and in the mean time maintain, untill they are of an age to maintain themselves, all the children, in what number so ever they may be, of whom it may happen to this continued union to be productive.

[074–132]

Here, then, from each pair are produced children in such numbers, as but for the variety of accidental causes from which the number reaching to such a prolific age as to become parents is subjected [to] defalcation would, at the end of a comparatively small number of generations, rise to a number prodigiously superior to the greatest ever actually exemplified under the most favourable circumstances. The average stock of necessaries, but more particularly of necessaries in the shape of food, that can be produced by a married couple in a given number of years not being by a great deal ade-quate to the maintenance of the average number of children begotten be-tween them in that space of time, a portion more or less considerable of the whole number of these children necessarily die: die for want of that support — partly in the shape of necessaries, partly in the shape of attendance — which, in a state of opulence, a married couple are both able and willing to procure for theirs. Since, then, if they come into life, quit it in early youth they must, the earlier the time at which they quit it, so much the better for all parties — the children themselves as well as their parents. The quantity of care and attendance bestowed in waste by the parents is so much the less, the pain of regret produced by the loss is so much the less, and on the part of the children themselves, so is the intermediate suffering produced by the deficiency of necessaries or attendance.

[074-133]

By consigning to an immediate and altogether imperceptible termination of existence all those who otherwise would perish sooner or later by a still untimely death, preceded by a long course of suffering in the shape of hunger, disease, and misery in an infinite variety of shapes, how prodigious is the quantity of suffering that might be saved in and to the world! Of this misery, under the Roman laws and customs no small proportion was doubtless saved. At all times the father was master of the life of his children: and though, doubtless, by one consideration or another — such as fondness for the mother — sympathy produced by the principle of association — many a life, which might have been made to terminate without suffering, was spared till it had for a length of time been embittered by a long-protracted course of suffering, yet still the number of those parents by whom use was made of the power given to them by the law used not to be inconsiderable.

[074-134]

If benevolence — sympathy for mankind — or rather for sensitive beings in all their forms — were in reality as common as it is supposed to be — the permission, the effect of which would thus beyond all possibility of dispute be the making, in so far as it was put to use, a defalcation, and that a very ample one, from the sum of human misery, would, in all civilized nations at least, be universally established by the non-enactment of the correspondent penal law in question.

Unhappily, of this salutary principle the quantity is far from being so great as that which some external appearances seem to indicate. To how deplorable an extent, either some other affection usurps the place of it, or, if it has place, being unaccompanied with reflection, it is upon the whole productive rather of mischief to mankind than benefit to mankind.

Thus in the case of infanticide, performed by the mother — to preserve her reputation from destruction. By an absurd and indiscriminating penal law, the mother is consigned to an ignominious death. This law, by what consideration has it been produced? — Partly by antipathy towards the mother produced by sympathy towards the infant, partly for want of the reflection by which this case would be shewn to have nothing but the mere physical appearance in common with those really mischievous acts which, under the name of murder, are punished with that same punishment.

[074-135]

If in the whole field of sensitive existence there be a proper object of sympathy, it is the mother: a being who, to the bodily agonies of parturition, adds the mental agony produced by the immediate prospect of everlasting infamy — of an ignominy to which no end is foreseen but that of life — the prospect of seeing affection, wheresoever she has been accustomed to experience it, on a sudden transformed into contempt — of seeing herself on a footing worse than that of a mere stranger with every person in whose company she had been in use to find a source of pleasure. Such is the being to whose cost, for no rational cause that can be mentioned, antipathy is in every breast substituted to the affection directly opposite.

If, in the whole field of sensitive existence, there be an unfit object of sympathy — at least in so far as regards the difference between life and death, it is the new-born infant of this same mother. From existence, if continued to it, it has every thing to fear: there can not be a sensitive being, and in particular there can not be a human being, in whose instance the probable ratio of unhappiness to happiness is so great — there can not be a human being to which, reckoning from birth to death, life is so likely to be a nuisance.

[074–137]

It possesses not as yet any such faculty as that of reflection: it has no anticipation of the future: it has no recollection of the past: scarcely can it be said to be possessed of so much as the faculty of consciousness. Of life it may, with unerring certainty, be deprived without any sense of suffering: for before it can have had time to suffer, all sensation is at an end. Of a hundred thousand new-born infants, the existence might be terminated without a quantity of suffering equal to that which is commonly produced by the drawing of one tooth. In the compass of a few hours, the same termination would be produced by mere neglect: but that neglect would indeed be cruelty: since in the compass of those few hours of undiscontinued existence and sensibility, suffering in no inconsiderable quantity will probably have been endured.

Yet, for a being thus conditioned is the whole stock of sympathy, genuine or fictitious, reserved.

Of this sympathy, what then is the real use to mankind? What being is there that can ever be the better for it? How immense is the multitude of beings who in any given space of time, suppose a year, are sufferers by it? and to how horrible an amount sufferers! To what praise is any one really entitled by the possession of it?

No, it is not by sympathy — it is by the want of real sympathy that is the cause of the system of conduct which on this occasion is so generally — so almost universally — maintained.

[074–138]

II. Second alledged mischief — *Enervation:* enervation of the bodily frame — detriment to health and strength.

That, from gratification afforded in this way to the sexual appetite, detriment may ensue, and to a considerable amount probably has ensued, can not reasonably be doubted. But under this head as under every other is — 1. in the first place, whether, supposing evil to be the result, the sum of that evil is in such quantity and value as to be preponderant over the good derived from the same source: 2. in the next place, if yes, whether the net balance or difference be to such amount as to justify the employing against it the force of penal law in general, and in particular of such penal laws of extreme vigour as those which, in the civilized world in general, and in the British empire in particular, have been in use to be employed against it. [074–139]

Of evil, in none of these its shapes, it is but too evident, can any exact measure be taken: on this as on so many other subjects, instead of the strong and steady lights to which all wishes ought to point, we must content ourselves with such glimmerings as can be collected.

By the appetite for *drink,* that, to a prodigious amount, destruction is continually resulting to health, to strength, to life, is matter of notoriety, though the exact amount is altogether unsusceptible of measurement. In respect of the insensible but not the less indubitable detriment to health and strength produced by the appetite for liquors containing any considerable proportion of ardent spirits — of the product of the vinous fermentation, the alledged mischief here in question would, supposing the allegation well grounded, be, in respect of quality, upon a footing of resemblance. But by the appetite for drink, when such is the nature of the instrument employed for the gratification of it, are produced, where the gratification is carried to a pitch of intoxication, certain and immediate disturbance and injury to the rational faculties, together with a chance of injury in every imaginable shape to the drunkard himself as well as to others: and from this mischief, the gratification here in question is altogether free. But for drunkenness taken by itself, and considered apart from any disorders of which it may happen to it to be productive, unless it be, in case of publicity, on the score of the pain of scandal inflicted or liable to be inflicted on the public mind by the exposure, what legislator was ever weak enough to employ against such weaknesses the force of penal law? [074–140]

For the purpose of determining whether, from a tendency to produce mischief in this shape, a ground for the application of punishment may be deducible, the direct course will be to compare in the respect in question the gratification derived to the appetite in question from this source with the gratification derived to the same appetite from the several other sources from which the like gratification is capable of being derived. These are: 1. in the first place, the regular social mode: 2. the solitary mode. The obnoxious mode in question may be considered as standing in competition with so many rival modes.

Compared with the first of these modes, and considered *a priori* on the grounds of physiological and pathological effect as deducible from medical observation, it seems not easy to say what difference there can be.

But to gratification in the regular mode, the danger of a carnal disease, communicated by contagion, stands attached: while upon the gratification of the same appetite in the irregular mode here in question, no danger approaching in point of probability to the danger that has place in the other case is found to attach. To persons altogether unacquainted with medical practice under this head, it might seem that from such contagion gratification sought in the irregular mode here in question were altogether exempt: but upon enquiry into the state of medical practice in countries in which the irregularity in question receives a sort of tacit and virtual toleration, he found the exemption comparative only, and not altogether absolute.
[074–141]

Compared in this respect with the solitary mode, whatsoever difference there is, is clearly and eminently in favour of the social.

That to their attachment to the solitary mode victims in large numbers, and of both sexes, are continually self-sacrificed is a proposition of which the practice of medical men, and even their advertisements, bear but too ample testimony. In the countries in which, as above, the social irregularity experiences a virtual toleration, no quantity of mischief in that shape approaching in any degree to that which is so well known to be attached to the solitary mode has ever been observed.

Comparisons of this sort are scarcely determinable by any observation or experience to which enumeration is applicable. But, by a single reflection bestowed on the obvious nature of the case, all demand for enumeration may well be regarded as superseded. In the case of the solitary mode, the source of gratification is always and uninterruptedly present: in the social case, it is present only by accident: the existence of the necessary opportunity depending upon the concurrence of contingencies: a concurrence which, where it does take place, may have place in any degree of unfrequency.

By the contemplation of the social mode, a person may be led into the practice of the solitary. True: but in that case the solitary is employed no otherwise than as a makeshift: the employment of it is, as it were, a work of necessity: exactly as in the incomparably more frequent case in which it is produced by the like contemplation of the social mode as practiced with the opposite and corresponding sex. By the contemplation of the superior mode, the inferior is therefore in a great degree put aside: put aside continually, unless and untill by the violence of the present temptation the impulse has become irresistible. On the other hand, suppose the social desire absent, the solitary desire finds nothing from this source to oppose it, and, therefore, unless efficiently opposed from other sources, becomes effective as often as it comes into existence.

[074–142]

This circumstance, were there no other in the case, would suffice to render it evident and indisputable that, in so far as depends upon mischief in this particular shape, it would be a point, and a point of no small importance, gained to human felicity, if, instead of the solitary mode, all persons who, for the gratification of this appetite, resort to irregular channels, would resort to the social mode. In the one case, the matter of temptation never can be absent: in the other case, it may, to any degree of unfrequency, be unfrequent.

If the one mode were rendered as free from punishment by institution as the other is by necessity — by the very nature of the case, the consequences could not but in this point of view be salutary. In this as in every other walk, the more acceptable mode of gratification has, in proportion to the difference, the effect of banish[ing] the less acceptable: the higher the value a man sets on the one, the more intensely he will disdain, the other.

As between the solitary mode and the regular, this effect is altogether beyond doubt. Many a man by whom, before the regular and social source is become accessible to him, the solitary is resorted to. By the same man, once accustomed to the social, the solitary is regarded with disgust: with disgust so conclusive, that where the source of the regular social mode has failed, absolute and perpetual continence has been the result.

[074–143]

In the Æneid the most preeminent exemplification of the union of bodily vigour with mental intrepidity is that exhibited by Nisus and Euryalus in the attack made by the two youths without other company upon the enemy's camp.[24] Of the bond of attachment by which the valorous pair were united in so desperate an enterprize, effectual intimation is given in three words — "*Nisus, amore pio pueri*"[25] Nay, (says somebody) you do them wrong: as if to guard, yet alas! how ineffectually, against such odious misrepresentations, the love by which they were bound together is carefully distinguished, and expressly declared to be no otherwise than of the *pious* kind. This of which you give intimation, could this have been the sort of love meant to be brought to view by the epithet *pious?* Pious indeed? — what could be more impious? Thus far the objector. Good, it may be answered, had Virgil been a disciple of Paul or even of Moses: but Virgil was no such thing. Applied to Nisus, as to his leader Æneas, that which was expressed and meant to be expressed by the word *pious* was neither more nor less than the sort of affection or emotion excited in the poet by the contemplation of the general character of his hero. Good, in his view, could not have been the *tree* of which such qualities were the *fruits.* In love thus applied could there in his view have been any thing *impious* — any thing so much as disreputable? Take the answer from himself. Note the pathos of his lamentations for the cruelty of the beautiful Alexis: and think in what sort of denial that cruelty manifested itself.[26]

[074–144]

By the considerations which thus present themselves *à priori,* the enquiring mind is prepared for the reception of particular matter of fact.

Of all associations of men of whom any memorial has been handed down to us by history, the one most celebrated for personal courage is the *Theban band.* This preeminence is stated as being the known result of a particular bond of union: and this bond is mutual love — love operating in this irregular shape.[27]

After a case thus notorious, it would be lost labour to bring to view the heroes of classic lore of whose participation in this propensity particular intimations happen to have reached the present times: the Themistocles's, the Aristides's, the Alexander's, the Cæsar's,[28] and their et cæteras.

In a case such as this, fiction in its nature affords more conclusive evidence than any particular realities: it shews the conclusion drawn by opinion from universal and continual experience.

Hercules was raised to the Godhead. By what? by his bodily vigour as well as by that intrepidity which was the fruit of it: of that vigour, his ravings at the loss of Hylas exhibit a proof of one of the uses which he made of it. He raved and kept as heavy a coil as Stout Hercules for loss of Hylas.[29]

[074–145]

When enervation, consumption, death, were the fruits of this appetite, of what species, according to these same antients, was the tree that bore it? It was the solitary tree: the *upas.*[h30] Ask Ovid else. To the solitary passion it was that the beautiful *Narcissus* fell a victim: himself alone the object of his love.[31]

[074–146]

h. | |[32]

In an intercourse of the sort in question, what is undeniable is — that if in any degree enervation be the consequence, it is only to the agent that it can apply. Yet when, being upon the look out for mischiefs to charge upon this taste, Montesquieu pitches upon this of enervation, it is not to the account of the agent's part, but on account of the patient's part, that he charges it.[33] By the same person, it may be said, may both these parts be played. True: but it is to the patient's part alone that the mischief is charged by Montesquieu. Hence it appears that it is by a hasty, and not a correct, view of the case that the observation of Montesquieu was suggested. Of those to whom the playing the patient's part was a sort of profession — a source of maintenance — it would naturally be the study to employ art to display those attributes for the exhibition of which the female sex stand not in need of art: the colours, gestures and language of the female sex would to them be objects of imitation. They would, in short, make themselves look as like to the female sex as possible: but in comparison of the male sex, the female is enervate. Thus it is that from the idea of effeminacy to that of enervation the transition is obvious. But all this is but the work of the imagination: the analogy is in nothing but the name. Neither in painting, curtseying or speaking in a feigned voice can any cause of weakness or ill-health be discovered.

[074–147]

III. [Third][34] alledged or supposed mischievous consequence — indifference as towards the opposite sex in the same species.

When an affection of any kind is upon the look-out for plausible grounds — such as may serve to justify, in the eyes of those among whom he lives, the person who entertains it — when it is upon the look-out for such grounds, and the nature of the case affords no substantial ones, the more vague and indeterminate the sort of ground is which a man has been able to pick up, the better the chance it affords of being made to answer his purpose. Why? because the more vague it is in its nature, the greater will be the difficulty of taking such hold of it as it is necessary to take for the refutation of it: and because the less manifest the nothingness of it is, the less the discredit attached to him whose conduct and discourse appear to have been governed by it.

Of this supposed or alledged mischief, it will be seen that there is not any real mischief at the bottom of it: and what will also be seen, that there exists a spring of action affording to him who is not himself a believer in the reality of it, an incentive — nor that an inconsiderable one, the tendency of which is to engage a man to take the requisite course for inducing other men to regard him as entertaining in relation to it the sort of persuasion which, by the supposition, has not in fact any place in his breast.

[074–148]

In the description here given of the alledged mischief, the widest extent conceivable was purposely assigned to the description of [the] obnoxious practice from which it can have been considered as liable to flow. But as the argument comes to be brought home to practice, then it is that, from the extent that will be assigned by it to the alledged mischief, large defalcation will require to be made.

1. By no man will, it is supposed, any such opinion be sincerely advanced, as that a human [being][35] in either sex is in any danger of experiencing a rival in any degree formidable in an animal of a different species. And thus it is that from one modification of sexual irregularity, viz. that in which it consists in the choice of an improper species, the imputation of mischievousness in this shape is struck off as inapplicable.

2. Little less likely it is that any such apprehension should be entertained as that of seeing to any sensibly mischievous or formidable extent, portions of the male sex rendered an object of indifference to the females of the human species by the like cause. It was not to any such notion that the fables concerning the Amazons owed their birth. It has been by the experienced tyranny of the male sex, not by any insensibility to their value in the character of instruments applicable to the gratification of sexual appetite, that the separation was produced according to the representation given of the case in those fables.

[074-149]

3. Remains, therefore, as the only remaining extent capable of being seriously ascribed to the alledged mischief — in the human species, indifference in the breast of the male sex as towards the female.

In this case as in any other, to constitute such a mischief as for the prevention of which the legislator would be justifiable in employing coercive measures, three things will be necessary — 1. that the mischief be shewn to have existence in some specific assignable shape, coming under a describable and described specific character: 2. that the practice by which it is produced be not attended with any beneficial effects capable, when taken together, of operating as an over-balance or exact counterpoise to it: 3. that the measures taken for the exclusion of it be not productive of evil to an amount superior or equal to the good resulting from the exclusion of it, in so far is it is excluded.

[074-150]

A notion which, on the face of it, is in so high a degree not only improbable and absurd, but contrary to the most extensively diffused and established notions as evidenced by the most abundantly expressed and common-place discourse, can not, though it be for the purpose of exposure, without great difficulty be taken in hand and brought to view. The magnitude of the influence exercised by the female sex over the male — the excessive and sinistrously applied influence — the follies, the vices, sometimes even the crimes which such influence has for its fruit — of the trivial lamentations and declamations of moralists and religionists, these are among the most common themes.

This being the case — the sort of apprehension here in question, where are the breasts by which it will be harboured? where are the tongues by which it will be expressed? By these same declaimers among whom the diametrically opposite disposition is so continually and so loudly deplored in the character of an abyss in which so large a portion of the species is continually finding its ruin? But if not in and by these, into what other breasts is it to find place? in and by what other tongues — what other pens — is it to find utterance?

[074–151]

The thus apprehended mischief — supposing it were to take place, it will assume some determinate shape. What will — what can — that shape be? Be it what it may, to one or other of two descriptions it will be found reducible: withholding from the sex in general such modes of behaviour as come under the denomination of *good* offices; using in relation to them such modes of behaviour as come under the denomination of evil offices. The good offices — in one word these *services* — thus withholden must be such the rendering of which is not at the time in question matter of legal obligation: for in so far as it is, for the mischief, such as it is, adequate provision may be, and naturally would be, made by law. The ill offices which, according to this notion, will be done to them will, for the same reason, be such and such alone the doing of which is left free by law: manifestation, for example, of aversion and contempt, by means and in modes not punishable.

[074–152]

In the support of the probability of any such result, not any the slightest consideration drawn either from the general principles of human nature or from any thing that is to be found in history has ever been deduced or ever can be deducible. In support of it, the utmost that can be said is that it is conceivable. Exactly on the same ground and with equal reason, in the character of a cause of general calamity, might the power of evil genii or fairies or witches be an object of apprehension. In the argument is necessarily involved this proposition — Whatsoever is conceivable is probable.

Against a proposition too palpably absurd to admit of serious refutation, an argument *ad hominem,* how inconclusive and irrelevant so ever when opposed to any rational one, may have its use. To suppose the existence of

any such danger, so far is the inclination towards the same sex from being susceptible of the appellation of *unnatural,* it is the inclination to the opposite sex that is the *unnatural* one; and that, being such, requires for the support of it, those sanguinary and inexorable laws which are actually so employed. Slight is the degree of preference which would suffice for the prevention of any such undesirable result. It is by majorities that fashions are established. On the part of a majority of the male sex, that degree of attraction for the female which at present is every where so observable would suffice to prevent those by whom it is felt from treating persons of the opposite sex with harshness or neglect, and their example would suffice to restrain the unsusceptible from any such barbarity and injustice.
[074–153]

The absurdity of any such apprehension will appear the more glaring, the more extensive and accurate the survey taken in this view of the field of history.

Of the strength of the influence exercised by the female sex over the male, exemplifications are to be found in abundance: sometimes with good, sometimes to evil purposes: of any such influence exercised over a person of the male sex by a male object of his concupiscence, an example is scarcely to be found. For the effects, if any, of the appetite directed towards the same sex, the nations to be looked to in preference will be those in which, no such sentiment as that of infamy being attached to the propensity, it felt itself at liberty to seek its gratification without restraint or disguise.

In the theatre at |ʌʌʌ| amidst the applauses of the assembly, if we may believe Quintus Curtius, the Eunuch Bagoas — Bagoas a young and beautiful Eunuch — Bagoas, a youth who, according to the custom of those ages and nations, to give the longer continuance to his beauty, had been deprived of the ensigns of virility — was covered with amorous kisses by the Macedonian Conqueror.[36] By the same blood-thirsty sensualist, Persepolis was consumed. But at whose instigation? Not at Bagoas's, but at Thais's.[37]
[074–154]

To which soever class of objects directed — those of his own sex or those of the opposite — the sensuality of Mark Anthony could not fail to furnish matter for the invectives of the hostile Orator:[i] but it was for Cleopatra, and

---

i. If among the Romans, as well as the Greeks, this propensity was so general and so far from being discreditable, how comes it, says a natural enough question, to have been taken by Cicero for the subject of invective. To Cicero himself, had any such question been put, his answer would have been ready: it was to the excess of the indulgence given to the appetite that the invective was meant to apply, not to the direction taken by it. Had it

not for Cario, or for any person from whom he received the same sort of accommodation which he afforded to Cario, that he lost the empire of the world.[38]

Disastrous to his people was indeed the attachment of James the first[39] to his minion Buckingham,[40] not to speak of other minions. But not less disastrous to the same country was the attachment of Charles the first[41] to the same worthless favourite, an attachment the excess of which could not, in the instance of the son, be referable to any such cause as that the influence of which was, in the instance of the father, so obvious.

Of the instances in which the religion of Jesus was indebted for its establishment to the influence of a wife over a royal husband, the multitude has been a frequent subject of remark: no religion, good or bad, is recorded as having derived any assistance from a male favourite.

[074–155]

Among the Eastern nations the prevalence of the propensity in question — the comparative multitude of the instances in which the appetite of the male looks for its gratification in the same sex — is and always has been matter of notoriety. Among the same nations, the ill-treatment which the weaker receives at the hands of the stronger sex, is a circumstance no less notorious than deplorable. But this ill-treatment, in what does it consist? in the restraints imposed upon personal liberty and in the inequality of that contract under which the entire person of the wife is given up in exchange for the fraction of a husband: a fraction which is the smaller, the larger the mass of his opulence — of that opulence of which, in every country in which justice is in honour, she enjoys an equal share. And this same ill-treatment, in what circumstance does it find its cause? Not in indifference, but in jealousy: not in the deficiency, but in the excess of the value set by male appetite upon female charms.

[074–156]

Neither among the Greeks nor among the Romans, any more than among those more Eastern nations, have any marks been ever manifested or betrayed themselves of any such supposed relative coldness and indifference.

The only nations in which, among the male part of the species, any ill-treatment resulting from any other cause than jealousy — in other words,

---

been otherwise, he would hardly have been at the pains of those bad verses of his, reported by Pliny the Younger, in which the memory of the bad direction taken by his own taste is perpetuated. But in Antony's case the great matter of reproach was that, in his intercourse with his own sex, he had borne that obsequious and servile part, the only one of the two which, by Grecian and Roman delicacy, was regarded as dishonourable.

than attachment carried to excess, have been such as come under the description of Savages: the Natives of the English part of North America,[j] and those of New South Wales,[k] may serve for example. Deplorable are the sufferings endured by the weaker sex of those parts of the globe from unfeeling negligence as well as active cruelty in the other. But in both of those regions instances of the harmless irregularity are, for any thing that has appeared, without example.

In the new-discovered Islands of the Pacific Ocean, the prevalence of the unprolific appetite, after having been concealed by the prudent delicacy of polished historiographers, has been revealed by the untutored and querulous zeal of pious missionaries. Prostitutes by profession, and that profession marked by peculiarity of attire, have there been observed among the male part of the species, as in other countries among the female. Yet neither in these any more than in other tropical regions has the treatment given by the stronger to the weaker sex been found to exhibit any marks of indifference. In neither sex does this appetite appear to [be] subjected to any of that privation to which, under the dominion of civilization, it has been doomed.
[074–157]

In politics, in literature, in business in general, the influence of the female sex has for a long time been more conspicuous in France than in England. Yet in France that propensity which in England is matter of ostentatious abhorrence, is a source of jest and merriment. In most persons an object of physical disgust, to many of religious abhorrence, to some of moral contempt, but scarce to any of moral abhorrence.

Neither in Italy nor in Germany have the female sex ever so much as fancied to themselves any cause either of complaint or apprehension on the score of indifference on the part of the male. Yet not only in Italy, but in Germany, the propensity in question is in general regarded with a degree of indifference, and even gratified with a degree of notoriety and security, the bare mention of which can not in England be endured with patience.
[074–158]

If from any degree of the influence of the unprolific appetite, any portion of the female sex had in any part of it any reason for being apprehensive of any such misfortune as that of becoming to the male sex, or any part of it, objects of indifference, it would not be the correct and regular portion, but the loose and prostitute. To be satisfied of this, it may be necessary, but it

j. l   l.[42]
k. Collins.[43]

will be sufficient, to [advert][44] to the footing on which the irregular and unprolific connection had place in the places and times in which it was tolerated, and indeed legalized.[1] Among the Romans, scarce ever at an age beyond that of twenty years was a person of the male sex regarded as an object of this appetite. The slaves who, having been applied to this use, had passed that age were distinguished by a particular name, *exoleti,*[45] signifying that they were no longer fit for it. So likewise among the Greeks, παιδεραστία not ἀνδρεραστία[46] was the name given to it. Not that in those days any more than the present — in those countries any more than in our own — the extension of it to a more advanced time of life was altogether without example.[m] But where it was observed to take effect, any such extension was, as it were, an irregularity mounted upon an irregularity — a still further and wider deviation from the ordinary course of nature.[n]

[074–159]

The observation has already been made above — it is not the sex in general — it is only that part of it which is unfortunate enough to seek for its subsistence in the practice of ministering to this appetite — it is only the prostitute part of it, if any, that can with any well-grounded apprehension behold in the most unbridled indulgence of the unprolific appetite any diminution of their influence. Where free from all restraint from law, or so much as from public opinion, it acted its part without reserve or mystery, the choice and competition was between pæderasty and fornication — not between pæderasty and marriage. Among the antient Greeks and Romans, among those of whose conversation, life, character and behaviour any memorials have been handed down by favour to the times in which we live, in the instance of a great part, perhaps the greater part, indications of the unprolific propensity may be found discernible: yet of these, few, if any, will be found of whom it appears that they died unmarried.

Jealous of his liberty, Socrates, in a conversation put into his mouth by his biographer and panegyrist Xenophon, declares of himself that he durst not trust himself under any such temptation as that in which he would be led by a kiss given to or received from a young person of his own sex.[50] Yet the

---

l. Nullus puer emptus libidinis causâ tam fuit domini potestate, quam tu in Curionis. Cicero in Marcum Antonium. Philippic.[47]

— agere intra viscera penem.
Legitimum. Juven.[48]

m. Imberbis barbatum (subintellecto verbo amavit).[49]

n. Among the persons tried for an offence of this description at Lancaster in the | | Assizes of the Year 18 | | is a man of the age of | |.

life he led under the Yoke of his wife Xantippe is notorious enough to afford the matter of a proverb.[51]

[074–097]

CHAPTER 7.

Ill-principled and unostensible causes of the proscription applied to certain of these modes

Sad is the task of him, who, by the nature and necessity of the case, is obliged to employ argument in combating arguments by which few or none of those before or against whom he is pleading have been swayed.

For shew alone have those arguments, or rather those discourses, which have as yet been subjected to examination, been employed and held up to public view — held up to view in the character of the considerations by which the practice or opinion of those by whom they have thus been employed have been determined.

In the following list may be seen the springs of action and considerations by the united force of which, viz. of some or all of them, have been produced the language and conduct of which the sort of propensity in question has been the subject and the object.

1. Antipathy — the unreflecting emotion and passion of antipathy.

2. Envy: viz. on the score of a species and fund [of] enjoyment in which the envying party has no share.

3. Self-complacency in the contemplation of the opportunity possessed of gratifying the passion of malevolence, without danger of punishment in any shape, or so much as the slightest degree of disrepute: in a word, without *self-denial* in any shape.

4. [Ditto] in the contemplation of the opportunity of encreasing a man's own reputation — of raising his place in the public estimation — by the same means by which one of his passions, viz. the passion of malevolence, receives its gratification.

[074–098]

As to antipathy.

That towards the act itself, under all the several forms under which it is wont to clothe itself, the antipathy is very general — and where it has place, it is seldom other than very strong — is what there seems little reason to doubt of.

But the antipathy — the only antipathy by which any effect of a mischievous nature is produced, is that antipathy which, through the act, directs itself against the agent. Of the antipathy towards the act, a like antipathy towards the agent, howsoever a frequent, is assuredly not a necessary and inseparable concomitant and consequence. That it is not so is a fact of the existence of which he by whom this page is writing stands assured by the most conclusive and satisfactory species of evidence.

Take the case of that species of sexual irregularity which consists of a sexual intercourse with an animal of a different species, whether of the same or of the opposite sex. To all persons but a comparatively small number, every act of this description has probably been an object of strong antipathy. But of whatsoever antipathy as towards the agent this antipathy towards the act is accompanied, the cause will be to be looked for in an aggregate of several circumstances. —

[074–099]

1. In the first place may be mentioned that antipathy of which every diversity of affection whatsoever may be the subject, especially where the subject is on any account of a nature to excite any considerable degree of interest.

2. In the next place may be mentioned that sentiment of *envy* which, in the breast of every man, the contemplation of an enjoyment of which it is out of his power to be partaker is apt to excite. That of *envy, antipathy,* in a degree of intensity more or less considerable, is an inseparable ingredient, seems not exposed to dispute. In case of active competition, in the breast of him whose success is assured[?], *Envy is emulation accompanied with antipathy:*[52] of envy, a definition more apposite than this will, in that case, hardly, it is believed, be found. Though to himself an intercourse of the kind in question would not be a source of enjoyment, yet to him in whose instance it has taken place, it can not but have been a source of enjoyment, else it could not have taken place: and [it is] by the contemplation of this enjoyment — enjoyment of a kind in which it is out of his power to participate, that the sentiment of envy is produced.

In this shape — in the shape of *envy* — antipathy, in so far as it has place, is altogether distinct from that simple antipathy which has place in the case just mentioned: and being thus distinct from it, operates in addition to it. By any difference of opinion on any subject belonging to any part of the field of politics, for example, or religion, nothing of envy is produced.

[074–100]

3. Opportunity of affording a safe gratification to the passion of antipathy.

Neither in the field of opinion nor on the ground of taste is there any where any the smallest spot, in which, by the manifestation of contrariety, ill-will is not — and that to an indefinite degree of intensity — capable of being excited. Ill-will — considered as in possession of the gratification which is the object of the correspondent desire, is called revenge or vengeance. Of vengeance, it is naturally understood that it supposes provocation: yet provided it be also understood that provocation is as capable of being afforded by contrariety of opinion or taste as by injury.

Produced by contrariety of opinion or of taste, the appetite of vengeance is even more difficultly to be satiated or appeased than when produced by injury: in case of contrariety, if appeased at all, it is by manifestation or declaration of conformity that it must be appeased.

[074–101]

If ill-will produced, and to a certain degree influenced, by contradiction, has any where and at any time been made to abstain from vengeance, it has not been for want of appetite: it has been because, unless it be on certain particular occasions, and within certain narrow limits, vengeance, not authorized by law, is every where punishable by law.

On the ground of opinion in general — on the ground of taste in general, vengeance excited by contradiction only has not been authorized by law, but has been made punishable by law: to the possessors of power, in whose breasts ill-will has been excited by provocation in either of these shapes — by contrariety of opinion — by contrariety of taste — pretence for vengeance to be taken by the hand of law has not seemed to be obtainable in sufficient force to ensure on the part of the people, under the affliction that would then[53] be administered, a certainty of a docile[?] patience sufficient to present the requisite assurance of safety on the part of their rulers.

In that part of the field of opinion, however, which regards religion, this sufficient stock of patience on the one part, and thence of vindictive activity on the other, has been found to have place.

Of that part of the field of taste, or in other words, of pleasure — in one part, viz. in that which regards the pleasures of the sexual appetite, under and in consequence of a favourable concurrence of circumstances, the requisite disposition in the mind of the subject many has either been found or produced.

[074–102]

Among the Greeks, of all the innoxious irregularities of this appetite, those of the innoxious class as above distinguished were in general left free. But in one of the states, however, viz. the Athenian, one species of this class was under certain circumstances treated as a punishable crime: where the irregularity being that which is such in respect of sex, and the sex on both parts the male, it was allowed in general, prohibited in particular excepted cases.[o] Pride, not antipathy, was at the bottom of the exceptions: where the

o. Potter II. 240.[54]

person by whom the active part was taken was in a state of servitude, the passive part was not to be taken by one who was free: and in this case, age perhaps as well as condition entered into the composition of the ground of difference. In the opposite case, every thing was as it should be.[55] Between the two cases, modern eyes would not descry a difference. Where a prohibition was established, religion had no concern in it: morality as little: antipathy, on any such footing as that of a generally prevalent sentiment, was altogether out of the question. To decline all opportunities of giving or receiving so much as a kiss where the other party was a young person of his own sex, was by Socrates made matter of merit: of merit on the ground of prudence: the philosopher fled from the temptation: to have given way to it might have been dangerous to his independence: it was inconsistent with the dignity of his situation to be a suitor for any thing to any body.[56]

[074–103]

It was among the Jews and in the days of Moses that religion, as it should seem, for the first time fixt her eye to this ground and took it for the theatre of her rigours. In the breast of Moses, the sentiment of antipathy found an object and an exciting cause in every sort of irregularity belonging to this class. Religion was at his command: in Religion, every caprice to which, in his fertile brain, imagination had ever given birth found a ready instrument, and that an irresistible one. In English the word impurity, in most other languages some other word or words that correspond to it, had been applied alike to objects unpleasant to sense, and offensive to imagination. In the head of tyranny, at the nod of caprice, physical impurities were converted into moral ones. Under Moses as under Bramah, the list of impurities thus created, sometimes out of nothing, sometimes out of physical impurities, was a labyrinth without an end. The more extensive and above all the more indefinite the system of penal law, the more transgressions on the part of the subject many: the more transgressions, the more fear: the more fear in the breast of the subject many, the more power in the hand of the ruling few. Wherever the people are in a shivering fit, the physician of their souls is absolute. Observation was made of physical impurities, discovery was made of moral, and then converted into religious impurities: for the cleansing of physical impurities water might serve: moral impurities required blood. With a person of the opposite sex, sexual intercourse at the time of her periodical indisposition required | |.[57] With a being of the same sex or of a different species, the like intercourse was found productive [of] a defilement not to be washed away but with blood.[58]

When for any other cause than that of production of pain or prevention of pleasure, actual or probable, punishment is allowed to be inflicted, no bounds can be assigned to the application of it: for any one cause man may be destroyed or consigned to death or misery as well as for any other: to keep some from being defiled, all may be destroyed.

[074–104]

On this whole field, on which Moses legislates with such diversified minuteness, such impassioned asperity and such unrelenting rigour, Jesus is altogether silent. Jesus, from whose lips not a syllable favourable to ascetic self-denial is, by any one of his biographers, represented as having ever issued. Jesus who, among his disciples, had one to whom he imparted his authority and another on whose bosom his head reclined, and for whom he avowed his love:[59] Jesus who, in the stripling clad in loose attire, found a still faithful adherent, after the rest of them had fled:[60] Jesus in whom the woman taken in adultery found a successful advocate:[61] Jesus, on the whole field of sexual irregularity, preserved an uninterrupted silence. Jesus was one person, Paul was another. The religion of Jesus was one thing, the religion of Paul another: where Jesus had been silent, Paul was vehement. He in whom, in that regular form in which it is necessary to the existence of the species, sexual intercourse had found an unwilling toleration and endurance, no wonder that in every irregular form it should in him have found an implacably condemning Judge.

The God of the universe is what he is. The God to whom man's worship is directed, is what each man's imagination makes.

[074–105]

A man's conduct may be said to be governed by the principle of asceticism in so far as, on any other consideration than that of a more than equivalent good considered as about to accrue either to himself or some other sensitive being or beings from the operation of any other than a supernatural cause, he subjects himself to pain in any shape, considered as pain, or avoids receiving pleasure in any shape, considered as pleasure.

By each of two very different springs of action has this same propensity been produced, viz. love of reputation, and desire of amity: love of reputation, or in other words, love of distinction: the desire of becoming to men in general an object of admiration on the score of a man's maintaining a line of conduct such as men in general do not maintain, and are thence regarded as incapable of maintaining: love of amity, viz. of the amity of an almighty being: in other words, the desire of ingratiating himself with that same being.

[074–106]

If the word *philosophy* be taken not in the sense in which it is frequently taken, viz. as synonymous to wisdom, but in its original and only proper sense, as synonymous to the love of wisdom, the sort of man in whom the propensity to asceticism has for its efficient cause the desire or love of reputation may be termed the *philosophical* ascetic:[p] he in whose breast it has for its efficient cause *the desire of ingratiating himself* with the almighty being, the *religious* ascetic.

Instead of the phrase desire of amity at the hands of the Almighty Being, or desire of ingratiating oneself with, or the desire or recommending himself to the favour of, the Almighty Being, some persons would naturally enough be disposed to say in one word *fear*. Why? Because the pains a man is acquainted with being much more intense and much more durable and much more easily producible than any pleasures which he is acquainted with, the Almighty Being at whose hands pains and pleasures in those several shapes are respectively capable of being expected is in many, not to say in most, human breasts naturally and commonly the source of a much greater portion of *fear* than *hope*. But though, in such a case, as between the two, *fear* is naturally the predominant affection, yet it is as surely not the only one: and if so, *fear* is not by itself a word sufficient[ly] indicative of the spring of action by which in this case the propensity in question — the propensity to embrace pain as pain, and to repulse pleasure as pleasure — is produced.

[074–107]

The being in whose breast any such desire exists as that of seeing any sensitive being, either without an adequate equivalent in any shape to himself or to any other, should either undergo pain or forego pleasure is *pro tanto* a malevolent being: and for whatsoever reason he can be regarded as such in any one case, for the same reason and with equal reason may he be so in every other.

The same person, who without scruple would represent the Almighty as desiring that, without equivalent, a man should forego pleasure to any amount or even undergo pain to any amount, would probably not endure that, to that same being, any such epithet as malevolent should be applied. Of an inconsistency more palpable than this, language is not capable. But in language there is not any imaginable inconsistency of which fear is not wont to be productive. Upon earth, the most cruel and unrelenting of tyrants have been, as it is altogether natural that they should be, those on whom the verbal expressions of love have with most profusion been lavished. In whichsoever situation he be placed, in the language employed to or in the hearing of the possessor of power regarded as absolute, the same cause will

p. Of this description were the Stoics.

of course be productive of the same effect: the more intensely his malevolence is feared, the more loudly his benevolence will be proclaimed.
[074–108]

It is easy to see that in imputing to the Almighty a desire to see a man
forego pleasure, accompanied moreover (for such is the notion of ascetics
of the religious cast) with an eventual determination to render them ever-
lastingly miserable in case of his ever omitting to forego it, the persuasion
of the religious ascetic that such is the determination taken by the Almighty
will be stronger — and indeed much stronger — in the case where the pleasure in question is attached to any more irregular gratification of the sexual
appetite than to any less irregular gratification of that same appetite. In the
case where the gratification is of the regular kind, it proceeds from that
modification of the appetite on which the species is completely dependent
for its continuance. But, notwithstanding the sort of discountenance rather
unguardedly thrown by St Paul on the most strictly regular mode of gratifying this appetite — a sort of oversight in which the institution of monastic
orders had its rise[62] — it seems, according to the reasoning of these religionists, not unreasonable to conclude, that in human beings at large the
gratification of the appetite in this productive mode may, notwithstanding
any pleasure with which it may happen to it to be unavoidably attended, be
tolerated: care being of course taken to separate and strain out the necessary
operation from the impure admixture, as effectually as [possible].[63] But in
the case of those modes of gratification of which a contribution[64] can not be
the accompaniment, there the cause of toleration has no place: in these
cases, therefore, the thus impure and inexcusable gratification remains a
just object of unbridled vengeance.
[074–109]

For had it been the desire of the Almighty that the species should be
extinct, that desire would before now have received its accomplishment.
Nor, on another account, can any such desire be consistently attributed to
him: for to this same Almighty being, by these same religionists, a habit is
ascribed — the habit, in which is necessarily included the desire — of consigning in an appropriate receptacle a great majority of the human race to
infinitely intense and infinitely lasting torture: and, as to so many of them as
might otherwise afford matter for the gratification of it, the desire would in
case of such extinction be frustrated.

In these considerations, in so far as the toleration in question is supposed
to have place, may be seen its supposed causes. But, in the instance of those
modes of gratification of which a contribution to the continuance of the
species can not, in any case, be the accompaniment, in this case the cause of

toleration has no place: in this case, therefore, the thus impure and inexcusable pleasure remains a just object of the unbridled and insatiable vengeance of the being in whose composition an infinity of power has for its accompaniment an infinity of benevolence.

[074–110]

Of this species of asceticism, viz. the religious, considered in itself alone, the effect should not go beyond the producing, on the part of the religionist, the determination to abstain for his own part from all such inexcusable gratifications: after producing antipathy towards the obnoxious act, there should it stop, and should not proceed so far onwards as to attach upon the agent. But in the case here in question, for its cause, the ascetic principle hath, as above,[65] the desire of ingratiating one's self to the favour of the Almighty: and for recommending one's self to any person's favour, no method more effectual can be found than the determination to take, and consequent habit of taking, for and treating as one's own enemies all that person's enemies. Where the person whose enemies are to be dealt with as our own is no more than a human being such as ourselves, Charity may interpose, and, to the disposition by which we are led thus to deal with them, apply a sort of bridle: but where that person is the Almighty himself, no such bridle is necessary or so much as proper and admissible. The being infinite, such ought to be our love, such consequently our hatred for his enemies — such consequently, in determination and efficiency, the acts in and by which that hatred is exercised, manifested, gratified, demonstrated.

Thus, then, we have an antipathy — an antipathy towards the persons[66] — naturally produced, and by the force of its efficient cause piety, wound up to the highest pitch.

[074–111]

On the part [of] the philosophic ascetics — in a word, among the *Stoicks* — in whose breasts the species of gratification in question being confounded with and in a manner undistinguished from numberless other modes of gratification, pleasures belonging [to] this appetite and clothed in these irregular forms seem scarcely to have been distinguished from the crowd of other pleasures. Contempt rather than hatred — contempt, and of that but a moderate degree, seems to be the sentiment and the only sentiment which, by the idea of the vulgar herd with their vulgar gratifications, was excited in the lofty bosoms of those self-exalted dogmatists. Of hatred, if any such sharp affection were any where discoverable in their works, it was not this gratification, but some other to which modern nations are more indulgent, that was the object of it. One species of sensual gratification there is against which the philosopher Lucian hurls the whole force of his overwhelming rhetoric: it is the gratification afforded by the sense of smell in the case where the matter by which it is afforded, instead of being left in the flower which affords it, has been extracted from it, and lodged in another place. [074–112]

4. Desire of the praise of virtue — desire of reputation on the ground of love of virtue.

If the cause of the violence of the antipathy which has for its object the species of irregularities in question is in a political point of view matter of importance, it is in respect of the appetite with which all antipathy [is] produced which, having persons for its objects, has the contemplation of any part of their conduct in any particular for its cause, viz. the desire of subjecting them, or seeing them subjected, to pain, and the intensity of that appetite a circumstance to which the quantity of pain, the production of which is endeavoured at, does of course proportion itself.

In the desire of *reputation* on the score of *virtue* may be seen, in addition [to] whatsoever degree of antipathy might otherwise be excited by the contemplation of the obnoxious sort of propensity in question, a circumstance the nature of which is to give encrease to the quantity of suffering of which, in virtue of this antipathy, a man would otherwise be disposed to use his endeavours for the production of, and thence by a natural association to give encrease to the intensity of the antipathy itself. [074–113]

Reputation — esteem — general   esteem — general   estimation — good repute — among those on the state of whose affections towards him, and consequently of their future conduct in relation to him, every man is sure to be more or less dependent for his comfort, is to every man, in every situation, to a greater or less degree, an object of desire. Of this esteem, the quantity a man possesses will depend upon the persuasion concerning the degree, if any, in which he is respectively possessed of various qualities and affections, chiefly mental, among which the love of virtue holds a conspicuous place: the love of virtue, in proportion to which the contemplation of the presence of the qualities productive of the esteem of persons in general towards the possessor of those qualities respectively is a source of pleasure to a man, the contemplation of the opposite qualities a source of displeasure and uneasiness.

If the being a lover of virtue be not exactly the same thing as the being one's self virtuous, at any rate the existence of the latter is in no inconsiderable degree probative of that of the former: and so it is that if there be scarce any man who would not gladly be thought himself virtuous, there is scarce any man who would not gladly be thought a lover of virtue in others. But if

not exactly the same affection, the love of any quality is at any rate intimately connected with, and in a high degree probative of, the hatred of the
opposite quality: in so much that, in so far as a man displays his hatred
toward any vice, he considers himself as making manifestation of his love
for the opposite and correspondent virtue.

[074–114]

In the idea of every thing that is ranked with propriety under the denomination of *virtue,* the ideal of *self-denial* is included. A virtuous conduct
is that which in its effect, or at least in its tendency, is subservient to general
utility, but which, without more or less of self-denial, can not in general be
maintained. Under and according to the principle of utility, in the idea of
virtue, the idea of utility general or special, and the idea of self-denial, are
both of them included. According to this principle, neither can utility without self-denial, nor self-denial without utility, amount to virtue. In the general utility of all imaginable sorts of act — those to which the individual is
continuously indebted for his preservation — and in particular eating and
drinking, occupy the highest place: but neither in eating and drinking is
there in any case any virtue: on the contrary, in some cases it is by abstaining from eating and by abstaining from drinking that virtue may be
exercised.

As little in self-denial standing alone can virtue have any existence: stript
of utility, all self-denial is folly and weakness: it is one of the two modifications of which asceticism is composed: self-tormenting being the other.

[074–115]

If to the exercise of virtue no self-denial were necessary, at the same time
that, notwithstanding the absence of this ingredient, it continued to be a
subject and cause of praise, all mankind would be uniformly and compleatly virtuous.

Occasions are not altogether wanting on which, and means by which,
without any expence in the article of self-denial, and consequently without
any expence in the article of virtue, the praise of virtue is, in a degree more
or less considerable, capable of being obtained. Of these means, among the
very cheapest is that of displaying the appearance, with or without the
reality, of anger and abhorrence towards any thing that possesses the reality
or appearance of vice — towards any practice or deportment that is or is
regarded as being *vitious:* towards the act itself and thence, in respect of it,
as a natural or even necessary consequence, as towards the agent — the
person whose act it is. For displaying this virtue-evidencing indignation,
the course a man takes is — in speaking of the practice, or of the person
considered as exercising the act, to employ those words and phrases as by

the use of which the mode of conduct in question, and any person or persons who are considered as exercising it, are marked out as being or as deserving to be objects of general hatred or contempt: and thus pointing down against the act and the agent the appearance and the effect of those hostile sentiments and affections.

[074–116]

If the obnoxious practice in question be of the number of those which the individual in question is known or thought or suspected to be or have been in the habit of engaging in or in the disposition to engage in, in so far as this is the case, by employing, in speaking of them, the language of abhorrence or contempt, a man exposes himself to the danger of drawing down upon himself the torment which it is or would be his endeavour to pour upon the head of the person thus marked out for the object of his hostility. But unfortunate indeed will a man be if, in the whole catalogue of these acts, habits and propensities which, with or without reasonable cause, are the objects of general disapprobation and reproach, he can not find out so much as a single one from the reproach of which he does not regard himself as being by abstinence, real or reputed, exempted and preserved. If so it be that any such obnoxious practices or propensities are found, so many as are found, against so many he finds himself at liberty to play off the artillery of invective without fear of any evil consequence to himself — without any danger or apprehension of self-injury. Of the persons in whose instance the appetite in question directs itself in search of gratification to an irregular source — whether it be to a wrong species or to the wrong sex, the number always has been, and always will be, comparatively small: this small number of persons excepted, all others will, in the sort of irregularity in question, find an occasion to put in, without any expence in the shape of self-denial, the appearance of the love of virtue, and, thereby, the appearance of virtue itself.

[074–117]

Among these will naturally be found — found in an indefinite degree of abundance — the most vitious and profligate of mankind: the more incapable of paying for the praise of virtue, in the shape of self-denial, the fair price, the more eager a man will naturally be to obtain it *gratis,* in so far as it is to be had upon such terms. Purchasing it at the fair price, he would have to keep in a state of subjection and restraint every inordinate appetite, every self-regarding and every dissocial affection: obtaining it at no higher price than that of adding his contribution to the torrent of unprovoked invective, he will not have to impose any restraint upon any self-regarding or any dissocial affection: on the contrary, to his dissocial passion he will, without any the least personal inconvenience or danger of inconvenience, afford a

feast such as [is] not to be derived from any other source. He will obtain for himself the sort of enjoyment which an ill-taught boy gives himself by tail-piping a dog, or an ill-taught man by bull-baiting, or an English Judge by consigning a man to the pillory for an offence which affords a hope of his having a jaw broken or an eye beat out by the surrounding populace.
[074–118]

Two opposite causes are alike capable of engaging a man to join in the cry of persecution-exciting invective: exemption from the obnoxious propensity, and the habit of giving the reins to it, coupled with the eventual apprehension of the imputation of it. In the breast of James the 1st, such was the violence of this passion, that, with the exception of such gratifications as admitted not by possibility of any unobnoxious construction, he could not restrain himself from giving loose to it in public. In one part of the literary and published works of this same King, published in his life-time, this same irregularity is numbered among, or set down as, one of the three crimes to which a King should on no account ever grant his pardon.[67] For the interpretation of this maxim, when considered in company with the before mentioned practice, another feature of the same Royal character may be proper to be kept in mind. According to the avowed principles of this same Royal head of the English Church, mendacity in discourse and deportment was, under the name of King-craft, among the choicest and indispensable endowments of which a King could pride himself upon the possession of.
[074–119]

Of the violence of that antipathy, whether real or affected, of which the propensities in question have, in the British isles, beyond all other countries, been the object — of the violence of that thirst which nothing less than the heart's blood of the intended victims marked out for slaughter by the dissocial appetite has hitherto been able to satisfy — the principal causes have now been brought to view: and in the view thus given of them it has been seen that, in the number of them, no such quality in it as that of a tendency to make in any shape a defalcation from the aggregate sum of human happiness has place: and that, in one word, in this dissocial and misery-engendering affection whatsoever fault there is has for its seat the breasts, not of those who are the objects of this antipathy, but of those who harbour it.[q]
[074–088]

q. As a cause of self-felicitation, Sir Thomas Browne, somewhere in his *Religio Medici* or else in his *Vulgar Errors,* mentions the reflection that, among the sins with the remembrance of which his conscience was loaded, there was not any that was without a name. If memory is not deceitful, for an exemplification of such a sin is thereupon

CHAPTER 8.

Forms of reproach in which the antipathy is wont to vent itself

[074–095r1]

Not inconsiderable is the number of Novels and other works having amusement for their object, in which the danger of loss by the introduction of a topic which no person charged with the care of the youth of either sex would naturally expose to the view of a pupil, much less feel disposed to satisfy the curiosity which the darkness of the allusion can not fail to excite, has not been insufficient to let slip the occasion of giving vent and encrease to the popular antipathy of which these propensities are the object.

1. In Smollet's life of *Roderic Random,*[69] the young Scotchman, on his arrival in London, having obtained an introduction to a Noble Countryman of his there resident, the Nobleman, being smitten with his appearance, forms projects upon his person, and for the purpose of sounding him, takes notice of the general prevalence of this taste among the Greeks and Romans of the classical times. With what indignation the hint thus given is received by the young adventurer, may easily be imagined.

Much about the time when the novel was first published, a Scotch Earl was detected in the consummation of an amour, after the manner of Tiberius,[70] with two of his servants at the same time. The affair getting [.ʌ.ʌ. ?], he found himself under the obligation of going off to the Continent, where, at the end of a long life, he died not many years since.[71]

[074–095r2]

2. In Fielding's *Life of Joseph Andrews,*[72] by one of the *dramatis personæ,* a similar proposal is made to Young Joseph — to this suppositious brother of the virtuous Pamela.[73] He comes not off so cheaply as the Scottish Earl: he gets a good drubbing for his pains.

3. In Wieland's *Agathon,*[74] the scene being in Greece, and the times the classic times, much notice is taken of the hero by a priest, at whose proposals a sort of horror is expressed as well adapted to the opinion of the time

---

mentioned, in the character of a practice having at one time place in Egypt, the taking for the object of sexual appetite a body the soul of which had left it.[68]

In this conceipt may be seen one out of the vast multitude of examples of the manner in which sins are created out of nothing by the conjunct force of a busy imagination, and the passion of fear when derived from a religious source — as if a practice of any kind was either the better or the worse for not having received a name.

and place at which the story was written, as ill-suited to that in which the same is laid.

4. In one of the numerous European imitations of which the original Oriental work known by the name of the Arabian Nights Entertainments has been the archetype — the Persian Tales is it not[75] — some horrible catastrophe is brought to view, and on the part of the people who are the subject of it, the sort of propensity here in question is the cause of it.

In the original itself, even in that English translation of it which is in every body's hands, one of the stories will, when once the idea is suggested, be seen to be the history of a *bonnes fortunes*[76] of this sort. In some subterraneous or other similarly sequestered spot, the subject of the Memoir finds himself shut up at the outset in a state of solitude. But though the confinement remains, from the solitude which at first accompanied it, he has the satisfaction of being relieved by the society of a beautiful youth of fifteen, in whose company his time passes so pleasantly, that the absence of all society of the opposite sex is never brought to view as a source of regret. This in a story-book in which the intercourse between the opposite sexes is almost the only source of whatever interest the story endeavours to create. [074–096]

5. In Socrates, if his own account of himself — or at any rate that which is given as his own account of himself by his pupil Xenophon — is to be believed, formed not in this respect any exception to the general rule. But this philosopher being to be represented, if not as a model of perfect virtue, as a model of the most perfect virtue that heathenism, unenlightened by the lights of Christian Revelation, admitted of, and the propensity in question leaving, according to common notions, all others at an immense distance below it in the abyss of vice, hence it was that, in spite of the clearest evidence, he was to be pronounced clear of it. By Aristophanes, in the dramatic composition of which the object and design was, by means of ridicule, to lower this philosopher in the estimation of his contemporaries, obsequiousness to this appetite of his is represented as the shape, or at least as one of the shapes, in which, by his pupils, a return used to be made for the instruction reaped by them from his lessons.[77] By the late Dramatist Mr Cumberland, in one of the numbers of his collection of Essays called *The Observer,* Socrates and Aristophanes are brought upon the carpet together, and the imputation thus cast by Aristophanes is treated as a most perfectly groundless calumny.[78]

In the same light is it mentioned somewhere by Bishop Warburton[79] in his usual style of positiveness and ignorance.

In addition to the conclusive evidence afforded, as above, by his admiring pupil, the circumstance is over and over alluded to as a matter of the utmost notoriety by passages without number in classical works of different posterior dates, nor is any passage importing either denial or doubt to be found in any one. No matter: it suited not the purposes of those moderns that it should be taken for true: therefore, it was not true.

[074–179]

CHAPTER 9.

Real Mischief from the punishment and restraint which have place in this same case

Thus far concerning imaginary evils: come we now to real ones.

Irregular — unnatural — call them by what names of reproach you will, in these innoxious gratifications taken in themselves nothing but good — pure good, if pleasure without pain be pure (mischief from excess being supposed out of the case) — will be to be found.

But if the act be pure good, punishment for whatsoever *purpose,* from whatsoever *source,* under whatsoever *name,* in which so ever *shape* and in whatsoever *degree* applied in consideration of it, will be not only evil, but so much pure evil.

In this mass of evil | | distinguishable parcels require to be brought to view. These are

1. Punishment belonging to the legal or political sanction — legal punishment.
2. Punishment belonging to the popular or moral sanction — infamy.
3. Punishment belonging to the religious sanction — fear of hell torment.
4. Punishment of the political sanction inflicted on the innocent under the notion of their being guilty: viz. in consequence of false evidence.
5. Fear of punishment and infamy on this score in the breasts of delinquents — thus self-banishment.
6. Fear of punishment and infamy on this score in the breasts of non-delinquents.
7. Loss of the gratification through the fear of punishment in its several shapes — negative evil of restraint: loss of enjoyment.
8. Positive pain produced from the violence of the restraint.

[074–180]

If, as above, the enjoyment be so much pure good, all punishment in whatever shape endured in consideration of it, the loss of it consequently and the oppressive sense of restraint produced by the forced abstinence so much pure evil, every man by whose instrumentality any such punishment, loss or restraint is produced is, to the amount of the quantity of gratification thus prevented from coming into existence, the author of the injury. By the absence of evil consciousness and thence by probity of intention, the imputation of improbity and thence the demand for punishment at the hands of the popular or moral sanction may, it is true, in a greater or less degree, be laid from the case. True: so long as it has place. But let warning, as here, have been given, by the man, whoever he be, who, being apprized of the alledged innoxiousness of these gratifications, and of the alledged existence of the fullest and clearest proof of it, persists in shutting his ears and eyes against these proffered proofs: by this man, ignorance of that which he ought to know — of that the means of knowing which are offered to him, operates not in any degree in the character of an extenuation of the injury: in proportion and to the amount of the evil of which, in so great a variety of shapes, he is the author, a tyrant and a persecutor.

[074–181]

In no shape can tyranny or persecution present a less title to sympathy and indulgence than in this. Here is ill-will without justifying cause: revenge — if the expression be not a contradiction in terms — revenge without provocation. Here is a frame of mind in which the dissocial affections — the dissocial appetites — bear sway: spite of warning and remonstrance, spite of assurance that what he is doing is wrong and unjustifiable, finding what to him appears a pretence for the exercise of it, a circumstance in which he flatters himself with the hope of finding shelter against popular indignation, he persists in the endeavour to administer gratification to this pernicious appetite.

Nothing in this case can be more false and groundless — nothing more hypocritical than the pretence of a love of virtue. In the suffering of no man, not even the most wicked and mischievous of mankind — in no such suffering, in no suffering in any shape considered by itself, considered in any other light than that of a necessary means of producing a more than equivalent good — of averting a more than equivalent evil, does a virtuous man, in so far as that appellation justly belongs to him, derive pleasure — regard it with any other feeling than that of pain: how much more incontestably is any such malignant enjoyment incompatible with virtue when the suffering from which it is reaped is the suffering of the innocent — when the conduct of the sufferer is pure from all moral guilt? No: the virtue of the persecutor is the virtue of him whose delight is in the inflicting of torture on such of his

fellow creatures as their weakness has put into his power: in throwing at a
cock while tied to a stake, driving a dog or cat to madness by a canister tied
to its tail, and so forth.

[074–185]

Of the act of him who, conscious of its being undue or having sufficient
reason to regard it as undue, contributes to the infliction of punishment in
any shape upon any other person, the guiltiness in a moral point of view is
universally recognized. But if in this case any such imputation as that of
guiltiness [is recognized], neither can he by whose act another person is laid
under *restraint,* in such sort as to be prevented from the enjoyment of any
gratification of which otherwise he might have had enjoyment, be altogether exempt from it. To deprive a man of a sum of money to any amount,
or to prevent him from making acquisition of it, is an injury, and the imputation of moral guiltiness attaches upon the commission of it. But on what
account? Either on none whatever, or else on account of pleasure in some
shape or other which, by means of it, he might have enjoyed or pain in some
shape or other he might have escaped: unless on one or other of these,
money, like every thing else, is without value. By every person who, by
pointing against them the force of the popular or moral sanction, contributes in any degree to restrain from a participation of any such gratification a
person by whom it would otherwise have been enjoyed — by every such
person the species of wrong or injury just spoken of is inflicted, and a
degree of moral guilt, proportioned to the value of the pleasure thus lost,
incurred. The amount being given, whether what is taken from a man be
money or money's worth makes not any the smallest difference.

[074–184]

If, with the attention to which they are so indubitably entitled, considerations of this nature were generally weighed, discourses of an ascetic tendency would not be uttered with that sort of carelessness of unreflecting
vehemence and virulence which is so commonly exemplified. A man could
no more hold himself guiltless in debarring another from the enjoyment of a
pleasure for the enjoyment of which he would have been glad to give a
guinea, than in picking his pocket of the guinea with which, but for the
theft, the pleasure would have been purchased. Without ever bestowing so
much as a moment's thought on the question whether the pleasure in question be or be not in any determinate way noxious, what more common than
for men to indulge themselves in railing at it without reserve: in the endeavour to cast odium in the first place on the pleasure itself, and then on him by
whom it is reaped.

[074–182]

Another evil of the most serious kind issuing from this source is that of which false accusation is the immediate cause. Deplorable is the facility afforded to men of profligate characters for ruining the reputation, and at the same time the pecuniary circumstances, of persons in whose instance an accusation of this sort would be altogether false and groundless.

Rarely in comparison does any such danger attach upon an offence productive of real mischief. Of an offence of which such are the effects, seldom does an instance occurr in which distinctly perceptible traces of it are not left behind by it: in which case, if no such traces are brought to light, a person accused has little or nothing to fear either in the shape of punishment or even in the shape of disrepute. In case of beating, the wound or bruize: in case of stealing, the removal of the goods: in case of rape, the marks of violence employed to overcome resistance. But in this case, violence not being any necessary accompaniment to the proposal, nor in case of consent to the act consummated in the attempt, any man who, for a certain length of time, was alone with any other may stand up and say, he made such or such an attempt upon me, or he acted in such or such a species of deportment towards me: and though the assertion should be compleatly false and groundless, the reputation of the man of whom this is said may receive such a wound as it may never recover from during life.

[074–183]

This being the case, how easy it is to fabricate out of the dread of an accusation of this nature an instrument of extortion is but too obvious and too notorious. Give me so much money, or I will say to such or such a person in conversation, or to such or such a person in writing, or in a word to every one in print, or even in the way of accusation to the Judge — that at such or such a place and time, you said so and so to me, or you comported yourself so or so — relative to me. Against a threat of this sort, what remedy does the nature of the case allow? Words or statements of deportment of this sort may by any person be at any time invented at pleasure, and without possibility of detection. Against mischief of this sort, who is there that can promise himself to be secure?

With the suffering of a man upon whom, to any such effect, an imputation altogether groundless has been cast, few are they who can altogether refuse their sympathy: few even of those whose fury, if they regarded [it] as true, would be most implacable: though in their instance it might be matter of curiosity to learn from themselves what number of persons, innocent in their eyes, they had rather see put to death than that any one who, in those same eyes, were guilty should escape. But, if in a case such as this sympathy had any thing to do with reason, who can dispute but that the claim to

sympathy were better grounded in the case w[h]ere an [act] of the prohibited sort in question *had* been committed by the man, than in the opposite case. For in the latter case, the man for his support has what in this
case will be called his conscience for his comfort and support; whereas in
the other case, this comfort is by the supposition wanting: for what has
never been done can never be discovered to have been done, whereas of
what a man has really done, seldom indeed can he have any satisfactory
assurance that [it] can never be discovered to have been done.
[074–188]

CHAPTER 10.

Beneficial tendencies of these modes

Supposing the tautogenous mode not pursued but abstained from, what,
in respect of the pursuit of pleasure, is the consequence of such abstinence?
The person in question, does he or does she abstain from sexual gratification altogether, or does he [or does she] reap it in any other and what mode?

The mode being by supposition the sexual, but without so much as the
potential prolifickness, the parties between whom the gratification is shared
may be either male and male or female and female. For the sake of clearness, first suppose it between male and male: it finds then in the language a
word by which it is distinguished: it is termed *pæderasty.*

Supposing pæderasty, then, being by supposition abstained from, sexual
pleasure either is pursued in some other shape or not pursued in any other
shape.

If pursued in another shape, in what other, then, is it pursued?

In the first place being pursued, the shape in which it is pursued will be
either a shape in which it is accompanied with injury to third persons, or a
shape in which it is not accompanied with any such injury.
[074–189]

For simplicity's sake, let it in the first place be consider[ed] as pursued in
a shape not accompanied with any such injury to third persons.

In respect of any ulterior effects with relation to the parties or party
concerned, pæderasty and bestiality seem to stand upon the same ground.
Mischief to health from excess being supposed absent, both seem equally
innoxious.

On the same supposition, on the same footing with both these modes of
gratification would stand the solitary act in either sex. But in this latter case,

as observed by Mr Bentham,^r the means of gratification being never want-ing, the supposition of absence of mischief to health by excess is not so likely to be verified.

[074–190]

Sexual intercourse between the opposite sexes without the sanction of marriage is productive of mischief and danger in a variety of shapes from which the like intercourse between two persons of the same sex, be it male or female, is free.

1. On the part of the female, loss of reputation, loss of the place she occupied in society — a mischief, when not actual, always probable.
2. For prevention of this loss, in case of pregnancy, measures taken for procuring abortion, and on failure of those measures, infanticide.

Of any of the known measures that can be employed to procure abortion, danger more or less considerable to health is an attendant consequence: and lest this danger should not be sufficiently severe, legislators, with their usual barbarity, have stept in and converted this measure of security into a crime.

The same barbarity has stept in to aggravate the still heavier sufferings of the female in case of infanticide. For the being which is endued with afflictive sensibility, and that in the most exquisite degree, they have no sympathy: of their stock of that article, the whole is carefully reserved for the being which itself has none. The physical image being in both cases the same, and they blind to the pathological effects, they confound this case with that of murder committed on an adult. Committed on an adult, murder is productive of the mischief distinguished by Mr Bentham under the name of mischief of the 2^d order:[81] according to the various shapes capable of being assumed by the case — shapes all of them capable of being distin-guished from each, murder is productive of danger or alarm or both in different degrees of extent to third persons. With no such consequences is infanticide attended when committed on a new-born child by the mother, or by the father with her consent, or by any other person with the consent of both parents.

[074–191]

It is thus that cruelty cloaths itself in the garb of mercy: vice in the garb of virtue. O men! &c.∧.∧.∧. who wilt then hear the voice of calm and unprejudiced reason?

Among the antient Romans, not only at the time of its birth, but at every

r. Dum.[80]

subsequent point of time during the life of the father, the life of the offspring was in the power of the father. All the admiration which the comparative earliness of the time in which their existence had place [has][82] procured for that nation has not preserved them on this occasion from reproach, and that in the usual undiscriminating stile, at the hands of the moderns. Infanticide committed by the father, so it be with consent of the mother, immediately or within a short time, say a few years after its birth, no alarm is impressed upon the mind of any other human being. But suppose the subject of the act to be a child already arrived at the age at which fear of death has taken place, the parent or parents at whose disposal their lives are placed being alive, children of the same or nearly the same age are capable of beholding in the power thus fatally exercised over that child a danger more or less pressing of an exercise of the like power over themselves.

Neither on the subject of abortion nor on that of infanticide, neither from Jesus nor from any one of his apostles, is any thing to be found. Yet to the account of their heathenism, i.e. to their unacquaintance with the religion of Jesus, is the power given under the Roman law to a father over his children ascribed as of course, and the fact of a prohibition issued by Jesus, where in truth none was issued by him, assumed with as little ceremony in this as in so many other cases.

[074–192]

If, on the part of the female, the violation of the law of chastity being discovered, by the loss of all reputable means of subsistence, the female finds herself under the necessity of continuing, as a source of subsistence, that course of interdicted gratification into which she had been led by sexual appetite, then comes what is called the habit of *prostitution,* and with it another train of evils. Dependency, the result of perpetually experienced contempt — disease from the excess — disease from the characteristic contagion — indigence — disease from that habit of intoxication which, under the pressure of the abovementioned miseries is so commonly resorted to as a palliative — by all this complicated cluster of evils, the thread of life is almost always cut short, and what remains of it is blackened by affliction. In this melancholy branch of trade, success, so far from leading as in other trades to affluence, is scarce ever for any continuance, bar the effect of warding off indigence. By the multitude of rivals, competition operates with a degree of ardour scarcely exemplified in any other instance: for the purchase of those means and those opportunities of display on which success is regarded as depending, not only the purse is kept empty, but credit kept constantly at the utmost stretch: the necessity of pleasing at any price — shining in such a degree of splendor as shall ensure a preference over the multitude of rival candidates — throws over the ambition natural to the sex, the gloss of necessary prudence.

[074–193]

Simple fornication — i.e. sexual intercourse with a prostitute of the opposite sex — has for its object the present gratification of sexual appetite — and no other: coitus with the same sex, if, in the judgment of the only competent judge, it affords though it be no more than equal gratification, is thus exactly upon a par with simple fornication. But of the evils to which, by simple fornication, one of the two parties, viz. the female, is exposed — evils by which, in so deplorably large a proportion of the whole number, that part of the population which is of that sex is actually afflicted, a view has just been given. From these evils, if, of the persons who, within any given space of time, have participated in the taking of this gratification, each one had taken for his or her mate, instead of a person of the opposite sex, a person of the same sex with itself, every one of them would have remained free.

[074–194]

How great and oppressive so ever the disrepute which at present attaches upon fornication on the part of the female, disrepute still greater and more oppressive attaches upon pæderasty: and this without discrimination as between the agent's part and the patient's. But if, in the whole of this field, the view taken by the public mind were correct, the disrepute attached to sexual intercourse with the same sex would vanish altogether. To the evils which, independently of the moral evil of disrepute — to the purely physical evils which, as above, attach upon the case of fornication, there exists not any thing that corresponds in the case of pæderasty. By the universal prevalence [of] a correct view taken of the nature of the case, the evils attached to pæderasty would be compleatly extirpated: but by no such means would the evils attached to fornication on the part of the female be done away. By fornication in the case of the female, the organs concerned undergo changes, by which the possessor is rendered less pleasing in the eyes of the opposite sex: but in the case of pæderasty, no correspondent change is produced. In the case of the female, chastity — not to speak of modesty — chastity in the eyes of all persons but those by whom expectations are entertained of profiting by the violation of it, has its value: in the male, it has no equal, if any, value.

[074–197]

Objection. Mischief — On the part of the male, diminution of sympathy for the female sex: i.e. of that affection the effect of which is to mitigate the rigour of the despotism which otherwise would, by the stronger sex, be exercised [over][83] the weaker, and which is accordingly so exercised among uncivilized nations. Or say —

Beneficial effect the |∧∧∧|[th.] Diminishing the mortification which, in case of a successful rival of her own sex, is experienced by a more or less neglected wife.

Where by the turn taken by sexual appetite a man is led to his own sex, it has been found by general experience that it is at the state of manhood that the faculty of giving excitation to this appetite terminates. Among the Romans (putting a certain number for an uncertain quantity — taking an average of the whole instead of a quantity which, from the nature of the case, could not but be exposed to variation upon a scale of very considerable length) twenty is the age spoken of in a variety of Latin writers as being the age at which this faculty has ceased. At this time of life, the change from one of the two opposite conditions to the other is marked by the word *exoletus.*

[074–198]

For marking the commencement of this same faculty, no such determinate age. Anterior as it is by so many years, it is to the age of compleat puberty, suppose it to be twelve years: twelve is by Tacitus mentioned as the age at which Germanicus[84] excited this appetite in the breast of .∧.∧. Here at the utmost is a reign of 8 years. But to the quality by which, in the breast of the male, this same appetite continues to be excited by the charms of the female, there are no such strict and determinate limits. If, therefore, it be the destiny of a wife to have a successful rival in the affections of her husband, she has much less to fear from one of his sex than from one of her own sex.

Accordingly, numerous are the instances in which history presents to view the powerful and so commonly the baneful effects of the influence exercised by the female over the male — instances of the like influence exercised over the male by the male are hardly to be found. Read Saint Simon and then say what mischiefs were not brought upon France by the thraldom in which Lewis the 14th was held by Madame Maintenon,[85] his unacknowledged but not the less all-powerful wife?[86]

[074–199]

Amidst the whole mass of the information which, by the classical writers of Greece and Rome, is furnished in relation to this subject, under so perfect a liberty of choice as the notions of the age and country afforded, scarcely will so much as a single instance be found in confirmation of any such notion as that, among males, occasional appetite for the same sex has any such effect as that of producing indifference towards the other. As to population, spite of wars, redundancy frequent, and, as proved by colonization, deficiency, except in case of sudden loss as once in Athens after the disaster of Sicily,[87] unexampled. It was at the expence, therefore, of fornication, not of marriage, that pæderasty took place: it was at the expence of the un-prolific and misery-producing, and not with the prolific and comfortable, intercourse with the opposite sex that sexual intercourse with the same sex used to take place.

It would, therefore, [be] too much to make sure of that, from pæderasty, population suffered any considerable check: thus much and no more could be said with confidence, viz. that if it were so to do, then for the reasons that have already been brought to view,[88] so much the better.

[074–206]

CHAPTER II.

Objections to the proposed freedom — with answers

To amount to any thing, these objections must consist in the allegation of evil in some specific shape stated as apt or liable to be produced by grati-fication in the mode in question.

The following are all which, on search, have been found alledged, or on consideration have been found capable of presenting themselves in this character.

1. Danger of diminution of sympathy on the part of the sex towards the other, in particular on the part of the male as towards the female.[89]

2. Danger of seduction of pupils by preceptors.

3. Danger of annoyance to the eyes and ears of third persons in the character of lovers of decency.

§ 1. Danger of the seduction of pupils by preceptors.

But the rising generation! how universal would be their contamination! In either sex, what chance of escape would there be for the tender flower of youth when, in every teacher, instead of a guardian, it might find a seducer?

Plausible at first as well as natural the objection: but on a closer view, it vanishes. To the dissipating of this illusion the same observation will serve by which so many others have been dissipated.

From the solitary gratification, with its attendant danger — the danger to health from excess — it is not in the nature of the case that the youth of either sex should be preserved by any guardianship, howsoever anxious and vigi-lant: but as hath been shewn already,[90] to any solitary mode whatever, any social mode is a salutary substitute.

To the temptations to excess to which, in the present state of public opinion, every youth of either sex remains encompassed, no new and clear addition could be made by the change in question. In neither sex can any youth be kept in a state of seclusion from those of his or her own sex and age. But, whether it be in the social mode or in the social practice of the solitary mode, a youth of the same age will always be a more tempting paramour than a person, such as a teacher, of more advanced age.
[074–207]

Neither in this nor in any shape, against the danger of excess can a person at the age of a pupil be reasonably expected to be so effectually upon his guard as a person at the age of a preceptor. So many fellow pupils, so many sources of stronger temptation than would have existence in the persons of an equal number of preceptors: and in relation to the same person at the pupil age, the number of persons officiating at the same time in the character of preceptors can not, generally speaking, be by a great deal equal to that of his or her associates of the same pupil age. Thus, by the danger in question, new as in some sort it may be, a greater danger is lessened: and of the addition thus made, the effect being not clear addition, but substitution, and of the substitution the effect being a clear substraction, the sum of danger will not be encreased, but diminished.
[074–208]

In so far as concerns progress in studies, by a connection of this sort, two opposite effects are both of them capable of being produced: an encrease in improvement, or a decrease.

How an encrease may come to be the result is obvious enough. Deriving from his intercourse with his pupil, in addition to whatever may be his remuneration in the ordinary form, remuneration in this extraordinary form, the preceptor, finding in the exercise of this his function pleasure in a sort and degree never in the present state of things experienced, may apply himself to it with a degree of zeal and assiduity correspondently encreased. The pupil on his part, experiencing, in stead of that moroseness and haughtiness which, from that commanding situation, is at present so frequently met with, a degree of attention and kindness so extraordinary, may find a pleasure in an occupation which otherwise would have been a painful and laborious one. In the case of a female pupil, if under the tuition of a fond mother learning goes on pleasantly and rapidly, with still more rapidity does it go on under the direction of a fond lover or a fond husband: and of that latter sort, by the supposition, will the relation be — the relation will have the same pleasure to cement it — the labour the same pleasure to sweeten it.

So far as this case is the case exemplified — so far the sexual connection has for its fruit no special evil, but on the contrary an additional and special good.

[074–209]

On the other hand, now suppose the sexual connection to be followed by the opposite effect — diminution in the degree of improvement. Of this diminution the cause will be, on the part of the preceptor towards the pupil, an undue degree of indiscriminating obsequiousness: on the part of the pupil, a disposition to make of that undue obsequiousness a sort of profit in the way of present pleasure, viz. the pleasure of idleness more than counterbalanced by the more or less distant but never ending evils which follow in the train of ignorance.

Here then, as far as it goes, will be a real mischief: but of this mischief the duration is not likely to be long. At present, the state of things in question is too rare to enter into calculation: no parent is upon his guard against it: in the supposed state of things it is, by the supposition, not too rare to enter into calculation: every parent will be upon his guard against it. In a state of the most perfect liberty in relation to this indulgence, the probability seems not great that among parents there should be any very considerable proportion to whom, even independently of any such apprehension on the subject of proficiency, a connection of this sort should be viewed with a contented eye. But even among those by whom, independently of any such apprehension, the connection should be an object of indifference, scarce will any one be to be found in whose mind any observation or suspicion of its being attended with any such mischievous effect would not be productive of such a degree of resentment as would be incompatible with the continuance of the preceptor in the trust which he had thus abused.

[074–210]

In this state of things, a preceptor in whose mind the seeds of any such propensity happened to have place would, therefore, either put an effectual and compleat restraint upon it, or on the supposition of his giving in some measure the reins to it, he would at least take care to keep it to such a degree under command as not to suffer it to be productive of the ill effect here in question. Either he would put upon present appetite an effectual restraint, or at any rate he would so far keep it within bounds as not to give up, for the gratification of the moment, [the] sort of reputation upon which he saw depending the provision and comfort of his whole life. In this species and degree of prudential restraint where would be the wonder, or comparatively speaking the difficulty? To the superior attraction of the charms of the opposite sex, every preceptor whose business brings him in contact with that sex finds himself exposed at present: and how seldom is that attraction found to be productive of the correspondent evil consequence? [074–211]

In the character of a ground of objection, the mischief here in question has been taken for the subject of consideration as being in itself, and so far as it extends, altogether inconsiderable. But when the numbers exposed to it are compared with the numbers of those to whom it has no application, it vanishes into nothing. Of the whole number of fathers and guardians in any country, small indeed is the number of those who are in a condition to provide for their children any such assistant as a private tutor: I say a private tutor: for as to preceptors in schools, whether large or small, any such connection between a preceptor and any one of his scholars would find in the jealousy of the rest such an obstacle as would in general be sufficient to divest the pursuit of all hope. Only in the darkness of the night, and in the vicinity produced by the allotment of two persons to one bed, could a preceptor in such a situation find an opportunity for the indulgence. While two Scholars in a bed is the common arrangement, a Master or Usher in the same bed with one of the Scholars is an arrangement at present by no means frequent, and in the state of things in question would probably be without example.[91]
[074–212]

§ 2. Wounds to the eyes of the lovers of decency.

What? shall our eyes, then, and our ears be continually assailed by the manifestations of this, to us at least, never otherwise than most vitious and abominable appetite?

Not more so than at present they are by those of the more usual form of it. Decency is among the inventions of civilized life which for one of its objects, and that which perhaps has been most compleatly attained, has had the preservation of pleasure: the preserving of those pleasures to which it applies [from][92] being sunk in their value by familiarity.[93]
[074–214]

CHAPTER 12.

Addition expectable from the proposed liberties to the sum of happiness

Speaking of the state of man in respect of happiness, Priestly,[94] in one of his works, declares his assurance that it will be paradisiacal beyond any thing that at present it is possible for any man to conceive. A class of men, to whom, abuse in all shapes being profitable, reformation in all shapes, and, by reason of the closeness of the alliance, improvement in all shapes, but more especially in the moral shape, is proportionably odious, set their faces against this benevolent hope, attacking it with accusations of hatred or contempt, as occasion serves. Bentham, acknowledging the well-groundedness of the hope if kept within rational limits, gives an indication of those limits. All happiness, says he, being composed of pleasures and accompanied [with] exemptions from pains, and all pleasures that are not of sense deriving their existence from the pleasures of sense, hence the sum of the pleasures in all shapes of which human nature is capable has its limits in the sum of the pleasures of sense of which the same nature is capable.

But by no possible contrivance can either the number of the senses in their character of intrinsic sources of pleasure, or the intensity of the sort of pleasure of which they are respectively the sources, be made to receive any considerable encrease.

[074–215]

Remains, therefore, two sources, and no more than two, from which the sum of happiness taken in all its shapes can receive encrease: one is diminution of the mass of pains; the other is removal of the obstacles which error and prejudice have opposed to the encrease of that stock of pleasures which every person has in his and her power.

Of the stock of pains to which human nature stands exposed, some are derived immediately from physical sources, others from moral sources. To lessen the stock of pains derived from physical sources is the business principally of the medical curator — of the branches of art and science that belong to medicine: to lessen the stock of pains derived from moral sources is the business of the moralist and the legislator.

But suppose, for argument sake, the whole stock of pain in all its other shapes removed for ever, still even by such a consummation no positive happiness — no pleasure — is produced: left destitute of pleasure, the condition of the living man, even after the removal of all pain, is not in the account of happiness left superior to that of a dead one. Still, therefore, every thing that belongs to the category of positive happiness — every thing positive that is worth having or working for — belongs to the category of pleasure: and, though there are pleasures that are not pleasures of sense, yet neither are there any pleasures which are not derived either from the pleasures of sense or from the absence of pains, and in that sense from the pains of sense.

[074–216]

Remains, therefore, two distinguishable senses as the only senses from which the sum of positive happiness can receive encrease: 1. the bringing within each man's reach pleasure in a quantity greater than that in which it would otherwise be within his reach: 2. the removing the obstacles which error and prejudice have hitherto with such fatal success opposed to his making use of those which have been lying within his reach.

But of the pleasures which, at any given point of time, lie within a man's reach, the number and value will depend upon that of the instruments or sources of pleasure the possession of which is necessary to the reaping of those same pleasures. But of these same instruments or sources, the aggregate stock is neither more nor less than the aggregate mass of the matter of wealth. The absolute mass of the matter of wealth in any community being given, the quantity and value of the average portion possessed by each member of the community will be in the exact inverse ratio as the number of the members of which that community is composed. But, such is the power of the sexual appetite, and such upon the whole, in comparison of all other modes, the superiority in intensity of that mode of gratifying it which has propagation for its effect, the number of the members of the community will always be at its maximum, and consequently the stock of the sources and instruments of pleasure in all shapes which are within each average man's reach at all times will be at its minimum.

[074–217]

Remains, therefore, as the only species of the elements of positive happiness — the only species of positive pleasure — which are susceptible of any considerable encrease — such of the pleasures of the sexual appetites as at present by public opinion, under the name and notion of irregularity, stand condemned.

These pleasures, though without excess and thence more than equivalent pain, not capable of being enjoyed for so great a proportion of man's time as all other pleasures of sense taken together, are by universal acknowledgment superior in intensity to all other pleasures of sense: they exclude not any other pleasures: they exclude not any other pleasures, whether pleasures of sense or pleasures not of sense.

But these are precisely the only pleasures of sense which are as fully and effectually within the reach of the most indigent — supposing them by whatever cause collected together in adequate numbers — as within the most affluent classes of mankind: they are equally within the reach of the subject many as of the ruling few.

[074–218]

Of the pleasures dependent upon wealth, the average mass enjoyed by a member of the subject many can never be rendered equal to the average mass enjoyed by a member of the ruling few: for though to the palate of the one his dry bread or his potatoes may be more savoury than to that of the other his turtle and his pineapple, yet of a sufficient quantity even of the bread or the potatoes — his coarse food — the eater of the bread or of the potatoes can not always be assured.

But of that pleasure which is not dependent upon wealth — not so at any rate in its nature, howsoever it may be by accident — the pleasure, to wit, of the sexual appetite — the mass enjoyed by the poorest member of the subject many may be equal to the mass enjoyed by the richest member of the ruling few. But of the pleasures of this class, to be in a condition to enjoy the greatest quantity that [the] accidental circumstances of his situation throw in his way, and that the constitution of his taste has happened to give him a relish for, it will be necessary that all those restraints which have been imposed by blind prejudice be removed: and by the removal of all this mass of prejudice, how prodigious the mass of pleasure that may be, as it were, created — brought into existence — by one single hand!
[074–219]

By one of the Roman collectors of anecdotes (Suetonius is it not?), one of the Roman Emperors (Nero is it not?) is said to have offered a premium for the invention of any new pleasure.[95] From the character of the person by whom this reward was offered, the nature of the wished-for pleasure being inferred, and the presumption being that it was of the sexual class at least, if not of the sexual genus, the advertisement has by the professors of tritical morality been numbered among the atrocities of the despot, and in the scale of guilt placed as usual above the most mischievous of them. Howsoever low the pleasure produced may stand in the scale of intensity, every new toy offered to the juvenile hand comes in species as clearly under the anathema thus pronounced as the most eccentric gratification offered to the sexual appetite.

Be it pleasure, be it pain — in the instance of a given pain, he who causes that to be experienced which but for him would not be experienced is as effectually the author of it as if with his own hand he had presented the instrument of it: to *remove* an *obstacle* may in point of effect be the same thing as to create a cause. By the removal of that cloud of prejudice by which this part of the field of morals has to this time been obscured, what calculation shall comprize the aggregate mass of pleasure that may be brought into existence — the value of the services that may be rendered to mankind — in a word, the mass of good that may be done? By this thought it is that the hand by which these pages have been penned, has been enabled to endure the disgust with which the subject was found encompassed — to go through the toil which the task required. *Non sibi sed toti!*[96] if ever there was a case in which this motto found its verification, it is this.

[074–221]

CHAPTER 13.

Benefit to genuine morality by the exclusion of the spurious morality by which the gratifications in question stand interdicted

If the abovementioned way of thinking on the subject be a just one — not only in a direct and an immediate way would the sum of happiness be encreased, viz. by encrease of the mass of pleasure and diminution of the mass of pain, but also in an indirect and unimmediate way, viz. by the extension given to genuine morality.

Scarcely can any extension be given to the mass of spurious morality, but it is at the expence of genuine. A notion very generally not to say universally prevalent is that of the utter impossibility of giving fulfilment to the whole stock of moral duties. Such at any rate is the notion universally prevalent under all the *established* forms of the religion of Jesus: more particularly under that which is established in the Church of England: of this proposition, not to look for any other evidence, a full proof is contained in that short prayer of the Anglican taken from the Romish Litany — Have mercy upon us miserable sinners.[97] Not only by the Laity from the Monarch to the beggar, but by the Clergy from the Archbishop to the Deacon, is this confession regularly and continually made. From this state, according to his own confession, not even is the holiest of the holy tribe preserved; not so much as by the Holy Ghost whom or which he received at his consecration, and of whom at every succeeding point of time he remains no less full than at the first moment.

[074–222]

Yet among these miserable sinners there remains, according to their own notion of the matter, a stock more or less considerable of good Christians — the same being also good men — good enough to pass for such and to be esteemed as such and loved and reputed as such among men, while in passage here on the way to heaven.

Of these two notions combined together, what then is the result? that the tighter-girt they are in this or that part of the field of duty — moral and religious together — the looser they may be, and that without prejudice to esteem in this world, and salvation in the other, on some other part of that same field.

Thus it is that the greater the regard to ceremonies and impractical points of faith taken together on the one hand, the less the regard to moral duties, spurious and genuine taken together, on the other: and as between spurious and genuine moral duties, the stricter the regard for spurious, the less strict the regard for the genuine.

From the well-known distich of the humorous Church-of-England poet, well has this rule received its illustration —

Compound for sins they are inclined to

By damning those they have no mind to.[98]

Thus to the once celebrated Essayist as well as physician Sir Thomas Brown, as declared in the *Religio Medici*, it was matter of consolation "that he had never been guilty of any sin without a name such as was that of the Egyptians." What he meant was the frolic of those embalmers who, applying to the softer sex the aphorism dead men tell no tales, would now and then take part payment for their trouble at the expence of that chastity which, as towards its possessor, had lost its use.[99]

NOTES

1. The first page of text is missing.

2. See I Corinthians 6: 9–10; I Timothy 1: 9–10.

3. The cross-reference here and in Bentham's next note is to a projected chapter entitled "State of English law and other laws in relation to this subject — its inconsistencies."

4. In the margin, Bentham has noted at this point: "In this case only on the male side could be the agency."

5. For Bentham's classification of offences, see *An Introduction to the Principles of Morals and Legislation*, ed. J. H. Burns and H. L. A. Hart (London, 1970), 187–91 [hereafter *IPML*], and *Traités de législation civile et pénale*, ed. É. Dumont, 3 vols. (Paris, 1802), i. 172–74.

6. Bentham left space in his manuscript to add an explanation of this and the remaining two points, but in the event failed to do so.

7. See chap. 2, pp. 37–38 above.

8. See chap. 5, pp. 43–49 below.

9. Frederick II (1712–86), king of Prussia from 1740.

10. William II (1650–1702), prince of Orange, king of England, Scotland, and Ireland, from 1689 is joint sovereign with Mary II (1662–94).

11. See chap. 8, p. 76 below.

12. MS "was."

13. MS "they were." Bentham means to refer to the God, rather than to the priests.

14. See chap. 7, p. 67 below.

15. A phrase used in William [Howley], bishop of London, *A Charge delivered to the clergy of the diocese of London* (London, 1814), 16.

16. In comment on this passage, Louis Crompton suggests that Bentham has confused two episodes: "On May 25, 1726, Benjamin Deschauffours was burned alive in the Place de Grèves for acts of sodomy. . . . Desfontaines had been threatened with the same fate in 1725 but was saved by the intercession of Voltaire." Crompton, *Byron and Greek Love* (Berkeley, 1985), 257n.

17. See Luke 18: 9–14.

18. Seneca (c. 4 BC–AD 65), Stoic philosopher.

19. See chap. 7, p. 68 below.

20. See *Erotes*, XII–XX, traditionally attributed to Lucian of Samosata (b. *c.* AD 120). The story concerned the statue of Aphrodite (Venus) at Cnidus.

21. In Ovid, *Metaphorphoses*, X, Pygmalion the sculptor falls in love with his statue, and the statue is brought to life by Venus.

22.The Athenian orators Aeschines (*c.* 397–*c.* 322 BC) and Demosthenes (384–322 BC) clashed in 343 and 330 BC over the relations of Athens and Macedon.

23. In what follows, Bentham does not deal with this third point.

24. For the attack on the Rutulians, see Virgil, *Aeneid*, IX. 176–458.

25. See ibid., v. 296: "Nisus, with a boy's devoted (*pio*) love."

26. The love of the shepherd Corydon for the boy Alexis is the subject of Virgil's second *Eclogue*.

27. According to Plutarch, the Sacred Band of Thebes, the elite force of the fourth-century BC Theban army, was formed of 150 homosexual pairs, whose mutual love led them to fight more fiercely.

28. Themistocles (*c.* 524–459 BC) and Aristides (d. *c.* 457 BC) were Athenian politicians; Alexander the Great (356–323 BC), king of Macedon from 336 BC; and Julius Caesar (100–44 BC), Roman general and politician.

29. See Samuel Butler, *Hudibras*, part 1, canto 3, 183–84. In Greek myth, Hylas, usually portrayed as the lover of Heracles, was taken on the voyage of the Argonauts by Heracles but was abducted by Nymphs at Cius in Mysia and never seen again. See Apollonius Rhodius, *Argonautica*, I. 1207–1357; and Theocritus, *Idyll*, XIII.

30. The legend of the upas of Java, poisoning everything for miles around it, was generated by a natural history article in the *London Magazine* of December 1783 and popularized by Erasmus Darwin in his *The Loves of the Plants (*London, 1789), canto 3.

31. See Ovid, *Metamorphoses*, III. 339–510.

32. Bentham has failed to provide a reference.

33. See Montesquieu, *Spirit of the Laws*, bk. 12, chap. 6.

34. MS "Second."

35. MS "species."

36. Quintus Curtius Rufus deals with the relationship of the eunuch Bagoas and Alexander the Great in *History of Alexander*, X. i. 25–42 but does not mention the precise incident referred to by Bentham.

37. Alexander the Great captured Persepolis, the capital of Persia, in 331 BC. In the summer of 330 BC, at the instigation of Thais, an Athenian woman, he allowed his soldiers to loot the city and burn its palaces. See Diodorus Siculus, *Library of History*, XVII. 71.

38. Marcus Antonius (83–30 BC) met Cleopatra VII (69–30 BC), queen of Egypt from 51 BC, at Tarsus in 41 BC. Cleopatra was often blamed for Marcus Antonius's defeat at the hands of Octavian. Cario was the boy lover of Marcus Antonius.

39. James VI (1566–1625), king of Scotland from 1567, and as James I, king of England and Ireland from 1603.

40. George Villiers (1592–1628), first duke of Buckingham.

41. Charles I (1600–49), king of England, Scotland, and Ireland from 1625.

42. Bentham has failed to provide a reference.

43. See David Collins, *An Account of the English Colony in New South Wales: with remarks on the dispositions, customs, manners, of the native inhabitants of that country*, 2 vols. (London, 1798–1802).

44. MS "adverse."

45. I.e., "grown-ups."

46. I.e., "love of boys not love of men."

47. See Cicero, *Philippic*, II. xviii. 45: "No slave boy bought for the sake of lust was so in the power of his master as you are in the power of Curio."

48. See Juvenal, *Satires*, IX. 43–44: "to drive the legitimate [i.e., lawfully procured] penis into the entrails." With this and the previous quotation Bentham is apparently noting not only the legitimacy of male same-sex relations in Rome, but the prevalence of practices not sanctioned by custom (Cicero and Juvenal both suggest that their *dominus* targets have played roles disparaged as submissive).

49. I.e., "The beardless youth (by an implied word loved) the bearded man." The phrase "imberbis barabatum" appears in the Latin version of Xenophon, *Anabasis*, II. vi., where Cyrus is said to have loved a bearded favorite called Tharypas before he had grown a beard himself.

50. Bentham possibly has in mind Xenophon, *Memorabilia of Socrates*, III. 8.

51. For Xanthippe's reputation as a scold, see Xenophon, *Symposium*, II. 10, and Shakespeare, *Taming of the Shrew*, I. ii. 68–69.

52. A view expressed by Thomas Hobbes (1588–1679): see *Leviathan*, ed. R. Tuck (Cambridge, 1991), chap. 6, p. 44.

53. MS "not then" appears to contradict the sense of the passage.

54. John Potter, *Archæologica Græca, or, the Antiquities of Greece*, 2d ed., 2 vols. (London, 1706), bk. 4, chap. 9.

55. An ironic echo of William Blackstone's phrase "Every thing is now as it should be," made in the context of a discussion of the law of heresy at *Commentaries on the Laws of England*, 4 vols. (Oxford, 1765–69), iv. 49, but which Bentham took to be characteristic of Blackstone's attitude to the British political system as a whole.

56. See chap. 6, p. 63 above.

57. See Leviticus 20: 18, where the punishment is banishment for both parties.

58. See Leviticus 20: 13 for homosexuality and 20: 15 for bestiality, where the punishment is death for all parties (including the beast).

59. See John 13: 23, 25.

60. See Mark 14: 51–2.

61. See John 8: 1–11.

62. Bentham perhaps had in mind I Corinthians 7: 8–9.

63. MS "impossible."

64. I.e., to the increase of population.

65. See chap. 5, pp. 43–47 above.

66. I.e., of the Almighty's enemies.

67. See "Religio Regis; or the Faith and Duty of a Prince. Written by King James I. being Instructions to his Son Prince Henry," in *The Prince's Cabala: or Mysteries of State* (London, 1715), 56: "But there are some horrible Crimes which you are bound in Conscience never to forgive; such as Witchcraft, wilful Murder, Incest, Sodomy, Poysoning, and false Coyning."

68. Sir Thomas Browne (1605–82) referred to this practice of the Egyptian embalmers in *Pseudoxia Epidemica, or Vulgar Errors* (London, 1646), chap. 19, where he commented, "We require a name for this." In his *Religio Medici* ([London], 1642), he remarked, "I thank the goodnesse of God I have no sinnes that want a name," which, according to John Keck, in his annotations to the fourth edition of *Religio Medici* (1656), was an allusion to the former passage. According to the Oxford English Dictionary, the first usage of the term "necrophilism" occurred in 1864.

69. Tobias Smollett's *The Adventures of Roderick Random* was first published in 1748.

70. Tiberius (42 BC — 37 AD), Roman emperor from 14 AD. See Suetonius, *Lives of the Twelve Caesars*, Tiberius. LXIII.

71. In the margin, Bentham has noted at this point: "Earl Finlater[?]." Possibly James Ogilvy (1750–1811), 7th earl of Findlater, landscape architect and philanthropist, who moved to the Continent in 1781.

72. Henry Fielding's *The History of the Adventures of Joseph Andrews and of His Friend Mr Abraham Adams* was first published in 1742.

73. Joseph Andrews was presented as the brother of the eponymous heroine of Samuel Richardson's *Pamela, or Virtue Rewarded*, which was first published in 1740.

74. C. M. Wieland, *The History of Agathon*, 4 vols. (London, 1773).

75. *The Thousand and One Days: Persian Tales. Translated from the French by Mr Ambrose Philips*, 3 vols. (London, 1783).

76. An allusion to Michel Baron's play *L'homme á bonnes fortunes* of 1686.

77. Aristophanes (d. *c.* 386 BC) ridiculed Socrates in his play *Clouds*.

78. See Richard Cumberland, *The Observer: being a collection of Moral, Literary and Familiar Essays*, 5 vols. (London, 1786–90), no. 76.

79. William Warburton (1698–1779), bishop of Gloucester.

80. I.e., Dumont's edition of *Traités de législation civile et pénale*, 3 vols. (Paris, 1802), iii, 10n.

81. See *IPML*, chap. 12.

82. MS "had."

83. MS "by."

84. In the text, Bentham has noted at this point: "→ Mention the relationship." For Tacitus's account of Germanicus (15 or 16 BC–AD 18), Roman general and adopted son of the emperor Tiberius, see *Annals*, bks. 1, 2.

85. Françoise d'Auloigné, marquise de Maintenon (1635–1719), was the morganatic second wife of Louis XIV (1638–1715), king of France from 1643.

86. Louis de Rouvroy, duc de Saint-Simon Vermanclois, *Mémoires, ou l'observateur véridique, sur le règne de Louis XIV*, 7 vols. (London, 1788–89).

87. I.e., the overwhelming defeat at Syracuse of the Athenian expedition of 415–413 BC.

88. See chap. 6, pp. 49–50 above.

89. This topic is dealt with in chap. 6, pp. 57–64 above.

90. See chap. 6, pp. 54–56 above.

91. In the text, Bentham has noted at this point: "→ Go on to observe that the chief use regards the most numerous classes, viz. as most numerous and as those in whom the keeping down the population is most desirable."

92. MS "by."

93. In the text, Bentham has noted at this point: "→ Go on to say that for the punishment of indecent exposure there will be the same demand as now."

94. Joseph Priestley (1733–1804), theologian and natural philosopher.

95. Bentham perhaps has in mind the creation by Tiberius of a new office with responsibility for pleasures, recorded in Suetonius, *Lives of the Twelve Caesars*, Tiberius. LXII.

96. I.e., "Not for oneself but for all."

97. The supplication is repeated several times by priest and congregation in the Litany of the Church of England.

98. Samuel Butler, *Hudibras*, part I, canto I, 213–14.

99. See chap. 7, pp. 75–76n. above.

II

Fundamentals of Jurisprudence

An Introduction to the Principles of Morals and Legislation

Preface and Chapters 1–5

Two editions of *An Introduction to the Principles of Morals and Legislation* were published during Bentham's lifetime, in 1789 and 1823. The book was first printed in 1780; Bentham added the preface in 1789 and added some notes in 1823. The preface provides a useful introduction to the treatise and to Bentham's jurisprudential ambitions as of 1789. For a comprehensive modern introduction to the work, see the essays by H. L. A. Hart and F. Rosen included in the paperback reissue of the *Collected Works* edition (Oxford University Press, 1996).

What follows is a reprint of the preface and the first five chapters (pages 1–50) of the *Collected Works* edition, which was prepared by J. H. Burns and H. L. A. Hart for the Athlone Press of the University of London (1970). The work, with full editorial apparatus, is reproduced here with the kind permission of the Bentham Committee, University College London. Scanning and formatting such a complex text proved challenging and involved many hands. Cross-references in the notes have been omitted or altered in bold; Bentham's marginal summaries have been omitted.

Preface

The following sheets were, as the title-page expresses, printed so long ago as the year 1780.[1] The design, in pursuance of which they were written, was not so extensive as that announced by the present title. They had at that time no other destination than that of serving as an introduction to a plan of a penal code *in terminis*, designed to follow them, in the same volume.

The body of the work had received its completion according to the then present extent of the author's views, when, in the investigation of some flaws he had discovered, he found himself unexpectedly entangled in an unsuspected corner of the metaphysical maze.[2] A suspension, at first not apprehended to be more than a temporary one, necessarily ensued: suspension brought on coolness, and coolness, aided by other concurrent causes, ripened into disgust.

Imperfections pervading the whole mass had already been pointed out by the sincerity of severe and discerning friends; and conscience had certified the justness of their censure. The inordinate length of some of the chapters, the apparent inutility of others, and the dry and metaphysical turn of the whole, suggested an apprehension, that, if published in its present form, the work would contend under great disadvantages for any chance, it might on other accounts possess, of being read, and consequently of being of use.

But, though in this manner the idea of completing the present work slid insensibly aside, that was not by any means the case with the considerations which had led him to engage in it. Every opening, which promised to afford the lights he stood in need of, was still pursued: as occasion arose, the several departments connected with that in which he had at first engaged, were successively explored; insomuch that, in one branch or other of the pursuit, his researches have nearly embraced the whole field of legislation.

Several causes have conspired at present to bring to light, under this new title, a work which under its original one had been imperceptibly, but as it had seemed irrevocably, doomed to oblivion. In the course of eight years, materials for various works, corresponding to the different branches of the subject of legislation, had been produced, and some nearly reduced to shape: and, in every one of those works, the principles exhibited in the present publication had been found so necessary, that, either to transcribe them piecemeal, or to exhibit them somewhere where they could be referred to in the lump, was found unavoidable. The former course would have occasioned repetitions too bulky to be employed without necessity in the execution of a plan unavoidably so voluminous: the latter was therefore indisputably the preferable one.

To publish the materials in the form in which they were already printed, or to work them up into a new one, was therefore the only alternative: the latter had all along been his wish, and, had time and the requisite degree of alacrity been at command, it would as certainly have been realised. Cogent considerations, however, concur, with the irksomeness of the task, in placing the accomplishment of it at present at an unfathomable distance.

Another consideration is, that the suppression of the present work, had it been ever so decidedly wished, is no longer altogether in his power. In the course of so long an interval, various incidents have introduced copies into various hands, from some of which they have been transferred, by deaths and other accidents, into others that are unknown to him. Detached, but considerable extracts, have even been published, without any dishonourable views, (for the name of the author was very honestly subjoined to them) but without his privity, and in publications undertaken without his knowledge.[3]

It may perhaps be necessary to add, to complete his excuse for offering to the public a work pervaded by blemishes, which have not escaped even the author's partial eye, that the censure, so justly bestowed upon the form, did not extend itself to the matter.

In sending it thus abroad into the world with all its imperfections upon its head, he thinks it may be of assistance to the few readers he can expect, to receive a short intimation of the chief particulars, in respect of which it fails of corresponding with his maturer views. It will thence be observed how in some respects it fails of quadrating with the design announced by it's original title, as in others it does with that announced by the one it bears at present.

An introduction to a work which takes for its subject the totality of any science, ought to contain all such matters, and such matters only, as belong in common to every particular branch of that science, or at least to more branches of it than one. Compared with its present title, the present work fails in both ways of being conformable to that rule.

As an introduction to the principles of *morals*, in addition to the analysis it contains of the extensive ideas signified by the terms *pleasure*, *pain*, *motive*, and *disposition*, it ought to have given a similar analysis of the not less extensive, though much less determinate, ideas annexed to the terms *emotion*, *passion*, *appetite*, *virtue*, *vice*, and some others, including the names of the particular *virtues* and *vices*. But as the true, and, if he conceives right, the only true ground-work for the development of the latter set of terms, has been laid by the explanation of the former, the completion of such a dictionary, so to style it, would, in comparison of the commencement, be little more than a mechanical operation.

Again, as an introduction to the principles of *legislation in general*, it ought rather to have included matters belonging exclusively to the *civil* branch, than matters more particularly applicable to the *penal*: the latter being but a means of compassing the ends proposed by the former. In preference therefore, or at least in priority, to the several chapters which will be found relative to *punishment*, it ought to have exhibited a set of propositions which have since presented themselves to him as affording a standard for the operations performed by government, in the creation and distribution of proprietary and other civil rights. He means certain axioms of what may be termed *mental pathology*, expressive of the connexion betwixt the feelings of the parties concerned, and the several classes of incidents, which either call for, or are produced by, operations of the nature above mentioned.[a]

The consideration of the division of offences, and every thing else that belongs to offences, ought, besides, to have preceded the consideration of punishment: for the idea of *punishment* presupposes the idea of *offence*: punishment, as such, not being inflicted but in consideration of offence.

Lastly, the analytical discussions relative to the classification of offences would, according to his present views, be transferred to a separate treatise, in which the system of legislation is considered solely in respect of its form: in other words, in respect of its *method* and *terminology*.

In these respects the performance fails of coming up to the author's own ideas of what should have been exhibited in a work, bearing the title he has now given it, viz. that of an *Introduction to the Principles of Morals and Legislation*. He knows however of no other that would be less unsuitable: nor in particular would so adequate an intimation of its actual contents have been given, by a title corresponding to the more limited design, with which it was written: viz. that of serving as an *introduction to a penal code*.

Yet more. Dry and tedious as a great part of the discussions it contains must unavoidably be found by the bulk of readers, he knows not how to regret the having written them, nor even the having made them public. Under every head, the practical uses, to which the discussions contained under that head appeared applicable, are indicated: nor is there, he believes, a single proposition that he has not found occasion to build upon in the penning of some article or other of those provisions of detail, of which a body of law, authoritative or unauthoritative, must be composed. He will venture to specify particularly, in this view, the several chapters shortly characterised by the words *Sensibility, Actions, Intentionality, Consciousness, Motives, Dispositions, Consequences*. Even in the enormous chapter

---

a. For example. — *It is worse to lose than simply not to gain. — A loss falls the lighter by being divided. — The suffering, of a person hurt in gratification of enmity, is greater than the gratification produced by the same cause.* These, and a few others which he will have occasion to exhibit at the head of another publication, have the same claim to the appellation of axioms, as those given by mathematicians under that name; since, referring to universal experience as their immediate basis, they are incapable of demonstration, and require only to be developed and illustrated, in order to be recognized as incontestable.

on the division of offences, which, notwithstanding the forced compression the plan has undergone in several of its parts, in manner there mentioned, occupies no fewer than one hundred and four closely printed quarto pages,[4] the ten concluding ones are employed in a statement of the practical advantages that may be reaped from the plan of classification which it exhibits. Those in whose sight the Defence of Usury has been fortunate enough to find favour,[5] may reckon as one instance of those advantages the discovery of the principles developed in that little treatise.

In the preface to an anonymous tract published so long ago as in 1776,[b] he had hinted at the utility of a natural classification of offences, in the character of a test for distinguishing genuine from spurious ones. The case of usury is one among a number of instances of the truth of that observation. A note at the end of Sect. 35 Ch. xvi of the present publication,[6] may serve to show how the opinions, developed in that tract, owed their origin to the difficulty experienced in the attempt to find a place in his system for that imaginary offence. To some readers, as a means of helping them to support the fatigue of wading through an analysis of such enormous length, he would almost recommend the beginning with those ten concluding pages.

One good at least may result from the present publication; viz. that the more he has trespassed on the patience of the reader on this occasion, the less need he will have so to do on future ones: so that this may do to those, the office which is done, by books of pure mathematics, to books of mixed mathematics and natural philosophy. The narrower the circle of readers is, within which the present work may be condemned to confine itself, the less limited may be the number of those to whom the fruits of his succeeding labours may be found accessible. He may therefore in this respect find himself in the condition of those philosophers of antiquity, who are represented as having held two bodies of doctrine, a popular and an occult one: but, with this difference, that in his instance the occult and the popular will, he hopes, be found as consistent as in those they were contradictory; and that in his production whatever there is of occultness has been the pure result of sad necessity, and in no respect of choice.

Having, in the course of this advertisement, had such frequent occasion to allude to different arrangements, as having been suggested by more extensive and maturer views, it may perhaps contribute to the satisfaction of the reader, to receive a short intimation of their nature: the rather, as, without such explanation, references, made here and there to unpublished works, might be productive of perplexity and mistake. The following then

b. A Fragment on Government, etc. reprinted 1822.[7]

are the titles of the works by the publication of which his present designs would lie completed. They are exhibited in the order which seemed to him best fitted for apprehension, and in which they would stand disposed, were the whole assemblage ready to come out at once: but the order, in which they will eventually appear, may probably enough be influenced in some degree by collateral and temporary considerations.

Part the 1st. Principles of legislation in matters of *civil*, more distinctively termed *private distributive*, or for shortness, *distributive*, *law*.

Part the 2d. Principles of legislation in matters *of penal law.*

Part the 3d. Principles of legislation in matters of *procedure*: uniting in one view the *criminal* and *civil* branches, between which no line can be drawn, but a very indistinct one, and that continually liable to variation.

Part the 4th. Principles of legislation in matters of *reward.*

Part the 5th. Principles of legislation in matters of *public distributive*, more concisely as well as familiarly termed *constitutional*, law.

Part the 6th. Principles of legislation in matters *of political tactics*: or of the art of maintaining *order* in the proceedings of political assemblies, so as to direct them to the end of their institution: viz. by a system of rules, which are to the constitutional branch, in some respects, what the law of procedure is to the civil and the penal.

Part the 7th. Principles of legislation in matters betwixt nation and nation, or, to use a new though not inexpressive appellation, in matters of *international* law.

Part the 8th. Principles of legislation in matters *of finance.*

Part the 9th. Principles of legislation in matters of *political economy.*

Part the 10th. Plan of a body of law, complete in all its branches, considered in respect of its *form;* in other words, in respect of its method and terminology; including a view of the origination and connexion of the ideas expressed by the short list of terms, the exposition of which contains all that can be said with propriety to belong to the head of *universal jurisprudence.*[c]

The use of the principles laid down under the above several heads is to prepare the way for the body of law itself exhibited *in terminis;* and which to be complete, with reference to any political state, must consequently be calculated for the meridian, and adapted to the circumstances, of some one such state in particular.

Had he an unlimited power of drawing upon *time*, and every other condition necessary, it would be his wish to postpone the publication of

---

c. Such as obligation, right, power, possession, title, exemption, immunity, franchise, privilege, nullity, validity, and the like.

each part to the completion of the whole. In particular, the use of the ten parts, which exhibit what appear to him the dictates of utility in every line, being no other than to furnish reasons for the several corresponding provisions contained in the body of law itself, the exact truth of the former can never be precisely ascertained, till the provisions, to which they are destined to apply, are themselves ascertained, and that *in terminis*. But as the infirmity of human nature renders all plans precarious in the execution, in proportion as they are extensive in the design, and as he has already made considerable advances in several branches of the theory, without having made correspondent advances in the practical applications, he deems it more than probable, that the eventual order of publication will not correspond exactly with that which, had it been equally practicable, would have appeared most eligible. Of this irregularity the unavoidable result will be, a multitude of imperfections, which, if the execution of the body of law *in terminis* had kept pace with the development of the principles, so that each part had been adjusted and corrected by the other, might have been avoided. His conduct however will be the less swayed by this inconvenience, from his suspecting it to be of the number of those in which the personal vanity of the author is much more concerned, than the instruction of the public: since whatever amendments may be suggested in the detail of the principles, by the literal fixation of the provisions to which they are relative, may easily be made in a corrected edition of the former, succeeding upon the publication of the latter.

In the course of the ensuing pages, references will be found, as already intimated, some to the plan of a penal code to which this work was meant as an introduction, some to other branches of the above-mentioned general plan, under titles somewhat different from those, by which they have been mentioned here. The giving this warning is all which it is in the author's power to do, to save the reader from the perplexity of looking out for what has not as yet any existence. The recollection of the change of plan will in like manner account for several similar incongruities not worth particularizing.[8]

Allusion was made, at the outset of this advertisement, to some unspecified difficulties, as the causes of the original suspension, and unfinished complexion, of the present work. Ashamed of his defeat, and unable to dissemble it, he knows not how to refuse himself the benefit of such an apology as a slight sketch of the nature of those difficulties may afford.

The discovery of them was produced by the attempt to solve the questions that will be found at the conclusion of the volume: *Wherein consisted the identity and* completeness *of a law? What the distinction, and where the separation, between* a penal *and a* civil *law? What the distinction, and where the separation, between the* penal *and* other branches *of* the law?

To give a complete and correct answer to these questions, it is but too evident that the relations and dependencies of every part of the legislative system, with respect to every other, must have been comprehended and ascertained. But it is only upon a view of these parts themselves, that such an operation could have been performed. To the accuracy of such a survey one necessary condition would therefore be, the complete existence of the fabric to be surveyed. Of the performance of this condition no example is as yet to be met with any where. *Common* law, as it styles itself in England, *judiciary* law, as it might more aptly be styled every where, that fictitious composition which has no known person for its author, no known assemblage of words for its substance, forms every where the main body of the legal fabric: like that fancied ether, which, in default of sensible matter, fills up the measure of the universe. Shreds and scraps of real law, stuck on upon that imaginary ground, compose the furniture of every national code. What follows? — that he who, for the purpose just mentioned or for any other, wants an example of a complete body of law to refer to, must begin with making one.

There is, or rather there ought to be, a *logic* of the *will,* as well as of the *understanding*: the operations of the former faculty, are neither less susceptible, nor less worthy, than those of the latter, of being delineated by rules. Of these two branches of that recondite art, Aristotle saw only the latter: succeeding logicians, treading in the steps of their great founder, have concurred in seeing with no other eyes. Yet so far as a difference can be assigned between branches so intimately connected, whatever difference there is, in point of importance, is in favour of the logic of the will. Since it is only by their capacity of directing the operations of this faculty, that the operations of the understanding are of any consequence.

Of this logic of the will, the science of *law*, considered in respect of its *form*, is the most considerable branch, — the most important application. It is, to the art of legislation, what the science of anatomy is to the art of medicine: with this difference, that the subject of it is what the artist has to work *with*, instead of being what he has to operate *upon*. Nor is the body politic less in danger from a want of acquaintance with the one science, than the body natural from ignorance in the other. One example, amongst a thousand that might be adduced in proof of this assertion, may be seen in the note which terminates this volume.

Such then were the difficulties: such the preliminaries: — an unexampled work to achieve, and then a new science to create: a new branch to add to one of the most abstruse of sciences.

Yet more: a body of proposed law, how complete soever, would be comparatively useless and uninstructive, unless explained and justified, and that in every tittle, by a continued accompaniment, a perpetual commentary of *reasons*[d]: which reasons, that the comparative value of such as point in opposite directions may be estimated, and the conjunct force, of such as point in the same direction, may be felt, must be marshalled, and put under subordination to such extensive and leading ones as are termed *principles*. There must be therefore, not one system only, but two parallel and connected systems, running on together, the one of legislative provisions, the other of political reasons, each affording to the other correction and support.

Are enterprises like these achievable? He knows not. This only he knows, that they have been undertaken, proceeded in, and that some progress has been made in all of them. He will venture to add, if at all achievable, never at least by one, to whom the fatigue of attending to discussions, as arid as those which occupy the ensuing pages, would either appear useless, or feel intolerable. He will repeat it boldly (for it has been said before him,) truths that form the basis of political and moral science, are not to be discovered but by investigations as severe as mathematical ones, and beyond all comparison more intricate and extensive. The familiarity of the terms is a presumption, but it is a most fallacious one, of the facility of the matter. Truths in general have been called stubborn things: the truths just mentioned are so in their own way. They are not to be forced into detached and general propositions, unencumbered with explanations and exceptions. They will not compress themselves into epigrams. They recoil from the tongue and the pen of the declaimer. They flourish not in the same soil with sentiment. They grow among thorns; and are not to be plucked, like daisies, by infants as they run. Labour, the inevitable lot of humanity, is in no track more inevitable than here. In vain would an Alexander bespeak a peculiar road for royal vanity, or a Ptolemy, a smoother one, for royal indolence. There is no *King's Road*, no *Stadtholder's Gate*, to legislative, any more than to mathematic science.

CHAPTER I

Of the Principle of Utility

1. Nature has placed mankind under the governance of two sovereign masters, *pain* and *pleasure*. It is for them alone to point out what we ought to do, as well as to determine what we shall do. On the one hand the

---

d. To the aggregate of them a common denomination has since been allotted — *the rationale*.[9]

standard of right and wrong, on the other chain of causes and effects, are fastened to their throne. They govern us in all we do, in all we say, in all we think: every effort we can make to throw off our subjection, will serve but to demonstrate and confirm it. In words a man may pretend to abjure their empire: but in reality he will remain subject to it all the while. The *principle of utility*[e] recognises this subjection, and assumes it for the foundation of that system, the object of which is to rear the fabric of felicity by the hands of reason and of law. Systems which attempt to question it, deal in sounds instead of sense, in caprice instead of reason, in darkness instead of light.

But enough of metaphor and declamation: it is not by such means that moral science is to be improved.

2. The principle of utility is the foundation of the present work: it will be proper therefore at the outset to give an explicit and determinate account of what is meant by it. By the principle[f] of utility is meant that principle which

e. Note by the Author, July 1822.

To this denomination has of late been added, or substituted, the *greatest happiness* or *greatest felicity* principle: this for shortness, instead of saying at length *that principle* which states the greatest happiness of all those whose interest is in question, as being the right and proper, and only right and proper and universally desirable, end of human action: of human action in every situation, and in particular in that of a functionary or set of functionaries exercising the powers of Government. The word *utility* does not so clearly point to the ideas of *pleasure* and *pain* as the words *happiness* and *felicity* do: nor does it lead us to the consideration of the *number,* of the interests affected; to the number, as being the circumstance, which contributes, in the largest proportion, to the formation of the standard here in question; the *standard of right and wrong,* by which alone the propriety of human conduct, in every situation, can with propriety be tried. This want of a sufficiently manifest connexion between the ideas of *happiness* and *pleasure* on the one hand, and the idea of *utility* on the other, I have every now and then found operating, and with but too much efficiency, as a bar to the acceptance, that might otherwise have been given, to this principle.

f. (Principle) The word principle is derived from the Latin *principium:* which seems to be compounded of the two words *primus,* first, or chief, and *cipium,* a termination which seems to be derived from *capio,* to take, as in *mancipium, municipium;* to which are analogous *auceps, forceps,* and others. It is a term of very vague and very extensive signification: it is applied to any thing which is conceived to serve as a foundation or beginning to any series of operations: in some cases, of physical operations; but of mental operations in the present case.

The principle here in question may be taken for an act of the mind; a sentiment; a

approves or disapproves of every action whatsoever, according to the tendency which it appears to have to augment or diminish the happiness of the party whose interest is in question: or, what is the same thing in other words, to promote or to oppose that happiness. I say of every action whatsoever; and therefore not only of every action of a private individual, but of every measure of government.

3. By utility is meant that property in any object, whereby it tends to produce benefit, advantage, pleasure, good, or happiness, (all this in the present case comes to the same thing) or (what comes again to the same thing) to prevent the happening of mischief, pain, evil, or unhappiness to the party whose interest is considered: if that party be the community in general, then the happiness of the community: if a particular individual, then the happiness of that individual.

4. The interest of the community is one of the most general expressions that can occur in the phraseology of morals: no wonder that the meaning of it is often lost. When it has a meaning, it is this. The community is a fictitious *body*, composed of the individual persons who are considered as constituting as it were its *members*. The interest of the community then is, what? — the sum of the interests of the several members who compose it.

5. It is in vain to talk of the interest of the community, without understanding what is the interest of the individual.[g] A thing is said to promote the interest, or to be *for* the interest, of an individual, when it tends to add to the sum total of his pleasures: or, what comes to the same thing, to diminish the sum total of his pains.

6. An action then may be said to be conformable to the principle of utility, or, for shortness sake, to utility, (meaning with respect to the community at large) when the tendency it has to augment the happiness of the community is greater than any it has to diminish it.

7. A measure of government (which is but a particular kind of action, performed by a particular person or persons) may be said to be conformable to or dictated by the principle of utility, when in like manner the tendency which it has to augment the happiness of the community is greater than any which it has to diminish it.

---

sentiment of approbation; a sentiment which, when applied to an action, approves of its utility, as that quality of it by which the measure of approbation or disapprobation bestowed upon it ought to be governed.

g. (Interest, &c.) Interest is one of those words, which not having any superior *genus,* cannot in the ordinary way be defined.

8. When an action, or in particular a measure of government, is supposed by a man to be conformable to the principle of utility, it may be convenient, for the purposes of discourse, to imagine a kind of law or dictate, called a law or dictate of utility: and to speak of the action in question, as being conformable to such law or dictate.

9. A man may be said to be a partisan of the principle of utility, when the approbation or disapprobation he annexes to any action, or to any measure, is determined by, and proportioned to the tendency which he conceives it to have to augment or to diminish the happiness of the community: or in other words, to its conformity or unconformity to the laws or dictates of utility.

10. Of an action that is conformable to the principle of utility, one may always say either that it is one that ought to be done, or at least that it is not one that ought not to be done. One may say also, that it is right it should be done; at least that it is not wrong it should be done: that it is a right action; at least that it is not a wrong action. When thus interpreted, the words *ought*, and *right* and *wrong*, and others of that stamp, have a meaning: when otherwise, they have none.

11. Has the rectitude of this principle been ever formally contested? It should seem that it had, by those who have not known what they have been meaning. Is it susceptible of any direct proof? it should seem not: for that which is used to prove every thing else, cannot itself be proved: a chain of proofs must have their commencement somewhere. To give such proof is as impossible as it is needless.

12. Not that there is or ever has been that human creature breathing, however stupid or perverse, who has not on many, perhaps on most occasions of his life, deferred to it. By the natural constitution of the human frame, on most occasions of their lives men in general embrace this principle, without thinking of it: if not for the ordering of their own actions, yet for the trying of their own actions, as well as of those of other men. There have been, at the same time, not many, perhaps, even of the most intelligent, who have been disposed to embrace it purely and without reserve.

There are even few who have not taken some occasion or other to quarrel with it, either on account of their not understanding always how to apply it, or on account of some prejudice or other which they were afraid to examine into, or could not bear to part with. For such is the stuff that man is made of: in principle and in practice, in a right track and in a wrong one, the rarest of all human qualities is consistency.

13. When a man attempts to combat the principle of utility, it is with reasons drawn, without his being aware of it, from that very principle itself.[h] His arguments, if they prove any thing, prove not that the principle is *wrong*, but that, according to the applications he supposes to be made of it, it is *misapplied*. Is it possible for a man to move the earth? Yes; but he must first find out another earth to stand upon.

14. To disprove the propriety of it by arguments is impossible; but, from

[h] "The principle of utility, (I have heard it said) is a dangerous principle: it is dangerous on certain occasions to consult it." This is as much as to say, what? that it is not consonant to utility, to consult utility: in short, that it is *not* consulting it, to consult it. Addition by the author, July 1822.

Not long after the publication of the Fragment on Government, anno 1776, in which, in the character of an all-comprehensive and all-commanding principle, the principle of *utility* was brought to view, one person by whom observation to the above effect was made was *Alexander Wedderburn,* at that time Attorney or Solicitor General, afterwards successively Chief Justice of the Common Pleas, and Chancellor of England, under the successive titles of Lord Loughborough and Earl of Rosslyn.[10] It was made — not indeed in my hearing, but in the hearing of a person by whom it was almost immediately communicated to me. So far from being self-contradictory, it was a shrewd and perfectly true one. By that distinguished functionary, the state of the Government was thoroughly understood: by the obscure individual, at that time not so much as supposed to be so: his disquisitions had not been as yet applied, with any thing like a comprehensive view, to the field of Constitutional Law, nor therefore to those features of the English Government, by which the greatest happiness of the ruling *one* with or without that of a favoured few, are now so plainly seen to be the only ends to which the course of it has at any time been directed. The *principle of utility* was an appellative, at that time employed — employed by me, as it had been by others, to designate that which, in a more perspicuous and instructive manner, may, as above, be designated by the name of the *greatest happiness principle.* "This principle (said Wedderburn) is a dangerous one." Saying so, he said that which, to a certain extent, is strictly true: a principle, which lays down, as the only *right* and justifiable end of Government, the greatest happiness of the greatest number — how can it be denied to be a dangerous one? dangerous it unquestionably is, to every government which has for its *actual* end or object, the greatest happiness of a certain *one,* with or without the addition of the comparatively small number of others, whom it is matter of pleasure or accommodation to him to admit, each of them, to share in the concern, on the footing of so many junior partners. *Dangerous* it therefore really was, to the interest — the sinister interest — of all those functionaries, himself included, whose interest it was, to maximize delay, vexation, and expense, in judicial and other modes of procedure, for the sake of the profit, extractable out of the expense. In a Government which had for its end in view the greatest happiness of the greatest number, Alexander Wedderburn might have been Attorney General and the Chancellor: but he would not have been Attorney General

the causes that have been mentioned, or from some confused or partial view of it, a man may happen to be disposed not to relish it. Where this is the case, if he thinks the settling of his opinions on such a subject worth the trouble, let him take the following steps, and at length, perhaps, he may come to reconcile himself to it.

(1) Let him settle with himself, whether he would wish to discard this principle altogether; if so, let him consider what it is that all his reasonings (in matters of politics especially) can amount to?

(2) If he would, let him settle with himself, whether he would judge and act without any principle, or whether there is any other he would judge and act by?

(3) If there be, let him examine and satisfy himself whether the principle he thinks he has found is really any separate intelligible principle; or whether it be not a mere principle in words, a kind of phrase, which at bottom expresses neither more nor less than the mere averment of his own unfounded sentiments; that is, what in another person he might be apt to call *caprice*?[11]

(4) If he is inclined to think that his own approbation or disapprobation, annexed to the idea of an act, without any regard to its consequences, is a sufficient foundation for him to judge and act upon, let him ask himself whether his sentiment is to be a standard of right and wrong, with respect to every other man, or whether every man's sentiment has the same privilege of being a standard to itself?

(5) In the first case, let him ask himself whether his principle is not despotical, and hostile to all the rest of human race?

(6) In the second case, whether it is not anarchical,[12] and whether at this rate there are not as many different standards of right and wrong as there are men? and whether even to the same man, the same thing, which is right today, may not (without the least change in its nature) be wrong to-morrow? and whether the same thing is not right and wrong in the same place at the same time? and in either case, whether all argument is not at an end? and whether, when two men have said, "I like this," and "I don't like it," they can (upon such a principle) have any thing more to say?

(7) If he should have said to himself, No: for that the sentiment which he proposes as a standard must be grounded on reflection, let him say on what particulars the reflection is to turn? if on particulars having relation to the

---

with £15,000 a year, nor Chancellor, with a peerage, with a veto upon all justice, with £25,000 a year, and with 500 sinecures at his disposal, under the name of Ecclesiastical Benefices, besides *et ceteras*.

utility of the act, then let him say whether this is not deserting his own principle, and borrowing assistance from that very one in opposition to which he sets it up: or if not on those particulars, on what other particulars?

(8) If he should be for compounding the matter, and adopting his own principle in part, and the principle of utility in part, let him say how far he will adopt it?

(9) When he has settled with himself where he will stop, then let him ask himself how he justifies to himself the adopting it so far? and why he will not adopt it any farther?

(10) Admitting any other principle than the principle of utility to be a right principle, a principle that it is right for a man to pursue; admitting (what is not true) that the word *right* can have a meaning without reference to utility, let him say whether there is any such thing as a *motive* that a man can have to pursue the dictates of it: if there is, let him say what that motive is, and how it is to be distinguished from those which enforce the dictates of utility: if not, then lastly let him say what it is this other principle can be good for?

CHAPTER II

Of Principles Adverse to That of Utility

1. If the principle of utility be a right principle to be governed by, and that in all cases, it follows from what has been just observed, that whatever principle differs from it in any case must necessarily be a wrong one. To prove any other principle, therefore, to be a wrong one, there needs no more than just to show it to be what it is, a principle of which the dictates are in some point or other different from those of the principle of utility: to state it is to confute it.

2. A principle may be different from that of utility in two ways: 1. By being constantly opposed to it: this is the case with a principle which may be termed the principle of asceticism.[i] 2. By being sometimes opposed to it,

---

i. (Asceticism) Ascetic is a term that has been sometimes applied to Monks. It comes from a Greek word which signifies *exercise*. The practices by which Monks sought to distinguish themselves from other men were called their Exercises. These exercises consisted in so many contrivances they had for tormenting themselves. By this they thought to ingratiate themselves with the Deity. For the Deity, said they, is a Being of infinite benevolence: now a Being of the most ordinary benevolence is pleased to see others make themselves as happy as they can: therefore to make ourselves as unhappy as

and sometimes not, as it may happen: this is the case with another, which may be termed the principle of *sympathy* and *antipathy*.

3. By the principle of asceticism I mean that principle, which, like the principle of utility, approves or disapproves of any action, according to the tendency which it appears to have to augment or diminish the happiness of the party whose interest is in question; but in an inverse manner: approving of actions in as far as they tend to diminish his happiness; disapproving of them in as far as they tend to augment it.

4. It is evident that any one who reprobates any the least particle of pleasure, as such, from whatever source derived, is *pro tanto* a partisan of the principle of asceticism. It is only upon that principle, and not from the principle of utility, that the most abominable pleasure which the vilest of malefactors ever reaped from his crime would be to be reprobated, if it stood alone. The case is, that it never does stand alone; but is necessarily followed by such a quantity of pain (or, what comes to the same thing, such a chance for a certain quantity of pain) that the pleasure in comparison of it, is as nothing: and this is the true and sole, but perfectly sufficient, reason for making it a ground for punishment.

5. There are two classes of men of very different complexions, by whom the principle of asceticism appears to have been embraced; the one a set of moralists, the other a set of religionists. Different accordingly have been the motives which appear to have recommended it to the notice of these different parties. Hope, that is the prospect of pleasure, seems to have animated the former: hope, the aliment of philosophic pride: the hope of honour and reputation at the hands of men. Fear, that is the prospect of pain, the latter: fear, the offspring of superstitious fancy: the fear of future punishment at the hands of a splenetic and revengeful Deity. I say in this case fear: for of the invisible future, fear is more powerful than hope. These circumstances characterize the two different parties among the partisans of

---

we can is the way to please the Deity. If any body asked them, what motive they could find for doing all this? Oh! said they, you are not to imagine that we are punishing ourselves for nothing: we know very well what we are about. You are to know, that for every grain of pain it costs us now, we are to have a hundred grains of pleasure by and by. The case is, that God loves to see us torment ourselves at present: indeed he has as good as told us so. But this is done only to try us, in order just to see how we should behave: which it is plain he could not know, without making the experiment. Now then, from the satisfaction it gives him to see us make ourselves as unhappy as we can make ourselves in this present life, we have a sure proof of the satisfaction it will give him to see us as happy as he can make us in a life to come.

the principle of asceticism; the parties and their motives different, the principle the same.

6. The religious party, however, appear to have carried it farther than the philosophical: they have acted more consistently and less wisely. The philosophical party have scarcely gone farther than to reprobate pleasure: the religious party have frequently gone so far as to make it a matter of merit and of duty to court pain. The philosophical party have hardly gone farther than the making pain a matter of indifference. It is no evil, they have said: they have not said, it is a good. They have not so much as reprobated all pleasure in the lump. They have discarded only what they have called the gross; that is, such as are organical, or of which the origin is easily traced up to such as are organical: they have even cherished and magnified the refined. Yet this, however, not under the name of pleasure: to cleanse itself from the sordes of its impure original, it was necessary it should change its name: the honourable, the glorious, the reputable, the becoming, the *honestum*, the *decorum*, it was to be called: in short, any thing but pleasure.

7. From these two sources have flowed the doctrines from which the sentiments of the bulk of mankind have all along received a tincture of this principle; some from the philosophical, some from the religious, some from both. Men of education more frequently from the philosophical, as more suited to the elevation of their sentiments: the vulgar more frequently from the superstitious, as more suited to the narrowness of their intellect, undilated by knowledge: and to the abjectness of their condition, continually open to the attacks of fear. The tinctures, however, derived from the two sources, would naturally intermingle, insomuch that a man would not always know by which of them he was most influenced: and they would often serve to corroborate and enliven one another. It was this conformity that made a kind of alliance between parties of a complexion otherwise so dissimilar: and disposed them to unite upon various occasions against the common enemy, the partisan of the principle of utility, whom they joined in branding with the odious name of Epicurean.

8. The principle of asceticism, however, with whatever warmth it may have been embraced by its partisans as a rule of private conduct, seems not to have been carried to any considerable length, when applied to the business of government. In a few instances it has been carried a little way by the philosophical party: witness the Spartan regimen. Though then, perhaps, it may be considered as having been a measure of security: and an application, though a precipitate and perverse application, of the principle of utility. Scarcely in any instances, to any considerable length, by the religious: for the various monastic orders, and the societies of the Quakers,

Dumplers,[13] Moravians, and other religionists, have been free societies, whose regimen no man has been astricted to without the intervention of his own consent. Whatever merit a man may have thought there would be in making himself miserable, no such notion seems ever to have occurred to any of them, that it may be a merit, much less a duty, to make others miserable: although it should seem, that if a certain quantity of misery were a thing so desirable, it would not matter much whether it were brought by each man upon himself, or by one man upon another. It is true, that from the same source from whence, among the religionists, the attachment to the principle of asceticism took its rise, flowed other doctrines and practices, from which misery in abundance was produced in one man by the instrumentality of another: witness the holy wars, and the persecutions for religion. But the passion for producing misery in these cases proceeded upon some special ground: the exercise of it was confined to persons of particular descriptions: they were tormented, not as men, but as heretics and infidels. To have inflicted the same miseries on their fellow-believers and fellow-sectaries, would have been as blameable in the eyes even of these religionists, as in those of a partisan of the principle of utility. For a man to give himself a certain number of stripes was indeed meritorious: but to give the same number of stripes to another man, not consenting, would have been a sin. We read of saints, who for the good of their souls, and the mortification of their bodies, have voluntarily yielded themselves a prey to vermin: but though many persons of this class have wielded the reins of empire, we read of none who have set themselves to work, and made laws on purpose, with a view of stocking the body politic with the breed of highwaymen, housebreakers, or incendiaries. If at any time they have suffered the nation to be preyed upon by swarms of idle pensioners, or useless placemen, it has rather been from negligence and imbecility, than from any settled plan for oppressing and plundering of the people.[j] If at any time they have sapped the sources of national wealth, by cramping commerce, and driving the inhabitants into emigration, it has been with other views, and in pursuit of other ends. If they have declaimed against the pursuit of pleasure, and the use of wealth, they have commonly stopped at declamation: they have not, like Lycurgus, made express ordinances for the purpose of banishing the precious metals.[14] If they have established idleness by a law, it has been not because idleness, the mother of vice and misery, is itself a virtue, but because idleness (say they) is the road to holiness. If under the notion of fasting, they have joined in the plan of confining their subjects to a diet,

j. So thought A° 1780 and 1789; not so A° 1814.[15]

thought by some to be of the most nourishing and prolific nature, it has been not for the sake of making them tributaries to the nations by whom that diet was to be supplied, but for the sake of manifesting their own power, and exercising the obedience of the people. If they have established, or suffered to be established, punishments for the breach of celibacy, they have done no more than comply with the petitions of those deluded rigorists, who, dupes to the ambitious and deep-laid policy of their rulers, first laid themselves under that idle obligation by a vow.

9. The principle of asceticism seems originally to have been the reverie of certain hasty speculators, who having perceived, or fancied, that certain pleasures, when reaped in certain circumstances, have, at the long run, been attended with pains more than equivalent to them, took occasion to quarrel with every thing that offered itself under the name of pleasure. Having then got thus far, and having forgot the point which they set out from, they pushed on, and went so much further as to think it meritorious to fall in love with pain. Even this, we see, is at bottom but the principle of utility misapplied.

10. The principle of utility is capable of being consistently pursued; and it is but tautology to say, that the more consistently it is pursued, the better it must ever be for human-kind. The principle of asceticism never was, nor ever can be, consistently pursued by any living creature. Let but one tenth part of the inhabitants of this earth pursue it consistently, and in a day's time they will have turned it into a hell.

11. Among principles adverse to that of utility, that which at this day seems to have most influence in matters of government, is what may be called the principle of sympathy and antipathy.[k] By the principle of

k. The following Note was first printed in January 1789.

It ought rather to have been styled, more extensively, the principle of *caprice.* Where it applies to the choice of actions to be marked out for injunction or prohibition, for reward or punishment, (to stand, in a word, as subjects for *obligations* to be imposed), it may indeed with propriety be termed, as in the text, the principle of *sympathy* and *antipathy.* But this appellative does not so well apply to it, when occupied in the choice of the *events* which are to serve as sources of *title* with respect to *rights:* where the actions prohibited and allowed the obligations and rights, being already fixed, the only question is, under what circumstances a man is to be invested with the one or subjected to the other? from what incidents occasion is to be taken to invest a man, or to refuse to invest him, with the one, or to subject him to the other? In this latter case it may more appositely be characterized by the name of the *phantastic principle.* Sympathy and antipathy are affections of the *sensible* faculty. But the choice of *titles* with respect to *rights,* especially

sympathy and antipathy, I mean that principle which approves or disapproves of certain actions, not on account of their tending to augment the happiness, nor yet on account of their tending to diminish the happiness of the party whose interest is in question, but merely because a man finds himself disposed to approve or disapprove of them: holding up that approbation or disapprobation as a sufficient reason for itself, and disclaiming the necessity of looking out for any extrinsic ground. Thus far in the general department of morals: and in the particular department of politics, measuring out the quantum (as well as determining the ground) of punishment, by the degree of the disapprobation.

12. It is manifest, that this is rather a principle in name than in reality: it

---

with respect to proprietary rights, upon grounds unconnected with utility, has been in many instances the work, not of the affections but of the imagination.

When, in justification of an article of English Common Law, calling uncles to succeed in certain cases in preference to fathers, Lord Coke produced a sort of ponderosity he had discovered in rights, disqualifying them from ascending in a straight line,[16] it was not that he *loved* uncles particularly, or *hated* fathers, but because the analogy, such as it was, was what his imagination presented him with, instead of a reason, and because, to a judgment unobservant of the standard of utility, or unacquainted with the art of consulting it, where affection is out of the way, imagination is the only guide.

When I know not what ingenious grammarian invented the proposition *Delegatus non potest delegare,* to serve as a rule of law, it was not surely that he had any antipathy to delegates of the second order, or that it was any pleasure to him to think of the ruin which, for want of a manager at home, may befal the affairs of a traveller, whom an unforeseen accident has deprived of the object of his choice: it was, that the incongruity, of giving the same law to objects so contrasted as *active* and *passive* are, was not to be surmounted, and that *-atus* chimes, as well as it contrasts, with *-are.*

When that inexorable maxim (of which the dominion is no more to be defined, than the date of its birth, or the name of its father, is to be found) was imported from England for the government of Bengal, and the whole fabric of judicature was crushed by the thunders of *ex post facto* justice, it was not surely that the prospect of a blameless magistracy perishing in prison afforded any enjoyment to the unoffended authors of their misery; but that the music of the maxim, absorbing the whole imagination, had drowned the cries of humanity along with the dictates of common sense.* *Fiat Justitia, ruat cœlum,* says another maxim, as full of extravagance as it is of harmony: Go heaven to wreck — so justice be but done: — and what is the ruin of kingdoms, in comparison of the wreck of heaven?

* Additional Note by the Author, July 1822.

Add, and that the bad system, of Mahometan and other native law was to be put down

is not a positive principle of itself, so much as a term employed to signify the negation of all principle. What one expects to find in a principle is something that points out some external consideration, as a means of warranting and guiding the internal sentiments of approbation and disapprobation: this expectation is but ill fulfilled by a proposition, which does neither

---

at all events, to make way for the inapplicable and still more mischievous system of English Judge-made law, and, by the hand of his accomplice Hastings, was to be put into the pocket of Impey — Importer of this instrument of subversion, £8,000 a-year contrary to law, in addition to the £8,000 a-year lavished upon him, with the customary profusion, by the hand of law. — See the Account of this transaction in *Mill's British India*.[17]

To this Governor a statue is erecting by a vote of East India Directors and Proprietors: on it should be inscribed — *Let it but put money into our pockets, no tyranny too flagitious to be worshipped by us.*

To this statue of the Arch-malefactor should be added, for a companion, that of the long robed accomplice: the one lodging the bribe in the hand of the other. The hundred millions of plundered and oppressed Hindoos and Mahometans pay for the one: a Westminister Hall subscription might pay for the other.

What they have done for Ireland with her seven millions of souls, the authorised deniers and perverters of justice have done for Hindostan with her hundred millions. In this there is nothing wonderful. The wonder is — that, under such institutions, men, though in ever such small numbers, should be found, whom the view of the injustices which, by *English Judge-made law,* they are compelled to commit, and the miseries they are thus compelled to produce, deprive of health and rest. Witness the Letter of an English Hindostan Judge, Sept. 1, 1819, which lies before me. I will not make so cruel a requital for his honesty, as to put his name in print: indeed the House of Commons' Documents already published leave little need of it.

So again, when the Prussian chancellor, inspired with the wisdom of I know not what Roman sage, proclaimed in good Latin, for the edification of German ears, *Servitus servitutis non datur,* (Cod. Fred. tom. ii. par. 2 liv. 2. tit. x. 6. p. 308.)[18] it was not that he had conceived any aversion to the lifeholder who, during the continuance of his term, should wish to gratify a neighbour with a right of way or water, or to the neighbour who should wish to accept of the indulgence; but that, to a jurisprudential ear, *-tus -tutis* sound little less melodious than *-atus -are.* Whether the melody of the maxim was the real reason of the rule, is not left open to dispute: for it is ushered in by the conjunction *quia,* reason's appointed harbinger: *quia servitus servitutis non datur.*

Neither would equal melody have been produced, nor indeed could similar melody have been called for, in either of these instances, by the opposite provision: it is only when

more nor less than hold up each of those sentiments as a ground and standard for itself.

13. In looking over the catalogue of human actions (says a partisan of this principle) in order to determine which of them are to be marked with the seal of disapprobation, you need but to take counsel of your own feel-

---

they are opposed to general rules, and not when by their conformity they are absorbed in them, that more specific ones can obtain a separate existence. *Delegatus potest delegare,* and *Servitus servitutis datur,* provisions already included under the general adoption of contracts, would have been as unnecessary to the apprehension and the memory, as, in comparison of their energetic negatives, they are insipid to the ear.

Were the inquiry diligently made, it would be found that the goddess of harmony has exercised more influence, however latent, over the dispensations of Themis, than her most diligent historiographers, or even her most passionate panegyrists, seem to have been aware of. Every one knows, how, by the ministry of Orpheus, it was she who first collected the sons of men beneath the shadow of the sceptre: yet, in the midst of continual experience, men seem yet to learn, with what successful diligence she has laboured to guide it in its course. Every one knows, that measured numbers were the language of the infancy of law: none seem to have observed, with what imperious sway they have governed her maturer age. In English jurisprudence in particular, the connexion betwixt law and music, however less perceived than in Spartan legislation, is not perhaps less real nor less close. The music of the Office, though not of the same kind, is not less musical in its kind, than the music of the Theatre; that which hardens the heart, than that which softens it: — sostenutos as long, cadences as sonorous; and those governed by rules, though not yet promulgated, not less determinate. Search indictments, pleadings, proceedings in chancery, conveyances: whatever trespasses you may find against truth or common sense, you will find none against the laws of harmony. The English Liturgy, justly as this quality has been extolled in that sacred office, possesses not a greater measure of it, than is commonly to be found in an English Act of Parliament. Dignity, simplicity, brevity, precision, intelligibility, possibility of being retained or so much as apprehended, every thing yields to Harmony. Volumes might be filled, shelves loaded, with the sacrifices that are made to this insatiate power. Expletives, her ministers in Grecian poetry, are not less busy, though in different shape and bulk, in English legislation: in the former, they are monosyllables*: in the latter they are whole lines.†

To return to the *principle of sympathy and antipathy:* a term preferred at first, on account of its impartiality, to the *principle of caprice.* The choice of an appellative, in the above respects too narrow, was owing to my not having, at that time, extended my views over the civil branch of law, any otherwise than as I had found it inseparably involved in the penal. But when we come to the former branch, we shall see the *phantastic*

ings: whatever you find in yourself a propensity to condemn, is wrong for that very reason. For the same reason it is also meet for punishment: in what proportion it is adverse to utility, or whether it be adverse to utility at all, is a matter that makes no difference. In that same *proportion* also is it meet for punishment: if you hate much, punish much: if you hate little, punish little: punish as you hate. If you hate not at all, punish not at all: the fine feelings of the soul are not to be overborne and tyrannized by the harsh and rugged dictates of political Utility.

14. The various systems that have been formed concerning the standard of right and wrong, may all be reduced to the principle of sympathy and antipathy. One account may serve for all of them. They consist all of them in so many contrivances for avoiding the obligation of appealing to any external standard, and for prevailing upon the reader to accept of the author's

---

principle making at least as great a figure there, as the principle of *sympathy and antipathy* in the latter.

In the days of Lord Coke, the light of utility can scarcely be said to have as yet shone upon the face of Common Law. If a faint ray of it, under the name of the *argumentum ab inconvenienti,* is to be found in a list of about twenty topics exhibited by that great lawyer as the co-ordinate leaders of that all-perfect system, the admission, so circumstanced, is as sure a proof of neglect, as, to the statues of Brutus and Cassius, exclusion was a cause of notice. It stands, neither in the front, nor in the rear, nor in any post of honour; but huddled in towards the middle, without the smallest mark of preference. (Coke Littleton. 11. a.).[19] Nor is this Latin *inconvenience* by any means the same thing with the English one. It stands distinguished from *mischief:* and because by the vulgar it is taken for something less bad, it is given by the learned as something worse. *The law prefers a mischief to an inconvenience,* says an admired maxim, and the more admired, because as nothing is expressed by it, the more is supposed to be understood.

Not that there is any avowed, much less a constant opposition, between the prescriptions of utility and the operations of the common law: such constancy we have seen to be too much even for ascetic fervour. (Supra, par. 10) From time to time instinct would unavoidably betray them into the paths of reason: instinct which, however it may be cramped, can never be killed by education. The cobwebs spun out of the materials brought together by "the competition of opposite analogies," can never have ceased being warped by the silent attraction of the rational principle: though it should have been, as the needle is by the magnet, without the privity of conscience.

* Μεν, τοί, γε, νῦν, &c. —

† And be it further enacted by the authority aforesaid, that — Provided always, and it is hereby further enacted and declared that — &c. &c.

sentiment or opinion as a reason and that a sufficient one[20] for itself. The phrases different, but the principle the same.[1]

15. It is manifest, that the dictates of this principle will frequently coincide with those of utility, though perhaps without intending any such thing. Probably more frequently than not: and hence it is that the business of penal

l. It is curious enough to observe the variety of inventions men have hit upon, and the variety of phrases they have brought forward, in order to conceal from the world, and, if possible, from themselves, this very general and therefore very pardonable self-sufficiency.[21]

1. One man (Lord Shaftesbury, Hutchinson, Hume, etc.)[22] says, he has a thing made on purpose to tell him what is right and what is wrong; and that it is called a *moral sense:* and then he goes to work at his ease, and says, such a thing is right, and such a thing is wrong — why? "because my moral sense tells me it is."

2. Another man (Dr Beattie)[23] comes and alters the phrase: leaving out *moral,* and putting in *common,* in the room of it. He then tells you, that his common sense teaches him what is right and wrong, as surely as the other's moral sense did: meaning by common sense, a sense of some kind or other, which, he says, is possessed by all mankind: the sense of those, whose sense is not the same as the author's, being struck out of the account as not worth taking. This contrivance does better than the other; for a moral sense, being a new thing, a man may feel about him a good while without being able to find it out: but common sense is as old as the creation; and there is no man but would be ashamed to be thought not to have as much of it as his neighbours. It has another great advantage: by appearing to share power, it lessens envy: for when a man gets up upon this ground, in order to anathematize those who differ from him, it is not by a *sic volo sic jubeo,* but by a *velitis jubeatis.*

3. Another man (Dr Price)[24] comes, and says, that as to a moral sense indeed, he cannot find that he has any such thing: that however he has an *understanding,* which will do quite as well. This understanding, he says, is the standard of right and wrong: it tells him so and so. All good and wise men understand as he does: if other men's understandings differ in any point from his, so much the worse for them: it is a sure sign they are either defective or corrupt.

4. Another man says, that there is an eternal and immutable Rule of Right: that that rule of right dictates so and so: and then he begins giving you his sentiments upon any thing that comes uppermost: and these sentiments (you are to take for granted) are so many branches of the eternal rule of right.

5. Another man (Dr Clark),[25] or perhaps the same man (it's no matter) says, that there are certain practices conformable, and others repugnant, to the Fitness of Things; and then he tells you, at his leisure, what practices are conformable and what repugnant: just as he happens to like a practice or dislike it.

6. A great multitude of people are continually talking of the Law of Nature; and then

justice is carried on upon that tolerable sort of footing upon which we see it carried on in common at this day. For what more natural or more general ground of hatred to a practice can there be, than the mischievousness of such practice? What all men are exposed to suffer by, all men will be disposed to hate. It is far yet, however, from being a constant ground: for

---

they go on giving you their sentiments about what is right and what is wrong: and these sentiments, you are to understand, are so many chapters and sections of the Law of Nature.

7. Instead of the phrase, Law of Nature, you have sometimes, Law of Reason, Right Reason, Natural Justice, Natural Equity, Good Order. Any of them will do equally well. This latter is most used in politics. The three last are much more tolerable than the others, because they do not very explicitly claim to be any thing more than phrases: they insist but feebly upon the being looked upon as so many positive standards of themselves, and seem content to be taken, upon occasion, for phrases expressive of the conformity of the thing in question to the proper standard, whatever that may be. On most occasions, however, it will be better to say *utility*: *utility* is clearer, as referring more explicitly to pain and pleasure.

8. We have one philosopher (Woolaston),[26] who says, there is no harm in any thing in the world but in telling a lie: and that if, for example, you were to murder your own father, this would only be a particular way of saying, he was not your father. Of course, when this philosopher sees any thing that he does not like, he says, it is a particular way of telling a lie. It is saying, that the act ought to be done, or may be done, when, *in truth,* it ought not to be done.

9. The fairest and openest of them all is that sort of man who speaks out, and says, I am of the number of the Elect: now God himself takes care to inform the Elect what is right: and that with so good effect, that let them strive ever so, they cannot help not only knowing it but practising it. If therefore a man wants to know what is right and what is wrong, he has nothing to do but to come to me.

It is upon the principle of antipathy that such and such acts are often reprobated on the score of their being *unnatural:* the practice of exposing children, established among the Greeks and Romans, was an unnatural practice. Unnatural, when it means any thing, means unfrequent: and there it means something; although nothing to the present purpose. But here it means no such thing: for the frequency of such acts is perhaps the great complaint. It therefore means nothing; nothing, I mean, which there is in the act itself. All it can serve to express is, the disposition of the person who is talking of it: the disposition he is in to be angry at the thoughts of it. Does it merit his anger? Very likely it may: but whether it does or no is a question, which, to be answered rightly, can only be answered upon the principle of utility.

Unnatural, is as good a word as moral sense, or common sense; and would be as good a foundation for a system. Such an act is unnatural; that is, repugnant to nature: for I do

when a man suffers, it is not always that he knows what it is he suffers by. A man may suffer grievously, for instance, by a new tax, without being able to trace up the cause of his sufferings to the injustice of some neighbour, who has eluded the payment of an old one.

16. The principle of sympathy and antipathy is most apt to err on the side

---

not like to practise it; and, consequently, do not practise it. It is therefore repugnant to what ought to be the nature of every body else.

The mischief common to all these ways of thinking and arguing (which, in truth, as we have seen, are but one and the same method, couched in different forms of words) is their serving as a cloak, and pretence, and aliment, to despotism: if not a despotism in practice, a despotism however in disposition: which is but too apt, when pretence and power offer, to show itself in practice. The consequence is, that with intentions very commonly of the purest kind, a man becomes a torment either to himself or his fellow-creatures. If he be of the melancholy cast (Dr Price),[27] he sits in silent grief, bewailing their blindness and depravity: if of the irascible (Dr Beattie),[27] he declaims with fury and virulence against all who differ from him; blowing up the coals of fanaticism, and branding with the charge of corruption and insincerity, every man who does not think, or profess to think, as he does.

If such a man happens to possess the advantages of style, his book may do a considerable deal of mischief before the nothingness of it is understood.

These principles, if such they can be called, it is more frequent to see applied to morals than to politics: but their influence extends itself to both. In politics, as well as morals, a man will be at least equally glad of a pretence for deciding any question in the manner that best pleases him, without the trouble of inquiry. If a man is an infallible judge of what is right and wrong in the actions of private individuals, why not in the measures to be observed by public men in the direction of such actions?[28] accordingly (not to mention other chimeras) I have more than once known the pretended law of nature set up in legislative debates, in opposition to arguments derived from the principle of utility.

"But is it never, then, from any other considerations than those of utility, that we derive our notions of right and wrong?" I do not know: I do not care. Whether a moral sentiment can be originally conceived from any other source than a view of utility, is one question: whether upon examination and reflection it can, in point of fact, be actually persisted in and justified on any other ground, by a person reflecting within himself, is another: whether in point of right it can properly be justified on any other ground, by a person addressing himself to the community, is a third. The two first are questions of speculation: it matters not, comparatively speaking, how they are decided. The last is a question of practice: the decision of it is of as much importance as that of any can be.

"I feel in myself," (say you) "a disposition to approve of such or such an action in a

of severity. It is for applying punishment in many cases which deserve none: in many cases which deserve some, it is for applying more than they deserve. There is no incident imaginable, be it ever so trivial, and so remote from mischief, from which this principle may not extract a ground of punishment. Any difference in taste: any difference in opinion: upon one subject as well as upon another. No disagreement so trifling which perseverance and altercation will not render serious. Each becomes in the other's eyes an enemy, and, if laws permit, a criminal.[m] This is one of the

---

moral view: but this is not owing to any notions I have of its being a useful one to the community. I do not pretend to know whether it be an useful one or not: it may be, for aught I know, a mischievous one." "But is it then," (say I) "a mischievous one? examine; and if you can make yourself sensible that it is so, then, if duty means any thing, that is, moral duty, it is your *duty* at least to abstain from it: and more than that, if it is what lies in your power, and can be done without too great a sacrifice, to endeavour to prevent it. It is not your cherishing the notion of it in your bosom, and giving it the name of virtue, that will excuse you."

"I feel in myself," (say you again) "a disposition to detest such or such an action in a moral view; but this is not owing to any notions I have of its being a mischievous one to the community. I do not pretend to know whether it be a mischievous one or not: it may be not a mischievous one: it may be, for aught I know, an useful one." — "May it indeed?" (say I) "an useful one? but let me tell you then, that unless duty, and right and wrong, be just what you please to make them, if it really be not a mischievous one, and any body has a mind to do it, it is no duty of yours, but, on the contrary, it would be very wrong in you, to take upon you to prevent him: detest it within yourself as much us you please; that may be a very good reason (unless it be also a useful one) for your not doing it yourself: but if you go about, by word or deed, to do any thing to hinder him, or make him suffer for it, it is you, and not he, that have done wrong: it is not your setting yourself to blame his conduct, or branding it with the name of vice, that will make him culpable, or you blameless. Therefore, if you can make yourself content that he shall be of one mind, and you of another, about that matter, and so continue, it is well: but if nothing will serve you, but that you and he must needs be of the same mind, I'll tell you what you have to do: it is for you to get the better of your antipathy, not for him to truckle to it."

m. King James the First of England had conceived a violent antipathy against Arians: two of whom he burnt.*[29] This gratification he procured himself without much difficulty: the notions of the times were favourable to it. He wrote a furious book against Vorstius, for being what was called an Arminian: for Vorstius was at a distance.[30] He also wrote a furious book, called "A Counterblast to Tobacco," against the use of that drug, which Sir Walter Raleigh had then lately introduced.[31] Had the notions of the times co-operated with

circumstances by which the human race is distinguished (not much indeed to its advantage) from the brute creation.

17. It is not, however, by any means unexampled for this principle to err on the side of lenity. A near and perceptible mischief moves antipathy. A remote and imperceptible mischief, though not less real, has no effect. Instances in proof of this will occur in numbers in the course of the work.[n] It would be breaking in upon the order of it to give them here.

18. It may be wondered, perhaps, that in all this while no mention has been made of the *theological* principle; meaning that principle which professes to recur for the standard of right and wrong to the will of God. But the case is, this is not in fact a distinct principle. It is never any thing more or less than one or other of the three before-mentioned principles presenting itself under another shape. The *will* of God here meant cannot be his revealed will, as contained in the sacred writings: for that is a system which nobody ever thinks of recurring to at this time of day, for the details of political administration: and even before it can be applied to the details of private conduct, it is universally allowed, by the most eminent divines of all persuasions, to stand in need of pretty ample interpretations; else to what

---

him, he would have burnt the Anabaptist and the smoker of tobacco in the same fire. However he had the satisfaction of putting Raleigh to death afterwards, though for another crime.

Disputes concerning the comparative excellence of French and Italian music have occasioned very serious bickerings at Paris. One of the parties would not have been sorry (says Mr D'Alembert†)[32] to have brought government into the quarrel. Pretences were sought after and urged. Long before that, a dispute of like nature, and of at least equal warmth, had been kindled at London upon the comparative merits of two composers at London; where riots between the approvers and disapprovers of a new play are, at this day, not unfrequent. The ground of quarrel between the Big-endians and the Little-endians in the fable,[33] was not more frivolous than many an one which has laid empires desolate. In Russia, it is said, there was a time when some thousands of persons lost their lives in a quarrel, in which the government had taken part, about the number of fingers to be used in making the sign of the cross. This was in days of yore: the ministers of Catherine II± are better *instructed*[34] than to take any other part in such disputes, than that of preventing the parties concerned from doing one another a mischief.

* Hume's Hist. vol. 6.

† Melanges Essai sur la Libérte de la Musique.

± Instruct, art. 474, 475, 476.

n. See Ch. XVI (Division) par. 42, 44 [**not included in this volume — S.E.**].

use are the works of those divines? And for the guidance of these interpretations, it is also allowed, that some other standard must be assumed. The will then which is meant on this occasion, is that which may be called the *presumptive* will: that is to say, that which is presumed to be his will on account of the conformity of its dictates to those of some other principle. What then may be this other principle? it must be one or other of the three mentioned above: for there cannot, as we have seen, be any more. It is plain, therefore, that, setting revelation out of the question, no light can ever be thrown upon the standard of right and wrong, by any thing that can be said upon the question, what is God's will. We may be perfectly sure, indeed, that whatever is right is conformable to the will of God: but so far is that from answering the purpose of showing us what is right, that it is necessary to know first whether a thing is right, in order to know from thence whether it be conformable to the will of God.[o]

19. There are two things which are very apt to be confounded, but which it imports us carefully to distinguish: — the motive or cause, which, by operating on the mind of an individual,[35] is productive of any act: and the ground or reason which warrants a legislator, or other by-stander, in regarding that act with an eye of approbation. When the act happens, in the particular instance in question, to be productive of effects which we approve of, much more if we happen to observe that the same motive may frequently be productive, in other instances, of the like effects, we are apt to transfer our approbation to the motive itself, and to assume, as the just ground for the approbation we bestow on the act, the circumstance of its

o. The principle of theology refers every thing to God's pleasure. But what is God's pleasure? God does not, he confessedly does not now, either speak or write to us. How then are we to know what is his pleasure? By observing what is our own pleasure, and pronouncing it to be his. Accordingly, what is called the pleasure of God, is and must necessarily be (revelation apart) neither more nor less than the good pleasure of the person, whoever he be, who is pronouncing what he believes, or pretends, to be God's pleasure. How know you it to be God's pleasure that such or such an act should be abstained from? whence come you even to suppose as much? "Because the engaging in it would, I imagine, be prejudicial upon the whole to the happiness of mankind"; says the partisan of the principle of utility: "Because the commission of it is attended with a gross and sensual, or at least with a trifling and transient satisfaction"; says the partisan of the principle of asceticism: "Because I detest the thoughts of it; and I cannot, neither ought I to be called upon to tell why"; says he who proceeds upon the principle of antipathy. In the words of one or other of these must that person necessarily answer (revelation apart) who professes to take for his standard the will of God.

originating from that motive. It is in this way that the sentiment of antipathy has often been considered as a just ground of action. Antipathy, for instance, in such or such a case, is the cause of an action which is attended with good effects: but this does not make it a right ground of action in that case, any more than in any other. Still farther. Not only the effects are good, but the agent sees beforehand that they will be so. This may make the action indeed a perfectly right action: but it does not make antipathy a right ground of action. For the same sentiment of antipathy, if implicitly deferred to, may be, and very frequently is, productive of the very worst effects. Antipathy, therefore, can never be a right ground of action. No more, therefore, can resentment, which, as will be seen more particularly hereafter, is but a modification of antipathy. The only right ground of action, that can possibly subsist, is, after all, the consideration of utility, which, if it is a right principle of action, and of approbation, in any one case, is so in every other. Other principles in abundance, that is, other motives, may be the reasons why such and such an act *has* been done: that is, the reasons or causes of its being done: but it is this alone that can be the reason why it might or ought to have been done. Antipathy or resentment requires always to be regulated, to prevent its doing mischief: to be regulated by what? always by the principle of utility. The principle of utility neither requires nor admits of any other regulator than itself.

CHAPTER III

Of the Four Sanctions or Sources of Pain and Pleasure

1. It has been shown that the happiness of the individuals, of whom a community is composed, that is their pleasures and their security, is the end and the sole end which the legislator ought to have in view: the sole standard, in conformity to which each individual ought, as far as depends upon the legislator, to be *made* to fashion his behaviour. But whether it be this or anything else that is to be *done*, there is nothing by which a man can ultimately be *made* to do it, but either pain or pleasure. Having taken a general view of these two grand objects (viz. pleasure, and what comes to the same thing, immunity from pain) in the character of *final* causes; it will be necessary to take a view of pleasure and pain itself, in the character of *efficient* causes or means.

2. There are four distinguishable sources from which pleasure and pain are in use to flow: considered separately, they may be termed the *physical*, the *political*, the *moral*, and the *religious*: and inasmuch as the pleasures and pains belonging to each of them are capable of giving a binding force to any law or rule of conduct, they may all of them be termed *sanctions.*[p]

3. If it be in the present life, and from the ordinary course of nature, not purposely modified by the interposition of the will of any human being, nor by any extraordinary interposition of any superior invisible being, that the pleasure or the pain takes place or is expected, it may be said to issue from or to belong to the *physical sanction.*

4. If at the hands of a *particular* person or set of persons in the community, who under names correspondent to that of *judge*, are chosen for the particular purpose of dispensing it, according to the will of the sovereign or supreme ruling power in the state, it may be said to issue from the *political sanction.*

5. If at the hands of such *chance* persons in the community, as the party in question may happen in the course of his life to have concerns with, according to each man's spontaneous disposition, and not according to any settled or concerted rule, it may be said to issue from the *moral* or *popular sanction.*[q]

p. *Sanctio,* in Latin, was used to signify the *act of binding,* and, by a common grammatical transition, *any thing which serves to bind a man*: to wit, to the observance of such or such a mode of conduct. According to a Latin grammarian,* the import of the word is derived by rather a far-fetched process (such as those commonly are, and in a great measure indeed must be, by which intellectual ideas are derived from sensible ones) from the word *sanguis,* blood: because, among the Romans, with a view to inculcate into the people a persuasion that such or such a mode of conduct would be rendered obligatory upon a man by the force of what I call the religious sanction (that is, that he would be made to suffer by the extraordinary interposition of some superior being, if he failed to observe the mode of conduct in question) certain ceremonies were contrived by the priests: in the course of which ceremonies the blood of victims was made use of.

A sanction then is a source of obligatory powers or *motives*: that is, of *pains* and *pleasures*; which, according as they are connected with such or such modes of conduct, operate, and indeed are the only things which can operate, as *motives*. See Ch. X (Motives) [**not included in this volume — S. E.**].

* Servius. See Ainsworth's Dict. ad verbum *Sanctio.*[36]

q. (Moral Sanction).[37] Better termed *popular,* as more directly indicative of its constituent cause; as likewise of its relation to the more common phrase *public opinion,* in French *opinion publique,* the name there given to that tutelary power, of which of late so much is said, and by which so much is done. The latter appellation is however unhappy and inexpressive; since if *opinion* is material, it is only in virtue of the influence it exercises over action, through the medium of the affections and the will.

6. If from the immediate hand of a superior invisible being, either in the present life, or in a future, it may be said to issue from the *religious sanction*.

7. Pleasures or pains which may be expected to issue from the *physical*, *political*, or *moral* sanctions, must all of them be expected to be experienced, if ever, in the *present* life: those which may be expected to issue from the *religious* sanction, may be expected to be experienced either in the *present* life or in a *future*.

8. Those which can be experienced in the present life, can of course be no others than such as human nature in the course of the present life is susceptible of: and from each of these sources may flow all the pleasures or pains of which, in the course of the present life, human nature is susceptible. With regard to these then (with which alone we have in this place any concern) those of them which belong to any one of those sanctions, differ not ultimately in kind from those which belong to any one of the other three: the only difference there is among them lies in the circumstances that accompany their production. A suffering which befalls a man in the natural and spontaneous course of things, shall be styled, for instance, a *calamity*; in which case, if it be supposed to befall him through any imprudence of his, it may be styled a punishment issuing from the *physical* sanction. Now this same suffering, if inflicted by the law, will be what is commonly called a *punishment*; if incurred for want of any friendly assistance, which the misconduct, or supposed misconduct, of the sufferer has occasioned to be withholden, a punishment issuing from the *moral* sanction; if through the immediate interposition of a particular providence, a punishment issuing from the *religious* sanction.

9. A man's goods, or his person, are consumed by fire. If this happened to him by what is called an accident, it was a *calamity*: if by reason of his own imprudence (for instance, from his neglecting to put his candle out) it may be styled a punishment of the *physical* sanction: if it happened to him by the sentence of the political magistrate, a punishment belonging to the *political* sanction; that is, what is commonly called a *punishment*: if for want of any assistance which his *neighbour* withheld from him out of some dislike to his *moral* character, a punishment of the *moral* sanction: if by an immediate act of *God's* displeasure, manifested on account of some *sin* committed by him, or through any distraction of mind, occasioned by the dread of such displeasure, a punishment of the *religious* sanction.[r]

r. A suffering conceived to befall a man by the immediate act of God, as above, is often, for shortness sake, called a *judgment*: instead of saying, a suffering inflicted on

10. As to such of the pleasures and pains belonging to the religious sanction, as regard a future life, of what kind these may be we cannot know. These lie not open to our observation. During the present life they are matter only of expectation: and, whether that expectation be derived from natural or revealed religion, the particular kind of pleasure or pain, if it be different from all those which lie open to our observation, is what we can have no idea of. The best ideas we can obtain of such pains and pleasures are altogether unliquidated in point of quality. In what other respects our ideas of them *may* be liquidated will be considered in another place.[s]

11. Of these four sanctions the physical is altogether, we may observe, the ground-work of the political and the moral: so is it also of the religious, in as far as the latter bears relation to the present life. It is included in each of those other three. This may operate in any case, (that is, any of the pains or pleasures belonging to it may operate) independently of *them*: none of *them* can operate but by means of this. In a word, the powers of nature may operate of themselves; but neither the magistrate, nor men at large, *can* operate, nor is God in the case in question *supposed* to operate, but through the powers of nature.

12. For these four objects, which in their nature have so much in common, it seemed of use to find a common name. It seemed of use, in the first place, for the convenience of giving a name to certain pleasures and pains, for which a name equally characteristic could hardly otherwise have been found: in the second place, for the sake of holding up the efficacy of certain moral forces, the influence of which is apt not to be sufficiently attended to. Does the political sanction exert an influence over the conduct of mankind? The moral, the religious sanctions do so too. In every inch of his career are the operations of the political magistrate liable to be aided or impeded by these two foreign powers: who, one or other of them, or both, are sure to be either his rivals or his allies. Does it happen to him to leave them out in his calculations? he will be sure almost to find himself mistaken in the result. Of all this we shall find abundant proofs in the sequel of this work. It behoves him, therefore, to have them continually before his eyes; and that under such a name as exhibits the relation they bear to his own purposes and designs.

---

him in consequence of a special judgment formed, and resolution thereupon taken, by the Deity.

s. See Ch. XIII (Cases unmeet) par. 2. Note [**not included in this volume — S.E.**].

CHAPTER IV

Value of a Lot of Pleasure or Pain, How to Be Measured

1. Pleasures then, and the avoidance of pains, are the *ends* which the legislator has in view: it behoves him therefore to understand their *value*. Pleasures and pains are the *instruments* he has to work with: it behoves him therefore to understand their force, which is again, in another point of view,[38] their value.

2. To a person considered *by himself*, the value of a pleasure or pain considered *by itself*, will be greater or less, according to the four following circumstances:[t]

1. Its *intensity*.
2. Its *duration*.
3. Its *certainty* or *uncertainty*.
4. Its *propinquity* or *remoteness*.

3. These are the circumstances which are to be considered in estimating a pleasure or a pain considered each of them by itself. But when the value of any pleasure or pain is considered for the purpose of estimating the tendency of any *act* by which it is produced, there are two other circumstances to be taken into the account; these are,

5. Its *fecundity*, or the chance it has of being followed by sensations of the *same* kind: that is, pleasures, if it be a pleasure: pains, if it be a pain.
6. Its *purity*, or the chance it has of *not* being followed by sensations of the *opposite* kind: that is, pains, if it be a pleasure: pleasures, if it be a pain.

These two last, however, are in strictness scarcely to be deemed properties of the pleasure or the pain itself; they are not, therefore, in strictness to

t. These circumstances have since been denominated *elements* or *dimensions* of *value* in a pleasure or a pain.

Not long after the publication of the first edition, the following memoriter verses were framed, in the view of lodging more effectually, in the memory, these points, on which the whole fabric of morals and legislation may be seen to rest.

> *Intense, long, certain, speedy, fruitful, pure* —
> Such marks in *pleasures* and in *pains* endure.
> Such pleasures seek, if *private* be thy end:
> If it be *public*, wide let them *extend.*
> Such *pains* avoid, whichever be thy view:
> If pains *must* come, let them *extend* to few.[39]

be taken into the account of the value of that pleasure or that pain. They are in strictness to be deemed properties only of the act, or other event, by which such pleasure or pain has been produced; and accordingly are only to be taken into the account of the tendency of such act or such event.

4. To a *number* of persons, with reference to each of whom the value of a pleasure or a pain is considered, it will be greater or less, according to seven circumstances: to wit, the six preceding ones; viz.

1. Its *intensity*.
2. Its *duration*.
3. Its *certainty* or *uncertainty*.
4. Its *propinquity* or *remoteness*.
5. Its *fecundity*.
6. Its *purity*.

And one other; to wit:

7. Its *extent*; that is, the number of persons to whom it *extends*; or (in other words) who are affected by it.

5. To take an exact account then of the general tendency of any act, by which the interests of a community are affected, proceed as follows. Begin with any one person of those whose interests seem most immediately to be affected by it: and take an account,

1. Of the value of each distinguishable *pleasure* which appears to be produced by it in the *first* instance.
2. Of the value of each *pain* which appears to be produced by it in the *first* instance.
3. Of the value of each pleasure which appears to be produced by it *after* the first. This constitutes the *fecundity* of the first *pleasure* and the *impurity* of the first *pain*.
4. Of the value of each *pain* which appears to be produced by it after the first. This constitutes the *fecundity* of the first *pain*, and the *impurity* of the first pleasure.
5. Sum up all the values of all the *pleasures* on the one side, and those of all the *pains* on the other. The balance, if it be on the side of pleasure, will give the *good* tendency of the act upon the whole, with respect to the interests of that *individual* person; if on the side of pain, the *bad* tendency of it upon the whole.
6. Take an account of the *number* of persons whose interests appear to be concerned; and repeat the above process with respect to each. *Sum up* the numbers expressive of the degrees of *good* tendency, which the act

has, with respect to each individual, in regard to whom the tendency of it is *good* upon the whole: do this again with respect to each individual, in regard to whom the tendency of it is *good* upon the whole: do this again with respect to each individual, in regard to whom the tendency of it is *bad* upon the whole. Take the *balance;* which, if on the side of *pleasure*, will give the general *good tendency* of the act, with respect to the total number or community of individuals concerned; if on the side of pain, the general *evil tendency*, with respect to the same community.

6. It is not to be expected that this process should be strictly pursued previously to every moral judgment, or to every legislative or judicial operation. It may, however, be always kept in view: and as near as the process actually pursued on these occasions approaches to it, so near will such process approach to the character of an exact one.

7. The same process is alike applicable to pleasure and pain, in whatever shape they appear: and by whatever denomination they are distinguished: to pleasure, whether it be called *good* (which is properly the cause or instrument of pleasure) or *profit* (which is distant pleasure, or the cause or instrument of distant pleasure,) or *convenience*, or *advantage*, *benefit*, *emolument*, *happiness*, and so forth: to pain, whether it be called *evil*, (which corresponds to *good*) or *mischief*, or *inconvenience*, or *disadvantage*, or *loss*, or *unhappiness*, and so forth.

8. Nor is this a novel and unwarranted, any more than it is a useless theory. In all this there is nothing but what the practice of mankind, wheresoever they have a clear view of their own interest, is perfectly conformable to. An article of property, an estate in land, for instance, is valuable, on what account? On account of the pleasures of all kinds which it enables a man to produce, and what comes to the same thing the pains of all kinds which it enables him to avert. But the value of such an article of property is universally understood to rise or fall according to the length or shortness of the time which a man has in it: the certainty or uncertainty of its coming into possession: and the nearness or remoteness of the time at which, if at all, it is to come into possession. As to the *intensity* of the pleasures which a man may derive from it, this is never thought of, because it depends upon the use which each particular person may come to make of it; which cannot be estimated till the particular pleasures he may come to derive from it, or the particular pains he may come to exclude by means of it, are brought to view. For the same reason, neither does he think of the *fecundity* or *purity* of those pleasures.

Thus much for pleasure and pain, happiness and unhappiness, in *general*. We come now to consider the several particular kinds of pain and pleasure.

CHAPTER V

Pleasures and Pains, Their Kinds

1. Having represented what belongs to all sorts of pleasures and pains alike, we come now to exhibit, each by itself, the several sorts of pains and pleasures. Pains and pleasures may be called by one general word, interesting perceptions. Interesting perceptions are either simple or complex. The simple ones are those which cannot any one of them be resolved into more: complex are those which are resolvable into divers simple ones. A complex interesting perception may accordingly be composed either, 1. Of pleasures alone: 2. Of pains alone: or, 3. Of a pleasure or pleasures, and a pain or pains together. What determines a lot of pleasure, for example, to be regarded as one complex pleasure, rather than as divers simple ones, is the nature of the exciting cause. Whatever pleasures are excited all at once by the action of the same cause, are apt to be looked upon as constituting all together but one pleasure.

2. The several simple pleasures of which human nature is susceptible, seem to be as follows: 1. The pleasures of sense. 2. The pleasures of wealth. 3. The pleasures of skill. 4. The pleasures of amity. 5. The pleasures of a good name. 6. The pleasures of power. 7. The pleasures of piety. 8. The pleasures of benevolence. 9. The pleasures of malevolence. 10. The pleasures of memory. 11. The pleasures of imagination. 12. The pleasures of expectation. 13. The pleasures dependent on association. 14. The pleasures of relief.

3. The several simple pains seem to be as follows: 1. The pains of privation. 2. The pains of the senses. 3. The pains of awkwardness. 4. The pains of enmity. 5. The pains of an ill name. 6. The pains of piety. 7. The pains of benevolence. 8. The pains of malevolence. 9. The pains of the memory. 10. The pains of the imagination. 11. The pains of expectation. 12. The pains dependent on association.[u][40]

u. The catalogue here given, is what seemed to be a complete list of the several simple pleasures and pains of which human nature is susceptible: insomuch, that if, upon any occasion whatsoever, a man feels pleasure or pain, it is either referable at once to some one or other of these kinds, or resolvable into such as are. It might perhaps have been a

4. (1) The pleasures of sense seem to be as follows: 1. The pleasures of the taste or palate; including whatever pleasures are experienced in satisfying the appetites of hunger and thirst. 2. The pleasure of intoxication.[41] 3. The pleasures of the organ of smelling. 4. The pleasures of the touch. 5. The simple pleasures of the ear; independent of association. 6. The simple pleasures of the eye; independent of association. 7. The pleasure of the sexual[42] sense. 8. The pleasure of health: or, the internal pleasurable feeling or flow of spirits (as it is called,) which accompanies a state of full health and vigour; especially at times of moderate bodily exertion. 9. The pleasures of novelty: or, the pleasures derived from the gratification of the appetite of curiosity, by the application of new objects to any of the senses.[v]

5. (2) By the pleasures of wealth may be meant those pleasures which a man is apt to derive from the consciousness of possessing any article or articles which stand in the list of instruments of enjoyment or security, and more particularly at the time of his first acquiring them; at which time the pleasure may be styled a pleasure of gain or a pleasure of acquisition: at other times a pleasure of possession.

(3) The pleasures of skill, as exercised upon particular objects, are those which accompany the application of such particular instruments of enjoyment to their uses, as cannot be so applied without a greater or less share of difficulty or exertion.[w]

6. (4) The pleasures of amity, or self-recommendation, are the pleasures that may accompany the persuasion of a man's being in the acquisition or the possession of the good-will of such or such assignable person or persons in particular: or, as the phrase is, of being upon good terms with him or

---

satisfaction to the reader, to have seen an analytical view of the subject, taken upon an exhaustive plan, for the purpose of demonstrating the catalogue to be what it purports to be, a complete one. The catalogue is in fact the result of such an analysis; which, however, I thought it better to discard at present, as being of too metaphysical a cast, and not strictly within the limits of this design. See Ch. XIII (Cases unmeet) Par. 2. Note [**not included in this volume — S.E.**].

v. There are also pleasures of novelty, excited by the appearance of new ideas: these are pleasures of the imagination. See infra 13.[43]

w. For instance, the pleasure of being able to gratify the sense of hearing, by singing, or performing upon any musical instrument. The pleasure thus obtained, is a thing superadded to, and perfectly distinguishable from, that which a man enjoys from hearing another person perform in the same manner.

them: and as a fruit of it, of his being in a way to have the benefit of their spontaneous and gratuitous services.

7. (5) The pleasures of a good name are the pleasures that accompany the persuasion of a man's being in the acquisition or the possession of the good-will of the world about him; that is, of such members of society as he is likely to have concerns with; and as a means of it, either their love or their esteem, or both: and as a fruit of it, of his being in the way to have the benefit of their spontaneous and gratuitous services. These may likewise be called the pleasures of good repute, the pleasures of honour, or the pleasures of the moral sanction.[x]

8. (6) The pleasures of power are the pleasures that accompany the persuasion of a man's being in a condition to dispose people, by means of their hopes and fears, to give him the benefit of their services: that is, by the hope of some service, or by the fear of some disservice, that he may be in the way to render them.

9. (7) The pleasures of piety are the pleasures that accompany the belief of a man's being in the acquisition or in possession of the good-will or favour of the Supreme Being: and as a fruit of it, of his being in a way of enjoying pleasures to be received by God's special appointment, either in this life, or in a life to come. These may also be called the pleasures of religion, the pleasures of a religious disposition, or the pleasures of the religious sanction.[y]

10. (8) The pleasures of benevolence are the pleasures resulting from the view of any pleasures supposed to be possessed by the beings who may be the objects of benevolence; to wit, the sensitive beings we are acquainted with; under which are commonly included, 1. The Supreme Being. 2. Human beings. 3. Other animals. These may also be called the pleasures of good-will, the pleasures of sympathy, or the pleasures of the benevolent or social affections.

11. (9) The pleasures of malevolence are the pleasures resulting from the view of any pain supposed to be suffered by the beings who may become the objects of malevolence: to wit, 1. Human beings. 2. Other animals. These may also be styled the pleasures of ill-will, the pleasures of the irascible appetite, the pleasures of antipathy, or the pleasures of the malevolent or dissocial affections.

12. (10) The pleasures of the memory are the pleasures which, after

x. See Ch. III (Sanctions).

y. See Ch. III (Sanctions).

having enjoyed such and such pleasures, or even in some case after having suffered such and such pains, a man will now and then experience, at recollecting them exactly in the order and in the circumstances in which they were actually enjoyed or suffered. These derivative pleasures may of course be distinguished into as many species as there are of original perceptions, from whence they may be copied. They may also be styled pleasures of simple recollection.

13. (11) The pleasures of the imagination are the pleasures which may be derived from the contemplation of any such pleasures as may happen to be suggested by the memory, but in a different order, and accompanied by different groups of circumstances. These may accordingly be referred to any one of the three cardinal points of time, present, past, or future. It is evident they may admit of as many distinctions as those of the former class.

14. (12) The pleasures of expectation are the pleasures that result from the contemplation of any sort of pleasure, referred to time *future*, and accompanied with the sentiment of *belief*. These also may admit of the same distinctions.[z]

15. (13) The pleasures of association are the pleasures which certain objects or incidents may happen to afford, not of themselves, but merely in virtue of some association they have contracted in the mind with certain objects or incidents which are in themselves pleasurable. Such is the case, for instance, with the pleasure of skill, when afforded by such a set of incidents as compose a game of chess. This derives its pleasurable quality from its association partly with the pleasures of skill, as exercised in the production of incidents pleasurable of themselves: partly from its association with the pleasures of power. Such is the case also with the pleasure of good luck, when afforded by such incidents as compose the game of hazard, or any other game of chance, when played at for nothing. This derives its pleasurable quality from its association with one of the pleasures of wealth; to wit, with the pleasure of acquiring it.

16. (14) Farther on we shall see pains grounded upon pleasures; in like manner may we now see pleasures grounded upon pains. To the catalogue of pleasures may accordingly be added the pleasures of *relief*: or, the pleasures which a man experiences when, after he has been enduring a pain of any kind for a certain time, it comes to cease, or to abate. These may of course be distinguished into as many species as there are of pains: and may give rise to so many pleasures of memory, of imagination, and of expectation.

z. In contradistinction to these, all other pleasures may be termed pleasures of *enjoyment*.[44]

17. (1) Pains of privation are the pains that may result from the thought of not possessing in the time present any of the several kinds of pleasures. Pains of privation may accordingly be resolved into as many kinds as there are of pleasures to which they may correspond, and from the absence whereof they may be derived.

18. There are three sorts of pains which are only so many modifications of the several pains of privation. When the enjoyment of any particular pleasure happens to be particularly desired, but without any expectation approaching to assurance, the pain of privation which thereupon results takes a particular name, and is called the pain of *desire*, or of unsatisfied desire.

19. Where the enjoyment happens to have been looked for with a degree of expectation approaching to assurance, and that expectation is made suddenly to cease, it is called a pain of disappointment.

20. A pain of privation takes the name of a pain of regret in two cases: 1. Where it is grounded on the memory of a pleasure, which having been once enjoyed, appears not likely to be enjoyed again: 2. Where it is grounded on the idea of a pleasure, which was never actually enjoyed, nor perhaps so much as expected, but which might have been enjoyed (it is supposed,) had such or such a contingency happened, which, in fact, did not happen.

21. (2) The several pains of the senses seem to be as follows: 1. The pains of hunger and thirst: or the disagreeable sensations produced by the want of suitable substances which need at times to be applied to the alimentary canal. 2. The pains of the taste: or the disagreeable sensations produced by the application of various substances to the palate, and other superior parts of the same canal. 3. The pains of the organ of smell: or the disagreeable sensations produced by the effluvia of various substances when applied to that organ. 4. The pains of the touch: or the disagreeable sensations produced by the application of various substances to the skin. 5. The simple pains of the hearing: or the disagreeable sensations excited in the organ of that sense by various kinds of sounds: independently (as before,) of association. 6. The simple pains of the sight: or the disagreeable sensations if any such there be, that may be excited in the organ of that sense by visible images, independent of the principle of association. 7.[aa] The pains resulting from excessive heat or cold, unless these be referable to the touch. 8. The

---

aa. The pleasure of the sexual sense seems to have no positive pain to correspond to it: it has only a pain of privation, or pain of the mental class, the pain of unsatisfied desire. If any positive pain of body result from the want of such indulgence, it belongs to the head of pains of disease.

pains of disease: or the acute and uneasy sensations resulting from the several diseases and indispositions to which human nature is liable. 9. The pain of exertion, whether bodily or mental: or the uneasy sensation which is apt to accompany any intense effort, whether of mind or body.

22. (3)[bb] The pains of awkwardness are the pains which sometimes result from the unsuccessful endeavour to apply any particular instruments of enjoyment or security to their uses, or from the difficulty a man experiences in applying them.[cc]

23. (4) The pains of enmity are the pains that may accompany the persuasion of a man's being obnoxious to the ill-will of such or such an assignable person or persons in particular: or, as the phrase is, of being upon ill terms with him or them: and, in consequence, of being obnoxious to certain pains of some sort or other, of which he may be the cause.

24. (5) The pains of an ill-name, are the pains that accompany the persuasion of a man's being obnoxious, or in a way to be obnoxious to the ill-will of the world about him. These may likewise be called the pains of ill-repute, the pains of dishonour, or the pains of the moral sanction.[dd]

bb. The pleasures of novelty have no positive pains corresponding to them. The pain which a man experiences when he is in the condition of not knowing what to do with himself, that pain, which in French is expressed by a single word *ennui,* is a pain of privation: a pain resulting from the absence, not only of all the pleasures of novelty, but of all kinds of pleasure whatsoever.

The pleasures of wealth have also no positive pains corresponding to them: the only pains opposed to them are pains of privation. If any positive pains result from the want of wealth, they are referable to some other class of positive pains; principally to those of the senses. From the want of food, for instance, result the pains of hunger; from the want of clothing, the pains of cold; and so forth.

cc. It may be a question, perhaps, whether this be a positive pain of itself, or whether it may be nothing more than a pain of privation, resulting from the consciousness of a want of skill. It is, however, but a question of words, nor does it matter which way it be determined.

dd. In as far as man's fellow-creatures are supposed to be determined by any event not to regard him with any degree of esteem or *good* will, or to regard him with a less degree of esteem or good will than they would otherwise; not to do him any sorts of *good* offices, or not to do him so many *good* offices as they would otherwise; the pain resulting from such consideration may be reckoned a pain of privation: as far as they are supposed to regard him with such a degree of aversion or disesteem as to be disposed to do him positive *ill* offices, it may be reckoned a positive pain. The pain of privation, and the positive pain, in this case run one into another indistinguishably.

25. (6)[ee] The pains of piety are the pains that accompany the belief of a man's being obnoxious to the displeasure of the Supreme Being: and in consequence to certain pains to be inflicted by his especial appointment, either in this life or in a life to come. These may also be called the pains of religion; the pains of a religious disposition; or the pains of the religious sanction. When the belief is looked upon as well-grounded, these pains are commonly called religious terrors; when looked upon as ill-grounded, superstitious terrors.[ff]

26. (7) The pains of benevolence are the pains resulting from the view of any pains supposed to be endured by other beings. These may also be called the pains of good-will, of sympathy, or the pains of the benevolent or social affections.

27. (8) The pains of malevolence are the pains resulting from the view of any pleasures supposed to be enjoyed by any beings who happen to be the objects of a man's displeasure. These may also be styled the pains of ill-will, of antipathy, or the pains of the malevolent or dissocial affections.

28. (9) The pains of the memory may be grounded on every one of the above kinds, as well of pains of privation as of positive pains. These correspond exactly to the pleasures of the memory.

29. (10) The pains of the imagination may also be grounded on any one of the above kinds, as well of pains of privation as of positive pains: in other respects they correspond exactly to the pleasures of the imagination.

30. (11) The pains of expectation may be grounded on each one of the above kinds, as well of pains of privation as of positive pains. These may be also termed pains of apprehension.[gg]

31. (12) The pains of association correspond exactly to the pleasures of association.

ee. There seem to be no positive pains to correspond to the pleasures of power. The pains that a man may feel from the want or the loss of power, in as far as power is distinguished from all other sources of pleasure, seem to be nothing more than pains of privation.

ff. The positive pains of piety, and the pains of privation, opposed to the pleasures of piety, run one into another in the same manner as the positive pains of enmity, or of an ill name, do with respect to the pains of privation, opposed to the pleasures of amity, and those of a good name. If what is apprehended at the hands of God is barely the not receiving pleasure, the pain is of the privative class: if, moreover, actual pain be apprehended, it is of the class of positive pains.

gg. In contradistinction to these, all other pains may be termed pains of *sufferance*.[45]

32. Of the above list there are certain pleasures and pains which suppose the existence of some pleasure or pain of some other person, to which the pleasure or pain of the person in question has regard: such pleasures and pains may be termed *extra-regarding*. Others do not suppose any such thing: these may be termed *self-regarding*.[hh] The only pleasures and pains of the extra-regarding class are those of benevolence, and those of malevolence: all the rest are self-regarding.[ii]

33. Of all these several sorts of pleasures and pains, there is scarce any one which is not liable, on more accounts than one, to come under the consideration of the law. Is an offence committed? it is the tendency which it has to destroy, in such or such persons, some of these pleasures, or to produce some of these pains, that constitutes the mischief of it, and the ground for punishing it. It is the prospect of some of these pleasures, or of security from some of these pains, that constitutes the motive or temptation, it is the attainment of them that constitutes the profit of the offence. Is the offender to be punished? It can be only by the production of one or more of these pains, that the punishment can be inflicted.[jj]

---

hh. See Ch. x (Motives) [**not included in this volume — S.E.**].

ii. By this means the pleasures and pains of amity may be the more clearly distinguished from those of benevolence: and on the other hand, those of enmity from those of malevolence. The pleasures and pains of amity and enmity are of the self-regarding cast: those of benevolence and malevolence of the extra-regarding.

jj. It would be a matter not only of curiosity, but of some use, to exhibit a catalogue of the several complex pleasures and pains, analyzing them at the same time into the several simple ones, of which they are respectively composed. But such a disquisition would take up too much room to be admitted here. A short specimen, however, for the purpose of illustration, can hardly be dispensed with.

The pleasures taken in at the eye and ear are generally very complex. The pleasures of a country scene, for instance, consist commonly, amongst others, of the following pleasures:

I. Pleasures of the senses

1. The simple pleasures of sight, excited by the perception of agreeable colours and figures, green fields, waving foliage, glistening water, and the like.

2. The simple pleasures of the ear, excited by the perceptions of the chirping of birds, the murmuring of waters, the rustling of the wind among the trees.

3. The pleasures of the smell, excited by the perceptions of the fragrance of flowers, of new-mown hay, or other vegetable substances, in the first stages of fermentation.

4. The agreeable inward sensation, produced by a brisk circulation of the blood, and

NOTES

1. This of course refers to the title page of the original 1789 edition. In 1823 the reference to 1780 was transferred to the verso of the title page. Bentham's correspondence shows that the work of printing was begun in April and continued until November 1780.

2. Cf. Introduction to *Of Laws in General* (in *CW*, xxxi ff.).

3. The only publication of this kind which has been traced took place in 1786, when Bentham's friend Francois-Xavier Schwediauer published in four volumes his *Philosophical Dictionary; or, the Opinions of modern philosophers on metaphysical, moral, and political subjects.* This compilation included ten brief extracts from the present work, drawn chiefly from its early chapters, together with six extracts from *A Fragment on Government.* But it seems doubtful whether this publication took place without Bentham's "privity": certainly Schwediauer told him that his name was to be "most honourably mentioned" in the *Dictionary* (Schwediauer to Bentham, 12 November 1784, Timothy L. S. Sprigge and Ian R. Christie, eds., *Correspondence*, iii [London: Athlone Press, 1968], 314, in *CW*, Letter 519; and cf. n. 5 to that letter, where the extracts from Bentham's works are identified).

4. Of the 1789 edition.

---

the ventilation of it in the lungs by a pure air, such as that in the country frequently is in comparison of that which is breathed in towns.

II. Pleasures of the imagination produced by association

1. The idea of the plenty, resulting from the possession of the objects that are in view, and of the happiness arising from it.

2. The idea of the innocence and happiness of the birds, sheep, cattle, dogs, and other gentle or domestic animals.

3. The idea of the constant flow of health, supposed to be enjoyed by all these creatures: a notion which is apt to result from the occasional flow of health enjoyed by the supposed spectator.

4. The idea of gratitude, excited by the contemplation of the all-powerful and beneficent Being, who is looked up to as the author of these blessings.

These four last are all of them, in some measure at least, pleasures of sympathy.

The depriving a man of this group of pleasures is one of the evils apt to result from imprisonment; whether produced by illegal violence, or in the way of punishment, by appointment of the laws.

5. Bentham's *Defence of Usury*, written in Russia in the spring of 1787, was published towards the end of that year and was well received.

6. P. 231, n. 13 below [**not included in this volume — S.E.**].

7. Bentham's reference is to paras. 58 ff. of the Preface to *A Fragment on Government*, *The Works of Jeremy Bentham*, ed. J. Bowring, 11 vols. (Edinburgh: William Tait, 1838–43), i. 237–38 [hereafter Bowring].

8. The references mentioned in this paragraph take for the most part such forms as "See B.I. tit. (Irrep. corp. injuries)," i.e., *Plan of a Penal Code*, book 1, title *Irreparable corporal injuries*.

9. Note added in the 1823 edition.

10. Alexander Wedderburn (1733–1805), Baron Loughborough 1780, Earl of Rosslyn 1801; solicitor-general 1771–78, attorney-general 1778–80, lord chief justice of the Common Pleas 1780–93, lord chancellor 1793–1801. Bentham met Wedderburn at the house of his friend John Lind in February 1777 (*Correspondence*, in *CW*, ii, 18) and it was most certainly Lind who told Bentham of Wedderburn's remark. See also Bentham's account of the matter in the "Historical Preface" (1828) to the *Fragment on Government*, para. V (Bowring i. 245–46).

11. The emphasis on the word *caprice* was suggested by Bentham in a MS entry in his copy of the 1789 edition, now in the British Museum. The suggestion was not followed in 1823.

12. Thus 1789 ed.; 1823 ed. has "anarchial."

13. *O.E.D.* does not list separately this name for the Church of the Brethren, or Dunkers, a German Baptist sect who, like the Quakers and Moravian Brethren with whom Bentham groups them, had settled in Pennsylvania. The Chicago *Dictionary of American English* cites for the term *Dumplers* a travel journal of 1778 not published until 1790 and a geographical work published in 1789, the year when Bentham's Introduction was first published. *O.E.D.*, s. v. *Dunker*, cites the second of these passages including the word *Dumpler*, but dates it 1796, from a later edition.

14. Like most statements about Lycurgus this is quite legendary.

15. This MS note was inserted by Bentham in his copy of the 1789 edition now in the British Museum. It was overlooked in 1823 but was inserted in the Bowring edition (i. 5n.).

16. *Coke upon Littleton*, 11a; part of chap. 1 "Fee Simple," sect. 3 (p): "It is a maxim in law that inheritance may literally descend, but not ascend . . . if the son purchase land in fee simple, and die without issue, living his father, the uncle shall have the land as heir to the son and not the father, yet the father is nearer of blood."

17. Warren Hastings (1732–1818), governor of Bengal 1772–4, governor-general under the Regulating Act 1774–85, was recalled to face impeachment in 1788 and partially acquitted in 1795. Sir Elijah Impey (1732–1809) was chief

justice of the Supreme Court at Calcutta from 1773 until 1783, when he was recalled to face charges made in the House of Commons that he had contravened the terms of his appointment by enlarging the court's jurisdiction. Cf. James Mill, *History of British India* (1818), ii, 585 ff.

18. Bentham is evidently referring to the work published at Halle in two volumes in 1749 and 1751 and compiled by the jurist Samuel von Cocceji (1679–1755). This provided much of the basis for the preparation by Johann von Carmer, Frederick the Great's chancellor from 1781, of what was eventually enacted, after Frederick's death, as the *Allgemeines Preussisches Landrecht*. A number of references in Bentham's papers reflect his interest in this major piece of codification. For a later reference in the present work, see below 306 [**not included in this volume — S.E.**].

19. Cf. n. 16 above. In this passage from *Coke upon Littleton* the tenth of twenty arguments cited is the argument "ab inconvenienti, from that which is inconvenient."

20. The words "and that a sufficient one" are an addition indicated in a list first printed in 1783, appended to the 1789 edition, but not followed in this instance by the 1823 edition. The insertion was duly made in the Bowring edition (i. 8).

21. The notes identifying the philosophers referred to in paragraphs 1, 2, 3, 5, and 8 below were inserted in MS by Bentham in the copy of the 1789 edition now in the British Museum. Written in 1819, the notes were first printed in the Bowring edition (1838). The misspellings of Hutcheson, Clarke, and Wollaston are Bentham's.

22. Anthony Ashley Cooper (1671–1713), 3rd Earl of Shaftesbury, used the phrase "Moral Sense" in his *Inquiry concerning Virtue* (1699). Francis Hutcheson (1694–1746) was a disciple of Shaftesbury, whose principles he expounded in his *Inquiry into the Original of our Ideas of Beauty and Virtue* (1720); he also wrote an *Essay on the Nature and Conduct of the Passions* (1728) and the posthumously published *System of Moral Philosophy* (1755). David Hume (1711–76) expounded his ethical theory principally in his *Enquiry concerning the Principles of Morals* (1751).

23. James Beattie (1735–1803) attacked Hume in his *Essay on the Nature and Immutability of Truth* (1770) and published *Elements of Moral Science* in 1790–93.

24. Richard Price (1723–91) first established his reputation by his *Review of the Principal Questions in Morals* (1758).

25. Samuel Clarke (1675–1729), whose most celebrated work was his *Discourse concerning the Being and Attributes of God*.

26. I.e., William Wollaston (1660–1724), whose principal work, *The Religion of Nature Delineated*, was privately printed in 1722 and published in 1724.

27. These insertions have the same origin as those explained in n. 21 above.

28. The text as printed in 1780 reads "of such actions of those individuals." In the list of errata appended to the 1789 edition the deletion of the last three words is indicated; but the 1823 edition (i, 33n.) followed by the Bowring edition (i. 9n.), mistakenly reads "of those actions."

29. Cf. David Hume, *History of Great Britain*, 1773 ed., v. 163: "Stowe says, that these Arians were offered their pardon at the stake, if they would merit it by a recantation." The executions took place in 1612.

30. Conrad Vorst (1569–1622) was accused of Arminianism after publishing in 1610 his *Tractatus Theologicus de Deo*. James I had the book burned in England and in 1612 published *A Declaration concerning the Proceedings with the States Generall, of the United Provinces of the Low Countreys, in the Cause of D. Conradus Vorstius.*

31. James I's *A Counterblaste to Tobacco* was published in 1604.

32. Cf. *Oeuvres Philosophiques, Historiques et Littéraires de d'Alembert,* 1805, iii, 337–409.

33. I.e., Swift's *Gulliver's Travels.*

34. Bentham had long been interested in Catherine the Great's *Instructions to the Commissioners for Composing a New Code of Laws* (1767; English translation, 1768): cf. *Correspondence*, in *CW*, ii. 99 and n. 4. The articles he refers to here read as follows: —

> "474. A Roman Governor wrote Word to an Emperor, that a Process was preparing against a Judge for High-treason, who had pronounced a Sentence contrary to the Ordinances of that Emperor; the Emperor replied, that, in his reign the Crimes of indirect High-treason were not to be admitted in the Courts of Judicature.
>
> "475. There was a Law among the Romans, which ordained, that whoever should throw anything, though by Accident, against the Images of the Emperors, should he punished as guilty of High-treason.
>
> "476. There was a Law in England, which declared all those guilty of High-treason who should foretell the Death of the King. In the last illness of that King, no Physician dared to inform him of the Danger he was in: We may presume, that they acted in the same Manner with respect to the cure."

Cf. W. F. Reddaway, *Documents of Catherine the Great* (1931), 286.

35. The 1789 edition here reads "by operating in a man's mind."

36. Robert Ainsworth (1660–1743) published his Latin dictionary between 1714 and 1736; it went through many later editions. The derivation of *sancio* is given as "à sanguis, quod fuso sanguine hostiae aliquid sanciretur — Servius." Bentham's reference to the noun *sanctio* is perhaps a slip or misprint for the verbal form.

37. This footnote was an addition made in January 1789. When it was inserted in the 1823 edition (i, 43n.) the bracketed words "Moral Sanction" (indicating, in accordance with Bentham's common practice, the subject of the note) were omitted, presumably because the text at the end of para. 5 (and the corresponding marginal heading) had been emended by inserting the words "or popular" after "moral."

38. The words "in another point of view" were substituted for "in other words" in the sheet of corrections and additions printed in 1783 and appended to the 1789 edition but were overlooked on this occasion in 1823 (i, 49). The correction was made in the Bowring edition (i. 16).

39. Note added in the 1823 edition. The mnemonic verses, headed "Memoriter Verses, expressive of the Elements or Dimensions of Value in Pleasures and Pains" were written by Bentham at the end of his copy of the 1789 edition, now in the British Museum. They are there dated "A° 1780," so that Bentham's reference in the present note to their composition "not long after the *publication* of the first edition" is probably a slip for "printing."

40. The last item in this list is an addition made in the 1823 edition.

41. This item was an insertion proposed in the 1783 sheet of corrections and additions, and made in 1823, the numbering of subsequent items being altered accordingly.

42. Here and in all subsequent instances, with one exception, the 1789 text reads "venereal" for 1823 "sexual."

43. Note added in 1783.

44. Note added in 1783.

45. Note added in 1783.

Place and Time

Edited by Philip Schofield and Stephen G. Engelmann

The following text is based on the original manuscripts located in the Bentham Papers, University College London Library, and has been edited according to the principles and techniques developed by the Bentham Project for the production of the new, authoritative edition of *The Collected Works of Jeremy Bentham.*

The text first appeared in French translation in *Traités de legislation civile et pénale,* edited by Étienne Dumont and published at Paris in three volumes in 1802 (see iii. 323–95). An English edition based on both the original manuscripts and Dumont's translation was edited by Richard Smith and published in *The Works of Jeremy Bentham,* ed. J. Bowring, 11 vols. (Edinburgh: William Tait, 1838–43), i. 168–94.

Both of these versions are deficient in a number of respects. It is hoped that the present text more faithfully represents Bentham's own intentions in relation to the structure and detailed presentation of the work. An authoritative text will appear in *The Collected Works of Jeremy Bentham.*

Thanks to Sunil Agnani, John French, and Allan Kershaw for help with the annotation.

The following symbols are used: | | gap in manuscript; [. . . ?] illegible word(s); thus[?] doubtful reading; [thus] editorial insertion. [088–002]

§ 1. Introduction

"Thus far, then," (I think I hear a reader say) "you have proceeded in your enquiries. Thus far you have determined or endeavoured to determine what is expedient to be done in the way of law. But *where* and *when* to be performed? for, some country and some period of time you must necessarily have had in view. If expedient in any country and at any time, it must be expedient in some individual country, at some individual period of time, that shall be assigned. Suppose, then, that country, suppose that period to have been assigned: let it have been your own or not your own: let it have been this or that or any other. Will the laws, then, which you propose for the given country (for, what concerns the article of time need not any longer be repeated) would they be equally good for every other? If not, what is the influence of place and time on the expediency of what you propose? to give the ques<tion> at once universal form, what is the influence of place and time on matters of legislation? What are the coincidences and what the diversities that ought to subsist between the laws established in different countries and at different periods, supposing them in each instance the best that can be established?"

I will reduce the question at once to that point of view in which the solution of it has the most immediate relation to practice, and, if just, will be productive of the most immediate benefit: and referring every thing to this standard, I enquire what are the deviations which it would be requisite to make from this standard in giving to another country such a tincture as any other country may receive without prejudice from English laws. I take my own <co>untry for the standard: I will suppose this country to be that given country: partly because to that country, if to any, I owe a preference: but chiefly because it is that with the circumstances of which I have the best opportunity to be informed.

This, then, is the hypothesis. The laws, then, which I would propose are established in this my country: and they are, of course, according to my conception of them, the best that can be devised. In this magnificent and presumptuous dream I must be allowed, for the purpose of the argument, to indulge myself.

This, then, is one term in the comparison: but there wants another. The problem, as it stands at present, is — the best possible laws for England being established in England, the variations which it would be necessary to make in those of another given country in order to render them the best laws possible with reference to that other country. But the problem, it is evident, must admitt of as many solutions as there are countries which, in the point in question, are different from England and from each other. To make the tour of the globe in this manner would evidently be an endless task. All that can be done here is to pitch upon some one country in particular for an example. To be as instructive as possible, this second country should, in

regard to the circumstances in question, form as strong a contrast with England as is possible. Such an example we seem to have in the province of Bengal.[1] Climate, face of the country, natural productions, present laws, manners, customs, religion of the inhabitants, every circumstance on which a difference in the point in question can be grounded, as different as can be. Add to which, that between these two countries, a transfer of the kind in question has actually been made or attempted to be made in reality. In regard to almost any two other examples that could have been chosen, the question would have been a mere question of speculation: in regard to these, whatever just remark may happen to be made is of direct use, and applies immediately to practice. To Bengal, then, let us turn the principal current of our attention: not precluding ourselves from [casting][2] every now and then, for the sake of variety, a transient glance towards other countries according as chance may present them to our view.
[o88–oo3]

These being the two countries between which the parallel is to be drawn, let us see upon what principles it is to be made. It is our destiny all along, as soon as ever we have got a glympse of perfection, to leave it by the way. Consummate perfection requires universal accuracy: universal accuracy requires infinite detail. It would be something, however, to trace, though it were ever so general, an outline of a perfect figure: and like Moses, the Jewish leader, to point out, though without conquering, the land of promise. To draw up in a perfect manner a statement of the difference between the laws that would be the best for England and the laws that would be the best for Bengal would require three things. First, the laws which, it is supposed, would be the best for England must be exhibited *in terminis*:[3] next, the leading principles upon which the differences between those and the laws for Bengal appear to turn must be display'd: lastly, these principles must be applied to practice, by making a methodical progress over the several laws which would require to be altered from what they are in the one case in order to accommodate them to the other. According to this plan, were it rigorously adhered to, a compleat code of laws [proposed] for England, accompanied with a collection of all the laws for Bengal which would require to be different from those which are for England, would form a part only of the matter belonging to the present head. The contents of all the succeeding books would, upon this plan, be wanted in order to help fill up the measure of the present chapter. The impracticability of this plan is such as need not be insisted upon. On this plan I would, notwithstanding, wish the reader to fix his eye: for though it be impossible to travel over the whole extent of it upon paper, he may, upon occasion, trace over any or every part of it, to what degree of minuteness he thinks proper, in his own mind. [088–004]

§ 2. Principles

The laws which would be the best for the country *from* which the laws are to be transferred being given, the next object of enquiry is the principles upon which the variations necessary to be made in those laws, in order to accommodate them to Bengal, the country *into* which they are to be transferred, are to be determined.

It hath already been shewn that the end and business of every law, being what they ought to be, may for shortness sake be reduced to this universal expression — the prevention of mischief. Now mischief, of whatever kind, is ultimately reducible to pain, or what may be deemed equivalent to it, loss of pleasure. What then? is the catalogue of pains and pleasures different in one country from what it is in another? have different countries different catalogues of pleasures and of pains? The affirmative, I think, will hardly be maintained: in this point at least human nature may be pronounced to be every where the same. If the difference lies not, then, in the pains and pleasures themselves, it must lie, if any where, in the things that are, or are liable to be, their causes. In this point, indeed, we shall find it to lie upon a little examination. The same event, an event of the same description, nay even the same individual event, which would produce pain or pleasure in one country, would not produce an effect of the same sort, or, if of the same sort, not in equal degree, as the same would have produced in another. Now the pathological powers of any exciting cause will depend upon two particulars: 1. upon the state and condition of the person himself whose interests are in question: 2. upon the state and condition of the external object the action of which is the exciting cause. Now the circumstances the assemblage of which constitutes the state and condition of a man in as far as he is liable to be affected by an exciting cause, as well as those which constitute the state and condition of any object which is exterior to him in as far as the action of such object is liable to become, with reference to him, an exciting cause, are the same circumstances of which the detail has been given under the title of *circumstances influencing sensibility.*[4] In the catalogue, then, of these circumstances we shall find the sum total of the principles of which we are in search — of the principles which, in our enquiry concerning the influence of place and time on matters of legislation, are to serve us as a guide.

The plan upon which this enquiry is to be conducted is already, then, compleatly drawn: the great task of invention has been performed: what remains is little more than manual labour. To assist him in the execution of it, a man should be provided with two sets of tables. Those of the first set would exhibit a number of particulars relative to the body of laws which has been pitched upon for a standard, as contemplated in different points of view: for example, a table of offences: tables of justifications, aggravations, extenuations, and exemptions: a table of punishments: a table of the titles of the civil code: a table of the titles of the constitutional code, and so on. Those of the other set will be: a general table of the circumstances influencing sensibility:[a] tables, or short accounts, of the moral, religious, sympa-

a. The Table of the circumstances influencing sensibility is of continual use. It is applicable to a variety of the most important purposes, of which this now before us is but one. It was first thought of as a necessary implement to the estimating the mischief of an offence: then for the purpose of adjusting the quantum of satisfaction: then again for estimating the force of a lot of punishment: in all these cases the country of the party injured, the party to whom satisfaction is due, and the party on whom punishment is to be inflicted, being given. Montesquieu had already taken the principal part of them into consideration with a view more or less explicit of giving a different adjustment to the laws in consideration of the different exigencies of the inhabitants of different countries: placing in the front of his enquiries those *secondary* circumstances, as I have stiled them, which operate not but by the medium of those others which I have termed *primary*.[5]

Before Montesquieu, a man who had a distant country given him to make laws for would have made short work of it. Name to me the people, he would have said, reach me down my Bible, and the business is done at once. The laws they have been used to, no matter what they are: mine will supersede them: manners, they shall have mine, which are the best in nature: religion, they shall have mine too, which is all of it true, and the only one that is so. Since Montesquieu, the number of documents which a legislator would require is considerably enlarged. Send the people (he will say) to me, or me to the people: lay open to me the whole tenor of their life and conversation: paint to me the face and geography of the country: give me as close and as minute a view as possible of their present laws, their manners and their religion.

M[r] Verelst, treading in the steps of Montesquieu, and availing himself of the opportunities afforded him by the important functions he had been engaged [088–006] in, has confirmed the speculations of the French philosopher by examples taken from actual observation.[*6] The accounts given by M[r] Verelst have received addition and confirmation from various succeeding writers, but above all from that vast and most authentic body of intelligence which, in the course of the years 1772, 1773 and 1781, has been laid before the British House of Commons.[7] The succeeding pages will serve to shew in what manner

thetic and antipathetic biases of the people for whose use the alterations are to be made: a set of maps as particular as possible: a table of the productions of the country, natural and artificial: tables of the weights, measures and coins in use: tables of its population, and the like.[b] These tables, if [088–005] a man would work with accuracy, he should have, not metaphorically only, but literally and materially, before his eyes.

Upon the plan thus chalked out, I proceed to exhibit the alterations above spoken of, following the order of the matters in the original code which is supposed to be the standard. In this course, it can not, for the reasons assigned already, be expected that I should travel long: nor even that I should glean up the whole of the matter that lies in view as I go. All that can consistently be done is to give a set of examples which, in point of order, shall exemplify the method that has been chosen, and, in point of multitude of variety, shall afford a tolerably satisfactory illustration of the principles under the direction of which they have been brought to light. I proceed, then, according to the order of the offences.

[088–007]

§ 3. Place

1.[9] Simple corporal injuries.

These would not require many modifications on account of the difference of place. Mere corporal sensibility, whatever differences it may admitt of in degree, is in specie[10] much the same all the world over. Yet a wound in a hot and unhealthy climate may be much more dangerous than the same wound would be in a temperate and healthy climate.[c] Stripping a man stark

---

the abovementioned theory and observations accord with the plan which has been exhibited, and the principles which have been laid down, in the course of the present volume.

* Mr Verelst had filled various stations in the province of Bengal during a course of |ᴧᴧᴧ| years, for the last |ᴧᴧᴧ| of which he had been Governor. His [View of the Rise, Progress and Present State of the English Government in Bengal] was published in 177|ᴧᴧᴧ|.

b. For a list of articles or heads comprising a statement of the wealth and commerce of any country or district, see the Abbé Morellet's Prospectus d'un nouveau dictionaire de commerce. p. 45. Paris. 1769. 8vo.[8]

c. In |ᴧᴧᴧ| the slightest scratch is oftentimes followed by the *tetanus* or locked jaw: a symptom which generally proves mortal. See Dr Lind's *Essay* on the diseases incident to hot climates.[11]

naked might be death in Siberia in circumstances in which it would be only play in the East Indies.

2. Irreparable corporal injuries.

Under this head it would be necessary to consider whether any and what indulgence should be given to the practice of depriving males of their virility. Such indulgence, it should seem, would stand on better grounds where the attendance of persons thus mutilated is looked upon as a necessary guard to female conjugal fidelity, than where the only use of them is to afford a somewhat higher gratification than could perhaps otherwise be procured to the ear of a musical *dilettante*.[12]

3 and 4. Simple injurious restrainment and multiple injurious compulsion.

See Simple mental injuries, and offences against person and reputation.

5. Wrongful confinement and wrongful banishment.

The effects of these two injurious acts are liable to receive great variation through differences in point of climate, manners, or religion.

A night's confinement in the prison called the Black hole in the hot climate of Calcutta was productive of the most excruciating torments to |∧∧∧| persons who were all that survived it out of |∧∧∧|.[13] In a winter's night in Siberia, the same number of persons might perhaps have undergone a confinement of the same length in the same space without any very remarkable inconvenience.

Confinement inflicted upon a Gentoo[14] might, under certain circumstances, be attended with the forfeiture of his *caste*: a possession much dearer to him than life. Even banishment, if the effects of it were to seclude him from the necessary apparatus for his religious rites, might be attended with a similar effect. Either species of co-ercion might at any rate wound his conscience, inflicting thereby a simple mental injury of the severest kind. The Gentoo seems to stand at the summit of the climax of sensibility in this line. Descending we find the Mahometan,[15] the Jew, the Greek Christian, the Catholic Christian, all exposed to suffer from similar causes according to their respective notions of religious duty. The Mahometan by being hindered from performing his ablutions, or forced upon a diet inconsistent with his fasts. The Jew in like manner by being forced at any time into a forbidden diet: the Greek by being put under a coercion of the same kind during any of his times of fasting. The catholic from a similar cause, or from the being prevented from hearing mass. Even the pious Protestant might suffer in some degree by finding himself deprived for a length of time of the comforts of a spiritual communion.

[088–008]

6. Menacement.

Under this head nothing in particular need be remarked. Whatever injury, if actually inflicted, would come under any of the preceding heads, belongs to this head so long as it is but threatened.

7. Simple mental injuries.

Those sights, those discourses, which would give pain to the inhabitant of one country would not, in every instance, be productive [of] a similar sensation to the inhabitant of another. This difference too, like so many others, turns upon the point of religion. The sectary of every religion, at least the vulgar that is the great bulk of every sect, is exposed to the dread of invisible agents: but the names and attributes of those agents are different. The mind of a Gentoo nurse or of her nurseling may be filled with unspeakable terror by being made to apprehend a visit from Peshush:[16] while a Christian knows no other objects of like terror than witches, devils, ghosts or vampires.

The votary of every sect may receive a cruel wound from any discourse or exhibition which tend[s] to reflect contempt on any of the objects of his veneration. But Protestants feel little in comparison but for Christ Jesus, and for that blessed spirit whom we are taught to figure to ourselves under the image of a dove. The Catholic, to the list of divine persons, adds the Blessed Virgin, and every martyr and every saint who comes to be added to the sacred catalogue makes an almost equal addition to the sphere of his sensibility. The Mahometan has his apostles besides Mahomet: and the Gentoo his deities besides Bramha.

Among the higher classes of Mahometans and Gentoos, for a man to introduce himself into the presence of a married woman, would to the husband be an unpardonable injury: a bare request to see her, an affront. Such injuries, to which the European would be insensible, might in Asia, with perfect propriety, be referred to the denomination now before us.

More than this, the idea which it would be proper to annex to these several offences, will vary much in different countries in virtue of the various circumstances to which it will be respectively proper to give the effect of justification, exemption, extenuation or aggravation.

The differences of castes in Hindostan furnish a copious stock of extenuations and aggravations to different classes of offences.

The extraordinary extent, if one may so say, of the surface of their moral as well as religious sensibility, exposes them to a proportional variety of injuries: hence so many peculiar occasions of *defence* and *provocation*. It is said that were a Hallachore[17] but to touch a man of a superior tribe, and in the transport of his indignation for the injury, the offended person were to draw his sabre and cut down the offender on the spot, he would think himself hardly dealt with if this act of summary justice, as it would seem to him, were imputed to him as an offence. We are told, that "on the Malabar side of the coast,[18] if a Hallachore chances to touch a man of superior tribe, he draws his sabre, and cuts him down on the spot, without any check from his own conscience, or from the laws of the country."[d] Such prejudices, should it be possible to avoid giving way to them altogether, would at least require to be attended to.

The power of the husband, the father, the mother, the guardian is cons[t]ituted, as far as regards the person of the subordinate relative, by justifying the superior in the exercise of those acts of authority over the inferior which, were it not for the justification, would come under one or other of the heads of offence above enumerated.[20]

[088–009]

8. *Semi-public offences through calamity.*

In countries which are nurseries of the *plague,* many precautions may be requisite which in other countries would be needless against that horrible distemper. Such precautions would give rise to a correspondent train of offences.

In Great Britain it would scarcely be in the power of any authority short of the supreme to do any thing, in the way of engrossing or otherwise, towards producing or enhancing the calamity of *famine.* In islands of less extent and fertility, or under governments more liable to abuse, the danger might not be so ideal. In Bengal, the famine by which so many millions were swept off in the year 1769,[e] was owing, let us hope, to no other cause than the inclemency of the seasons, or the insuperable difficulties attending a new system of government.[21] But without legislative precautions, a similar effect might perhaps be produced by the abuse of delegated power in that distant member of the Empire.

In mountainous countries great mischief is some times done by falls of snow which in the neighbourhood of the Alps are called *avalanches,* and by which whole villages are sometimes overwhelmed. A sudden concussion given to the air, by means so inconsiderable as the discharge of a pistol, will sometimes, it is said, be sufficient to give rise to a catastrophe of this sort. I forget what traveller it is who says on this account the discharge of fire arms is made penal in some parts of that mountainous region.[f]

d. Scrafton: *Reflections on the government of Indostan.*[19] Verelst's View of the English government in Bengal.

e. Verelst, p. 72. E. India Reports of the H. of Commons, 1772.

f. I can find no such regulation, however, in the Sardinian Code.[22]

In maritime countries the *coasts* of which consist of a loose sand, there are often found plants chiefly of the *rush* kind, which, by the matted contexture of their roots, communicate to the soil a degree of tenacity by means of which it is enabled to afford a more effectual resistance to the encroachments of the element. By the laws of various countries in Europe, the destruction of such plants is prohibited under penalties which would be altogether useless in different situations.

In the Dutch and Flemish provinces, the extreme vigilance with which it is necessary to guard against the incursions of the sea will naturally give occasion to various regulations for which there would be no use in a more elevated situation.

In towns where the coldness of the climate requires that the houses should be substantial, and the dearness of ground-rent renders the stile of building lofty, the danger that may attend the fall of such as happen to be ruinous gives occasion to regulations which would be unnecessary in those sultry regions where an ordinary house is little more than a large umbrella.

In some parts of Spanish America, the fear of Earthquakes prevents the inhabitants, it is said, from giving to their buildings that degree of solidity which, on other accounts, they would deem eligible. In such harzardous situations the superintending care of the legislator might perhaps be no improper second to the prudence of the individual.

9. *Semi-public offences of mere delinquency.*

Simple corporal injuries.

In hot climates the letting in to a country a mass of stagnant water might, in certain situations, be productive of an injury to public health from which the inhabitants of more temperate regions are in a great measure secure.

Sicily and other parts of Italy are exposed to a wind called the Sirocco which, by the excessive heat and languor it occasions, is extremely troublesome.[g] Certain parts of the East are occasionally afflicted with a wind called Samiel,[h] [23] the influence of which is said to be almost instantaneously fatal. If in any of those countries there were a wood, or a hill, or even a wall, which could in any degree answer the purpose of screening the neighbourhood from the blast, the removal of such a fence might be guarded against by penalties which, in our temperate regions, would have no such utility to justify them.

[o88–o10]

In Arabia and other countries where water is scarce, the poisoning or

g. |∧∧∧|[24]

h. See Ives's *Voyage.*[25]

dissipating the water of a single spring might expose thousands to perish with thirst, and render the communication between one district and another almost impracticable.

In Russia, the destroying or pulling down a few inns might be productive of effects almost equally destructive. In England, hundreds of much better houses of the like sort are put down every year without occasioning the least sensation.

Simple mental injuries.

In some parts of France it is the custom to carry corpses to the grave without a coffin, exposed to public view. In England, I have heard a story related with great horror of an instance when the funerals of paupers have been so carelessly performed, that the light might be discover'd through their coffins. What would have been the feelings of the neighbourhood, had the French state of interment been employ'd?

Self-regarding offences against person.

In the northern climates, drunkenness makes men stupid: in the southern, mad: in the one it is folly; in the other, wickedness. To speak at random, in the one situation penalties against drunkenness should be slight; in the other, they should be severe. In Mahometan countries, the strict prohibition supposed to be laid by the Koran against the use of intoxicating liquors,[i] makes some amends, perhaps, for the mischievous effects of that barbarous religion.

10. *Offences against reputation.*

Defamation.

Among the Greeks the insinuation of a mistake made with regard to sex would have passed but for a joke: Xenophon tells a story of that sort of himself.[j] Even now, wherever the Mahometan religion prevails, such practices seem to be attended with scarce any disrepute. Things are even said to be on a footing nearly similar in some of the southern, and even northern, parts of Europe. I will not be more particular, fearing to do them wrong. In England, not only the letter of the law makes them capital, as in other parts of Europe, but the law is carried into execution with a degree of zeal which no other species of criminality is sufficient to inspire. But were it even altogether unpunishable by law, a groundless imputation of this nature would be an injury scarcely less atrocious than at present: since the consequence of being reputed guilty would be attended with a degree of infamy

---

i. |∧∧∧|[26]

j. Anabasis |∧∧∧| and see the memorabilia.[27]

which can be compared to nothing so properly as that which attends forfeiture of caste among the Hindoos.

[088–011]

In England, to say of a farmer he had sown rye-grass and clover in the
same field would be of as little prejudice to him as to say that he had sown
either of those plants alone. In Judea, while the Mosaic institutions were in
vigour, such an imputation would have been a very serious injury.[k] A Spanish grazier would as soon hear of his having bred a mule as of his having
bred a horse: the purity of a Jewish grazier would have been shocked at the
imputation.

Universally, the degree of damage which a man sustains by an act of
defamation depends not at all upon the aspect borne by the dictates of utility
to the practice he is charged with, but to the aspect which is borne to it by
the political, moral, and religious sanctions: by the moral, principally and
immediately: and by the other two, chiefly in virtue of the degree in which
the moral is subject to their influence.

[088–013]

Extortion.

Different political situations may occasion considerable varieties in the
definition of this offence. Were a clerk in a counting-house to send his
compliments to the first Lord of the treasury[28] with an intimation that a
present of £l∧∧∧l would not be unacceptable, if the sender of the message
did not profit much, as little would the receiver suffer.

In Hindostan, such a message might not be a matter of altogether so
much indifference. When a message equally civil came, or was thought to
have come, from some of the factors of the company of English merchants
trading to that country, to Mahomed Reza Cawn,[29] it appears not to have
been altogether wholly unattended to.[l]

Under the Gentoo, the Mahometan, the Catholic religions, a field of
extortion is open, which in Protestant countries has been shut up. If the
priest will conduct me [on] the road to heaven, (says the Protestant) it is
well: if not, I must go without him.

[088–013]

11. *Offences against property.*

It is evident that these are liable to infinite diversity, in as far as the

k. Leviticus Ch. 19. v. 19. Thou shalt not let thy cattle gender with a diverse kind: thou
shalt not sow thy field with mingled seed: neither shall l∧∧∧l

l. E. India Reports of the H. of Commons. 1772.

events which it is expedient should be admitted into the list of those con-stitutive of title are liable to differ. Other differences will necessarily arise from a thousand sources too tedious to particularize. To enlarge upon this head would be impossible without engaging prematurely in the intricacies of the civil branch of jurisprudence.

The name of Usury will in different countries, according to the greater or less plenty of money, be given to contracts of very different descriptions. In England, six per cent is deemed excessive: in Bengal, 12 per cent is deemed moderate; just as it was formerly among the ancient Romans.
[o88–o12]

12. *Offences against person and reputation together.*

It is evident enough that the idea annexed to the denomination of a lascivious injury must be liable to considerable variation, according as the manners of the people in this respect are more or less reserved. It would be different in Spain, in France, in England. An Englishman, on his travels upon the continent, after being disgusted with the kisses of his own sex, is mortified at being denied that freedom with the other, in countries where it has been the subject of serious controversy whether the bosom of the peni-tent might or might not be free to the hand of the confessor. In Mahomedan countries it is an affront to a woman of any rank, and still more to her husband, to look her in the face. Different parts of the female body in different countries are veiled with different degrees of care.

I forget what was said of the Spartans, I think, to express their hardiness — they were said to be face all over. A Mahometan woman is obscure all over.

The idea of obscenity, how strange soever it may appear, seems not to be invariably annexed to the same parts and the same functions. Among let-ter'd nations, indeed, men's notions in this respect seem to be pretty uni-form. But among unletter'd, however civilized in other respects, the case is different. In Otaheite,[30] whatever little symptoms of modesty are discover-able seem to be transferred from the functions by which the species is continued to those by which the individual is preserved.

Atkins the traveller observed an instance of this among a tribe of Ne-groes.[m] As often as the King drank, two of his attendants "held up a cloth before his face that he might not be seen." Wine, however, is no friend to modesty: when his majesty had "got drunk, this respect was laid aside."

The same notions of delicacy have been established in other African tribes, if we may give credit to several more antient travellers who are

m. *Voyage to Guinea &c.* 8vo 2^d edit. 1737. p. 199.[31]

quoted by Barbeyrac in *his* notes on Puffendorf.[n][32] "The inhabitants of
Senega," they tell us, "are as much ashamed of their mouth, as of any other
part of the body: and, therefore, they ordinarily go with a cover upon it,
which they only take off on account of eating."[33]

[100–031]

13. *Offences against condition.*

The powers annexed to conditions of the domestic kind on the side of the
superior are constituted by justifications annexed to various offences: to
speak more explicitly, by exceptive clauses subjoined to the laws relative to
most[?] of the offences against person, reputation and property, establishing
the circumstances constitutive of the party's title to the condition in question as circumstances justificative of such acts as, were it not for such
exceptions, would be unlawful.

In most Christian countries it must be some very extraordinary behaviour on the part of a wife that can render it allowable in a husband to
keep her under confinement. To a mahometan (I speak always of those who
are rich enough to live in this stile) not to be allow'd to keep his wives under
confinement would be intolerable.

Look over the catalogue of the offences to which the matrimonial conditions are exposed upon the Christian plan of matrimony, we shall find few or
none which will not require to be created under the Mahometan, scarce any
but what may require a different description in the one case from what they
do in the other. Among Christians, on the part of the husband, polygamy is an
offence: so is it among mahometans. But among the former, such polygamy
consists in the having more wives at a time than one: among the latter, in the
having more than four: concubines not reckoned.[34] In certain Christian
countries, polygamy on both sides, for want of a proper police in this behalf,
happens but too often. With regard to the wife, in mahometan countries, the
manner of living is of itself sufficient to render such an incident much less
likely to take place. It is [evident][35] that the grand distinction between the
nature of the offences of this class upon the Christian plan, and that of the
offences of the same denominations upon the mahometan, turns upon the
different shares of regard shewn by the legislator to the two contracting
parties. In *most* European nations, the regard shewn to the wife is not much
inferior to that shewn to the husband: among the Mahometans, the interests
of the wife seem to have been sacrificed almost entirely. In Asia, the husband
is more the master than the guardian of the wife: and that sort of master
whose servant is a slave. In Europe, the husband is as much the guardian as

n. B. vi. Ch. I. 31.[33]

the master. Of course among mahometans, all the offences in the creation of which the husband is the party favoured° take a deeper die: those in which the wife is the party favoured are almost invisible.

When we come to guardianship, we find relations of this nature established in eastern countries with regard to persons between whom no such relation is established in the western. In Hindostan, among the mahometans at least, the next heir of the deceased husband is the guardian of the widow: and without the privileges of the husband he succeeds to the authority of the jailor.P

I have said among *most* European nations. In Spain, we find a slight tincture of Asiatic manners, left by foreign conquerors after the religion that seems to have introduced them had been extirpated: a tincture originally foreign, and now almost worn out. In Russia, we find manners originally Asiatic, softening by culture into European.

[100–029]

Conditions of mastership and servitude.

Where absolute slavery is established without limitation, as hath already been observed, there is no such thing as an abuse of mastership. In other respects, under every state of government and manners, the offences to which these conditions are exposed will come under the same plan of denomination, while the analysis descends not to any stage of division lower than that to which the names here made use of were adapted.

[100–032]

Thus much concerning offences of a private, semi-public and self-regarding nature; together with offences by falshood and offences against trust in as far as they stand included under the former. Thus much also concerning the civil branch of the legal system; in as far as it is envelopped in and interwoven with the penal. At this period I make a necessary pause: nor will it be possible to travel farther, even in the hasty and superficial stile in which I have come thus far. There remains the subject of public offences, the subject of constitutional law, and that of procedure. On the two former topics, the influence exerted on the standard of expediency by local circumstances, as on the one hand it seems to be more generally recognized, so on the other hand it could not in so striking a manner be brought to view: and with regard to the province of procedure, the latter reason at least holds good, if not the former.[37]

[088–015]

o. v. Ch. IᴧᴧᴧI {Parties.}[36]

p. H. of Commons Rep. see E. India affairs a° 1781.

§ 4. Regard to be paid to subsisting institutions[38]

Looking over the examples above given, we shall find reason for dividing them into two classes: the first, consisting of those in which the influence of the circumstances operating as a ground of variation is, in point of possibility, unsurmountable: the other, consisting of those in which that influence is not necessarily and absolutely unsurmountable, however difficult or inexpedient or unsafe it may be to act in opposition to it. In the former predicament stand all those cases in which the ground of variation is brought about by causes purely physical: causes which produce their effect independently of any influence they may exercise on the faculties of man, and, in spite of any exertion that can be given to those faculties, must continue to produce it: causes which neither need the concurrence of human powers, nor can be controuled by [the] opposition of those powers. Of this nature are the circumstances of climate and texture of the earth, in as far as the condition of things exterior to man is determined by them. In countries where the soil is sandy and there is water ready to encroach, the encouragement of plants calculated to give tenacity to the soil is an object which countries, where the land is already sufficiently tenacious, can never have occasion to propose to themselves. In the parched deserts of Asia and Arabia, the preservation of the scanty supply of water which nature or art may happen to have afforded requires a degree of anxiety which can never be necessary in the cool and well-water'd territory of Great Britain. There can never be any use in a tax or a bounty upon the growth of rice or sugar in Great Britain: nor upon the cultivation of apples or grapes in the West Indies. The truth of these propositions is matter of intuition; because in these countries the climate is an unsurmountable obstacle to the growth of the respective articles.

Of the opposite nature come the circumstances of government, religion, and manners, including the several primary circumstances through the intervention of which these secondary ones display their efficacy. A bad form of government may, while it subsists, render it ineligible to introduce a set of laws *in populum*[39] — laws of the penal or civil class — which under a good government would be consummately beneficial: the same thing may be said of a bad religion, and a bad system of manners. Now it should be observed that the examples above given in the preceding section belong some of them to the one, others to the other, of these classes. But it is not physically impossible, at least for any reason that strikes one at first sight, but that a bad form of government, a bad set of opinions on matters of religion, or a bad system of manners, may be changed into a better. It is true that the articles of climate and texture of the earth, but particularly the former, have a certain influence over the articles of government, manners and religion: but is that influence any where a pernicious one? and if it be, is it absolutely unsurmountable by legislative policy? or what comes to the same thing, not to be surmounted without the introduction of such a mass of evil as would compensate or more than compensate for that which it may have driven out?

These are questions of great nicety and importance.

[088–016]

Without waiting for the discussion of these |∧∧∧| questions, there are some who would be apt to go on questioning in a bolder and more impatient strain.[40]

Take the form of government in the country to be regulated and compare it with that of the standard country in any point whatsoever: that of the former is in the point in question either exactly upon a par with the latter, or superior to it, or inferior. That the former should be superior is scarce consistent with the supposition: for then the law of the standard country is not in that point what it is supposed to be in every point, the best imaginable. If the former be inferior, then comes in the question, which is likely to be the greater evil? the evil depending upon such inferiority, or the evil, if any, which might be produced by the measures requisite to remove the other? the evil of the disease, or the evil of the remedy? But the evil of the remedy is, perhaps, likely to be but temporary: while the evil of the disease, and thence the benefit of the remedy, is likely to be perpetual. Here, then, comes in another question: what portion of present comfort is it worth while to sacrifice for the sake of any and what chance of future benefit? and the magnitude of each being given, for what length of time is it worth while to sacrifice a present comfort of the given magnitude to a given chance of succeeding benefit?

That in many instances it must be extremely difficult to ascertain to which of these cases the expediency of a given law belongs, and that to arrive at entire certainty may be absolutely impossible, is not to be denied: but the use of reducing the case into these several subordinate cases is not the less unquestionable. It is always something to see where the difficulty lies, although it should be insuperable: and to point out the only means by which the best solution can be given, although that solution should not be so satisfactory as could be wished. It is something to get certain principles, leaving facts in the uncertainty that belongs to them. By shewing the real uncertainty of the most conclusive arguments that can be offered on the subject, it will prevent us from giving to less conclusive arguments more than their due weight: it will [088–017] enable us to unravel the web of sophistry, and to humble the imperiousness of declamation: it will be of service in as far as the caution that accompanies a salutary doubt is preferable to the rashness that may be the fruit of misconception. Such sort of instruction indeed brings little thanks to him who gives it. To be in doubt is to be unsatisfied: to be unsatisfied is to be uneasy. People in general had rather be peremptory in the wrong, than in the right and undecided. Declamation has here, then, as on so many other topics, the advantage over argument; and a man's chance of persuading will be in proportion rather to the energy of his expressions than to the justness of his views.

That even in regard to the forms of government there should be many points that are indifferent may easily be conceived. In this respect, a law with relation to a given point in the country to be regulated may be different from the law relative to the same point in the standard country, and yet be upon a par with it notwithstanding. The case may be the same with regard to religion, as to every thing that concerns the temporal interests of society. It is still more evident that the case may be easily the same with regard to manners. It may even happen that the law which prevails in the country to be regulated shall be better for that country than it would be in the standard country: while the law that obtains with relation to the same point in the standard country is better for that country than it would be in the country to be regulated. Thus suppose that in the standard code it were found advisable that, in such part as relates to procedure, a set of institution[s] somewhat similar to those at present in force in England concerning Juries should have place: it might happen that in Bengal such a plan could not in any part of it be adopted with any advantage, or that if it could, yet in several points a variety of additions, defalcations or alterations would require to be made. Why? because in England, in certain causes, the requisite degree of impartiality and intrepidity together might with better reason be expected from a Jury than in a Judge: whereas in Bengal, in the same causes, the same degree of those qualities taken together might with better reason be expected from a Judge than from a Jury, at least if constituted in precisely the same way as in the former case. This difference, however, would depend in good measure upon a certain inferiority which at present there appears to be in Bengal with respect to the form of government on the one hand, and the national manners on the other: insomuch that were the time ever to come when that inferiority shall disappear, the reason for this difference between the institutions would become less forcible, and perhaps vanish altogether. At present, it has been said, the passion of avarice has given birth to two evil propensities which are become in a manner epidemical among the inhabitants of English race: a propensity to practice extortion to the prejudice of the subjected Asiatics, and a propensity to practice peculation to the prejudice of the public revenue. Hence arises a sort of tacit convention and combination on the part of every man to support, assist and protect every other in the practice of the like enormities. A Jury, then, if taken at hazard from the body of English inhabitants would never convict a man of either of those offences how manifest soever were his guilt. But a Judge, not having any such concerns with the natives as could lead to the practice of extortion, nor being invested with any such trust as could give room to peculation, having the eyes of mankind fixed upon every part of his conduct and being raised by his rank and fortune above the level of ordinary society, would have no adequate motives to induce him, and at the same time strong motives to restrain him, from engaging in any such combination. So long, then, as such a state of manners [088–018] continues, you must either have no laws against extortion or peculation, or no Juries, or Juries *de medietate*[41] composed partly of English and partly of Asiatics, if a mixture of that sort can, by any set of expedients, be made practicable and eligible upon the whole. Whether the facts be as is here suggested — I pretend not to enquire: I state them merely in the way of illustration, to answer the purpose of a feigned case, for which purpose the truth of them is altogether immaterial: it is sufficient if they have such a colour of truth, as not to appear utterly improbable.

If this be allow'd, it is, then, not a case utterly improbable that the standard of perfection in matters of law may, with regard to certain points, be different in different countries, for a time at least, even where the influence of physical grounds of variation is out of the question. The case may be the same with regard to religion politically considered; but is more particularly apt to be so with regard to those ordinary and continually repeated points of behaviour which come under the head of manners and way of life. It may be better that in Bengal, at least among people of Asiatic race, the husbands should be disposed to expect that their wives should keep confined, and that the women should be disposed to submitt to such confinement: while in England it may be better that the husband should not be disposed to entertain any such expectation, nor the wife to comply with it. If that be the case, there will be no reason why, by any new laws, we should seek to make an alteration in these antient manners.

I state this again hypothetically, as before. Montesquieu seems to be decided in the affirmative. "Thou who read," says he,[q] "of the treacheries,

q. Liv. 16. c. 11.[42]

assassinations, poisonings, and all sorts of enormities, which the liberty of the female sex is the occasion of at Goa, and in the other settlements of the Portugueze in the Indies, where religion allows but of one wife, comparing them at the same time with the innocence and purity of manners that characterizes the same sex in Turkey, Persia, the Mogal empire, China and Japan, will be satisfied that it is oftentimes as necessary to separate them from men where a man has but one of them as where he has a number."

How the case may have stood among the Portugueze I can not say: but the English have also their settlements in that country; and English wives have at least as much liberty as could possibly have been enjoyed by Portugueze: yet who ever heard of any such abominations as Montesquieu has been speaking of among the former?
[o88–o19]

Thus much must be allow'd at any rate, that in order to judge of the regard that ought to be paid to subsisting institutions, these institutions must be examined: and in order to be examined, they must be brought to light. In such a detail, then, there are two questions which are constantly to be kept in view: what are the present institutions relative to the point in question; and how far the expediency of giving them continuance follows from their existence. These two questions, distinct as they are, are very difficult to keep clear. For why mention them, it will be said, if it be not in this view? The very circumstance of their being mentioned as existing and as capable of furnishing a ground for continuing things upon their present footing: to mention them where it is known to be in the view to such a purpose is the same thing as to approve them. Now the more these points are in danger of being confounded, the greater is the care that ought to be taken to keep them distinct: in the first place in one's own mind, in the next place in the language made use of to express it: the τὸ ὄν and the τὸ καθῆκον[43] as they would be called in Greek. Unfortunately, nothing has been more common amongst writers than to confound them.[r] Indeed, it is next to impossible so to turn the

---

r. [100–005] This distinction is in truth the great stumbling block of a certain class of writer. The question of fact and the question of propriety are incessantly confounded. Sometimes it is the latter that is put for the former: of this an example may be seen in Sir W. Blackstone's *Commentaries*. See *Fragm. on Government*. Ch. ⎰ΛΛΛ⎱. Sect. ⎰ΛΛΛ⎱.[44] More frequently, the former for the latter: as in the instances quoted above from Montesquieu. The books that have been written on the pretended law of nature have scarce any other foundation than this mistake. There are accordingly two sorts of propositions which are produced indiscriminately under the character of laws of nature: the one declaring how things are, the other how they ought to be. Parents are disposed to maintain their

phrase as to keep them separate in each case: all that one can do is, after exhibiting a number of them together, then to give warning of the distinction once for all. Accordingly, this very source of misapprehension could not but occur in the course of the examples given in the last preceding section: but being now noticed, it is to be hoped it will be removed. I there gave them as circumstances the influence of which required to be attended to: without meaning to determine whether it were advisable to give way to it without reserve. There being such and such laws already subsisting, it deserves consideration how far a new set of laws inconsistent with them ought to be established: there being such and such notions about religion and state of manners already prevailing to which the new laws would be repugnant, it deserves consideration how far the institution of such laws is to be wished for. This was a question I meant in many instances merely to bring to view without deciding upon it: and to this purpose the language I employ'd will, I believe, be found not unsuitable. Whatever a writer's meaning be on this point, he will do well to declare it in the most explicit terms: otherwise his meaning from the first to the last will be obscure.

To shew how natural it is to fall into this confusion, I will take an instance out of Montesquieu; which, however, is but one out of a thousand. "When a country," says he,ˢ "is so circumstanced, that the climate of itself produces more inhabitants than the country can support, it is idle to make laws for the sake of promoting population." Here, then, he lays down a rule: immediately on the back of it he produces three examples: for the purpose, one should naturally suppose, of justifying the rule. As the rule which he has given is conformable to his sentiments, one should think that the examples

---

children: Parents ought to maintain their children. Whatever truth there is in the latter of these propositions, it is widely different from, nor is it a consequence of, the former. So again, Kings have been used to make slaves of those whom they have taken in war. It is not wrong in Kings to make slaves of those whom they have taken in war.

Mr Hume seems to be the first who has remarked the propensity there is in writers to slip in a proposition of the latter of these kinds instead of one of the former.[45] His was a real and most important discovery in moral philosophy. Writers, however, have not made that profit from it which they might. Germany more especially is still full of writers and lecturers on the *jus naturæ*[46] who do not know yet what it is they are writing or reading about, history or policy: the moral history of man, or the arts of government and legislation. Expose to light the partition that distinguishes between these two objects and the phantom of the law of nature vanishes.

s. |ᴧᴧᴧ|[47]

he gives of what has been done in conformity to that rule are so too. But in the instances I am about to mention one can hardly imagine this to have been the case. In China and Tonquin, a father is permitted to expose his new-born children. In China and Tonquin again, the father is permitted to sell his daughters, though at a marriageable age. In Formosa (supposing the account to be true, which most probably it is not), a woman, before she is five-and-thirty, is not permitted to bear children, though able and willing to support them: it being the duty of the Priestess to search all women under this age who are suspected of the crime of pregnancy, and, if found guilty, to force [o88–o2o] an abortion by stamping on their bodies.[48] How immense the distance between the policy of the rule and the policy of these several laws which are brought to view, as if they were so many applications of the rule? Judging from the rule itself, it is folly, by turning a pleasure into a task, to render the lives of the present race uncomfortable, for the sake of giving birth to contingent beings who would be produced without it. Judg[ing] from the first example, (to which that of the Greeks and Romans might have been added) it is right to permit a parent to take away life from a being who can not suffer from the apprehension of the loss of it, and to whom, if he retained it, it would only be a burthen. Judging from the second example, (to which that of the Romans might also have been added) it is right to permitt a parent to consign his daughter, to whom expectation has moderated the bitterness of such a change, to the arms of a man whom it is uncertain whether she will like. Judging from the third, a stranger is permitted or required to invade the peace of a family to violate the person of a woman and endanger her life by a most cruel outrage, and all without a motive. The first was law among the Greeks and Romans, and if the opposite law be the more eligible, it is only as a measure of indirect legislation against a cruelty of disposition which might be fatal to persons[49] who are in a condition to suffer from the apprehension of a like catastrophe. The second was law among the Romans, and, under sanction of the law, is virtually the practice of those Christian parents who, by coercive methods, induce their daughters to accept the hand of a wealthy lover. The last is too foolish and too atrocious to have the force of law in any country under the sun.
[o88–o23]

The following rules, if given for the purpose of information, would be idle: but in the way of *memento* they may have their use. They are chiefly a recapitulation of the preceding disquisitions.

1. No law should be changed, no prevailing usage should be abolished, without special reason: without some specific assignable benefit [which] can be shewn as likely to be the result of such a change.

2. The changing of a custom repugnant to our own manners and sentiments, for no other reason than such repugnancy, is not to be reputed as a benefit.

3. In all matters of indifference, let the political sanction remain neuter: and let the authority of the moral sanction take its course.

4. The easiest innovation to introduce is that which is effected merely by refusing to a coercive custom the sanction of the law, especially where the coercion imposed upon one individual is not attended with any profit to another.

Thus, supposing what is said of the Formosan custom to be true, there could certainly be no hardship to the Formosan women at large in saving them from having their bellies trod upon unless they liked it: but from the benefit of this innovation there would be to be deducted the loss of the satisfaction, if any, which the Priestesses had been used to have in treading upon them: the mortification, if any, which the Priestesses might feel at not having that amusement continued to them any longer.

An Hindoo woman every now [and] then takes it into her head to burn herself upon the death of her husband: if the act is altogether voluntary and she is persuaded she shall find her account in it, I can see no reason why she should not be indulged: but such permission should not be granted till after she had undergone an examination and the fact of her consent were indubitably ascertained.

5. The clear utility of the law will be as its abstract utility, deduction made of the dissatisfaction and other inconvenience occasioned by it.

6. The *value* of that dissatisfaction will be in the compound ratio of:

1. The *multitude* of the persons dissatisfied.

2. The *intensity* of the dissatisfaction in each person.

3. The duration of the dissatisfaction on the part of each.[t]

7. As a means of obviating such dissatisfaction, indirect legislation should be preferred to direct: gentle means to violent: example, instruction and exhortation should precede, or follow, or if possible stand in the place of, law.

8. The slowness of its operation is *pro tanto*[50] an objection to a measure: but if this slowness may be a means of obviating a dissatisfaction which expeditious measures would excite, the former may be preferable.
[088–025]

When the prejudices of the people are violent and obstinate, the legislator is in great danger of running into extremes. One extreme is, to shock

t. See Ch. lʌʌʌl {Value}.[51]

those prejudices by unnecessary violations; the other is, to suffer them to be made a pretence for eluding the force of those obligations by means of which society is kept together.

These prejudices generally have some *salvo* for good government; as the most pernicious tracts in religion have frequently (it has been observed)[u] some *salvo* for good morals. Find out this salvo then, if there is one, and make use of it: and in the mean time, if it be worth while, try what instruction and other gentle means will do towards getting the better of the prejudice.

But if nothing of this kind will do, and it be found impossible to untie the Gordian knot, do like Alexander and cut it.[52] The welfare of all must not be made a sacrifice of to the obstinacy of a few; nor the happiness of ages to the quiet of the day.

Prejudices that appear unsurmountable at first view may be got over by a little management.

Among the Gentoos of Hindostan, a man of a certain rank would think himself eternally dishonoured were he obliged to make his appearance in a court of justice. What does that signify? persons of that description are always rich: send a special commission to examine them, and make them be at the expence.

Among the Hindoos, persons of a certain rank would sooner submitt to any inconvenience than take an oath. What does that signify? persons of that description may as well be trusted upon their word as those who take oaths upon their oath. Do they say what is not true? it is as easy to punish them for simple falshood as to punish others for perjury. Do not Quakers depose upon their affirmation? and do not Peers, in certain cases, depose upon their honour?

Neither Mahometans nor Gentoos can bear that any officer of justice, any more than any other person of the male sex, should visit the apartments, much less the persons, of their women. Justice, in their account, is not worth purchasing at such a price. What does that signify? appoint women to the office.[v]

An English woman would cry out, and with equal justice, against the tyranny of subjecting her person to the brutal inquisitiveness of male examiners. Deriving protection against such treatment from the odium which it would excite, she returns from Calais to Dover swaddled up with laces like an

u. Priestly on Government.[53]

v. [100–005] If in Bengal physicians were paid by the public as in Russia, some of them should be of the female sex. This would require an establishment for the instruction of females in the business of that profession.

Egyptian mummy. But is it absolutely necessary that, because female delicacy is not to be violated, the public should be defrauded and modesty should be turned into a cloak for avarice? Either the payment of a tax on these luxuries ought not to be commanded, or the non-payment ought not to go unpunished. [o88–o26]

Among the various casts or tribes of the Hindoos there is one of which the members are called *Decoits*. To these Decoits,[54] Brama has revealed that it is proper they should steal every thing they can lay their hands on, and, if necessary, rob and murder every body that comes in their way. What is to be done with them? Are they, out of respect to their consciences, to be permitted to labour in this vocation? No, verily: for if it was the pleasure of Brama that these people should apply their industry to robbery, it was also the pleasure of Brama that they should bear the consequences of the industry that shall have been employed by honest men to save themselves from being robbed.[w]

In the IΛΛΛI century, near IΛΛΛI, lived a tribe of people from whom the word *Assassin* has its name. If one of these was commanded by their chief (who found frequent occasion to issue such commands) to go and cut the throat of any one he named, obedience was sure to follow. The terror of this titled murderer spread far and near: kings were not safe upon their thrones. But at last a Tartar chief found means to apply the only remedy that probably occurred to him against such a public pestilence, possibly the only one it admitted of, and the whole race of them was exterminated.

M[r] Hastings,[55] in considering how to deal with the Decoits, recommends a milder yet not less effectual remedy. Let the men and their families, says he,[x] be made slaves. Domestic slavery, considered as a punishment, has little severity in it (as Montesquieu already had observed) in a country

w. The Judges of the supreme Court found out another way of dealing with these people, which was to turn them loose when [by] the hand of justice, or at least of what in that country had been used to pass for justice, they were caught, and re-instate them in the exercise of their vocation. There was prophecy in the history of Don Quixote and the galley-slaves.

By this they unbound the hands of villainy: by another they had tied the hands of justice. By a third they had laid the ax to the root of the revenue. By these decisions they had given the natives to understand that no man's property is secure against any hand but that of justice. By the proscription of Nuncomar they shew'd that no man's life is secure against their own[?].[56]

x. IΛΛΛI[57]

where political freedom is unknown: as a preventive remedy, nothing could be more effectual.

[088–027]

Montesquieu says[y] that, for changing customs and manners, customs and manners only should be employ'd, not laws. Why? because, says he, laws are the particular institutions of the legislator; customs and manners, those of the nation in general. The maxim itself has some truth in it: but the reason is good for nothing. For what act or what habit is it that a law can be made against, and that might not be the act of the nation in general were it not for the law? To understand what there is of truth in the maxim, and what are the true reasons of it, let us turn to his examples: for without his examples one should seldom know what to make of his rules.

Peter the Great[58] made a law obliging the Russians to cut off their beards and wear their cloaths short like Europeans: and to enforce it, he posted guards to dock the skirts of all passengers who were observed to contravene it. The measure, says Montesquieu afterwards, was tyrannical: the change which he wanted to bring about, he should have effected not by making a law, but by setting an example.

In the making of this law his object was either to gratify his own taste merely, by putting the people into a dress he liked to see instead of one he did not like to see, or it was to polish them, that is to bring the national character as near as he could to the European, which he looked upon as better calculated to make them happy. The latter supposition is the more probable as well as the more honourable: and it is that in which Montesquieu himself seems disposed to acquiesce. In the former supposition, the law, being a coercive one, is improper: the punishment annexed to it and the hardship produced by it being *groundless:* and the law may well indeed be stiled what Montesquieu stiles it, a tyrannical one. On the other supposition, it is a measure of indirect legislation: levelled at all those mischievous points of behaviour to which he imagined his subjects would be the less prone were they to propose to themselves the maxims of Europeans for their model. The proposed change being effected, he might then have to say to the nobles and the leading people that were about him: Ye are Europeans. This is now an European country — see every thing about you is European: look even at the common people: their countenances, their dresses, are European. In short, Ye yourselves are Europeans — behave yourselves, then, like Europeans. Ye are European husbands: treat your wives, then, as

y. Esprit des loix. l. 19. ch. 14.

European gentlemen treat their's. Ye are European landlords: treat your vassals, then, as European gentlemen treat their tenants. Ye are European gentlemen: think it, then, as great a disgrace for any of you to be seen drunk, as it is to an European gentleman. Ye are European gentlemen: betake yourselves, then, to the profitable studies, the innocent and elegant amusements, of European gentlemen. Much more might he have added in the same strain.

Could he have effected the desired change of character without effecting this change in dress? could he have effected the change in dress merely by dressing himself as he wished to see his subjects dress, or by other means less coercive than this law? In either of these cases, the law and the hardship attendant upon it was, not useless indeed as Montesquieu calls it, (*inutile*) but, however, needless. Was the benefit attendant upon the proposed change of manners, or rather of so much of that change as was owing solely to the change of dress, worth the purchasing at the expence of all that hardship? If not, the law was then *unprofitable*. Such is the slow and minute, but sure and conclusive, method of estimating the tendency of a law upon the principle of utility.

In such, as indeed in most, matters, the cautious Statesman will avoid the tone of peremptoriness and decision: his conclusions will always in the first instance be hypothetical. *If* such and such events are the likeliest to take place? But are they? this is a matter which ought to be stated as accompanied with the degree of uncertainty that belongs to it. Beware of those who, by the confidence of their predictions, make up for the weakness of their reasons.

Whatever degree of advantage the law in question was calculated to purchase, the price paid for that benefit must be acknowledged to have been a high one. The observances prescribed being constant and habitual, the image of compulsion would be incessantly before their eyes: and this coercion could not but appear tyrannical, as it would seem to be imposed either for no reason at all, or for a reason which would seem worse than none. [o88–o29]

§ 5. Laws appear the worse for being transplanted[59]

We have seen the danger that attends the introduction of a large body of laws at once into any country, those laws being the best imaginable: we have seen the cautions which, in the management of such a business, require to be observed. The danger and the caution which will be requisite in surmounting it will, of course, be greater in proportion to the diverging of the laws in question from the line of perfection. But, where the new laws are such as are already in force in another nation, this is not all: the danger, in short the mischief, for it is more than danger, is much greater.

Would you see the worth of any established body of law in its genuine colours, transplant it into a foreign clime. The vitious parts of it, (that is, speaking of any system as yet in being, the great bulk of it) no longer veiled by partiality, will display themselves in their genuine weakness and impropriety.

The people of every country are attached to their own laws: to those parts of them at least under which they have [been] bred and to which they have been taught to pay an habitual acquiescence. If the people are not, the lawyers are: whose voice, in a matter of this sort, goes the greatest part of the way towards forming what appears to be the voice of the people. They were born under them: they have been used to them: they know no better. If they know but little of their own laws, they know nothing at all of any others. Whatever benefits they derive from political society, they derive from them: and the benefits that are not to be had from them are looked upon as unattainable. They are assiduously taught, and the people are ready enough to believe, that the oppressions they suffer from the same quarter, are the necessary price of these benefits. The patience of nations under the abuses which are the growth of their own country, and their impatience under whatever are imported from a foreign country, have their source in the natural and unavoidable mixture of ignorance and prejudice. They will endure abuses they have been accustomed to, but they will not endure new ones: they will sit easy under the yoke of their own prejudices; but they will not sit easy under the prejudices of another people.

When a body of very imperfect laws, that is when such as are the best of those of which the groundwork has been laid in barbarous ages, is imported in the lump from one country into another, it will be found that opposite judgments will be entertained of it by the two nations: the one will be disposed to think a great deal better of it, the other, if possible, a great deal worse of it, than it deserves.

To a man who has learnt by rote what the law in such or such a case happens to be without considering why or whether and for what reason it ought to be so, such is the whole together, such is every individual part: abuses and defects the most flagrant are equally sacred with institutions the most salutary and indispensable.

The constitutional branch of the law of England, taking it in it's leading principles, would probably be found by far the best beyond comparison that has hitherto made its appearance in the world: resting at no very great distance, perhaps, from the summit of perfection. Thus it stands at least [in] the opinion of judicious and impartial minds; which, I believe, will appear the more just, the longer it is considered, more particularly when considered with reference to the circumstances and situation of that favoured people whose happiness it is to have stumbled upon so invaluable a possession. Between this [088–030] part of the law and some of the principles that govern the system of procedure, particularly in what concerns criminal matters, there is a pretty strict connection and dependence. The honour due to this part, which, however superior in importance, [is][60] in point of truth but as one out of a hundred, [is][61] extended by an easy process of the imagination to the other ninety-nine. Examine it piece by piece, we should find it a vast bundle of inconsistencies: the wisdom of one page being continually disgraced by the folly of the next. But this incongruity does not shew itself to the distant and admiring multitude, against whose censure its very immensity, which is one of its greatest blemishes, forms a most effectual defence. Do you comprehend the whole of it? — No. — Then pretend not to judge of any part of it. Such is the rebuke which the sage professor is ever ready to give to the uninformed layman: such is the opiate which the uninformed layman is ever ready to administer to himself.

This predilection, how well soever it may have veiled from the eyes of Englishmen the defects of English laws while the dominion of those laws has been confined within the limits of the country which gave them birth, is not so strong, but that the experience of their effects when transplanted into Bengal has been able to overcome it. Experience too fatal not to be severely felt, and too manifest to be dissembled, has demonstrated their incompetency. Those, however, who have seen the ineptitude of that system because they could not fail to see it, and who have cried out under it because the burthen of it was become intolerable, complaining of it as unfit to be established *there,* have scarce ventured to go farther. Bad as they found it there, they have not ventured to insinuate, scarcely perhaps have they so much as allowed themselves to suspect, that it was chargeable [with] any intrinsic defects, that it was bad with reference to the country which gave it birth. The most striking feature in the government of that distant country is the arbitrariness of its leading principles: the most striking feature in that of the English government is the strictness of its procedure. From this observation, an expedient has been formed for reconciling the experienced incompetency of the English laws as applied to Bengal, with [their][62] supposed competency as applied to England. Laws which are fit for a free country are, for that very reason, incompetent for a country where the government is arbitrary and despotical. That this observation is just as applied to certain parts of the law will not be denied: but that it is applicable to the greater part of them, or even to more than a very small part, is what I am much disposed to question.

In opposition to these notions I would venture to lay down the following propositions: 1. That the English law is, a great part of it, of such a nature as to be bad every where. 2. but that it would not only be, but appear, worse in Bengal than in England. 3. that a system might be devised which, while it were better for Bengal, would also be better even for England at the same time.

To enable us to form a judgment of the truth of these propositions, let us take a general, though rapid, view of the English law with a view to the following particulars:

1. the manner in which it has taken its rise:

2. the nature and texture of it as it shews itself at present in England:

3. the effects which it either promised to have or has been found to have in consequence of the attempts that have been made to introduce it into Bengal.

These several points can not always be kept distinct in the mode of treating them: but it will be proper that the distinction there is between them should be constantly kept in view.

[088–031]

The English law, like every other body of law which has concreted without a plan, is distinguishable into statute law and customary. The statute law, framed with great attention to the circumstances and for the most part with great regard to the welfare of England, was framed without any regard to the circumstances [and] welfare of countries the acquisition of which had never been foreseen. The customary or as it is called the common law, in which accident rather than design has mixed in a few principles which are inestimable, has been made up with very little regard for the welfare of any country, even of that which has given it birth. To prove this (for a proof that shall be suited to the present purpose must be given in a few lines or not at all) I shall not dig into the dark ruins of remote antiquity; nor send my readers to wander among the jarring elements of British, Saxon, Danish, Norman and Roman jurisprudence. One strong lineament is sometimes sufficient to paint in just and striking colours the character of an individual: the same thing may be said of a body of laws. To find out and learn the general complexion of it, let us interrogate the venerable sage who stands generally recognized as the oracle of that law. Sr Edward Coke, in the first volume of his institutes,[63] has furnished us with a list of the topics or heads of argument which, according to him, furnish the several grounds of decision which are received in the courts of justice. They are in number lᴧᴧᴧl: of these |ʌʌʌ| the principle of utility, the *argumentum ab inconveniente*[64] as he phrases it, [it] must be confessed, is one. But how is it introduced? It stands neither in the van nor in the rear, nor in any post of honour: it is shuffled in without distinction towards the middle. To judge from this account, what is the chance, then, that the rule of law on which the decision is grounded in any given instance, shall be of the number of those in the framing of which the welfare of the people has been kept in view? it should be as one to twenty. The further any one were to penetrate into the texture of the law (taking but utility for [his][65] guide) the better he would be convinced that the account given of it by this its warmest panegyrist is not an unsuitable one: and that, for the greater part of it, it is a piece of cobweb work spun out of phantastic conceits and verbal analogies, rather than a mass of substantial justice cast in the mould of reason.

That the assertion may not appear entirely gratuitous, let us run over a few of the most prominent points in it with a rapid pace, considering with ourselves all along how far it answers what ought to be the purposes of its institution in England, and thence or otherwise how far it is likely to answer the like purposes in Bengal.

I shall say nothing here of the numerous defects and inconsistencies of the penal branch of the law: of the total want of symmetry that prevails throughout the whole: of the want of names for so many extensive and important heads of delinquency: of the total want of authoritative definitions for the few [. . . ?] offences that have a name: of the multitude of crying injuries which are left without redress: of the impunity of so many mischievous practices, and the unmerited punishment annexed to so many acts of which the mischief is slight or indiscernible: of the utter want of plan in the adjustment of punishments to offences: of the neglect of every rule of proportion: of the want of variety and appositeness in the species of punishment that are employ'd: of the lavish and unnecessary use that is made of the unvariable, unequable, uncommensurable, uncharacteristic, unfrugal, uncompensating, unpopular, irremissible punishment of death: the total want of method and comprehension in the very imperfect attention that is paid to the several grounds of justification, aggravation, extenuation, and exemption: the want of fixed and settled principles for ascertaining the quantity and quality of the compensation or other satisfaction which the several sorts of injuries have a claim to. These particulars [088–032] would lead me into too wide a field for the present volume, and would plunge me into a premature anticipation of the next: add to which, these are defects in which the ruder penal systems already established in Bengal would probably enough be found to possess a still more ample share. The points I would rather choose for examples are those in which the ineptitude of the English law must appear the more striking in as much as the practice of the Asiatic courts in relation to those points is, or for any thing that hinders may be, less unconformable to the rules of reason. A few of these points I shall now run over, keeping the method I have pitched upon in view, but without confining myself to the obligation of touching upon every head, or of marking out the connection between one head and another. The defects I shall have occasion to bring to view will be found to arise from various causes: in some instances from the deformities which grew up with the law in its cradle; sometimes from the additional vices which have been produced in it by the circumstances which have happen'd to accompany its migration.[66] [100–018]

Specific things irrecoverable.

Such is the excellence of the English law, say its panegyrists, that there is no right but has its remedy.[z] This is true: and to prove it, where there is no remedy, deny the right. That done, there is no one specific thing in England, land excepted, that the owner has a right to. If, in answer, a man sees any thing of another that he likes, gets it or keeps it, and stands trial, the worst that can happen is to pay the price which a jury may chance to put upon it. The price paid, he takes his choice: if the price suits him, he takes the thing: if not, he parts with it. Upon these terms the property of every man is the prey of every other. The quiet of the people under such laws depends partly upon habit, partly upon prejudice, but chiefly upon ignorance. The antiquary little thinks that his Otho may be taken from him for the price of the copper,[67] the connoisseur that his Raphael[68] may be carried off upon paying for it by the yard, the lover that the miniature of his absent mistress may be torn by a rival from his bosom at the price a broker would give for it or sell it for. Change the scene now to Hindostan. What would be the feelings of an Indian Rajah to find that his god, the pledge of his eternal happiness, [may be taken from him] at the instigation of an hostile Rajah, by the profane hands of some follower of Mahomet, for a price to be set upon it by an unbelieving Christian?

Want of survivorship in Damages.

By the law of England, if you committ an outrage against a man's person, restraining yourself however within some bounds so as to spare his life, he may obtain a pecuniary amends at the price which will be taken notice of by and by, if the lottery of litigation should be in his favour. But to stop there would be bad management: you should go on without flinching:

z. *Comm.*[69]

you should pursue him to his grave: and then the law takes your purse into its protection.

If, then, you have any purpose of revenge or avarice to answer by keeping a man in confinement, do so: but let the place be unhealthy, and keep him there to his death. Choose rather an old man than a young one, a sickly man than a healthy, the tender sex rather than the robust. Should the life of a man stand in the way of your avarice or your vengeance — in short, if you have an opportunity in any way of making your fortune by murdering a man, the law allows you so to do: only let his death be slow. Should matters be precipitated, the dose of poison or of torment operate too quick, your [. . . ?] may chance to pay for it: even then, you may comfort yourself with the having ruined his family, and enriched your own.[aa]

Should he slip through your fingers before his business is quite done, do not despair. You know, or if you do not know there are enough to tell you, how the law abhors dispatch: months, perhaps years, are yet your own. Witnesses may be silenced or kept out of the way in more ways than one. Though you should be convicted, do not give it up: till judgment is signed, you are safe. Should judgment even go against you, what then? your design upon his fortune has by this time taken effect: you quit the field to him, and you enjoy the profits of your ingenuity in a foreign country. There you must amuse yourself for a month or two, or at most a year or two, when an act of insolvency calls you home. At this price, if [100–017] you are a tradesman, by throwing in a few lies, you may have got your rival's trade from him: if a candidate for preferment or a legacy, his preferment or his legacy: if a lover, his mistress and her fortune.

Under the protection of this law, what a scope does an Asiatic climate afford for the exercise of Asiatic ingenuity? The days how broiling, the nights how damp, the Peons how obedient, the marshes of the Ganges how conveniently pestilential![bb]
[088–033]

aa. Hodgson's case.[70]

bb. Few men, I suppose, whose private experience has not brought examples to their view in which ingenuity has triumphed under cover of this law: but in general, as there is no redress to be had, there is no injury proved, and the public never hears any thing of the matter. And to cite examples of this sort without the sanction of the law would neither be safe nor proper. I will take a known transaction or two, and by substituting in the room of some of the circumstances, other circumstances equally possible, shew how easily they might have come under the present case.

Every body has heard of the fate of Lord Pigot, Governor of Madras, who in the year

Compensation.

"The more atrocious the crime, the more remediless the party injured."
Take a lawyer unawares, propose this maxim to him on a sudden, and ask
him whether he ever heard of any thing more obviously unjust, he will be
ready enough perhaps [to] answer without hesitation in the negative. A
maxim like this, he would perhaps tell you, was fit only for that imaginary

---

177|ΛΛΛ|, after a struggle for power occasioned by the inexplicitness of the laws, was
deposed by a majority of his council, and confined at the Mount |ΛΛΛ| where he died.[71]
Whatever may have been their demerits otherwise, a severe scrutiny acquitted the delinquents of every thing that savoured of an intention to produce the catastrophe that ensued.
No hardship: no want of room for exercise: Madras one of the healthiest spots in India:
and the scene of his confinement, one of the healthiest spots about Madras. But though
they intended a part only of the mischief, they reaped the full benefit of the whole. That
their own fortunes should not have been benefited by the revolution is difficult to suppose.
That Lord Pigot's was impaired by it, and that the fortune which devolved upon his
representatives was thereby lessened by it, it is impossible to doubt. But as Lord Pigot
was dead, his representatives had no remedy.

At some future time, without any violent breach of probability, the scene of a similar
transaction may be supposed to be laid in the unwholesome neighbourhood of Calcutta:
and the actors may be to such a degree exasperated, as to seek one another's death.

At various times, various individuals have been forcibly sent home from India for
various real or pretended misdemeanours: always to the great diminution, sometimes to
the total ruin, of their fortunes. The conduct of the government has in some of these
instances been justified by law, and in all of them, I believe, by policy and good intention.
But if at one time twenty or thirty men in inferior stations were in the wrong, so at another
time may two or three in a higher: and then, if the sufferers die, their families are reduced
from affluence to indigence and the oppressors triumph.

The influence of this rule of law extends to a multitude of cases besides that in which a
corporal injury is the cause of the pecuniary wrong. I know an instance where a young
woman recover'd a thousand pounds of a man for breach of a promise of marriage: he
died a day or two after judgment: had he died a few days sooner, the remedy would been
lost. I know an officer, who, by a false suggestion of absence, has been supplanted in his
office. The damage to his fortune he reckons at something between twenty and thirty
thousand pounds. What the profit of the wrongdoer is does not appear. Whether any
redress is to be had by law depends upon their joint lives. If it had been a matter of honest
difference in the way of trade, the law would not have made the representatives of the one
irresponsible, nor left those of the other without redress. It is only when the suffering is
occasioned by villainy that it manifests its indifference.

scene of things, depictured for the amusement of children, in which the pig is roasting the cook, and the thief hanging the judge. Yet to this maxim a real and very extensive deference is paid by the law of England. If a man gives you a black eye, you may make him pay for it: but if he puts it out, you get nothing, and whatever is taken from him, goes nominally to the King, really to John Stiles, or Jack Nokes,[72] who has no concern at all in the matter. If a man kills a pig of your's, you get the value of it: but if he kills your child, you don't get any thing: if any thing is got out of him, it goes to a stranger as before. A man sets your house on fire: if by misfortune, you receive amends: if through malice, you receive nothing.[cc]

Lawyers (for what will not bigotry defend?) defend this as they would any thing: "for," say they, "so long as satisfaction is made, what signifies who gets it?" To know whether they are sincere, pass a law, that whosoever owes any thing to these reasoners shall pay it to the King.

The Mahometan law, bad as it is, is at least unsullied [by] this abomination. It inclines in certain cases towards the opposite extreme: substituting satisfaction to punishment instead of superadding it. Let a Gentoo or a Mahometan wife have been made a widow by the rashness or wickedness of an Englishman: and see whether a page of Blackstone's *Commentaries* will be an opiate to her sorrow.

The experiment, as every one knows, had like to have been made on the wife of the unfortunate |∧∧∧| whom an English Attorney shot through the body, in the prosecution of the attempts of the English Court of Justice to overturn the Country judicatures.[73]

In a country where there is no King, who is it gets the forfeiture? This

cc. [100–016] This is the case wherever the offence is punished with that complicated sort of punishment which denominates it a felony. Part of this punishment if the felony be as the phrase is, without clergy, consists in death: other part in universal forfeiture. This forfeiture is given nominally to the King: whose privilege it is on all occasions to trample on the concurrent rights of subjects. It were well if it were so in reality: for the King of the present constitution, who is the reverse of the grim idol of that name fashioned out by the hands of antient judges, would probably pay obedience to the laws of universal justice. This, however, the old law has taken care for the most part to prevent: by giving the forfeiture in the metropolis and the populous county of Middlesex in reality to the Sheriffs, a set of men who, being plunder'd by the public, have a sort of equitable title of plunder in their turn.

In cases of theft and robbery, the law upon certain conditions restores a man his goods, if they happen to be forthcoming: it would have been too great a stretch of thought, to have comprehended the case of their being destroy'd or otherwise made away with.

would make a curious question: as lawyers feelingly call it, wherever the legislator has left the print of his improvidence. Had the death of Lord Pigot been deemed murder, the forfeitures of the delinquent Council would have afforded a rich bone of contention. What became of the spoils of the Bramin Nindocomar,[74] whom the English Judges hanged on pretence that a set of men in London had made forgery a felony without the benefit of English Braminship?

[o88–035]

Procedure.

You are the father of a family: you call on me and say: two of my children disagree: my eldest son has taken a couple of oranges which he says his brother gave him: this my youngest son denies. Advise me, then: what shall I do to settle the matter between them: what shall I do to come at the truth? I look grave and answer you as follows. I fear, indeed, there is something wrong on one side or the other: I am afraid that one or other of them does not speak truth: falshood should not be permitted to gain its ends: if I were in your place, I would endeavour to sift the matter to the bottom. I will tell you, then, how you shall manage. You must not think of sending for either of them and examining him unawares: nor of bringing them face to face: so far from it, should either of them happen to come into the room where you are of his own accord, you must take care and not say a syllable to him about the matter. I'll tell you what you must do: let your youngest son tell his story upon paper, putting what questions to his brother he thinks proper: give the other boy a reasonable time to contrive his answer: first six weeks, then a month, then three weeks, then a fortnight: if his answers should be evasive, then go on the same course with him again: perhaps the youngest may by this time think of some questions which he omitted to put the first time, or a fresh string of questions may be made requisite by the answers to the first: this will make another string of adjournments necessary. Mean time the eldest, perhaps, will be for telling his story and putting his questions in return: by this means the time for deliberation will be doubled. When affairs are come to this pass, you may either read what they have written yourself, or you may desire their uncle to enquire of the people of the family whether any body heard any thing of what passed: taking care not to speak to either of the boys themselves: when their uncle has told you what he has learnt, then the matter will be ripe for your decision. By this time, twice as much as the money in dispute will have been spent in pens and paper: all memory of what passed at the time when the dispute arose will be at an end: your children will have become skilled in the evils of falshood and evasion: the time of the servants will have been taken up in carrying messages and letters backwards and forwards: your own time will have been wasted in poring over all this idle scrawl: a fixt enmity will have taken root between your children: your relations and servants will have taken their parts on one side or the other: and thus the truth will be fully brought to light, and the whole family will [live] in uninterrupted peace and harmony. My speech concluded, would not you think me in a delirium? From the beginning to the end of it, would [you] think there were the least particle of common sense? This, however, is without the least sophistication the exact progress of what is called a suit in equity: a suit which, unless justice were denied,[dd] might be brought for a pecuniary demand as trifling as that which has been here supposed. When I say exact, I mean as far as it goes: but according to a very simple pattern, stripped of a thousand incidents, by fewer or more of which a suit can scarce fail to be diversified. Not a syllable here of pleas, replications, demurrers, bills of interpleader, bills of reviver, exceptions to reports, rehearings, motions, and the like. In the patriarchal government, no type could be found of mysteries like these. I know very well that a state is larger than a family: I know very well that a Judge is not to be expected to feel the same impartial tenderness for suitors, as a father for his children: but it lies upon those who think they can defend the current practice to shew why the same methods which are seen to defeat the purposes of justice in the one case are necessary to effect them in the other. This system of possible equity and certain injury has also been imported into Bengal. To whose method of proceeding does the method of a Turkish Cadi[75] or a Bengal Cawzee[76] bear the nearest resemblance, that of a father all the world over, or that of a Chancellor in England? I would venture to answer, to the father's.[77]

[100–015]

If the absurdity of the course of procedure can receive any additional proof from the confession of those under whose authority it is carried on, neither is this proof wanting. Would one think it? With all this anxiety of arbitrary rules to exclude arbitrary discretion, conjunctures will every now and then turn up in the hurly-burly of this chaos, which lay the parties at the mercy of the judge. A suitor, in his attempts to draw his antagonist into one

---

dd. In fact where the demand does not exceed ten pound, this species of justice is denied; and that openly and without shame.* Ask a man of equity for what reason? his answer is, *de minimis non curat lex:*†[78] the subsistence of a family for half a year is an object not worth caring about.

  * I∧∧∧I

  † I∧∧∧I[79]

of those pitfalls which the law has sown so thick in the track of justice, falls into it himself. He then cries to the Judge to help him out. Yes, says the Judge, with an honest exultation: but now I have you, I will make terms with you. The laws I am obliged to act under are a heap of folly; let us think no more of them. They have set up an insurmountable barrier between truth and me: suffer me to pull it down: I will exact from your antagonist a similar compliance. He durst not, any more than you, refuse me: should he be obstinate, I grant you what you ask without reserve. Let me see you, then, for the first time face to face: he shall make his appearance likewise, and I will set you face to face. You shall answer whatever questions shall be put to you: he shall do the same. On the other hand, you shall be at liberty to tell your own story; just as he will be to tell his. Open your bureau to him; he shall open his to you: produce your papers; he shall produce his.

When a cause takes this turn, every thing is as it should be: the misfortune is that this is the case only about one time in a hundred, and at the end of a suit instead of the beginning. When the parties have had more trouble than would [have] carried them through the suit, had it been properly begun: and when the auxiliaries, in dipping into the purses of their principals, find nothing there.

[100–013]

Procedure — Juries.

Could an institution any way resembling that of juries in England with any prospect of advantage be established in favour of the natives under the government of the English in Bengal? This is a question on which, without a very particular study of the subject, I would not take upon me to pronounce. But thus much I would take upon me to say, that it could not without very considerable deviations from the form in which it subsists in England. The following may serve as a loose and imperfect sketch of them.

In England, a man has, unless by accident, nothing at all to fear, and never much to fear, from the consequences of his verdict: in Bengal, a native would have, or, what would be much at one, would [fancy][80] he had, every thing to fear.

The first point is to determine the qualifications which shall entitle and oblige a man to accept of the office of a Juror: that is the classes of persons out of whom Jurymen are to be taken. Let these be as numerous as is consistent in the first place with a convenient vicinity of their residence: 2. with the degree of wealth and reputation which is deemed necessary for the purpose of responsibility. The larger the number out of whom the selection is to be made, the greater proportion will that of the unbiassed be likely to bear to that of the biassed.

Out of this same total number, let at least three times the number of those who are to serve be drawn by lot: let this triple number, for instance, be 27. Out of these let the plaintiff strike out one third, and the defendant one third more: there will remain *nine*. Let these nine be the triers.

If the conflict of interests is between an European and an European, between a Mussalman and a Mussalman, between a Gentoo and a Gentoo, the jurors returned may be all of the religion of the parties. If it should lie [between] a Mahometan and a Gentoo, they may be taken as equally as can be from both religions; determining by lot which religion shall have the odd one, or taking for the odd one an European.

If an European and a Mahometan, or an European and a Gentoo, the turn of the scale might, if it should be thought necessary, be given to the European. In this case, number returned should be 12 Mahometans or Gentoos, and 15 Europeans.

In civil cases, the majority should decide. In criminal cases, two-thirds might in general be sufficient to convict: though perhaps some variations in the number might be grounded on the nature of the crime and the magnitude of the punishment.

With regard to the power of recusation, the exercise of it should not be permitted only, but compelled: in order that, in the discharge of this invidious task, the parties might have to say, they could not help it. The Mahometan or Gentoo should accordingly be compelled to strike off his [100–014] proportion of Europeans. To effect this compulsion, the [plaintiff],[81] if he would not strike out his number upon its being proposed to him by the officer of the court, should lose his cause. This would not always do for the defendant, on account of the uncertainty of the quantum of the demand. If he refused to strike out his number, the plaintiff should be obliged to do it for him.

The verdict of each should be given secretly, into the hands either of the Judge or of some inferior officer, or rather of two or more. In the first place it should be determined, in the common way of ballotting, whether the verdict be for the one party or the other. Where the demand is uncertain, this will not suffice.[82]

[100–012]

Offences against the Sovereignty.

The standing principle of the good old English common law is that the King is every thing: and that if the welfare of the people is worth attending to, it is because they are his property. Is a criminal to be punished? it is because he has broken the King's peace. Is civil justice to be administer'd? it is that the care of Majesty may find rest. Does this immortal personage chance to die? All delegated power sinks with him into the grave. Is the peace of the Kingdom any longer worth preserving? Yes, provided the successor should chance to think so.

In conformity to these principles, treason, so long as it touch not the person of the King, is unimpeachable: so that if a faction were to conspire *with* or *for* the King against the other members of the sovereignty, in order to punish them, you must say they conspired *against* him: and the most mischievous of all treasons is that which Judges, of their own authority, have created so in contradiction to the positive letter of the statute law. Now, in Bengal there is no King: there is consequently no treason. It is not then without reason that Bengal is called the Paradise of nations: treason, the earliest of sins and the greatest of crimes, will no more harbour in it than venomous insects in Hibernia.[83]

Should a military man enter into the service of the enemy: should a party conspire to depose a governor; should a governor plant the standard of independency, what have they to fear? not a hair of the head of any of them can be touched.

But if in Bengal there is no king, and by consequence no treason, in England, however, there is a trading company. This company is allow'd to say to its servants, Bengal is our warehouse; and should any of you set this warehouse of our's on fire, then, do ye, if ye can catch him, turn him out.

Should a servant, then, subvert the government and by that means, or by other means, acquire the sum he wishes to come home with, he may be sent for home. If, then, he comes home, and chooses to live at home, and party runs high against him, and he is prosecuted, and that criminally, and the fortune of law is adverse to him, and judges are severe, he refunds a fiftieth or a hundredth part of his gains: if he chooses to live abroad, judges may do as they please, he keeps the whole.

Of this sort are the means which the English law affords at present for the maintenance of government in Bengal.

If the country has hitherto escaped absolute destruction, if the lust of power and the thirst of riches have hitherto been kept within any tolerable bounds, to what causes is this blessing due? we must attribute it to the force of the moral sanction, not to that of the political: to manners, not to laws.

[100–010]

Constitutional Law.

Under the head of Treason we have seen the provision that the Anglo-Bengali law as it stands at present affords for the maintenance of subjection on the part of the people to what is there the ruling power. Let us see how the matter stands with respect to the subjection of the ruling power there to the ruling power here, and with respect to the consistency established between the two great branches of the ruling powers there as between themselves.

By the first act, the supreme legislative authority there is vested in the Governor and 4 Councillors: the Governor having a casting vote: reserving to the King a negative, and the laws are not to be *repugnant* to the laws of England or to the orders of the Company. I am Governor-General: my duty to his Majesty is unimpeachable: he shall have his negative, and let him see what he will make of it. I am Governor-General. I have two Councillors on my side: or death or ill-health rids me of an opponent's vote, and doubles the value of my own. The last ship is sailed for England. I make a law. I am a cautious and a prudent man. I make it only for a year: it is only a measure of experiment. Half-a-year after, the first ship sails. I transmitt the law to England; it takes six months in its passage: the King disapproves the law and kills it with his negative: in half-a-year more the act of disallowance comes from England: this is 1 1/2 year after the birth of the law: but half-a-year before it is thus slain, it has died a natural death: it has completed the term prescribed for its continuance. In the mean time, finding the good effects of it by experience, I pass another law to the same tenor or the same purport, or if that be too much, to the same effect as the foregoing: but success has not begotten in me that presumption which it might in the breast of another man: my caution is persevering. I give the second law the same short-lived continuance as the first. In due time comes the disallowance of the second law. But in the mean time the beneficial effects of this second law have been confirmed: I have made a third. O king! *devota pedem oscula.*[84]

I shift my character and enter again upon the stage. I am Chief Justice (Lord Chief Justice it seems I am) of the supreme Court. The Governor-General has made a law: but I don't like the Governor-General, or I don't like his law. It regards nothing but the happiness of these barbarians. It trenches on Magna Charta: I can find no precedent for it in Lord Coke: shall the servant of those merchants carry his point against the servant of the great King? Forbid it honour. The Governor and Council have given it their *fiat:* but is that all? to be valid, must it not be register'd, and register'd in my court? Why to be register'd under me, if I am not to judge of it? How can it be register'd without my allowance? Are not the Register-books mine, are not the officers at my command? Why register it under me, if I am not to judge of it? Why not register it in the Council-books? Let me look around. How is it in France? How is it in the French Courts of Justice which are called Parliaments? Does not the power of registration there confer a negative? Might may overcome right, and consent may be extorted: but is validity ever imputed to a law untill that consent be given? The French Courts of justice, then, have a negative upon the laws: and in a legal government like ours, shall the rights of justice be less ample than in that arbitrary one? Was it meant that the King's supreme independent Court of justice should sub-mitt without remedy or reserve to laws enacted by their own suitors?

To quit these borrow'd characters. The Supreme Council have power to enact laws in all cases whatsoever, saving the rights of the King, of the Parliament, and of the Company: and let the power of registration in the Supreme Court confer no negative. Let us examine these powers a little farther and see how they harmonize. In the Supreme Council there is the supreme legislative power; in the Supreme Court the judicial. As incident to this judicial power, a legislative power in matters of procedure is conferred on the Supreme Court. Is this independent of the legislative power of the Supreme Council? [100–011] Yes, say the Supreme Court: for else what becomes of our power or our independence: to what purpose attempt to stretch the hand of authority over those our suitors? Besides, upon whom is it that the legislature has conferred this power? upon us, or upon them?

No, say the Supreme Council: for it is of the essence of the judicial power to be subordinate to the legislative. To you is given the power of making laws in these cases in particular, for these purposes in particular: to us the power of making laws in all cases whatever, saving our subordination to the authorities in England. What the Parliament is in England, we are in Bengal: what the Courts of Justice, you. Are not the British Courts of Justice subordinate to the British Parliament? Would any validity remain to regulations of the Court of King's Bench which the High Court of Parlia-ment should rescind?

To settle these points would, I think, be much easier than to say how it is they are settled already.
[088–037]

§ 6. Influence of time

We now come to speak of the influence of time on the expediency of a law or set of laws. The question on this head divides itself into two. The laws that are the best possible for a given place at the time present being found, would the same laws, had they happen'd to be found in time past, [have] been the best possible for that time past: and the like with relation to time future? This we see, when consider'd with a view to any direct influence it can have, is a mere question of speculation: nobody can transfer our present laws to time past; *we* can not transfer them to time future. Nevertheless, as a right way of thinking on this head may contribute, perhaps, in a manner more or less remote, to guard us against mistakes in practice, a few words on this head also may not be altogether thrown away.

Time, as we have already had occasion to observe, is nothing of itself. To learn what influence it possesses, we must enquire what influence may be exercised by those causes of a superior order into which it is resolvable. In regard to causes purely physical, the field of variation, at least as to any correspondent variation of influence, can not be very considerable. As to the texture of the soil, lands once marshy may be drained: lands once dry may be overflow'd. Rivers which formerly poured into the sea may, in very particular situations, be intercepted and dissipated in their course: from lakes communication may be open'd to the sea. Peninsulas may by nature or by industry be converted into islands: and continents may be intersected by canals. The higher parts of mountains may crumble down by their own weight or be washed down by rivers. At the mouths of rivers, islands may be formed, or the continent lengthen'd out by the opposition of the sea. Volcanos, when constant, may tend to reduce mountains to a level: occasional, they may raise it into hills, sink beds in it for lakes, or throw up islands in the sea. Ports may be deserted, or new ones hollow'd out by the caprices of the ocean. All these alterations may give occasion for correspondent changes in regard to the individual places that are the objects of certain laws: principally those laws to which semi-public offences against a neighbourhood, offences against the public force, offences against the public wealth and offences against the national wealth respectively, owe their birth.[ee] But the generical denominations of those offences and the general nature of those laws will be still the same: and, at any rate, whatever variations on this head are made requisite by time will be such and such only as are made requisite by place.

It is the same thing with regard to climate and those peculiarities in respect of animal and vegetable produce which are the consequence partly of this circumstance and partly of the former. Partly by means of cultivation, partly by means of other causes of which the operation is less known, the quantity of sensible heat diffused over the surface of the earth appears to have a tendency by slow degrees to verge towards an equilibrium: hot climates become perhaps a little cooler: more certainly, cold climates become a little warmer. Rome, for instance, is become as warm as some other place that is now warmer was at a former period.[ff] Partly from this meliora-

ee. v. Ch. 16. {Division} 33 Note (h) and 54 n. (m).[85]

ff. See Barrington's Ob. on the Statutes.[86]

tion of the climate, partly from the simple importation of a new article into a region already prepared by climate to receive it, a vast variety of productions of both the living kingdoms, but especially of the vegetable, find their way in process of time into places in which they were unknown before. But these mutations make none in what ought to be the generical description of the offences and consequently the general tenor of the laws of which such things are respectively the subjects. Potatoes, which are now the food of Britain and the bread of Ireland, two centuries ago were not known to either: speaking, then, of potatoes simply, there was not that demand for a law against the stealing of potatoes that there is now. But so long as men have been men, there has always been occasion for laws against stealing: for laws against stealing any thing whatsoever: and if the laws which there were against stealing did not include potatoes, it was owing to the blindness or indolence of the legislators of that time, [o88–038] not to any difference between the laws that were fit for that time and those that are fit for this. If there was no such word, then, in the language as potatoe (there being no such sort of thing as is signified by the word potatoe known), there was, however, the word vegetable; there was the word *moveable:* there was at any rate the word *thing.* If there was no such word as *guinea fowl,* there was the word *fowl*; the word *bird*; the word *animal*; the word *moveable* again; and the word *thing.*[87] It is the nature of these generic terms to open up and let in the import of the subalternate specific ones as fast as they are formed.

So far, then, as the texture of the soil and the nature of its productions are concerned, a succession of time may give occasion to a demand for some of the alterations to which a change of place may give occasion. But this does not extend to those variations which are made requisite by correspondent varieties in the mental or moral qualities of men. The changes which time may bring on in respect of heat and cold will never be considerable enough to give one zone the temperature of another.[88]

[o88–044]

It is a saying attributed to Solon[89] that the laws he had given to the Athenians were not the best in themselves, but the best they were capable of receiving. This would hold good in the greatest degree in regard to the constitutional branch of their laws, the principles of which have most in them that is arbitrary and of which the utility depends upon the likings and dislikings that happen to have gained footing among the people. In this there was doubtless somewhat of truth, considering the turbulent and jealous disposition of the people to whom it was applied. But that it was strictly true, one may venture without much hesitation to deny.

There could not have been a more convenient maxim for saving the credit of a legislator: and those who have had a legislator to defend have not failed to make the most of it. But there are few maxims, perhaps, that have been carried so much beyond the mark: and it has been frequently cited in cases where it has been erroneous in itself, and perhaps not altogether innocent in its consequences.

Whatever Athenian arrogance may pretend, it will not easily gain credit in a discerning mind, that at so early a period of society, the best of all possible laws should have presented themselves to view. It will not be believed, that among a people whose character disqualified them from receiving any better laws than those which Solon gave them, there should have existed a man who, in his own mind, had carried that most difficult of sciences to so high a pitch of perfection that it will never be possible for any other man to carry it higher.

This sort of apology, what degree of truth soever there may have been in it in the instance in which it has been made, has since been much abused: and it has been employ'd to gain a reputation of expediency and wisdom for many a mischievous and many a foolish law. The law, such as it is, lies before you: yet foolish as you may think it, the lawgiver may, for aught that we know, have been the wisest of mankind. But such as the author is, such are his works: since, then, the lawgiver is wise, the law itself may perhaps be a wise one too, how foolish soever it may appear to you. It may have had its use, though you and I don't see it. Let the law, then, stay where it is: to abolish it is dangerous: a mischief may ensue which we are not able to foresee. Such is the circle in which many a man who, insensible to the force of truth, has nothing to guide him but the prejudices he has conceived in favour of antiquity scruples not to run. If any one has a mind to see how far a legislator was entitled to the benefit of this plea, let him consider in what channel the prejudices of the people are likely to have run, and of what nature the coercion is which it is natural they should have imposed upon the legislator. It is natural enough they should have opposed any important change he might have been inclined to make in the article of religion: and yet we have seen religions overthrown by the legislator and others set up in their stead. It is natural enough they should have opposed the investing men with new powers, or making a new distribution of the old: and yet in this way too we have seen great changes made by legislators with little or no opposition on the part of the people. It is natural enough they should oppose any wishes he might express or might be suspected to entertain of subjecting them to new and irksome restraints or obligations: although among the most necessary restraints and obligations we shall find some of the most irksome. — But a supposition that is not by any means a natural one is that, by dint of menaces and clamour, they should have forced him to fetter their own freedom by a heap of idle, trifling and ridiculous obligations and restraints. When a code, amidst all its redundancies, is defective, and regulations of the most obvious use and necessity — regulations which, from the fundamental principles of human nature, we know must have been as necessary at one time as at another — are looked for in it in vain, it is not a mere *ipse dixit*[90] that will warrant [us] to give credit for utility to institutions in which not the least trace of utility is discernible.

* * *

[088–042]

Take an intelligent Mahometan, if an intelligent Mahometan be to be found, press him upon the absurdity of the laws of Mahomet, drive him to his last shifts, he will say, True: consider'd with regard to their application to the purposes of the present life they are not indeed altogether what they might have been, if made now: but consider the time: consider the state of the people, the state of knowledge at that time. Such laws as a man might make now would not have been understood. They were excellent for the time: they were excellent for the people. Such laws as a man might make now either would not then have been expressed or could not have been understood.

To this argument there is a short answer. The words that Mahomet made use of we know: to those words the same ideas, or ideas that were the same to all material purposes, were annexed then, that are annexed now: so at least we must suppose in as far as we pretend to understand them. Give me, then, the words of the Koran: give me the ideas that belong to them: I ask no more. Out of them and them alone I will undertake to produce you a code which shall contain a hundred times the useful matter there is in that, without any of those absurdities, the existence of which, upon comparison made with the ideas of utility we have at present, you can not but acknowledge.

But better laws, though they could have been written at that time and would have been understood, would not have been received, for the people were an ignorant, a prejudiced, a stubborn, a head-strong people. This argument may also be demolished without much difficulty.

Ignorant, prejudiced and stubborn as they were, did not your prophet tear them from their most rivetted, their most sacred prejudices. Were they not polytheists, and did [he][91] not make them unitarians? did [he][92] not tear out of the calendar the whole sacred catalogue of the daughters of God? did not he search out with the severest diligence the crimes and vitious propensities they were most addicted to? Throughout the whole of his system and of his proceedings is any want of firmness, any of audacity, discernible? If not, there is but one want to which the imperfection of his system can any longer be attributed, the want of wisdom. A want of a share of wisdom, on the part of a man who you say was taught by God himself, the want of a share of wisdom equal to what may be found at present in a man of the most ordinary level.

* * *

[088–043]

My people will not endure even the most necessary restraints: I have, therefore, heaped upon them a vast multitude of restraints that are of no use. Such logic may pass upon some minds, but they must first of all have been prepared by a pretty ample dose of prejudices. Now to be accounted for — the energy of character necessary to enable a man to lead mankind influences as well the intellectual faculties as the affections. The character to which we have given the name of enthusiasm is made up of a determined courage and a rambling imagination. No coward, no man even of selfish prudence, was ever a founder of [a] new system of legislation. *Nemo unquam vir magnus sine aliquo afflatu divino unquam fuit,*[93] says Cicero: the plain truth of this, as far as it is true, is, that the energy of the head, in the degree in which it is necessary to constitute a legislator, I mean always an enterprizing legislator, is always accompanied with a more than common degree of energy in the heart.

The Alcoran[94] is stuffed with a heap of institutions, the bulk of them not of the least conceivable use. Mahomet, it may be said, was a man of divine and consummate wisdom. The people he had to deal with were a foolish people: and he was forced to accommodate himself to their folly. — Specious enough this, while we keep to generals. — But come to particulars with him, and see what he will say then. The people were a foolish people. — I believe it. But what folly on their part could have laid him under the necessity of producing such institutions as we see? What was it that obliged him to &c.[95]

* * *

[088–040]

On this occasion we must once more bring to view the distinction between the matter of fact and the matter of right, or rather of expediency: between what has taken place, and what ought to have taken place.[96] That in rude ages the tenor of the laws hath always been very wide of what would be the standard of perfection for the present age is clear enough. That it could not but have been so without a miracle is also pretty clear. But ought it so to have been? Were the imperfect laws which obtained then better for that time than the most perfect which we can imagine now would have been for the same time. The affirmative is what seems to have been insinuated, but, as it should seem, without sufficient cause.

There are two classes of people from whom this notion seems to have gained countenance. The one consisting of those who, from indolence or timidity or less pardonable motives, have found it convenient to set their faces against every proposal that savours of improvement or reformation. To people of this description, it must have seemed the happiest contrivance imaginable, if from the very excellence of a system of laws they can raise an argument, and that a conclusive one, against it's fitness. Such an argument, when sifted to the bottom, will indeed be found to be a contradiction in terms; but how few are they by whom such arguments can be sifted to the bottom. If they can get such an argument to apply to the laws of past times, the next step is to transfer it to the present. Get such an argument to pass muster in the first case in which there is but little reason in it, and perhaps you may get it received in the other case in which there is no reason in it at all.

The other class of people are those who have a system to defend, which, without some such expedient, would be indefensible. This is the case with the votaries of all those absurd and false religions which have descended into the details of legislation. Viewed by the light of polished reason, the defects of our code are too glaring to be dissembled. Say, then, that from causes peculiar to that age, it could not have been better. That to invest it with the authority of law in present times would appear to be a measure equally ridiculous and destructive is not to be denied. That this pretended emanation of divine wisdom would be found worse than the worst of those which are in force in polished nations, is scarcely to be disputed. What is to be done? there is but one thing: take the blame off the shoulders of the legislator, and lay it upon the people. Say they were stupid, stubborn, prejudiced, intractable: this will put you at your ease. You may then acknowledge, and acknowledge with safety, that in a certain sense the laws were bad: and this will entitle you to maintain that in another sense they were good. They were bad in theory, but they were good in practice: they were bad in appearance, but they were the best possible in effect.

The plea is plausible enough, while it keeps to generals: and as there is no other, it must be made the most of. Distress of argument forced it from minds engrossed by prejudice, and it may pass, as any thing else would pass, upon those who are prejudiced the same way. But come to particulars, the illusion vanishes. Take what nation you will, give them what character you please, where could have been the advantage that injuries should have been left without redress: that the liberty of men should be teazed and perplexed by a chain of minute and [088–041] frivolous obligations: that punishments, perhaps of the severest kind, should be heaped on them for acts from which no mischievous consequences can be traced: that when the act which is forbidden happens to be of the number of those that are pernicious, no account should be taken of the various grounds of justification, aggravation, extenuation and exemption which are pertinent to the case? that punishments should be inflicted without measure and without choice? that no enumeration should be given of the grounds of right, nor any compleat set of principles established for the decision of claims to property: that the business of judicial procedure should be abandoned to arbitrary discretion: and that where power of any other sort is given, no care should be taken to shape it to its end by the necessary apparatus of obligations, qualifications and exceptions?

If there be any ground for denying the truth of the position, that the laws which are the best for a civilized would also have been the best for a rude age, in any case, it is in the case of such part of the law as concerns punishments, and such part of it as concerns the laws *in principem*.[97] In a very rude age, it is possible that punishments in point of quantity might require to be somewhat greater than it were necessary they should be in a civilized one. In a rude age, the religious sanction has commonly given but little assistance to the political: the force of the former, though much greater in a rude than in a civilized age, being diverted into other channels: hence one reason why the quantum of punishment provided by the political sanction may require to be somewhat greater in the former period than the latter. In a rude age, the moral sanction has less force than in a civilized one: hence another reason for adding something to the magnitude of the punishment provided by the political. In a rude period of society, the people are not yet broke in to the habit of lending spontaneously their assistance to the laws: hence a third reason. The differences, however, that may be occasioned by these circumstances can at the utmost be but very slight: especially if the maxim laid down in a former chapter be just, that even in a civilized age the whole complement of punishment that is judged necessary must be taken from the political sanction, and that the auxiliary sanctions alone can not safely be depended upon for any part of it.

* * *

[142–212]

Then again with regard to that branch of the laws of which the office is to set bounds to the power of the prince. As to this matter, thus much may be true, that in a rude age, a perfect system of laws on this head would probably not be so regularly observed as in a civilized one. For the regard paid to laws of this class depends upon habit; upon an habitual train of sentiments and turn of disposition on the one part and on the other: upon the part of the people, on a disposition to express dissatisfaction and even if necessary to go to farther lengths in case of the violation of such laws: upon the part of the prince, on the habit of feeling shame at the thoughts of such a violation and of apprehending, in the light of a punishment, the discontents that may ensue. Now habits of this sort take a certain time to form. But what does all this prove? only that in a rude age a perfect system of laws in this behalf would not be so well observed, nor produce such good effects, as in a civilized one: not that a less perfect system would produce better.gg

The next question is, it being allow'd that a perfect system of laws, according to the conception we may be able to form of such a system, would have been better for any past time than any of which men had any examples then, how stands it with regard to future times? Is there not reason to think that the most perfect of what we are able to form a conception of at present may be as much inferior to the most perfect which in process of time men may be able to form a conception of, as they are superior to the most imperfect of which we have any trace in history? Are there any and what bounds to the progress of improvement in this line? are we arrived, in prospect at least, at that *ne plus ultra* of perfection, beyond which it is not in the nature of things for us to go?

The Chevalier de Chastellux is clear in his opinion that from the beginning of things to the present time the condition of man has gone on improving; or at least what is all that is to the purpose, that this condition is much better at the present than at any former period, and that it is likely to be better and better still: a comfortable doctrine, which he has supported by a train of the clearest proofs that history can afford.[98] Dr Priestly goes farther still: giving it as his opinion that in process of time the world will arrive at a state so paradisiacal as to surpass any thing which at present we [142–213]

gg. It may be said that in the most civilized states of which we have as yet had experience, standing armies have been established, which the prince has had at his command: and that where this is the case, laws in principem can not be expected to have any effect. But the circumstance of a large standing army is no necessary concomitant to the other circumstances which constitute civilization: as the example of Great Britain is sufficient to demonstration. But even notwithstanding this immense augmentation of the power of the prince, it may perhaps be doubted whether the privileges of the people are not in general better observed at present, than they were in those rude ages which preceded the establishment of standing armies: the sense of shame and the principle of benevolence acting more powerfully now than the fear of popular vengeance acted then.

can conceive.[99] In this general improvement of every thing that concerns the condition of mind, that of the laws must be included as of course: the improvement of the laws being at once the consequence and the cause of those improvements in point of manners and encrease of knowledge, on which felicity more immediately depends. But to say this, if it be meant in a literal sense, seems to be going rather too far: nor does it seem possible that so long [as] man is man, the degree of his felicity can rise to any higher standard, than what we are and must be perfectly well able to measure and see to the end of, even without any other lights than we possess at present.

But how extensive soever may be the exceptions from the general rule that laws which would be the best for the present would have been so for any former [age], the argument of those religionists will never be the better for it. Their systems, if examined with ever so moderate a degree of discernment and impartiality, will present examples in abundance of laws which never could have been good, omissions which never could have been eligible, defects in point of method and composition which never could have been otherwise than of pernicious consequence in any age.

Nor would it be of any avail to them to say, the notions and language of men did not at the time of the publication of these codes admitt of any higher degree of perfection in the laws than what is there exhibited. This plea, when canvassed with ever so moderate a degree of attention, will vanish into air.

To pass a peremptory reprobation upon a proposition of the nature in question may seem at first sight to carry with it an air of solecism. For in order to prove, if it be capable of proof, that the condition of human nature at the period in question will not carry with it any such felicity as we are not now able to conceive, we must begin with supposing ourselves able to conceive the greatest measure of felicity that can belong to it, which is taking for granted the very matter in dispute. But in effect it is only taking that for granted which any one who should be on the opposite side must, in the very statement of the question, be necessitated to grant. For it states the sort of being who is the subject of the question to be man: man living in the state in which we see him live: endued with the sensibilities with which we feel him to be endued: surrounded by the objects with which we see him to be surrounded: drawing his enjoyments and his sufferings from the sources from which we see him draw them. Knowing, then, these sensibilities, these objects and these sources, we know the *ne plus ultra* as well of his enjoyments as of his sufferings. Give him a new sense indeed, the objection ceases: but then he is no longer the being whom we have agreed to take for the subject of our question: he is not man, but something better: and what

tendency has time, or the best laws which it can disclose, what tendency has
it, I say, to put a man in possession of a new sense? This is what it lies upon
our antagonists to shew, who may be inclined towards the opinion we are
now disputing.

[142–211]

The purpose of these observations is neither more nor less than to exon-
erate from the charge of presumption the pretension of having been able to
mark out even now the limits of perfection in this line of government. Untill
the grand principle which alone can give a right direction to our researches
could be held up to view, and cleared from the false principles with which it
was entangled[?], untill the several ends and objects as pointed out by that
principle could be ascertained and followed up throughout the whole course
of their ramifications, untill the whole apparatus of the means conducive to
the attainment of those ends could be survey'd and put in order, all notions
of perfection could not but be inadequate and premature. But if these points
should be found at length to have been accomplished, the idea of perfection
is no longer too mighty for our grasp, and though no man now living must
expect himself to gain entrance into this state of promised happiness, he
may, however, like Moses on the top of Pisgah,[100] console himself with the
having ascended to that eminence from whence the whole extent of it lies
open to his view.

* * *

[142–200]

The perfection of the law will be at its *acme,* and the condition of
mankind, as far as depends upon the law, will be at its *optimum,* when the
following signs are visible: when palpable injuries are unknown except by
means of the laws by which they stand prohibited: when no acts to which
man's nature is prone, are included in the catalogue of offences, that do not
deserve to be so: when the rights and duties of the various classes of
subjects are so well defined by the civil code that there are no longer any
controversies upon the point of law: when the code of procedure is so
framed that the few controversies which arise purely out of the matter of
fact are terminated without any unnecessary expence or delay: when courts
of justice are seldom filled, though always open without intermission: when
the military forces of nations being broken down by mutual stipulations, not
by mutual impotence, the burthen of taxes is render'd imperceptible: when
trade is so far free, that no branch which might be carried on by many is
confined to few, nor any branch pinched by the pressure of taxes into a
smaller compass than it would otherwise assume: when for the encouragement of such branches of industry as require positive encouragement,

positive encouragement is given, and liberty, perfect liberty, to such as require nothing more: when the constitutional law is settled on such a footing, and the rights, powers and duties of the servants of the public are so distributed and circumstanced, and the dispositions of the people to submission and to resistance so temper'd and adjusted, that the prosperity resulting from the preceding circumstances is fixed: lastly, when the law which is the rule of men's actions is concise, intelligible, unambiguous, and in the hands of every man. But to what does all this felicity amount: only to the absence of a certain quantity of evil: to the absence of a part of the various mass of evil to which human nature is now subject. That the accession of felicity would be great and the prospect comfortable is not to be denied: but still there is nothing in it that is mysterious and unknown: nothing but what the imagination of man at the present period is perfectly competent to conceive. Fire will burn, frost pinch, thirst parch, hunger gripe, as heretofore: toil even as now must be the prelude to subsistence: that the few may be wealthy, the many must be poor: all must be tantalized more or less with the prospect of joys or supposed joys which they are out of hope of tasting: and how much lighter soever coercion may sit than it does now, coercion must still be felt, that all may be secure.

Sense, which is the basis of every idea, is so of every enjoyment; and so long as man remains man, the stock of sources, those sources more or less remote, of every thing that is called enjoyment, never can encrease. In the regions of poetry, painting, music and their sister arts, the mines of novelty will in a few centuries be exhausted: and if the instruments of enjoyment are more exquisite, taste will be more severe. If this be paradise, paradise is but at best what the Asiatics meant by it, a garden: it is still, however, a very pleasant garden to look to in comparison of the wilderness of evils and abuses in which we have as yet been wandering.
[o88–o45]

§ 7. Immutability, in what sense to be attributed to laws[101]

Before a period is put to this chapter, it may naturally be expected that some notice should be taken of the immutability which many have been so fond of attributing to certain laws or pretended laws, as also of the much talked of distinction between *mala in se* and *mala prohibita*[102] with reference to actions: a notion which seems analogous to the former. These and abundance of other such notions, or rather of other such phrases, seem to have been the result of the abortive efforts made by the imagination to raise the understanding out of its state of darkness.

How mighty in every branch of science, and in the moral branch in particular, how mighty and how universal is the force of words! How many questions, even of those of which one would least expect it, would, if examined with attention, be found to turn upon nothing else! Who would have thought it? even the question concerning the immutability of certain laws is of the number! The same act which ought to be forbidden in one age and country, ought it to be forbidden in every other? Yes and no: yes, if in pronouncing the word *act* we have in view a large and general class of acts: no, if a narrow and particular one.

The plain truth of the matter is this: there are certain acts that admitt of laws which, if worded in a certain manner, may stand good and be equally applicable to all places and times: while there are other acts for which no such laws can be devised. Under the former predicament come those acts of which the name is included in a single word: such as murder, theft, adultery, perjury and the like. Let no one committ murder; let no one committ theft; let no one committ adultery; let no one committ perjury; and so on. Upon this plan one might make a variety of laws, of which the expediency might without impropriety be termed universal and immutable.

[088–046]

But laws, while confined to terms so loose and so extensive, will never be found precise and clear enough for service. The act thus vaguely described must, before it can be perfectly distinguished and understood, be broken down into species: the law relating to it must accordingly be broken down into a multitude of laws: the phrase, pure as it stands now, must be transformed into others in which provisions of an expository, limitative or exceptive nature will be necessary. Now, among these qualifying provisions will in every case be some the effect of which is to except out of the general prohibition certain cases in which the act is either commanded or allowed by some other branch of the body of law. Now, of these qualifying provisions, some, it will be found, ought in point of expediency to be variable: different in one country from what they are in another: different in the same country at one time from what they are [at][103] another: this is what becomes of the immutability and universality of these immutable and universal laws. Let no man take that which is not his own: but the description of what is and what is not each man's own depends upon the laws of the place, and is changing every day: let no man kill, except those whom, at the command of a magistrate of such or such a description or on some other account, he is allow'd to kill: but the laws by which such magistrate is described are different in every town and may be alter'd every day.

[100–028]

Let no man carnally know the wife of any other man: but who is to be reputed each man's wife depends in like manner upon laws which are equally subject to variation. Let no man give false testimony in violation of a promise he has given to bear true testimony before a magistrate: but the description of this magistrate depends upon laws of a local and temporary nature, as before. Universal laws of which the universality, immutable laws of which the immutability, depends upon the manner in which they are worded: laws universally and immutably expedient, of which the expediency and immutability is altogether dependent upon other laws which not only are, but ought to be, liable to continual variations. Laws of divine authority (for this also is said of them) of which the very substance and materials varies with every variation that takes place in this or that branch of a code of human laws.

There are certain laws, then, in a form in which they are capable of occupying a place in an authoritative code, and which are capable of being so worded as to be capable of serving without variation for all places and all times: that is as far as they go: at the same time that the texture of them is, then, so loose and general, as to require, before they can answer the purposes they are designed for, to be fitted up, as it were, with an apparatus of expository provisions, many of which will require to be of a different tenor in different times and places. On the other hand, there are certain other laws (and these indeed are by far the most numerous) to the expediency of which this degree of universality and permanency can not by any contrivance be communicated. Will it be expected that an enumeration shall be given of those of the former class? will it be even so much as expected, that a line shall be drawn between the [100–026] one class and the other, and a criterion given by which they may be distinguished? Both these tasks are no more than persons of a certain description may with reason be expected to fulfill: those, I mean, who talk so much, and with so much pomp, of the eternal and immutable laws of God and nature: laws from which those of human stamp derive all their efficacy, which they are not to be permitted to contradict, and which, if they do presume to contradict, they are *ipso facto* void. Since, then, God has given us, as you say, these laws, you, who it seems are in the secret and are so sure of it, ought to know what it is that God has given us: for else of what laws is it that you are speaking all the while? Shew us, then, these immutable and eternal laws: write them down for us that we may read them: count them for us that we may know when it is that we have got them all and that none of them may escape us. This is what any man is entitled to demand of these makers or interpreters or professors or whatever else they pretend to be of divine yet unrevealed immutable and eternal laws. But to perform it will be found, if it is not seen already to be, palpably impossible. For what, in short, does the number of them depend upon? It depends upon two things: upon the local nature and accidental idiom of the language: and upon the manner in which that language is managed and employ'd. In the language of one nation you shall have more of these universal laws; in that of another, fewer: in the same language, one man shall be able to make more of them; another, fewer: and unless he were to try for it, a man would perhaps make none at all. If a man wants to know how many laws of this stamp there are in a given language, and in a body of laws drawn up upon a given plan and in a given stile, he must stay till the laws are made: if they are well made, by running over the whole collection, he may then very probably pick out here and there no inconsiderable number of the sort of laws which he is in search for.

Should, then, the body of laws of which this is the introduction come up to what it is designed for, I may arrogate to myself avowedly what others have arrogated to themselves implicitly, the privilege of having made immutable universal laws: and should any body ask me where and which they are, I might lay my finger on the book, and answer, they are there. But far from a sincere and candid [enquiry][104] after truth be all this quackery, not to say this blasphemy, this imposture: and let him remember that, if there be one person who could be justified in thinking it no robbery to be equal with God, there is but one.[hh]

[088–049]

hh. [100–027][105] Montesquieu, who has shewn in so convincing a manner how rare it is for any large portion of law that is suited to the circumstances of one age or country to be exactly suitable to those of another age or country, Montesquieu himself appears not to have been altogether exempt from the illusion of these notions, notwithstanding the discovery he makes of the falsity of them when he comes to consider the matter in the detail. Not content with an eternity *a parte post,* as the logicians phrase it, he is for giving to his laws of nature an eternity *a parte ante.*[106] In his opening chapter, which from the beginning to the end is utter darkness, there were laws, he says, for men, before there was such a creature as man existing: do you doubt of this? that you may doubt no longer, know then, that the radii of a circle were all equal before there was such a thing in nature as a circle.[107]

He goes on and gives instances: and his examples thicken the mist excited by his rule. The first of these eternal laws is, obey all sorts of human laws as they happen to be established, an instance of which seems to be a flat contradiction to the rule: obey them without exception, for he makes none, whether conformable or not to the invariable and irreversible laws of nature. The second is, if you have received a benefit from another being, be grateful for it: a proposition which means next to nothing untill it be shewn in

Were I to choose to what I would be most ready to attribute these magnificent prerogatives so often spoken of, it should rather be to certain grounds of law, than to the laws themselves: to the principles on which they should be founded, to the subordinate reasons deducible from those principles, and to the plan — the best plan — upon which they can be put together: to the considerations by which it is expedient the legislator should suffer himself to be governed; rather than to any laws which it is expedient he should make, for the government of those who stand committed to his care.

On this ground, then, a man engaged in a design like that which is the object of this work might lay claim to the attributes of universality and eternity for the rectitude of his doctrines with as little arrogance as he could impute to the most confin'd and temporary expediency: provided that, in the execution of his plan, he has boldness and strength enough to make the division in his mind — to set apart all along whatsoever is peculiar to particular times and places, and, circumscribing what is general, and setting aside what is particular, to raise his imagination to that elevated point from which the whole map of human interests and situations lies expanded to his view.[108]

The rules concerning the cases that are respectively meet and unmeet for punishment and for reward — the rules concerning the proportion proper to be observed between offences and punishments, between acts of merit and reward — the rules concerning the properties to be wished for in a lot of punishment or reward — the principles in which the division of offences has its foundation — the principles on which the various methods of attacking offences by indirect or far-fetched means — all these, if they are just and proper now, would at any time have been so, and will be so every where and to the end of time. They will hold good, so long as pleasure is pleasure, and pain pain: so long as steel wounds, fire burns, water seeks a level, bread nourishes, inanition destroys, so long as the tooth of the slanderer keeps its venom: so long as difference of sex attracts, so long as neighbour needs the

---

what shape the gratitude is to shew itself, in what cases it is to be exerted, and what lengths it is to go. The third is, being a created being, don't think to make yourself independent of the being who created you: a law which seems to be levelled against those and those only who were concerned in building the tower of Babel. The fourth establishes the eternal invariable obligation of the rule of retaliation in all cases, and that not on the ground of utility, and so far as it has utility to recommend it, but on the ground of I know not what title that a wrongdoer has to undergo this sort of punishment, on the score of having deserved it.[109]

help of neighbour, so long as men derive credit or fortune from their ancestors, or are bound by the ties of affection to their children.

[088–047]

The notion concerning the essential distinction between *mala in se* and *mala prohibita* is a sort of counterpart and consequence of the former. *Mala in se* are the offences that are forbidden by the laws that are immutable: *mala prohibita* such as are prohibited by laws that are not immutable. This is a labyrinth into which the greatest part of writers have been tempted to plunge on one occasion or another: though none can travel in it two steps together without losing themselves. Accordingly, we have no great reason to be surprized when we find the same writer in the same book ranking the same act by the same name at one time under the one of these opposite divisions, and at another time under the other.[ii]

The common notion of this distinction (as far as a distinction which has no clearness in it is capable of an explanation) seems to be this. *Mala in se,* which, I suppose, is put instead of *mala per se,* are acts which are evil of themselves: that is, although there be no political law by which they stand prohibited: *mala prohibita* are such acts as are indeed evil, but would not have been so had it not been for the law by which they stand prohibited. According to this account of the matter, the mischievousness, if that be what is meant by evil, of acts of the former class is altogether independent of the laws: that of acts of the latter class so dependent on those laws as to owe its existence to them altogether. The former would be mischievous though there were no laws by which they were prohibited; and they would still be mischievous, although there were laws by which they were commanded. The latter, till there were laws which prohibited them, were innocent: laws prohibiting them were made, and then they became pernicious. Thus much for the distinction itself: suspicions may have already arisen from the stating of it, that the foundation of it is none of the clearest: but to throw some little matter of light upon all this darkness, the following observations may be of use.

If any act can with propriety be termed pernicious, it must be so in virtue of its consequences: this has been clearly shewn already: therefore, no act can, strictly speaking, be in itself pernicious; nor even of or by itself; any farther than the words *of* or *by* may be understood to exclude the influence of certain laws. So far for *mala in se.* Now, then, as to *mala prohibita.* Why is it that any act is prohibited, if prohibited with good cause? Because it is

---

ii. This is what S[r] W. Blackstone in his *Commentaries* has done with regard to theft. In the |ʌʌʌ| it is a *malum in se:* in |ʌʌʌ| it is a *malum prohibitum.*[110]

pernicious. Let it be otherwise than pernicious, and the law and whatever punishment it is sanctioned by are groundless, and thence improper.[jj]

The distinction pretends abstraction to be made of subsisting political laws: but in fact no such abstraction is ever made. Of the number of these *mala in se,* theft, I suppose, is one. But what is theft? Is it the same with taking? No: is it the taking of a thing in any circumstances? No: it is the taking in certain cases only. In what cases, then? In the cases in which, amongst others, this circumstance occurs, viz: that the act of taking, as on the part of the person in question, stands prohibited: prohibited, then, by what? by the subsisting laws: else how can the act be theft?

If theft be not a *malum in se,* murder, at least, will, I suppose, be allow'd to be. What, then, is murder? Is it the same with killing? No, surely: for if that were the case, it would be murder to kill one in order to save the lives of [a] thousand; it would be murder to kill a seaman who was running with a torch in his hand to set fire to the powder-room. It is, then, the killing [o88–048] in certain cases only. In what cases, then? in the cases in which, amongst other circumstances, there occurs this, viz: that of the absence of every ground of extenuation or justification, of which that of a command given by persons authorized by the laws is one.

As to the affair of an act's being render'd mischievous by the laws, thus much, however paradoxical it may seem, is true. The paradox, however, will cease when we revert to what has been said already on a former occasion of the case where the mischief of an act may be contingent, and to the examples by which that observation is illustrated, to wit that of the withholding of a contribution which should have been given to the public. Under the head of mischievous acts may be placed, as hath already been observed, for the sake of comprehension and conciseness, not only such acts as are attended with a positive mischief, but also such acts as consist in the negation or non-performance of acts from whence a positive good would have ensued. Now it is perceived that a benefit will ensue if my share of a tax is paid, provided a sufficient number of other persons pay their shares likewise: provided the officer to whom it is paid by me and by them pays it over to his superiors; and so on. The benefit which the act commanded by the law imposing on me the tax *would* produce were it performed is antecedent to the tax (for the benefit would be the same were the contribution paid voluntarily and without the law) and it is the prospect of it that is the ground and justifying reason of the law. Therefore, it is not by this law in particular, the very law by which the act of not paying the tax stands

jj. v. Ch. 13 {Cases unmeet}.[111]

prohibited, that the mischief of such act is produced. Still, however, the production of it is the result of law: of that cluster of laws, to wit, by the concurrence of which that body of obligations is produced in virtue of which the whole produce of the tax is applied to those beneficial purposes for which it stands appropriated.

But this *malum prohibitum,* this act which becomes mischievous merely in consequence of the establishment of certain laws, is the mischief of it less real than that of a *malum in se,* of an act which stands not in need of the concurrence of any laws to render it mischievous? No, certainly: the evil of such an act enters into the composition of a mass of evil which, taken together, may far exceed the evil even of an act of murder. Let the deficiency in the contributions of the people rise to a certain amount, an enemy breaks in, and among the consequences of the irruption are many thousand homicides which, if they have not the name, may have the effect, of murder.

NOTES

1. Bengal: a province of the Mughal empire controlled by the British East India Company at this time, comprising much of the vast Ganges river delta and surroundings in the northeastern part of the Indian subcontinent.

2. MS "catching."

3. I.e., "at length."

4. See *An Introduction to the Principles of Morals and Legislation*, ed. J. H. Burns and H. L. A. Hart (London, 1970), chap. 6, pp. 51–73 [hereafter *IPML*].

5. Charles de Secondat, baron de Montesquieu (1689–1755); Bentham is acknowledging the importance of the comparative approach of his 1748 *De l'Esprit des Lois* (*The Spirit of the Laws*).

6. Harry Verelst (1734–85), East India company administrator, governor of Bengal from 1767 to 1769.

7. Bentham refers here to Reports from Committees of the House of Commons on East India (1772 and 1773) and the East Indies (1781), as the British government increased its involvement through successive scandals over company rule.

8. André Morellet (1727–1819), French philosophe, member of the Academy from 1785.

9. Bentham's enumeration of the subheadings within this section appears to be both incomplete and inconsistent. The enumeration has, therefore, been editorially supplied.

10. I.e., "in kind."

11. James Lind (1716–94), naval surgeon and physician, *An Essay on Diseases Incidental to Europeans in Hot Climates* (London, 1768).

12. Here Bentham compares the demand for European castrati unfavorably to that for Middle Eastern eunuchs.

13. Black Hole of Calcutta: temporary prison during Bengali takeover of the city in 1756, made legendary by John Zephaniah Holwell's sensational *A Genuine Narrative of the Deplorable Deaths of the English Gentlemen, and others, who were suffocated in the Black Hole in Fort-William, at Calcutta* . . . (London, 1758).

14. I.e., Hindu.

15. I.e., Muslim.

16. Peshush: probably a variant transliteration of Pishacha, a kind of demon. See especially the first entries for "Pisachee" in Henry Yule and A. C. Burnell, *Hobson-Jobson: A Glossary of Colloquial Anglo-Indian Words and Phrases* . . . , ed. William Crooke (London, 1903), 714.

17. I.e., an individual of very low caste.

18. I.e., the southwest side.

19. Luke Scrafton (1732–70?), East India Company administrator, *Reflections* published in London, 1763.

20. In the margin, Bentham has noted in relation to this paragraph: "Postpone this."

21. I.e., the Bengal Famine of 1769–70, when between a quarter and a third of the population of Bengal, more than ten million people, died of starvation.

22. The alpine duchy of Savoy was under the civil code of Sardinia through much of the eighteenth century.

23. Literally "poison wind" (Arabic and Turkish); also known as simoom; both it and the sirocco are potentially fierce hot winds.

24. Bentham has failed to provide a reference.

25. Edward Ives (d. 1786), naval surgeon and traveler, *A Voyage from England to India in the Year MDCCLIV* (London, 1773), 274.

26. Bentham has failed to provide a reference.

27. Bentham possibly has in mind Xenophon's mention of his "boy" at *Anabasis* 7.3.20 and his identification with Kritoboulos's desire (for the son of Alcibiades) during the discussion in *Memorabilia of Socrates* 1.3.8–15. See Clifford Hindley, "Xenophon on Male Love," *Classical Quarterly*, new series, 49:1 (1999), 81–82.

28. MS orig. "Ld North (I write in 1782)." Frederick North (1732–92), chancellor of the exchequer from 1767 to 1782 and prime minister from 1770 to 1782.

29. Muhammad Reza Khan (c. 1717–91), Mughal administrator of Bengal. Bentham alludes to the circumstances of the dubious corruption charges used by Governor Warren Hastings to first remove Khan from office in 1772, in an attack on the system of dual rule in the province.

30. I.e., Tahiti.

31. John Atkins (c. 1685–1757), naval surgeon; Bentham's quotation is almost exact.

32. Jean Barbeyrac (1674–1744), Huguenot jurist who published a French translation of Samuel Pufendorf (1632–92), *De Jure Naturae et Gentium*, with his own substantial editorial apparatus. This work was in turn translated into English.

33. See Pufendorf, *Of the Law of Nature and Nations* (Oxford, 1710), 470n. Bentham's quotation is almost exact.

34. In the margin, in relation to the following two sentences, Bentham has noted, "Qu.," i.e., "Quere?"

35. MS "even" appears to be a slip.

36. See Bentham, *Of the Limits of the Penal Branch of Jurisprudence*, ed. Philip Schofield (Oxford, 2010), section 8 (corresponds to *Of Laws in General*, ed. H. L. A. Hart [London, 1970], chap. 6).

37. Bentham did in fact compose the following fragment on "Offences against Religion" (see Bentham Papers, University College London Library, c. 19 [hereafter UC]), which constituted a public offence, but did not integrate it into the text for this section:

"Offences against Religion.

"It is held by Lord Chief Justice Coke [7. Rep. 176 Calvin's case. Shower's Parl. Cases 31.] before the conquest of Bengal, and by Justice Blackstone since, that laws which 'are against the law of God, as in the case of an infidel country,' do, upon the conquest of that country by 'christians, become void.' [1 Comm. 105, second quotation is a gloss] If this does not mean persecution, what does it mean? Such doctrines require either to be explained or to be expunged.

"In England the bulk of the people are prone to toleration: without the least propensity to do injury to the consciences of any, except Catholics, under whose forefathers their forefathers have smarted. But divines have been intolerant, and lawyers have been divines.

"Happily our Eastern conquerors, whatever other censure they may have merited, have kept clear from the infection of these doctrines.

"Ld Chief Justice |ʌʌʌ|, in giving judgment on a man whose offence consisted in a free examination into the truth of the Christian history, justified himself by saying, that 'Christianity is part of the laws of the land.' What is it we are to understand by this loose and declamatory expression? That when a thief takes your cloak from you, you are bound to give him your coat? that criminals taken in the fact are not to be punished till you can find a spotless executioner? that when a man is seen to be of a church different from the christian, or of no church at all, you are to compel him to come in? Here then we have another dictum which should either be explained or be expunged.

"Such are the lights which are to be collected from the common law of England for the ordering of the religious concerns of a million of Mahometans added to nine million of Gentoos.

"By a statute of William the third, extorted by a bigotted party from that enlighten'd prince, the severest punishments are denounced against him who shall deny any of the persons of the blessed trinity to be God, and against him who shall maintain that there are more Gods than one. Is this one of the English laws which have authority in Bengal? I know not: but this we know — that a Gentoo nobleman of the very first rank in the country was hanged for offending against another English law, by an act committed nine years before there was any pretence for saying that any English law had any force over the natives of that country [see note 56 below].

"At length, indeed, such as do not submitt to the yoke of English laws, by an act which is looked upon as voluntary, are no longer to be proscribed — but of the endless heap of laws which it is impossible to know, has any line been drawn between those which they are and those which they are not to suffer by? May not the laws which concern religion be placed in the former class as well as in the latter? Lord Coke hath said delegata potestus non potest delegare [i.e., "a delegated power cannot be delegated"]: the same Lord Coke hath said, that laws contrary to the law of God are void, and that the laws of an infidel country are contrary to the laws of God. Would not the one maxim be as convenient as the other? Is not religion as good a cloak as justice? Can any consideration be a check to those to whom the infamy of a proscription ex-post-facto opposed none? Can any security be reaped by the Gentoo by prohibitions hobbling on at two years' distance in the footsteps of misrule?"

In the margin, in relation to this final paragraph, Bentham has noted: "Is murder in its call for vengeance less loud than forgery?

"And the Bramin who assists the self-devoted widow in her sacrifice, can he, in the eyes of an English lawyer, be any thing than a murderer: and is not a law which authorizes murder repugnant to the laws of God?"

38. An alternative, but apparently superseded, draft of the beginning of this section is at UC c. 6.

39. I.e., addressed to the people.

40. Bentham appears to abandon the paragraph at this point.

41. Or, Jury de medietate linguae; a jury of which half is composed of natives and half of foreigners.

42. De l'Esprit des Lois, (London, 1768), ii, 112 (Bentham's translation).

43. I.e., the "that which is" and the "that which is proper"; Bentham has neglected to put the accents on his Greek.

44. William Blackstone (1723–80), jurist; his monumental *Commentaries on the Laws of England* was published in four volumes between 1765 and 1769. Ben-

tham attended Blackstone's Oxford lectures in the early 1760s and published *A Fragment on Government* anonymously in 1776. Bentham is probably referring here to chapter 4, section 10 of the *Fragment*; see *A Comment on the Commentaries and A Fragment on Government*, ed. J. H. Burns and H. L. A. Hart (London, 1977), 478.

45. David Hume (1711–76) discusses the slip from "is" to "ought" in his *A Treatise of Human Nature*, vol. iii (London, 1740) (III.i.I).

46. I.e., "natural law."

47. Bentham has failed to provide a reference.

48. See Montesquieu, *De l'Esprit des Lois* xxiii, 16. The passage in quotation marks above is not found in the French; Bentham appears to be paraphrasing here. Tonquin is Tonkin, the northernmost part of modern-day Vietnam; Formosa is modern-day Taiwan.

49. MS orig. and del. "the lives of adults."

50. I.e., "to this extent only."

51. *IPML*, chap. 4, pp. 38–41 (pp. 136–39 above).

52. I.e., take swift and drastic action to solve an otherwise intractable problem. Legend has it that whoever would untie the Gordian knot would rule Asia, and that as a young man Alexander the Great (356–323 BC) simply took out his sword and cut it.

53. See Joseph Priestly (Joseph Priestley, 1733–1804), *An Essay on the First Principles of Government* (Dublin, 1768), 120–21, or Priestley, *Political Writings*, ed. Peter Miller (Cambridge, 1993), 55.

54. I.e., dacoits, or bandits; Bentham seems to have in mind those purportedly religiously motivated gangs of robber-murderers who would become known as Thugs.

55. Warren Hastings (1732–1818), governor-general of Bengal from 1773 to 1785. Hastings was impeached by the British House of Commons on several charges in 1787; he was acquitted in 1795.

56. With this note Bentham heaps contempt on the proceedings of the Supreme Court of Judicature, established in 1774 to bring Bengal under English law (see also note k to chapter 2 of *IPML*, pp. 122–23n above). In Cervantes's *Don Quixote* (part 1, chap. 22), the hero farcically meddles in the local administration of justice by freeing a group of prisoners who later attack him. Nandakumar (1705?–75) was the defendant in the supreme court's most famous case, one that would become notorious as a judicial murder. An Indian aristocrat and enemy of Warren Hastings (see previous note), he was tried and hanged on a conviction for forgery after charging Hastings with bribery.

57. Bentham has failed to provide a reference.

58. Peter I, tsar and emperor of Russia from 1682 to 1725.

59. An alternative, but apparently superseded, draft of the beginning of this section is at UC lxxxviii. 21.

60. MS "are."

61. MS "are."

62. MS "it's."

63. Sir Edward Coke (1552–1634), jurist; *Institutes of the Lawes of England* appeared in four parts between 1628 and 1644.

64. I.e., "reasoning from inconvenience" (noting the harm that would be created by a particular construction of the law). See the first part of the *Institutes* (Coke upon Littleton) 11a, and Bentham's discussion in the addendum to note k of chap. 2 of *IPML*, p. 125n.

65. MS "our."

66. Bentham composed a number of passages illustrating the deformity of English law but failed to indicate the order in which they should appear. The following ordering is, therefore, conjectural. The subheadings have been taken from the marginal subheadings on the text sheets.

Related fragments headed "Law and Equity" are at UC c. 8–9; "Fiction" at UC c. 20–21; "Better there — fictions dropt" at UC c. 22; and "Charter" at UC c. 23.

67. "(Copper) Otho": exceedingly rare coin (Otho, Roman emperor from January to April 69 AD).

68. Raphael (1483–1520), Italian Renaissance painter.

69. See Blackstone, 2 Comm. 55–56.

70. It is unclear which Hodgson's case Bentham has in mind.

71. George Pigot (1719–77), governor of Madras (now Chennai) in southeastern India in 1755–63 and again in 1775–76. Following the coup of 1776 he was imprisoned in relative comfort at St. Thomas's Mount outside the city but died before orders resolving the conflict reached India.

72. "John Stiles, or Jack Nokes": generic names used in law; similar to John Doe and Richard Roe.

73. Attempts to trace this incident have been unsuccessful.

74. I.e., Nandakumar; see note 56 above.

75. I.e., *qadi*: a judge in a Shari'a (Islamic law) court.

76. I.e., *qazi*, a South Asian variant of *qadi*; see previous note.

77. A related fragment on "Procedure" is at UC c. 14a.

78. I.e., "the law does not care about little things."

79. Bentham has failed to provide references.

80. MS "fancied."

81. MS "Plff."

82. The following related fragment, headed "Puncta attendenda" (i.e., "Points

to be considered"), is at UC c. 7: "Shall the duties the non-observance of which becomes an offence, the duties of performance as well as of forbearance, be with regard to all these three races the same? If not, in what instances shall they differ? Shall the same circumstances which *abolish*, *aggravate* or *extenuate* the offence on the part of the one be admitted to abolish, aggravate, or extenuate it on the part of the two others? shall the punishments inflicted on these three different classes of men be throughout in specie as well as in quantity the same? Shall the same circumstances which exempt one of those classes from punishment exempt the others? Shall the events from the various proprietary and other rights with which men are made investible date their commencement, and those from which they date their termination, be the same with regard to one of these races as with regard to another? shall the laws of inheritance, the laws of partnership, the laws of insolvency, the laws of conveyance, be the same? Shall the one be bound by every contract by which the rest are bound, or shall contracts be binding on one which shall not be binding on another? Shall the contract of the one receive in all cases the same interpretation with the contract of another? shall the obligations which, in consequence of a contract, the law in it's prudence imposes upon the parties or those connected with them, in addition to the individual obligations created by the contract itself, be in every case the same? Shall the legal relations which are respectively established between the master and the servant, between the husband and the wife, between the parent and the child, between the guardian and the ward, be the same to which ever of these races the parties belong in whom these relations are respectively to be found? Shall the same magistrate who, for a given purpose, has authority over one of these classes have in every instance the same authority over the other two? Shall the course of procedure where a person of the one of these classes is plaintiff or defendant be the same in every point as where a person of either of the other classes appears in the same legal character? Shall notice of the laws on the observance of which their respective fates are made to depend be forwarded to all alike, or to some only, or to none? shall all, or shall some, or shall none, be punished for not paying obedience to mandates of the existence of which it was impossible for any of them to be apprized?"

83. I.e., Ireland. The following two paragraphs, which appear in the text at this point, have been marked by Bentham for deletion:

"But in England there is a trading company of merchants: and this company is allowed to say, Bengal is my ware-house: and when a man shall have set it on fire, he shall be turned out. Such is the provision which the law of England affords, as it stands at present, for the preservation of Sovereignty in Bengal.

"Does it follow from hence that the English laws against treason, if fitted to their end, would be improper in Bengal? by no means: for those which there are in England are not fitted for their end. From such premises, I say, the proposition does not follow: whether it be true in itself is a question to[o] complicated to be discussed here."

84. Bentham possibly intends "*devote pedem osculo*," i.e., "devotedly I kiss your foot."

85. See *IPML*, 225n, 262–63.

86. Daines Barrington (1727/8–1800), English judge; see *Observations on the Statutes, chiefly the more ancient* . . . , 2d ed. (London, 1766), 189–90n.

87. In the margin, Bentham has noted in pencil at this point: "Make here a note on British[?] supineness."

88. Bentham composed a number of passages intended for the remainder of this section but failed to indicate the ordering of the text. The order adopted here is, therefore, conjectural. The breaks between the various passages are indicated by three asterisks.

89. Solon (c. 640–c. 560 BC); Athenian statesman, legendary archaic lawgiver for the classical age.

90. I.e., an unproven assertion, *ipse dixit* meaning "he himself said"; Bentham would eventually coin "ipsedixitism" to label the principle of sympathy and antipathy discussed in *IPML*, pp. 121–32 above.

91. MS "you."

92. MS "you."

93. I.e., "No man ever became great without some measure of divine inspiration." From Cicero's *De Natura Deorum* (II, 66).

94. I.e., the Qur'an.

95. In the text, Bentham has noted at this point, "here give examples. — " but did not, in the event, go on to give any such examples.

96. An abandoned alternative to this passage is at UC lxviii. 39:

"It seems to be a common notion that those laws which are the best with reference to a civilized nation would not have been so with reference to the circumstances of a rude and ignorant nation. On the contrary, that rude nations must have rude and simple, that is imperfect, laws: I mean not only that in point of fact the laws of a rude nation will have been rude, but that in point of expediency it was proper they should be so. The former of these propositions is undeniable: the latter I deny."

In the text, Bentham has noted at this point:

"Solon &c by way of introduction.

"Afterwards interrogate with respect to all the points of perfection — all offences forbidden &c."

Solon is discussed at p. 195 above.

97. I.e., addressed to the sovereign.

98. Francois-Jean Beauvoir, Chevalier de Chastellux (1734–88), French sol-

dier and aristocrat who made this argument in his 1772 *De la Félicité Publique* (*An Essay on Public Happiness* [London, 1774]).

99. See Priestley, *Political Writings*, 10.

100. Pisgah: in Deuteronomy 34: 1–4, the peak from which Moses sees the promised land before his death.

101. Related fragments, headed "Laws of Taxation" and "Laws how render'd permanent in absolute monarchies," are at UC c. 25.

102. I.e., between "things bad in themselves" and "things bad by virtue of being prohibited." See Bentham's discussion, p. 209 ff. below.

103. MS "in."

104. MS "enquirer."

105. Bentham did not indicate precisely where in this section this footnote should appear. Its placement here is conjectural.

106. Eternity conceived as everlastingness is divided into two aspects: an infinite stretch of time before the present (*a parte ante*), and an infinite stretch of time after the present (*a parte post*). See the entry for "Eternity" in Dagobert D. Runes, ed., *The Dictionary of Philosophy* (New York, 1942).

107. Montesquieu, *De l'Esprit des Lois* i. 1.

108. The following paragraph, which appears in the text at this point, has been marked by Bentham for deletion:

"Offences, that is acts which are fit to be so denominated, are here distinguished according to the nature of the mischief which it is their tendency to produce. Mischief consists in pain or in what is equivalent, loss of pleasure, actual or contingent: but pleasures and pains are in themselves the same at all times and all the world over."

109. Ibid. i. 2.

110. See Blackstone, 1 Comm. 54 and 4 Comm. 230.

111. See *IPML*, 158–64.

Rationale of Judicial Evidence, Specially Applied to English Practice
Book 1, Chapter 1

The material for this huge text—it takes up nearly two volumes of Bowring's dense, posthumous eleven-volume *Works*—was composed by Bentham in three drafts, mostly from 1803 to 1812. It was first published as a two-volume recension by Etienne Dumont (*Traité des preuves judiciaires* [Paris, 1823]); then, when Dumont returned the manuscripts, Bentham asked the young John Stuart Mill to prepare a more complete edition. He did so starting in late 1824 or early 1825 and working solidly for a year, then seeing the work through to press in the five-volume edition published in London in 1827. The manuscripts were then destroyed (as was standard practice); the Bowring edition reproduces Mill's work and includes his excellent notes (marked "Editor" to distinguish them from Bentham's).

What follows is a very small excerpt from the Russell and Russell reprint of the Bowring edition (1962), the chapter on "evidence in general" (vi. 208–9). This does not contain the main argument of the work, which aims to substitute a "natural arrangement" for the "technical arrangement" of the English common law; nor does it give any sense of Bentham's views on procedure and "adjective law" more generally. But much else besides is buried in the *Rationale*; this excerpt is included here for its broader philosophical and political significance.

Book I. — Theoretic Grounds

CHAPTER I.

On Evidence in General

EVIDENCE is a word of relation: it is of the number of those which in their signification involve, each of them, a necessary reference to the import expressed by some other; which other must be brought to view at the same time with it, or the import cannot be understood.

By the term evidence, considered according to the most extended application that is ever given to it, may be, and seems in general to be, understood, any matter of fact, the effect, tendency, or design of which, when presented to the mind, is to produce a persuasion concerning the existence of some other matter of fact — a persuasion either affirmative or disaffirmative of its existence.[a]

Of the two facts thus connected with each other, the latter may, for the purpose of expressing the place it bears in its relation to the other, be distinguished by the appellation of the *principal* fact, or matter of fact: the other, by that of the *evidentiary* fact, or matter of fact.[b]

Taking the word in this sense, questions of evidence are continually presenting themselves to every human being, every day, and almost every waking hour of his life.

Domestic management turns upon evidence. Whether the leg of mutton now on the spit be roasted enough, is a question of evidence; a question of which the cook is judge. The meat is done enough; the meat is not done enough: these opposite facts, the one positive, the other negative, are the principal facts — the facts sought: evidentiary facts, the present state of the fire, the time that has elapsed since the putting down of the meat, the state of the fire at different points during that length of time, the appearance of the meat, together with other points perhaps out of number, the development of

a. In the word evidence, together with its conjugates, *to evidence, evidencing, evidenced,* and *evidentiary,* the English language possesses an instrument of discourse peculiar to itself: at least as compared with the Latin and French languages. In those languages the stock of words applicable to this purpose is confined to the Latin verb *probare* and its conjugates: a cluster of words with which the English language is provided, in addition to those which, as just observed, are peculiar to itself.

b. When the persuasion, if any, which is thus produced, is complete, and at its highest point, the principal fact may, in a more expressive way, be termed the fact proved: the evidentiary, the probative fact. But of this pair of appellatives, the range occupying but a point in the scale, the use will, comparatively speaking, not be frequent.

which might occupy pages upon pages, but which the cook decides upon in the cook's way, as if by instinct; deciding upon evidence, as Monsieur Jourdan talked prose,[1] without having ever heard of any such word, perhaps, in the whole course of her life.

The impression, or something like an impression, I see in the grass — the marks of twisting, bending, breakage, I think I see in the leaves and branches of the shrubs — the smell that seems to present itself to my nostrils — do they afford sufficient evidence that the deer, that the enemy, I am in chase of, have passed this way? Not polished only, but even the most savage men — not human kind only, but even the brute creation, have their *rules* — I will not say, as Montesquieu[2] would have said, their *laws* — of Evidence.[c]

If all *practice*, much more must those comparatively narrow branches of it, which are comprehended under any such names as those of *art* and *science*, be grounded upon evidence.

Questions in natural philosophy, questions in natural history, questions in technology in all its branches, questions in medicine, are all questions of evidence. When we use the words *observation*, *experience*, and *experiment*, what we mean is, facts observed, or supposed to be observed, by ourselves or others, either as they arise spontaneously, or after the bodies in question have been put, for the purpose, into a certain situation.

Questions even in mathematics are questions of evidence. The facts, the evidentiary facts, are feigned; but the question concerning the inference to be drawn in each instance, from the feigned existence of the evidentiary facts, to the existence of the facts sought — the question whether, in the way of analogy, the supposed evidentiary facts afford a sufficient ground for being *persuaded* of the corresponding existence of the principal facts — is not the less a question of evidence. The matter of fact, which, presented to the mind in one point of view, is called by this one name, is it the *same* matter of fact which, when presented in another point of view, is called by this other name? Do two and two make four? and for example, the two apples on the right-hand side of the table, added to the two apples on the left-hand side of the same table, are they the same apples, and the same number of apples, that constitute all the apples now lying before me upon the table? In this question of identity — in this question of nomenclature disguised under scientific forms, we see a question of evidence.[d]

c. Esprit de Lois, L. I. ch. 1.

d. The difference, in respect of evidence, between questions of mathematics and questions of purely experimental science — of chemistry, for example — is merely this: that the evidence applicable to the former, is that description of evidence which is

The first question in natural religion is no more than a question of evidence. From the several facts that have come under my senses relative to the several beings that have come under my senses, have I or have I not sufficient ground to be persuaded of the existence of a being distinct from all those beings — a being whose agency is the cause of the existence of all these, but whose separate existence has never at any time, by any perceptible impressions, presented itself, as that of other beings has done, to the cognizance of the senses?

Evidence is, in every case, a means to an end — a particular branch or article of knowledge, considered in respect of its subserviency towards a course of action in which a man is called upon to engage, in the pursuit of some particular object or end in view.

In the case of a branch of science — physical science — cultivated by a private individual, that object may be the producing some physical effect, whether of a customary or of a new complexion; or perhaps nothing more than the general advancement of the science — the making an addition to the mass of knowledge, applicable in common to the production of useful effects, customarily produced, or newly discovered, as it may happen.

On this ground, a great part of the business of science in general may be resolved into a research after evidence. The usefulness of it, with reference to the interests of mankind in general, will be in proportion to that of the department of science to which it belongs, and to the place it occupies in that department.

When the conduct to which the evidence in question is subservient — the conduct for the guidance of which the facts in question, and the knowledge obtainable in relation to them, are searched after — when the conduct thus at stake is the conduct of government as such — of men occupied, on the occasion in question, in the exercise of the powers of government, — the importance of the evidence, and of the conduct pursued in relation to it, take a proportionate rise.

In the map of science, the department of judicial evidence remains to

---

founded upon general reasoning; while the evidence applicable to the latter, is evidence of that description which is derived immediately from matters of fact, presenting themselves to our senses. To point out the peculiar properties of these two kinds of evidence, and to distinguish them from one another, belongs rather to a treatise on logic than to a work like the present; which, considering evidence almost exclusively in regard to its connexion with judicature, excludes all general speculations which have no immediate bearing upon that subject. — *Editor.*

this hour a perfect blank. Power has hitherto kept it in a state of wilderness: reason has never visited it.

In the few broken hints which, in the form of principles, may be picked up here and there in the books of practice, little more relevant and useful information is to be found, than would be obtainable by natural philosophy from the logicians of the schools.

The present work is the result of an attempt to fill up this blank, and to fill it up with some approach towards completeness. Not the minutest corner has been left unexplored: the dark spots have not been turned aside from, but looked out for.

Among the subjects here treated of are several concerning which not any the slightest hint is to be found in any of the books of practice.

Should this endeavour be found successful, it may be regarded as a circumstance not disadvantageous to the science, that the survey of the subject happened to be postponed to so mature a period in the history of the human understanding. So much the less rubbish to clear away: so much the less prejudice to contend with.

Should it happen to this work to have readers, by far the greater part of the number will be composed of those for whose use it was not intended — those to whom, were it not for the predilection produced by professional interest in favour of the best customer, Injustice, and her handmaid Falsehood, — justice and injustice, truth and falsehood, would be objects of indifference.

The class of men for whose use it is really designed, is a class composed as yet of those, among whom a personal or other private interest, hostile to that of the public, will prevent it, if not from finding readers, from finding other than unwilling and hostile readers — readers whose object in reading the work will be, to consider by what means, with the fairest prospect of success, the work and the workman may be endeavoured to be crushed.

The species of reader for whose use it was really designed, and whose thanks will not be wanting to the author's ashes, is the legislator; the species of legislator who as yet remains to be formed — the legislator who neither is under the dominion of an interest hostile to that of the public, nor is in league with those who are.

NOTES

1. I.e., Monsieur Jourdain, oafish protagonist of Molière's *Le Bourgeois Gentilhomme* (The Bourgeois Gentleman), 1670; see act II, scene iv.

2. Charles de Secondat, baron de Montesquieu (1689–1755); author of *De l'Esprit des Lois* (*The Spirit of the Laws*), 1748.

Constitutional Code Rationale
Chapters 1 and 2

What follows is the first two of the seven chapters of "Constitutional Code Rationale," an essay written by Bentham in 1822. The essay is one of his early attempts to write an introduction for the *Constitutional Code*. Bentham published volume 1 of his *Constitutional Code* in 1830, but he did not include this material. A portion of the material was incorporated into the posthumous Bowring version of the *Code*. The essay was published complete and according to Bentham's arrangement when Philip Schofield edited it and three companion pieces for *First Principles Preparatory to Constitutional Code*, a *Collected Works* volume published by Oxford University's Clarendon Press in 1989.

The text and annotation are reproduced here with permission of Oxford University Press. Included is the material from pages 229–43 of the original. For more on this essay, see Schofield's editorial introduction to *First Principles*, especially xv–xix and xxii–xxv.

CHAPTER I.

First Principles Indicative of the Foundation of This Proposed Constitutional Code[1]

§ 1. First principles described in general terms

To whatever portion of the field of thought and action the literary work in question belongs, it has been found convenient, and is accordingly usual, to place at the beginning of it some opinion or opinions, embracing in their extent the whole of the portion in question, or as large a portion of it as may be.

On this occasion a number of mutually related expressions are found needful or convenient, and accordingly in fact are usually employed.

Take for example — First principles — Leading principles — First lines — Outlines — Positions — Axioms — Aphorisms.

If in writing, in the composition of the work, the design be to recommend a certain course of action as ought to be, or say proper to be, pursued for the attainment of a certain end, thereupon come certain other words and phrases of correspondently extensive import. Of this sort are Ends — Objects of pursuit — Means — Obstacles — Helps — Counterforces acting in opposition to the obstacles.

Where the object of the inquiry and discussion is what is the course of action which with relation to the field in question is proper to be pursued, a necessarily concomitant object of regard throughout is — the course actually pursued: pursued in the community which the writer has in view.

If the course actually pursued is on all points the same with the course proper to be pursued, it is well: and unless on the supposition that in default of apposite warning and instruction a departure, to an extent more or less considerable, may have place, any work on the subject in question would be useless, and by him in whose opinion such coincidence has place can not consistently be undertaken.

In regard to some of the above expressions — viz. ought to be done — ought not to be done — is proper to be done — is not proper to be [done] — one matter of fact there is which on every occasion it may be of use to the reader to have in mind. This is that every thing of which any such expression can be in an immediate way the expression is a certain state of mind on the part of him by whom the expression is employed: the state of his mind with relation to the subject matter of the discourse whatsoever it happens to be.

This state of mind will be the state of one or more of his intellectual faculties — in one word his understanding — or the state of his sensitive faculties — in one word feelings — or the state of his volitional faculties — in one word his will, his desires, his wishes.

Thus in the case at present on the carpet. When I say the greatest happiness of the whole community ought to be the end or object of pursuit in every branch of the law — of the political rule of action — and of the constitutional branch in particular — what is it that I express — this and no more: namely that it is my wish, my desire, to see it taken for such by those who in the community in question are actually in possession of the powers of government: taken for such, in such sort that on the occasion of every arrangement taken by them in the exercise of such their powers, their endeavour shall be to render such their course of action contributory to the attainment of that same end, conducive to that same end, contributory to the obtainment of it. Such then is the state of that faculty in me which is termed the will: such is the state of those particular acts or modifications of that faculty which are termed wishes or desires, and which have their immediate efficient causes in corresponding feelings — in corresponding pleasures and pains such as on the occasion in question the imagination brings to view.

In making this assertion I make a statement relative to a matter of fact, namely that which at the time in question is passing in the interior of my own mind: how far this assertion, this statement, is correct, is a matter on which it belongs to the reader, if it be worth his while, to form his judgment.

If, admitting the existence of this desire on my part, it be his desire to learn from me how it happens to have place, in other words what are the efficient causes, I am ready to give him the information he desires, if in his estimate it be worth his while to receive it.[2]

Such then being the desire, truly or falsely expressed by me, but at any rate expressed by me — in his breast has that same desire a place? If so, then may it be worth his while to apply his intention to the course herein marked out by me under the notion of its being correspondent, and contributory and conducive to the attainment of that same end. On the other hand, if so it be that that same desire has no place in his breast, on that supposition, generally speaking, it will be a useless trouble to him to pay any further attention to any thing contained in it.

To this observation one exception it is true there is, and it is this: namely that, if the end in view which it is his wish to see pursued is different from this, it may be of use to him to take note of the arrangements here proposed as conducive to the end pursued by me, for the purpose of taking or rec[om]mending such different and opposite arrangements as may prevent the attainment of the end proposed by me and procure or promote the attainment of that other end, be it what it may, which is more agreable to his wishes: say for example, the greatest happiness of some one member of the community in question, or of some other number smaller than the majority of the whole number of the members.

So again when I say — in the breast of every ruler, on the occasion of the arrangements taken by him in the field of government, the actual end or object of pursuit has, in the instance of every such arrangement, been his own greatest happiness, and that in such sort as that wherever in his judgment there has been a competition between his happiness and that of all the other members of the community in question taken together, he has on each occasion given to his own happiness the preference over theirs, and used his endeavours to give encrease to his own happiness, in whatsoever degree the aggregate of their happiness may in his judgment be lessened by it, — in saying thus, what I have been doing [is] exhibiting the state of my own mind viewed in another point of view: viewed as it were in another part of it — my judgment, the judicial faculty. I have given that as my opinion: an opinion of which I am prepared to bring to view the efficient causes.[a]

§ 2. First principles enumerated

1. Position — Axiom. The right and proper end of government in every political community is the greatest happiness of all the individuals of which it is composed.

Say in other words, the greatest happiness of the greatest number.

In speaking of the correspondent first principle, call it the greatest-happiness principle.

a. While I am a-doing, I observe another law-writer who, on the score of my so doing, taxes me with egotism, or to use another word, with Dogmatism: meaning by dogmatism the doing something which it is his wish, his desire, should not be done.[3]

In answer to this charge what I say is — that either a man must do thus, or he must forbear to write at all: for that it is not possible for man to write without doing thus.

But on this occasion what I say is not confined to self-defence against the charge of Dogmatism — it has for its object the giving warning against that form of discourse on which the imputation expressed by the word Dogmatism does really and properly attach.

In saying as above the proper end of government is the greatest happiness of all or, in case of competition and to the extent of the competition, the greatest happiness of the greatest number, it seems to me that I have made a declaration of peace and good will to all men.[4]

On the other hand were I to say the proper end of government is the greatest happiness of some one, naming him, or of some few, naming them, it seems to me that I should be making a declaration of war against all men, with the exception of that one or of those few.

Be the subject what it may, unless it be allowed to me to say what in relation to that subject are my judgments, my feelings or my desires, I can not say any thing in relation to it: and as to my judgment on each occasion, not giving it as on every occasion I do for more than it is worth, it seems to me that it is on my part no unreasonable claim to be allowed — free from every imputation conveyed or endeavoured to be conveyed by the word Dogmatism — to be allowed to give it.

This being the basis on which all legislation and all morality rests, these few words written in hopes of clearing it of all obscurity and ambiguity, of all doubts and difficulties, will not, I hope, be regarded as misapplied or applied in waste. On no other occasion shall any thing said by any other writer be taken by me for the subject matter of disputation.

In speaking of this end of government, call it the right and proper end of government.

2. Position — Axiom. The actual end of government is in every political community the greatest happiness of those, whether one or many, by whom the powers of government are exercised.[5]

In general terms the proof of this position may be referred to particular experience, as brought to view by the history of all nations.

This experience may be termed *particular* inasmuch as the particular class of rulers is the only class concerned in it to which it bears reference: this may be called the experimental or practical proof.

For further proof reference may be made to the general, indeed the all-comprehensive, principle of human nature. The position which takes this fact for its subject may be termed an axiom and the expression given to it is as follows.

In the general tenor of human life, in every human breast, self-regarding interest is predominant over all other interests put together. More shortly thus, self-regard is predominant: or thus, self-regarding interest is predominant over all other interests put together: or thus, self-preference has place every where.

This position may to some eyes present itself in the character of an axiom: as such self-evident, and not standing [in] need of proof. In other [eyes] as a position or proposition which, how clearly so ever true, still stands in need of proof.

To deliver a position in the character of an axiom is to deliver it under the expectation that either it will not be controverted at all, or that he by whom it is controverted will not, in justification of the denial given by him to it, be able to advance any thing by which the unreasonableness of his opinion or pretended opinion will not be exposed. Of this stamp are the axioms laid down by Euclid.[6] In the axioms so laid by him, nothing of dogmatism will, it is believed, be found.

For the satisfaction [of] those by whom this last account of it is preferred, reference may be made to the *existence* of the species as being of itself a proof — and *that* a conclusive one. For, after exception made of the case of children not arrived at the age at which they are capable of going alone, or adults reduced by infirmity to a helpless state, take any two individuals, A and B, and suppose the whole care of the happiness of A to be confined to the breast of B, A himself not having any part in it, and the whole care of the happiness of B confined to the breast of A, B himself not having any part in it — and this to be the case throughout, it will soon appear that in this state of things the species could not continue in existence, and that a few months, not to say weeks or days, would suffice for the annihilation of it.

Of all modes in which, for the governance of one and the same individual, the two faculties could be conceived as placed in different seats, sensation and consequent desire in one breast, judgment and consequent action in another, this is the most simple. If, as has with less constant truth been said of the blind leading the blind, both would in such a state of things be continually falling into the ditch,[7] much more frequent and more speedily fatal would be the falls supposing the separation to have place upon any plan more complex: suppose the care of the happiness of A, being taken altogether from A, were divided between B and C: the happiness of B and C being provided for in the same complex manner: and so on, the greater the complication, the more speedy, could there be any difference, would the destruction be, and the more flagrant the absurdity of a supposition assuming the existence of such a state of things.[8]

Note that if in the situation of ruler the truth of this position held good in no more than a bare majority of the whole number of instances, it would suffice in the character of a ground for practice: in the character of a consideration by which the location of the several portions in the aggregate mass of political power should be determined: for in the way of induction, it is only by the greater, and not [by][9] the lesser, number of instances that the general conclusion can reasonably be determined: in a word, mathematically speaking, the probability of a future contingent event is in the direct ratio of the number of past instances in which an event of the same sort has happened to the number of those in which it has not happened — it is in this direct ratio, and not in the inverse.

If human beings were so circumstanced, if such were the condition of human beings, that the happiness of no one being came in competition with that of any other — that is to say, if the happiness of each or of any one could receive encrease to an unlimited amount without having the effect of producing decrease in the happiness of any other, then the above expression might serve without limitation or explanation. But on every occasion the happiness of every individual is liable to come into competition with the happiness of every other. If, for example, in a house containing two individuals, for the space of a month there be a supply of food barely sufficient to continue for that space of time the existence of one of them — not merely the happiness of each but the existence of each stands in competition with, and is incompatible with, the existence of the other.

Hence it is, that to serve for all occasions, instead of saying the greatest happiness of all, it becomes necessary to say the greatest happiness of the greatest number.

If however instead of the word *happiness* the word *interest* is employed, the phrase universal interest may be employed as corresponding indifferently to the interest of the greatest number as to the interest of all.[10]

In the eyes of every impartial arbiter, writing in the character of legislator, and having exactly the same regard for the happiness of every member of the community in question as for that of every other, the greatest happiness of the greatest number of the members of that same community can not but be recognized in the character of the right and proper, and sole right and proper, end of government: end, or say object of pursuit.

For the designation of the opposite or reverse of what is right and proper, the adjunct sinister may, in consideration of the mutual relation borne to each other by the two terms taken in the original physical sense, be expressed.

Accordingly, in so far as between the happiness of the greatest number and the happiness of any lesser number any competition and incompatibility has place, if the greatest happiness of the greatest number be taken for the only right and proper end of government, the happiness of any lesser number, coming into competition and being incompatible with the happiness of the greatest number, may be stiled a *sinister* end of government: end, or say object of pursuit.[11]

If, as above, so it be, that, in the situation of a ruler, whatsoever that situation be, the conduct of no man can at any moment reasonably be expected to be determined by any interest that at that same moment stands in opposition to that which in his conception is his own individual interest, [it][12] follows that for causing it to take any direction in which it will be subservient to the universal interest, the nature of man, the nature of the case, affords no other method than that which consists in the bringing of the particular interest of rulers into accordance with the universal interest.

Here then we have a third principle of the first rank in addition to the two former ones.

Call it the Means-prescribing, or Junction-of-interests prescribing, principle.

To make a third, e'en join the former two.

The first declares what ought to be: the next, what is: the last, the means of bringing what is into accordance with what ought to be.

Meantime this junction of interests, how can it be effected? The nature of the case admitts but of one method, which is the destroying the influence and effect of whatever sinister interest the situation of the individual may expose him to the action of: this being accomplished he will thereby be virtually divested of all such sinister interest: remains as the only interest whereby his conduct can be determined, his right and proper interest: that interest which consists in the share he has in the universal interest, which is the same thing as to say that interest which is in accordance with the universal interest taken in the aggregate.

Be the act what it may, there are two modes in either of which a man may be divested of the interest requisite to his performance of it: one is the over-powering the force of whatsoever body of interests may be acting on him in a direction tending to engage him in the performance of it, in other words destroying the effect of all sinister interests by the application of a prepon-derant right and proper interest: this is the direct mode. The other is — the divesting him of the power of performing that same act. For that which in his own eyes it is not in a man's power to perform, it can not in his own eyes be his interest to endeavour to perform: it can never be a man's interest to expend time and labour without effect. Considered in its application to a man's interest, this mode may be termed an *indirect* mode.

Thus it is that by one and the same arrangement, application may be made to both the will and the power: at the same time and in either mode, the requisite junction of interests is capable of being effected or secured.

A question that now immediately presents itself: [how] is it that to any individual, supposing him invested by the Constitution in question with the supreme power, any inducement can by that same Constitution be applied of sufficient force to over-power any sinister interest to the operation of which, by his situation, he stands exposed? Inducements operating on inter-ests are all of them reducible to two denominations — punishment and re-ward. Punishment in every shape his situation suffices to prevent his stand-ing exposed to: so likewise reward. For being by the supposition invested with supreme power, the matter of reward can not be applied to him in any shape in which he has not already at his command whatsoever it would be in the power of the Constitution by any particular arrangement to confer on him. To him who has the whole, it is useless to give this or that part.

To a question to this effect, the only answer that can be given is suffi-ciently manifest. By reward an individual so situated can not be acted upon: for there exists no other individual in the community at whose hand he can receive more than he has in his own. By punishment, as little — for there exists no individual at whose hands he is obliged to receive or will receive any such thing.

The result is that in a Monarchy no such junction of interests can be effected, and that therefore by no means can Monarchy be rendered conducive to the production of the greatest happiness of the greatest number: nor therefore, according to the greatest happiness principle, be susceptible of the denomination of a good form of government.[13]

CHAPTER 2.

The Junction of Interests, How Effected: Or Sinister Interests, How Overpowered

For the effecting of this junction — for the removal of those obstacles to the greatest happiness of the greatest number — the following are the expedients which the nature of the case presents to view.

1. Rendering the possessors of supreme operative power eventually punishable for any abuse of it: i.e. for any act whereby the sinister sacrifice is to any amount effected or endeavoured to be effected.

This expedient supposes the existence of another: namely the lodging of the supreme operative power in more hands than one: the taking it, considered as a whole or aggregate, into shares: and that in such sort as to give to one individual one share, to other individuals in whatever number, to each of them another share, in other words to break this integer into fractions: or say in a single word, to *fractionalize* or fractionize it.

If it be in such sort fractionized as that an individual whose share is so large as to preserve him at one time from being subjected to punishment may at another time have no power at all, or at any rate no power such as to preserve him from exposure to punishment, the problem is accomplished. And in such an arrangement there is nothing either unexampled or peculiarly difficult: nothing but what is familiar in practice.

Resource 2. Placing, to the greatest possible extent, in the situation of rulers those over whom rule is to be exercised.

Could this expedient be employed — employed and with advantage throughout — no need would there be of recourse to any other. But this would be — not government, but the absence of all government. For a time at least it might serve for hundreds: it could never serve for millions.

Two circumstances are seen at once, either of which suffices to render it physically impossible.

1. To act in concert, it would be necessary the whole multitude should at the same time be in the same place, and that in such sort that each one should be within sight and hearing of all the rest.

2. It would be necessary for them to give to the business of government, and in particular the business which consists in settling in what manner the matter of subsistence and abundance, in proportion as it comes into

existence, shall be disposed of, the time necessary to the bringing it into existence.

Hence the need of *deputation*: an operation by which the supreme operative power and the supreme constitutive power are detached from one another: the supreme operative being committed to the individuals deputed, deputed to exercise it in the character of trustees: the supreme constitutive, exercisable with relation to these same possessors of the supreme operative power, being reserved in the hands of those over all whom, individually taken, this same supreme operative power may notwithstanding be exercised.

In the supreme constitutive power may be considered as comprized two perfectly distinct and instantly distinguishable powers — the supreme locative and the supreme dislocative: the power of placing in the situation in question the individual in question, and the power of displacing him — of removing him out of it. In point of fact, the power of displacing is capable of being lodged in hands different from those in which the power of placing the individual in question is reposed. It is even capable of being withheld altogether from every human hand: in which case it is exercised by death. But in point of expediency, how inadequate to the purpose of the required junction of interests the first of these powers can not but be, unless accompanied by the other, and that other placed in the same hands, is sufficiently evident.

In this way is done upon an all-comprehensive scale, that which is every where permitted to be done upon the smallest scale. In the instance of no individual, the case of acknowledged imbecility excepted, infancy for example or insanity, is any objection made to the permitting any individual to place the management of his affairs in the hands of another in quality of trustee, and thus to place them at one time, and take them out again at any other time. That which is unquestionably right in the case of each — why it should be otherwise than right in the case of all, it rests with him to say who in this latter case takes upon him to condemn it.

In the case of Monarchy, the locative function is placed in the hands of blind chance under the name of *birth*, the dislocative in no other hands than those of death. Why in the one case blind chance, in the other case death, should be regarded as affording a better probability of relative aptitude than is afforded by human judgment, judgment exercised by those who have the strongest interest in the correctness of it, is among those questions which look for an answer.

Objections will be considered in another place.[14]

On the scale of private life, only on one or other of two suppositions is either the power of location or the power of dislocation with reference to a trustee denied to the principal. The one is — that of mental infirmity on his part: and on that supposition, regard for his own happiness requires that both the one and the other power should be refused to him. The other, that of moral untrustworthiness: and on that supposition, whether the power of location has or has not been possessed or exercised by him, regard for the interest of those for whose sake the power of location has been exercised requires that the power of dislocation — at any rate the absolute power — should not be exercised by the same hands. Why? because if it were, the application of the power given to the trustee to the purpose in question could not be secured. This is the case where, for the purpose of securing the liquidation of a debt, the property of a debtor is placed in the hands of trustees one or more, till the liquidation shall have been accomplished.

By the division thus made of the power, the will is likewise operated upon — and the junction of interests, the bringing of the personal interest of the functionary into accordance with the universal interest, promoted. In so far as his situation is an object of value in his eyes, and in so far as his continuance in it or his return to it or to a similar one is felt by him to be dependent on those of whose interest the universal interest is composed, in so far is his individual interest brought into accordance with the universal interest.

On what occasion soever applied, for what purpose soever applied, to whomsoever applied, whether it be punishment or reward that is applied — either this junction of interest is effected — either the separate interest of the individual is brought into accordance with the universal interest, and thereby with his share in it, or the purpose whatsoever it be, so far as concerns the effect meant to be produced on the conduct of that same individual, is not effected.

Expedient 3d. Confining and keeping confined within the narrowest limits consistent with its sufficiency with relation to the right and proper all-comprehensive end of government, the mass of supreme operative power possessed when, as above, separated from, and placed in subordination to, the supreme constitutive power. Say — minimizing supreme operative power.

In what distinguishable shapes supreme operative power exists or is capable of having existence will be seen in due place.

So likewise, in what distinguishable ways it is capable of being confined, as above.[15]

Reasons. The less the quantity of power with which a functionary is armed, the more easily will it be for the legislator to deal with him, in such sort as to keep his individual interest in a state of accordance with the universal interest: the less easy will it be for him to find accomplices for any measures adverse to the universal interest; and the more sensibly will he feel [his] dependence on the good opinion and good will of those whose interest composes the universal interest.

Expedient the 4th. Corroborating and employing to the utmost advantage every such force as the nature of the case renders it possible to employ in the character of a counterforce serving as a check upon the legal power lodged in the official hands in question: viz. the power of the popular, or say moral, sanction: the power of the functionaries in question being the power of the political, including that of the legal, sanction: the power of the popular, or say the moral, sanction as applied by the fictitious tribunal denominated the public opinion tribunal.

All human sources of power being already brought upon the carpet, the force here brought to view in the character of a counterforce to that of the possessors of the supreme operative power can not be any thing else than the power of those whose interest composes the universal interest: their power considered under a somewhat different point of view, and designated accordingly under another name.

In the situation of possessors of the supreme constitutive power with relation to the possessors of the supreme operative power, those whose interest composes the universal interest were brought to view in the character of legislators: in the situation here in question, the same persons, the same functionaries if such they may be stiled, are presented to view in the character of judges. Neither of the one power nor of the other, nor of both together, though lodged in the same hands, is there in this case any danger of abuse: in the case of [each]16 power, making the most of it for the advancement of their own interest is in this case the very course that is most desirable.

When of this natural counterforce such advantage is made as is capable of being made, the effect is that in case of misdecision or misrule in any shape an appeal has place, has place of itself and without formality, delay, vexation or expence, from the possessors of the supreme operative power to their creators, the possessors of the supreme constitutive power, in the character of Judges.

Even in the very sink of corruption, where all functionaries are corrupt — rendered necessarily so by the very form of government — even in such an atmosphere, this tribunal, fictitious as it is, is not altogether without force: by this force it is, and no other, that all that evil has been prevented which as yet remains undone: if in so pestilential an atmosphere, in which what is called religion has its effect, and understanding and will labour under the avowedly desired prostration of strength, this antiseptic is not without its effect, what would it be under a pure one?

How to employ this counterforce to most advantage will form a particular subject of enquiry in another place.[17]

Expedients for effecting the junction of interests recapitulated:[18]

1. To those whose interest composes the universal interest give or leave as much power as possible.

2. To those whose interest is not the universal interest but in its very nature adverse to the universal interest give as little power as possible.

3. Keep on foot, in the character of a power prepared when occasion calls, a power superior to their own, the power of those whose interest is the universal interest, in readiness to act upon them in the character of Judges and punish them with dishonor and loss of office in their character of legislators.

When these things are accomplished, all things are accomplished by which any thing can be done towards keeping the interest of the possessors of supreme operative power in accordance with the universal interest: that is to say, if the word *duty* be worth employing, in accordance with their *duty*.

To this same denomination — viz. bringing the less principal interest into accordance with the more principal interest — is referable whatsoever in private trusts is done in the view of securing probity on the part of trustees.

So likewise whatsoever is done for the purpose of minimizing the evil produced by the misdeeds of those against whom, under the general denomination of malefactors or say criminals, the force of punishment under the name of punishment is applied by that branch of the aggregate mass of law which is distinguished by the name of penal law. Were it not for the punishment, the particular and sinister interest, correspondent to and created by the appetite whatsoever it be in which the misdeed had its source, would stand unopposed, and produce conduct opposite in the way in question to the universal interest. Comes the legislator with his penal law: punishment being attached to the misdeed, the sinister interest finds itself thereupon encountered and opposed by another interest operating in a direction favorable, or at least supposed to be favorable, to the universal interest — to the universally right and proper interest. If, at the moment of decision, in the eyes of the individual in question, in all dimensions or elements of value taken together — namely intensity, duration, propinquity, certainty, purity and fecundity — the value of the mass of looked for pleasure which constitutes the temptation is greater than the value of the punishment opposed to it by the penal sanction added to the force of the other sanctions, the misdeed is committed notwithstanding: if not so great, the particular and sinister interest is overpowered and rendered inefficient by the united force of the sanctions, and conduct is determined by that interest which is in accordance with the universal interest, as above.

NOTES

1. An earlier draft of this chapter, dated 26–27 July 1822, is at Bentham Papers, University College London Library UC xxxvi. 80–85 [hereafter UC]. Other related fragments are at UC xxxvi. 78–79 (21 July 1822) and clx. 237 (22 July 1822).

2. Bentham added at this point, "Here give in a Note the three efficient causes," but none appears to have been written.

3. The author in question was Jean Baptiste Antoine Hyacinthe Blondeau (1784–1854), the French jurist who in his work *Essais sur quelques points de Législation et de Jurisprudence* (Paris, 1819), 47n., had written, "Cet auteur [Bentham], qui, dans le chapitre II de ses *Principes généraux de Législation*, combat avec tant de force les Dogmatiques, nous paraît avoir lui-même admis, comme un dogme, ce principe: *les Lois doivent avoir pour but l'intérêt général.*" The essay "Principes généraux de Législation" formed the first part of *Traités de législation civile et pénale* (i. 1–145); Blondeau may, however, have had in mind chapter 3, see esp. i. 21.

4. Luke 2: 14.

5. In the marginal summary, Bentham added. "Corresponding principle: Rulers' object-indicating principle. Corresponding end or object: sinister end or object."

6. The celebrated geometrician, who lived at Alexandria during the reign of the first Ptolemy (323–283 BC).

7. Matthew 15: 14; Luke 6: 39.

8. Bentham noted at this point, "See Appendix No. 1. Dissertation on Self-preference: proving the necessity of it in the human and every other sensitive being," but no material under this heading appears to have been written.

9. MS "in."

10. Bentham noted at this point: "☞ Insert relation between the import of the word *happiness* and the import of the word *interest*." For a discussion of this relation, see, for instance, *An Introduction to the Principles of Morals and Legislation*, ed. J. H. Burns and H. L. A. Hart (London, 1970) *(CW)*, 12–13 **[pp. 113–14 above — S.E.]**.

11. There is no text corresponding to the following marginal summary, which belongs here: "Correspondently every particular interest the advancement of

which is incompatible with ditto of the universal ditto, a sinister [interest]. The sacrifice of every such sinister interest to the right and proper interest, the right and proper sacrifice. The sacrifice of the right and proper interest to any sinister ditto, a sinister sacrifice."

12. MS "in."

13. The marginal summary expands on the text at this point: "Under a pure Monarchy, the sinister sacrifice is unintermittingly performed. The greatest happiness of one is the end constantly aimed at: the greatest happiness of the greatest number constantly sacrificed. The force of his share in the universal interest continually mastered by ditto of his separate and sinister interest. The sinister sacrifice constantly performed to an indefinite amount. To an indefinite extent, Misrule substituted to Good Rule."

14. In the margin, Bentham noted at this point: "See | | ." For further discussion of Bentham's views on monarchy, see "Supreme Operative," 149–226 above **[not included in this volume — S. E.]**.

15. In the margin, Bentham noted at this point: "See | | ." For a discussion of this topic, see "Economy as applied to Office," chap. 4, pp. 30–39 above **[not included in this volume — S. E.]**.

16. MS "every."

17. See chap. 5, pp. 283–98 below **[not included in this volume — S. E.]**.

18. This phrase is taken from the marginal summary.

Pannomial Fragments

Until the very end Bentham was working on his Pannomion, or complete code of laws. These notes of his are dated from 1828 to 1831, so they comprise Bentham's most mature reflections on the foundations of jurisprudence. The papers were edited for Bowring by Richard Smith. A spot check of the manuscripts, which are deposited in the British Library, confirms that Smith's transcription work is sound, thorough, and unembellished; only the arrangement of the materials is suspect.

What follows is taken from pages 211–30 of volume iii of the 1962 Russell and Russell reprint of *The Works of Jeremy Bentham,* ed. J. Bowring, 11 vols. (Edinburgh: William Tait, 1838–43). The editor's note (p. 211) reads as follows: "The MSS. from which the following Chapters are extracted, were written at sundry times, and are in an unfinished state; — the author appears to have designed ultimately to have worked up the sketches he has thus left into an Introduction to a Pannomion, or Complete Code of Laws. Some of the latest sheets are dated June 1831."

In addition to some light annotation, the Bowring text has been slightly altered and corrected for ease of reading. Original editorial notes (Bentham's and Smith's) are lettered; additions are numbered.

This material has not yet appeared in the *Collected Works of Jeremy Bentham.*

CHAPTER I

General Observations

By a Pannomion, understand on this occasion an all-comprehensive collection of law, — that is to say, of *rules* expressive of the will or wills of some person or persons belonging to the community, or say society in question, with whose will in so far as known, or guessed at, all other members of that same community in question, whether from habit or otherwise, are regarded as disposed to act in compliance.

In the formation of such a work, the sole proper all-comprehensive end should be the greatest happiness of the whole community, governors and governed together, — the *greatest-happiness principle* should be the fundamental principle.

The next specific principle is the *happiness-numeration principle.*

Rule: In case of collision and contest, happiness of each party being equal, prefer the happiness of the greater to that of the lesser number.

Maximizing universal security; — securing the existence of, and sufficiency of, the matter of subsistence for all the members of the community; — maximizing the quantity of the matter of abundance in all its shapes; — securing the nearest approximation to absolute equality in the distribution of the matter of abundance, and the other modifications of the matter of property; that is to say, the nearest approximation consistent with universal security, as above, for subsistence and maximization of the matter of abundance: — by these denominations, or for shortness, by the several words *security, subsistence, abundance,* and *equality,* may be characterized the several specific ends, which in the character of means stand next in subordination to the all embracing end — the greatest happiness of the greatest number of the individuals belonging to the community in question.

The following are the branches of the pannomion, to which the ends immediately subordinate to the greatest-happiness principle respectively correspond: —

To constitutional law, the axioms and principles applying to equality.

To penal law, the axioms and principles applying to security; viz. as to —
1. Person; 2. Reputation; 3. Property; 4. Condition in life.

The principle presiding over that branch of the *penal code,* which is employed in the endeavour to arrest, or apply remedy to offences considered as being and being intended to be productive of suffering to one party, without producing enjoyment, otherwise than from the contemplation of such suffering, to the other, is the *positive-pain-preventing principle.*

Rule: Let not any one produce pain on the part of any other, for no other purpose than the pleasure derived from the contemplation of that same pain.

The persons for the regulation of whose conduct the *positive-pain-preventing principle* applies are —

1. The subject citizens, taken at large.

2. The sovereign, in respect of the quantity, and thence the quality of the subsequentially preventive, or say punitive, remedy applied by him against any offence.

To civil law, more particularly, apply the axioms relating to security as to property. Sole principle — *the disappointment-preventing principle.*

Rule applying to the aggregate, composed of the several sources of positive good or happiness, elements of prosperity, objects as they thus are of general desire: Among a number of persons, competitors actually or eventually possible, for the benefit or source of happiness in question, exceptions excepted, give it to that one in whose breast the greatest quantity of pain of disappointment will have place, in the event of his not having the thing thenceforward in his possession, or say, at his command.

The exception is when, by any different disposition, happiness in greater quantity, probability taken into account, will be produced.

Of any such exception the existence ought not to be assumed: if it exist, the proof of its existence lies upon him by whom its existence is asserted.

To political economy apply the axioms and principles relating to subsistence and abundance. To political economy — that is to say, to those portions of the penal and civil codes in the rationale of which considerations suggested by the art and science of political economy are applicable and have place: considerations over and above and independent of the sensations produced by loss and gain.

By axioms of moral and political pathology, understand so many general propositions, by each of which statement is made of the pleasure or pain (chiefly of the pain) produced by the several sorts of evils, which are the result of human agency on the part of the several individuals respectively affected by them; to wit, by means of the influence exercised by them on the quantity or degree in which the benefits expressed by the fore-mentioned all important words, are by the respective parties, agents and patients, enjoyed, or the opposite burthens constituted by the absence of them endured.

Of these propositions, it will be observed that they divide themselves into *groups*; — one group being relative to security, another to subsistence, a third to abundance, the fourth and last to equality: the first bringing to view the enjoyment derived from the undisturbed possession of security at large — security in the most comprehensive application made of the word, contrasted with the enjoyment producible by the breach of it, — the second group bringing to view the subject of subsistence; — the third group bringing to view the subject of abundance, — and the fourth group bringing to view the subject of equality, and stating the evil consequence of any legislative arrangement by which a defalcation from the maximum of practicable equality is effected.

In each of the axioms, the antagonizing, or say competing, interests of two parties are conjointly brought to view: — in those which relate to security, these parties are, the maleficent agent, or say wrongdoer, and the patient wronged: — in those which relate to subsistence, abundance, and equality, they are the parties whose interests stand in competition, no blame being supposed to have place on either side. By the legislator, preference should be given to that interest by preference to which the happiness of the greatest number will be most augmented.

To the first of the three stages of the progress made in society by the good or evil flowing from a human act, belong the effects of which indication is given in and announced by these same four groups of axioms.

The principles which form the groundwork of the here proposed system, correspond to the above-mentioned *specific* ends, immediately *subordinate* to the all-comprehensive *end,* expressed for shortness by the *greatest-happiness principle,* — and have their foundation in *observations* on the pathology of the human mind as expressed in the above-mentioned *propositions,* to which, in consideration of their supposed incontrovertibility and extensive applicability, have been given, for distinction sake, the name of axioms.

As to these principles, the names by which expression is given to them have for their object and purpose *conciseness* — the conveying, by means of these several compound substantives, a conception of the several groups of pathological effects in a manner more concise, and thence more commodious, than by a repetition made each time of the several groups of axioms to which they correspond, and which they are employed to recal to mind.

Correspondent to the axioms having reference to security, will be found the principles following: —

I. Principle correspondent to security, and the axioms thereto belonging, is the *security-providing principle.*

Of the security-providing principle, the following modifications may be brought to view, corresponding to the several *objects* respecting which security requires to be afforded: —

1. The objects for, or say in respect of which, security is endeavoured, are these —

i. Person: the person of individuals on the occasion of which body and mind require to be distinguished.

ii. Reputation: the reputation of individuals or classes, or say the degree of estimation in which they are respectively held.

iii. Property: the masses of the matter of wealth respectively belonging to them, and possessed by them in the shape of capital, or in the shape of income.

iv. Power: the portions of power respectively belonging to them, for whose sake soever, or say to whose benefit soever exerciseable, whether for the sake and benefit of the individual power-holder himself — or for the sake of other persons, one or more, in any number; in which case the power is styled a *trust,* and the power-holder a *trustee,* and the person or persons for whose benefit it is exercised, or designed to be exercised, entitled *bene-fitee,* and the person or persons by whom the trust was created a *trustor.*

v. Rank: or say factitious reputation or estimation, — the source of factitious reputation or estimation put into the possession of the individual by a series of delusions operating on the imagination.

vi. Condition in life, in so far as beneficial: the aggregate benefits included in it will be found composed of the above objects, two or more of them.

N. B. The four last-mentioned objects may, for conciseness sake, be spoken of as so many modifications of the matter of prosperity.

vii. Miscellaneous rights: including exemptions from burthensome obligations.

2. The maleficent acts, or say offences, against which the endeavour is used to apply the appropriate punitive and other remedies.

3. The contingently maleficent agents, against whose maleficent acts the endeavour will be used to employ the several remedial applications. These may be —

i. External, or say foreign governments and subjects, considered as liable to become adversaries. Code in which provision is made against evil from that source, the Constitutional. Ch. &c. Defensive Force[1] — sub-departments of the administration department, those of the army and the navy ministers.

ii. Internal; viz. fellow-citizens; as distinguished into — a. Fellow-citizens at large, or say non-functionaries; b. Functionaries considered in respect of the evil producible by them in such their several capacities.

4. The several classes of persons to *whom,* by the several arrangements employed, the security is endeavoured to be afforded. These may be distinguished into — i. Citizens of the state in question; distinguished into — a.

Persons considered in their individual capacities: correspondent offences —
private offences. b. Persons considered in classes: correspondent offences
— semi-public offences. c. Functionaries as such considered in the aggregate: correspondent offences — public offences, such as are purely public in
contradistinction to such as are privato-public; offences affecting their individual capacity, but constituted public offences by the indefinable multitude
of the individuals liable to be affected. ii. Foreigners with reference to the
state in question; — governments and subjects as above included.

A modification of the security-providing principle, applying to security in respect of all modifications of the matter of property, is the
disappointment-preventing principle. The use of it is to convey intimation
of the reason for whatever arrangements come to be made for affording
security in respect of property and the other modifications of the matter of
prosperity, considered with a view to the interest of the individual possessor. In the aggregate of these are contained all the security-requiring
objects, as above, with the exception of *person.*

II. Subsistence-securing principle: correspondent subordinate end in
view — subsistence. The use of it is to convey intimation of the reason for
whatever arrangements come to be made for the purpose of securing, for the
use of the community in question, a sufficient quantity of the matter of
subsistence.

III. Abundance-maximizing principle: the use of it is to convey intimation of the reasons for whatever arrangements may come to be made in
contemplation of their conduciveness to the accomplishment of that end.

IV. Equality-maximizing, or say, more properly, inequality-minimizing
principle: the use of it is to convey intimation of the reasons for whatever
arrangements come to be made, in contemplation of their conduciveness to
this end.

CHAPTER II

Consideranda

Subjects of consideration on the present occasion are the following: —
Pleasures and pains — happiness and unhappiness — good and evil — ends
and means — rules and principles — axioms of pathology, physical, and
mental — or say psychological — observation and experiment. Of these,
many are mutually correlative, — all are intimately connected with, and
give and receive explanation to and from each other.

Happiness is a word employed to denote the sum of the pleasures experienced during that quantity of time which is under consideration, deduction made or not made of the quantity of pain experienced during that same quantity of time.

Unhappiness is a word employed to denote the sum of pains experienced during the quantity of time which is under consideration, deduction made or not made of the quantity of pleasure experienced during that same quantity of time.

Good is a word employed to denote either pleasure, or exemption from pain — and the cause efficient, and more or less effective, of either.

Evil is a word employed to denote either pain or loss of pleasure, or a cause efficient, and more or less effective, of either.

In regard to good and evil, consider —

I. Their *condition* or import as to existence and non-existence.

Their *existential character,* or say character or mode of designation in regard to existence, or say logical character: — this is either *positive* or *negative.*

Positive good, is that which assumes not the existence of evil, and which accordingly might have place if there were no such thing as evil.

Negative good, is that which is constituted by the non-existence of evil on the occasion in question.

Positive evil, is that which assumes not the existence of good, and which accordingly might have place, if there were no such thing as good.

II. In regard to each, their *quality.*

By good, understand either pleasure, or the absence — or say, on the occasion in question, the non-existence — of *pain.* Pleasure is positive good; absence of pain — negative good.

By evil, understand either pain, or the absence — or say, on the occasion in question, the non-existence — of pleasure. Pain is positive evil; absence of pleasure — if arising from loss — negative evil.

III. Their relation in respect of causality.

Understand by *good,* either actual pleasure, or absence of pain, or anything considered as the cause of pleasure, or the absence of pain.

Understand by *evil,* either actual pain, or absence of pleasure, or anything considered as the cause of pain or of the absence of pleasure.

IV. Their quantity, in respect of — 1. Intensity; 2. Duration; 3. Extent.

V. Their productiveness — or say fecundity — 1. Direct; 2. Inverse.

VI. Part taken by human action in the production of them.

1. Wish, or say desire; 2. Direction to action in consequence — or say, in pursuance of such wish.

End is a word employed to denote a good, the prospect of eventually experiencing which, operates as a motive tending to produce at the hands of any sensitive being, some good which is an object of human desire and hope.

Means is a word employed to denote any substance, state of things, or matter, considered as contributing to the attainment of the good, which on that same occasion is regarded as an end.

Pleasures and exemptions from pains, with their respective correlatives, happiness and exemption from unhappiness, are the ultimate ends of action.

As between *good* and *evil,* good alone is an ultimate end of the action of a sensitive being.

Good and *evil,* both are means in their nature capable of being made conducive to the attainment of the ultimate end — the net maximum of happiness; and accordingly by men in general, and by men in the situation of legislators in particular, are employed in that view, and for that purpose.

Of good or evil, one and the same portion is capable of acting, on one and the same occasion, in the character of an *end,* and in that of a *means:* — of a means in relation to some antecedent end or state of things — of an end in relation to some eventually subsequent state of things.

Remedy, in all its shapes, is an instrument having for its use the exclusion of wrong in all its several shapes — or say, the exclusion of maleficence in all its several shapes.

Of remedy in every shape, the application made is attended with and productive of burthen.

The application of remedy, instead of excluding wrong, is productive of wrong, if and in so far as it is productive of burthen outweighing the benefit.

In this way may effects and causes be seen linked together, as it were, in a chain composed of links in indefinite number, and, taken in the aggregate, of correspondent length.

So much for the matter of good, being that the production of which is, or at least ought to be the object, or say end in view, of everything which passes under the denomination of law — or a law: — and so much for good and evil, — both of them employed as means, and the only means employable, for the attainment of that end.

But what is a law, and what are laws themselves? Before this is explained, must be brought to view that species of matter which on each occasion is occupied in passing judgment on the aptitude of the law in question, considered as a *means* employed in and for the attainment of that end. To this purpose comes the need of the ideas, expression to which is given by the two mutually and intimately connected words *rule* and *principle.*

Correspondent to every rule you may have a principle: correspondent to every principle you may have a rule.

Of these two, a rule is the object which requires first to be taken into consideration and presented to view. Why? Because it is only by means of a rule that any moving force can be applied to the active faculty, or any guide to the intellectual — any mandate can be issued — any instruction given.

A *rule* is a *proposition* — an entire proposition: a *principle* is but a *term*: True it is, that by a principle instruction may be conveyed. Conveyed? Yes: but how? No otherwise than through the medium of a proposition — the corresponding proposition — the proposition which it has the effect of presenting to the mind. Of presenting? Yes: and we may add, and of bringing back; for only in so far as the rule has been at the time in question, or some anterior time present to the mind, can any instruction, any clear idea be presented to the mind by a principle.

A principle, therefore, is as it were an abridgment of the corresponding rule; — in the compass of a single term, it serves to convey for some particular present use, to a mind already in possession of the rule, the essence of it: it is to the rule, what the essential oil is to the plant from which it is distilled.

So it does but answer this purpose, its uses are great and indisputable.

1. It saves words, and thereby time.

2. By consisting of nothing more than a single term, and that term a noun-substantive, it presents an object which, by an apt assortment of other words, is upon occasion capable of being made up into another proposition.

So, it is true, may a rule — but only in a form comparatively embarrassing and inconvenient. This will appear by taking in hand any sentence in which a principle has place, and instead of the principle employing the corresponding rule.

Upon occasion, into any one sentence principles in any number may be inserted: and the greater the number, the stronger will be the impression of the embarrassment saved by the substitution of the principles to the rules.

A principle, as above, is no more than a single term; but that term may as well be composite, a compound of two or more words, as single. Of these words one must be a noun-substantive; the other may be either a noun-adjective or a participle; including under the appellation of a noun-adjective, a noun-substantive employed in that character, in the mode which is so happily in use in the English language, and which gives it, in comparison with every language in which this mode is not in use, a most eminently and incontestably useful advantage.

By an *axiom* is meant a sort of rule, of which by certain properties, the combination of which is peculiar to it, the usefulness is pre-eminent in comparison with other rules. These properties are —

1. Incontestableness.

2. Comprehensiveness.

3. Clearness.

As to axioms, the axioms that belong to this subject are axioms of mental pathology. The facts they are enunciative of, are facts enunciative of certain sensations, as being produced by certain events or states of things operating as their efficient causes.

By a *reason* for any act, is conveyed the idea of its supposed addition, actual or probable, to the greatest happiness. This effect may be produced either — 1. Immediately; 2. Through an intervening chain of any number of links.

A *law* is a word employed in three different senses, which require to be distinguished: but in each of them it imports that the *will* to which it gives expression either emanates from the supreme authority in the state, or has that same authority for its support.

In one sense it denotes an entire command, — the whole matter of a command. Call this the *integral* sense, and the sort of law a *complete law*.

In the second sense it contains no more than a portion of a command; and the matter of the command may be to an indefinite extent voluminous, containing laws of the first-mentioned sort in any number: in this sense it has for its synonym the word enactment: call the law in this sense a *fractional* or *incomplete* law.

In the third sense it designates the aggregate body of the enactive paragraphs to which it happens to have received the token of their being expressive of the will of the person or persons invested with the supreme authority in the political state, or of some person who acts in this behalf, under, and by virtue of that same authority.

By *power of classification* a species of legislative power is exercised. Thus when an enactment to any effect has been framed, if by any proposition bearing the form of a command or a rule, enlargement or retrenchment is applied to the genus, or say class of objects which contribute to constitute the subject-matter of the command; — by this means, in a sort of indirect way, by and with the help of the other words which enter into the composition of the enactment, is produced the effect of a different enactment: one of the classes of which that same subject-matter is composed receives thereby *contraction* or enlargement, and a fresh classification is made thereby.

Note here — in the giving existence to an enactment, three distinguishable parts are capable of being taken — or say, functions are capable of being performed; viz. the *institutive*, the *constitutive*, and the *consummative;* and this whether by one and the same authority, or by so many different authorities: by exercise given to the power of classification in any instance, a different consummation as it were is given to the several enactments, in the matter of which, the generic words in question are any of them contained.

Of this same function — of this same power, exercise is made by any functionary, or set of functionaries, belonging to a department other than, and thence inferior to, the *legislative;* for in no other way can classes be filled up by individuals, and reality given to general ideas. Call this power, power of location, or say *locative* power. But what difference there is between this case and the preceding consists in this: in the former case, by no other authority than the legislative can the power be exercised — the effect produced: in the latter case it is produced in virtue of a general authorization given by the legislative authority, and by that authority is never produced, unless it be in consequence of some extraordinary occurrence.

So much for particular laws, and small masses of particular laws. Now for the divisions of the all-comprehensive aggregate in which they are all of them at all times comprised.

The Pannomion may be considered as composed of two branches — the effective and the constitutive.[a]

In the effective branch may be considered as contained the portion of the matter which is more immediately occupied in giving direction to the conduct of the members of the community of all classes.

The constitutive is occupied in determining who those persons in particular are, by whom the powers belonging to the effective branch shall be exercised.

Considered with relation to its connexion with good and evil employed in the character of punishment and reward for the purpose of giving direction to human conduct, the Pannomion is distinguished and divided into two branches — the directive and the sanctionative.

By the directive part, indication is given of the course which it is the desire of the law-giver that upon the occasion in question the subject-citizens should pursue.

By the sanctionative pact, information is given to them of the inducement which they will find for the pursuing of those same courses.

The matter of which this inducement is composed, is either the matter of good as above, or the matter of evil. Where and in so far as it is of the matter

---

a. It may also be considered as divided into substantive and adjective. The substantive branch of the law has for its business the giving direction and effect to human conduct; — the adjective has for its business the giving execution and effect to substantive law.

of good, *remunerative* is the name that may be given to the law: where and in so far as it is the matter of *evil*, penal is the name commonly given to the law — *punitive*, a name that may be given to it.

These two branches of a law are addressed to different descriptions of persons; — the *directive* to persons at large — the *sanctionative* to the members of the official establishment.

By the sanctionative, provision is made of the inducement, to which the legislator trusts for the compliance he seeks and expects to find on the part of those to whom the directive branch of the law is addressed. This inducement is the eventual expectation of either good or evil in the mind of those to whom the directive branch of the law is addressed: — if it be *good*, the law in that branch of it is styled a *remunerative* law: if *evil* a penal law.

The persons to whom a remunerative law is addressed are those functionaries belonging to the administrative department, by whom disposal is made of the money, or whatever else the matter of good employed consists of, directing them eventually to bestow the article in question on the person in question in the event of his having complied with the directive law in question, and thereby rendered the service desired at his hands.

The persons to whom a penal law is addressed, are the official persons belonging to the judiciary department, presided over and directed by the judges.

Of the matter to which it may be convenient to give insertion in the civil code, and to which accordingly insertion is given in it, there are two different sorts: one of which may be styled the *directive* as above — the other the expositive.

To the directive belongs that sort of matter, of which, under that name, mention has been already made — the directive, without the addition of the sanctionative, and in particular the punitive.

Not that, without the addition of the sanctionative, the directive could in general without absurdity be trusted to. Of a correspondent eventual punishment, including, where applicable, satisfaction, to be administered in case of non compliance, the existence must all along thereby be assumed. But in relation to punishment, this is the whole of that which naturally here finds its place: — in the penal code will be inserted all denunciation of extra punishment, together with what belongs to the mode in which the application made of the matter of punishment is brought about; — leaving to the civil code, the direction of the mode in which satisfaction, and in particular that branch of it which consists in the allotment of compensation for wrong, shall be administered.

The expositive matter belongs in common to, constitutes and forms part and parcel of, the directive part of the matter of the civil code, and the penal code.

Among the words and locutions, of which exposition is given in it, may be seen this or that word, in the exposition of which a prodigious quantity of matter is employed.

Take, for instance, the word *title* or the word *right*, when employed as synonymous with and equivalent to it. Exposition of it is alike necessary to the completion of any enactment belonging either to the civil or the penal code.

Take, in the first place, the *civil*. The principal part of it is occupied in the declaration of to what person or persons each subject-matter of property, each object of general desire, shall belong, in such sort as to be styled his or their own — who he is or they are, to whom it belongs — or say, who have title to it. Now, then, be the subject-matter what it may — who is it that has *title* to it? Who but he in whose favour some one in the list of completely collative events or states of things has place; no event or state of things having, with relation to that same title, an ablative effect, having at the same time place in the disfavour of that same individual.

So much for the portion in question — the portion of the matter of the civil code.

But not less necessary is reference made in the penal code to that same matter.

Take, for instance, in offences severally considered, offences affecting property, — the offence of *theft*. To the conveying of an accurate conception of the nature of this offence, mention of title is indispensable. Why? Answer: Because, when it is under the persuasion of his having a title to the thing in question, where it is under this persuasion that the man took it, — by no one will he be regarded as having committed the offence thus denominated: thence so it is, that in any well-adapted definition of this offence, averment of the non-existence of any such persuasion must be contained.

Not that in the idea of the offence it is necessary that the idea of any portion of that same matter in particular — the idea, for example, of any one collative event more than another — should have place.

Merely expositive, and mixed: of the one sort or the other will be found to be every particle of the matter which will with most convenience be aggregated to the matter of the civil code.

Constitutive of the mixed matter will be — 1. Matter of general concernment; 2. Matter of particular concernment.

CHAPTER III

Expositions

Only with reference to language can the attribute denoted by the word universal be with propriety attributed to the subject of *law*.

In each country, at each point of time, it is matter of accident whether a law to a given effect is in force; though, consideration had of the general effect, and not of the particular tenor, in no inconsiderable quantity, masses of the matter of law might be found, such as are not likely to be wanting in any country that has the use of letters. A mass of the matter of language expressive of law might be found, of which the equivalent cannot be wanting, in any country, among any assemblage of human beings, in the presence of each other, for any considerable length of time. This may be styled the language of universal law.

Follows the exposition of some of these terms, the use of which exposition upon this occasion is not so much to teach as to fix their import: —

1. *Obligation.* — Obligations may exist without rights; — rights cannot exist without obligations.

Obligation — a fictitious entity, is the product of a law — a real entity.

A law, when entire, is a command; but a command supposes eventual punishment; for without eventual punishment, or the apprehension of it, obedience would be an effect without a cause.

Reward — eventual reward, is not capable of securing obedience to will signified, — is not capable of giving to will the effect of a command: — apprehension of the abstraction of reward already in possession or expectancy may do it. Yes: but though *reward* alone be the word employed in the description of the case, the operation signified is of the nature of punishment; — the effect of it not enjoyment, but suffering.

Obligation has place, when the desire on the part of the superior, the obliger, being signified to the obligee, he understands at the same time, that in the event of his failing to comply with such desire, evil will befal him, and that to an amount greater than that of any evil which he could sustain in compliance with that desire.

2. *Right.* — Otherwise than from the idea of obligation, no clear idea can be attached to the word *right*.

The efficient causes of right are two —

1. Absence of correspondent obligation. You have a *right* to perform whatever you are not under obligation to abstain from the performance of. Such is the right which every human being has in a state of nature.

2. The second efficient cause of right is, presence of correspondent obligation: This obligation is the obligation imposed upon other persons at large, to abstain from disturbing you in the exercise of the first-mentioned sort of right. The first-mentioned right may be termed a naked kind of right; — this second-mentioned right, a vested or established right.

The word right, is the name of a fictitious entity: one of those objects, the existence of which is feigned for the purpose of discourse, by a fiction so necessary, that without it human discourse could not be carried on.[b]

A man is said to have it, to hold it, to possess it, to acquire it, to lose it. It is thus spoken of as if it were a portion of matter such as a man may take into his hand, keep it for a time and let it go again. According to a phrase more common in law language than in ordinary language, a man is even spoken of as being invested with it. Vestment is clothing: invested with it makes it an article of clothing, and is as much as to say is clothed with it.

To the substantive word are frequently prefixed, as adjuncts and attributives, not only the word political, but the word natural and the word moral: and thus rights are distinguished into natural, moral, and political.

From this mode of speech, much confusion of ideas has been the result.

The only one of the three cases in which the word right has any determinate and intelligible meaning is that in which it has the adjunct political attached to it: in this case, when a man is said to have a right (mentioning it), the existence of a certain matter of fact is asserted; namely, of a disposition on the part of those by whom the powers of government are exercised, to cause him, to possess and so far as depends upon them to have the faculty of enjoying, the benefit to which he has a right. If, then, the fact thus asserted be true, the case is, that amongst them they are prepared on occasion to render him this service: and to this service on the part of the subordinate functionaries to whose province the matter belongs, he has, if so it be, a right; the supreme functionaries being always prepared to do what depends upon them to cause this same service to be rendered by those same subordinate functionaries

Now, in the case of alleged natural rights, no such matter of fact has place — nor any matter of fact other than what would have place supposing no such natural right to have place. In this case, no functionaries have place — or if they have, no such disposition on their part, as above, has place; for if it have, it is the case of a political right, and not of a merely natural right. A man is never the better for having such natural right: admit

b. Though fictitious, the language cannot be termed *deceptious* in intention at least, whatsoever in some cases may without intention be the result.

that he has it, his condition is not in any respect different from what it would be if he had it not.

If I say a man has a right to this coat or to this piece of land, meaning a right in the political sense of the word, — what I assert is a matter of fact; namely, the existence of the disposition in question as above.

If I say a man has a natural right to the coat or the land — all that it can mean, if it mean any thing and mean true, is, that I am of opinion he ought to have a political right to it; that by the appropriate services rendered upon occasion to him by the appropriate functionaries of government, he ought to be protected and secured in the use of it: he ought to be so — that is to say, the idea of his being so is pleasing to me — the idea of the opposite result displeasing.

In the English language, an imperfection, perhaps peculiar to that language, contributes to the keeping up of this confusion. In English, in speaking of a certain man and a certain coat, or a certain piece of land, I may say it is right he should have this coat or this piece of land. But in this case, beyond doubt, nothing more do I express than my satisfaction at the idea of his having this same coat or land.

This imperfection does not extend itself to other languages. Take the French, for instance. A Frenchman will not say, *Il est droit que cet homme ait cet habit*: what he will say is, *Il est juste que cet homme ait cet habit. Cet appartient de droit a cet homme.*

If the coat I have on is mine, I have a *right* by law to knock down, if I can, any man who by force should attempt to take it from me; and this right is what in any case it can scarcely be but that a man looks to when he says, *I have a right* to a constitution, to such or such an effect — or a right to have the powers of government arranged in such manner as to place me in such or such a condition in respect of actual right, actually established rights, political rights.

To engage others to join with him in applying force for the purpose of putting things into a state in which he would actually be in possession of the right, of which he pretends to be in possession, is at bottom the real object and purpose of the confusion thus endeavoured to be introduced into men's ideas, by employing a word in a sense different from what it had been wont to be employed, and from thus causing men to accede in words to positions from which they dissent in judgment.

This confusion has for its source the heat of argument. In the case of a political right, when the existence of it is admitted on all sides, all dispute ceases. But when so it is that a man has been contending for a political right which he either never has possessed, or having in his possession, is fearful of losing, he will not quietly be beaten out of his claim; but in default of the political right, or as a support to the political right, he asserts he has a natural right. This imaginary natural right is a sort of thread he clings by: — in the case in question, his having any efficient political right is a supposed matter of fact, the existence of the contrary of which is but too notorious; and being so, is but too capable of being proved. Beaten out of this ground, he says he has a natural right — a right given him by that kind goddess and governess Nature, whose legitimacy who shall dispute? And if he can manage so as to get you to admit the existence of this natural right, he has, under favour of this confusion, the hope of getting you to acknowledge the existence of the correspondent political right, and your assistance in enabling him to possess it.

It may, however, be said, to deny the existence of these rights which you call imaginary, is to give a *carte blanche* to the most outrageous tyranny. The rights of man anterior to all government, and superior as to their authority to every act of government, these are the rampart, and the only rampart, against the tyrannical enterprises of government. Not at all — the shadow of a rampart is not a rampart; — a fiction proves nothing — from that which is false you can only go on to that which is false. When the governed have no right, the government has no more. The rights of the governed and the rights of the government spring up together; — the same cause which creates the one creates the other.

It is not the rights of man which causes government to be established: — on the contrary, it is the non-existence of those rights. What is true is, that from the beginning of things it has always been desirable that rights should exist — and *that* because they do not exist; since, so long as there are no rights, there can only be misery upon the earth — no sources of political happiness, no security for person, for abundance, for subsistence, for equality: — for where is the equality between the famished savage who has caught some game, and the still more famishing savage who is dying because he has not caught any?

Law supposes government: to establish a law, is to exercise an act of government. A law is a declaration of will — of a will conceived and manifested by an individual, or individuals, to whom the other individuals in the society to which such will has respect are generally disposed to obey.

Now government supposes the disposition to obedience: — the faculty of governing on the one part has for its sole efficient cause, and for its sole measure, the disposition to obey on the other part.

This disposition may have had for its cause either *habit* or *convention*: a convention announces the will of one moment, which the will of any other moment may revoke; — habit is the result of a system of conduct of which the commencement is lost in the abyss of time. A convention, whether it have ever yet been realized or not, is at least a conceivable and possible cause of this disposition to obedience, from which government, and what is called political society, and the only real laws, result. Habit of obedience is the cause, a little less sure — the foundation, a little less solid, of this useful, social, disposition, and happily the most common.

The true rampart, the only rampart, against a tyrannical government has always been, and still is, the faculty of allowing this disposition to obedience — without which there is no government — either to subsist or to cease. The existence of this faculty is as notorious as its power is efficacious.

Shall this habit of obedience be continued unbroken, or shall it be discontinued upon a certain occasion? Is there more to be gained than to be lost in point of happiness, by its discontinuance? Of the two masses of evil, — intensity, duration, certainty, all included — which appears to be the greatest, that to which one believes one's self exposed from continued obedience, or that to which one believes one's self exposed by its discontinuance?

On which side is the greatest probability of success? On the side of the satellites of the tyrant, who will endeavour to punish me in case of disobedience? or on the side of the friends of liberty, who will rally around me to defend me against oppression?

It is an affair of calculation: and this calculation each one must make for himself according to circumstances. It is also a calculation that no one can fail to make, either ill or well, whatever may be the language he employs, or whosoever he may be.

But this calculation is not sufficiently rapid for those who choose for their amusement the destruction and reconstruction of governments. Rights of men strongly asserted, but ill-defined, never proved; rights of men, of which every violation is an act of oppression — rights ready to be violated at every moment — rights which the government violates every time it does anything which displeases you — right of insurrection ready to be exercised the first moment that oppression occurs; — this is the only remedy which suits those who would make equality to flourish at any rate, by taking the power of governing for themselves, and leaving obedience for all others.

It is the weakness of the understanding which has given birth to these pretended natural rights; it is the force of the passions which has led to their adoption, when, desirous of leading men to pursue a certain line of conduct which general utility does not furnish sufficient motives to induce them to pursue, or when, having such motives, a man knows not how to produce and develope them, yet wishes that there were laws to constrain men to pursue this conduct, or what comes to the same thing, that they would believe that there were such laws, — it has been found the shortest and easiest method to imagine laws to this effect.

Behold the professors of natural law, of which they have dreamed — the legislating Grotii[2] — the legislators of the human race: that which the Alexanders and the Tamerlanes endeavoured to accomplish by traversing a part of the globe,[3] the Grotii and the Puffendorffs[4] would accomplish, each one sitting in his arm chair: that which the conqueror would effect with violence by his sword, the jurisconsult would effect without effort by his pen. Behold the goddess Nature! — the jurisconsult is her priest; his idlest trash is an oracle, and this oracle is a law.

The jurisconsult in his arm-chair is an individual sufficiently peaceable: he lies, — he fabricates false laws in the simplicity of his heart; — desirous of doing something, ignorant how to do better, hoping to do well, he would not willingly injure any one. From his hands the instruments he employs have passed into hands of a far different temper.

The invention was fortunate: it spared discussion — it saved research and reflection — it did not require even common sense — it spared all forbearance and toleration: — what the oath is on the part of the footpad who demands your purse,[5] the rights of man have been in the mouth of the terrorist.

Those who govern allege legal rights — the rights of the citizen — real rights: those who wish to govern allege natural rights — the rights of man — counterfeit rights — rights which are sanctioned by the knife of the assassin, as well as the gibbet and the guillotine.

Those to whom the faculty of making these imaginary laws, instead of real laws, has been transferred, have not much trouble in making them. Constitutions are made as easily as songs: they succeed each other as rapidly, and are as speedily forgotten.

For the making of real laws, talent and knowledge are requisite: for making real laws good or bad, labour and patience are requisite: but for the making of forgeries sources of the rights of man, nothing more is required than ignorance, hardihood, and impudence.

Rights of men, when placed by the side of legal rights, resemble assignats, whether false or genuine, placed by the side of guineas or Louis dor.[6]

Two passions have laid claim to the giving birth to the declarations of rights — to the substitution, of the declaration of particular rights to the preparation of real laws — vanity and tyranny: vanity, which believes it can lull the world asleep, by being the first to do what all the world has always had before its eyes — tyranny, glad of finding a pretext for punishing all opposition, by directing against it the force of public hatred. Rights, there you have them always before your eyes: to deny their existence, is either to exhibit the most notorious bad faith or the most stupid blindness; the first a vice which renders you deserving of the indignation of all men — the other a weakness which consigns you to their contempt.

It is because without rights there can be no happiness, that it is at any rate determined to have rights: but rights cannot be created without creating obligations: it is that we may have rights, that we submit to obligations; and in respect to obligations, not to those alone which are strictly necessary for the establishment of the rights of which we feel the want, but also obligations such as those which may result from all the acts of authority exercised by government, which the general habit of obedience allows it to exercise.

The end of all these acts of authority should be to produce the greatest possible happiness to the community in question.

This is the true, and the only true end of the laws. Still, of the operations by which it is possible to conduct men towards this end, the effect — the constant, necessary, and most extensive effect, is to produce evil as well as good; to produce evil, that good may be produced, since upon no other conditions can it be produced.

The mystic tree of good and evil, already so interesting, is not the only one of its kind: life, society, the law, resemble it, and yield fruits equally mixed. Upon the same bough are two sorts of fruits, of which the flavour is opposite — the one sweet and the other bitter.

The sweet fruits are *benefits* of all kinds — the bitter and thorny fruits are burthens. The benefits are *rights*, which under certain circumstances are called *powers* — the burthens are *obligations* — *duties*.

These products, so opposed in their nature, are simultaneous in their production, and inseparable in their existence. The law cannot confer a benefit, without at the same time imposing a burthen somewhere; — it cannot create a right, without at the same time creating an obligation — and if that right be of any value, even a numerous train of obligations.

But if among these moral as well as among physical products, the sweet cannot exist without the bitter, — the bitter can exist — it exists too often — without the sweet. Such is the case with those obligations which may be called pure or barren, which are not accompanied by rights, those benefits, those advantages, which sweeten and conceal the bitterness: — obligations which are fulfilled by useless efforts or sufferings, the fruit of every law produced by tyranny, neglecting or despising the counsels of utility, and yielding to the suggestions of caprice — unless the gratification of this caprice can be considered as a benefit.

Benefits being in themselves good, the well-instructed legislator (I mean, directed by utility) would create and confer them freely with pleasure. If it depended upon himself, he would produce no other fruits: if he could produce them in infinite quantity — he would accumulate them in the bosom of society; but as the inexorable law of nature is opposed to this course, and he cannot confer benefits without imposing burthens, all that he can do is to take care that the advantage of the benefit exceed the disadvantage of the burthen, and that this advantage be as great, and the disadvantage as small, as possible.

When, in order that a burthen may produce its effect — that the advantage expected from it may be produced, it is necessary that its weight be felt, it is called punishment.

It is thus that the non-penal branch of the law and the penal are both of them occupied in the establishing and securing every man in possession of his rights of all sorts. These rights are so many instruments of felicity — they are the instruments of whatsoever felicity a man can derive from government.

A man's political rights are either his private rights, or his constitutional rights. Under every form of government, every man has his private rights; — but there are forms of government, in which no man but one, or some other comparatively small number, have any constitutional rights.

Of private rights these five sorts have been distinguished: — 1. Rights as to person; 2. Rights as to property; 3. Rights as to power; 4. Rights as to reputation; 5. Rights as to condition in life.

All these rights have for their efficient cause certain services, which by a general and standing disposition on the part of the functionaries of government in the supreme grade are understood to have been rendered to every man, and which, in consequence, on each particular occasion the functionaries of judicature, and upon occasion the functionaries belonging to the army, hold themselves in readiness to render to him. These services consist in the giving execution and effect to all such ordinances of the government as have been made in favour and for the benefit of every individual situated in the individual situation in which in all respects he is situated.

In virtue and by means of that same standing and all-comprehensive service, the supreme rulers have given the name of *wrong*, and the name, quality, and consequence of an *offence*, to every act by which any such right is understood to have been broken, infringed, violated, invaded. In giving it the name of an offence, they have made provision of pain under the name of punishment, together with other means of repression, for the purpose of preventing the doing of it, or lessening as far as may be the number of instances in which it shall be done.

Rights are, then, the fruits of the law, and of the law alone. There are no rights without law — no rights contrary to the law — no rights anterior to the law. Before the existence of laws there may be reasons for wishing that there were laws — and doubtless such reasons cannot be wanting, and those of the strongest kind; — but a reason for wishing that we possessed a right, does not constitute a right. To confound the existence of a reason for wishing that we possessed a right, with the existence of the right itself, is to confound the existence of a want with the means of relieving it. It is the same as if one should say, *everybody is subject to hunger, therefore everybody has something to eat.*

There are no other than legal rights; — no natural rights — no rights of man, anterior or superior to those created by the laws. The assertion of such rights, absurd in logic, is pernicious in morals. A right without a law is an effect without a cause. We may feign a law, in order to speak of this fiction — in order to feign a right as having been created; but fiction is not truth.

We may feign laws of nature — rights of nature, in order to show the nullity of real laws, as contrary to these imaginary rights; and it is with this view that recourse is had to this fiction : — but the effect of these nullities can only be null.

3. *Possession.* — "Better," says a maxim of the old Roman, called civil law — "better (meaning in comparison with that of any other person), is the condition of the possessor"[7] — better his condition, that is to say, better the ground and reason which a person in his situation is able to make for the enjoyment of the thing, than any that can be made by any one else.

Of the propriety and reasonableness of this notion, scarcely by any one who hears of it, how far soever from being learned, can a sort of feeling fail of being entertained — by no one, even of the most learned, has expression, it is believed, been ever given to it. This omission the greatest-happiness principle, and that alone, can supply. In the case of loss of the possession, he who has the possession would feel a pain of privation — or say, regret, more acute — than a man of the same turn of mind, whose expectation of obtaining it was no stronger than the possessor's expectation of keeping it, would, in the event of his failing to obtain possession of it.

Of so many hundred millions of persons, each of whom, in case of his having had possession of the thing and then lost it, would upon the losing of it have felt pain in a certain shape proportioned to the value of the thing, not one feels pain in any shape at the thoughts of not having it: not one of them but might, in the shape in question, feel pain in any quantity more or less considerable, if after having the thing in possession, he were, without receiving or expecting any equivalent for it, to cease to have it.

The horse you have bred, and still keep in your stable, is yours. How is it constituted such — constituted by law? Answer: The naked right — the right of making use of it, the law has left you in possession of; — to wit, by the negative act of forbearing to inhibit you from using it: the established right, the law has conferred upon you by the order given to the judge to punish every person who shall disturb or have disturbed you in the use of it.

The horse which was yours, but by the gift you have made of it is become the horse of a friend of yours, — how has it been constituted such — constituted by law? Answer: By a *blank* left as it were in the command to the judge, — that blank being left to be filled up by you in favour of this friend of yours, or any other person to whom it may happen to be your wish to transfer the horse, either gratuitously or for a price.

So long as the law in question has this blank in it, it is an incompleted, an imperfect law — it waits an act on your part to render it a perfect one. The law in its completed state is the result of two functions, into which the legislative function in this case is divided — the initiative to it, and the consummative. By the legislator, the initiative is exercised — by you, the consummative.

In the same way in which, according to this example, rights and powers are given to individual persons, they may be and are given to classes of persons. On classes of persons, the correspondent obligations not only may, but must be imposed: in short, exceptions excepted, they must be imposed on all persons of all classes; — for supposing but a single person excepted from the obligation, your right is not entire, — it is shared by you with the person so excepted. If, for example, in transferring the horse to your friend, you kept yourself from being included in the obligation to abstain from the use of the horse — if, in a word, you kept yourself excepted from the obligation imposed on other persons in general, the horse is not your friend's alone, any more than yours; but, in the language of English law, you and he are joint tenants of the horse.

4. *Power.* — In common speech, the word power is used in two senses; — to wit, the above sense, which may be called the proper and legal sense — and another sense more ample, which may be styled the popular sense.

In the strictly legal sense, which is used in the penal and civil branches of law — in the popular sense, which is used in the constitutional branch.

In both cases, the fruit of the exercise of the power is looked to, and that fruit is compliance: on the part of the person subject to power, compliance with the wishes expressed, or presumed to be entertained, by the person by whom the power is possessed. For convenience of discourse, say in one word the *power-holder.*

The force of the remunerative sanction, it has above been observed, is not sufficient to constitute an obligation; it is, however, in a certain sense, sufficient, as everybody knows, to constitute power: the effect of power is produced, in so far as, by the will declared or presumed of him who in this sense is the power-holder, compliance is produced.

Power may be defined to be the faculty[c] of giving determination either to the state of the passive faculties, or to that of the active faculties, of the subject in relation to and over which it is exercised; — say the correlative subject.

Power is either coercive or allocative.

Coercive power is either restrictive or compulsive.

Of the correlative subject, the passive faculties are either insensitive or sensitive.

If merely insensitive, it belongs to the class of inanimate beings, and is referred to the still more general denomination of things.

If sensitive, to the class of animals.

If the animals of the class in question are considered as belonging to the class of reasonable beings, the correlative subject is a person — including human beings of both sexes and all ages.

If considered as irrational, it has hitherto by lawyers been confounded with inanimate beings, and comprehended under the denomination of things.

In so far as the power is exercised with effect, the possessor of the power — say the power-holder — may, relation had to the correlative subject, be termed the *director* — the correlative subject the *directee.*

c. In this form, the exposition is of the sort styled *definition,* in the narrowest sense of the word, — *definitio per genus et differentiam:* — exposition effected by indication given of the next superordinate class of objects in which the object in question is considered as comprehended, together with that of the qualities peculiar to it with reference to the other objects of that same class.

The import of the word *faculty* being still more extensive than that of the word power, as may be seen by its assuming the adjunct passive, the word power is, in a certain sense, not unsusceptible of the definition *per genus et differentiam:* but to complete the exposition, an exposition by periphrasis may perhaps require to be added.

5. *Command.* — An instrument which as above has been mentioned as necessary to the generation of the fictitious entities, called a right and a power, is, as has been seen, a command. But a command is a discourse, expressive of the wish of a certain person, who, supposing his power independent of that of any other person, and to a certain extent sufficiently ample in respect of the subject-matters — to wit, persons, things moveable and immoveable, and acts of persons, and times — is a legislator; — say a legislator in the singular: for simplicity sake, the case of a division of the legislative power among divers persons or classes of persons, may on this occasion be put aside.

6. *Quasi Commands.* — Now then comes a doubt, and with it a question: — in the state of things you have hitherto been supposing, the law in question is of that sort called statute law: and in the case of statute law the print of a command is sufficiently visible. But obligations are created — rights established, not only by statute law, but by another species of law called common law: Where in this case is the command? — where is the person by whom it has been issued? — where, in a word, is the legislator? The judge is not a legislator. Far from claiming so to be, he would not so much as admit himself to be so: he puts aside, if not the function, at any rate the name.

Hitherto we have been in the region of realities: we are now of necessity transported into the region of fictions. In the domain of common law, everything is fiction but the power exercised by the judge.

On each occasion the judge does, it is true, issue a command: — this command is his decree; but this decree he on every occasion confesses he would not on any occasion have the power of issuing with effect, were it not for a command, general in its extent, and in such sort general as to include and give authority to this individual decree of his.

To be what it is, a command, general or individual, must be the command of some person. Who in this case is this person? Answer: Not any legislator; for if it were, the law would be a statute law. A person being necessary, and no real one to be found, hence comes the necessity of a fictitious one. The fictitious one, this fictitious person, is called the common law — or more generally, that he may be confounded with the real person in whose image he is made, *the law.*

To warrant the individual decree which he is about to pronounce, the judge comes out with some general proposition, saying, in words or in effect, *thus saith* THE LAW. On the occasion of the issuing of this sham law, the pretext always is, that it is but a copy of a proposition, equally general, delivered on some former occasion by some other judge or train of successive judges.

In this proposition there may be or may not be a grain of truth, but whether there be or be not, the individual decree has in both cases alike the effect of a law — of a real law — issued by a legislator avowing himself such, and acknowledged as such.

A command being the generic name of the really existing instrument of power called *a law,* let *a quasi command* be the name of that counterfeit instrument feigned to answer the purpose of it, to produce the effects of it, for the purpose of enabling the judge to produce, in the way of exacting compliance, the effect of a law.

Of this appellation the use and need will be seen in the procedure code, on the occasion of the formula called the demand paper, provided for the purpose of giving commencement to a suit in that same code.[d]

Supposing the connexion between a command in the mandatory form, and a proposition in the assertive form, made out and explained: whatsoever proposition would, if emanating from the legislator, have constituted an apposite ground for the *demand* — to wit, the demand made in the *demand paper,* elsewhere spoken of — a proposition to that same effect might equally well serve, if stated as being a proposition conformable to the doctrine of the common law. In the one case, the proposition would be a reality, in the other case a fiction: in the one case, what were the proper words of it could not be a subject-matter of dispute; in the other case it might, and would frequently be the subject-matter of dispute: still, however, in the character of a ground of inference, it would in both cases be equally intelligible.

Be this as it may — not to the plan here proposed would the imperfections of this part of the instrument of demand with propriety be ascribable. The root of the imperfection is in the very nature of the common law. To its supreme inaptitude, by the proposed instrument, such remedy as the nature of the case admitted is applied, and the use thus made of the common law is the result — not of choice, but of unresistible necessity. How sadly inadequate a portion of this fictitious law is, in the character of a succedaneum, to a correspondent and equivalent portion of real law, would on each occasion be visible to every eye; and as often as it came under the eye, so often would the urgency of the demand for the substitution of real to sham law be forced upon the attention. What would be in the power of the legislature to do at any time, and in the compass of a day, is to substitute this plain speaking form of demand to the existing absurd and deceptious one: what it is not in his power to do in the compass of a day, nor perhaps till at the end of some

d. See *Principles of Procedure,* Vol. II. p. 65, Ch. XII. 4.[8]

years, is the complete substitution of real to sham and impostor's law, — substitute, and audacious rival of the only genuine law.

CHAPTER IV

Axioms

§ 1. Axioms of Mental Pathology — a necessary ground
for all legislative arrangements

By an axiom of mental pathology, considered as a ground for a legislative arrangement, understand a proposition expressive of the consequences in respect of pleasure or pain, or both, found by experience to result from certain sorts of occurrences, and in particular from such in which human agency bears a part: in other words, expressive of the connexion between such occurrences as are continually taking place, or liable to take place, and the pleasures and pains which are respectively the results of them.

Practical uses of these observations, two: — 1. With regard to pleasures, the learning how to leave them undisturbed, and protected against disturbance — (for as to the giving increase to them by the power of the legislator to anything beyond a very inconsiderable amount, it is neither needful nor possible); 2. With regard to pains, the learning how on each occasion to minimize the amount of them in respect of magnitude and number — number of the individuals suffering under them — magnitude of the suffering in the case of each individual.

Arithmetic and medicine — these are the branches of art and science to which, in so far as the maximum of happiness is the object of his endeavours, the legislator must look for his means of operation: — the pains or losses of pleasure produced by a maleficent act correspond to the symptoms produced by a disease.

Experience, observation, and experiment — these are the foundations of all well-grounded medical practice: experience, observation, and experiment — such are the foundations of all well-grounded legislative practice.

In the case of both functionaries, the subject-matter of operation and the plan of operation is accordingly the same — the points of difference these: — In the case of the medical curator, the only individual who is the subject-matter of the operations performed by him, is the individual whose sufferings are in question, to whom relief is to be administered. In the case of the legislator, there are no limits to the description of the persons to whom it may happen to be the subject-matter of the operations performed by him.

By the medical curator, no power is possessed other than that which is given either by the patient himself, or in case of his inability, by those to whose management it happens to him to be subject: — by the legislatorial curator, power is possessed applicable to all persons, without exception, within his field of service; each person being considered in his opposite capacities — namely, that of a person *by whom* pleasure or pain, or both, may be experienced, and that of a person *at whose hands* pleasure or pain, or both, may be experienced.

Axioms of *corporal* pathology may be styled those most extensively applicable positions, or say propositions, by which statement is made of the several sorts of occurrences by which pleasure or pain are or have place in the human body: — as also, the results observed to follow from the performance of such operations as have been performed, and the application made of such subject-matters as have been applied for the purpose of giving increase to the aggregate of pleasure, or causing termination, alleviation, or prevention, to have place in regard to pain.

Axioms of *mental* pathology may be styled those most commonly applicable propositions by which statement is made of the several occurrences by which pleasure or pain is made to have place in the human mind: — as also, the results observed to follow from the performance of such operations as have been performed, and the application of such subject-matters as have been applied for the purpose of effecting the augmentation of the aggregate of the pleasures, or the diminution of the aggregate of the pains, by the termination, alleviation, or prevention of them respectively, when individually considered.

Security — subsistence — abundance — equality — *i.e.* minimization of inequality: — by these appellatives, denomination has been given to the particular ends which stand next in order to the universal, and the greatest happiness of the greatest number. This being admitted, these are the objects which will be in view in the formation of the several axioms of pathology which present themselves as suitable to the purpose of serving as guides to the practice of the legislatorial curator.

Unfortunately, on this occasion, the imperfection of language has produced an embarrassment, which it does not seem to be in the power of language altogether to remove: all that can be done, is to lessen and alleviate it. Subsistence — abundance — equality, — these three immediately subordinate ends are conversant about the same matter; to wit, the matter of wealth. But security, besides a matter of its own, is conversant with that same matter, with which, as above, they are conversant; to wit, the matter of wealth: security for the matter of wealth — or say, to each individual, security for that portion of the matter of wealth which at the time in question belongs to him, and is called his. Security is accordingly security against all such maleficent acts by which any portion of the matter of wealth which ought to be at the disposal of the individual in question, is prevented from being at his disposal at the time in question. Now, the not having at his disposal at the time in question a certain portion of the matter of wealth, is indeed one efficient cause of pain to the individual in question, be he who he may, but it is but one out of several. In addition to the matter of wealth, sources of pleasure, and of exemption from pain, are certain others which have been found reducible under the following denominations; to wit, power, reputation, and condition in life: — condition in life, to wit, in so far as, reference had to the individual whose it is, the effect is considered as beneficial — this complex subject-matter including in it the three subject-matters above mentioned — that is to say, the matter of wealth, or in two words, power and reputation.

Correspondent to these several subject-matters of security are so many classes of offences — of maleficent acts, by the performance of which such security is disturbed. Offences affecting property — offences affecting power — offences affecting reputation — offences affecting condition in life.

But all these subject-matters are, with reference to the individual in question, distinct from him, and exterior to him; — and in a more immediate way — and otherwise than through the medium of any of these out-works, he stands exposed to be made to suffer pain, as well of mind as of body, by the agency of every other individual, in whose instance a motive adequate to the purpose of producing an act by which it will be inflicted, has place. Thus, then, in addition to offences affecting property — offences affecting power — offences affecting reputation — offences affecting condition in life, — we have offences affecting person, considered with reference to its two distinguishable parts, body and mind.

So many of these classes of maleficent acts, so many branches of security: in which list, as being the most obviously and highly important, and most simple in the conception presented by it, security *against* maleficent acts affecting *person* — more shortly, security for person, presents itself as claiming to occupy the first place; after which, security for property, and so forth, as above.

§2. Axioms applicable to Security for Person

Axioms forming the grounds for such legislative arrangements as have for their object and their justification, the affording security for person against such maleficent acts, to which it stands exposed.

1. The pleasure derivable by any person from the contemplation of pain suffered by another, is in no instance so great as the pain so suffered.

2. Not even when the pain so suffered has been the result of an act done by the person in question, for no other purpose than that of producing it.

Hence, one reason for endeavouring to give security against pain of body or mind, resulting from human agency, whether from design or inattention.

Now, suppose the pain to be the result of purely natural agency, — no human agency having any part in the production of it — no human being deriving any satisfaction from the contemplation of it, — the result is still the same.

Hence one reason for endeavouring to give security against pain of body or mind resulting from casualty, or as the word is, when the evil is considered as having place upon a large scale, — *calamity.*

Axiom indicative of the reasons which form the grounds of the enactments prohibitive of maleficent acts, productive of evil, affecting persons — that is to say, either in body or mind — in any mode not comprised in one or other of the modes of maleficence from which the acts constituted offences in and by the penal code receive their denomination, viz. Offences produced by the irascible appetite: —

When by one person, without gratification sought other than that derived from the contemplation of suffering in this or that shape, as about to be produced on the part of that other gratification in a certain shape, is accordingly produced in the breast of such evil doer, — call the gratification the pleasure of *antipathy satisfied* — or of *ill-will satisfied.*

If this antipathy has had its rise in the conception that by the party in question (say the victim), evil in any shape has been done to the evil doer, — the pleasure of antipathy gratified takes the name of the pleasure of *vengeance* — or say *revenge.*

Axiom. In no case is there any reason for believing that the pleasure of antipathy gratified is so great as the pain suffered by him at whose expense, as above, the pleasure is reaped.

Offences to which the axiom applies are — 1. Offences affecting body; 2. Offences affecting the mind other than those belonging to the other classes; 3. Offences affecting reputation — the reputation of the sufferer — other than those by which the reputation of the evil doer is increased; 4. Offences affecting the condition in life of the sufferer, other than those by which the reputation of the evil doer is increased or expected to be increased.

For justification of the legislative arrangements necessary to afford security against maleficent acts affecting the person, what it is necessary to show is, that by them pain will not be produced in such quantity as will cause it to outweigh the pleasure that would have been produced by the maleficent acts so prevented.

For this purpose, in order to complete the demonstration and render it objection-proof, in certain cases, it will be necessary to take into account not only the evil of the first order, but the evil of the second order likewise.

First, then, considering the matter on the footing of the effects of the first order on both sides, — Axioms bearing reference to the effects of the first order on both sides, are the following: —

Axioms serving as grounds and reasons for the provision made by the legislator for general security; — to wit, against the evils respectively produced by the several classes and genera of offences.

Case 1. An offence affecting person, or say corporal vexation, in any one of its several shapes — offender's motive, ill-will or spite — the enjoyment of the offender will not be so great as the evil of the first order, consisting in the suffering experienced by the party vexed.

Case 2. So if the offence be an offence productive of mental vexation — and the motive the same.

Case 3. So if the offence be an offence affecting reputation.

Case 4. So, exceptions excepted, in the case of every other class or genus of offences, the motive being ill-will or spite, as above.

Case 5. Exceptions are among offences affecting person and reputation jointly, the offences having for their motive sexual desire; to wit — 1. Sexual seduction, allurative, or say enticitive; 2. Sexual seduction compulsory; 3. Rape; 4. Vexatious lascivious contrectation.[9]

In any of these cases, what may happen is — that the enjoyment of the offender may be equal or more than equal to the suffering of the party wronged; in either of which cases the evil of the first order has no place. But to all other persons, the suffering of the one part will present itself as being to an indefinite degree greater than the enjoyment of the offender and proportioned to the apparent excess will be the actual alarm on the part and on behalf of persons exposed to the like wrong from the same cause: and thence, so far as regards alarm, will be the evil of the second order.

Addendum to security axioms: —

Be the modification of the matter of prosperity what it may, by losing it without an equivalent, a man suffers according to, and in proportion to, the value of it in his estimation — the value by him put upon it.

Value may be distinguished into — 1. General, or say value in the way of *exchange;* and 2. Special, or say idiosyncratical — value in the way of *use* in his own individual instance.

Note, that the value of a thing in the way of exchange arises out of, and depends altogether upon, and is proportioned to, its value in the way of use: — for no man would give anything that had a value in the way of use in exchange for anything that had no such value.

But value in the way of use may be distinguished into *general*, which has place so far as, and no further than, the thing is of use to persons in general — and *special* or idiosyncratical, which has place in so far as, in the case of this or that person in particular, the thing has a value in the way of use over and above the value which it has in the case of persons in general: of which use, that of the *pretium affectionis*, the *value of affection*, is an example.

Definition: When from any cause — human agency or any other — a mass of the matter of wealth, or of the matter of prosperity in any other shape, is made to go out of an individual's possession or expectancy without his consent, the pain produced in his breast by contemplation of its non-existence, or say by the loss of it, call *the pain of disappointment*: he being disappointed at the thought of the good which, it having been in his possession or expectancy, he has thus lost.

Among the objects of law in every community, is the affording security against this pain in this shape.

Axiom: The pleasure of antipathy or revenge produced in the breast of the evil-doer by the contemplation of a pain of disappointment produced in the breast of the sufferer, is not in any case so great in magnitude as that same pain.

To this axiom corresponds, as being thereon grounded, a fundamental principle entitled the *disappointment-preventing principle.*

Operation necessary for the establishment and continuance of security, — Fixation of the text of the laws.

For leading expectation, the law need only be exhibited, provided that it be clear, and not too vast for comprehension. But that it may be exhibited, it is necessary that it exist. The greatest and most extensive cause of regret respecting English law, is, — that as respects a large portion, it has no existence. Instead of laws, it cannot even be said that we possess shadows of law: — shadows imply substances by which they are formed; — all that we possess is a *phantom*, conjured up by each one at his pleasure, to fill the place of the law. It is of these phantoms that *common law, unwritten, judge-made* law, is composed.

A discussion upon a point of unwritten or common law has been defined *a competition of opposite analogies.* In giving this definition, the most severe and well-deserved censure was passed both upon this species of law, and upon the carelessness of the legislators who have tolerated its per-nicious existence — who have allowed the security of their fellow-citizens to remain without foundation, tossed about by the interminable and always shifting competition of opposite analogies, — who have left it upon a quick-sand, when they might have placed it upon a rock.

§ 3. Axioms pathological, applicable to Subsistence

Axiom 1. Though to each individual his own subsistence be, by the nature of man, rendered the chief object of his care, and during his infancy an object of care to the author of his existence, yet a considerable portion of the aggregate number of the members of the community there will always be, in whose instance a subsistence cannot have place (without the legislator's care) without provision made by the legislator to that effect.

2. For the subsistence of all, and accordingly of these, provision will to a certain degree have been made by the provision for security in all its shapes, and for security of property in particular: as also for abundance; for abun-dance, because of the abundance possessed by some is composed a stock, a fund, out of which matter is capable of being taken applicable to the pur-pose of affording, whether immediate or through exchange, subsistence to others. But for the subordinate end to the purpose here in question, the utmost of what can be done for these two other subordinate ends, taken together, will not of itself be sufficient.

Of the nonpossession of the matter of subsistence in such quantity as is necessary to the support of life, death is the consequence: and such natural death is preceded by a course of suffering much greater than what is atten-dant on the most afflictive violent deaths employed for the purpose of punishment.

Rather than continue to labour under this affliction, individuals who are experiencing it will naturally and necessarily, in proportion as they find opportunity, do what depends upon them towards obtaining, at the charge of others, the means of rescuing themselves from it: and in proportion as endeavours to this purpose are employed, or believed to be intended to be employed, security for property is certainly diminished — security for per-son probably diminished on the part of all others.

By the coercive authority of the legislator provision cannot be made for the indigent, otherwise than by defalcation from the mass of the matter of abundance possessed by the relatively opulent, nor yet, without a correspondent defalcation more or less considerable, from security for property on their part.

In every habitable part of the earth, people, so soon as they behold themselves and their eventual offspring secured against death for want of the matter of subsistence, which security cannot be afforded otherwise than by correspondent defalcation from the matter of abundance in the hands of the relatively opulent, will continue to effect addition to the number of its inhabitants. But this augmentation thus produced will proceed with much greater rapidity than any addition that can be made to the quantity of the matter of subsistence possessed, as above, by the indigent, by defalcation made at the expense of security for property, as well as from the matter of abundance, by correspondent defalcation from the matter of abundance in the hands of the relatively opulent.

The consequence is, that sooner or later, on every habitable part of the earth's surface, the community will be composed of three classes of inhabitants: — 1. Those by whom, with the addition of more or less of the matter of abundance, the matter of subsistence is possessed in a quantity sufficient for the preservation of life and health; — 2. Those who, being in a state in which they are perishing for want of the matter of subsistence, are on their way to speedy death; — 3. Those who to save themselves from impending death are occupied in waging war upon the rest, providing the means of subsistence for themselves at the expense of the security of all, and the matter of subsistence and abundance in the possession of all.

So long as by arrangements taken for the purpose by government, the thus redundant part of the population can be cleared off by being conveyed from the habitable part of the globe in question to some other part, these two classes of quickly perishing individuals may be prevented from receiving formation, or if formed, from receiving increase. But in no one part of the habitable globe can this be done by government without expense, nor the matter of expense be obtained without defalcation made from security, and suffering from loss, by forced contribution as above; and sooner or later, in proportion as property and security for property establishes itself, the whole surface of the habitable globe cannot but be fully peopled, in such sort, that from no one spot to any other could human creatures be transplanted in a living and about to live state.

Human benevolence can, therefore, hardly be better employed than in a quiet solution of these difficulties, and in the reconciliation of a provision for the otherwise perishing indigent, with this continual tendency to an increase in the demand for such provision.

§ 4. Axioms applying to Abundance

1. Included in the mass of the matter of abundance, is the mass of the matter of subsistence. The matter of wealth is at once the matter of subsistence and the matter of abundance: the sole difference is the quantity; — it is less in the case of subsistence — greater in the case of abundance.

2. If of two persons, one has the minimum of subsistence without addition, — and the other, that same minimum with an addition, — the former has the matter of subsistence, the latter the matter of abundance: — understand, in comparison with him who has nothing beyond the minimum of the matter of subsistence, — the term abundance being a comparative, a relative term.

3. The matter of subsistence being, in the instance of each individual, necessary to existence, and existence necessary to happiness, — suppose a quantity of the matter of wealth sufficient for the subsistence of 10,000 persons, at the disposition of the legislator; more happiness will be producible, by giving to each one of the 10,000 a particle of the matter of subsistence, than by giving to 5000 of them a portion of the matter of abundance composed of two particles of the matter of subsistence, and then giving none to the remaining 5000: since, on that supposition, the 5000 thus left destitute would soon die through a lingering death.

4. But suppose that, after giving existence to the 10,000, and to each of them a particle of the matter of subsistence, the legislator have at his disposal a quantity of the matter of wealth sufficient for the subsistence of another 10,000 persons, and that he have the option — of either giving existence to an additional number of persons to that same amount, with a minimum of the matter of subsistence to each, — or instead, without making any addition to the first 10,000, of giving an addition to the quantity of wealth possessed by them, — a greater addition to the aggregate quantity of happiness would be made by dividing among the first 10,000 the whole additional quantity of wealth, than by making any addition to the number of persons brought into existence. For, supposing the whole 10,000 having each of them the minimum of the matter of subsistence on any given day, — the next day, in consequence of some accident, they might cease to have it, and in consequence cease to have existence: whereas, if of this same 10,000, some had, in addition to his minimum of the matter of subsistence, particles one or more of the matter of abundance, here would be a correspondent mass of the matter of wealth, capable of being by the legislator so disposed of as to be made to constitute the matter of subsistence to those who, otherwise being without subsistence, would soon be without existence.

5. Not that, as between the matter of subsistence, and the matter of abundance, the identity is other than virtual — identity with reference to the purpose here in question, to wit, the effect on happiness; — and this virtuality depends upon the facility of obtaining one of the sorts of matter necessary to subsistence, in exchange for matter neither necessary, nor so much as contributing to subsistence — potatoes, for example, in exchange for coin; but so far as is necessary to the guidance of the legislator's practice, this virtual identity always has had, and is likely always to have place.

6. Thus it is that the matter of abundance, as contradistinguished from the matter of subsistence, is contributory to happiness, in three distinguishable ways or capacities: — 1. As contributing in a direct way to enjoyment, in a degree over and above what could be contributed by the mere matter of subsistence; 2. As contributing in an indirect way to security, to wit, by its capacity of serving, in the way of exchange, for the obtainment of the efficient instruments of security in any of these shapes; 3. As eventually contributing, in the same indirect way, to subsistence.

§ 5. Axioms applying to Equality,[e] in respect of wealth

I. Case or state of things the first. — The quantities of wealth in question, considered as being in a quiescent state, actually in the hands of the two parties in question: neither entering into, nor going out of the hands of either.

1. *Cæteris paribus,* — to every particle of the matter of wealth corresponds a particle of the matter of happiness. Accordingly, thence,

2. So far as depends upon wealth, — of two persons having unequal fortunes, he who has most wealth must by a legislator be regarded as having most happiness.

3. But the quantity of happiness will not go on increasing in anything near the same proportion as the quantity of wealth: — ten thousand times the quantity of wealth will not bring with it ten thousand times the quantity of happiness. It will even be matter of doubt, whether ten thousand times the wealth will in general bring with it twice the happiness.[f] Thus it is, that,

4. The effect of wealth in the production of happiness goes on diminishing, as the quantity by which the wealth of one man exceeds that of another goes on increasing: in other words, the quantity of happiness produced by a particle of wealth (each particle being of the same magnitude) will be less

e. See also *Principles of the Civil Code,* ch. 6, Vol. I. p. 304.[10]

f. In England a disproportion still greater than this is actually exemplified.

and less at every particle; the second will produce less than the first, the third than the second, and so on.

5. Minimum of wealth, say £10 per year; — greatest excess of happiness produced by excess in the quantity of wealth, as 2 to 1: — magnitude of a particle of wealth, £1 a year. On these data might be grounded a scale or table, exhibiting the quantities of happiness produced, by as many additions made to the quantity of wealth at the bottom of the scale, as there are pounds between £10 and £10,000.

II. Case, or state of things the second, — the particles of wealth about to enter into the hands of the parties in question.

1. Fortunes unequal: — by a particle of wealth, if added to the wealth of him who has least, more happiness will be produced, than if added to the wealth of him who has most.

2. Particles of wealth at the disposition of the legislator, say 10,000; — happiness of the most wealthy to that of the least wealthy, say (as per No. 5), as 2 to 1: — by giving to each one of 10,000 a particle of wealth, the legislator will produce 5000 times the happiness he would produce by giving the 10,000 particles to one person.

3. On these data might be grounded a scale, exhibiting the quantities of happiness produced, by so many additions made as above to the minimum of wealth, to the respective happiness of any number of persons, whose respective quantities of wealth exceed one another, by the amount of a particle in each instance.

III. Case, or state of things the third, — the particles of wealth about to go out of the hands of the parties.

1. By the subtraction of a particle of the matter of wealth, a less subtraction from happiness will be produced, if made from the wealth of him who has the matter of abundance, than if from the wealth of him who has the matter of subsistence only.

2. So, if from the wealth of him who has a larger portion of the matter of abundance, than if from the wealth of him who has not so large a portion of the matter of abundance.

3. Fortunes equal, and the aggregate sum subtracted being given, the greater the number of the persons from whose wealth the subtraction is made, the less will be the subtraction thereby made from the aggregate of happiness.

4. Fortunes unequal, still less will be the subtraction of happiness, if it be in the ratio of their fortunes that the subtraction is made, the greatest quantity being subtracted from those whose fortunes are greatest.

5. A quantity of the matter of wealth may be assigned, so small, that if

subtracted from the fortune of a person possessed of a certain quantity of the matter of abundance, no sensible subtraction of happiness would be the result.

6. The larger the fortune of the individual in question, the greater the probability that, by the subtraction of a given quantity of the matter of wealth, no subtraction at all will be made from the quantity of his happiness.

7. So likewise, if the ratio of the sum to be subtracted, to the aggregate mass from which it is to be subtracted, be so great, that by the subtraction of it, subtraction of a quantity, more or less considerable, cannot but be made from the aggregate of happiness, — still the larger, in the case of each individual, the aggregate of wealth is from which the subtraction is made, the less will be the quantity of happiness so subtracted, as above.

IV. Case, or state of things the fourth, — the particles of wealth about to go out of the hands of the one party into the hands of the other.

1. Fortunes, equal: — take from the one party a portion of the matter of wealth and give it to the other, — the quantity of happiness gained to the gainer of the wealth will not be so great as the quantity of happiness lost to the loser of the wealth.

2. Fortunes unequal: — the poorer the loser, the richer the gainer: greater in this case is the diminution produced in the mass of happiness by the transfer, than in the last mentioned case.

3. Fortunes again unequal: — the richer the loser, the poorer the gainer: the effect produced on happiness by the transfer may in this case be either loss or gain.

Whether it be the one or the other, will depend partly upon the degree of the inequality, partly upon the magnitude of the portion of wealth transferred. If the inequality be very small, and the wealth transferred also small, the effect produced on the sum of happiness may be loss. But if either be — much more if both be other than, very small, the effect on happiness will be gain.

4. Income of the richer, say £100,000 a-year — income of the less rich, say £99,999 a-year: wealth taken from the first, and transferred to the less rich, £1 a-year: — on the sum of happiness the effect will be on the side of loss; — more happiness will be lost by the richer than gained by the less rich.

Hence one cause of the preponderance produced on the side of evil by the practice called gaming.

5. Income of the richer loser, £100,000 a-year; — income of the less rich gainer, £10 a-year; — wealth lost to the richer, gained by the less rich, £1 a-year: — on the sum of happiness the effect will be on the side of gain.

More happiness will be gained by the less rich gainer, than lost by the more rich loser.

Thus it is, that if the effects of the first order were alone taken into account, the consequence would be, that, on the supposition of a new constitution coming to be established, with the greatest happiness of the greatest number for its end in view, sufficient reason would have place for taking the matter of wealth from the richest and transferring it to the less rich, till the fortunes of all were reduced to an equality, or a system of inequality so little different from perfect equality, that the difference would not be worth calculating.

But call in now the effects of the second and those of the third order, and the effect is reversed: to maximization of happiness would be substituted universal annihilation in the first place of happiness — in the next place of existence. Evil of the second order, — annihilation of happiness by the universality of the alarm, and the swelling of danger into certainty: — Evil of the third order, — annihilation of existence by the certainty of the non-enjoyment of the fruit of labour, and thence the extinction of all inducement to labour.

Independently of the destruction which would thus be produced by carrying, or even by the known intention of carrying to its utmost possible length the equalization, or say levelling system, as above, diminution would be effected in the aggregate of happiness, by the extinction of the fund afforded by the matter of abundance for keeping undiminished the stock of the matter of wealth necessary for subsistence.

On consideration of what is stated above, it will be found that the plan of distribution applied to the matter of wealth, which is most favourable to universality of subsistence, and thence, in other words, to the maximization of happiness, is that in which, while the fortune of the richest — of him whose situation is at the top of the scale, is greatest, the degrees between the fortune of the least rich and that of the most rich are most numerous, — in other words, the gradation most regular and insensible.

The larger the fortunes of the richest are, the smaller will be the number of those whose fortunes approach near to that high level: the smaller, therefore, the number of those from whose masses of property the largest defalcation could by possibility be made: — and, moreover, the larger those masses, the greater would be the difficulty which the legislator would experience as to the obtaining at their charge such defalcation as the nature of the case would not exclude the possibility of making.

Thus, for example, it would, in case of over population, be easier in

England, or even in Ireland, to ward off famine for a time, than it would be in British India.

Equality requires, that though it be at the expense of all the other members of the community, the income of those whose income is composed of the wages of labour be maximized. Reason: Of these are composed the vast majority of the whole number of the members of the community.

Exceptions excepted, equality requires that the profits of stock be minimized. Reason: Because the net profit of stock is composed of the mass, or say portion remaining to the employer of the stock, after deduction made of the wages of the labour applied to it.

Exception will be — if this supposed case be really exemplified — where the possessors of the wages of labour are so many, and the possessors of the profits of stock so few, that by a small addition to the one, no sensible defalcation will be made from the other.

§ 6. Axioms relating to Power, Rank, and Reputation

By axioms relating to power, understand self-serving power, exempt from the obligation by which it is converted into trust.

As between individual and individual, the pleasure to the superior, to the power-holder, from the possession and exercise of the power, is not so great as the pain experienced by the party subjected.

Therefore, only when converted into extra-benefiting by appropriate obligation, can it be conducive to greatest happiness.

The same observations will equally apply to rank, and factitious estimation produced by rank.

So also to extra reputation, or say estimation, unless when acquired by service rendered to others.

The principle corresponding to these axioms, as to equality, is *the inequality-minimizing principle*.

NOTES

1. See *The Works of Jeremy Bentham*, ed. J. Bowring, 11 vols. (Edinburgh: William Tait, 1838–43), ix. 333–428 [hereafter Bowring].

2. Hugo Grotius (1583–1645); author of *De jure belli ac pacis* (*On the Law of War and Peace*), 1625, a founding text of natural rights theory.

3. Alexander (356–323 BC) and Tamerlane (i.e., Timur, 1336–1405) were both highly successful conquerors.

4. Samuel von Pufendorf (1632–94), author of *De jure naturae et gentium* (*On*

the Law of Nature and Nations), 1672 and its 1673 abridgement, *De officio hominis et civis juxta legem naturalem* (*On the Duty of Man and Citizen According to Natural Law*).

5. In contemporary letters, footpads — robbers who worked on foot — were often portrayed as being foul-mouthed.

6. Assignats were paper monies issued by the French revolutionary government; Louis d'ors were gold coins first minted under Louis XIII in 1640.

7. Bentham is probably referring to usucapion, or ownership from possession in early Roman law. On usucapion and its revisions, see Justinian's *Institutes*, Lib. II Tit. VI.

8. The editor cites Bentham's discussion of the "demand paper," a proposed device for replacing multiple criminal and civil procedures with a single form by means of which any public or private "pursuer" could bring charges directly before a judge; Bowring, ii. 65–72.

9. I.e., sexual molestation.

10. The editor cites Bentham's discussion of the "Propositions of Pathology Upon Which the Advantage of Equality is Founded"; Bowring, i. 304–07.

III

Politics, Policy, and Political Economy

Panopticon, or, the Inspection-House
Letters 1, 2, and 6

The body of *Panopticon* was written as a series of letters on Bentham's only extended trip abroad, visiting his brother Samuel in Russia in 1786–87. The letters were first published, with additional postscripts, in Dublin and London in 1791.

Bentham was passionate about *Panopticon*. The opening of his preface reads as follows: "*Morals reformed — health preserved — industry invigorated — instruction diffused — public burthens lightened — Economy seated, as it were, upon a rock — the Gordian knot of the Poor Laws not cut, but untied — all by a simple idea in architecture!*"

Although the principle of and design for the Inspection House are of wide application — it is no less than "a new mode of obtaining power of mind over mind"[1] — Bentham's project in the 1790s was to build a penitentiary on this plan. Contracts were signed and sites established; through several years of false hopes and delays before full and final rejection, Bentham's experience with the authorities left him embittered. (For the history, see Janet Semple, *Bentham's Prison* [Oxford, 1993].)

What follows is a very small sample of *Panopticon*, but the hope is that these three letters are sufficient to introduce the work. They are taken from the 1962 Russell and Russell reprint of Bowring's *Works*, iv. 40–41, 45–46.[2] Letters 1 and 2 describe the scheme; Letter 6 is of broad theoretical import and illustrates the intimate connection between *Panopticon* and Bentham's near-contemporary work on publicity in legislative assemblies, presented in the next chapter.

Panopticon has yet to appear in the *Collected Works of Jeremy Bentham*.

LETTER I

Idea of the Inspection Principle

Crecheff in White Russia,
— 1787.

Dear * * * *,[3] — I observed t'other day in one of your English papers, an advertisement relative to a HOUSE OF CORRECTION therein spoken of, as intended for * * * * * * *. It occurred to me, that the plan of a building, lately contrived by my brother, for purposes in some respects similar, and which, under the name of the *Inspection House*, or the *Elaboratory*, he is about erecting here, might afford some hints for the above establishment.[a] I have accordingly obtained some drawings relative to it, which I here inclose. Indeed I look upon it as capable of applications of the most extensive nature; and that for reasons which you will soon perceive.

To say all in one word, it will be found applicable, I think, without exception, to all establishments whatsoever, in which, within a space not too large to be covered or commanded by buildings, a number of persons are meant to be kept under inspection. No matter how different, or even opposite the purpose: whether it be that of *punishing the incorrigible, guarding the insane, reforming the vicious, confining the suspected, employing the idle, maintaining the helpless, curing the sick, instructing the willing* in any branch of industry, or *training the rising race* in the path of *education:* in a word, whether it be applied to the purposes of *perpetual prisons* in the room of death, or *prisons for confinement* before trial, or *penitentiary-houses*, or *houses of correction*, or *work-houses*, or *manufactories*, or *mad-houses*, or *hospitals*, or *schools*.

It is obvious that, in all these instances, the more constantly the persons to be inspected are under the eyes of the persons who should inspect them, the more perfectly will the purpose of the establishment have been attained. Ideal perfection, if that were the object, would require that each person should actually be in that predicament, during every instant of time. This being impossible, the next thing to be wished for is, that, at every instant, seeing reason to believe as much, and not being able to satisfy himself to the

---

a. The sudden breaking out of the war between the Turks and Russians, in consequence of an unexpected attack made by the former on the latter, concurred with some other incidents in putting a stop to the design. The person here spoken of, at that time Lieutenant-Colonel Commandant of a battalion in the Empress's service, having obtained a regiment and other honours for his services in the course of the war, is now stationed with his regiment in a distant part of the country.[4]

contrary, he should *conceive* himself to be so. This point, you will immediately see, is most completely secured by my brother's plan; and, I think, it
will appear equally manifest, that it cannot be compassed by any other, or to
speak more properly, that if it be compassed by any other, it can only be in
proportion as such other may approach to this.

To cut the matter as short as possible, I will consider it at once in its
application to such purposes as, being most complicated, will serve to
exemplify the greatest force and variety of precautionary contrivance. Such
are those which have suggested the idea of *penitentiary-houses*: in which
the objects of *safe custody*, *confinement*, *solitude*, *forced labour*, and *instruction*, were all of them to be kept in view. If all these objects can be
accomplished together, of course with at least equal certainty and facility
may any lesser number of them.

LETTER II

Plan for a Penitentiary Inspection-House

Before you look at the plan, take in words the general idea of it.

The building is circular.

The apartments of the prisoners occupy the circumference. You may call
them, if you please, the *cells*.

These *cells* are divided from one another, and the prisoners by that
means secluded from all communication with each other, by *partitions* in
the form of *radii* issuing from the circumference towards the centre, and
extending as many feet as shall be thought necessary to form the largest
dimension of the cell.

The apartment of the inspector occupies the centre; you may call it if you
please the *inspector's lodge*.

It will be convenient in most, if not in all cases, to have a vacant space or
area all round, between such centre and such circumference. You may call
it if you please the *intermediate* or *annular* area.

About the width of a cell may be sufficient for a *passage* from the
outside of the building to the lodge.

Each cell has in the outward circumference, a *window*, large enough, not
only to light the cell, but, through the cell, to afford light enough to the
correspondent part of the lodge.

The inner circumference of the cell is formed by an iron *grating*, so light
as not to screen any part of the cell from the inspector's view.

Of this grating, a part sufficiently large opens, in form of a *door*, to admit the prisoner at his first entrance; and to give admission at any time to the inspector or any of his attendants.

To cut off from each prisoner the view of every other, the partitions are carried on a few feet beyond the grating into the intermediate area: such projecting parts I call the *protracted partitions*.

It is conceived, that the light, coming in in this manner through the cells, and so across the intermediate area, will be sufficient for the inspector's lodge. But, for this purpose, both the windows in the cells, and those corresponding to them in the lodge, should be as large as the strength of the building, and what shall be deemed a necessary attention to economy, will permit.

To the windows of the lodge there are *blinds*, as high up as the eyes of the prisoners in their cells can, by any means they can employ, be made to reach.

To prevent *thorough light*, whereby, notwithstanding the blinds, the prisoners would see from the cells whether or no any person was in the lodge, that apartment is divided into quarters, by *partitions* formed by two diameters to the circle, crossing each other at right angles. For these partitions the thinnest materials might serve; and they might be made removeable at pleasure; their height, sufficient to prevent the prisoners seeing over them from the cells. Doors to these partitions, if left open at any time, might produce the thorough light. To prevent this, divide each partition into two, at any part required, setting down the one-half at such distance from the other as shall be equal to the aperture of a door.

These windows of the inspector's lodge open into the intermediate area, in the form of *doors*, in as many places as shall be deemed necessary to admit of his communicating readily with any of the cells.

Small *lamps*, in the outside of each window of the lodge, backed by a reflector, to throw the light into the corresponding cells, would extend to the night the security of the day.

To save the troublesome exertion of voice that might otherwise be necessary, and to prevent one prisoner from knowing that the inspector was occupied by another prisoner at a distance, a small *tin tube* might reach from each cell to the inspector's lodge, passing across the area, and so in at the side of the correspondent window of the lodge. By means of this implement, the slightest whisper of the one might be heard by the other, especially if he had proper notice to apply his ear to the tube.

With regard to *instruction*, in cases where it cannot be duly given without the instructor's being close to the work, or without setting his hand to it by way of example before the learner's face, the instructor must indeed here as elsewhere, shift his station as often as there is occasion to visit different workmen; unless he calls the workmen to him, which in some of the instances to which this sort of building is applicable, such as that of imprisoned felons, could not so well be. But in all cases where directions, given verbally and at a distance, are sufficient, these tubes will be found of use. They will save, on the one hand, the exertion of voice it would require, on the part of the instructor, to communicate instruction to the workmen without quitting his central station in the lodge; and, on the other, the confusion which would ensue if different instructors or persons in the lodge were calling to the cells at the same time. And, in the case of hospitals, the quiet that may be insured by this little contrivance, trifling as it may seem at first sight, affords an additional advantage.

A *bell*, appropriated exclusively to the purposes of *alarm*, hangs in a *belfry* with which the building is crowned, communicating by a rope with the inspector's lodge.

The most economical, and perhaps the most convenient, way of *warming* the cells and area, would be by flues surrounding it, upon the principle of those in hot-houses. A total want of every means of producing artificial heat might, in such weather as we sometimes have in England, be fatal to the lives of the prisoners; at any rate, it would often times be altogether incompatible with their working at any sedentary employment. The flues, however, and the fire-places belonging to them, instead of being on the outside, as in hot-houses, should be in the inside. By this means, there would be less waste of heat, and the current of air that would rush in on all sides through the cells, to supply the draught made by the fires, would answer so far the purpose of ventilation. But of this more under the head of Hospitals.

* * *

LETTER VI

Advantages of the Plan

I flatter myself there can now be little doubt of the plan's possessing the fundamental advantages I have been attributing to it: I mean, the *apparent omnipresence* of the inspector (if divines will allow me the expression), combined with the extreme facility of his *real presence*.

A collateral advantage it possesses, and on the score of frugality a very material one, is that which respects the *number* of the inspectors requisite. If this plan required more than another, the additional number would form an objection, which, were the difference to a certain degree considerable, might rise so high as to be conclusive: so far from it, that a greater multitude than ever were yet lodged in one house might be inspected by a single person; for the trouble of inspection is diminished in no less proportion than the strictness of inspection is increased.

Another very important advantage, whatever purposes the plan may be applied to, particularly where it is applied to the severest and most coercive purposes, is that the *under* keepers or inspectors, the servants and subordinates of every kind, will be under the same irresistible controul with respect to the *head* keeper or inspector, as the prisoners or other persons to be governed are with respect to *them*. On the common plans, what means, what possibility, has the prisoner, of appealing to the humanity of the principal for redress against the neglect or oppression of subordinates in that rigid sphere, but the *few* opportunities which, in a crowded prison, the most conscientious keeper *can* afford — but the none at all which many a keeper *thinks* fit to give them? How different would their lot be upon this plan!

In no instance could his subordinates either perform or depart from their duty, but he must know the time and degree and manner of their doing so. It presents an answer, and that a satisfactory one, to one of the most puzzling of political questions — *quis custodiet ipsos custodes*?[5] And, as the fulfilling of his, as well as their, duty would be rendered so much easier, than it can ever have been hitherto, so might, and so should, any departure from it be punished with the more inflexible severity. It is this circumstance that renders the influence of this plan not less beneficial to what is called *liberty*, than to necessary coercion; not less powerful as a controul upon subordinate power, than as a curb to delinquency; as a shield to innocence, than as a scourge to guilt.

Another advantage, still operating to the same ends, is the great load of trouble and disgust which it takes off the shoulders of those occasional inspectors of a higher order, such as *judges* and other *magistrates*, who, called down to this irksome task from the superior ranks of life, cannot but feel a proportionable repugnance to the discharge of it. Think how it is with them upon the present plans, and how it still must be upon the best plans that have been hitherto devised! The cells or apartments, however constructed, must, if there be nine hundred of them (as there were to have been upon the penitentiary-house plan), be opened to the visitors, one by one. To do their business to any purpose, they must approach near to, and come almost in contact with each inhabitant; whose situation being watched over according to no other than the loose methods of inspection at present practicable, will on that account require the more minute and troublesome investigation on the part of these occasional superintendents. By this new plan, the disgust is entirely removed, and the trouble of going into such a room as the lodge, is no more than the trouble of going into any other.

Were *Newgate* upon this plan, all Newgate might be inspected by a quarter of an hour's visit to Mr. Akerman.[6]

Among the other causes of that reluctance, none at present so forcible, none so unhappily well grounded, none which affords so natural an excuse, nor so strong a reason against accepting of any excuse, as the danger of *infection* — a circumstance which carries death, in one of its most tremendous forms, from the seat of guilt to the seat of justice, involving in one common catastrophe the violator and the upholder of the laws. But in a spot so constructed, and under a course of discipline so insured, how should infection ever arise? Against every danger of this kind, what private house of the poor, one might almost say, or even of the most opulent, can be equally secure?

Nor is the disagreeableness of the task of superintendence diminished by this plan, in a much greater degree than the efficacy of it is increased. On all others, be the superintendent's visit ever so unexpected, and his motions ever so quick, time there must always be for preparations blinding the real state of things. Out of nine hundred cells, he can visit but one at a time, and, in the meanwhile, the worst of the others may be arranged, and the inhabitants threatened, and tutored how to receive him. On this plan, no sooner is the superintendent announced, than the whole scene opens instantaneously to his view.

In mentioning inspectors and superintendents who are such by office, I must not overlook that system of inspection, which, however little heeded, will not be the less useful and efficacious: I mean, the part which individuals may be disposed to take in the business, without intending, perhaps, or even without thinking of, any other effects of their visits, than the gratification of their own particular curiosity. What the inspector's or keeper's family are with respect to *him*, that, and more, will these spontaneous visitors be to the superintendent, — assistants, deputies, in so far as he is faithful, witnesses and judges, should he ever be unfaithful, to his trust. So as they are but there, what the motives were that drew them thither is perfectly immaterial; whether the relieving of their anxieties by the affecting prospect of their respective friends and relatives thus detained in durance, or merely the satisfying that general curiosity, which an establishment, on various accounts so interesting to human feelings, may naturally be expected to excite.

You see, I take for granted as a matter of course, that under the necessary regulations for preventing interruption and disturbance, the doors of these establishments will be, as, without very special reasons to the contrary, the doors of all public establishments ought to be, thrown wide open to the body of the curious at large — the great *open committee* of the tribunal of the world. And who ever objects to such publicity, where it is practicable, but those whose motives for objection afford the strongest reasons for it?

NOTES

1. *The Works of Jeremy Bentham*, ed. J. Bowring, 11 vols. (Edinburgh: William Tait, 1838–43), iv. 39.

2. Because of space constraints, I have omitted the intricately detailed note on toilet and plumbing design that concludes letter II.

3. The letters were addressed to Bentham's father, Jeremiah Bentham (1712–92).

4. The reference here is to the outbreak of the Russo–Turkish War of 1787–92; the Ottoman empire attempted to recover territory lost, including the Crimean Peninsula on the northern coast of the Black Sea, during the Russo–Turkish war of 1768–74. Bentham's brother Samuel (1757–1831) served as a Russian military officer and superintendent of shipbuilding in the Crimea; Bentham is here acknowledging that the Inspection-House was initially Samuel's idea.

5. I.e., "who will guard the guardians?" or "who will keep the keepers?" See Juvenal, *Satires*, VI.347.

6. Richard Akerman (1722–92); keeper of Newgate prison in London from 1754 until his death.

Of Publicity

"Of Publicity" is from *Essay on Political Tactics*, Bentham's essay on parliamentary procedure, drafted mostly in the spring of 1789 for the May convening of the French Estates-General on the eve of the Revolution. Although an excerpt (not this one) was printed in 1791, "Of Publicity" was not published until 1816, when Étienne Dumont included it in *Tactiques des assemblées législatives, suivi d'un traités des sophismes politiques* (Geneva and Paris). Bentham's own plan was consulted for the posthumous Bowring edition, but much of this text, including the present chapter, was simply retranslated from Dumont's French. The manuscript is almost completely lost, and the *Collected Works* version of *Political Tactics* (ed. Michael James, Cyprian Blamires, and Catherine Pease-Watkin [Oxford, 1999]) was forced to rely substantially on the Bowring (see its fine introduction for the complex provenance of each edition of this work).

What follows, only slightly changed and lightly annotated, is chapter 2, "Of Publicity," from the 1962 Russell and Russell reprint of *The Works of Jeremy Bentham*, ed. J. Bowring, 11 vols. (Edinburgh: William Tait, 1838–43), ii. 310–17, edited by Richard Smith (who signs his notes "*Ed.*"). This is the only selection in this volume that is not confirmed "real Bentham," but it is well worth including. "Of Publicity" is not only a fine statement of Enlightenment faith in print culture and the power of public opinion; it is also Bentham's early formulation of publicity as a technology of government, which would be generalized in his late constitutional writings. Many of its flourishes are, however, pure Dumont, and Bentham was not involved in its preparation for press. As such, it gives the reader of this volume a sense of the Bentham who was known to his contemporaries: ironically, as David Lieberman has noted, this figure, not the "authentic" one being excavated from manuscript, *is* the historical Bentham.[1]

Before entering into the detail of the operations of the assembly, let us place at the head of its regulations the fittest law for securing the public confidence, and causing it constantly to advance towards the end of its institution.

This law is that of *publicity*. The discussion of this subject may be divided into six parts: — 1. Reasons for publicity; 2. Examination of objections to publicity; 3. Exceptions to be made; 4. The points to which publicity should extend; 5. The means of publicity; 6. Observations on the practice established in England.

§ 1. Reasons for Publicity

1. To constrain the members of the assembly to perform their duty.

The greater the number of temptations to which the exercise of political power is exposed, the more necessary is it to give to those who possess it, the most powerful reasons for resisting them. But there is no reason more constant and more universal than the superintendence of the public. The public compose a tribunal, which is more powerful than all the other tribunals together. An individual may pretend to disregard its decrees — to represent them as formed of fluctuating and opposite opinions, which destroy one another; but every one feels, that though this tribunal may err, it is incorruptible; that it continually tends to become enlightened; that it unites all the wisdom and all the justice of the nation; that it always decides the destiny of public men; and that the punishments which it pronounces are inevitable. Those who complain of its judgments, only appeal to itself; and the man of virtue, in resisting the opinion of to-day — in rising above general clamour, counts and weighs in secret the suffrages of those who resemble himself.

If it were possible to abstract one's self from this tribunal, who would wish so to do? It without doubt would be neither the good nor the wise man, since in the long run these have nothing to fear, but everything to hope. The enemies of publicity may be collected into three classes: the malefactor, who seeks to escape the notice of the judge; the tyrant, who seeks to stifle public opinion, whilst he fears to hear its voice; the timid or indolent man, who complains of the general incapacity in order to screen his own.

It may perhaps be said, that an assembly, especially if numerous, forms an internal public, which serves as a restraint upon itself. I reply, that an assembly, how numerous soever, will never be sufficiently large to supply the place of the true public. It will be most frequently divided into two parties, which will not possess, in reference one to another, the qualities necessary for properly exercising the function of judges. They will not be impartial. Whatever the conduct of an individual may be, he will almost always be secure of the suffrages of one party, in opposition to the other. The internal censure will not be sufficient to secure probity, without the assistance of external censure. The reproaches of friends will be little dreaded, and the individual will become insensible to those of his enemies. The spirit of party shut up within narrow limits, equally strips both praise and blame of its nature.

2. To secure the confidence of the people, and their assent to the measures of the legislature: —

Suspicion always attaches to mystery. It thinks it sees a crime where it beholds an affectation of secrecy; and it is rarely deceived. For why should we hide ourselves if we do not dread being seen? In proportion as it is desirable for improbity to shroud itself in darkness, in the same proportion is it desirable for innocence to walk in open day, for fear of being mistaken for her adversary. So clear a truth presents itself at once to the minds of the people, and if good sense had not suggested it, malignity would have sufficed to promulgate it. The best project prepared in darkness, would excite more alarm than the worst, undertaken under the auspices of publicity.

But in an open and free policy, what confidence and security — I do not say for the people, but for the governors themselves! Let it be impossible that any thing should be done which is unknown to the nation — prove to it that you neither intend to deceive nor to surprise — you take away all the weapons of discontent. The public will repay with usury the confidence you repose in it. Calumny will lose its force; it collects its venom in the caverns of obscurity, but it is destroyed by the light of day.

That a secret policy saves itself from some inconveniences I will not deny; but I believe, that in the long run it creates more than it avoids; and that of two governments, one of which should be conducted secretly and the other openly, the latter would possess a strength, a hardihood, and a reputation which would render it superior to all the dissimulations of the other.

Consider, in particular, how much public deliberations respecting the laws, the measures, the taxes, the conduct of official persons, ought to operate upon the general spirit of a nation in favour of its government. Objections have been refuted, — false reports confounded; the necessity for the sacrifices required of the people have been clearly proved. Opposition, with all its efforts, far from having been injurious to authority, will have essentially assisted it. It is in this sense that it has been well said, *that he who resists, strengthens*: for the government is much more assured of the general success of a measure, and of the public approbation, after it has been discussed by two parties, whilst the whole nation has been spectators.

Among a people who have been long accustomed to public assemblies, the general feeling will be raised to a higher tone — sound opinions will be more common — hurtful prejudices, publicly combated, not by rhetoricians but by statesmen, will have less dominion. The multitude will be more secure from the tricks of demagogues, and the cheats of impostors; they will most highly esteem great talents, and the frivolities of wit will be reduced to their just value. A habit of reasoning and discussion will penetrate all classes of society. The passions, accustomed to a public struggle, will learn reciprocally to restrain themselves; they will lose that morbid sensibility, which among nations without liberty and without experience, renders them the sport of every alarm and every suspicion. Even in circumstances when discontent most strikingly exhibits itself, the signs of uneasiness will not be signs of revolt; the nation will rely upon those trustworthy individuals whom long use has taught them to know; and legal opposition to every unpopular measure, will prevent even the idea of illegal resistance. Even if the public wish be opposed by too powerful a party, it will know that the cause is not decided without appeal: hence persevering patience becomes one of the virtues of a free country.

The order which reigns in the discussion of a political assembly, will form by imitation the national spirit. This order will be reproduced in clubs and inferior assemblies, in which the people will be pleased to find the regularity of which they had formed the idea from the greater model. How often, in London, amid the effervescence of a tumult, have not well-known orators obtained the same attention as if they had been in parliament? The crowd has ranged itself around them, has listened in silence, and acted with a degree of moderation which could not be conceived possible even in despotic states, in which the populace, arrogant and timid alternately, is equally contemptible in its transports and its subjection. Still, however, the régime of publicity — very imperfect as yet, and newly tolerated, — without being established by law, has not had time to produce all the good effects to which it will give birth. Hence have arisen riots, for which there was no other cause than the precipitation with which the government acted, without taking the precaution to enlighten the people.[a]

3. To enable the governors to know the wishes of the governed.

In the same proportion as it is desirable for the governed to know the conduct of their governors, is it also important for the governors to know the real wishes of the governed. Under the guidance of publicity, nothing is more easy. The public is placed in a situation to form an enlightened opinion, and the course of that opinion is easily marked. Under the contrary régime, what is it possible to know with certainty? The public will always proceed, speaking and judging of everything; but it judges without information, and even upon false information: its opinion, not being founded upon facts, is altogether different from what it ought to be, from what it would be, if it were founded in truth. It ought not to be believed that government can dissipate at pleasure, those errors which it would have been easy to prevent. Late illumination does not always repair the evil of a previously erroneous impression. Have the people, from the little which has transpired respecting a project, conceived sinister apprehensions? We will suppose them unfounded; but this does not alter the case: they become agitated; they murmur; alarm is propagated; resistance is prepared. Has the government nothing to do but to speak — to make known the truth, in order to change the current of the public mind? No; without doubt: confidence is of slow growth. The odious imputations exist; the explanations which are given of necessity, are considered as the acknowledgements of weakness. Hence improvement itself produces a shock, when improperly introduced, and when it is opposed to the inclinations of the people. The history of the Emperor Joseph II would furnish a multitude of examples.[2]

To these major considerations may be joined others, which ought not to be neglected.

4. In an assembly elected by the people, and renewed from time to time, publicity is absolutely necessary to enable the electors to act from knowledge.

For what purpose renew the assembly, if the people are always obliged to choose from among men of whom they know nothing?

To conceal from the public the conduct of its representatives, is to add inconsistency to prevarication: it is to tell the constituents, "You are to elect or reject such or such of your deputies without knowing why — you are forbidden the use of reason — you are to be guided in the exercise of your greatest powers only by hazard or caprice."

a. For example, the riots in London in 1780.[3]

5. Another reason in favour of publicity: — To provide the assembly with the means of profiting by the information of the public.

A nation too numerous to act for itself, is doubtless obliged to entrust its powers to its deputies. But will they possess in concentration all the national intelligence? Is it even possible that the elected shall be in every respect the most enlightened, the most capable, the wisest persons in the nation? — that they will possess, among themselves alone, all the general and local knowledge which the function of governing requires? This prodigy of election is a chimera. In peaceful times, wealth and distinguished rank will be always the most likely circumstances to conciliate the greatest number of votes. The men whose condition in life leads them to cultivate their minds, have rarely the opportunity of entering into the career of politics. Locke, Newton, Hume, Adam Smith,[4] and many other men of genius, never had a seat in parliament. The most useful plans have often been derived from private individuals. The establishment of the sinking fund by Mr. Pitt, it is well known, was the fruit of the calculations of Dr. Price, who would never have had the leisure requisite for such researches, if his mind had been distracted by political occupations.[5] The only public man, who from the beginning of the quarrel with the American colonies had correct ideas upon the subject, and who would have saved the nation from war if he had been listened to, was a clergyman, excluded by this circumstance from the national representation.[b] But without entering into these details, it may easily be conceived how effective publicity is, as a means of collecting all the information in a nation, and consequently for giving birth to useful suggestions.

6. It may be thought descending from the serious consideration of this subject, to reckon among the advantages of publicity, *the amusement which results from it*. I say amusement by itself, separate from instruction, though it be, in fact, not possible to separate them.

But those who regard this consideration as frivolous, do not reason well. What they reckon *useful*, is what promises an advantage: amusement is an advantage already realized; and this kind of pleasure in particular, appears to me sufficient by itself to increase the happiness of any nation, which would enjoy much more than those nations who know it not.

Memoirs are one of the most agreeable parts of French literature, and there are few books which are more profound: but memoirs do not appear till long after the events which they record have happened, and they are not in the hands of every one. English newspapers are memoirs, published at the moment when the events occur; in which are found all the parliamentary

b. Dean Tucker.[6]

discussions — everything which relates to the actors on the political theatre; in which all the facts are freely exhibited, and all opinions are freely debated. One of the Roman emperors proposed a reward for the individual who should invent a new pleasure:[7] no one has more richly deserved it, than the individual who first laid the transactions of a legislative assembly before the eyes of the public.[c]

§ 2. Objections to Publicity

If publicity be favourable in so many respects to the governors themselves — so proper for securing them against the injustice of the public, for procuring for them the sweetest reward of their labours — why are they so generally enemies of this régime? Must it be sought in their vices? in the desire of the governors to act without responsibility — to withdraw their conduct from inspection — to impose upon the people — to keep them in subjection by their ignorance? Such motives may actuate some among them; but to attribute them to all, would be the language of satire. There may be unintentional errors in this respect, founded upon specious objections: let us endeavour to reduce them to their just value.

First objection — "The public is an incompetent judge of the proceedings of a political assembly, in consequence of the ignorance and passions of the majority of those who compose it."

If I should concede, that in the mass of the public there may not be one individual in a hundred who is capable of forming an enlightened judgment upon the questions which are discussed in a political assembly, I shall not be accused of weakening the objection; and yet, even at this point, it would not appear to me to have any force against publicity.

This objection would have some solidity, if, when the means of judging correctly were taken from the popular tribunal, the inclination to judge could be equally taken away: but the public do judge and will always judge. If it should refrain from judging, for fear of judging incorrectly, far from deserving to be charged with ignorance, its wisdom would deserve to be admired. A nation which could suspend its judgment, would not be composed of common men, but of philosophers.

But the increase of publications, it will be said, will increase the number of bad judges in a much greater proportion than the good ones.

To this it may be replied, — that for this purpose it is necessary to distinguish the public into three classes: The first is composed of the most

c. See Paley's Moral Philosophy, b. vi. Ch. 6, in which this subject is treated in a manner to which there is nothing to add.[8]

numerous party, who occupy themselves very little with public affairs — who have not time to read, nor leisure for reasoning. The second is composed of those who form a kind of judgment, but it is borrowed — a judgment founded upon the assertions of others, the parties neither taking the pains necessary, nor being able, to form an opinion of their own. The third is composed of those who judge for themselves, according to the information, whether more or less exact, which they are able to procure.

Which of these three classes of men would be injured by publicity?

It would not be the first; since, by the supposition, it would not affect them. It is only the third: these judged before — they will still judge; but they judged ill upon imperfect information; they will judge better when they are in possession of the true documents.

Whilst in respect of the second class, we have said that their judgments are borrowed, they must therefore be the echo of those of the third class. But this class being better informed, and judging better, will furnish more correct opinions for those who receive them ready made. By rectifying these, you will have rectified the others; by purifying the fountain, you will purify the streams.

In order to decide whether publicity will be injurious or beneficial, it is only necessary to consider the class which judges; because it is this alone which directs opinion. But if this class judge ill, it is because it is ignorant of the facts — because it does not possess the necessary particulars for forming a good judgment. This, then, is the reasoning of the partisans of mystery: — "You are incapable of judging, because you are ignorant; and you shall remain ignorant, that you may be incapable of judging."

Second objection — "Publicity may expose to hatred a member of the assembly, for proceedings which deserve other treatment."

This objection resolves itself into the first, — the incapacity of the people to distinguish between its friends and its enemies.

If a member of a political assembly have not sufficient firmness to brave a momentary injustice, he is wanting in the first quality of his office. It is the characteristic of error to possess only an accidental existence, which may terminate in a moment, whilst truth is indestructible. It requires only to be exhibited, and it is to effect this that everything in the region of publicity concurs. Is injustice discovered? — hatred is changed into esteem; and he who, at the expense of the credit of to-day, has dared to draw for reputation on the future, is paid with interest.

As regards reputation, publicity is much more useful to the members of an assembly than it can be hurtful: it is their security against malignant imputations and calumnies. It is not possible to attribute to them false discourses, nor to hide the good they have done, nor to give to their conduct an unfair colouring. Have their intentions been ill understood? — a public explanation overturns the false rumours, and leaves no hold for clandestine attacks.

Third objection — "The desire of popularity may suggest dangerous propositions to the members; — the eloquence which they will cultivate will be the eloquence of seduction, rather than the eloquence of reason; — they will become tribunes of the people, rather than legislators."

This objection also resolves itself into the first, — that is, the incompetence of the people to judge of their true interests, to distinguish between their friends and their flatterers.

In a representative state, in which the people are not called upon to vote upon political measures, this danger is little to be apprehended. The speeches of the orators, which are known to them only through the newspapers, have not the influence of the passionate harangues of a seditious demagogue. They do not read them till after they have passed through a medium which cools them; and besides, they are accompanied by the opposite arguments, which, according to the supposition, would have all the natural advantage of the true over the false. The publicity of debates has ruined more demagogues than it has made. A popular favourite has only to enter parliament, and he ceases to be mischievous. Placed amid his equals or his superiors in talent, he can assert nothing which will not be combated: his exaggerations will be reduced within the limits of truth, his presumption humiliated, his desire of momentary popularity ridiculed; and the flatterer of the people will finish by disgusting the people themselves.

Fourth objection — "In a monarchy, the publicity of the proceedings of political assemblies, by exposing the members to the resentment of the head of the State, may obstruct the freedom of their decisions."

This objection, more specious than the preceding, vanishes when it is examined, and even proves an argument in favour of publicity. If such an assembly be in danger from the sovereign, it has no security except in the protection of the people. The security arising from secret deliberations is more specious than real. The proceedings of the assembly would always be known to the sovereign, whilst they would always be unknown to those who would only seek to protect it, if the means were left to them.

If, then, a political assembly prefer the secret régime, by alleging the necessity of withdrawing itself from the inspection of the sovereign, it need not thus deceive itself: this can only be a pretence. The true motive of such conduct must rather be to subject itself to his influence, without too much exposing itself to public blame; for by excluding the public, it only frees itself from public inspection. The sovereign will not want his agents and his spies: though invisible, he will be, as it were, present in the midst of the assembly.

Is it objected against the régime of publicity, that it is a system of *distrust*? This is true; and every good political institution is founded upon this base. Whom ought we to distrust, if not those to whom is committed great authority, with great temptations to abuse it? Consider the objects of their duties: they are not their own affairs, but the affairs of others, comparatively indifferent to them, very difficult, very complicated, — which indolence alone would lead them to neglect, and which require the most laborious application. Consider their personal interests: you will often find them in opposition to the interests confided to them. They also possess all the means of serving themselves at the expense of the public, without the possibility of being convicted of it. What remains, then, to overcome all these dangerous motives? what has created an interest of superior force? and what can this interest be, if it be not respect for public opinion — dread of its judgments — desire of glory? — in one word, everything which results from publicity?

The efficacy of this great instrument extends to everything — legislation, administration, judicature. Without publicity, no good is permanent: under the auspices of publicity, no evil can continue.

§ 3. Objects to which publicity ought to extend

The publication of what passes in a political assembly ought to embrace the following points: —

1. The tenor of every motion.
2. The tenor of the speeches or the arguments for and against each motion.
3. The issue of each motion.
4. The number of the votes on each side.
5. The names of the voters.
6. The reports, &c. which have served as the foundation of the decision.

I shall not stop to prove that the knowledge of all these points is necessary for putting the tribunal of the public in a condition for forming an enlightened judgment. But an objection may be made against the publicity of the respective number of the voters. By publishing these, it may be said, the authority of the acts of the assembly will be in danger of being weakened, and the opposition will be encouraged when the majority is small.

To this it may be replied, that it is proper to distinguish between illegal and legal opposition. The first is not to be presumed; the second is not an evil.

The first, I say, is not to be presumed. The existence of a government regulated by an assembly, is founded upon an habitual disposition to conformity with the wish of the majority: constant unanimity is not expected, because it is known to be impossible; and when a party is beaten by a small majority, far from finding in this circumstance a motive for illegal resistance, it only discovers a reason for hope of future success.

If afterwards a legal opposition be established, it is no evil; for the comparative number of suffrages being the only measure of probability as to the correctness of its decisions, it follows that the legal opposition cannot be better founded than when guided by this probability. Let us suppose the case of a judicial decision; — that there have been two judgments, the one given by the smallest majority possible, the other by the greatest: would it not be more natural to provide an appeal against the first than against the second?

But the necessity of appeal in judicial matters is not nearly of the same importance as in matters of legislation. The decisions of the judges apply only to individual cases: the decisions of a legislative assembly regulate the interests of a whole nation, and have consequences which are continually renewed.

Do you expect that you will obtain greater submission by concealing from the public the different numbers of the votes? You will be mistaken. The public, reduced to conjecture, will turn this mystery against you. It will be very easily misled by false reports. A small minority may represent itself as nearly equal to the majority, and may make use of a thousand insidious arts to deceive the public as to its real force.

The American Congress, during the war of independence, was accustomed, if I am not deceived, to represent all its resolutions as unanimous. Its enemies saw in this precaution the necessity of hiding an habitual discord. This assembly, in other respects so wise, chose rather to expose itself to this suspicion, than to allow the degrees of dissent to the measures which it took, to be known. But though this trick might succeed in this particular case, this does not prove its general utility. The Congress, secure of the confidence of its constituents, employed this stratagem with their approbation, for the purpose of disconcerting its enemies.

The names of the voters ought to be published, not only that the public may know the habitual principles of their deputies, and their assiduity in attending, but also for another reason. The quality of the votes has an influence upon opinion, as well as their number. To desire that they should all have the same value, is to desire that folly should have the same influence as wisdom, and that merit should exist without motive and without reward.

§ 4. Exceptions to the rule of Publicity

Publicity ought to be suspended in those cases in which it is calculated to produce the following effects: —

1. To favour the projects of an enemy.
2. Unnecessarily to injure innocent persons.
3. To inflict too severe a punishment upon the guilty.

It is not proper to make the law of publicity absolute, because it is impossible to foresee all the circumstances in which an assembly may find itself placed. Rules are made for a state of calm and security: they cannot be formed for a state of trouble and peril. Secresy is an instrument of conspiracy; it ought not, therefore, to be the system of a regular government.

§ 5. Means of Publicity

The following are the means of publicity which may be employed, either in whole or in part, according to the nature of the assembly, and the importance of its affairs.

1. Authentic publication of the transactions of the assembly upon a complete plan, including the six points laid down in the preceding article: —

2. The employment of short-hand writers for the speeches; and in cases of examination, for the questions and answers.

3. Toleration of other non-authentic publications upon the same subject.

4. Admission of strangers to the sittings.

The employment of short-hand writers would be indispensable in those cases in which it would be desirable to have the entire tenor of the speech. But recourse need not be had to this instrument, except in discussions of sufficient importance to justify the expense. In England, in an ordinary trial, the parties are at liberty to employ them. In the solemn trial of Warren Hastings,[9] the House of Commons on the one side, and the accused on the other, had their short-hand writers; — the House of Lords, in character of judge, had also its own.

With regard to non-authentic publications, it is necessary to tolerate them, either to prevent negligence and dishonesty on the part of the official reporters, or to prevent suspicion. An exclusive privilege would be regarded as a certificate of falsity. Besides, the authentic publication of the proceedings of the assembly could only be made with a slowness which would not give the public satisfaction, without reckoning the evil which would arise in the interval from false reports, before the authentic publication arrived to destroy them.

Non-official journals completely accomplish this object. Their success depends upon the avidity of the public, and their talent consists in satisfying it. This has in England reached such a point of celerity, that debates which have lasted till three or four o'clock in the morning, are printed and distributed in the capital before mid-day.

The admission of the public to the sittings is a very important point; but this subject requires explanations, which would not here be in their place. It will be treated separately.

The principal reason for this admission is, that it tends to inspire confidence in the reports of the journals. If the public were excluded, it would always be led to suppose that the truth was not reported, or at least that part was suppressed, and that many things passed in the assembly which it did not know. But independently of this guarantee, it is very useful for the reputation of the members of the assembly to be heard by impartial witnesses, and judged by a portion of the public which is changed every day. This presence of strangers is a powerful motive to emulation among them, at the same time that it is a salutary restraint upon the different passions to which the debates may give rise.[d]

§ 6. State of things in England

In order to form a just idea of the state of things in England relative to publicity, it is necessary to pay attention to two very different things — the rules, and the actual practice. The following are the rules: —

1. All strangers (that is to say, all who are not members of the assembly) are prohibited from entering, under pain of *immediate imprisonment*. Introduction by a member forms no exception to the prohibition, nor any ground of exemption from the punishment. This prohibition, established during the stormy times of the civil war in 1650, has been renewed seven times, under circumstances which furnish neither this excuse nor any other.[e]

2. Prohibition, as well of others as of the members themselves, to report

d. In the Swiss cantons, no strangers are admitted to the debates in their representative councils, nor are any accounts of their proceedings published.

e. 26th Feb. 1688,   15th Nov. 1705,
   21st Nov. 1689,   26th Jan. 1709,
   2d April 1690,   and
   31st Oct. 1705,   16th March 1719.

anything that passes in the House, or to publish anything on the subject without the authority of the House.

This regulation, which dates from the commencement of the civil war, has been renewed thirty times, and for the last time in 1738, in an order in which passion appears carried to its greatest height. The language of the proudest despots is gentle and moderate, in comparison with that of this popular assembly.

3. Since 1722, there has been published by the House of Commons, what are called the Votes of the House; that is, a kind of history of its proceedings, meagre and dry, containing the formal proceedings, with the motions and decisions; and in cases of division, the numbers for and against, but without any notice of the debates.

Before this period, this publication only took place occasionally.

These votes, collected and republished at the end of the year, with an immense mass of public laws and private acts, form what are called the Journals of the House. These journals were formerly given to each member, but not sold to the public.[f]

4. Projects of laws before they are passed by parliament. These projects, called *bills*, are not printed under a general rule, but the printing is ordered upon special motion, and for the exclusive use of the members; so that no one can know what they contain, unless he obtain one of these privileged copies through a member. It is, however, of more importance that the public should be made acquainted with these, than with the votes.

How singular soever it may be thus to see the deputies of the people withdrawing themselves with so much hauteur from the observation of their constituents, the principles of a free government are as yet so little known, that there has been no general complaint against a conduct which tends to destroy all responsibility on the part of the representatives, and all influence on the part of the nation.

But since public opinion, more enlightened, has had greater ascendency, and principally since the accession of George III.,[10] though these anti-popular regulations are still the same, a contrary practice has prevailed in many particulars. It is doubtless to be regretted, that whatever improvement has taken place in England has been accomplished through a continual violation of the laws; but it is gratifying to observe that these innovations insensibly tend to the general perfection.

The House of Commons has allowed a small portion of the public to be

f. All the papers published by the House of Commons are now allowed to be sold (1838) — *Ed.*

present at its sittings — about one hundred and fifty strangers can be accommodated in a separate gallery. Unhappily, this indulgence is precarious. That the House ought to be able to exclude witnesses in the cases of which we have spoken, is conceded; but at present it is only necessary that a single member should require the observation of the standing order, which being always in force, is irresistible.

As to the contents of the debates and the names of the voters, there are numerous periodical publications which give account of them. These publications are crimes; but it is to these fortunate crimes that England is indebted for her escape from an aristocratic government resembling that of Venice.[11]

These publications would not have obtained this degree of indulgence, if they had been more exact. At one time, if a stranger were discovered in the gallery with a pencil in his hand, a general cry was raised against him, and he was driven out without pity. But at present, connivance is more extended, and short-hand writers, employed by the editors of the public newspapers, are tolerated.[g]

Among the Lords, the regulations are nearly the same, but the tone is more moderate. No admission to strangers — (order 5th April 1707). No publication of debates allowed — (order 27th February 1698). It was, however, among them, that in our times the plan of indulgence which at present reigns was commenced.

This House has one custom, which gives to one set of its opinions a publicity of which no example is found in the other.

I refer to *protests*. These are declarations, made by one or many members of the minority, of the reasons for their dissent from the measures adopted by the majority, and inserted in the journals. These protests are printed and circulated, in opposition to the regulations. There results from this publication a singularity which ought to lead to consideration, if consideration were within the province of routine. It is, that the only reasons presented to the public in an authentic form, are those which are opposed to the laws.

The House of Lords, in permitting a portion of the public to attend its sittings, has rendered this favour as burthensome as possible. There are no seats. The first row of spectators intercepts the view, and injures the hearing of those who are behind. Some of the more popular members have at different times proposed to give the public more accommodation; but the

g. They have in the present House of Commons a gallery appropriated to themselves (1838) — *Ed.*

proposition has always been refused by the majority of their colleagues, either from considering that a painful attitude is more respectful, or from an absolute horror of all change.[h]

NOTES

1. D. Lieberman, "Economy and Polity in Bentham's Science of Legislation," in *Economy, Polity, and Society: British Intellectual History 1750–1950*, ed. S. Collini, R. Whatmore, and B. Young (Cambridge: Cambridge University Press, 2000), 108. On Dumont and this historical Bentham see Cyprian Blamires, *The*

h. By the French constitution of the year 1814, it was directed, that "all the deliberations of the Chamber of Peers[12] should be secret."

I can discover no good reason for this secresy. If publicity be dangerous, it appears to me that there is least danger for the peers, who are the least exposed to the danger of popular ambition.

Non-publicity appears to me particularly disadvantageous to the peers. They require publicity as a bridle and a spur; as a bridle, because in virtue of their situation they are thought to have interests separate from the body of the people — as a spur, because their immoveability weakens the motives of emulation, and gives them an absolute independence.

I suppose that the Chamber of Peers is considered as being, or about to become, eminently monarchical, as being the bulwark of royalty against the attacks of the deputies of the people. But in this point of view, is not the secresy of their deliberations a political blunder? Public discussion is allowed to those who by the supposition are enemies of the royal authority, or at least too much inclined to democracy; and those who are considered the hereditary defenders of the king and his dominion, are shut up to secret discussion. Is not this in some manner to presume that their cause is too feeble to sustain the observation of the nation, and that to preserve the individuals from general disapprobation, it is necessary they should vote in secret?

When a proposition in the Chamber of Deputies has obtained great popular favour, is it not desirable that the arguments by which it has been opposed should be known? that the body which has rejected it should have the right of publicly justifying its refusal? that it should not be exposed to the injurious suspicion of acting only with a view to its own interest? that it ought not to be placed in so disadvantageous a position in the struggle which it has to sustain? The body which speaks in public, and whose debates are published, possesses all the means of conciliating to itself numerous partisans, whilst those who deliberate in secret can only influence themselves. It would therefore seem that this secresy, so flattering to them, had been invented as a means of taking from their influence over opinion, more than was given to them in superiority of rank.

French Revolution and the Creation of Benthamism (New York: Palgrave Macmillan, 2008).

2. Emperor Joseph II (1741–90) was Holy Roman Emperor from 1765 to 1790; his reforming zeal — in pursuit of Enlightenment goals such as centralization of government, religious toleration, emancipation of the peasantry, etc. — was met with fierce resistance.

3. Bentham refers here to the Gordon riots, named after Lord George Gordon (1751–93); the riots were triggered by his Protestant Association's agitation to repeal the Papists Act of 1778, which had taken initial steps toward Catholic emancipation.

4. John Locke (1632–1704), Isaac Newton (1643–1727), David Hume (1711–76), and Adam Smith (1723–90). Among the most prominent European thinkers of their time, Locke and Newton would become associated with the English Enlightenment and Hume and Smith with the Scottish.

5. William Pitt (Pitt the younger, 1759–1806), British prime minister from 1783 to 1801 and 1804 to 1806. In 1786 he established a sinking fund, in which governmental revenues are held in order to accumulate interest used to pay the national debt. For this he relied on the advice of Richard Price (1723–91), who made the relevant calculations in *An Appeal to the Public, on the Subject of the National Debt*, first published in 1772.

6. Josiah Tucker (1713–99), dean of Gloucester cathedral from 1758. He advocated separation from the American colonies as early as 1766, fearing that the course of British policy there would only fuel war and political unrest.

7. Bentham mentions this proposal in a few places, recalling elsewhere that it was Nero's. It would, it seems, become a staple of nineteenth-century letters; other authors mention Tiberius and Elagabalus, all without citation. Such a proposal is actually attributed to Xerxes of Persia by Cicero in *Tusculan Disputations* V.vii.

8. William Paley (1743–1805) wrote a long paragraph on the satisfactions of following and discussing the political news; see *The Principles of Moral and Political Philosophy*, 4th ed. (London, 1787), ii. 184–86.

9. Warren Hastings (1732–1818), governor-general of Bengal, was impeached by the British House of Commons in 1787 and acquitted in 1795 after a long trial in the House of Lords.

10. George III (1738–1820), king of Great Britain and Ireland from 1760 to 1801; king of the United Kingdom of Great Britain and Ireland from 1801 to 1820.

11. Venice's aristocratic republic is also compared unfavorably to England by Montesquieu; see *De l'Esprit des Lois (The Spirit of the Laws)* (1748), bk. 9, chap. 6.

12. The restoration of the Bourbon monarchy in France in 1814 created a bicameral legislature, composed of a hereditary and appointed Chamber of Peers and an elected Chamber of Deputies.

Manual of Political Economy
Chapters 1 and 2

Having enjoyed great success with his *Defence of Usury* (1787), Bentham apparently intended to publish an introductory text on political economy. The *Manual* seems to have been composed in the early 1790s, but it was never published as such during Bentham's lifetime. Some of its material found its way into Étienne Dumont's recension, *Théorie des peines et des récompenses* (1811); this same material was retranslated by Richard Smith for the *Rationale of Reward* in 1825. According to its modern editor, Werner Stark, the *Manual* was garbled and mixed up with Bentham's later *Institute of Political Economy* in the Bowring edition.

What follows is Bentham's text as given in pages 223–31 of W. Stark, ed., *Jeremy Bentham's Economic Writings*, vol. 1 (London: George Allen and Unwin, 1952). I have not reproduced Stark's editorial apparatus, which remains under copyright. This is a tiny sample of the *Manual* and a tinier sample of Bentham's substantial work on political economy, intended only to introduce the reader to some fundamental principles. Those who are interested should consult all three volumes (1952–54) of Stark's edition and his valuable notes and commentary. Bentham's political economy has yet to appear in the *Collected Works of Jeremy Bentham*, although work is now underway, and two volumes on the Poor Laws, edited by Michael Quinn, have been produced.

[PART ONE: GENERAL OBSERVATIONS]

1. Introduction

THIS little treatise is meant to serve as a manual of political economy. Political economy may be considered as a science or as an art. But in this instance, as in others, it is only as a guide to the art that the science is of use.

Political economy, considered as an art exercisible by those who have the government of a nation in their hands, is the art of directing the national industry to the purposes to which it may be directed with the greatest advantage.

The object of this little treatise is to shew in a general way, what ought to be done in the way of political economy, and what ought not to be done.

The general result is that of the much that has been done in this way and with these views scarce any thing ought to have been done: and that of what ought to be done, as matters stand, almost the whole consists in undoing what has been done, and in obviating the inconveniences that would result from the carrying on this process of undoing in an abrupt and inconsiderate manner.

It will naturally occur to some as an objection to this work, in short to any work on this subject, that it has already been treated of by Dr. Adam Smith;[1] that Dr. Smith is a writer of great and distinguished merit, and that this subject has been treated of by him very copiously. The objection will naturally appear the stronger in proportion as it is observed that the principles here laid down concurr with those laid down by that illustrious writer.[a]

In answer to this objection I offer the following observations:

1. The design of this work is different from that of his. His had two objects, the το ον and the τὸ πρέπον.[2] But the το ον is evidently the

a. Be the doctrine true or false, this concise sketch will serve at any rate to give a view of the state of the question upon all the topics of political economy that can come under the consideration of the legislature. To this doctrine, the habitual practice of the legislature is in many, I may say in most points, in diametrical opposition. If the doctrine be erroneous, exhibited as it is here, it will not be difficult to correct the error: if it be just, those who may be disposed to make use of it for the correction of the errors that guide the present practice, may now do so with little trouble.

Concise as it is, it will be found not more concise than comprehensive. It was designed to embrace the whole of the subject, [and] as far as I can trust my conceptions, it does so. It certainly embraces all the topics and all the arguments touched upon by Dr. Smith: and it as certainly embraces several topics, as well as several arguments, which he has not touched upon.

principal: the other comes in incidentally as it were. In this, the sole object is the το πρεπον. His object was the science: my object is the art. By him the art is touched upon incidentally only and piecemeal, and as it were without intending it, in treating of the science: by me it is treated of directly and professedly. His views seem scarcely to have carried him beyond the science: by me the science is considered only as a means to an end: and as no otherwise worth occupying one's self about than in proportion to its subserviency to that end. This work is to Dr. Smith's, what a book on the art of medicine is to a book of anatomy or physiology.

2. He has not made the utmost of his argument.

3. He has not embraced the whole of the subject.

4. He has not compressed his argument within the smallest compass.

5. He has not given it the most advantageous method.

6. With matters belonging to political economy, he has mixed matters foreign to that subject.

7. He has not taken for the sole or for the principal, or even for any part of the professed object of his enquiry, the question how, with regard to all these matters, the law ought to be: he has considered principally the science: what he has said of the art has come in rather incidentally than professedly.

8. Along with the matter employed in the enquiry what the law ought to be, [is] intermixed matter employed in the description of the course that human industry takes abstractedly from the consideration of law. This matter, instead of being *censorial* [i.e.] critical with regard to the state of the law, [is] *expository* or descriptive with regard to the actual course of nature. And of this expository matter by far the greatest part of his book is composed.

The great object, the great *desideratum*, is to know what ought and what ought not to be done by government. It is in this view, and in this view only, that the knowledge of what is done and takes place without the interference of government can be of any practical use. Otherwise than in this view the knowledge of what spontaneously takes place is matter of curiosity rather than use. The only use of the science is the serving as a foundation to the art. For what purpose does it concern us to know how [. . . ?] things are? Only in order that we may know how to deal with them, and to dispose of ourselves in respect of them.

9. He has not employed in argument the position which I make use of as the groundwork of the whole: viz. the limitation of industry by the limitation of capital. If he had, it might have spared him some inconsistencies and mistakes: a position which, [if] I am not very much mistaken, draws the

argument into a very small compass, and places the whole subject, at the very outset, in a very clear point of view.

10. In combating error, or what has appeared to him in that light, instead of taking opinions one by one, he has taken them in the lump and made them up into systems: a mode of proceeding which is never favourable to perspicuity, and scarce ever perfectly reconciliable to truth.[b]

At any rate, this treatise, whether better upon the whole than Dr. Smith's or not so good, is in point of method very different. If some there are, who find it easier to gain instruction from that book, others there may be who find it easier to gain it from this. Although not better, yet if not much worse, it will therefore at any rate in virtue of that difference have its use, as giving two chances for the easiest mode of instruction instead of one.

2. Fundamental principles

Under the general name of *wealth* is comprised every object which, being within the reach of human desires, is within the grasp of human possession, and as such either actually subservient, or capable of being made subservient, to human use.

The wealth of any community is the sum of the portions of wealth belonging to the several individuals of which that community is composed.

All wealth is the joint result or product of land and labour: of human

b. By making propositions into systems and representing such systems as being adopted not only by individuals, but by whole parties, a man virtually asserts and renders it incumbent on him to prove that there are large assemblages of known individuals by every one of whom the propositions in question are every one of them embraced: that every man of the party maintains every one of the propositions: a position which is seldom true, which is never worth proving, which is very apt to be disputed, and which, if disputed, is scarcely capable of being proved. Taking this course, a man can scarcely avoid giving into the error which Aristotle in his catalogue of fallacies characterizes by the name of the fallacy *secundum plures ut unum.*[3]

While he reasons feebly, the proposition, erroneous or not erroneous, stands its ground, and he fails that way: if he attacks the proposition forcibly, and so forcibly that nobody can find any thing to say in its defence, nobody owns it: if he finds no owner for it, he is charged with beating the air: if he finds one, he is charged with calumny and injustice.

In exposing errors, or what are taken for such, the best way therefore both for reader and writer is to take them separately, and exhibit them one by one. Both the nature of the proposition, and its erroneous quality, if it be erroneous, are thus distinctly brought to view: and if it be embraced generally, there can scarcely be any difficulty of finding some one writer who has fathered it, and in whose words it may be exhibited.

labour operating either immediately upon land, or upon something issuing more or less immediately from land.

The ends or uses of wealth may be all comprized under the four following terms: 1. subsistence: 2. enjoyment: 3. security: 4. encrease.[c]

As wealth can not be put to any of its uses without consumption, the stock subsisting at any given period, far from being augmented, can not so much as be kept up without continual encrease.

Wealth considered as flowing in at successive periods is stiled *income* or *revenue*.

All wealth issuing either immediately or mediately from land, the produce of which renews itself for the most part periodically, in virtue of the influence of the seasons,[d] income or revenue is accordingly for the most part *periodical*, i.e. flowing in at stated periods, owing to the vicissitude or successive recurrence of the same seasons.

A portion of wealth considered as employed for the purpose of encrease is stiled *capital*.[e]

A man, while he is employed in any way in giving encrease to wealth, must have 1. *materials* to work upon: 2. *instruments* to work with: 3. a *place* to work in: 4. a place to be in, when not at work: 5. food, and other consumable means of subsistence, to maintain him. All these, considered as directed to the end in question, viz. the giving encrease to wealth, come under the denomination of capital.

Capital may be distinguished into *fixed*, and *outgoing*. Under the denomination of *outgoing* may be comprehended: 1. the consumable means of subsistence: 2. the materials above mentioned, before they have received the portion of labour destined to be applied to them by the individual in question, [i.e., before] they have been prepared for use: 3. of the instruments in question, such, if any, as have been compleatly consumed before

c. Equality is a [further] end which law ought to propose to itself, as far as [it] is consist[ent] with the others: but what has been done, or may be done, with this view, will hardly be thought to come within the pale of political economy. As far as it concerns wealth, it will hardly be reckoned an object distinct from opulence: since the end in view, in whatever may be done in the design of favouring equality, is nothing but the making those who would otherwise be poorer richer, [or] rather that the poorer should be less poor rather than that the richer should be less rich.

d. Vegetables immediately — Animals, through vegetables — Minerals, not.

e. Land, in as far as it is necessary, may be considered as coming under the head of capital, especially as far as concerns any improvement it has received from industry. The original unimproved land is a portion of capital furnished by nature.

the article in question has been prepared for use. All the other modifications of capital may be referred to the denomination of *fixed*.

The article, whatever it be, in the production of which the encrease given to wealth consists, may be distinguished by the general appellation of *finished work*.

An article of finished work, if instead of being consumed or kept for use by him by whom or for whom it is made, or by or for some one else to whom he gives it *gratis*, is given in exchange for something else, becomes an article of *sale*, an article or object of *trade, commerce, traffic*, or *merchandize*.

In all communities that have made any sort of progress in the career of civilisation, a class of men has formed itself, who derive a livelihood from buying goods of the maker, in order to sell [them] again to the consumer who wants them for use.

The makers of goods for sale may be termed, in contradistinction to those who sell them without making them, *manufacturers*: and the latter, in contradistinction to the former, *venders*.

Among venders there is a distinction which, on several accounts, comes often to be noticed. The most numerous are those who sell goods retail as well as wholesale, in small quantities as well as in large, therefore more frequently to him who wants them for use, than to him who buys them only to sell again, exposing them accordingly in most instances to the indiscriminate view of the public passengers in a *shop*. A few there are in comparison who can find their account in selling goods in large quantities only, accordingly to those chiefly or exclusively who buy them to sell again, and thence without the necessity of exposing them purposely to the indiscriminate view of the public in a shop or otherwise. Such persons are termed in contradistinction to the former [the shopkeepers], *merchants*.

As it is necessary for some purposes that these different classes of men should in the way of speaking of them be kept distinct, so is it for other purposes that they should be comprehended under one denomination which, without confining itself to any one of the classes, shall include them all. — *traders*, and *commercial men* are terms which may be exclusively appropriated to this purpose.[f]

The business of selling and making for sale may accordingly be comprehended under the common denominations of *trade* and *commerce*.

As labour can in no instance be bestowed upon any object in any considerable quantity without capital, the quantity of labour that can be bestowed

---

f. In law, *trader* does this, *tradesman* includes manufacturers without including merchants.

upon any object will be limited by the quantity of capital that can be bestowed upon it.

The quantity of capital employed in a community being given, the quantity of encrease given to the stock of wealth within a given period will be in proportion to the degree of advantage with which that capital is applied, in other words, in proportion to the advantageousness of the direction given to it.

The degree of advantage with which a quantity of capital is applied being given, the quantity of encrease given to the stock of wealth within a given period will be in proportion to the quantity of capital which the community has had at command and employed within that period.

The encrease of wealth made in any community within a given period, depends then upon two things: 1. upon [the] quantity of capital: 2. upon the advantageousness of the direction given to it.

The possible ways then, in which any extraordinary degree of encrease can be given to the quantity of wealth in any community within a given period, are all reducible to these two: [1.] adding to the quantity of capital employed in it: 2. adding to the degree of advantageousness with which the capital, whatever there be of it, is employed.

Except in as far as a more advantageous direction is given to the capital of the community than would have been given to it otherwise, it is therefore impossible by any means or efforts whatsoever to add any thing to the encrease that would otherwise have been given to the stock of wealth in a community, without making an addition to the quantity of capital employed in it: and all measures taken by government or individuals in any such view must necessarily be unavailing.

The advantageousness of the direction given to a quantity of capital in any instance depends upon two things: 1. the choice of the trade itself: 2. the choice of the mode of carrying it on.

In both cases the chance which there is of the best choice relative to both points will be [1.] in proportion to the degree of interest which he, by whom the choice is made, has in making the best possible: 2. in proportion to the chance he has of possessing the faculties of knowledge and judgment in relation to the business in the highest degree possible.

The chance there is of a man's possessing in this superior degree the faculties of knowledge and judgment depends itself in great measure on the degree of interest he has in the concern: since the degree in which those faculties are possessed depends, as far as temperament and opportunity are given, in great measure upon the measure of attention bestowed on the business, which [in its turn] depends on the degree of interest he takes, and is likely to take in it.

The interest which a man takes in the affairs of another, a member of the sovereignty for example in those of a subject, is not likely to be so great as the interest which either of them takes in his own: still less where that other is a perfect stranger to him.

Judgment depends partly upon *natural faculties*, partly upon *acquired faculties*, partly upon *acquired knowledge*: knowledge depends partly upon *opportunity*, partly upon measure of *attention*: measure of attention depends partly upon *intensity* of attention, partly upon the quantity of *time* bestowed in it. Opportunity depends partly upon causes *within the power* of the man in question, partly upon causes *out of his power*.

In not one of these particulars is the statesman likely to be more than upon a par with the individual whose choice relative to the subjects in question he is so ready to controul: in almost all of them he is constantly and necessarily inferior beyond all measure.

A first Lord of the Treasury for instance, or other Member of Parliament, or a first Lord of Trade, is not likely to have had so many opportunities of acquiring knowledge relative to farming as a farmer, relative to distilling as a distiller, relative to manufacturing of stuffs as a manufacturer of stuffs, relative to the selling of the produce of any of those trades at home or abroad as one who has made the selling of them the business of his life.

A first Lord [of the Treasury, or other Member of Parliament, or a first Lord of Trade] is not likely to have bestowed attention for so great a length of time on the business of farming as a farmer, on that of distilling as a distiller, on that of manufacturing stuffs in all its branches as a manufacturer of stuffs.

A first Lord of the Treasury, or of Trade, or any other Member of the Legislature, is not likely, during the time he is bestowing attention, to bestow it with equal energy on the business of farming as a farmer, on that of distilling as a distiller [and so on].

A first Lord of the Treasury, or of Trade, or any other Member of the Legislature, is therefore not likely to possess either so much knowledge or so much judgment relative to the business of farming as a farmer [or relative to the business of distilling as a distiller, and so on].

A first Lord of the Treasury therefore, or of Trade, or any other Member of the Legislature, is not likely in the instance of any one of the many thousand trades that exist in the world, to form relative to the best mode of carrying on that trade a choice so good as that which would be formed by a person embarked, or intending to be embarked, on the trade in question: still less in the instance of every one of those trades.

But the choice of the most advantageous among a number of trades depends among other things on the knowledge of the most advantageous mode in which each of those trades respectively can be carried on: it is only by knowing the utmost degree of advantage that can be reaped from each, each being carried on in the most advantageous mode, that it can be known which of them, and in what degree, is more advantageous than another.

A first Lord of the Treasury therefore, or of Trade, or any other Member of the Legislature is still less likely to make a better choice in regard to the option to be made of one out of the many thousand trades existing or capable of existence, and in that sense in regard to the most advantageous direction to be given to capital, than in regard to the mode of carrying on any one in particular of those trades, and in that other sense in regard to the advantageousness of the direction to be given to capital.

Though a first Lord of the Treasury or of Trade or any other Member of Parliament happened by any accident or industry to be apprised of a circumstance demonstrating that this or that particular sort of trade, or this or that mode of carrying on a particular sort of trade, would be particularly advantageous, and though it were sure that in that particular, and by that accident, the statesman were better acquainted with the interest of the trader than the trader himself, yet even this would not afford them any sufficient warrant for endeavouring to employ the power of government in inducing any individual or individuals to embark in such branch of trade, unless the statesman had also a stronger regard for the interest of the trader than the trader himself, in other words, loved every man better than any man loves himself: for in that case simple information would be sufficient to produce the effect without any exercise of power: and so sure [it is] that the information is true, so sure is it that the exercise of power would be unnecessary, and to no use.

The quantity of capital existing in the world at the end of a certain period, depends not upon the quantity of wealth produced down to that period, but upon the difference between the whole quantity that has been produced, and that part which has been consumed.

The quantity of capital in the world can therefore receive an encrease by the care of man in one way only which is by *frugality*.

The quantity of capital in any particular community may receive encrease in either of two ways: 1. by frugality: or 2. by importation from some other community.

Capital imported into a community may be imported either with the proprietors, or without the proprietors: if without the proprietors, either with or without an equivalent: if without an equivalent, either with or without consent: if with consent, that consent may have been forced or free: if with an equivalent, with an equivalent preceeding, or one to come: that is, either in the way of plunder, tribute, gift, payment, or loan.

NOTES

1. Adam Smith (1723–90), author of *An Inquiry into the Nature and Causes of the Wealth of Nations* (1776).

2. I.e., the "that which is" and the "that which is fitting."

3. I.e., "treating the many as one." Bentham is quite clear about the problem here, but the reference to Aristotle's fallacies appears confused (none goes by this name, and none exactly fits this case).

Nonsense Upon Stilts,

Or Pandora's Box Opened, Or the French Declaration of Rights Prefixed to the Constitution of 1791 Laid Open and Exposed— With a Comparative Sketch of What Has Been Done on the Same Subject in the Constitution of 1795 . . .

Right the child of Law.

This essay, formerly known as "Anarchical Fallacies," is the most famous of Bentham's writings on France. Its fierce attack on natural rights amplifies Bentham's earlier attacks on the doctrine, for example, his critique of American declarations in the long concluding footnote to *An Introduction to the Principles of Morals and Legislation* (see *IPML*, ed. J. H. Burns and H. L. A. Hart [London, 1970], 309–11). Étienne Dumont published a recension of these materials in 1816 under the title "Sophismes Anarchiques." The "Anarchical Fallacies" (*The Works of Jeremy Bentham*, ed. J. Bowring, 11 vols. [Edinburgh: William Tait, 1838–43], ii. 489–534) departed substantially from Dumont in its greater fidelity to Bentham's composition; what follows is the bulk of the *Collected Works of Jeremy Bentham* edition, reconstructed in accordance with the protocols of the Bentham Project.

Bentham wrote "Nonsense Upon Stilts" in 1795, provoked by the appearance of a new French Declaration of Rights prefacing the third constitution since the Revolution. Because of space constraints, I have omitted the third part of the essay (the critique of Sieyès), but the last section — "On the Use and Abuse of the Word *Right*" — is included in full. The text is

reproduced with the permission of Oxford University Press from *Rights,*
Representation, and Reform, ed. Philip Schofield, Catherine Pease-Watkin,
and Cyprian Blamires (Oxford, 2002), 317–88 and 398–401. Cross-
references have been omitted or altered.

Preliminary Observations

The Declaration of Rights, I mean the paper published under that name by
the French National Assembly on the | | of | | 179 | |,[1] assumes for its
subject-matter a field of disquisition as unbounded in point of extent as it is
important in its nature. But the more ample the extent given to any proposition, or string of propositions, the more difficult it is to keep the import of it
confined without deviation within the bounds of truth and reason. If, in the
smallest corner of the field it ranges over, it fails of coinciding with the line
of rigid rectitude, no sooner is the aberration pointed out, than (in as much
as there is no medium between truth and falshood) its pretensions to the
appellation of a truism are gone, and whoever looks upon it must recognize
it to be false and erroneous, and if as here political conduct is the theme[?],
so far as the error extends and fails of being detected, pernicious. In a work
of such extreme importance with a view to practice, and which throughout
keeps practice so closely, and immediately, and professedly in view, a single
error may be attended with the most fatal consequences. The more extensive the propositions, the more consummate will be the knowledge, the
more exquisite the skill indispensably requisite to confine them on all points
within the pale of truth. The most consummate ability in the whole nation
would not have been too much for the task: one may venture to say it would
not even have been equal to it. But that on the sanctioning of each proposition the most consummate ability should happen to be vested in the heads of
the sorry majority in whose hands the plenitude of power happened on that
same occasion to be vested, is an event against which the chances are
almost as infinity to one. Here then is a radical and all-pervading error — the
attempting to give to a work on such a subject the sanction of government:
especially of such a government, a government composed of members so
numerous, so unequal in talents, as well as discordant in inclinations and
affections. Had it been the work of a single hand, and that a private one, and
in that character given to the world, every good effect would have been
produced by it that could be produced by it when published as the work of
government, without any of the bad effects which in case of the smallest
error must result from it when given as the work of government.

The Revolution, which threw the government into the hands of the penners and adopters of this declaration, having been the effect of insurrection, the grand object is evidently to justify the cause. But by justifying it they invite it: in justifying past insurrection, they plant and cultivate a propensity to perpetual insurrection in time future. They sow the seeds of anarchy broadcast: in justifying the demolition of existing authorities, they undermine all future ones, their own consequently in the number. — Shallow and reckless vanity! They imitate in their conduct the author of that fabled law according to which the assassination of the prince upon the throne gave to the assassin a title to succeed him.[2] *People, behold your rights*: *let a single article of them be violated, insurrection is not your right only*, *but* "the most sacred of your duties." — Such is the constant language, for such is the professed object, of this source and model of all laws — this self-consecrated oracle of all Nations.

The more *abstract* — that is the more *extensive*, the proposition is, the more liable to involve a fallacy. Of fallacies, one of the most natural modifications is that which is called *begging the question*: — the abuse of making the abstract proposition resorted to for proof, a cover for introducing, in the company of *other* propositions that are nothing to the purpose, the very proposition which is admitted to stand in need of proof.

Is the provision in question fit in point of expediency to be passed into a law for the government of the French Nation? That was the proper question to have been put in relation to each provision proposed to enter into the composition of the body of French Laws: that *mutatis mutandis* would have been the question put in England. Instead of that, as often as the utility of a provision appeared (by reason of wideness of its extent, for instance) of a doubtful nature, the way taken to clear the doubt was to affirm it to be a provision fit to be made law for all men: for all Frenchmen, and for all Englishmen, for example, into the bargain.[3]

Hasty generalization, the great stumbling-block of intellectual vanity! hasty generalization, the rock that even genius itself is so apt to split upon! hasty generalization, the bane of prudence and of science!

In the British Houses of Parliament, more especially in the most efficient house for business,[4] there prevails a well-known jealousy of and repugnance to the voting of abstract propositions. This jealousy is not less general than reasonable. A jealousy of abstract propositions is a jealousy of impertinence — I mean the original and strictly proper sense of impertinence. An aversion to abstract propositions is an aversion to whatever is beside the purpose: an aversion to impertinence.

The great enemies of public peace are the selfish and the hostile passions: necessary as they are, the one to the very existence of each individual, the other to his security. On the part of these affections, a deficiency in point of strength is never to be apprehended: all that is ever to be apprehended in respect of them, is to be apprehended on the side of their excess. Society is held together only by the sacrifices that men can be induced to make of the gratifications they demand: to obtain these sacrifices is the great difficulty, the great task of government. What has been the object, the perpetual and palpable object, of this Declaration of pretended Rights? To add as much force as possible to these passions already but too strong: to burst the cords that hold them in: to say to the selfish passions, there — every where, is your prey: to the angry passions, there, every where, is your enemy.

Such is the morality of this celebrated composition rendered famous by the same qualities that gave celebrity to the incendiary of the Ephesian temple.[5]

The logic of it is of a piece with the morality of it: a perpetual vein of nonsense flowing from a perpetual abuse of words. Words having a variety of meanings where words with single meanings were equally at hand: the same word used in a variety of meanings in the same page: words used in meanings not their own where proper words were equally at hand: words and propositions of the most unbounded signification turned loose without any of those exceptions or modifications which are so necessary on every occasion to reduce their import within the compass not only of right reason, but even of the design in hand, of whatever nature it may be. The same inaccuracy, the same inattention, in the penning of this cluster of oracles on which the fate of nations was to hang, as if it had been an oriental tale or an allegory for a magazine: stale conceits instead of necessary distinctions: figurative language preferred to simple: sentimental conceits as trite as they are unmeaning preferred to apt and precise expressions: frippery ornament preferred to the majestic simplicity of sound sense: the acts of the senate loaded and disfigured by the tinsel of the play-house.

In a play or a novel an improper word is but a word: and the impropriety, whether noticed or no, is attended with no consequences. In a body of laws, especially of laws given as constitutional and fundamental ones, an improper word may be a national calamity: and civil war may be the consequence of it. Out of one foolish word may start a thousand daggers.

Imputations like these may appear general and declamatory; and rightly so, if they stood alone: but they will be justified even to satiety, by the details that follow. Scarce an article which, on rummaging it, will not be found a true Pandora's Box.[6] Were this to be taken for the standard, not a law, good or bad, past, present or future — real or imaginable — that would not find its condemnation in some part or other of this tabernacle of the laws of nature. Not a law ever has been or would be passed here or any where against which insurrection would not be the most sacred [. . . ?].

In running over the several articles I shall, on the occasion of each article, point out in the first place the errors it contains in theory, and thence in the second place the mischiefs it is pregnant with in practice.

The criticism is verbal: true — but what else can it be? Words — words without a meaning — or with a meaning too flatly false to be maintained by any body, are the stuff it's made of. Look to the letter, you find nonsense: — look beyond the letter, you find nothing.

Art. 1. Men (all men) are born and remain free and equal in respect of rights. Social distinctions can not be founded but upon common utility.[7]

In this article are contained (we see) two distinct sentences, grammatically speaking. The first is full of error, the other of ambiguity.

In the first are contained four distinguishable propositions. All of them false, all of them notoriously and undeniably false.

1. That all men are born free. —

2. That all men remain free. —

3. That all men are born equal in rights. —

4. That all men remain (i:e: remain for ever, for the proposition is indefinite and unlimited) equal in rights.

1. & 2. All men born free?

All men remain free? — No, not a single man. Not a single man that ever was, or is, or will be. All men, on the contrary, are born in subjection, and the most absolute subjection: the subjection of a helpless child to the parents on whom he depends every moment for his existence. In this subjection every man is born, in this subjection he continues for years, for a great number of years — and the existence of the individual and of the species depends upon his so doing.[8]

What is the state of things to which the supposed existence of these supposed rights is meant to bear reference? A state of things prior to the existence of government or a state of things subsequent to the existence of government? If to a state of things prior to the existence of government, what would the existence of such rights as these be to the purpose, even if it were true, in any country where there is such a thing as government?

If to a state of things subsequent to the formation of government, if in a country where there is a government, in what single instance — in the instance of what single government — is it true? Setting aside the case of parents and child, let any man name that single government under which any such equality exists, in which any such equality is recognized.[9]

All men born free? — absurd and miserable nonsense! when the great lamentation, a complaint made perhaps by the very same people at the same time, is that so many men are born slaves. Oh, but when we acknowledge them to be born slaves, we refer to the laws in being: which laws being void, as being contrary to those laws of nature which are the efficient causes of these rights of man that we are declaring, the men in question are slaves in one sense, though free in another: slaves and free at the same time: free in respect of the laws of nature, slaves in respect of the pretended human laws, which though called laws are no laws at all, as being contrary to the laws of nature. For such is the difference, the great and perpetual difference, betwixt the good subject, the rational censor of the laws, and the anarchist: between the moderate man and the man of violence. The rational censor, acknowledging the existence of the law he disapproves of, proposes the repeal of it. The anarchist, setting up his will and fancy for a law before which all mankind are called upon to bow down at the first word — the anarchist, trampling on truth and decency, denies the validity of the law in question, denies the existence of it in the character of a law, summoning all mankind to rise up in a mass and resist the execution of it.

Whatever is, is — was the maxim of Des Cartes, who looked upon it as so certain as well as so instructive a truth that every thing else that goes by the name of knowledge might be deduced from it.[10] The philosophical vortex-maker, who, however mistaken in his philosophy and his logic, was harmless enough at least, the manufacturer of identical propositions and celestial vortexes little thought how soon a part of his own countrymen, fraught with pretensions as empty as his own and as mischievous as his were innocent, would contest with him even this his favourite and fundamental maxim by which every thing else was to be brought to light. *Whatever is, is not* — is the maxim of the anarchist, as often as any thing comes across him in the shape of a law which he happens not to like.

Cruel is the Judge, says Lord Bacon, who, in order to enable himself to torture men, applies torture to the laws.[11] Still more cruel is the anarchist, who, for the purpose of effecting the subversion of the laws themselves as well as the massacre of the legislators, tortures not only the words of the law but the very vitals of the language.

3. All men are born equal in rights. The rights of the heir of the most indigent family equal to the rights of the heir of the most wealthy. In what sense is this true? I say nothing of hereditary *dignities* and *powers*.

Inequalities such as these being proscribed under and by the French government in France,[12] are consequently proscribed by that government under every other government, and consequently have no existence any where. For the total subjection of every other government to French government is a fundamental principle in the law of universal independence, the French Law. Yet neither was this true at the time of issuing this Declaration of Rights, nor was it meant to be so afterwards. The 13th Article, which we shall come to in its place,[13] proceeds on the contrary supposition. For, considering its other attributes, inconsistency could not be wanting to the list. It can scarcely [be] more hostile to all other laws than it is at variance with itself.

4. All men (i:e: all human creatures of both sexes) remain equal in rights. All men, meaning doubtless all human creatures. The apprentice then is equal in rights to his Master: he has as much liberty with relation to the Master as the Master has with relation to him. He has as much right to command and punish the Master, as the Master has to command and punish him. He is as much Owner and Master of the Master's house, as the Master himself is. The case is the same as between Ward on the death of a Father, and Guardian. So again, as between Wife and Husband. The Madman has as good a right to Confine any body else as any body has to confine him. The Idiot has as much right to govern every body as any body can have to govern him. The Physician and the Nurse, when called in by the next friends of a sick man seized with a delirium, have no more right to prevent his throwing himself out of the window than he has to throw them out of it. All this is plainly and incontestably included in this article of the declaration of rights: in the very words of it and in the meaning, if it has any meaning. Was this the meaning of the Authors of it? Or did they mean to admitt this explanation as to some of the instances, and to explain the article away as to the rest. Not being Idiots, nor Lunatics, nor under a delirium, they would explain it away with regard to the madman and the man under a Delirium. Considering that a child may become an orphan as soon as it has seen the light, and that in that case, if not subject to government, it must perish, they would explain it away, I think, and contradict themselves, in the case of Guardian and Ward. In the case of Master and Apprentice, I would not take upon me to decide. It may have been their meaning to proscribe that relation altogether. At least, this may have been the case as soon as the repugnancy between that institution and this Oracle was pointed out. For the professed object and destination of it is to be the standard of truth and falshood, of right and wrong, in every thing that relates to government. But to this standard and to this article of it, the subjection of the Apprentice to the Master is flatly and diametrically repugnant. If it does not proscribe this

servitude, this inequality, it proscribes none. If it does not do this mischief, it does nothing.

So again in the case of Husband and Wife. Amongst the other abuses which this Oracle was meant to put an end to may, for aught I can pretend to say, have been the institution of marriage. For what is the subjection of a small and limited number of years in comparison of the subjection of a whole life? Yet without subjection and inequality no such institution can by any possibility take place: for of two contradictory wills, both can not be done at the same time.

The same doubts apply with regard to the case of Master and hired servant. Better a man should starve than hire himself, better half the species starve than hire itself out to service. For where is the compatibility between liberty and servitude? For how can liberty and servitude subsist in the same person? For what good citizen is there that would hesitate to die for liberty? And as to those who are not good citizens, what matters it whether they live or starve? Besides that every man who lives under this constitution, being equal in rights, equal in all sorts of rights, is equal in respect to rights of property. No man therefore can be in any danger of starving: no man can have so much as that motive, weak and inadequate as it is, for letting himself out to service.

Sentence 2$^{d.}$

Social distinctions can not be founded but upon common utility. This proposition has two or three meanings. According to one of them the proposition is notoriously false: according to another it is irreconcileable to the four propositions that preceded it in the same sentence.

What is meant by *social distinctions*? — what is meant by *can*? What is meant by *founded*?

What is meant by *social distinctions*? Distinctions not respecting equality? — then they are nothing to the purpose. — Distinctions in respect of equality? — then, consistently with the preceding propositions in this same article, they can have no existence: not existing, they can not be founded upon any thing. The distinctions above exemplified, are they in the number of the social distinctions here intended? — Not one of them (as we have been seeing) but has subjection, not one of them but has inequality, for its very essence.

What is meant by *can*? can not be founded but upon common utility? — Is it meant to declare what *is* established or what *ought to be* established? Does it mean that no social distinctions but those which it approves of as having the foundation in question *are* established any where, or simply that none such *ought to be* established any where, or that if the establishment or maintenance of such distinctions by the laws is attempted any where, such laws ought to be treated as void, and the attempt to execute them to be resisted? For such is the poison that lurks under such words as *can* and *can not* when set up as a check upon the laws. They present all these three so perfectly distinct and widely different meanings. In the first, the proposition they are inserted into referrs to practice, and makes appeal to observation: —to the observation of other men in regard to a matter of fact: in the second, it is an appeal to the approving faculty of others in regard to the same matter of fact: in the third, it is no appeal to any thing or to any body, but a violent attempt upon liberty of speech and action on the part of others by the terrors of anarchical despotism rising up in opposition to the laws. It is an attempt to lift the dagger of the assassin against all individuals who presume to hold an opinion different from that of the orator or the writer, and against all governments who presume to support any such individuals in any such presumption. In the first of these imports, the proposition is perfectly harmless: but it is commonly so untrue, so glaringly untrue, so palpably untrue, even to drivelling, that it must be plain to every body it can never have been this meaning that was intended. In the second of these imports, the proposition may be true or not, as it may happen, and at any rate is equally innocent: but it is such as will not answer the purpose: for an opinion that leaves others at liberty to be of a contrary one will never answer the purpose of the passions: and if this had been the meaning intended, not this ambiguous phraseology, but a clear and simple one presenting this meaning and no other would have been employ'd. The different imports seem to be designed for different classes of persons: the third, which may not improperly be termed the ruffian-like or threatening import, is the meaning intended to be presented to the weak and timid, while the two innocent ones, of which one may even be reasonable, are held up before it as a veil to blind the eyes of the discerning reader and screen from him the mischief that lurks beneath.

Can and *can not* when thus applied, *can* and *can not* when used instead of *ought* and *ought not*, *can* and *can not* when applied to the binding force and effect of laws—not of the acts of individuals, nor yet of the acts of subordinate authority, but of the acts of the supreme government itself, are the disguised cant of the Assassin: after them, there is nothing but *do him* betwixt the preparation for murder and the attempt. They resemble that instrument which in outward appearance is but an ordinary staff, but which within that simple and innocent semblance conceals a dagger. — These are the words that speak daggers, if daggers can be spoken: they speak daggers, and there remains nothing but to use them.[14]

Look w[h]ere I will, I see but too many laws the alteration or abolition of which would, in my poor judgment, be a public blessing. I can conceive some, to put extreme and scarcely exampled cases, to which I might be inclined to oppose resistance, with a prospect of support such as promised to be effectual. But to talk of what the law — the supreme legislature of the country, acknowledged as such — *can* not do! — to talk of a *void* law, as you would of a void order or a void judgment! — the very act of bringing such words into conjunction is either the vilest of nonsense, or the worst of treason: — treason — not against one branch of the sovereignty, but against the whole: — treason not against this or that government, but against all governments.

Art. 2. The end in view of every political association is the preservation of the natural and imprescriptible rights of man. These rights are, liberty, property, security, and resistance to oppression.[15]

Sentence 1. The end in view of every political association is the preservation of the natural and imprescriptible rights of man.

They can scarcely be said to have a meaning: but if they have, or rather if they had, a meaning, these would be propositions either asserted or implied.

1. That there are such things as rights anterior to the establishment of governments: for *natural* as applied to rights, if it means any thing, is meant to stand in opposition to *legal* — to such rights as are acknowledged to owe their existence to government, and are consequently posterior in their date to the establishment of government.

2. That these rights *can not* be abrogated by government: for *can not* is implied in the form of the word imprescriptible, and the sense it wears when so applied is the cut-throat sense above explained.

3. That the governments that exist derive their origin from formal meetings or what are now called *conventions*: associations entered into by a partnership contract, with all the members for partners: entered into at a day prefixed for a predetermined purpose, the formation of a new government. For as to formal meetings holden under the controul of an existing government, they are evidently out of question here. In which it seems again to be implied in the way of inference, though a necessary and unavoidable inference, that all governments (that is self-called governments, knots of persons exercising the powers of government) that have had any other origin than an association of the above description are illegal — that is no governments at all — resistance to them and subversion of them lawful and commendable, and so on.

[1.] Such are the notions implied in this first part of the article. — How stands the truth of things? — that there are no such things as natural rights — no such things as rights anterior to the establishment of government — no such things as natural rights opposed to, in contradistinction to, legal — that the expression is merely figurative — that the moment you attempt to give it a literal meaning, it leads to error, and to that sort of error that leads to the extremity of mischief.

We know what it is for men to live without government, and living without government to live without rights — we know what it is for men to live without government: for we see instances of such a way of life in abundance — we see it in many savage nations or rather races of mankind: for instance among the savages of New South Wales, whose way of living is so well known to us.[16] No habit of obedience, and thence no government: no government, and thence no laws nor any such things as rights. No security, no property: liberty, as against regular controul, the controul of laws and government, perfect: but as against all irregular controul, the mandates of stronger individuals, none. In this state, at a time earlier to the commencement of history, in this same state, judging from analogy, we, the inhabitants of the part of the globe we call Europe, were. No government, consequently no rights: no rights, consequently no property: no legal security, no legal liberty. Security not more than belongs to beasts: forecast and sense of insecurity keener: consequently, in point of happiness, below the level of the brutal race. In proportion to the want of happiness resulting from the want of rights, a reason for wishing that there were such things as rights. But reasons for wishing there were such things as rights, are not rights: a reason for wishing that a certain right were established, is not that right: wants are not means:[17] hunger is not bread.

2. That which has no existence can not be destroy'd: that which can not be destroy'd can not require any thing to preserve it from being destroy'd. Natural rights is simple nonsense: natural and imprescriptible rights, rhetorical nonsense, nonsense upon stilts. But this rhetorical nonsense ends in the old strain of mischievous nonsense. For immediately a list of these pretended natural rights is given, and these are so expressed as to present to view legal rights. And of these rights, whatever they are, there is not, it seems, any one of which any government *can* (in the cut-throat sense of the word *can) can* upon any occasion whatever abrogate the smallest particle.

So much for Terrorist language. What is the language of reason and plain sense upon this same subject? — That in proportion as it is *right* or *proper* — i:e: advantageous to the society in question — that this or that right, a right to this or that effect, should be established and maintained, in that same proportion it is *wrong* that it should be abrogated: but that as there is no *right* which ought not to be maintained so long as it is upon the whole advantageous to the society that it should be maintained, so there is no right which, when the abolition of it is advantageous to society, should not be abolished. To know whether it would be more for the advantage of society that this or that right should be maintained or abolished, the time at which the question about maintaining or abolishing it must be given, and the circumstances under which it is proposed to maintain or abolish it: the right itself must be specifically described: not jumbled with an undistinguishable heap of others under any such vague general terms as property, liberty and the like. One thing in the midst of all this confusion is but too plain. They know not what they are talking of under the name of natural rights, and yet they would have them imprescriptible: proof against all the power of the laws: pregnant with occasions summoning the members of the community to rise up in resistance to the laws. What then was their object in declaring the existence of imprescriptible rights, and without specifying a single one by any such mark as it could be known by? This and no other, to excite and keep up a spirit of resistance to all laws, a spirit of insurrection against all governments. Against the governments of all other nations, instantly: against the government of their own nation, against the government they themselves were pretending to establish, soon: that is as soon as their own reign should be at an end. In us is the perfection of virtue and wisdom: in all mankind besides the extremity of wickedness and folly. Our will shall consequently reign without controul and for ever: reign now we are living, reign when we are no more. All nations, all future ages, shall be, for they are predestined to be, our slaves.

Future governments will not have honesty enough to be trusted with the determination what rights shall be maintained, what abrogated: what laws kept in force, what repealed. Future subjects (I should say future citizens, for French government does not admitt of subjects) will not have wit enough to be trusted with the choice whether to submitt to the determinations of the government of their time or to resist it: governments, citizens, all to the end of time, all must be kept in chains.

Such were their maxims: such their premises: for it is by such premises only that the conclusion of imprescriptible rights and unrepealable laws can be supported. What is the true source of these imprescriptible rights, these unrepealable laws? — Power turned blind by looking from its own height: self-conceit and tyranny exalted into insanity. No man was to have any other man for a servant: yet all men were for ever to be their slaves. Making laws on pretence of declaring them: giving for laws, any thing that came uppermost and those unrepealable ones, on pretence of finding them ready made. — Made by what? — Not by a God, they allow of none: but by their Goddess, Nature.

[3.] The origination of governments from a contract is a pure fiction, or in other words a falshood. It never has been known to be true in any instance: the allegation of it does mischief by involving the subject in error and confusion, and is neither necessary nor useful to any one good purpose upon earth.

All governments that we have any account of have been gradually established by habit, after having been formed by force: unless it be in the instance of government formed by individuals that have been emancipated or emancipated themselves from governments already formed, the governments under which they were born: a rare case, and from which nothing follows with regard to the rest. What signifies it how governments were formed? Is it the less proper, the less conducive to the happiness of society, that the happiness of society should be the one object kept in view by the members of the government in all their measures? Is it less the interest of men to be happy, less to be wished that they may be so, less the moral duty of their governors to make them so as far as they can, at Mogador than in Philadelphia?

Whence is it but government that contracts derive their binding force? Contracts came from government, not government from contracts. It is to the habit of enforcing contracts and seeing them enforced that governments are chiefly indebted for whatever disposition they have to observe them.

Sentence the 2$^{d.}$ These rights (these imprescriptible as well as natural rights) are liberty, property, security and resistance to oppression.

Observe the extent of these pretended rights, each of them belonging to every man, and all of them without bounds. — Unbounded liberty: that is, amongst other things, the liberty of doing or not doing on every occasion as each man pleases: unbounded property, that is the right of doing with every thing around [him][18] (with every *thing* at least, if not with every *person)* whatever he pleases, communicating that right to any body, and withholding it from any body he pleases: unbounded security, that is security for such his liberty, for such his property, and for his person, against every danger to which any of those possessions can be exposed: unbounded resistance to oppression, that is an unbounded exercise of the faculty of guarding himself against whatever unpleasant circumstance may present itself to his imagination or his passions under that name. — Nature, say some of the interpreters of the pretended law of nature, Nature gave to each man a right to every thing:[19] which is in effect but another way of confessing, Nature has given no such thing to any body: for in regard to most rights it is as true that what is every man's right is no man's right, as that what is every man's business is no man's business. Nature gave, gave to every man, a right to every thing: be it so: and thence the necessity of human government and human laws to give to every man his own right, without which no right whatever would amount to any thing. Nature gave every man a right to every thing before the existence of laws, and in default of laws. This nominal universality and real nonentity of right set up provisionally by nature in default of laws, the French oracle lays hold of and perpetuates it under the laws and in spite of laws. These anarchical rights that Nature had set out with, shot down as so many rough materials out of which the fabric of society might be reared, art, Democratic art, attempts to rivet down and declares them indefeasible.

Unbounded liberty: I must still say, unbounded liberty. For though the next article but one returns to the charge, and gives such a definition of liberty as seems intended to set bounds to it, yet in effect the limitation amounts to nothing: and where as here no warning is given of any exception in the texture of the general rule, every exception that turns up is, not a confirmation but a contradiction of the rule. Liberty without any preannounced or intelligible bounds — and as to the other rights, they remain unbounded to the end — Rights of man composed of a system of contradictions and impossibilities!

In vain would it be said that though no bounds are here assigned to any of these rights, yet it is to be understood as taken for granted and tacitly admitted and assumed that they are to have bounds: viz: such bounds as it is understood will be set them by the laws. Vain, I say, would be the apology: for the supposition would be contradictory to the plain words of the article itself, and would be in the teeth of the very object which the whole declaration has in view. It would be self-contradictory because these rights are, in the same breath in which their existence is declared, declared to be imprescriptible: and imprescriptible, or as we in England should say indefeasible, means nothing unless it excludes the interference of the laws.

It would be not only inconsistent with itself, but inconsistent with the declared and sole object of the declaratory decree, if it did not exclude the interference of the laws. It is against the laws themselves and the laws only that this Declaration is levelled. It is for the hands of the legislator and all legislators and none but legislators that the shackles it provides are intended: it is against the apprehended encroachments of legislators that the rights in question, the liberty and property and so forth, are intended to be made secure: it is to such encroachments and damages and dangers that whatever security it professes to give has respect. Pretious security for rights against legislators, if the extent of those rights in every direction were purposely left to depend upon the will and pleasure of those very legislators!

Nonsensical or silly[20] — and in both cases mischievous — such is the alternative.

So much for all these pretended indefeasible rights in the lump: their inconsistency with each other, as well as the inconsistency of them in the character of indefeasible rights with the existence of government and all peaceable society, will appear still more plainly when we examine them one by one.

1. Liberty then is imprescriptible — incapable of being taken away — out of the power of every government ever to take away: liberty, that is every branch of liberty: every individual exercise of liberty: for no line is drawn, no distinction, no exception made. What these instructors as well as governors of mankind seem if possible not to know is that all rights are made at the expence of liberty: all laws by which rights are created or confirmed. No right without a correspondent obligation. Liberty as against the coercion of the law may, it is true, be given by the simple removal of the obligation by which that coercion was applied, by the simple repeal of the coercing law. But as against coercion applicable by individual to individual, no liberty can be given to one man but in proportion as it is taken from another. All coercive laws therefore (that is all laws but constitutional laws and laws repealing or modifying coercive ones), and in particular all laws creative of liberty, are, as far as they go, abrogative of liberty: not here and there a law only, not this or that possible law, but almost all laws are therefore repugnant to these natural and imprescriptible rights: consequently null and void, calling for resistance and insurrection; and so on, as before.

2. Property.[21] Property then, proprietary rights, are in the number of the natural and imprescriptible rights of man: of the rights which a man is not indebted for to the laws, and which can not be taken from him by the laws. Man, that is every man, (for a general expression given without exceptions is an universal one) has a right to property, to proprietary rights, and which can not be taken away from him by the laws. To proprietary rights — good — but in relation to what subject? for, proprietary rights without a subject to which they are referable, without a subject on or in relation to which they can be exercised, will hardly be of much value — will hardly be worth taking care of with so much solemnity. In vain would all the laws in the world have ascertained that I have a right to have something: if this is all they have done for me, if there be no specific subject in relation to which my

proprietary rights are established, I must either take what I want without right or starve. As there is no such subject specified with relation to each man or to any man (indeed how could there be?) so that the proposition is left as indefinite with regard to the designation of the subject of property as with regard to the designation of the owners, the necessary inference (taking the passage literally) is, that every man has all manner of proprietary rights with relation to every subject of property without exception: in a word that every man has a right to every thing.[22]

It will probably be acknowledged that, according to this construction, the clause in question is equally ruinous and absurd: and thence the inference may be, that this was not the construction, this was not the meaning, in view. But by the same rule every possible construction that the words employ'd can admitt of might be proved not to have been the meaning in view: nor is this clause awhit more absurd or ruinous than all that goes before it, and a great deal of what comes after it. And in short, if this be not the meaning of it, what is? Give it a sense, give it any sense whatever, it is mischievous: to save it from that imputation there is but one course to take, which is to acknowledge it to be nonsense.

Thus much would be clear, if any thing were clear in it, that according to this clause whatever proprietary rights, whatever property, a man once has, no matter how, being imprescriptible, can never be taken away from him by any law: or of what use or meaning is the clause? so that the moment it is acknowledged in relation to any article that that article is my property, no matter how or whence it became so, that moment it is acknowledged that it can never be taken away from me: therefore, for example, all laws and all judgments, whereby any thing is taken away from me without my free consent, all taxes for example and all fines, are void, and as such call for resistance and insurrection, and so on as before.

3. Security. Security stands the third in the list of those natural and imprescriptible rights which laws did not give and which laws are not in any degree to be suffered to take away. Under the head of security, liberty might have been included, so likewise property: since security for liberty or the enjoyment of liberty may be spoken of as one branch of security: security for property or the enjoyment of proprietary rights as another. Security for person is the branch that seems here to have been understood: security for each man as against all those hurtful or disagreable impressions (exclusive of those which consist in the mere disturbance of the enjoyment of liberty) by which a man is affected in his person, which have a man's person for their subject: loss of life — loss of limbs — loss of the use of limbs — wounds, bruizes and the like. All laws are null and void then which on any

account or in any manner seek to expose the person of any man to any risk: which appoint capital or other corporal punishment: which expose a man to personal hazard in the service of the military power against foreign enemies, or in that of the judicial power against delinquents: all laws which, to preserve the country from pestilence, authorize the immediate execution of a suspected person in the event of his transgressing certain bounds.

4. Resistance to oppression. Fourth and last in the list of natural and imprescriptible rights, resistance to oppression: meaning, I suppose, the right to resist oppression. What is oppression? power misapplied to the prejudice of some individual. What is it that a man has in view when he speaks of oppression? some exertion of power which he looks upon as misapplied to the prejudice of some individual: to the subjecting on the part of such individual some suffering [to] which (whether as forbidden by the laws or otherwise) we conceive he ought not to have been subjected. But against every thing that can come under the name of oppression, provision has been made already, in the manner we have seen, by the recognition made of the three preceding rights: since no oppression can fall upon a man which is not an infringement of his rights in relation to liberty, rights in relation to property or rights in relation to security, as above described. Where then is the difference? — to what purpose this fourth clause after the three first? — to this purpose: the rights they seek to establish — the mischief they seek to prevent — are the same, the difference lies in the nature of the remedy endeavoured to be applied. To prevent the mischief in question, the endeavour of the three former clauses is to tie the hand of the legislator and his subordinates by the fear of nullity, and the remote apprehension of general resistance and insurrection: the aim of this fourth clause is to raise the hand of the individual concerned to prevent the apprehended infraction of his rights at the moment when he looks upon it as about to take place. Whenever you are about to be oppressed, you have a right to resist the oppression: therefore, whenever you conceive yourself to be oppressed, conceive yourself to have a right to make resistance, and act accordingly. In proportion as a law of any kind, any act of power supreme or subordinate, legislative, administrative or judicial, is disagreable to a man, especially if, in consideration of such its unpleasantness, his opinion is that such act of power ought not to have been exercised, he of course looks upon it as oppressive. As often as any thing of this sort happens to a man, as often as any thing happens to a man to inflame his passions, this article, for fear his passions should not be sufficiently inflamed of themselves, sets itself to work to fan the flame, and urges him to resistance. Submitt not to any decree or other act of power of the justice of which you are not yourself

perfectly convinced. If a Constable calls upon you to serve in the militia, shoot the Constable, and not the enemy. If the Commander of a Press-Gang troubles you, push him into the sea: if a Bailiff, throw him out the window. If a Judge sentences you to be imprisoned or put to death, have a dagger ready, and take a stroke first at the Judge.

Art. 3. The principle of every sovereignty (government) resides essentially in the nation. No body of men, no single individual, can exercise any authority which does not issue from thence in an express manner.[23]

Of the two sentences of which this article is composed, the first is perfectly true, perfectly harmless and perfectly uninstructive. Government and obedience go hand in hand. Where there is no obedience, there is no government: in proportion as obedience is paid, the powers of government are exercised. This is true under the broadest democracy: this is equally true under the most absolute Monarchy. This can do no harm any where: nor any good. I speak of its natural and obvious import taken by itself, and supposing the import of the word *principle* to be as clear and unambiguous as it is to be wished it were, that is taking it to mean *efficient cause*. Of power on the one part, obedience on the other is most certainly every where the efficient cause.

But being harmless it would not answer the purpose, as declared by the immediately succeeding sentence: being harmless, this meaning is not that which was in view. It is meant as an antecedent proposition, on which the next proposition is grounded in the character of a consequent. No body of men, no individual, *can* exercise any authority which does not issue from the nation in an express manner. Can: still the ambiguous and envenomed *can*. What can not they in point of fact? can not they exercise authority over other people if and so long as other people submitt to it? This can never be the meaning. This can not be the meaning not because it is an untrue and foolish one, but because it contributes nothing to the declared purpose. The meaning must be here as elsewhere, that of every authority not issuing from the nation in an express manner every act is void: consequently ought to be treated as such, resisted, risen up against, and overthrown. Issuing from the nation in an express manner is having been conferred by the nation by a formal act in the exercise of which the nation, i:e: the whole nation, joined. An authority issues from the nation in one sense, in the ordinary implied manner, which the nation submitts to the exercise of, having been in the habit of submitting to it, every man as long as he can remember, or to some superior authority from which it is derived. But this meaning it was the evident design of the article to put a negative upon: for it would not have answered the disorganizing purpose all along apparent and more than once avowed. It is accordingly for the purpose of putting a negative upon it that the word *expressément, in an express way or manner*, is subjoined. Every authority usurped to which a man has been appointed in any other mode than that of popular election: and popular election made by the nation, that is the whole nation (for no distinction or division is intimated) in each case.

And this is expressly declared to be the case — not only in *France*, under the government of France, but *every where*, and under every government whatsoever. Consequently all the acts of every government in Europe, for example, are void, excepted perhaps, or rather not excepted, two or three of the Swiss Cantons: the persons exercising the powers of government in those countries, usurpers: resistance to them and insurrection against them, lawful and commendable.

The French government itself not excepted: whatever is, has been or is to be the Government of France. Issue from *the* nation: that is from the *whole* nation, for no part of it is excluded. Women consequently included and children: children of every age. For if women and children are not part of the nation, what are they? Cattle? Indeed, how can a single soul be excluded, when all men, all human creatures, are and are to be equal in regard to rights? in regard to all sorts of rights, without exception or reserve.

Art. 4. Liberty consists in being able to do that which is not hurtful to another: therefore the exercise of the natural rights of each man has no other bounds than those which insure to the other members of the Society the enjoyment of the same rights. These bounds can not be determined but by the law.[24]

In this article three propositions are included.

Proposition the 1st. Liberty consists in being able to do that which is not hurtful to another. — What in that and nothing else? is not the liberty of doing mischief liberty? if not, what is it? and what word is there for it in the language, or in any language, by which it can be spoken of? — How childish, how repugnant to the ends of language, is this perversion of language! To attempt to confine a word in common and perpetual use to an import to which nobody ever confined it before, or will continue to confine it. And so I am never to know whether I am at liberty or no to do or to omitt doing an act till I see whether or no there is any body that may be hurt by it? till I see to the whole extent of all its consequences! Liberty? — what liberty? as against what power? — as against coercion from what source? — as against coercion issuing from the law? then, to know whether the law has left me at liberty in any respect in relation to any act, I am to consult not the words of the law, but my own conception of what would be the consequences of the act: if among these consequences there be a single one by which any body would be hurt, then, whatever the law says to me about it, I am not at liberty to do it. If an officer of justice is ordered to cause a thief to be whipped, to know whether he is at liberty to cause the sentence to be executed, he must know whether whipping would hurt the thief: if it would, then the officer is not at liberty to inflict the punishment which it is his duty to inflict.

Proposition 2$^{d.}$ And so the exercise of the natural rights of each individual has no other bounds than those which insure to the other members of the Society the enjoyment of those same rights. — Has no other bounds? — where is it that it has no other bounds? in what nation? under what government? — If under any government, then the state of legislation is in a state of absolute perfection. If there be no such government, then, by a confession necessarily implied, there is no nation upon earth in which this definition is conformable to the truth.

[Proposition]^{25} 3$^{d.}$ These bounds can not be determined but by the law. — More contradiction, more confusion. What then? this liberty, this right which is one of four rights that existed before laws and will exist in spite of all that laws can do, owes all the boundaries it has, all the extent it has, to the laws. Till you know what the laws say to it, you don't know what there is of it, nor what account to give of it: and yet it existed, and that in full force and vigour, before there were any such things as laws: and so will continue to exist, and that for ever, in spite of any thing which laws can do to it. Still the same inaptitude of expression: still the same confusion of that which, it is supposed, *is*, with that which, it is conceived, *ought to be*.

What says plain truth upon this subject? what is the sense the most approaching to this nonsense?

The liberty which the law *ought* to allow of and leave in existence, leave uncoerced, unremoved, is the liberty which concerns those acts only by which, if exercised, no damage would be done to the community upon the whole: that is either no damage at all, or none but what promises to be compensated by at least equal benefit.

Accordingly the exercise of the rights allowed to and conferred upon each individual ought to have no other bounds set to it by the law than those which are necessary to enable it to maintain every other individual in the possession and exercise of such rights as the regard due to the interests or greatest possible happiness of the whole community taken together admitt of his being allowed. The marking out of these bounds ought not to be left to any body but the legislator acting as such, to any body but him or them who are acknowledged to be in possession of the sovereign power: that is it [ought] not to be left to the occasional and arbitrary declaration of any individual, whatever share he may possess of subordinate authority.

The word *autrui*, another, is so loose, making no distinction between the community and individuals, as, according to the most natural construction, to deprive succeeding legislators of all power of repressing, by punishment or otherwise, any acts by which no individual sufferers are to be found, and to deprive them beyond a doubt of all power of affording protection to any man, woman or child against his or her own weakness, ignorance or imprudence. Acts of a pernicious tendency, acts fit to be placed by government in the catalogue of offences, may be divided into four great classes: acts prejudicial in the first instance to assignable individuals, acts prejudicial to individuals unassignable but included within the bounds which mark out a division of the community, acts prejudicial to the community in general, acts prejudicial to the agent himself: acts which, when respectively aggregated to the list of offenses, are referable to the several classes of offences against individuals, offences against a neighbourhood or other particular class of men, offences against the community at large, or offences against a man's self.[26]

Art. 5. The law has no right to forbid any other actions than such as are hurtful to Society. Whatever is not forbidden by the law can not be hindered, nor can any individual be compelled to do that which the law does not command.[27]

Sentence the 1st. The law has no right (*n'a le droit*) to forbid any other actions than such as are hurtful to society. The law has no right (*n'a le droit*, not *ne peut pas*). This for once is free from ambiguity. Here the mask of ambiguity is thrown off. The avowed object of this clause is to preach constant insurrection, to raise up every man in arms against every law which he happens not to approve of. For take any such action you will, if the law has no right to forbid it, a law forbidding it is null and void, and the attempt to execute it, an oppression, and resistance to such attempt and insurrection in support of such resistance legal, justifiable and commendable.

To have said that the law ought not to forbid any act that is not of a nature prejudicial to society would have answered every good purpose, but would not have answered the purpose which is intended to be answered here.

A government which should fulfill the expectations here held out would be a government of absolute perfection. The instance of a government's fulfilling these expectations never has take[n] place, nor till men are Angels ever can take place. Against every government which fails in any degree of fulfilling these expectations, it is the direct object of this manifesto to excite insurrection: here as elsewhere it is therefore its direct object to excite insurrection at all times against every government whatsoever.

Sentence 2. Whatever is not forbidden by the law can not be hindered, nor can any individual be compelled to do that [which] the law does not command.

The effect of this law, for want of the requisite exceptions or explanations, is to annihilate for the time being and for ever all powers of command, all power the exercise of which consists in the issuing and enforcing obedience to particular and occasional commands: — domestic power, judicial power, power of the police, military power, power of superior officers in the line of civil administration over their subordinates. If I say to my son, do not mount that horse which you are not strong enough to manage, if I say to my daughter, don't go to that pond where there is a young man a-bathing, they may set me at defiance, bidding me shew them where there is any thing about mounting unruly horses, or going where there are young men a-bathing, in the laws. By the same clause they may each of them justify themselves in turning their back upon the lesson I have given them, while my apprentice refuses to do the work I have given him, and my wife, instead of providing the supper I had desired her to provide for ourselves and family, thinks fit to go and sup with another man whose company is more to her taste. In the existing order of things under any other government than that which was here to be organized, whatever is commanded or forbidden in virtue of a power which the law allows of and recognizes, is virtually and in effect commanded and forbidden by the law itself, since, by the support it gives to the persons in question in the execution of their respective authorities, it shews itself to have adopted those commands and considered them as its own before they are issued, and whatever may be the purport of them, so long as they are confined within the limits which it has marked out. But all these existing institutions, being fundamentally repugnant to the rights of man, are null and void, and incapable of filling up this or any other gap in the texture of this new code. Besides this right of not being hindered from doing any thing which the law itself has not forbidden, nor compelled to do any thing which it has not itself commanded, is an article in the list of natural, inalienable, sacred and imprescriptible rights over which political laws have no sort of power: so that the attempt to fill up the gap, and to establish any such power of commanding or forbidding what is not already commanded or forbidden by the laws, would be an act of usurpation, and all such pretended establishment of powers, null and void. And how can any such powers subsist in a society of which all the members are free and equal in point of rights?

Admitt however that room is given for the creation of the powers in question by the spirit, though not by the letter, of this clause, what follows? — that in proportion as it is harmless it is insignificant, and incapable of answering its intended purpose. This purpose is to protect individuals against oppressions to which they might be subjected by other individuals possessed of powers created by the law in the exercise or pretended exercise of those powers. But if these powers are left to the determination of succeeding and, according to the plan of this code, inferior legislatures, and may be of any nature and to any extent which these legislatures may have thought fit to give them, what does the protection here given amount to, especially as against such future legislatures, for whose hands all the restraints which it is the object of this declaration to administer are intended? Mischievous or nugatory — still the old alternative.

The employ of the improper word *can* instead of the proper word *shall* is not unworthy of observation. *Shall* is the language of the legislator knowing what he is about, carrying on his business, and aiming at nothing more. *Can*, when properly employ'd in a book of law, is the language of the private commentator or expositor drawing inferences from the text of the law, from the acts of the legislator, or what takes the place of the acts of the legislator, the practice of the courts of justice.

Art. 6. The law *is* the expression of the general will. Every citizen has a right of concurring in person, or by his representatives, in the formation of it. — It ought to be the same for all, whether it protects, or whether it punishes. All the citizens being equal in its eyes, are equally admissible to all dignities, public places and employments, according to their capacity, and without any other distinction than that of their virtues and their talents.[28]

This article is a hodge-podge containing a variety of provisions, as wide from one another as any can be within the whole circuit of the law: some relating to the constitutional branch, some to the civil, some to the penal: and in the constitutional department, some relating to the organization of the supreme power, others to that of the subordinate branches.

Proposition 1. *The* law is the expression of the general will. *The* law? — what law? *is* the expression of the general will? — where is it so? In what country? at what period of time? In no country: at no period of time? In no other country than France: nor even in France. As to general, it means universal: for there are no exceptions made: women, children, madmen, criminals: for these, being human creatures, have already been declared equal in respect of rights. Nature made them so: and even were it to be wished they were otherwise, nature's work being unalterable, and the rights unalienable, it would be to no purpose to attempt it.

What is certain is, that in any other nation at any rate no such a thing as a law ever existed to which this definition could be applied. But that is nothing to the purpose: since a favourite object of this effusion of universal benevolence is to declare the governments of all other countries dissolved and to persuade the people that the dissolution has taken place.

But any where, even in France, how can the law be the expression of the universal, or even the general, will of all the people, when by far the greatest part have never entertained any will at all about the matter, and of those who have, a great part (as is the case with almost all laws made by a large assembly) would rather it had not taken place?

Sentence 2. All the citizens *have a right* to concurr in person or by their representatives in the formation of it. — Here the language changes — from the enuntiation of the supposed practice, to the enuntiation of the supposed right. — Why does it change? After having said so silly a thing as that there is no law any where but what was the expression of the will of every body, what should have hindered its going on in the same silly strain and saying that every body did concurr, did join, in the formation of it? — However, as the idea of right is in this second sentence at any rate presented by its appropriate term, the ambiguity diffused by the preceding sentence is dissipated, and now it appears beyond a doubt, that every law in the formation of which any one citizen was debarred from concurring either in person or by his representatives, is and ever will be, here and there and every where, a void law.

To characterize proxies the French language, like the English, has two words, representatives and deputies: the one liable to misconstruction, the other not: to misconstruction, and to such misconstruction as to be made expressive of a sense directly opposite to that which appears here to have been intended: the one tainted with fiction as well as ambiguity, the other expressing nothing but the plain truth. — Being so superior to imitation, so free to choose, not tied down by usage as people in Britain are, how come they to have taken the English word representatives, which has given occasion to so many quibbles, instead of their own good word Deputies, which can not give occasion to any thing like a quibble? The King of Great Britain is acknowledged to be the representative of the British nation in treating with foreign powers, but does the whole nation ever meet together and join in signing an authority to him so to do? The King of Great Britain is acknowledged in this instance to represent the British Nation: but is he in this instance ever pretended to have been deputed by it? The Parliamentary electors have been said to represent the non-electors, and the members of Parliament to represent both: but did any body ever speak of either Members or Electors as being the deputies of the non-electors? Using the improper word representatives instead of the proper word deputies, the French might be saddled with the British Constitution for any thing there is in this clause to protect them from so horrible a grievance. Representatives sounded better perhaps than Deputies. Men who are governed by sounds sacrifice every thing to sound. They neither know the value of precision, nor are able to attain it.

Sentence 3. It (the law) ought to be the same for all whether it protects, or whether it punishes: i:e: as well in respect of the protections it affords, as in respect of the punishments it inflicts.

This clause appears reasonable in the main, but in respect to certain points it may be susceptible of explanations and exceptions, from the discussion of which it might have been as well if all posterity had not been debarred.

As to protection, English law affords a punishment which consists in being put out of the protection of the law: in virtue of which a man is debarred from applying for redress from any kinds of injuries.[29] For my own part I do not approve of it: but perhaps they do who, having it in their power to abrogate it, retain it. In France, I suppose, it is approved of where, in a much severer form than the English, it has been so much practised.[30] This species of punishment is inhibited for ever, by the letter at least of this clause. As to [the] spirit of it, one of the ruling features of this composition from end to end is that the spirit of it is incomprehensible.

Under the English law, heavier damages are given in many instances to the Ministers of Justice acting as such in case of ill-founded prosecutions against them for supposed injuries to individuals than would be given to individuals aggrieved by prosecutions for the same injuries.[31] The notion evidently is that the servants of the public, not having so strong an interest in defending the rights of the public as individuals have in defending their own, the public man would be apt to be deterred from doing his duty if the encouragement he has to do it were no greater than the encouragement which the individual has to defend his right. These examples, not to plunge further into details, appear sufficient to suggest a reasonable doubt whether, even in this instance, the smack smooth equality which rolls so glibly out of the lips of the rhetorician be altogether compatible with that conformity to every bend and turn in the line of utility which ought to be the object of the legislator.

As to punishment, a rule as strictly subordinate to the dictates of utility as the doctrine of undeviating equality is congenial to the capricious play of the imagination, is not in any instance to employ more punishment than is necessary to the purpose. Where as between two individuals there is a known difference in point of sensibility, the result of their respective situations, a punishment which in name, that is according to every description which could be given of it in and by the law, would be equal in the two instances, would in effect be widely different. Fifty lashes may in the estimatation of the law be equal to fifty lashes: but it is what no man can suppose, that the suffering that a hard-working young man, or even a young woman of the hard-working class, would undergo from the infliction of so many lashes, could be really equal in intensity to that which must have been endured from the same nominal punishment (were even the instrument and force applied the same) by the Countess Lapuchin, till then one of the fairest ornaments of the Court of a Russian Empress.[32] Banishment would upon the face of the law be equal to banishment: but it is not altogether so certain that to a servant of the public who happens to have nothing to live upon but a salary requiring residence, it would be no greater punishment than to the sturdy labourer who in one country as well as in another may derive an equal livelihood from the labour of his hands.

Those, if any such there are, to whom distinctions such as these would appear consonant to reason and utility, might perhaps regard them as not irreconcileable with the language of this clause. But others might think them either not reasonable, or though reasonable not thus reconcileable. And were any such distinctions to be engrafted onto the law by any succeeding legislature, those who did not approve of the alteration would, if at all actuated by regard to the tenor and spirit of this code, raise a cry of aristocracy, and pronounce the alteration void: and then comes resistance and insurrection and so on as before.[a]

a. D[r] Hunter, the celebrated Anatomist, used to tell a story in his lectures,[33] which shews the power of the imagination, and how widely its suggestions are apt to differ from those of reason and utility. A Surgeon, being called in to a patient who had hurt his hand, found all the fingers but the little one injured beyond recovery: he accordingly cut them off: and when they were dispatched, seeing the little finger standing up so awkwardly above the rest of the hand, after the others were gone, that he went on cutting, and dispatched that likewise. Imagination was quicker than Reason, and shut the door against her.

Sentence 4. The citizens being all of them equal in its sight, are all of them admissible to all dignities, public places and employments, according to their capacity, and without any other distinction than that of their talents and their virtues.

This is one of the few clauses, not to say the only one, which does not seem liable to very serious objection: nothing to the general spirit, though perhaps something to the expression. As to classes of men in general, it were to be wished that no class of men should stand incapacitated with regard to any object of competition by any general law: nor can any thing be said in favour of those hereditary incapacitations which suggested and provoked this clause. Yet as governments are constituted, and as the current of opinion runs, there may be cases where some sort of incapacitations in regard to Offices seem called for by the object which operated as the final cause in the institution of the Office. It seems hardly decent or consistent, for example, to allow to a Jew the faculty of nominating to a Christian benefice with cure of souls: though by a judgment of no very antient Date, the law of England was made to lend its sanction to an appointment of this sort.[34] As inconsistent does it appear to admitt of a Catholic patron's presenting to a Protestant, or a [Protestant to a Catholic][35] benefice: at least so long as diversities in matters of religion are regarded as a matter of importance, or those diversities continue to have ill-will for their accompaniment. Ecclesiastical patronage in the hands of individuals is indeed one of the abuses, or supposed abuses, which it was the object of this code to eradicate: and since then the maintenance of an Ecclesiastical establishment of any kind at the expence of the state has in France been added to the catalogue of abuse.[36] But at the time of the promulgation of this code the spirit of subversion had not proceeded this length: Ecclesiastical offices were still kept up, though in relation to these together with as well all other offices the right of nomination was given to assemblies of the people.[37] The incongruity of admitting the professor of a rival religion to the right of suffrage would therefore be the same in this instance as in the case where the nomination centered in a single breast, though the danger would seldom be of equal magnitude. It would be like admitting an enemy's general to contract for the supply of arms and ammunition.

Madmen and criminals of the worst description are equally protected against exclusion from any office or the exercise of any political right. As to offices which under this system a man can not come into possession of but by election, the inconvenience, it may be said, can not be great: for though not incapable of being elected, there is no danger of his being so. But this is not the case with regard to any of those political privileges which this system gives a man in his own right, and as a present handed over to him from the hands of nature: such as the right of suffrage with regard to Offices. Were an assassin covered with the blood of the murdered person and ordered for execution on the 2^d of the month, or what is doubtless worse a Royalist convicted of adherence to the government under which his country had flourished for so many hundred years, to put in his claim for admittance to give his suffrage in the election of a Deputy to the Convention or of a Mayor of the Paris Municipality, I see not how his claim could be rejected without an infringement of this clause: indeed if this right like all the others is, as we are told over and over again, a present of the Goddess Nature and proof against all attacks of law, what is to be done, and what remedy can be administered, by the laws? Something it is true is said of talents and of virtues: and the madman, it may be said, is deficient in point of talents and the criminal in point of virtues. But neither talents nor virtues are mentioned otherwise than as marks of pre-eminence and distinction recommending the possessors to a proportionable degree of favour and approbation with a view to preference: nothing is said of any deficiency in point of talent or of virtue as capable of shutting the door against a candidate outright: distinction is the word, not exception — distinction among persons all within the list, not exception excluding persons out of the list.

So far from admitting the exclusion of classes of men however incompetent, the provision does not so much as admitt of the exclusion of individuals from any office. An individual or a knot of individuals, bent upon affording a constant obstruction to all business and selected perhaps for that very purpose, might be returned to the supreme Assembly or any other, nor could they be got rid of without a breach of the natural and inviolable rights of man as declared and established by this clause.

What makes the matter still the clearer is, that this particular provision is given in the character of a consequence of, that is as being already included in, the preceding article declaring the perfect and unchangeable equality of mankind in respect of all manner of rights. — The citizens being all of them equal in her sight, are all of them equally admissible and so forth: as the general proposition therefore admitts of no exception made to it, no more can this particular application of it. Virtues and Talents sound prettily, and tickle the imagination, but in point of clearness, had that been the object, the clause, such as it is, would have been all the better had it ended with the words public places and employments, and had so much as is said about capacity and distinction and virtues and talents been left out.

Art. 7. No one can be accused, arrested or detained but in the cases determined by the law, and according to the forms prescribed by the law. Those who sollicit, issue, execute or cause to be executed arbitrary orders, ought to be punished: but every citizen summoned or arrested in virtue of the law, ought to obey that instant: he renders himself guilty by resistance.[38]

Sentence 1st No one can be accused, arrested or detained but in the cases determined by the law and according to the forms prescribed by the law.

Here again we have the improper word *can* instead of *ought*. Here however the power of the law is recognized and passes unquestioned: the clause therefore is in so far not mischievous and absurd, but only nugatory and beside the purpose. The professed object of the whole composition is to tie the hands of the law, by declaring pretended rights over which the law is never to have any power: liberty, the right of enjoying liberty, at the head of them. Here this very liberty is left at the mercy and good pleasure of the law. As it neither answers the purpose it professes to have in view, so neither does it fulfill the purpose which it ought to have had in view, and might have fulfilled, the giving the subject, or to speak in the French stile the citizen, that degree of security which, without attempting to bind the hands of succeeding legislators, might have been given him against arbitrary mandates. There is nothing in this article which might not be received, and without making any alteration, into the constitutional codes of Prussia, Denmark, Russia or Morocco. It is or is not law (no matter which for I put it so only for supposition's sake). It *is* law, let us say, in those countries that upon order signed or issued by any one of a certain number of persons, suppose Ministers of state, any individual may be arrested at any time and detained in any manner and for any length of time, without any obligation on the part of the person issuing the order to render account of the issuing of it or of the execution of it to any body but the Monarch. If such was the law in these countries respectively before the establishment of such a law as this clause imports, such may it remain, and that without effecting any abridgement of the powers of the Minister in question, or applying any check to the abuses of those powers, or affording the subject any security or remedy against the abuses of those powers, after the introduction of such article. The case in which it is determined by the law that a man may be so arrested and detained is the case of an order having been issued for that purpose by any one in such a list of Ministers, and the form in which the order for that purpose must be conceived is the wording the order in the form in which orders to the purpose in question have been in use to be worded, or in short any other form which the Minister in question may be pleased to give it. If to this interpretation any objection can be made, it must be grounded on the ambiguity of the import of the word *the law*, an ambiguity derived from the definition above given of it in this declaratory code. If the laws are all of them *ipso facto* void, as this manifesto has by the preceding article declared them in all countries where the laws are made by any other hand than that of the whole body of the people, then indeed the security intended to be afforded is afforded: because in that case no arrest or detention can be legal till the ground and form of it has been pre-ordained by a law issuing from that source. On the contrary, if that article is to be explained away, and countries foreign to France are to be left in possession of their laws, then the remedy and security comes to nothing for the reason we have seen. Mischievous or nugatory, such is the alternative every where else, such is the option here.

Sentence 2$^{d.}$ Those who sollicit, issue, execute or cause to be executed arbitrary orders, ought to be punished.

Yes, says a Moullah of Morocco after the introduction of this article into the Morocco code. Yes, if an order to the prejudice of the liberty of the subject is illegal, it is an arbitrary order, and the issuing of it is an offence against the liberty of the subject, and as such ought to be and shall be punished. If one dog of an infidel presumes to arrest or detain another dog of an infidel, the act of arrest and detention is an arbitrary one, and the law requires that than which nothing can be more reasonable, viz: that the presuming dog be well bastonaded. But if one of the faithful, to every one of whom the sublime Emperor, crowned with the Sun and Moon, has given the command over all dogs, thinks fit to shut up this or that dog in a strange kennel, what is there of arbitrariness in that? It is no more than one of the customs which the laws allow of where the true Believers have dogs under them.

The security of the individual in this behalf, depends, we see, upon the turn given to that part of the law which occupies itself in the establishing of the powers necessary to be established for the furtherance of justice. Had the penners of this Declaration been contented with doing what they might have done consistently with reason and utility in this view, they might have done thus: addressing themselves to succeeding legislators, they might have warned and instructed them to be particular in the indication of the cases in which they should propose to create such powers, and in the indication of the forms according to which the powers so created should be exercised: for instance, that no man should be arrested but for some one in the list of cases enumerated by the law as capable of warranting an arrest, nor without the specification of that case in an instrument executed for the purpose of warranting such arrest: nor unless such instrument were signed by an Officer of such a description; and so on — not to attempt to exhibit a code of such importance and extent and nicety in the compass of a parenthesis. In doing so, they would have done what would at least have been innocent, and might have had its use: but in doing so they would not have prosecuted their declared purpose: which was not only to tutor and lecture their more experienced and consequently more enlightened successors, but to tie their hands, and keep their fellow-citizens in a state of constant readiness to cut their throats.

Sentence 3$^{d.}$ But every citizen summoned or arrested in virtue of the law, ought to obey that instant: — he renders himself guilty by resistance.

This clause is mighty well in itself: — the misfortune is, that it is beside the purpose. The title of this code is the Declaration of Rights, and the business of it is accordingly, in every other part of it, to declare such rights, real or supposed, as are thought fit to be declared. But what is here declared is for once a *duty*: the mention of which is some how or other slipt in as it were through inadvertance. The things that people want most to be reminded of are, one would think, their duties: for their rights, whatever they may be, they are apt enough to attend to of themselves. Yet it is only by accident, under a wrong title, and as it were through mistake[?], and in this single instance, that any thing is said that would lead the body of the people to suspect, that there were any such things appertaining to them as *duties*.

He renders himself guilty by resistance. — Oh yes, certainly — unless the law for the infringement of which he is arrested or attempted to be arrested is an oppressive one: or unless there is any thing oppressive in the behaviour of those by whom the arrest or detention is performed. If, for instance, there be any thing of the insolence of Office in their language or their looks: if they lay hold of him on a sudden, without leaving him time to run away: or if they offer to pinion his arms while he is drawing his sword, without waiting till he has drawn it: if they lock the door upon him, or put him into a room that has bars before the window: or if they come upon him the same night while the evidences of his guilt are about him and all fresh, instead of waiting on the outside of the door all night till he has destroy'd them.^{b} In any of these cases,

b. By a recent decree of the Convention this silly provision has actually been made law, under the notion of favouring liberty.[39] The liberty of doing mischief it certainly does favour, as certainly as it disfavours the liberty of preventing it. Ask for a reason, *a man's house,* you are told, *is his Castle.*[40] Blessed liberty! where the trash of sentiment pass for reasons, and poetry sets the rule to law. But if a man's house is his castle by night, why not by day? — and if a house is a castle to the owner, why not to every body else in whose favour the owner chooses to make it so? By day or by night, is it less hardship to a

as well as a thousand others that might be mentioned, can there be any doubt about the oppression? but by article 2$^{d.}$ of this same code, an article which has already been established and placed out of the reach of cavil, the right of resistance to oppression is in the number of those rights which Nature hath given, and which it is not in the power of man to take away.

Art. 8. The law ought not to establish any other punishments than what are strictly and evidently necessary, and no one can be punished but in virtue of a law established and promulgated before the commission of the offence, and applied in a legal manner.[41]

Sentence 1$^{st.}$ The law ought not to establish any other punishments than what are strictly and evidently necessary. —

The lesson administered by this clause is not great: so far however [it] is well that the purpose declared in this instrument is departed from, and nothing but instruction is here attempted to be given which succeeding legislators may be governed by or not as they think fit. It is well indeed that penal laws not conforming to this condition are in it included in the sentence of nullity so liberally dealt out on other occasions, since if they were it might be difficult enough to find a penal law any where that would stand the test, from whatever source, pure or impure, democratical, aristocratical or monarchical, it were derived. No rules of any tolerable degree of particularity and precision have ever yet been laid down for adjusting either the quantum or the quality of punishments, or at least none that could have been in the contemplation of the framers of this code: and even supposing such rules laid down and framed with the utmost degree of particularity and precision that the nature of the subject is susceptible of, it would still be seen in most instances, if not in every instance, that the offense admitted optionally of a considerable variety of punishments of which, though any one might perhaps be more proper than the one at present annexed to the offence, yet no one could be made [to] appear to be strictly and evidently necessary to the exclusion of the rest. As a mere memento then of what is fit

---

suspected person to have his house searched than to an unsuspected one? Here we have the mischief and the absurdity of the antient Ecclesiastical asylums, without the reason.

The course of justice in England is still obstructed to a certain degree by this silly epigram, worthy of the age which gave it birth. Delinquents, like foxes, are to have law given them: that is chances of escape, given them on purpose, as if it were to make the better sport for the lawyers by and for whom the hunt is made.[42]

to be attended to, a clause to this effect may be very well: but as an instruction, calculated to point out in what manner that which is so fit to be attended to may be accomplished, nothing can be more trifling or uninstructive: it is even erroneous and fallacious, since an assumption it makes, and that by necessary implication, is that it is possible in the case of every offence to find a punishment of which the strict necessity is capable of being made evident, which is not true. The order of the King who sent the Princess his daughter up the hill in quest of the singing-water, supposed the existence of the singing-water.[43] The existence of the singing-water had as much truth in it as the existence of the order by which the Princess was dispatched in quest of it: but the existence of a system of punishments of which the absolute necessity is capable of being made evident with reference to the offences to which they are respectively annexed is not altogether so clear as the existence of the article by which succeeding legislators are sent in quest of such a system by these their masters and preceptors. One thing is but too evident — that the attention bestowed by the penner of this article on the subject on which he gives the law to posterity so much at his ease was [something][44] less than strict. It was the Utopia created by the small talk of Paris that was dancing before his eyes, and not the elementary parts of the subject-matter he was treating of, the list of possible punishments confronted with the list of possible offences. He who writes these observations has made, he believes, a closer and more detailed inquiry into the subject than any body that has been before him: he has laid down a set of rules, by which, as he conceives, the disproportion but too generally prevalent between punishments and offences may be reduced within bounds to an extent much narrower than it occupies any where at present in any existing code of law:[45] and what he would undertake for is — to make evident not a list of such strictly necessary punishments, but the impossibility of its existence.

Sentence 2. No one can be punished but in virtue of a law established and promulgated before the commission of the offence, and applied in a legal manner.

This clause, if instead of the insurrection-inviting *can* the word *ought* had been employ'd as in the preceding clause of this same article, would as far as it goes have been well enough. As it is, while on the one hand it not only tends to bring on the everlasting danger of insurrection, on the other hand it leaves a considerable part of the danger against which it is levelled uncovered and unprovided against.

Many are the occasions on which sufferings as great as any that, being inflicted with a view to punishment and even the same in kind, go under the

denomination of punishment may be inflicted without any such view—
without a view to punishment—for a purpose different from that of punishment. These cases a legislator who understood his business would have
collected and given notice of, for the purpose of marking out the boundaries
and confines of the instruction in question, and saving it from misapplication. *Laying an embargo*, for instance, is a species of *confinement*, and were
a man subjected to it with a view to punishment might in many cases be a
very severe punishment: yet if the providence of the legislator happens not
to have provided a general law empowering the executive authority to lay
an embargo in certain cases, the passing of a special law for that purpose
after the conjuncture that calls for it has taken place may be a very justifiable and even necessary measure, for instance to prevent intelligence from
being communicated to a power watching the moment to commence hos-
tilities, or to prevent articles of subsistence or instruments of defence of
which there is a deficiency in the country from being carried out of it. Banishment must in a certain sense be admitted to be equally penal, whether
inflicted for the purpose of punishment, or only by way of precaution, for
the purpose of prevention, and without any view to punishment. Will it be
said that there is no case in which the supreme government of a country
ought to be trusted with the power of removing out of it, not even for a time,
any persons, not even foreigners, from whom it may see reason to apprehend enterprizes injurious to its peace?—So in the case of imprisonment, which though in some instances it may be a severer, may in others be
a less severe infliction than banishment. Even death, a suffering which if
inflicted with a view to punishment is the very extremity of punishment,
and which according to my own conception of the matter neither need nor
ought to be inflicted in any instance for the purpose of punishment, may
in some instances perhaps be highly necessary to be inflicted without any
view to punishment—for example to prevent or stop the diffusion of the
plague. Thus it is, that while the clause passing censure on *ex post facto*
penal laws (a censure in itself, and so it confines itself to the cases strictly
within its declared subject, so highly reasonable) is thus exhibited with the
insurrection-compelling *can* in it, and without the explanations necessary
as we have seen to guard it against misapplication, the country is exposed to
two opposite dangers: one, that an infliction necessary for the purpose of
prevention should be resisted and risen up against by individuals under the
notion of its being included in the prohibition given by this clause; the
other, that the prohibitive measure, how necessary soever, should be abstained from by the legislature through apprehension of such resistance.

As to the concluding addition *and legally applied*, it might have been spared without much loss. If the law referred to in justification of an act of power has not been legally applied in the exercise of that act of power, the act has not been exercised in virtue of that law.

Art. 9. Every individual being presumed innocent untill he has been declared guilty, if it be judged necessary to arrest him, every act of rigour which is not necessary to the making sure of his person, ought to be severely inhibited by the law.[46]

This article being free from the insurrection-exciting particle, and confining itself to the task of simple instruction, is so far innocent: the purpose of it is laudable: but the purport of it might have been expressed with more precision.

The maxim it opens with, though of the most consummate triviality, is not the more conformable to reason and utility, and is particularly repugnant to the regulation in support and justification of which it is adduced. That every man *ought* to be presumed innocent (for *"is"* presumed innocent is nonsense) untill he has been *declared* (that is adjudged) guilty is very well so long as no accusation has been preferred against him, or rather so long as neither that nor any other circumstance appears to afford reason for suspecting the contrary, but irrational afterwards — after such a ground for supposing he may have been guilty has been brought to light. The maxim is more particularly absurd when applied to the case where it has been judged proper (on sufficient grounds we are to suppose) to put him under arrest, to deprive a man of his liberty of loco-motion: suppose him innocent, and the defalcation made from his liberty is injurious and unwarrantable. The plain truth of the matter is, that the only rational ground for empowering a man to be arrested in such a case, is its not being yet known whether he is innocent or guilty: suppose him guilty, he ought to be punished: suppose him innocent, he ought not to be touched. But the unsophisticated truth and common sense does not answer the purpose of poetry or rhetoric: and it is from poetry and rhetoric that these tutors of mankind and sovereigns of futurity take their law. A clap from the galleries is the object, not the welfare of the state.

As to the expression of passion, *"ought to be severely* repressed" (by punishment I suppose) it is as well calculated to inflame (the general purpose of this effusion of matchless wisdom) as it is ill-calculated to instruct. A rather more simple and instructive way of stating it would have been to say, in relation to every such exercise of rigour as goes beyond what appears necessary to the purpose in question — that of the making sure of the person, that not coming within the ground and sole ground of justification taken from that source, it remains upon the footing of an offence of that description whatever it be — of an injury of the species in question whatever it may be. The satisfaction and punishment annext to it will come of course to be of the same nature and extent as for an injury of the same nature and extent having no such circumstance to give occasion to it. Should the punishment in such case be greater or less than the punishment for the same injury would be if altogether unfurnished with the justification which covers the remainder of the unpleasant treatment? Should the punishment of the servant of justice exceeding his authority be greater or less than that of the uncommissioned individual doing the same mischief without any authority? On some accounts it should be greater: on other accounts, not so great. But these are points of minute detail which might surely as well have been left to the determination of those who may have time to give them due examination, as determined upon at random by those who had no such time. The words here seem to intimate that the punishment for the abuse of power of the minister of justice[47] exceeding his authority ought to be the greater of the two. — But why so? — You know better where to meet with the minister of justice than with an offending individual taken at large: the officer has more to lose than the individual: and the better the assurance you have that a delinquent in case of accusation will be forthcoming, in readiness to afford satisfaction in the event of his being sentenced to afford it, the less the alarm which his delinquency inspires.

Art. 10. No one ought to be molested (meaning probably by government) for his opinions, even in matters of religion, provided that the manifestation of them does not disturb (better expressed perhaps by saying except in as far as the manifestation of them disturbs or rather tends to the disturbance of) the public order established by the law.[48]

Liberty of publication with regard to opinions, with or without exceptions, is a liberty which it would be highly proper and useful to establish, but which can receive but a very precarious establishment from an article thus worded. *Disturb the public order* — what does that mean? Lewis 14th. need not have hesitated about receiving an article thus worded into his code. The public order of things in this behalf was an order in virtue of which every religion but the Catholic, according to his edition of it, was proscribed.[49] A law is enacted, forbidding men to manifest, to express, a particular opinion or set of opinions relative to a particular point in religion: forbidding men to express any of those opinions in the expression of which the Lutheran doctrine, for example, or the Calvinistical doctrine, or the

354 Politics, Policy, and Political Economy

Church-of-England doctrine, consists: in a prohibition to this effect consists the public order established by the law. Spite of this a man manifests an opinion of the number of those which thus stand prohibited as belonging to the religion thus proscribed. The act by which this opinion is manifested, is it not an act of disturbance with relation to the public order thus established? Extraordinary indeed must be the confidence of him who could take upon him to answer in the negative.

Thus nugatory, thus flimsy, is this buckler of rights and liberties in one of the few instances in which any attempt is made to apply it to a good purpose.

What should it have done then? — a question this the answer to which is scarcely within the province of these sheets. The opinion I set out with declaring, the proposition I set out with, is, not that the Declaration of rights should not have existed[?] in this shape, but that nothing under any such name or with any such design should have been attempted.

A word or two however may pass in the way of supererogation — that opinions of all sorts may be manifested without fear of punishment — that no publication should be deemed to subject a man to punishment on account of any opinions it may be found to contain, considered as mere opinions; at the same time that the plea of manifesting religious opinions or of practising certain acts supposed, in virtue of certain religious opinions, to be enjoined or recommended as proper or necessary to be practised should not operate as a justification for either exercising or prompting men to exercise any act which the legislature, without any view or reference to religion, has already thought fit or may hereafter think fit to insert into the catalogue of prohibited acts or offences.

To instance two species of delinquency, one of the most serious, the other of the slightest, nature — acts tending to the violent subversion of the government by force — acts tending to the obstruction of the passage in the streets. An opinion that has been supposed by some to belong to the Christian religion is that every form of government but the Monarchical is unlawful. An opinion that has been supposed by some to belong to the Christian religion, by some at least of those that adhere to that branch of the Christian religion which is termed the Catholic, is that it is a duty or at least a merit to join in processions of a certain description to be performed on certain occasions. What then is the true sense of the provision in question in relation to these two cases? What ought to be the conduct of a government that is neither monarchical nor catholic with reference to the respective manifestation of these two opinions?

First, as to the opinion relative to the unlawfulness of a government not monarchical? The falsity or erroneousness which the members of such a government could not but attribute in their own minds to such an opinion is a consideration which, according to the spirit and intent of the provision in question, would *not* be sufficient to authorize their using penal or other coercive measures for the purpose of preventing the manifestation of them. At the same time, should such manifestation either have already had the effect of engaging individuals in any attempt to effect a violent subversion of the government by force, or appear to have produced a near probability of any such attempt, in such case the engagement to permitt the free manifestation of opinions in general, and of religious opinions in particular, is not to be understood to preclude the government from restraining the manifestation of the opinion in question in every such way as it may have been deemed likely to promote or facilitate any such attempt.

Again, as to the opinion relative to the meritoriousness of certain processions. By the principal part of the engagement government stand precluded from prohibiting publications manifesting an opinion in favour of the obligatoriness or meritoriousness of such processions. By the spirit of the same engagement they stand precluded from prohibiting the performance of such processions, unless a persuasion of a political inconvenience as resulting from such practice, a persuasion not grounded on any notions of their unlawfulness in a religious view, should come to be entertained: as if, for example, the multitude of the persons joining in the procession, or the crowd of persons flocking to observe it, should fill up the streets to such a degree or for such a length of time and at intervals recurring with such frequency as to be productive of such a degree of obstruction to the free use of the streets for the purposes of business as in the eye of government should constitute a body of inconvenience worth encountering by a prohibitive law.

It would be a violation of the spirit of an engagement to this effect if government, not by reason of any view it entertained of the political inconveniency of these processions (for example, as above) but for the purpose of giving an ascendancy to religious opinions of an opposite nature (actuated, for example, by a Protestant antipathy to Catholic processions), were to make use of the real or pretended obstruction to the free use of the streets as a pretence for prohibiting these processions.

These examples, while they serve to illustrate the ground and degree and limits of the liberty which it may seem proper on the score of public tranquillity and peace to leave to the manifestation of opinions of a religious nature, may serve at the same time to render apparent the absurdity and perilousness of every attempt on the part of the government for the time being to tie up the hands of succeeding governments in relation to this or any other spot in the field of legislation. Observe how nice, and incapable of being described beforehand by any particular marks, are the lines which mark the limits of right and wrong in this behalf, which separate the prudent course from the imprudent, the useful from the pernicious! how dependent upon the temper of the times, upon the events and circumstances of the day! with how fatal a certainty persecution and tyranny on the one hand, or revolt and civil war on the other, may follow from the slightest deviation from propriety in the drawing of such lines: and what a curse to the country a legislator may be who, with the purest intentions, should set about set-tling the business to all eternity by inflexible and adamantine rules drawn from the sacred and inviolable and imprescriptible rights of man and the primæval and everlasting laws of nature!

I give the preference, for the purpose of exemplification, to one of those points in relation to which it would give me pleasure to see liberty estab-lished for ever as it could be established consistently with security and peace. My persuasion is that there is not a single point with relation to which it can answer any good purpose to attempt to tie the hands of future legislators: and as there is not a single point, not even of my own choosing, in relation to which I would endeavour to give any such perpetuity to a regulation even of my own framing, it is still less to say, strong as it may appear to say, that were it to depend upon me — were the power of sanction-ing in my hands — I would sooner give my sanction to a body of laws of any body else's framing, how bad soever it might appear to me, free from any such perpetuating clause, than a body of laws of my own framing, how well soever I might be satisfied with it, if it must be encumbered with such a clause.

Art. 11. The free communication of thoughts and opinions is one of the most pretious rights of man: every citizen may therefore speak, write, and print freely, provided always that he shall be answerable for the abuse of that liberty in the cases determined by the law.[50]

The logic one meets with in this composition is altogether of a piece with the policy of it: when you meet with a *therefore*, when you meet with a consequence denounced, with one proposition denounced as conclusion and consequence drawn from the one immediately preceding it, assure yourself, whether the propositions themselves are as propositions true or false, as ordinances reasonable or unreasonable, expedient or inexpedient,

that the consequent is either in contradiction with the antecedent, or has nothing at all to do with it.

The liberty of communication for opinions is one branch of liberty: and liberty is one of the four natural rights of man over which human ordinances have no power. There are two ways in which liberty may be taken away: by physical or bodily coercion and by moral coercion or denuntiation of punishment: the one applied before the time for exercising the liberty, the other to be applied after it in the shape of punishment in the event of its not producing its intended effect in the shape of prohibition. What is the boon granted in favour of liberty, of the branch of liberty here in question, by this article? It saves it from succeeding legislators in one shape: it leaves it at their mercy in the other. Will it be said, that what it leaves exposed to punishment is only the abuse of liberty? Be it so: what then? Is there less of liberty in the abuse of liberty than in the use of it? Does a man take less liberty when he makes use of the property of another than when he confines himself to his own? Then liberty and confinement are the same thing, synonymous terms. What is an abuse of liberty? — it is that exercise of liberty, be it what it will, which a man who bestows that name on it does not approve of. Every abuse of this branch of liberty is left exposed to punishment; and it is left to future legislatures to determine what shall be regarded as an abuse of it! What is the security worth that is thus given to the individual as against the encroachments of government? what does the barrier pretended to be set up against government amount to? a barrier which government is expressly called upon to set up where it pleases? Let me not be mistaken — what I blame the constitution-makers for is — not the having omitted to tie the hands of their successors tight enough, but the suffering themselves to harbour a conceit so mischievous and so foolish as that of tying them up at all: and in particular, for supposing that were they weak enough to suffer themselves to be so shackled, a phrase or two of so loose a texture could be capable of doing the[?] business to any purpose.

The general notion in regard to offences, a notion so general as to have become proverbial, and even trivial, is that *prevention is better than punishment.*[51] Here prevention is abjured, and punishment embraced in preference. Once more, let me not be mistaken. In the particular case of the liberty of communication for opinions there most certainly are reasons for giving up the object of prevention and confining the operations of the legislator in the choice of means of repression to punishment, to the application of punishment, which do not apply to other offences. A word or two to this purpose, and to justify the seeming inconsistency, would have been rather more instructive than most of those other instructions of which the authors of this code are so profuse.

Not only is the consequent of the two propositions, when clogged with the proviso at the tail of it, repugnant to the antecedent, but in itself it extends a vast way beyond what is intended as a covering for it. The free communication of thoughts and opinions (*thoughts* and *opinions* I presume are here put as synonymous terms, nor is *thoughts* intended to mean any thing more than is intended to be meant by *opinions*) the free communication of opinions, says the antecedent, is one of the most valuable of the rights of man — of these unalienable rights of man. — What says the consequent of it? — not only that a man is to be at liberty to communicate opinions without the possibility of being prevented — but that he is to be at liberty to communicate what he will without the possibility of being prevented, and in any manner — false allegations to the prejudice of the reputation of the individuals — in a word slander of all sorts — and that in all manner of ways, by speech, by word of mouth, by writing and even in the way of printing, without the possibility of stopping his mouth, destroying his manuscript or breaking up the press.

What then? does it follow that because a man ought to be left at liberty to publish opinions of all sorts subject not to previous prevention, but only to subsequent punishment, that therefore he ought to be left at equal liberty to publish allegations of all sorts, false as well as true, allegations known by him to be false as well as allegations believed by him to be true, attacks which he knows to be false upon the reputation of individuals as well [as attacks which he knows to be true]? — Far is it from my meaning to contend in this place, especially in a parenthesis, much more to take for granted, that the endurance [of] even these mischiefs, crying as they are, may not be a less evil than the subjecting the press to a previous censure under any such restrictions on the exercise of that power as could be devised, at any rate under any such as have ever hitherto been proposed. All I mean to say is that whether a man ought or ought [not] to be left at liberty to publish private slander without the application of any thing to stop the progress of it, it does not follow that it ought to be left in his power to do this — to publish such allegations — because it ought to be left in like manner in his power to publish whatever can come under the denomination of opinions. As for the word thoughts, which is put in a line with the word opinions as if [it was][52] meant for something different from opinions, I shall lay it out of the question altogether till I can find somebody who will undertake to satisfy me in the first place that it was meant to denote something in addition to opinions, and in the next place that that something was meant to include allegations, true and false, in relation to matters of fact.

Is it, or is it not, a matter to be wished, in France for example, that measures were taken by competent authority, whatever authority be deemed competent, to draw the line between the protection due to the useful liberty and the restraint proper for the pernicious license of the press? — What a pretious task would the legislator find set for him by this declaration of sacred, inviolable and imprescriptible rights! The protectors of reputation on one side of him: the idolators of liberty on the other. Each with the rights of man in his mouth and the dagger of assassination in his hand, ready to punish the smallest departure from the course marked out in his heated imagination for this unbending line.

Art. 12. The guarantee of the rights of the man and of the citizen necessitates a public force: this force *is* therefore instituted for the advantage of all, and not for the particular utility of those to whom it is intrusted.[53]

The general purpose of the whole performance taken together being pestiferous and pestilential, this article has thus much to recommend it, that it is nothing to the purpose: no declaration of inviolable rights: no invitations to insurrection. As it stands it is a mere effusion of imbecillity: a specimen of confused conception and false reasoning. With a little alteration it might be improved into a common-place memento, as stale and consequently as useless as it is unexceptionable: to wit that the employment given to the public force, maintained as it is at the expence of the public, ought to have for its object the general advantage of the whole body of the public taken together, not the exclusive private advantage of particular individuals.

This article is composed of two distinct propositions: in the first, after throwing out of it as so much surplusage the obscure part about the warranty or maintenance of the rights of the man and the citizen, there will remain a clear and intelligible declaration of opinion asserting the necessity of a public force: to this is hooked on in the shape of an inference, of a logical conclusion, an unqualified assertion, in the way of statement, of an historical matter of fact, which may have been true in one place, and false in another, the truth of which is incapable of being ascertained in any instance, an operation the labour of which may be spared with the less loss from its being nothing to the purpose.

This matter of fact is neither more nor less than the main end in view which happened to be present in the minds of the several persons to whose co-operation the public force was respectively indebted for its institution and establishment in the several political communities in the world, and which officiated in the character of a final cause in every such instance. This final cause, the penner of this article, such is his candour and good opinion of mankind, pronounces without hesitation or exception to have been the pure view of the greatest good of the whole community, public spirit in its purest quality and in its most extensive application. Neither Clovis, Pepin nor Hugh Capet had the smallest preferable regard to the particular advantage of themselves or their favourites in laying the foundations of the public force in France, nor any other consideration in view than what might be most conducive to the joint and equal advantage of Franks, Gauls and Gallo-Romans upon the whole.[54] As little partiality existed in the breast of William the Conqueror in favour of himself or any of his Normans on the occasions of his sharing out England among those Normans, and dividing it into Knight's fees: freemen and villains, Barons and Yeomen, Normans, Danes and English, collectively and individually, occupying an equal place in his affections and exercising an equal portion of his sollicitude.[55]

According to this construction, the inference, it must be confessed, may be just enough. All you have to suppose is that the greatest Good of the whole community taken together was in every instance the ruling object of consideration in the breast of the institutors of the public force: the pursuit of that greatest good in a certain shape not perfectly explained being the ruling object with these worthy men, as they did institute this public force it seems to follow pretty accurately that the attainment of that general advantage was the end in view in every instance in which that force was instituted.

Should the two proposition[s], the position and the inference in this [their][56] genuine signification, appear too silly to be endurable, the way to defend [them][57] may be to acknowledge that the man that penned [them][58] knew no difference between a declaration of what he supposes was or is the state of things with regard to this or that subject, and a declaration of what he conceives ought to have been or ought to be that state of things: and this being the case, it may be supposed that in saying such was the end in view upon the several occasions in question, what he meant was that such it ought to have been. If this were really his meaning, the propositions are such, both of them, as we may venture to accede to without much danger. A public force is necessary, we may say: and the public is the party for whose advantage that force ought to be employ'd. The propositions themselves are both of them such, that against neither of them surely can any objection be produced: as to the illative particle by which they are strung together, if the application made of it be not exactly of the clearest nature, you have only to throw it out, and every thing is as it should be[59] and the whole article is rendered unexceptionable.

Art. 13. For the maintenance of the public force, and for the expences of administration, a common contribution is indispensable: it ought to be equally divided among all the citizens in proportion to their faculties.[60]

In the first part of this article two propositions are contained. One is that a common contribution is indispensable for the maintenance of the public force. If by this is meant, that raising money upon all for the maintenance of those whose individual forces go to the composition of the public force, I see no reason to dispute it. If the meaning be that this is the only possible way of maintaining a public force, it is not true. Under the feudal system those whose individual forces composed the public force were maintained not at the expence of the community at large, but at their own expence.

The other proposition is — that a common contribution is indispensable for the expences (meaning the other expences) of administration. Indispensable? Yes certainly: so far as these other branches of administration can not be carried on without expence, if they are carried on, the defraying of that expence is indispensable. But are these nameless branches of administration necessary? — for if they are not, neither is a common contribution for the defraying of the expence of them. Are they then necessary? These unnamed and unindicated branches of administration which in this secret manner are put down on the list of necessary ones, is their title to be placed upon it a just one? This is a question to which it is impossible to find an answer: yet till an answer be found for it, it is impossible to find a sufficient warrant for admitting this proposition to be true. From this proposition, as the matter stands upon the face of it, it should seem that one of these sacred and inviolable and imprescriptible rights of a man consists in the obligation of contributing to an unknown mass of expence, employ'd upon objects not ascertained.

Proposition 3ᵈ· It (the common contribution in question) ought to be equally divided amongst all the citizens, in proportion to their faculties.

Partly contradiction, — a sequel to, or rather repetition of, preceding contradictions — partly tyranny under the mask of justice.

By the first article, human creatures are, and are to be all of them, on a footing of equality in respect to all sorts of rights. By the second article, property is of the number of those rights. By the two taken together, all men then are and are to be upon an equal footing in respect to property: in other words all the property in the nation is and is to be equally divided, divided into equal portions. At the same time, as to the matter of fact, what is certain is that at the time of passing this article no such equality existed, nor were any measures so much as taken for bringing it into existence. This being the case, which of the two states of things is it that this article supposes? the old and really existing inequality, or the new and imaginary equality? In the first case the concluding or explanatory clause is in contradistinction with the principal one: in the other case it is tautological and superfluous. In the first case the explanatory clause is in contradiction with the principal one: for from unequal fortunes, if you take equal contributions, the contributions, the defalcations, are not proportional. If from a fortune of one hundred pounds you take a contribution [of] ten pounds, and from a fortune of two hundred pounds, ten pounds and no more, the proportion is not a tenth in both cases, but a tenth in the one and only a twentieth in the other. In the second case, that is if equality in point of property be the state of things supposed, then indeed equality of contribution will be consistent with the plan of equalization as also consonant to justice and utility: but then the explanatory clause, in proportion to their faculties, will be tautologous and superfluous: and not only tautologous and superfluous, but obscure and perplexing: for proportionality in point of contribution is not consistent with equality in point of contribution on more than one out of an infinity of suppositions, viz: that of equality in point of fortune: nor in point of fact was the one consistent with the other in the only state of things which was in existence at the time.

Men's faculties too? what does that word mean? This, if the state of things represented as actually existing as well as always having existed, and for ever about to exist, had been any thing more than a sick man's dream, would have required to be determined, had it been at all a matter of concern to prevent men from cutting one another's throats, and must have been determined before this theory could have been reduced to practice. In the valuation of men's faculties is it meant that their possessions only, or that their respective wants and exigencies as well as their ways and means, should be taken into account? — In the latter case what endless labour! in the former case what injustice!

In either case, what tyranny! An inquisition into every man's exigencies and resources, an inquisition which to be adequate to its object must be perpetual, an inquisition into every man's circumstances, one of the pillars[?] of this fabric of liberty! To an English reader, to a reader who should put an English construction upon this plan of taxation (masked by the

delusive term contribution as if voluntary contributions could be a practicable substitute for compulsory), to a reader who should collect from the
state of things in England the construction to be put upon this plan of
taxation, the system here in view would not shew itself in half its blackness.
To an English reader it might naturally enough appear that all that was
meant was that the weight of taxation in general should bear in a loose sense
as equally, or rather as equitably, that is as proportionably, as it could
conveniently be made to do: that taxes, a word which would lead him
directly and almost exclusively to taxes upon consumption, should be imposed, for example, upon superfluities in preference to the necessaries of
life. — Wide indeed would be his mistake. — What he little would suspect is
that taxes on consumption, the taxes and from whence arise the only contributions that in plain truth and not in a sophistical sense are voluntary on the
part of the contributor, are carefully weeded out by French financiers, deluded by the term *indirect*, a sort of term of proscription, invented by a set of
muddy-headed metaphysicians.[61] Little does he think that the favourite
species of taxation in that country of perfect liberty is a species of imposition and inquisition which converts every man who has any property into a
criminal in the first instance, which sends the tax gatherer into every nook
and corner of a man's house, which examines every man upon interrogato-
ries, and of which a double or treble tithe would be an improved and
mollified modification.[62]

Art. 14. All the citizens have the right to ascertain by themselves or by
their representatives, the necessity of the public contribution, to give their
free consent to it, to follow up the application of it, and to determine the
quantity of it, the objects on which it shall be levied, the mode of levying it
and getting it in, and the duration of it.[63]

Supposing the author of this article an enemy to the state, and his object,
to disturb the course of public business, and set the individuals of it together by the ears, nothing could [have] been more artfully or more happily
adapted to the purpose. Supposing him a friend, and his object to administer
either useful instruction or salutary controul, nothing more silly or childish
can be imagined.

In the first place, who is he speaking of? what does he mean by all the
citizens? — Does he mean all collectively acting in a body, or every citizen,
any individual, that is any one that pleases? This right of mine, is it a right
which I may exercise by myself, at any time, whenever it happens to suit
me, and without the concurrence of any body else, or which I can only

exercise if and when I can get every body else, or at least the major part of every body else, to join me in the exercise of it? The difference in a practical view is enormous: but the penners of this declaration, by whom terms expressive of aggregation and terms expressive of separation are used, to all appearance, promiscuously, shew no symptoms of their being aware of the smallest difference. If in conjunction with every body else, I have it already by the sixth article.[64] Laws imposing contributions are laws. I have already then a right of concurring in the formation of all laws whatever: what do I get by acquiring the right of concurring in the formation of the particular class of laws which are employ'd in imposing contributions? As a specification, as an application of the general provision to this particular subject, it might be very well. But it is not given as a specification but as a distinct object. What marks the distinction the more forcibly, is the jumbling in this instance, and in this instance only, acts of another nature with acts of legislation: the right of examining into the necessity of the operation, and of following it up when performed, with the right of performing it: the right of observing and commenting on the manner in which the powers of government are exercised, with the right of exercising them.

Make what we will of it, what a pretty contrivance for settling matters and putting an end to doubts or disagreements. This, whatever it is, is one of the things which I am told I have a right to do, that is either by myself or by certain persons alluded to under the denomination of my representatives — either in one way or the other, but in which? — This is exactly what I want to know, and this is exactly what it does not tell me. Can I do it by myself: or only by my representative: that is to say, in the latter case by a deputy in whose election I have perhaps had a vote, perhaps not, perhaps given the vote, perhaps not: perhaps voted for, perhaps voted against, and who, whether I voted for or against him, will not do either this, or any one other act whatsoever, at my desire?

Have I, an individual, have I in my individual capacity, a right when I please to ascertain, that is to examine into, the necessity of every contribution established or proposed to be established? Then have I a right to go whenever I please, to any of the offices in the department of the revenue, to put all the business of the office to a stand, to take all the people I find under my command, to make them answer all my questions, to make them furnish me with as many papers or other documents as I choose to have. You, my next neighbour, who are as much a citizen as I am, have as much of this right as I have. It is your pleasure to take this same office under your command to the same purpose at the same time. It is my pleasure the people should do what I bid them and not what you bid them: it is your pleasure they should do what you bid them and not what I bid them — which of us is to have his pleasure? — The answer is he who has the strongest lungs, or if that won't do, he who has the strongest hand. To give every thing to the strongest hand is the natural result of all the tutoring and all the checking and controuling of which this lecture on the principles of government is so liberal: but this is the exact result of that state of things which would have place, supposing no government at all, nor any such attempt as this to destroy government under the notion of directing it.

The right of giving consent to a tax — the right of giving consent to a measure — a curious mode of expression for the right of signifying assent or dissent as a man thinks proper! that a man professing and pretending to fix words, to fix ideas, to fix laws, to fix every thing, and to fix it to all eternity, should fix upon that expression of all others, which, since the French language is ill-constructed enough and unhappy enough to afford such an expression, denotes an efficient right of the sort in question in no other way than by presenting in the first instance a nugatory and illusive one: the right of giving consent instead of the right of giving a vote: the right of giving consent and consent only instead of the right of giving consent or dissent or neither as a man thinks proper.

Art. 15. The society has a right to demand from every agent of the public an account of his administration.[65]

The society? — what is the meaning, what is the object here? Different where it ought to be identical, identical where it ought to be different, ever inexplicit, ever indeterminate, using as interconvertible expressions which, for the purpose of precision and right understanding, require the most carefully to be set and kept in opposition, such is the language from the beginning of this composition to the end!

Is it that superiors in office have a right to demand such an account of their subordinates? Not to possess such a right would be not to be a superior: not to be subject to the exercise of it would be not to be a subordinate. In this sense the proposition is perfectly harmless, but equally nugatory. Is it that all men not in office have this right with respect to all men or every man in office? Then comes the question as before, — each in his individual capacity, or only all together in their collective? If in their collective, whatever this article or any other article drawn up in the same view does or can do for them amounts to nothing: whatever it would have them do, it gives them no facility for doing it which they did not possess without it. Whatever it would have them do, if one and all rise for the purpose of doing it, bating what hindrance they may receive from one another, there will be nobody to hinder them. But is there any great likelyhood of any such rising's ever taking place? and were such a thing to happen as it's taking place, would there be any great use in it?

If the right is of the number of those which belongs to each and every man in his individual capacity, then comes the old story over again of mutual obstruction and the obstruction of all business, as before.

The right of demanding an account? — what means that too? the right of simply putting the question, or the right of compelling an answer to it? — and such an answer as shall afford to him that puts it the satisfaction he desires? In the former case the value of the right will not be great: in the latter case he who has it, and who by the supposition is not in office will in fact be in office, and as every body has it and is to have it, the result is that every body is in office: and those who command all men are under the command of every man.

Instead of meaning stark nonsense, was the article meant after all simply to convey a memento to those who are superiors in office to keep a good look out after those who are under them? If this be the case, nothing can be more innocent nor unexceptionable. Neither the child that is learning wisdom in his horn-book, nor the old woman who is teaching him, need blush to own it. — But what has it to do in a composition, the aggregate of the wisdom of the nation, and of which the object is throughout and exclusively to *declare rights*?

Silly or pestilential, such, as usual, is here the alternative. In the shape of advice, a proposition may be instructive or trifling, wholesome or insipid. But be it the one or the other, the instant it is converted or attempted to be converted into a law, of which those called legislators are to be the objects, and those not called legislators to be the executors, it is all sheer poison, and of the rankest kind.

Art. 16. Every Society in which the warranty of rights is not assured "*la garantie des droits n'est pas assurée*" nor the separation of powers determined, has no constitution.[66]

An exhibition this, such as no nation under the sun but the French could give: — self-conceit inflamed into insanity. Legislators turned into turkey-cocks: the less important operation of constitution-making, interrupted for the more important operation of bragging. Had the whole human species, according to the wish of the tyrant, but one neck,[67] it would find in this article a sword designed to sever it. This constitution, the blessed constitution of which this heaven-born declaration forms the base, the constitution of France, is not only the most admirable constitution of the world, but the only one.

That no other country but France has the happiness of possessing the sort of thing, whatever it be, called a constitution, is a meaning sufficiently convey'd. This meaning the article must have, if it has any: for other meaning, other meaning most assuredly, it has none. *Has the nation*, you say, *has the nation I belong to got such a thing as a constitution belonging to it or not?* — if you want to know, look whether a declaration of rights, word for word the same as this, forms part of it. Every society in which the warranty of rights is not assured, for *Toute Societé dans laquelle la garantie des droits n'est pas assurée*, is, it must indeed be confessed, most rueful nonsense. But if the translation were not exact it would be unfaithful: and if it were not nonsensical, it would not be exact. What is meant to be insinuated, not expressed (for by nonsense nothing is expressed), is, a constitution having a Declaration of rights such as this, set by authority in the character of an introduction at the head of the collection of its laws.

As to the not absolutely nonsensical but only very obscure clause about a society's having the separation of powers determined, it seems to be the result of a confused idea of an extended application of the old maxim *divide et impera*:[68] the governed are to have the governors under their governance by having them divided amongst themselves. A still older maxim is that a house divided against itself can not stand,[69] and supposing both maxims applied to this one subject, I am inclined to think a truer one. On the existence of two perfectly independent and fighting sovereignties, or three such fighting sovereignties (for what it is supposed is, or rather what it is supposed *is not* but *ought to be*, the state of things in Britain seems here to be the example in view), the perfection of good government, or at least of whatever approach to good government can subsist without the actual adoption *in terminis* of a declaration of rights such as this, is supposed to consist. And in short, though Britain has no such thing as a constitution belonging to it at present, yet if during a period of any length, five or ten years for example, it should ever happen that neither House of Commons nor House of Lords had any confidence in the King's Ministers or any of them, nor any disposition to endure their taking the lead in legislation (the House of Commons being all the while, as we must suppose, peopled by universal suffrage), possibly in such case (for it were a great deal too much to affirm) Britain might be so far humoured as to be allow'd to suppose herself in possession of a constitution — a sort of a thing which, though of inferior stuff, might pass under the name of a constitution, even without having this French Declaration of rights to stand at the head of it.

That Britain possesses at present any thing that can bear that name has by Citizen Payne, *following* or *leading* (I really remember not which, nor is it worth remembering), at any rate *according* with this Declaration of Rights, been formally denied.[70]

According to general import, supported by etymology, by the word *constitution* something *established*, something *already* established, something possessed of *stability*, something that has given *proofs* of stability, seems to be implied. What shall we say if, of this most magnificent of all boasts, not merely the simple negative but the direct converse should be true? and if, instead of France's being the only country that has a constitution, France should be the only country that has none! Yet if government depends upon obedience, the stability of government [upon] the permanence of the disposition to obedience, and the permanence of that disposition [upon] the duration of the habit of obedience, this most assuredly must be the case. And if, instead of saying you can't have a constitution unless you make it, it would be much nearer the truth, or rather it would be the plain truth and the only truth, that you can't have a constitution, if you attempt to make one. Your posterity may, if they have good fortune and very good fortune indeed: but you yourselves, the makers of it, can not with propriety be said to have it. So that which has been said of nobility (nobility by descent) in the way of sarcasm may be said of a constitution in good and very good earnest, the way to make it is to sit quietly for so many years in your chair.

Art. 17. Property being an inviolable and sacred right, no one can be deprived of it, unless it be when public necessity, legally established, evidently requires it (i:e: the sacrifice of it), and under the condition of a just and previous indemnity.[71]

Here we have the finishing piece in this pile of contradictions: it does not mismatch the rest. By the first article all men are equal in respect of all sorts of rights: and so are to continue for evermore, spite of every thing that can be done by laws. By the second article property is of the number of those rights. By this seventeenth and last article no man can be deprived of his property, no not of a single atom of it, without an exact equivalent. All men are equal in respect of property while John has £50,000 a year, and Peter nothing. All men are to be equal in respect of property, and that for everlasting, at the same [time] that he who has a thousand times as much as a thousand others put together, is not to be deprived of a single farthing of it, without having first received as much from God knows where. The author could not lay down his pen without finishing as he began, decorating once more this legislative composition with the flowery word sacred, so useful in poems, plays and college declamations. In the language of antient religion consecration often meant destruction. In this sense this declaration of rights may be allowed to have made property sacred, even as Jephthah conceived himself bound to make his daughter sacred by cutting her throat.[72]

Nonsense and contradiction apart, the topic touched upon here is one of those questions of detail that require to be settled, and is capable of being settled, by considerations of utility deducible from quiet and sober investigation, to the satisfaction of sober-minded men, but as much beneath the attention of these creators of the rights of man, as the care of changing a foul shirt for a clean one would be beneath the attention of a straw-crowned King of Bedlam.[73] Necessity? what means necessity? for of the superlatives of all sorts with which this prose run mad is so liberally crammed, there is no making any sense whatever till they have been struck out and such expressions of sober import as come nearest to them, inserted in their room. Does necessity order the making of new streets, new roads, new bridges, new canals? A nation which has existed for so many ages with the stock of water-roads which it received from nature, is any addition to that stock *necessary* to the continuation of its existence? — If not, there is an end to all improvement in every one of those lines. In all these cases there are disadvantages on one side, there are advantages on the other: but what are all the advantages in the world when set against the sacred and inviolable rights of man, derived from the unenacted and unrepealable laws of nature!

Here comes in the distinction between species susceptible and species not susceptible of the *value* of *affection*: between losses in relation to which the adequacy of indemnification may be reduced to a certainty, and losses in respect of which it must remain exposed to doubt; and the question in what cases a more than equivalent gain to one individual will warrant the subjecting another individual, with or without compensation, to a loss. All these distinctions are capable of being made: all these questions are capable of receiving a solution to the satisfaction of a man who thinks it worth his while to be at the pains of comparing the feelings on one side to the feelings on the other, and to judge of regulations by their effect on the feelings of those whom they concern, instead of pronouncing on them by the random application of epithets and phrases taken from plays and declamations.

Declaration of the Rights and Duties of the Man and the Citizen.
A°. 1795.

Rights

Art. 1. The Rights of man in society are liberty, equality, security and property.[74]

Comparing this Declaration of 1795 with its predecessor of 1791 we may observe it open with a specimen of legislative shuffling: on the one hand a sense of the absurdity of its predecessor and the mischief that had been the fruit of it: on the other hand a determination not to acknowledge it.

The sorts of rights which this second Declaration as well as the first sets out with the intention of declaring are of two sorts, those of the man and those of the citizen: those which it proceeds immediately to declare are neither the one nor the other but something between both — *the rights of man in society*.

This difference is not a mere affair of words. The rights declared by the first Declaration were declared to be natural, unalienable and imprescriptible: such rights against which all laws that should at any time presume to strike would become *ipso facto* void. If no distinction were to be recognized between the rights of the man and the rights of the citizen, one of the expressions must be acknowledged to be unmeaning, and the insertion of it a dangerous impertinence: if a distinction between them be to be recognized, it must be this: that the rights of the man, the rights of the man as existing in a state antecedent to that of political society, antecedent to the state of citizenship, are the only one of the two sorts to which the character of inalienable and imprescriptible can be understood to belong: those of the citizen, growing out of the laws by which the state of citizenship is constituted, are the produce of the law itself and may be trusted to remain at the disposal of the law which gave them birth, and may continue to depend for their existence on the law from which they received it.

This second Declaration, leaving the doubt in its full force whether there are or are not a certain description of rights over which laws have no power, a description of rights which, as we have seen, covers the whole field of legislation, shutting the door against every thing that can present itself under the name of law, consequently whether such laws as they are about to enact are or are not capable of possessing any binding force, varnish[es] it over by a subterfuge. — Obliterating the distinction so carefully made and so recently recognized between the man and the citizen, they produce, instead of the two, a sort of neutral or double man, who is neither the one nor the other, or else both in one.

Comparing the list of rights whoever they belong to (whether of the man or the citizen or the man in society), we shall find that between the year 1791 and the year 1795, unalienable as they are, they have undergone a change. Indeed for a set of unalienable rights they must be acknowledged to have been rather of the unsteadiest. At the time of the passing the 1st. Article of the Declaration of [1791][75] they were but two of them, liberty and equality. Between that first article and the next to it in the same Declaration, three new ones had started up in addition to liberty: viz: property, security and resistance to oppression: total, four sorts of rights: not five, for in the same interval an accident had happened to equality, and some how or other it was not to be found. In the interval between 1791 and 1795 it has been found: accordingly in the list of 1795 we may observe equality occupying an elevated station above every thing but liberty, with security and property lying at its feet. Looking for resistance against oppression, we may observe it kicked out of doors: and like the images of two illustrious Romans mentioned by Tacitus, the more observable for not being to be seen.[76] To account for this exclusion we must recollect that between 1791 and 1795, in short from the moment of his naturalization (for it was in America that he had his birth),[77] Citizen Resistance-against-oppression had been playing strange tricks: he had been constantly flying in the face of the powers in being, whatever were the powers in being: he had rendered himself a perfect nuisance, and so strong an one that it was high time for him to be sent to Coventry. He has accordingly been sent to Coventry, where he remains in a state of constant requisition, ready to present himself at the call of patriotism wherever a King is to be assassinated, or a riot to be kicked up. He had been discovered at length to be a most dangerous enemy to security after a four years' experience of his activity in that line: two years before his naturalization in France I had taken the liberty to denounce him as such in a book which found its way into the hands of Condorcet and others:[c] but my denuntiation was not heard.

As to the rest, the nonsensicalness and mischievousness of this article has been pointed out in the observations on the corresponding article of the Declaration of [1791].[78]

Art. 2. Liberty consists in the power of doing that which hurts not {the rights} of others.[79]

---

c. Introduction to the Principles of Morals and Legislation, 1789, page the last.[80]

The same as the commencement of Art.4 in the Declaration of [1791],[81] except as to the insertion of the words {*the rights*}.

Art. 3. Sentence 1: Equality consists in this — that the law is the same for all, whether it protects, or whether it punishes.

Sentence 2: Equality admitts not any distinction of births, any hereditary succession of powers.[82]

In Art. 6 of the Declaration of [1791][83] we saw this given in the character [of] a maxim, in which quality the propriety of it has been discussed:[84] the maxim is now turned into a definition of equality. This is equality certainly as far as it goes: but is it to be understood as stopping here, or is it to go any farther and how much farther? These questions are not answered: apparently because the Declaration-makers were afraid to answer them. Mean time thus much is certain: there is nothing in this Declaration of Rights to stop it: therefore on it must go in its own course: which course can never have found its end, till it has laid every thing smack smooth, not leaving such a thing as any one stone in the whole fabric of property above another.

That equality should leave no hereditary succession of powers is natural and consistent enough: but how does it contrive to leave any powers at all? Where is the equality between him who has powers, and him who has none? The exclusion of the hereditary succession of powers excepted, it turns out then that people are not the more at a par for the possession of this blessing, and that in short, to speak correctly, equality and inequality are the same thing.

No distinction of births — no distinction in point of birth? — how is that managed? Are all men in France to be born of the same mother? are all men in France to be got by the same father? Will democratic omnipotence prevent the Montmorencys from being descended from a known line of ancestors beginning under the Capets, or I forget what other family from a line beginning under Clovis?[85] What they probably meant to say is that no distinction in point of rights should be suffered to depend on any distinction in point of birth: but as epigrams are at least as necessary in a French book of legislation as laws, the paradoxical turn of expression was preferred as being to their conceptions the most natural.

Art. 4. Security results from the concurrence of all in the making secure {in the giving security for} the rights of each.[86]

An epigram upon Security — a definition imitated from the *Malade ima-ginaire*. The property which opium has of laying men to sleep results from its soporific quality.[87] Now, Citizen, if you don't know what security is, f . . . b. . . . [88] you deserve to have your house knocked down about your ears.

Concurrence of all on one hand — rights of each on the other. From this antithesis we learn that wherever security happens to be conferred by the exertions of any number less than all (as for instance if infants at the breast or lying-in-women take no part in the operation), it is no security at all.

Art. 5. Property is the right of enjoying and disposing of one's goods, of one's revenues, of the fruit of one's labour and one's industry.[89]

Another definition in the soporific stile, but perhaps not quite so inno-cent. Property is the right of enjoyment *and* disposal. Let a man then have ever so much of either right, yet if he has not the other, he has no property. It is perhaps owing to this definition of property that what the *ci-devant* Clergy of France had to live upon was not their property, and consequently there was no harm in robbing them of it.[90] In England, tenant for life of a settled estate conceives himself to be a man of property: this article informs him that he knows nothing about the matter. In England, a woman who has an advowson conceives the advowson to be her property. Let her consult a French legislator, he will tell her f. . . . it is no such thing, since she can't give herself the living.[91]

Declaration of the Duties of Man.
A°-1795.

Right being one of the fruits of Law, and *Duty* another, it occurred to the second set of Constitution-makers, that a *Declaration of Rights* would be but a *lap-sided* job, without a *Declaration of Duties*, to match it on the other side. A first Declaration of Rights having driven the people mad, a Declara-tion of duties, it was hoped, might help bring them to their senses. Whatever were their notions about the matter, thus much must be admitted to be true — that if poison *must* be taken, an antidote may have its use: but what would be still better, would be — to throw both together, poison and anti-dote, into the fire. Every medicine that is good for any thing, say the physicians, is a poison.[92] The political medicine we have now to analyse forms no exception to the rule.

What seems to have been no better understood by the second set of constitution-makers than the first, is that rights and duties are inseparable —

that so sure as rights are created, duties are created too, and that though you may make duties without making rights (which is in fact the result of the alas! but too numerous catalogue of laws by which nobody is the better), yet to make rights without making duties is impossible. As deep judges in legislative as Master Jourdan in colloquial composition, what seems to have escaped their sagacity is, that while making rights on pretence of dealing them out ready made, they have been making duties without knowing any thing about the matter.[93]

The Declaration of Rights (says the preamble or introductory sentence) contains the obligations of legislators: the maintenance of society requires that those who compose it know and fulfill equally *their* duties.[94] Whether by *duties* in the latter part of the sentence were meant exactly the same thing as by *obligations* in the first, I will not take upon me absolutely to determine: if it were, it will furnish one amongst so many other proofs how insensible these masters of legislation are of the value of useful precision, in comparison to that of fancied elegance.[95]

Art. 2. All the duties of the Man and the Citizen are derived from these two principles engraven by Nature in the hearts of all men.

Do not to another that which you would not men should do to you.

Do constantly to others the good which you would receive from them.[96]

The known source of this precept is the Gospel — Whatsoever ye would that men should do unto you, do ye even so unto them[97] — Do as you would be done by, says the abridged expression of it as given by the English proverb. What improvement the precept has received from the new edition given of it by the anti-christian hands will presently appear.

A division is here made of it into two branches, a negative and a positive: the tendency of the negative, placed where it is, is pernicious: the tendency of the positive branch, worded as it is, is absurd and [a] clumsy departure from the spirit of the original: the former, for want of the limitations necessary to the application here made of it, is mischievously extensive: the latter, by the tail clumsily tacked on to it, is made too narrow.

In what country is it, that it is the wish of accusers to be accused, of Judges to be condemned, of Guilotiners to be guillotined? In Topsy-turvy land, where Cooks are roasted by pigs, and hounds hunted by the hare. In that same land a law thus worded might do no harm and government might go on as well with it as without it. In France thus much is clear, that whatsoever individual prosecutes a delinquent, whatsoever Judge condemns him, whatsoever subordinate Minister of Justice executes the sentence of a

Judge, is a transgressor of this law, this fundamental law given without reservation or exception, said to be engraven just as we see it in all hearts, and placed first in the list of duties.

Morality, not affecting precision, addresses itself to the heart: Law, of which precision is the life and soul, addresses itself to the head.

The positive branch of the precept, under the necessity it should seem of rounding the period and making the line run well, is so worded as to shut the door against generosity. — Do to a man that good — what good? — why exactly and "constantly" just that very good which you want him to do to you. — And if you happen not to want any thing of him, what then? — why then, let him want and welcome — there is nothing in this rule of law that can afford him a handle to take hold of should he be inclined to accuse you of a breach of this fundamental duty. If you want a twopenny loaf, for example, go to the baker and give him either a twopenny loaf or two-pence: in the former case you fulfill the letter, in the latter the spirit, of the law. Should you happen to see a man starving for want of such a loaf let him starve and welcome: you want nothing of him, not you: neither the two-penny loaf nor the two-pence: let him starve on, he can not indict you upon this law.

Art. 4. No one is a good citizen if he is not a good son, a good father, a good brother, a good friend, a good husband.[98]

Good, as good as any other good thing that has been said a thousand times over, in a novel or a play — silly as a law, scarce reconcileable to the next preceding article, and not altogether reconcileable to the interests of the community at large.

The word civil gives name to one class of duties: the word domestic to another. Is it impossible to violate one law without violating another? Is there no distinction between duties? Is there no distinction between laws? does a man by beating his wife defraud the revenue? Does a man by drinking smuggled coffee beat his wife? Brutus, the elder Brutus, who, under a government where the father had the power of life and death over the child, put his sons to death for conspiracy against the government,[99] was he a bad citizen? or does goodness in a father consist in putting his children to death?

A friend of Lord Monteagle's was engaged with Guy Fawkes and others in a conspiracy for blowing up the legislature.[100] Under this fourth article and the third,[101] what should Monteagle have done? The third bids him discover the plot, for it bids him defend and serve the society and the laws thus threatened with destruction by the plot. The fourth bids him say nothing about the matter: for what could he say about it that would not endanger the safety of his friend? If Monteagle had happened to have been a well-wisher to the conspiracy, and desirous of concealing it, what could he have desired for his security better than such a clause?

Art. 5. No man is a good man if he is not frankly and religiously an observer of the laws.[102]

Of *the* laws? — of what laws? — of all laws? of all laws present and to come? whatsoever they may forbid, whatsoever they may enjoin? — a religious observer of the laws which forbid his religion, the only religion he thinks true, and bid him drag to judicial slaughter those who exercise it? To talk of religion, except in the way of rhetorical flourish in the stile which is here conceived to be the proper stile for law, may perhaps be deemed on this occasion an abuse of words. Well then, the men of September, or since they are out of power, the men of the 10[th.] of August,[103] were they good men? were they frank and religious observers of the law declaring and enacting the inviolability of the King?[104] — The question may seem puzzling: but a former passage will help us to a solution. By Art. [6] of the Declar[n.] of Rights, a law is no law unless made by democracy run mad — made by men, women and children, convicts, madmen — mediately or immediately — and so on.[105] Here then we have a clue: in a democracy run mad, goodness means submission to the laws: under every other sort of government, goodness means rebellion.

Art. 6. He who openly violates the laws, declares himself in a state of war with society.[106]

More very decent *clappable* matter for the stage: in a book of law, pretiously childish, and not a little dangerous.

To be in a state of war, is to be in that state in which the business of each party is to kill the other.

In kindness to one set of Button-makers we have a silly law in England condemning the whole country to wear now and for everlasting a sort of buttons they don't like.[107] A sillier law can scarcely be imagined: but laws of a similar stamp are but too plenty in Great Britain, and France will have good luck indeed, if laws of similar complexion do not, in spite of every exertion of democratic wisdom, find their way into France. In London you may see any day, in any street, men, women and children violating these and other such wholesome laws, knowingly or unknowingly, with sufficient openness. Since all these wicked, uncivic button wearers have declared war against society, what would the Citizen penner of this Declaration say — what say you, Citizen Legal-epigram-maker — to a few four and twenty pounders filled with grape shot, to clear the streets of them?

Art. 7. He who, without openly infringing the laws, eludes them by cunning or address, wounds the interests of all: he renders himself unworthy of their benevolence and of their esteem.[108]

As to the truth of this proposition, whether the eluding the observance of a law is or is not prejudicial to any body depends upon the nature of the law: if the law be one of those which are of no use to any body, the eluding of it does no harm to any body: if it be one of those which are of use to this or that description of persons and that only, the eluding of it may be a prejudice to them, but does no harm to any body else.

Were the law of libels as it stands in England to be obey'd without infraction, there would be no more liberty of discourse on political subjects in England than there is on religious subjects in Spain: were it executed in every instance of its being infringed, there would not be a man or a woman in England who had eyes or ears out of a jail. The law of England, taking it with all its faults, is probably at least as near perfection upon the whole as the law of any other country: at the same time, were any good to come of it, I would engage to find laws in it by dozens and by scores any one of which, if generally obey'd or at least if duly executed, would be enough to render the country as miserable as France.

Things being in this state, there seems unhappily no help for it, but that it must be left to each man's conscience in respect to what laws he shall be forward, and to what backward, to pay obedience, and lend his hand to execute. While matters are in this imperfect state, indiscriminate obedience is no more to be insisted on with regard to laws in any country, than under a limited Monarchy passive obedience is with regard to Kings.

To judge by these three last articles of the Declaration of Duties of the man and the citizen, the compositor seems to have been rather hard put to it to cover the requisite quantity of paper. Rights of man present themselves in sufficient plenty: but when he comes to Duties it becomes apparent that when a man has said it is your duty to obey the laws, he has said all that is to be said about the matter. Accordingly the contents of these three articles are — not any addition to the list of duties, but observations on the subject, consisting of a string of epigrams and fine speeches out of plays.

In regard to offences, the great difficulty is, and the great study ought to be — to distinguish them from one another: the business of this article is to confound them. In England simple disobedience is one thing, rebellion (technically but rather improperly called treason) another: the punishment of the one, where no special punishment is appointed, is a slight fine or a short imprisonment; that of the other, capital. In France under the auspices of this Declaration, these trifling differences are not thought worth noticing: disobedience and rebellion are discovered to be the same thing. The state of the laws in France must be superior not only to what it has ever been during the revolutionary anarchy, but to what it ever has been during the best times of French history or of the history of any other country of considerable extent, if there be a single day in any year in which scores of laws have not been transgressed, and that openly, by thousands and tens of thousands of individuals. If this be true, the effect of this single article must be, that after the restoration of peace and the perfect establishment of the best of all possible constitutions, the habitual state of France will be a state of civil war.

In the Codes of other countries, the great end of government is to quiet and repress the dissocial passions: in France the great study is to inflame and excite them: it does so when it talks of declaring rights: it does so still, even when declaring duties. Under this code, to be a true Frenchman a man must be for ever in a passion: never without a knife in his hand in readiness for his next neighbour's throat or his own. Whatever subject my pen begins upon, says Anacreon, changes into love.[109] Among French Constitution-makers, whatever subject a man begins upon, changes into anarchy.

A Frenchman knows no difference between a tragedy and a law: fine sentiments, epigrams upon stilts, *chaleur mouvement*, are equally indispensable in both. A tragedy, to be interesting, must be levelled at some law. Every law ends in a tragedy — every law must read like one.

Art. 8. On the maintenance of property (properties) rests the cultivation of the lands, all the productions, every means of labour, and the whole {fabrick of} social order.[110]

The article, as thus worded, reads bold enough, and if it were less so, it would not be faithful.

This article presents a striking picture of the distress of the penman. His subject is exhausted, his budget of duties, and what is more, even of fine speeches, emptied: he knows not what more to say, and yet so fond is he of hearing himself talk, he can never persuade himself to have done. To come back to *property* — what is it I can say to you that can persuade you to respect property? If you have no regard for property, what is it you have a regard for? — Do you like country-work? do you like good things in general? do you like work in general? — or — to keep the best to the last — if work won't tempt you, what say you to a little social order? — the very quintessence of all good things! you can't conceive how good it is!

Art. 9 and last in this list of *duty-declaring* articles. Every citizen owes his services to the country, to the maintenance of liberty, equality and property, as often as the law calls upon him to defend them.[111]

The conclusion of this short but superfluous composition is of a piece with the beginning: full of uncertainty, full of inconsistency, full of danger.

Every citizen owes his services to the country, to the [maintenance][112] and so forth, as often as he [is] called upon to defend them — Owes services? — *what* services? for what time, and upon what terms? — Military services? for soldier's pay and for life? If this was *not* meant, nothing can be easier than for any legislature, any administration — any administrator — any recruiting serjeant — to give it that meaning. — *Property* we have seen already secured by double and treble tithe:[113] *liberty* is here secured by a system of universal *crimping*. In England pressing is still looked upon as a hardship, though the custom of pressing is as old as the practice of navigation, and though no man is liable to be pressed who has not voluntarily embarked in a profession which he knows will subject him to it. What should we say in England were an Act of Parliament to be passed in virtue of which all men without exception, of all ages and professions, sick and well, able and decrepit, hearty and infirm, married and single, housekeepers and lodgers, lawyers, clergymen, and quakers, were liable to be pressed for soldiers? — Women perhaps into the bargain: since in France women's necks have been found to fit the guillotine as well as men's, and in England, thanks to the sages of the law, women make good constables.[114]

Equality too then is to be maintained, as well as property, equality without limitation, and that by every body at the call of every body. The distribution of property being at the time of issuing this declaration prodigiously unequal, as much at least as in many a monarchy, how are equality and property to be maintained there at the same time?

To choose which of the two shall be maintained — since both can not be maintained together — seems to be left to the wisdom of the Citizens: rich or poor, industrious or idle, full or fasting, as occasion may arise. To a considerable majority, the maintenance of equality will probably be the pleasanter task of the two as well as the more profitable.

On the Use and Abuse of the Word Right.

It is right I should continue to possess the coat I have upon my back, and so on with regard to every thing else I look upon as my property, at least till I choose to part with it.

It is right I should be at liberty to do as I please — I should be better if I might be permitted to add — whether other people were pleased with what it pleased me to do or not: but as that is hopeless I must be content with such a portion of liberty, though it is the least I can be content with, as consists in the liberty of doing as I please, subject to the exception of not doing real mischief to other people.

It is right I should be secure against all sorts of damage.

It is right I should be upon a par with every body else — upon a par at least — and if I can contrive to get a peep over other people's heads, where will be the harm in it?

But if all this is right now, at what time was it ever otherwise? it is then naturally right. — And at what future time will it be otherwise? it is then unalterably right, right for everlasting.

As it is right I should possess all these blessings, I have a right to all of them.

But if I have a right to the coat on my back, I have a right to knock any man down that attempts to rob me of it — else what signifies my having a right to it?

For the same reason, if I have a right to be secure against all sorts of harm, I have a right to knock any man down who attempts to harm me.

For the same reason, if I have a right to do whatever I please subject only to the exception of not doing mischief to other people, it follows that, subject only to that exception, I have a right to knock any man down who attempts in any instance to prevent my doing as I please.

For the same reason, if I have a right to be upon a par with every body else in every respect, it follows that should any man take upon him to raise his house higher than mine, rather than it should continue so, I have a right to pull it down about his ears, and to knock him down if he attempts to hinder me.

Thus easy, thus natural, under the guidance of the selfish and antisocial passions, thus insensible, is the transition from the language of peace to the language of destruction. — Transition did I say? what transition? — from right to right? the propositions are identical — there is no transition in the case. — Certainly, as far as words go, scarce any — no more than if you were to trust your wife with a man for a week or so, and he were to return her violated or poisoned — it was your wife you trusted to him, it is your wife you have received again: what you had trusted to him, you have received.

It is in England rather than in France that the discovery of the *Rights of Man* ought naturally to have taken its rise: — it is we, we English, that have the better *right* to it. It is in the English language that the transition is more natural than perhaps in most others: at any rate more so than in the French. It is in English and not in French that we may change the sense without changing the word, and, like Don Quixote on the enchanted horse, travel as far as the moon and farther without ever getting off the saddle.[115] One and the same word right, that most enchanting of all words, is sufficient for operating the fascination. The word is our's, that magic word, which by its single powers compleats the fascination. In its adjective shape it is as innocent as a dove: it breathes nothing but morality and peace. It is in this guise that, passing in at the heart, it gets possession of the understanding: then it assumes its substantive shape, and, joining itself [to] a band of suitable associates, it plants the banner of insurrection and lawless violence. It is right men should be as near upon a par with one another in every respect as they can be made consistently with general security — here we have it in its adjective form synonymous with desirable, proper, becoming, consonant to general utility, and the like. I have a right to put myself upon a par with every body in every respect — here we have it in its *substantive* sense — forming with the other words a phrase equivalent to this — wherever I find a man who will not let me put myself on a par with him in every respect, it is right and proper and becoming that I should knock him down, if I have a mind to do so, and if that won't do, knock him on the head and so forth.

The language of the French is fortunate enough not to possess this mischievous abundance. But a Frenchman will not be kept back from his purpose by any want of words. The want of an adjective *right*, of an adjective composed of the same letters as the substantive *right*, is no loss to him. Is, has been, ought to be, shall be, can, all are put for one another, all are pressed into the service, all made to answer the same purpose. By this inebriating compound we have seen all the elements of the understanding confounded, every fibre of the heart inflamed, the lips prepared for every folly, and the hand for every crime.

Our right to this pretious discovery, such as it is, of the rights of man must, I repeat it, have been prior to that of the French. It has been seen how peculiarly rich we are in materials for making it. I will prove its filiation. It shall be seen, how from *real* laws come *real* rights: and then it will be seen, how from *imaginary* laws, come imaginary ones. *Right*, the substantive *right*, is the child of law: and when once brought into the world, what more natural than for poets, for rhetoricians, for all dealers in moral and intellectual poisons, to give the child a spurious parentage, to lay it at Nature's door, and set it up in opposition against the real author of its birth. Then comes a bastard brood of monsters, "Gorgons and Chimæras dire."[116] And thus it is that from *legal rights*, the offspring of law and friends of peace, come *anti-legal rights*, the mortal enemies of law, the subverters of government and the assassins of security.

Will this antidote to the second French disease[117] have its effect? will this preservative for the understanding and the heart against the fascination of sounds find lips to take it? This is almost too much — in any great degree, in point of speedy or immediate efficacy at least, it is certainly too much to hope for. Alas! how dependent are opinions upon sounds! what Hercules shall break the chains by which opinions are led captive by sounds? By what force of words shall connections between words and ideas be dissolved, connections coeval with the cradle? By what authority shall this original vice in the structure of the language be corrected? by what | | shall a mode of expression which has taken root in the vitals of the language be expelled? by what detergent shall a word in continual use be deprived of half its signification, an article of necessary use to the body politic be purged of half its properties? The language of plain and strong sense is difficult to learn: the language of smooth nonsense, easy and familiar. The one requires a force of attention capable of stemming the tide of usage and example: the other requires nothing but to swim with it. It is for *education* to do what can be done: and in education is, though unhappily the slowest, the surest as well as earliest resource. The recognition of the nothingness of the laws of nature, and of the rights of man that have been grounded on them, is a branch of knowledge of as much importance to an Englishman, though a negative one, as the most perfect acquaintance that can be formed with the existing laws of England.

It must be so — Shakespeare,[118] whose plays were filling English hearts with rapture, while the Drama of France was not superior to that of Caffraria,[119] Shakespeare, who had a key to all the passions and to all the stores of language, could never have let slip an instrument of delusion of such superior texture. — No it is not possible, that the rights of man — the natural, Pre-adamitical, ant*e*-legal and ant*i*-legal rights of man — should have been unknown to Shakespeare. — How could the Macbeths, the Jaffeirs, the Iagos,[120] do without them? they present a cloak to every conspiracy — they hold out a mask to every crime — they are every villain's armory — every spendthrift's treasure.

But if the English were the first to bring the rights of man into the closet from the stage, it is to the stage and the closet that they have confined them. It was reserved to France, to France in her days of degradation and regeneration, in those days in comparison of which the worst of her days of fancied tyranny were halcyon ones, to turn debates into tragedies, and the senate into a stage.

The mask is now taken off, and the following [is] the language by which the anarchist may be recognized.

Asserting *rights* of any kind — acknowledging them at the same time not to be recognized by government.

Using instead of *ought* and *ought not*, the words *is* or *is not*, *can* or *can not*.

In former times, in the times of Grotius [and] Puffendorf, these expressions were little more than improprieties in language, prejudicial to the interests of knowledge: at present, since the French Declaration of Rights has adopted them and the French Revolution display'd their import by a practical comment, the use of them is already a *moral* crime, and not undeserving of being constituted a legal crime, hostile to the public peace.

NOTES

1. The Declaration of the Rights of Man and the Citizen, initially adopted by the National Assembly on 26 August 1789, was prefixed in a slightly amended form to the Constitution of 1791, which was published on 2 September 1791 (see *Archives parlementaires*, xxx. 151–68), declared to be complete the following day and accepted by Louis XVI on 14 September 1791.

2. In Roman times the priest of the sacred grove of Diana at Aricia was known as *rex nemorensis*, i.e., "King of the Wood." The priesthood was open only to runaway slaves, and to succeed to the title the contender had to kill the incumbent in single combat, using as weapon a branch broken from a tree in the grove. See Servius, *In Vergilii Carmina Commentarii*, on *Aeneid*, VI. 136; Strabo, *Geography*, V. iii. 12; and Suetonius, *De vita Caesarum*, IV. xxxv.

3. Bentham has marked the remainder of the paragraph for deletion: "This medium of proof was but too alluring: to the advantage of removing opposition was added the pleasure, the sort of titillation so exquisite to the sense [?] of vanity in a French heart, the satisfaction — to use a homely but not the less apposite proverb — of teaching grandmothers to suck eggs. Hark ye Citizens of the other side of the water: can you tell us what rights you have yet belonging to you? No; that you can't. It's *we* that understand rights: not our own only, but your's into the bargain: while you, poor simple souls! know nothing about the matter."

4. I.e., the House of Commons.

5. Erostratus, or Herostratus, set fire to the temple of Artemis, at Ephesus in 356 BC, on the same night that Alexander the Great was born. Erostratus confessed that his aim had been to immortalize himself by the deed.

6. In classical mythology, Pandora, the first woman, brought with her from heaven a box containing every kind of human misery and ill, which escaped and spread out all over the earth when she opened it.

7. "Les hommes naissent et demeurent libres, et égaux en droits. Les distinctions sociales ne peuvent être fondées que sur l'utilité commune." The Articles of the Declaration of the Rights of Man and the Citizen are reproduced from *La Constitution Française, Présentée au Roi le 3 Septembre 1791, et acceptée par Sa Majesté le 14 du même mois* (Paris, 1791), 2–8.

8. Bentham has marked the remainder of the paragraph for deletion: "To forget that man is born young — to forget the condition in which they themselves and their own children were, on their coming into the world, such are the qualifications which these legislators produce for being the instructors of nations."

9. Bentham has marked the remainder of the paragraph for deletion: "Oh, but it ought to be recognized, for the rights in question are not only natural but unalienable: and being unalienable, whatever infractions are made on them are illegal and void, the governments that make them tyrannical, abusive, in fact no governments at all, but knots of usurpers whose orders ought to meet with nothing but resistance. No government but what perpetually violates these rights: therefore no government but what ought to meet with perpetual resistance. No government against which insurrection is not a duty. Such is the practical consequence of the magnificent theory, invented and promulgated, as itself declares, for the support of government as well as for the happiness and the instruction of all mankind. So far is this from misrepresentation or exaggeration, that accordingly it is become the avowed and general doctrine in France that all governments but that of France (meaning the government of the day whatever it be) are usurpations."

10. Bentham's attribution of the maxim "whatever is, is" to Descartes seems somewhat polemical. Descartes' view was that humans were warranted in ascribing existence only to objects which were clearly and distinctly perceived, and that all knowledge was founded on the proposition *cogito ergo sum*, i.e., "I am thinking, therefore I exist": see "Discourse on the Method of rightly conducting one's reason and seeking the truth in the sciences" (first published in French in 1637), part 4, p. 32, in *The Philosophical Writings of Descartes*, i. 127. Descartes, as Bentham goes on to state, did, however, suggest "that the whole of the celestial matter in which the planets are located turns continuously like a vortex with the sun at its centre": see "The Principles of Philosophy," part 3, art. 30, p. 92, in ibid., i. 253.

11. Francis Bacon (1561–1626), first Baron of Verulam and first Viscount Saint Alban, philosopher and writer, lord chancellor 1618–21, had written, "*Judges* must beware of Hard Constructions, and Strained Inferences; For there is no Worse Torture, than the Torture of Lawes": see *The Essayes or Counsels, Civill and Morall*, ed. M. Kiernan (Oxford, 1985) (first published 1597–1625), essay 56, "Of Judicature," 166.

12. The National Assembly had abolished the hereditary nobility and hereditary titles by a decree of 19 June 1790, and the abolition was reiterated in the Preamble to the Constitution of 1791.

13. See pp. 361–63 below.

14. The following paragraph appears to have been added to the text in 1801.

15. "Le but de toute association politique est la conservation des droits naturels et imprescriptibles de l'homme. Ces droits sont la liberté, la propriété, la sûreté, et la résistance à l'oppression."

16. Descriptions of the aborigines of New South Wales and their environment had appeared, for instance, in *A Journal of a Voyage round the World, In his Majesty's Ship Endeavour, In the Years 1768, 1769, 1770, and 1771* (London, 1771), 111–16, 122–23; John Hawkesworth, *An Account of Voyages undertaken by the order of his present Majesty for making Discoveries in the Southern Hemisphere, and successively performed by Commodore Byron, Captain Wallis, Captain Carteret, and Captain Cook, in the Dolphin, the Swallow, and the Endeavour*, 3 vols. (London, 1773), iii. 481–543, 566–86, 622–49; and Sydney Parkinson, *A Journal of a Voyage to the South Seas, in his Majesty's Ship, The Endeavour* (London, 1773), 132–53. These accounts were based upon the explorations of Captain James Cook (1728–79), who had landed in New South Wales in 1770 during his circumnavigation of the globe between August 1768 and June 1771.

17. MS orig. "want is not supply."

18. MS "me."

19. This view was perhaps most clearly expressed by Thomas Hobbes (1588–1679) in *Leviathan* (first published in 1651), part 1, chap. 14, [64] but was also discussed by Hugo Grotius (1583–1645), Benedict de Spinoza (1632–77), and Samuel Pufendorf (1632–94). See, for instance, Grotius, *De jure belli ac pacis* (first published in 1625), lib. 1, cap. 2, 5; Spinoza, *Tractatus theologico-politicus* (first published in 1670), chap. 16; and Pufendorf, *De jure naturae et gentium* (first published in 1672), lib. 1, cap. 7, 13.

20. MS orig. "nugatory."

21. An alternative draft of this section appears at Bentham Papers, University College London Library, cxlvi. 91: "2. Second species of natural and imprescriptible rights: rights of property. Laws creative of these rights lye again under the same curse. How is property given? by restraining liberty: that is by taking it away

so far as is necessary for the purpose. How is your house made yours? — by my being debarred from the liberty of entering it without your leave."

22. Bentham marked the remainder of the paragraph for deletion, presumably because it repeated the argument at pp. 330–32 above: "Accordingly *Natura dedit unicuique jus ad omnia*, says I forget what interpreter of the pretended law of Nature. Unfortunately in most matters of property what is every man's right is no man's right: so that the effect of this part of the Oracle, if observed, would be not to establish property but to extinguish it, and, as this is one of the rights declared to be imprescriptible, unchangeable, to render it impossible ever to be revived." For the view that "Nature has given to each man a right to every thing," see n. 19 above.

23. "Le principe de toute souveraineté réside essentiellement dans la Nation. Nul corps, nul individu ne peut exercer d'autorité qui n'en émane expressément."

24. "La liberté consiste à pouvoir faire tout ce qui ne nuit pas à autrui. Ainsi, l'exercice des droits naturels de chaque homme n'a de bornes que celles qui assurent aux autres membres de la société la jouissance de ces mêmes droits. Ces bornes ne peuvent être déterminées que par la loi."

25. MS "Sentence."

26. In the margin, Bentham has noted at this point: "Exemplify or give in a note a list of the offences to which impunity is here insured." Bentham did not go on to consider this topic in "Nonsense Upon Stilts," but for an extended discussion, see *An Introduction to the Principles of Morals and Legislation*, ed. J. H. Burns and H. L. A. Hart (London, 1970) (*CW*), chap. 13, pp. 158–64 [hereafter *IPML*].

27. "La loi n'a le droit de défendre que les actions nuisibles à la société. Tout ce qui n'est pas défendu par la loi ne peut être empêché; et nul ne peut être contraint à faire ce qu'elle n'ordonne pas."

28. "La loi est l'expression de la volonté générale. Tous les citoyens ont droit de concourir personnellement, ou par leurs représentans, à sa formation. Elle doit être la même pour tous, soit qu'elle protége, soit qu'elle punisse. Tous les citoyens étant égaux à ses yeux, sont également admissibles à toutes dignités, places et emplois publics, selon leur capacité, et sans autre distinction que celle de leurs vertus et de leurs talens."

29. For outlawry under English law, see Blackstone, *Commentaries on the Laws of England* (Oxford, 1765–69), iii. 283–84, iv. 314–15.

30. The sanction of "civil death" under the ancien régime in fact had similar consequences to English outlawry. Although the practice was officially ended with the Constitution of 1791, the émigrés were declared to be "civilly dead" by a Decree of the National Convention of 28 March 1793. They were banished for life on pain of death should they return to France, and their property was confiscated by the Republic. This latter was perhaps the "severer form" which Bentham had in mind.

31. By 7 Jac. I, c. 5 (1609), made perpetual by 21 Jac. I, c. 12 (1623), justices of the peace and other officials were allowed double costs if they successfully defended an action brought against them for anything done in virtue of their office.

32. Countess Lapuchin, or Lapukhina, a celebrated beauty at the court of Elizabeth (1709–62), empress of Russia from 1741, suffered the punishment of the knout and had her tongue cut out on 31 May 1744, and was then banished to Siberia, until recalled by Peter III (1728–62), emperor of Russia in 1762. An account appeared in M. L'Abbé D'Auteroche, *Voyage en Sibérie, fait par ordre du roi en 1761*, 4 vols. (Paris, 1768), i. 227–28, translated into English as *A Journey into Siberia, made by order of the King of France by M. L'Abbé Chappe D'Auteroche* (London, 1770), 338–39.

33. Probably William Hunter (1718–83), first professor of anatomy at the Royal Academy 1768–83, who began lecturing in London on surgery and anatomy in 1746 and quickly established a reputation for eloquence and for the apposite use of illustrative examples. That Bentham attended the lectures of William, rather than those of his brother John Hunter (1728–93), who joined William as an assistant lecturer in 1754, formed his own class for anatomy and surgery in 1763, and commenced public lectures on the theory and practice of surgery in 1773, is indicated in Bentham to Thomas Foley, 5 June 1822, *The Correspondence of Jeremy Bentham*, vol. xi, ed. C. Fuller (Oxford, 2000) (*CW*), 91.

34. The judgment to which Bentham refers has not been traced, but it may have been delivered by Lloyd Kenyon (1732–1802), first Baron Kenyon, master of the rolls 1784–88, chief justice of King's Bench 1788–1802. In the later case of *Mirehouse v. Rennell* (1833), reported in Richard Bligh, *New Reports of Cases Heard in the House of Lords*, 10 vols. (London, 1829–38), vii. 241–324, at 322, such an opinion was ascribed to Kenyon by William Draper Best (1767–1845), first Baron Wynford, justice of King's Bench 1818–24, chief justice of Common Pleas 1824–29.

35. MS "Catholic to a Protestant."

36. State subsidies to religious institutions were renounced by the National Convention in a decree of 18 September 1794.

37. By the Civil Constitution of the Clergy of 12 July 1790, the National Assembly had established a new salary scale for the clergy and had delegated the power of making appointments to benefices to the enfranchised "active citizens."

38. "Nul homme ne peut être accusé, arrêté ni détenu que dans les cas déterminés par la loi, et selon les formes qu'elle a prescrites. Ceux qui sollicitent, expédient, exécutant ou font exécuter des ordres arbitraires, doivent être punis; mais tout citoyen appelé ou saisi en vertu de la loi, doit obéir à l'instant: il se rend coupable par la résistance."

39. Bentham presumably had in mind the Constitution of 5 Fructidor, Year III

(22 August 1795), tit. 14, art. 359: "La maison de chaque citoyen est un asyle inviolable: pendant la nuit, nul n'a le droit d'y entrer que dans les cas d'incendie, d'inondation, ou de réclamation venant de l'intérieur de la maison."

40. The doctrine *domus sua cuique est tutissium refugium*, or "Every man's house is his castle," was quoted in *Semayne's Case* (1604) and reported in *The Fifth Part of the Reports of Sir Edward Coke Kt.* (Savoy, 1738), 91–93.

41. "La loi ne doit établir que des peines strictement et évidemment nécessaries; et nul ne peut être puni qu'en vertu d'une loi établie et promulguée antérieurement au délit, et légalement appliquée."

42. For Bentham's comments on what he termed "the fox-hunter's reason" for excluding "self-disserving evidence" in English law, see *Rationale of Judicial Evidence, specially applied to English practice*, 5 vols. (London, 1827), vol. v, bk. 9, pt. 3, chap. 3, 3, pp. 238–40 (*The Works of Jeremy Bentham*, ed. J. Bowring, 11 vols. [Edinburgh: William Tait, 1838–43], vii. 454).

43. Bentham appears to have garbled the story of Princess Parizade or Farizade, who, having been maliciously separated from her father, the Sultan, and her mother at birth, is sent by a holy woman in search of a talking bird, a singing tree, and golden water, an adventure which results in her recognition by her father. A version of the story appears in *The Arabian Nights' Entertainment*, 4 vols. (Dublin, 1728), iv. 255–308.

44. MS "nothing" contradicts the evident sense of the passage.

45. See *IPML*, chap. 14, pp. 165–74.

46. "Tout homme étant présumé innocent jusqu'à ce qu'il ait été déclaré coupable, s'il est jugé indispensable de l'arrêter, toute rigueur qui ne seroit pas nécessaire pour s'assurer de sa personne, doit être sévèrement réprimée par la loi."

47. MS "of the justice."

48. "Nul ne doit être inquiété pour ses opinions, même religieuses, pourvu que leur manifestation ne trouble pas l'ordre public établi par la loi."

49. The Revocation of the Edict of Nantes by Louis XIV in October 1685 deprived the Huguenots, or French Protestants, of all civil and religious rights.

50. "La libre communication des pensées et des opinions est un des droits les plus précieux de l'homme. Tout citoyen peut donc parler, écrire, imprimer librement; sauf à répondre de l'abus de cette liberté dans les cas déterminés par la loi."

51. Perhaps the most famous statement of this principle was to be found in Beccaria, *An Essay on Crimes and Punishments* (London, 1767), chap. 41, p. 164: "It is better to prevent crimes, than to punish them." A similar point had been made in Montesquieu, *The Spirit of Laws* (London, 1750), bk. 6, chap. 9, i. 118, in the context of a discussion of "moderate governments": "a good legislator is less bent upon punishment than preventing crimes; he is more attentive to inspire good morals than to inflict punishments."

52. MS "they were."

53. "La garantie des droits de l'Homme et du Citoyen nécessite une force publique. Cette force est donc instituée pour l'avantage de tous, et non pour l'utilité particulière de ceux auxquels elle est confiée."

54. These three figures were important early rulers of France. Clovis (c. 466–511), king of the Salian Franks from 481 or 482, converted to Christianity c. 498. Pépin d'Héristal (d. 714) became mayor of the palace of Austrasia in 679, and following his victory at Terty over the mayor of the palace of Neustria became sole mayor of the palace over all the Franks in 687. Hugh Capet (936–96), king of France from 987, was the founder of the Capetian dynasty, the direct line of which ruled France until 1328, when Philip VI (1293–1350), from a collateral branch of the family, succeeded to the throne, inaugurating the Valois dynasty.

55. William I or the Conqueror (1027 or 1028–87), king of England from 1066, having led the Norman Conquest of England in 1066, had by the end of his reign replaced all the great Anglo-Saxon landholders with his own followers.

56. MS "its."

57. MS "it."

58. MS "it."

59. An echo of Blackstone's phrase, "Every thing is now as it should be," made in the context of a discussion of the offence of heresy at *Commentaries on the Laws of England*, iv. 49, but which Bentham took to be characteristic of Blackstone's attitude to the British political system as a whole.

60. "Pour l'entretien de la force publique, et pour les dépenses d'administration, une contribution commune est indispensable. Elle doit être également répartie entre tous les citoyens, en raison de leurs facultés."

61. The French system of taxation was overhauled at the end of 1790 and beginning of 1791, with all indirect taxes being suppressed and three new direct taxes introduced: the *contribution foncière*, or land tax, was created on 23 November 1790 and came into effect on 1 January 1791; the *contribution mobilière*, or tax on personal property, was created on 13 January 1791 and imposed retrospectively from 1 January 1791; and the *patentes*, or tax on commerce and industry, was created on 2 March 1791, came into effect on 1 April 1791, and, though suppressed in 1793, was revived in 1795.

62. The new system of taxation required a vast state machinery, under the control of the local authorities, whose duty it was to levy the taxes. In principle, significant intrusion into each man's private affairs was necessary during the period of assessment of tax liability, when financial records and other measures of income, wealth, and profits had to be made available for scrutiny. See Camille Bloch, *Les contributions directes* (Paris, 1915).

63. "Tous les citoyens ont le droit de constater par eux-mêmes, ou par leurs

représentans, la nécessité de la contribution publique; de la consentir librement; d'en suivre l'emploi; et d'en déterminer la quotité, l'assiette, le recouvrement et la durée."

64. See p. 340 above.

65. "La société a le droit de demander compte à tout agent public de son administration."

66. "Toute Société dans laquelle la garantie des Droits n'est pas assurée, ni la séparation des Pouvoirs déterminée, n'a point de Constitution."

67. When the audience at the Circensian games favored a party in opposition to him, Gaius, better known as Caligula (12–41), Roman emperor from 37, threatened them with the words *utinam populus Romanus unam cervicem haberet*, i.e., "I wish the Roman people had but one neck": see Suetonius, *De vita Caesarum*, IV. xxx; and Cassius Dio, *Roman History*, LIX. xiii. 6.

68. I.e. "divide and rule."

69. Matthew 12: 25; Mark 3: 25.

70. See Thomas Paine (1737–1809), *Rights of Man: being an answer to Mr. Burke's attack on the French Revolution* (London, 1791), 54: "I readily perceive the reason why Mr. Burke declined going into the comparison between the English and French constitutions, because he could not but perceive, when he sat down to talk, that no such thing as a constitution existed on his side [of] the question." Paine's allusion is to Burke's *Reflections on the Revolution in France*, first published on 1 November 1790: see *The Writings and Speeches of Edmund Burke*. Volume 8: *The French Revolution 1790–1794*, ed. L. G. Mitchell (Oxford, 1989), 53–293.

71. "La propriété étant un droit inviolable et sacré, nul ne peut en être privé si ce n'est lorsque la nécessité publique, légalement constatée, l'exige évidemment, et sous la condition d'une juste et préalable indemnité."

72. See Judges 11: 29–40.

73. An allusion to the Bethlehem Royal Hospital, founded as a priory in 1247 and granted by Henry VIII (1491–1547), king of England from 1509 and king of Ireland from 1541, to the City of London as a hospital for the insane in 1547.

74. "Les droits de l'homme en société sont la liberté, l'égalité, la sûreté, la proprieté." The Articles of the "Déclaration des droits et des devoirs de l'homme et du citoyen" are reproduced from *Constitution de la République Française, proposée au peuple Français par la Convention Nationale* (Paris, An III [1795]), 3–6.

75. MS "1795."

76. See Tacitus, *Annales*, III. 76: *Sed praefulgebant Cassius atque Brutus eo ipso quod effigies eorum non visebantur*, i.e., "But Cassius and Brutus were shining all the more because their images were not to be seen." The context of this

remark was a funeral procession in the time of Tiberius (42 BC–37 AD), emperor of Rome from 14 AD, when images of illustrious Romans were carried. However, images of Cassius (d. 42 BC) and Brutus (c. 85–42 BC), the slayers of Julius Caesar (100–44 BC), were not part of the procession, as public display of enemies of the state was proscribed.

77. Bentham presumably had in mind the Declaration of Independence of 4 July 1776, which stated that governments were instituted to secure the rights of "Life, Liberty and the pursuit of Happiness," and that "whenever any Form of Government becomes destructive of these ends, it is the Right of the People to alter or to abolish it, and to institute new Government," and that in the circumstances "it is their right, it is their duty, to throw off" the government of the king of Great Britain.

78. MS "1795." See pp. 327–35 above.

79. "La liberté consiste à pouvoir faire ce qui ne nuit pas aux droits d'autrui."

80. See *IPML* (*CW*), 308–11, where Bentham criticized "attempts to limit the powers of supreme representative legislatures," though he did not specifically mention "resistance against oppression." Bentham considered sending a copy of this work to Condorcet in the spring of 1789: see Bentham to André Morellet, 28 April 1789, *Correspondence* (*CW*), iv. 50n.

81. MS "1795." See p. 336 above.

82. "L'égalité consiste en ce que la loi est la même pour tous, soit qu'elle protège, soit qu'elle punisse. L'égalité n'admet aucune distinction de naissance, aucune hérédité de pouvoirs."

83. MS "1795."

84. See pp. 342–45 above.

85. The earliest named individual from whom the Montmorency family claimed descent was Bouchard I (d. 1007), comte de Vendôme from 980, who served as advisor to Hugh Capet. The second family referred to by Bentham was also the Montmorency family, since they also claimed descent from the first baron who followed Clovis in his conversion to Christianity around 498.

86. "La sûreté résulte du concours de tous pour assurer les droits de chacun."

87. See Moliere, *Le malade imaginaire* (first performed in 1673), act I, scene i: "un julep hépatique, soporatif, et somnifère, composé pour faire dormir Monsieur."

88. I.e., "foutre bleu."

89. "La propriété est le droit de jouir et de disposer de ses biens, de ses revenus, du fruit de son travail et de son industrie."

90. Bentham presumably had in mind the decree of the Constituent Assembly of 2 November 1789 that all ecclesiastical benefices were at the disposal of the nation.

91. In the margin at this point, Bentham has noted: "These flowers are not essential to the compositions of a French legislator: but they are indispensable ingredients to his conversations. See the trial of Carrier and all other minutes of conversations under the reign of liberty." Jean Baptiste Carrier (1756–94), having been sent to Nantes by the National Convention in October 1793 to suppress local opposition, had been responsible for an estimated ten thousand deaths, including the so-called *noyades* of Nantes, when rebel prisoners had been drowned in the Loire. Having been recalled to Paris on 8 February 1794 by the Committee of Public Safety, he was eventually brought before the Revolutionary Tribunal for trial on 11 November 1794, and was executed on 16 December 1794. Bentham does not comment on the remaining seventeen of the twenty-two articles which constituted that part of the "Déclaration" dealing with "Droits."

92. Cf. Ovid, *Tristia*, II. 20: *res eadem vulnus opemque feret*, i.e., "The same thing will both cure and harm me."

93. See Molière, *Le bourgeois gentilhomme* (first performed in 1670), act II, scene iv, where M. Jourdain asks a philosophy teacher for a definition of prose writing. On hearing the answer he exclaims: "il y a plus de quarante ans que je dis de la prose sans que j'en susse rien."

94. I.e., Article 1: "La déclaration des droits contient les obligations des législateurs: le maintien de la société demande que ceux qui la composent connaissent et remplissent également leurs devoirs."

95. In the margin, Bentham has noted in pencil at this point: "Continue." However, no continuation of this discussion has been identified.

96. "Tous les devoirs de l'homme et du citoyen dérivent de ces deux principes gravés par la nature dans tous les coeurs:

"Ne faites pas à autrui ce que vous ne voudriez pas qu'on vous fît.

"Faites constamment aux autres le bien que vous voudriez en recevoir."

97. Matthew 7: 12; Luke 6: 31.

98. "Nul n'est bon citoyen s'il n'est bon fils, bon père, bon frère, bon ami, bon époux."

99. Lucius Iunius Brutus, one of the first two consuls in 509 BC, executed two of his sons for their involvement in a plot to restore the Tarquins as kings of Rome. See Livy, *Ab urbe condita*, II. v. 5–9.

100. The Gunpowder Plot was a conspiracy of Roman Catholics, including Guy Fawkes (1570–1606), to blow up the Houses of Parliament during the State Opening on 5 November 1605, and thereby to kill James I. Fawkes was discovered in the cellars beneath the Houses of Parliament following a warning sent from another of the conspirators, Francis Tresham (1567?-1605), to his Protestant brother-in-law, William Parker (1575–1622), fourth Baron of Monteagle, advising him to avoid the ceremony.

101. "Les obligations de chacun envers la société, consistent à la défendre, à la servir, à vivre soumis aux lois, et à respecter ceux qui en sont les organes."

102. "Nul n'est homme de bien s'il n'est franchement et religieusement observateur des lois."

103. I.e., the persons responsible for the so-called September Massacres of 1792 and for the attack on the Tuileries of 10 August 1792 respectively.

104. See the Constitution of 1791, tit. 3, chap. 2, 1, art. 2 "La personne du Roi est inviolable et sacrée."

105. See p. 340 above.

106. "Celui qui viole ouvertement les lois, se déclare en état de guerre avec la société."

107. The importation or sale of foreign buttons had been prohibited, and the materials from which buttons were permitted to be made restricted, by a series of statutes: see 13 & 14 Car. II, c. 13; 4 Will. III, c. 10; 8 Ann., c. 6; and 4 Geo. I, c. 7.

108. "Celui qui, sans enfreindre ouvertement les lois, les élude par ruse ou par adresse, blesse les intérêts de tous; il se rend indigne de leur bienveillance et de leur estime."

109. See *Anacreontea*, 23: "I want to tell of the sons of Atreus, I want to sing of Cadmus, my lyre strings only sing of love." The *Anacreontea* were, until the early nineteenth century, attributed to Anacreon (b. c. 575–570 BC), the Greek lyric poet, though they were not in fact composed until many centuries later, at various times between the first century BC and the sixth century AD.

110. "C'est sur le maintien des propriétés que reposent la culture des terres, toutes les productions, tout moyen de travail, et tout l'ordre social."

111. "Tout citoyen doit ses services à la patrie et au maintien de la liberté, de l'égalité et de la propriété, toutes les fois que la loi l'appelle à les défendre."

112. MS "country."

113. See pp. 361–63 above.

114. In *R. v. Stubbs*, decided in the Court of King's Bench on 21 April 1788, it was held by William Henry Ashurst or Ashhurst (1725–1807), justice of King's Bench 1770–99, that a woman was competent to serve in "the office of high chamberlain, high constable, and marshal; and that of a common constable," though he added that "where there are a sufficient number of men qualified to serve the office, they are certainly more proper." See Charles Durnford and Edward Hyde East, *Reports of Cases Argued and Determined in the Court of King's Bench, from Trinity Term, 27th George III. to Michaelmas Term, 29th George III. both inclusive*, 3d ed., 8 vols. (London, 1789), ii. 406.

115. Don Quixote and Sancho Panza are blindfolded and tricked by a duke and his wife, the Dulcinea del Toboso, into believing that they are flying into the region

of fire between the moon and heaven on the back of an enchanted wooden horse named Clavileño: see *Don Quixote*, part 2, bk. 2, chap. 41.

116. See Milton, *Paradise Lost* (first published in 1667), ii, 626–28:

> . . . and worse
> Than fables yet have feigned, or fear conceived,
> Gorgons and Hydras, and Chimeras dire.

117. The first "French disease" was, of course, syphilis.

118. William Shakespeare (1564–1616), dramatist and poet.

119. Caffraria, or Kaffraria, in the northeast of present-day South Africa.

120. These three figures are conspirators. Macbeth appears in the play of the same name, and Iago in *Othello, the Moor of Venice*, by Shakespeare, while Jaffeir appears in *Venice Preserv'd, or, A Plot Discover'd*, first performed in 1682, by Thomas Otway (1652–85).

On Retrenchment

Bentham wrote this essay in June 1828 for a collection of papers on bureaucratic reform, a supplement to his work on the *Constitutional Code*. He decided not to include it in the volume published in 1830 entitled *Official Aptitude Maximized; Expense Minimized*. It is possible that he was planning a separate short work on the subject of retrenchment. For more on the history of this text and companion materials, see the editorial introduction to *Official Aptitude Maximized; Expense Minimized*, ed. Philip Schofield (Oxford 1993), especially xvii, xli–xliii, and xlviii–xlix.

The essay was first published in 1993 as an appendix to the *Collected Works of Jeremy Bentham* edition of *Official Aptitude*. It includes a digression on the history of political thought and the emergence and meanings of utility that Bentham had marked for exclusion, as well as a broader discussion of justice as the prevention of disappointment. With the permission of Oxford University Press, what follows is a reproduction of appendix B to *Official Aptitude*, 342–67, with only cross-references omitted or altered (in bold).

§ 1. Disappointment-prevention principle — what: its connection with Greatest happiness principle

1. Proportioned to profusion is the demand for retrenchment.

2. For the conduct of this operation, one subordinate principle, and that the only one justifiable, is presented by the all-ruling and all-comprehensive principle — the greatest happiness principle.

3. Undenominated as yet, though so extensively acted upon, is this

alike unobjectionable principle. Call it the *Disappointment-prevention* principle.[a]

4. Corresponding proposition, this proposition or say *aphorism*: this aphorism fit to serve as an *axiom*:

In the distribution made and maintained of the several separable portions of the aggregate subject-matter of property in the state, let the object or end in view be, on each occasion, *minimization*, and so far as possible *exclusion*, of the sensation of *disappointment*.

5. *Reason*. Never can any such sensation have place without being accompanied with a correspondent *pain*: call it the *pain of disappointment*.

6. Possession or expectancy — in either of those two relative situations will be the subject-matter in question: and in every case it will be in either the one or the other.

7. Correspondent to the import attached to the word *disappointment* is the import attached to the word *loss*. By the word *loss* is denoted that state of things which, reference to the happiness of the individual in question, has place when, after having been the object of his expectation, any thing considered in the light of [a][1] benefit fails of actually being, or of being about to be, in his possession.[b]

a. Use of the principle, bringing to view the axiom: contributing — to *conciseness*, by the difference between the number of words entering into the composition of the substantive with its compound adjective; to clearness, by the employment of a locution constantly the same instead of one for the expression of which assemblages of words indefinite in number and diversity are liable to be employed: and as often as the assemblages of words are different, doubts will be liable to arise whether so many different imports may not have been intended to be expressed by them.

By this same principle, so far as regards the modification of justice termed civil in contradistinction to penal — justice applied to cases called *civil* in contradistinction to cases called *penal* — may moreover be attached, also for the first time, a clear idea to the denominations *justice* and *principle*, say rather *principle* of *justice*.

b. N.B. Disappointment can not have place without loss or belief of loss on the part of the individual said to be disappointed. Loss may have place without disappointment: it actually has place in so far as the benefit lost had not been an object of expectation antecedently to the loss. Where, antecedently to the loss, no expectation had place, the result is — not *disappointment*, but *regret*: and the pain, whatever it be, which in the breast of the loser is produced by contemplation of the loss, is termed a pain — not a *pain of disappointment*, but a *pain of regret*. But of the case where regret without disappointment has place the exemplification being so unfrequent in comparison of that where dis-

8. Proportioned to the value of the interest in the subject-matter in the breast of the individual in question will be, in each of the two cases, the pain of disappointment. As to the circumstances on which that value depends, they belong not, in any especial manner, to the present purpose.

9. With few exceptions, by this principle, under the existing system, are the allotments made of the several subject-matters of property regulated. By this principle, notwithstanding its not having till now been ever heard of: and by this undenominatedness are called to mind the species of contract termed innominative in Rome-bred law, and the Bible text *Quem vobis ignoranter colitis hunc vobis annuncio*.[2]

§ 2. Offences in the case of which this principle constitutes the sole reason for constituting them such

10. On looking over the several sorts of acts regarded as maleficent, and on that account by appropriate prohibitions, by the laws of civilized nations, generally speaking inserted in the catalogue of *offences*, and combated by punishment and the appropriate remedies, the sole reason for so dealing by them, though that an amply sufficient one, may be seen to be the pain denominated as above: the pain of which, by every one who [puts][3] to himself the question, and [deduces][4] the answer to it from his own feelings and experience, it may be seen and felt to be productive.

11. Offences affecting the use of a corporeal subject-matter of property, moveable or immoveable: but not the title thereto, otherwise than in so far as title, defeasible or indefeasible, is conferred by simple *possession*.

i.[5] Wrongful *detention*, or say *detainer*, applicable alike to moveables and immoveables.

ii. Wrongful asportation — applicable to moveables alone.

iii. Wrongful destruction — applicable to moveables alone.

iv. Wrongful deterioration — applicable to moveables and immoveables.

v. Wrongful disturbance of occupation — applicable to moveables and immoveables.

vi. Wrongful interception of occupation.

vii. Wrongful occupation.

viii. Theft: i.e. wrongful asportation without supposition of title.

ix. Embezzlement: i.e. wrongful detention without supposition of title.

---

appointment is the result, it seems scarcely worth while to establish a separate principle for the case where regret, without disappointment, is the result.

x. Fraudulent obtainment: i.e. obtainment of the subject-matter with consent obtained by deception.

xi. Peculation: i.e. obtainment of benefit in any shape by a trustee, accompanied with loss to the intended benefitee.

xii. Wrongful damnification: i.e. wrongful production of loss in any shape, from any source, to the party wronged.

xiii. Wrongful interception of profit in any shape, from any source, to the party wronged.[c]

xiv. Extortion: i.e. wrongful obtainment of a corporeal subject-matter of property, or of profit, in any shape to the loss of the party wronged by means of intimidation: i.e. production of fear of eventual evil in any other shape than that of corporal vexation: in which case the offence is called *robbery*.

12. Offences affecting title to subject-matters of property, or to a benefit in any other shape.

i. Wrongful non-collation of title.

ii. Wrongful ablation of title.

iii. Usurpation of title.

iv. Wrongful transference of title.

v. Wrongful interception of title.

vi. Wrongful depretiation of title.

13. Offences of these same denominations have place with regard to *condition in life* in so far as beneficial, or considered as such.

Conditions in life are:

i. Domestic.

ii. Profit-seeking occupations.

iii. Power-conferring situations.

iv. Rank- or Dignity-conferring situations.

14. Domestic conditions are those of:

i. Husbandship.

ii. Wifeship.

iii. Fathership.

iv. Mothership.

v. Sonship.

vi. Daughtership.

vii. Natural Relationship in remoter degrees.

c. ☞ In these two cases, though by previous non-expectation coupled with subsequent non-information, disappointment is excluded, and with it the evil of the first order, yet ditto of $2^{d.}$ order has place.[6]

viii. Guardianship,

ix. Wardship.

15. Offences affecting the enjoyments from condition in life considered as beneficial.

i. Wrongful detention of Child, Ward, Servant, or Wife.

ii. Wrongful asportation of ditto.

iii. Wrongful disturbance of beneficial occupation of ditto.

iv. Wrongful occupation of ditto: wherein of *adultery* in the case of wife.

v. Wrongful disobedience on the part of ditto.

vi. Wrongful desertion, or say elopement, on the part of ditto.

16. Offences affecting property and reputation: property, by means of reputation.

i. Usurpation of inventorship: in particular in the case of any profitable or profit-seeking invention.

ii. Usurpation of fabricatorship: as where in regard to a certain corporeal subject-matter of property, a man pretends that it was made by him, whereas it was not: or that in the making of it he bore a certain part, whereas he did not.

iii. Wrongful ascription of fabricatorship: as where a man sells, as fabricated by another fabricator whose reputation as such is superior to his, a subject-matter made by him, or by some other fabricator of inferior reputation.

iv. Usurpation of vendorship: as where a subject-matter is offered to sale and sold as if belonging to the stock of a vendor superior in reputation, whereas the stock it belonged to was that of a vendor inferior in reputation.

In all these several cases, the benefit by the loss of which the disappointment is produced consists of profit — pecuniary or quasi-pecuniary profit — or of relative and appropriate reputation, or of both.

17. When the benefit in question has for its efficient cause human service in this or that particular shape, the rendition of that service being the subject-matter of obligation, and the obligation having for its efficient cause agreement of two or more parties one with another, promising the one to render to the other service in this or that shape, the other to render to the former, in consideration of service in that same shape, service in this or that other shape — in this state of things the species of *convention* called a contract has place: in which case in so far as a benefit, the expectation of which was produced by the making of the contract, fails of being received, correspondent loss, actual or supposed, with correspondent disappointment takes place.[7]

Thus it is that under the direction of the greatest happiness principle the practice of compelling the fulfilment of contracts has for its sole reason, though that, exceptions excepted, a sufficient one, the disappointment produced by the non-fulfilment.

As to the exceptions, it is in like manner to the greatest happiness principle that a benevolent mind will address itself for such exceptions as the nature of things furnishes.

The period during which the imaginary *original contract* was by liberalists in general resorted to as affording the sole reason why what was regarded as good government should be instituted or maintained, may be considered as constituting a special period in the history of the progress of society in civilization — in the arts of life.

Since the bringing to view the greatest happiness principle, whether under this its name or under that of the principle of utility, that period may be considered as having terminated, and this other as having succeeded it.

The time is now come when the utter inaptitude of the original contract principle in the character of a ground and source of practice in the constitution of government has been placed and stands in a light too clear and strong to be resistible. For:

1. The alledged fact of the formation of such a contract is a mere fiction.

2. The formation of such a contract, supposing it to have had place, would not, in the eyes of a being endowed with self-regard and sympathy, be upon consideration accepted as being *of itself* a fit ground for and source of practice. For:

3. Suppose, be the contract what it may, to the community in general, more happiness from the breach than [from][8] the observance — more unhappiness from the observance than from the breach[9] — what human being, endowed with feeling self-regarding and sympathetic, would, after due consideration, say — "Let the contract, however, be observed"?

Accordingly under all existing systems of law, cases are found — cases ample in extent and number — in which, without difficulty, the Legislator, or in his place the Judge, has said — "Let not this contract be observed." And of this inhibitory exception, what has been the ground — the declared ground? always evil, in this or that particular shape, stated as eventually about to have place, if, of the whole contract in question, or of this or that clause in it, observance should happen to have place.

Correspondent to the several subject-matters of the several species of contract will be the evils of which, but for the requisite and appropriate inhibition, observance given to the contract would to a certainty, or with more or less probability, as supposed, be productive. Accordingly under the head of every such species of transaction, one sub-head requisite to be inserted is that of Cases of exception as to observance.

And note that where for the purpose of securing observance, the application of the power of the government is not thought fit to be made, either of two courses may be taken by it.

1. The option between observance and non-observance may be left to the free choice of the party in question: or,

2. The observance of it may be made the subject-matter of positive interdiction.

Obvious are the sorts of cases in which the demand for positive interdiction has place. Witness the case in which the subject-matter of the contract is — an act of homicide in a case in which the act has received the appellation of an act of murder. General Rule: whatsoever act is by the law treated on the footing of an offence, observance of a contract for the bearing a part in the commission of such offence is neither compelled nor so much as permitted, but inhibited: inhibited, and accordingly dealt with on the footing of an act of *co-delinquency* with relation to such offence.

Note well the course taken by human reason in this track.

Assuming that in every political community it is right and proper that all but one should be, at all times and in respect of all acts, subject to the will of that one, Filmer held up to view, in the character of an adequate ground, reason or justificative cause, the fictitious fact, the existence of which is asserted by the proposition — Of this community (naming it) all the members but one were begotten by that one.[10]

To this reason, the mind of Locke, having taken it into due consideration, found itself unable to subscribe.[11] Of the arrangement in question, according to him, the propriety was still to be assumed. But, for the support of it on the ground of reason, some other principle was to be assumed, and was assumed accordingly. That principle, what was it? The *original contract*.

Here then for the overthrow of one phantom — not Reason, but Imagination was to be applied to. The champion furnished by Imagination was of course — not a truth, but another such phantom — another fiction. Resorted to by this philosopher was the device employed, as the story goes, by an ingenious Law-adviser: who, when by his client information was given to him of a document which presented itself as a forgery, said, "Don't set about making proof of the forgery: but, what will be much less trouble to you — forge a release."

The philosopher having had for his patron Sir Anthony Ashley Cooper, who, being originally a lawyer, became, with the title of Earl of Shaftesbury, Lord High Chancellor,[12] hence a probability that it was from lawyercraft that this fiction was borrowed. Fiction, the most efficient of all the instruments invented by lawyercraft, was an instrument of all work, presenting itself to every hand that had boldness enough to take it up.

Bad as compared to the greatest happiness principle, compared with Filmer's fiction, and the correspondent principle, the principle adopted by Locke, though from lawyercraft, was good. Under Filmer's principle, the propriety of submission to the absolute sway of one admitted not of any exceptions. Not so under the original contract principle. For, the existence of a contract being admitted, remained to be settled — settled by so many fictions of detail — the terms of that same contract. But in the settling of those terms, the interest of the subject many [is][13] the interest which would of course be taken for the object of endeavour on the part of the subject many — that is to say of all who were not, by the power of corruption or that of delusion, engaged in the path of absolutism. Here then, and thus far, in a sort of twilight, the greatest happiness principle, though not under that name or under any name, would be taken for a guide: so many occasions for the application of it, so many imaginary clauses in the imaginary contract.

But what sort of an argument is that for the explosion of which two words are, at any time on each occasion, sufficient — *Not true!*

Feign a reason for the support of your position? why be at the trouble of any such expedient? As well might you claim the liberty of feigning the truth of your position, whatever it be, as that of feigning the truth of any other position adduced by you for the support of it.

The original contract had not only taken possession of that part of the public mind at large which, adhering to Monarchical Government, had not adopted it in its purest form but looked for limitations and checks to it, but had even been adopted by the new Government — the Whig Government, which took place on the occasion of the Revolution of 1688.

As to the partisans of a Republic, from no such fiction could their purpose receive support. Whether they had any fixt principle with a determinate name to it does not appear. As an avowed member of that party, till comparatively of late years no man had ever ventured to shew himself.

It was at the very conclusion of a small pamphlet, title at present not remembered, that in the character of the only defensible end in view in government Joseph Priestly held up in view "the greatest happiness of the greatest number." Date of that same pamphlet, 1767, or a few years before or after.[14]

In the year 1776 was published, by the author of these pages, the 8[vo.] Volume intituled *Fragment on Government etc.*[15] In that work the principle expressed as above by Priestly was taken in hand and employed in form in waging war against the *Original Contract* principle.

But the denomination there employed was not an exactly apt one. The denomination given to it was that which had presented itself to his view as being established: not only as one that was found established by authority too respectable to be opposed: but as one the aptness of which had been exemplified and demonstrated by the instructive and useful application that had been made of it.

In France the denomination of the principle of Utility had by Helvetius, in his work intituled *de l'Esprit*,[16] been given to this same principle. Clearness had at the same time been given to the import of it: the import of the word happiness had been brought down from the region of vague generalities, anchored on *terra firma* by means of its relation to that of the words pain and pleasure: in happiness he viewed a compound — composed of the presence of pleasure in any of its forms coupled with the absence of pain in all its forms, the mass of pleasure being at the same time regarded as being in a considerable degree *intense*. This being established, he proceeded, as the course of instruction required, to frame a catalogue of the several observable modifications of pleasure on the one hand, of pain on the other: but had not travelled far in that track when he stopt. After his death a work of his was published — a posthumous work under the title of *De l'Homme*.[17] But in this, but little if any advance was made beyond that which, as above, had been [made] in his abovementioned first work.[d]

Some years before this, so long before as the year 1742, came out the *Essays* of David Hume. In this work the locution *the principle of Utility* presents itself. But by Hume, no such precise idea was attached to the word *Utility* as by Helvetius. Witness the title to one of those same *Essays* — namely, *Why Utility pleases?*[21] Attached in his mind to the word *utility* appears to have been the idea of *conduciveness to an end*, whatsoever it

d. By the author of these, Anno 18., the investigation of the several distinguishable modifications of pleasure and pain of which human nature is susceptible having been pursued, the catalogue of them has (it is believed) been rendered little, if any thing, short of completion; and in conjunction with it have been given lists of the several other names of fictitious entities the import of which [have][18] for [their][19] basis the respective imports of so many correspondent modifications of pleasure or pain: that is to say *interests, desires,* and *motives:* by which means has been given what by no other means could be given — a correspondently fixt and precise import to these same additional names of fictitious psychological entities.[20]

might happen to that end to be productive of: pleasure indeed if pleasure: but production of positive pain, if so it happened that *such* was the end in view: or another meaning capable of being attached to it was — that of conduciveness to a more valuable future contingent, in preference to less valuable present or speedily expected, pleasure.

So far was this appellative from being the most apt one, that by thinking men in considerable proportion (so it has fallen in the way of the author of these pages from time to time to hear) the import attached to it has been understood to be confined to that of a principle employed for the purpose of prescribing the giving preference to future pleasure of greater value or exclusion of future pain of greater value, or both, to present pleasure or exemption from pain, or both.

In particular, in the case of a lady of great celebrity, notice having been taken that the principle of utility was to her an object of declared distaste, a reason or efficient cause that had been assigned for such distaste was — that it had been wont to present itself to her view as putting an exclusion upon *pleasure*.

Long after the publication of the *Fragment* as above, Dr Paley, in his work on Morals,[22] took up and employed the locution *principle of Utility*. But for reasons too obvious to need explanation, it did not suit his purpose to make any such particular application of it as had been made of it, nor therefore to attach any such clear and precise import to it as had been attached to it by Helvetius.

Impressed by the above considerations with the persuasion of its comparative inaptitude, for several years past the author of these pages has, in his writings, substituted to the locution *the principle of utility* that of *the greatest happiness principle*.

For some time however, and indeed till very lately, the catalogue of his aberrations from the line of exact propriety was not yet at an end. As occasion called, to the locution *greatest happiness* he had substituted the locution (copied as above from Priestley) *the greatest happiness of the greatest number* (always understood of the members of the community in question): regarding the longer locution as the apt expression in its compleat state, and the shorter as nothing different from an abridgment of it.

Lately however — by it is not remembered what particular incident — a closer degree of attention having been called down upon the subject, a conviction was obtained that by this mode of expression, if applied to practice, effects widely different from those intended — in a word mischief to an almost indefinite amount — might be produced. For, note what is capable of being understood to be the result.

Bring to view in supposition two communities. Number of the individuals — in the one, 1,000: in the other, 1,001: of both together, 2,001. By the greatest happiness, the arrangement prescribed would be that by which the greatest happiness of all together would be produced. But wide indeed from this effect might be the effect of the application of the principle, if the arrangement productive of the greatest happiness of the greatest number — no regard being shewn to the happiness of the smallest number — were understood to be the arrangement prescribed by that same principle.

So long as the greatest number — the 1,001 — were in the enjoyment of the greatest degree of comfort, the greatest possible degree of torment might be the lot of the smallest of the two numbers — the 1,000: and still the principle stating as the proper object of endeavour the greatest happiness of the greatest number be actually conformed to — not contravened.[23]

§ 3. Evil of 2$^{d.}$ order from disappointment

Hitherto no *other* consequences have been brought into consideration — no other evil consequences of an arrangement considered as liable to be productive of disappointment have been brought into account. But before the account can with propriety be closed — before the instructions for the application to be made to practice of the disappointment-prevention principle can be presented as compleat — the consequences of the *2$^{d.}$ order* — the *evil consequences of the 2$^{d.}$ order* — must be brought to view.[e]

For this purpose a distinction will require to be made between the cases where, in the breast of the party in whose instance the disappointment is regarded as having place, his title to the subject-matter of loss is, by supposition, *out* of doubt, and those in which it is capable of being the subject-matter of doubt.

Take for instance the case of *theft*. In this case, at the time of the theft, the lawful proprietor, from whom the thing was taken, was in the undisturbed expectation of continuing, as long as he should be so pleased, to derive from it whatsoever benefit it presented itself to him as affording to him in his situation the means of deriving from it. In these circumstances, no sooner is the loss of it discovered by him, than the disappointment, with the pain inseparable from it, is experienced by him. On his part, from the first to the last of the time during which his possession of the thing had had place, an assurance had had place, not only that such means as it was in the power of the law to afford him for the continuing of the thing in the state in which it would be at his disposal would, upon occasion, be afforded to him, but that

e. See Bentham per Dumont, *Traités de Législation &c.*[24]

such means would be effectual: excepting always the cases in which it might happen to his possession to be cut short by any one of those accidents of which the one in question (loss by theft) is one: accidents the occurrence of which is comparatively so rare, that by the contemplation of the whole assemblage of them put together the strength of the assurance as to the continuance of the possession experiences, in the ordinary state of things, no more than a scarcely sensible degree of diminution.

Not so in the cases where, as between a party on one side and a party on the other, the title to the thing is the subject of doubt: each of them regarding himself as having the right to the possession of, and benefit derivable from, the thing, to the exclusion of the other as well as of all besides. In this case a natural question is — in what way is it that, in this case, the disappointment-prevention [principle] can afford a sufficient indication of the course which, consistently with the conceptions associated with the word *justice*, justice requires to be taken? — for in this case, by the very supposition, whatsoever of the two opposite courses it may be that is taken, disappointment will take place: to both the contending parties the thing can not be allotted, and in the breast of that one of them, whichsoever it be, to whom it is not allotted, the sensation of loss will be experienced, and that of disappointment will, by the supposition, be sure to have place.

Answer. The object, or say end in view, which the Judge, acting in conformity to his duty, will have in view and his endeavours directed to the attainment of — at any rate the main object is — the prevention, or at least the termination, of that evil of the 2^d order, which, in the breasts of such other members of the community to whose cognizance it might happen to the case to come, might naturally be expected to have place in the event of an allotment made of the thing in question different from that which would be dictated by the conception commonly attached to the word justice, but without correspondent consciousness, directed by the idea of the eventual *disappointment*.

This, let it be observed, is the *main* object. For, as to the evil of the first order, it *has* already taken place, and can not, by the Judges or any other human power, be made *not* to have taken place: what remains, generally speaking, possible is the administering to the sufferer in some shape or other *good — benefit* — in satisfaction and compensation for it. But whether in the nature of the case such satisfaction can be afforded depends upon the circumstances of the individual parties, and other particular circumstances, such as are apt to be different, one from another, in each individual case: whereas, by apt judicial arrangements, the evil of the 2^d order is in every case capable of being either prevented or any rate in a considerable degree diminished: and, by the extent of which it is susceptible, this in other cases remediable evil is in the scale of importance much superior to that other which is in such a degree liable to prove irremediable.

Under these circumstances, for the purpose of doing what the conceptions attached to the word *Justice* require to be done, what is the course which a well-intentioned Judge will take? Answer. He will take into joint consideration, and compare the one with the other, the respective situations which the two parties present themselves to his conception as being respectively in as to strength of expectation with reference to the possession of the thing — of expectation as likely to have had place in their respective breasts with regard to the enjoyment of the mass of benefit which the proprietorship of the thing is capable of conferring. He will put himself in idea successively into the two relative situations which present themselves to him as being occupied by the two parties: this done, he will put a question to himself, and the question will be — on which of the two sides, were you on that side, would your expectation of being ultimately in possession of the thing be the strongest? To this question let an answer [have]²⁵ been given, so will thereby an answer have been given to the question, to which of the two parties does the disappointment-prevention principle require that the ultimate possession of the thing be allotted: for, in exact proportion to the strength of the expectation of the benefit derivable from the thing, will be that of the disappointment produced by the loss of it.

§ 4. Estimate of loss — difficulties attending it

Two cases require here to be distinguished: that in which graduation as between quantity and quantity has no place, and that in which such graduation has place. Of the case where graduation has not place, an example is afforded by the case where the question is which of the two parties it is that has a right to the benefit — say the thing moveable or immoveable in dispute. Of the case where graduation has place, an example is afforded by the case where the question is concerning the *quantum* of the damage done to the subject-matter in question, to wit person, subject-matter of property, moveable or immoveable, and the like. In the non-graduation-exhibiting case, the task of the Judge, under the guidance of the disappointment-prevention principle, will be a comparatively easy one: nothing of idiosyncrasy in regard either to persons or to things will have place, perplexing the judgment with degrees indefinite perhaps in number, between all which, without any criterion exclusively applying to any one of them, he will have to decide. In the graduation-exhibiting case he will have to labour under this same difficulty.

In respect to the degree of this difficulty two cases require again to be distinguished: 1. that in which, whether in respect of mind or body, person is the subject-matter of the damage; 2. that in which some thing, corporeal or incorporeal — moveable or immoveable, is the subject-matter of the damage. The case where the difficulty is at its maximum is that in which *mind* is the subject-matter of the damage. For in this case are liable to have place, each of them presenting a demand for mensuration, the several circumstances affecting sensibility:[f] and of the whole number of these, a great part, perhaps the greater,[27] will be found exposed to exaggeration — either on the side of infra-appretiation,[28] or on the side of super-appretiation,[29] or on both sides.

§ 5. For estimation of loss, parties' attendance needful

To this case bears reference one of the many circumstances by which the importance of the appearance of parties in the presence of the Judge, in contradistinction to the appearance of their respective advocates, is established. Where the personal condition of the party himself is present to the perception of the Judge, the probability of deception on the one part by misrepresentation on the other is at its minimum: not only is evidence capable of being checked immediately without the intervention of any refracting medium, but deportment — a circumstance speaking so strongly in explanation of reported evidence — is presented to the observation of the Judge. In this case, where the object presented to the senses of the Judge is the party, the object so presented is the original itself: in the case where it is the professional representative of the party, it is but the picture of that same original: and that a picture in the painting of which the utmost skill and energy of the experienced artist will be employed in effecting the utmost degree of misrepresentation possible: the consequence is that in each individual case, taken individually, the probability of misrepresentation and consequent and correspondent deception is at its maximum: and in the aggregate of the whole number of individual cases the degree of probability as to success between the best cause and the worst approach[es] to a level with a degree of propinquity depending conjunctly on the degree of appropriate aptitude on the part of the advocate, and the degree of deficiency in

---

f. For a detailed list and explanation of them see *Introduction to Morals and Legislation*, Ch. | |.[26]

respect of appropriate aptitude, and in particular in respect of *judicial* aptitude, on the part of the Judge. Think in this case of the chance which an ordinary Jury has for the not being deceived by a first-rate Advocate opposed by an inferior Advocate of ordinary rate.

True it is — that, in this case, [in] the breast of the party, there is the particular and sinister interest operating with greater strength than in the breast of his Advocate. But, on the other hand, supposing on the part of the Judge a sincere desire to come at the truth, the efficiency of the power he has for eliciting the truth in spite of concealment and misrepresentation, and at the same time for detecting and exposing falshood, will be much greater where the subject-matter on which it operates is the unexperienced and unskilled individual than where it is the well-experienced and well-skilled advocate. In case of wilful misrepresentation, on the part of the Advocate no such sensibility to the sudden reproach of contradictory conscience has place as that which has place commonly in the breast of the party.

§6. Existing system — *peculiar case of* Vested rights

Vested rights! vested rights! On an occasion on which an arrangement is proposed having for its object the exsiccation of a source of expence regarded as needless, if the case be such that on the part of the present possessors of a benefit derived from the expence the locution *vested rights* is regarded as being applicable, strong is the reliance placed on the influence and effect expected from it. Here then we have two sorts of rights, vested and unvested, in opposition to one other. Practical effect of the distinction this. Of a possessor of a vested right, in case of extinction, altogether indisputable is the claim of the possessor to compensation, and *that* altogether an adequate one. Of the possessor of a right not coming under the denomination of a vested right, it may happen to the claim to be sufficiently grounded or not sufficiently grounded, according to circumstances.

This being the case, and supposing it admitted that in case of competition a vested right possesses a claim to compensation operating in preference to any which can be possessed by a right not vested — this admitted, what, under the guidance of the greatest happiness principle, is the ground capable of being assigned for such preference? Answer. This, beyond dispute. Under the circumstances under which a vested right is understood to have place, the expectation is regarded as being more intense than in the other case, so therefore the correspondent disappointment.

Set aside the ill effects to which the disappointment-prevention principle bears reference, wheresoever, on the ground of the needlessness of the official situation to which the service, if any, is attached, the situation is abolished, no compensation at all ought to be allowed: so much money employed in compensation, so much money expended in waste. Take into account those same evil effects, thereupon comes in the demand for compensation, and that compensation an adequate one.

In the so frequently exemplified case where, for the use of the public, property in immoveables is taken out of the hands of the proprietor, and lodged in the hands of government, the propriety of the demand for compensation, and that to an amount fully adequate, is universally acknowledged. Between this case and that of an official situation regarded as the subject-matter of a vested right, is there, in any and what respect, a difference? Answer. So far as regards the evil of the $1^{st.}$ order, expectation of situation being regarded as equally strong, disappointment in case of loss correspondent and proportionable, none.

To the evil effects of the $2^{d.}$ order bears reference what difference has place between the two cases: proportioned to the extent of the class on which the evil of the $2^{d.}$ order — the danger and alarm — applies itself is the magnitude of this branch of the evil. The class to which it extends in the case where it is land that is thus, and by the supposition without compensation, taken into the hands of government, is the class composed of all who have any interest in land. The class to which it extends in the case in which it is official profit that is thus, and on the same terms, taken into the hands of government, is the class composed of those alone who are in possession of such official profit, and among these of those alone in whose instance the interest possessed is understood to come under the denomination of a *vested interest*.[30]

§7. Creation of needless Offices for compensation in contemplation of revolutionary retrenchment — how to obviate

Two cases require now to be put in conjunction.

Case $1^{st.}$ The progress of depredation, corruption and waste so rapid, as to have driven on the vessel of government to a near-approaching revolution: understand by a revolution, the sudden substitution of a system in which equal regard is paid to the interest of all, to the existing system in which the interest of the many, of the vast majority, is made a constant sacrifice of to the particular and sinister associated interest of the one and the few.

Case $2^{d.}$ In contemplation of the vastness of the burthen thus fastened or sought to be fastened on the shoulder of the community, those who take the lead in the reform-seeking enterprize have in contemplation the suppression of the alledged needless offices, or some of them, without compensation.

Note that, in the natural course of things, the profused institution of needless lucrative offices is at once a cause and an effect of the sort of change in question. In the character of an efficient and not improbably effective cause, it has long been in progress: and of whatsoever efficient causes may be found assignable, it presents itself as the most strongly operative.[31]

On the other hand, suppose such a change to present itself, to those whose interest is bound up with the existing system, as in a *paulo-post-futurus*[32] state, nothing is more natural than that, by observation made of the punctuality of the regard paid to vested interests, they should take instruction from the proverb by which the policy of making hay while the sun shines is recommended.

A design of this sort being (by supposition) acted upon, — for defeating it, here would be a case in which the evil produced by disappointment applied to the expectations thus generated would lie outweighed by the evil that would be produced by the giving effect to the design: and [by] the apprehension of the appropriate remedy, that is to say the resumption, the peculation [which] the supposed design has for its object would naturally be, if not altogether prevented, at any rate checked.

§8. Quantity of emolument given, gradations in value in respect of certainty — Offices considered with a view to compensation on abolition

In a state of things by supposition presenting an irresistible demand for retrenchment, two classes of functionaries, placed in strongly contrasted situations, have now been brought to view: possessors of situations the interest in which passes under the denomination of a *vested interest*, and possessors of situations to which no such favour-conferring denomination is attached.

Thus far, as to supposition. In point of fact, among the former are to be found at all times, and will naturally be found, the possessors of needless offices, useless offices, overpaid offices, and sinecure offices — offices these last in which no labour whatever, serviceable or unserviceable, being performed, the possession of the office is but a pretence for receiving the emolument attached to it, the act of receiving that same emolument being accordingly an obtainment of money on false pretences to every effect but that of being dealt with in consideration of it [on] the footing of a criminal delinquent—that which in the language of existing penal law is *visited* (as the word is) with punishment in a variety of shapes, all of them having the effect of imprinting infamy. This class being composed of persons coming under the description of the ruling few, themselves possessors of political power in this or that shape, or retainers of those who are, the class they belong to may be distinguished by the appellation of the aristocratical class.

To the latter of the two classes belong those by whom in no instance is emolument received without labour performed, and in whose instance the quantity of labour is maximized, the quantity of remuneration minimized. The individuals thus situated being neither themselves possessors of power, nor by any community of particular interest linked with the possessors of power, the class they belong to may be distinguished by the appellation of the democratical class.

To this class belong the sort of Clerks denominated Writing Clerks: functionaries whose functions consist in little or nothing more than writing and performing the operations of common arithmetic. Upon these plebeians, in any number, without a thought of any such thing as a Retired allowance, when retrenchment is the order of the day, the process of elimination, it is believed, [has] been commonly performed with as little scruple or hesitation as upon privates in Army or Navy service.

Consistently with the greatest happiness principle—consistently with its immediate subordinate, the disappointment principle—can this distinction thus acted upon be defended? Let him who thinks he can without exposure to the imputation of inconsistency—and in consequence to merited disapprobation, answer in the affirmative.

As applied to this class, as between adequate compensation and no compensation at all, a sort of middle course presents itself as not being, in appearance at least, altogether destitute of ground for its support—ground derived from the greatest happiness principle. These, it may be said, possess an attainment for which other occupations besides official ones present a demand: eliminated from their official situations they will accordingly have it [in] their power to obtain other situations in the service of individuals. This case being realized, of the utmost pay they will find obtainable, in point of quantity and certainty of continuance taken together, the value will not be so great as that of the pay attached to their respective official situations—"Give them then the amount of the difference: such is the allowance prescribed by justice."

True: provided always that, and in so far as, the correct value of that same difference shall have been ascertained. But can it be ascertained? how it can be seems not very easy to determine.

So far as, an allowance being proposed, the individual in question prefers the acceptance of it to the continuing in the service, it is well: no disappointment produced; no injustice suffered. But suppose this is not the case? In this case, on his being disbanded from the service, disappointment will have place; to defend the arrangement from the imputation of injustice does not present itself as practicable.

In return for his labour, will he have it in his power to obtain any pay at all? Even of this, if the number thus eliminated at once is to a certain degree considerable, scarcely can any adequate assurance be had: at any rate in that state of over-population, the pressure of which seems destined to indefinite encrease.

Supposing the attainment of the proper temperament not absolutely impracticable, the accomplishment of it can not but necessitate a minute enquiry into idiosyncratical circumstances. In a word, nothing less than a judicial enquiry, carried on by a judicatory acting in the way of antitechnical procedure, could answer the purpose: and, under the existing system, where is any such judicatory to be found? at any rate a judicatory capable of being applied to this same purpose?

§ 9. Existing System — gradations as to dislocability, thence as to value as depending on certainty

Under the existing system, gradations may be observed in the value of regard considered as due to the claim for compensation. At the head of the scale stands the sort of office on which vested rights are rivetted: next to that, the office holden during good behaviour: lowest, the office holden during pleasure.

Not so great in reality and effect as in shew is the difference between Office with vested rights and Office during good behaviour. Office held during good behaviour is, in plain English, Office held unless and until removal shall take place at the suit of the King by sentence of the King's own Bench: and unless the prosecution were carried on in pursuance of the known wishes of the Right Honorables who govern in his Majesty's name, supposing remorse to have produced in the breast of a delinquent possessor of such an office a desire, with a view to atonement, to see himself convicted, it would not be a matter altogether easy to him to find the means of giving accomplishment to so pious a purpose. Under matchless Constitution, functionaries of the highest order have a vested interest in the impunity of all subordinates under them, in the impunity, that is to say, at any hands but their own.

Witness the case of a Justice of Peace who, for giving encrease to the value of a publick House of his own, refuses to grant or continue a licence to the occupant of a neighbouring house. Under Lord Tenterden's law in particular, no punishment without a corrupt motive, no knowing that a corrupt motive has had place unless the party accused makes declaration to that effect.[33] Be the gain ever so enormous, no defensible reason assigned or assignable, if his wish is to be put upon his trial, the worshipful Gentleman must make affidavit, and say my motive for refusing the licence was corrupt: and even [then] might be found to remain a question garnished with great doubts — the question whether the rule *nemo tenetur seipsum [accusare]*[34] might not be found applicable to this case.

No accusation, no conviction: no conviction, no dislocation, no punishment. Be the place a place during good behaviour or only during pleasure, in rebellion to those who govern in the King's name, will a man in a subordinate office dare to prefer accusation, or so much as to give information, against the occupants of a superordinate authority in a certain higher sphere? If, on the part of this informant, a peccadillo can, by an appropriate microscope, be discovered, how vast so ever the mass of waste, depredation and corruption proved in the higher regions, how extensive the conspiracy by which it has been effected, [. . . ?] will be [the] lot of the informant, a peerage that of the arch-delinquent. A case which may at any rate be consulted for illustration, may be seen in the letters of Mr Sedgwick and the Reports of the Committee which had for Chairman the Right Hon. | | Wallace:[35] whether for proof, would be for any person to answer to whom it should appear worth his while, for any practical purpose, to give perusal to those instructive documents.

At any rate one thing is still wanting in that case; for Mr Wallace's Noble relative Lord Melville, an advancement in the peerage.[36]

So far as regards strength of expectation, small in some situations is the difference between tenure during good behaviour, and tenure during pleasure. In name no longer than during pleasure, in effect (says the man to himself) my tenure is during life: for, during life, I shall, for I will, continue to please.

§ 10. Existing System, custom as to self-dislocation
on dislocation of patrons

Always be it remembered, however, that, on the present occasion, the behaviour of the individual does not come in the question, belongs not to the subject under consideration. This subject is dislocation in the wholesale way for the purpose of frugality: not dislocation in retail, with a view to appropriate aptitude.

In the entire list of Offices held during pleasure, instances however are found, in no small number and of no small value, in which, upon the dislocation of a superordinate, subordinates, one or more, go out of course. In this case the dislocation has for its efficient cause — in some instances the act of a superior paramount to both, in others the act of the dislocatee himself. In this latter case, the suicidal act has for its internal cause, in outward shew gratitude, or a sense of honour: in reality, most commonly self-regarding prudence — if of my own accord I follow my patron in his retirement, the consequence is — that in the event of his reinstatement I shall by him be reinstated with him: if I stay behind, I may be ejected at any time by those by whom he is ejected; in which case I shall not be reinstated with him: serving under the banners of his adversaries, I shall be regarded as hostile to his interests, or at best indifferent.

In no small degree curious and instructive would be a list of these Official situations, accompanied, confronted and contrasted by a correspondent list of situations in regard to which the efficient cause of mortality has not had place.[g] Thereupon an object for enquiry, proof, and explanation, would be — the *principle* in which the distinction has had its source.

g. Pitt the first it was who for the first time placed in office the Earl of Shelburne of that day, afterwards Marquis of Lansdowne, constituting him one of the Secretaries of State.[37] Shelburne being at that time a personal favorite of George the third — as such he has often spoken of himself to the author of these pages — with whom the choice originated can not be affirmed with any degree of assurance. Shelburne, when he became Minister-in-Chief in the situation of First Lord of the Treasury, constituted Pitt the second, son of Pitt the first, his Vice-Minister, in the situation of Chancellor of the Exchequer.[38] When, in 1783, upon the conclusion of the peace, the Whig Aristocracy, of which the Marquis of Rockingham was the head, Edmund Burke the life and soul, out-voted the Earl of Shelburne and thus rendered his resignation necessary, the simultaneous resignation of his protegé and locatee, Pitt the second, was looked for by him as a matter of course.[39] Pitt the second, young as he was, was not so young as not to see that on the part of his patron the chance of reintegration was = o — the Whigs of that time being a strong, numerous, well-compacted and disciplined phalanx, while Shelburne had scarce any adherents besides personal ones; [he] accepted the offer made him by the Royal master and to the Vice-Ministership added the Ministership-in-chief.[40] Perfidy and ingratitude — perfidy by breach of a virtual contract — were the stains cast by this conduct upon the character of the young Statesman. So, at least, was the conception of the Ex-Premier, as more than once expressed by him, and with no slight energy, in discourse with, or in the hearing of, the author of these pages.

§ 11. Existing System. Inconsistencies as to undislocability and dislocability of Judges

Among the boasts of matchless Constitution is the undislocability, so delusively termed the independency, of the Judges. This quality being a declared indispensable requisite to and of upright judicature, it accordingly has place in the case of the 12 high-seated Common Law Judges and one of the three highest-seated Equity Judges, to wit the Master of the Rolls. At the same time, either it is not an indispensable requisite to upright judicature, or upright judicature is not necessary to good government or to the well-being of the community. For it has not *place* in the situation of Lord High Chancellor, nor in that of Justice of the Peace: and the said Chancellor is, amongst other things, head of the law, the functionary by whom, to so vast an extent, the proceedings of all the other great Judges are controuled, and at whose recommendation the occupants of their several situations are located. As little has it place in the case of the situation of Justice of the Peace: a situation of which there [are] at all times several thousands in existence — situations in which some scores or perhaps hundreds as many suits, of one sort or other, are heard and determined as by all the Judges of the superior class put together. Thus it is that, for instances in which the boast is consistent with truth, instances there are to the amount of scores or hundreds in which it is repugnant to truth. It is [untrue][41] in regard to the top and bottom of the scale; it is [true][42] in regard to the intermediate degrees of the scale.

From a recent occurrence, to the list of the cases in which either that which goes by the name of independence is not necessary to upright judicature — or upright judicature is not necessary to the well-being of the community, it appears that addition must be made of the situation of Judge Advocate.[43]

In the person of the Judge Advocate may be seen a mongrel in another form. Impartiality is an indispensable quality in a Judge: partiality is an inseparable quality in an Advocate. Accordingly, in the person of every Judge Advocate, as the very appellation declares and acknowledges, the two qualities, each of them the negation of the other, are united. But here too comes into action the King's Prerogative, the universal solvent of all difficulties. In each case that comes before them, let my Judges be every one of them impartial; let my Attorney General be partial; let my Judge Advocate be at once impartial and partial, both in the most perfect degree. So saith the royal worker of all needful miracles; so saith he, and the miracle is wrought according to his word.

Not that in this case the arrangement is in so high a degree absurd as, upon the face of the statement, it may naturally be supposed to be. In military service, as in every branch of service, high in the scale of importance stands *justice*: but in military service, still higher, it may be said, stands *obedience*. For the anomaly, from this same plea, so it is that excuse may be found derivable: excuse, yes: but justification, not. For the necessary obedience, provision equally, or rather still more, effectual might be made by other arrangements, and those standing clear from an objection so palpable, placing upon the arrangement the imputation of inconsistency with so strong a glare.

§ 12. Existing System. Inconsistencies as to the union of Law and Equity Jurisdiction in one person

Among official situations, some pairs of situations may be seen which ought to be and are said to be to each other as oil and vinegar: vinegar occup[y]ing the under, oil the upper: mixture of the two, but for some intermediate substance, for example a hard egg, serving as a bond of unity, impracticable.

Thus are circumstanced in relation to one another Common Law and Equity law: Common Law the vinegar, Equity the Oil. But in this case the King's Prerogative possesses the virtue, and performs the function, of the hard egg. Accordingly, in the case of each one of the four Judges called Barons of the Exchequer Judicatory, Common Law and Equity law may at all times be seen condensed in equal perfection and perfect union.

NOTES

1. MS "the."

2. This passage from the Vulgate is properly rendered, "Quod ergo ignorantes colitis, hoc ego annuntio vobis," and appears in the Authorized Version as, "Whom therefore ye ignorantly worship, him declare I unto you" (Acts 17: 23). These were Paul's words to the Athenians, after seeing the altar dedicated to the unknown God.

3. MS "putting."

4. MS "deducing."

5. For the sake of clarity, in the enumeration of these subcategories, Bentham's Arabic numerals have been replaced by Roman numerals.

6. For the distinction between evil of the first and evil of the second order, see §3, p. 405 and n. 24 below.

7. A passage at Bentham Papers, University College London Library, cxii. 145 (3 June 1828) [hereafter UC], which Bentham inserted in the text but which interrupts the sense of the essay and appears to have been abandoned in midsentence, is

reproduced here: "As a test of the propriety of the above-mentioned theory — and of the usefulness of the denomination thence given to so indisputably influential a principle, let any one make upon himself the following experiment. Let him take in hand any arrangement, existing or proposed, which to him is an object of disapprobation, and if his disapprobation have not for its efficient cause and ground the notion of its being detrimental in respect of national subsistence, national abundance, or national equality, let him see whether, in his view of it, the effect of it will not be the production of the pain of disappointment somewhere. Different (it may be said) — widely different — the quantities of pain produced in different breasts by the same loss. True: but, notwithstanding all this diversity, if for any purpose, on any occasion, an estimate is preferable to blind caprice, and the making of it a duty incumbent on government."

8. MS "for."

9. An echo of *Hamlet*, I. iv. 15–16: "it is a custom More honour'd in the breach than the observance."

10. See Filmer's *Patriarcha*, first published in 1680.

11. In his *Two Treatises of Government*, first published in 1690, Locke attempted to refute Filmer's views.

12. Anthony Ashley Cooper (1621–83), first Baron Ashley and first Earl of Shaftesbury, was lord chancellor in 1672–73.

13. MS "being."

14. See Joseph Priestley, *An Essay on the First Principles of Government; and on the nature of Political, Civil, and Religious Liberty* (London, 1768), 17: "The good and happiness of the members, that is the majority of the members of any state, is the great standard by which every thing relating to that state must finally be determined." The pamphlet in fact had 191 pages.

15. See *A Comment on the Commentaries and A Fragment on Government*, ed. J. H. Burns and H. L. A. Hart (London, 1977) (*CW*), esp. 439–48.

16. *De l'Esprit* had been first published in 1758.

17. Helvétius's posthumous *De l'Homme, de ses facultés intellectuelles et de son éducation*, was first published, in two volumes, in 1773.

18. MS "has."

19. MS "its."

20. See *A Table of the Springs of Action*, first published in 1817, in *Deontology* (Oxford, 1983) (*CW*), 79–115.

21. David Hume (1711–76) had published the first version of his *Essays, Moral and Political* in two volumes in 1741–42. However the "essay" to which Bentham refers is in fact section 5 of *An Enquiry concerning the Principles of Morals*, first published in 1751.

22. In the margin, Bentham noted at this point: "☞ Quere the title of it?"

William Paley had first published *The Principles of Moral and Political Philosophy* in 1785.

23. On the corresponding marginal summary sheet at UC cxii. 77, Bentham made the following "Addendum" dated 10 June 1828: "Note that, to be at once appropriate and all-comprehensive, a deontological principle designed for giving direction to human conduct should apply alike to conduct in public and private life.

"This does the greatest happiness principle: — *original contract*, not.

"Original contract, if good for any thing, would have been applicable to private life."

24. The distinction between evil of the first and evil of the second order is discussed in *Traités de législation*, 3 vols. (Paris, 1802), ii. 251–55. See also *An Introduction to the Principles of Morals and Legislation*, ed. J. H. Burns and H. L. A. Hart (London, 1970) (*CW*), 143 [hereafter *IPML*], where Bentham defines "primary mischief" as that "sustained by an assignable individual, or a multitude of assignable individuals," and "secondary mischief" as that "which, taking its origin from the former [i.e., primary mischief], extends itself either over the whole community, or over some other multitude of unassignable individuals."

25. MS "being."

26. See *IPML* (*CW*), chap. 6, "Of Circumstances Influencing Sensibility," 51–73.

27. In the margin, Bentham noted at this point: "☞ Examine."

28. MS orig. "depretiation."

29. MS orig. "ultra-pretiation."

30. The text continues with the following paragraph, which Bentham appears to have abandoned in midsentence: "Among those whose interest is commonly understood to come under the denomination of a *vested interest* are the possessors of offices, the existence of which belongs to the catalogue of the most mischievous of established nuisances: offices, that is to say, by which, in proportion to the amount of the fees attached to them and."

31. The sense of the marginal summary (see the marginal summary sheet in Bentham's hand at UC cxii. 78) differs from that of the text at this point: "Creation of Needless Offices is the natural cause of a revolution: suppression of them the natural effect."

32. I.e., "a little in the future."

33. The Court of King's Bench would not proceed against a justice of the peace for an alleged illegal act unless it appeared that he had been influenced by a partial, corrupt, or malicious motive. This applied to the granting of alehouse licences. It is unclear, however, what Bentham means by "Lord Tenterden's law": it does not appear that Tenterden (as Abbott had been created in April 1827) made any innovations, either in Parliament or on the bench, in this area of the law.

34. I.e., "no one is compelled to accuse himself."

35. Thomas Wallace (1768–1844), first Baron Wallace, lord of the admiralty in 1797–1800, commissioner of the Board of Control 1800–1806, 1807–16, 1828–30, vice-president of the Board of Trade 1818–23, master of the mint in Ireland 1823–7, was chairman of the Commission of Inquiry into the Collection and Management of the Revenue, whose Thirteenth and Fourteenth Reports dealt with the Board of Stamps, recommending substantial alterations to its organization and procedures (see *Commons Sessional Papers* (1826) x. *passim*). In particular, the commissioners were critical of the inadequate supervision and control exercised over officials in Scotland by the board, especially its chairman, James Sedgwick (1775–1851), who had been appointed to the office in 1817. As a result, the Treasury decided to dismiss the existing board and appoint a new one, giving allowances in compensation to all the members except Sedgwick (see the Treasury Minute of 6 October 1826 in *Commons Sessional Papers* (1826–27) xvii. 1–14.) Sedgwick vigorously defended himself in a series of letters published in the *Morning Chronicle* and republished in three pamphlets: *Twelve Letters addressed to the Right Hon. Thomas Wallace, M.P. Chairman of the Commission of Revenue Inquiry* (London, 1826); *Letter the Thirteenth* (London, 1826); and *Letter the Fourteenth* (London, 1827).

36. In 1814 Wallace had married Jean, Lady Melville (1766–1829), second wife and widow of Henry Dundas, first Viscount Melville, and stepmother of Robert Dundas, second Viscount Melville. Sedgwick had criticized the system of patronage in Scotland, in which Melville, Lord Privy Seal of Scotland 1814–51, had considerable influence. Bentham was perhaps unaware that Wallace himself had been raised to the peerage in February 1828 as Baron Wallace.

37. William Petty (1737–1805), second Earl of Shelburne and first Marquis of Lansdowne, had in fact been appointed to office as first lord of trade (April–September 1763) by George Grenville (1712–70), first lord of the Treasury, 1763–65, before serving under Chatham (Pitt was raised to the peerage as Earl of Chatham in August 1766) as secretary of state for the Southern Department from July 1766 to October 1768.

38. Pitt was chancellor of the exchequer in Shelburne's administration from July 1782 to April 1783.

39. Shelburne was defeated in the House of Commons on 17 and 21 February 1783 on the preliminary articles of peace, agreed with the United States of America, France, and Spain, at the conclusion of the American War of Independence. After several weeks of negotiation, George III eventually accepted the resignation of Shelburne and, with him, Pitt, whereupon the Fox–North Coalition came into office. Rockingham had in fact died in July 1782.

40. When forming his own ministry in December 1783, Pitt took the offices of

first lord of the Treasury and chancellor of the exchequer, but did not give office to Shelburne.

41. MS "true." Bentham meant to say that the "boast" was "untrue" in its application to the lord chancellor and justices of the peace, "true" in its application to the twelve "high-seated Common Law Judges" and the master of the rolls.

42. MS "untrue."

43. This paragraph appears to supersede a previous passage at UC cxii. 173: "A curious enough particular is — that among these situations in regard to which, according to the practice of matchless Constitution, dislocation in retail ought to be expected to ensue in the event and in virtue of the dislocation in gross termed a change of Ministry or a change of administration, a sort of judicial office is one. This is the Office of the *Judge-Advocate*, Justice Minister of the Army — of the Land-branch of the Defensive Force." The judge advocate general had not traditionally been a political appointment. However upon the formation of Canning's administration in April 1827, the incumbent judge advocate general, John Beckett (1775–1847), MP for Cockermouth 1818–21, Haslemere 1826–32, and Leeds 1835–37, had been replaced by James Abercromby (1776–1858), later first Baron Dunfermline, MP for Midhurst 1807–12, Calne 1812–30, and Edinburgh 1832–39, speaker of the House of Commons 1835–39. Abercromby retained his place during Goderich's administration (September 1827–January 1828) but was in turn dismissed, and Beckett reinstated upon the formation of Wellington's administration.

Essays

Jeremy Bentham, the Principle of Utility, and Legal Positivism

PHILIP SCHOFIELD

I

In *Principia Ethica,* published in 1903, G. E. Moore argued that Bentham, like most other philosophers, had been guilty of committing a "naturalistic fallacy." The "naturalistic method," or "Naturalism," according to Moore, consisted in "substituting for 'good' some one property of a natural object or of a collection of natural objects; and in thus replacing Ethics by some one of the natural sciences." A "natural object" was an object which existed now, had existed, or was about to exist, whereas "good" was a property of certain natural objects but was not itself a natural property. Natural properties existed independently of the objects of which they were properties, whereas good could not be imagined as existing by itself. "They [i.e., natural properties] are, in fact, rather parts of which the object is made up than mere predicates which attach to it. If they were all taken away, no object would be left, not even a bare substance: for they are in themselves substantial and give to the object all the substance it has."[1] The naturalistic method introduced a confusion into what Moore considered to be the fundamental question of ethics, namely "how 'good' is to be defined." The "true answer" to this question was that "good" could not be defined, in the same way that "yellow," for instance, could not be defined, for "good," like yellow, was "a simple notion," and a definition was "only possible when the object or notion in question is something complex." It was possible to define "*the* good," the substantive to which the adjective "good" applied, but as "*the* good" was that to which the adjective applied, it was necessarily something different from that adjective itself. In short, while "*the* good" was definable, "good itself" was indefinable.[2] Nevertheless, it had been a common mistake among philosophers to assume that, when they were identifying properties which belonged to those things which they considered good, "they were actually defining good." They thought that the properties in question were "absolutely and entirely the same with goodness," and this was to commit the "naturalistic fallacy."[3] Moore illustrated his point as follows. He noted that the statement "I am pleased" did not imply that "I" was the same thing as "having pleasure," but rather that "I" was "having the sensation of pleasure." Similarly, the statement that "pleasure is good" did not mean that "pleasure" was the same thing as "good," in other words that pleasure meant good, and that good meant pleasure. Indeed, it was meaningless to say "that pleasure is good, unless good is something different from pleasure." The fallacy was the same in both cases, though in the first case one natural object was confused with a different natural object, whereas in the second case good, "which is not in the same sense a natural object," was confused with a natural object, pleasure. This latter case, bearing reference to the field of ethics, constituted the naturalistic fallacy.[4]

According to Moore, Bentham's doctrine was "a very good illustration of [the naturalistic] fallacy, and of the importance of the contrary proposition that good is indefinable." Bentham had stated that the general happiness was "the *right* and proper *end* of human action." He had thereby adopted the position that right (or good) meant the same as "conducive to general happiness," which was "not an ethical principle at all, but either a proposition about the meaning of words, or else a proposition about the *nature* of general happiness, not about its rightness or goodness." To define good as the general happiness was to define good in terms of a natural property and therefore to commit the naturalistic fallacy. Bentham, suggested Moore, might have still been prepared to maintain that the general happiness was "the proper end of human action," in other words was *the* good, had he been made aware of the fallacy. Since "Naturalism" offered "no reason at all, far less any valid reason, for any ethical principle whatever," Bentham would then have had to seek other reasons in support of his utilitarianism. However, "had he sought for other reasons, he *might* have found none which he thought to be sufficient. In that case he would have changed his whole system — a most important consequence."[5]

The "naturalistic fallacy," as conceived by Moore, consisted in the attempt to define goodness in terms of a natural property, but the term was subsequently also applied to the attempt to derive an "ought" from an "is," that is, to derive an ethical standard from facts about the physical world. W. Frankena pointed out that there was "no essential connection" between these two versions of the naturalistic fallacy. Moore's naturalistic fallacy was a particular example of what Frankena termed the "definist fallacy," that is, "the process of confusing or identifying two properties, of defining one property by another, or of substituting one property for another," and which did not necessarily involve an infringement of "the bifurcation of the ethical and non-ethical."[6] For the sake of clarity, I will refer to Moore's naturalistic fallacy as the "definist fallacy" and to the attempt to derive an "ought" from an "is" as the "so-called naturalistic fallacy." Bentham was charged by Moore with committing the definist fallacy, but he has also standardly been charged with committing the so-called naturalistic fallacy — in other words, both with defining good as pleasure and with deriving an ethical standard, the principle of utility, from facts about the physical world, the existence of the sensations of pain and pleasure — and hence with committing philosophical errors of the gravest kind.[7] In response, a number of commentators have defended Bentham from the charge that he derived an "ought" from an "is," arguing that his ethical standard, the principle of utility, is, or may be seen to be, logically independent of human psychology. Rather than adopting this approach, however, I will argue that Bentham did indeed place ethics on a naturalistic basis, but that, from the point of view of Bentham's ontology, the whole notion of the so-called naturalistic fallacy is nonsense. For Bentham, the principle of utility was true just because it rested on a factual or naturalistic foundation; in other words, it was this factual or naturalistic foundation which distinguished the principle of utility from all other ethical principles, which, because they did not have this foundation, were false.[8] As far as the definist fallacy is concerned, I will argue, again from a consideration of Bentham's ontology and its associated theory of language, that to criticize Bentham on this ground is to misunderstand his position. Furthermore, an appreciation of Bentham's ontology has significant implications for our understanding of the nature of his legal theory and calls into question some aspects of H. L. A. Hart's influential interpretation of Bentham's legal positivism.[9] In particular, I will take issue with Hart's contention that one of Bentham's objectives was to offer a morally neutral definition of law.

II

My discussion assumes the validity of a distinction between a historical interpretation of Bentham's thought and a philosophical reconstruction of it.[10] I take these to be two different enterprises: the former is an attempt to recover the "historical Bentham";[11] and the latter an attempt to reconstruct Bentham's thought in its most satisfactory form. My historical interpretation of Bentham is not intended to call into question in any way the merits of the philosophical approach as such. This approach has produced some excellent Bentham scholarship in recent years and has led to reconstructions of Bentham's utilitarianism that, according to the lights of contemporary political and moral philosophy, are either more coherent, more consistent, or more plausible than a historical reading of the texts would allow.[12] However, I do take issue with the attribution to the "historical Bentham" of views he did not hold and could not have held. The reconstructions in question do, of course, take seriously the constraints imposed by a historical reading of Bentham's texts, but only up to a point: it would be helpful if the philosopher would be more explicit about when that point had been reached.

The two themes discussed above — namely, Bentham's commission of the definist and so-called naturalistic fallacies, and the distinction between the historical and philosophical approaches — may be illustrated by reference to A. J. Ayer's seminal essay on Bentham's principle of utility. In short, Ayer concedes that Bentham commits the fallacies in question, but he reconstructs Bentham's system in such a way that it is no longer vulnerable to the standard criticisms, yet at the same time attributes this reconstruction to the "historical Bentham." Having noted that Bentham "believed that morals and politics could be made into a branch of science," in other words, be given a naturalistic basis, Ayer carefully recounts Bentham's best-known statement of the principle of utility, which appears in the opening chapters of *An Introduction to the Principles of Morals and Legislation.* Bentham held "that pleasure is the only good and pain the only evil," "conceived of 'good' as the object of desire and 'evil' as the object of aversion," and accepted that "different things" were "good for different persons, in so far as in all matters of pleasure and pain, different persons have different tastes." The best judge of the value of any actual experience was the person who was having the experience, and in so far as it gave him pleasure it was good.[13] But what was good for a particular individual had to be distinguished from what was right for the community as a whole. The principle of utility as "a criterion of morals" directed that the right action was that which produced a greater quantity of happiness than any alternative.[14] Ayer writes, "The object of Bentham's definition is to give words like 'right' and 'wrong' a purely descriptive meaning. It is assumed that there are various possible ways of acting in any given situation, and that one has to decide which of them is right. But this is equivalent to asking which of them produces the greatest quantity of happiness; and this, according to the theory, is a plain question of fact. . . . And this might seem to justify Bentham's claim that he succeeds in putting morals onto a scientific basis."[15] Ayer then identifies and attempts to deal with objections to Bentham's position. The main objection is that "while Bentham may have succeeded in finding a descriptive meaning for the ethical terms that he uses, it appears to be at the cost of sacrificing their normative force." In other words, an action will be performed only if the agent considers it to be in his own interest to do so, but not if the agent, even though recognizing it to be right, considers it to be against his interest. All that Bentham has achieved, concedes Ayer, is "a new way of describing a certain class of actions" — those that are conducive to the greatest happiness of the community may be described as right — but an individual has no reason to do them unless he believes that the action which is conducive to the greatest happiness of the community is also that which is conducive to his own greatest happiness.[16] Bentham attempts to reconcile the interests of the individual and the community through the imposition of sanctions by the legislator and society generally, but this "solution" to the "difficulty" is "not so much theoretical as practical."[17]

Ayer goes on to suggest that Bentham "pursues his end" not only by making "the rewards of benevolence . . . appear as attractive as possible," but also "in a very much more subtle way," even though Bentham did not himself "appear to be aware" he was doing it. This is the point at which Ayer begins his reconstruction of Bentham's utilitarianism. He argues that Bentham's very definition of right action as that which promotes the greatest happiness of the greatest number provides a motive for people to perform it by persuading them to transfer the feelings of approval which they have about doing what is right to doing what is conducive to the greatest happiness. Bentham's definitions, then, were "not so much descriptive as persuasive. The principle of utility is not a true, or even a false, proposition; it is a recommendation." If it were meant as a true or false proposition, "then its validity would turn on the question how words like 'right' and 'wrong' were actually used," which would merely tend to reflect "more or less arbitrary sentiments of approval or disapproval." Bentham's concern was not to discover how exactly these words were used, but "to *give* them a meaning": "What he was trying to do, whether he was aware of it or not, was to make the best of two worlds; to turn judgments of value into judgments of fact and at the same time to retain their emotive force, so that they would actually cause people to do what they were understood to describe. Unless the use of words like 'right' and 'wrong' was primarily emotive, this aim would not be achieved. And that is why I said that Bentham's definitions were not so much descriptive as prescriptive."[18] On the one hand, Ayer admits that this is a strategy which the "historical Bentham" did not intend, but, on the other hand, he is prepared to attribute it to Bentham "whether he was aware of it or not."

Ayer then considers what he calls the "stock objection to Bentham's system," that not all human action is purposive, and not all purposive action is aimed at promoting happiness. If one responds that whatever a man does is done in order to promote his happiness, then this is to assert a tautology. If one responds that every man who acts purposively does that action from which he expects to derive most pleasure, then it is psychologically false. Ayer considers this latter argument against Bentham to be "valid" but not "fatal," for one could still hold that pleasure is the only good in itself, while giving up the contention that it is the only thing which is ever actually desired. However, most people will still wish to argue, claims Ayer, that while pleasure is one value, it is not the only value, and that while pleasure should sometimes be aimed at, on other occasions it should not. Instead of maintaining Bentham's proposition that everyone seeks happiness as a psychological generalization, Ayer suggests that "a more subtle way of preserving the essential part of Bentham's system" is simply to identify happiness with the ends which a man pursues, whatever those ends happen to be: "Then Bentham's principle of utility becomes the principle that we are always to act in such a way as to give as many people as possible as much as possible of whatever it is that they want. I think that this interpretation preserves the essence of Bentham's doctrine, and it has the advantage of making it independent of any special psychological theory."[19] Ayer accepts, therefore, that Bentham's attempt to place ethics on a naturalistic basis is problematic, if not erroneous. He sympathetically reconstructs "Bentham's doctrine" in terms of prescription and preference satisfaction, in order to rescue it from both the definist fallacy (Bentham's description of "right" as equivalent to "conducive to general happiness") and the so-called naturalistic fallacy (Bentham's attempt to make morals into a branch of science). The question of whether Bentham's attempt to create a science of morals led him to commit these fallacies — namely, that in his attempt to prove the principle of utility he committed the definist fallacy by identifying good with pleasure, and that in deriving a normative principle from a statement of fact about the natural world he committed the so-called naturalistic fallacy — is also addressed in a more recent and similarly sympathetic reconstruction of Bentham's utilitarianism advanced by P. J. Kelly. Kelly points out that critics of Bentham have argued that he commits the definist fallacy by assuming that pleasure and good are conceptually identical, so that an action that produces the greatest amount of pleasure is equivalent to that which produces the greatest amount of good. Similarly, he assumes that statements about what is the right action or what ought to be done are descriptive statements about what action results in the greatest amount of pleasure. This means that when Bentham states that to do right is to do that which results in the greatest amount of pleasure, he is merely asserting a tautology — namely, to do right (that is, to do that which results in the greatest amount of pleasure) is to do that which will result in the greatest amount of pleasure (that is, to do right).[20] Kelly does not, however, follow Ayer in reconstructing Bentham's thought in terms of prescription and preference satisfaction; rather, he denies that there is any convincing textual evidence that Bentham does define good and right in terms of pleasure — that he regarded good and right as synonymous with pleasure — and recategorizes the principle of utility as a metaethical principle. Kelly argues that instead of defining good and right in terms of pleasure, Bentham gives "a philosophical explanation of the meaning of these moral terms" which "involves establishing the framework for their effective employment." This framework is provided by the principle of utility, which constitutes an "objective criterion" for assessing moral judgments, in other words, "a metaethical principle which provides the criterion of meaningfulness for moral judgements, and for the terms of moral discourse." Bentham appreciates that "moral judgements reflect approval and disapproval" and are not therefore "merely descriptive judgements." Such judgments make sense only in terms of the effect of the conduct in question on the happiness of the community as a whole: "The principle of utility which links moral judgements with the effect of conduct on the well-being of the community is a metaethical principle because it provides the criterion of meaningfulness of moral terms. This is not the same as providing analytical definitions of the terms of moral discourse." Since Bentham does not treat the terms "good" and "pleasure" as synonyms, he does not commit the definist fallacy.[21] Nor does Bentham commit the so-called naturalistic fallacy, a charge to which Bentham may be open, admits Kelly, if the principle of utility is treated as a normative principle, in other words, as indicating which actions ought to be done. However, since the principle of utility, according to his recategorization, is a metaethical principle, in other words "provides the criterion of meaningfulness for moral judgments," and not a normative principle, the criticism misses the point. Bentham, states Kelly, explicitly rejects the attempt "to prove the principle of utility as the sole criterion of meaningfulness in moral discourse, and as the criterion of moral judgement," though he did provide "some indirect support for this claim."[22] Kelly's point seems to be that if Bentham does not even attempt to prove the truth of the principle of utility, then he cannot be said to attempt to prove it by deriving it from facts about the natural world.[23]

In the course of his discussion Ayer reconstructs in several significant respects what he takes to be Bentham's doctrine, yet writes as if his reconstruction is attributable to the "historical Bentham." He begins by showing that Bentham attempts to place morality on the descriptive basis of psychological fact but goes on to argue that his system is best interpreted as a prescriptive theory, exhorting individuals to perform those actions which the standard claims to be right. Moreover, while Bentham's standard recommends the promotion of the greatest happiness in terms of maximizing pleasure, Ayer's reconstructed standard recommends the maximization of preference satisfaction. Just as forcefully as Ayer before him, Kelly, viewing the principle of utility not as a guide to practical action but as a meta-ethical standard of evaluation, is more concerned to reconstruct Bentham's utilitarianism in a way which meets the standard philosophical criticisms than in providing a historical interpretation of Bentham's thought.[24]

III

The strategy of both Ayer and Kelly, in their reconstructions of Bentham's thought, is to draw a conceptual distinction between Bentham's psychology and his ethics. Bentham does not derive his ethical theory, encapsulated in the principle of utility, from his hedonistic account of human psychology and thereby commit the so-called naturalistic fallacy of deriving an "ought" from an "is." But these philosophical reconstructions do not dispose of the question of what the "historical Bentham" meant by the principle of utility. In order to answer this question, instead of drawing on modern philosophical categories which were unknown to him, it is necessary to look more closely at his own philosophical views and in particular at his ontology, which was characterized by the distinction he drew between the names of real entities and the names of fictitious entities.[25] Bentham did not accept any ultimate ontological distinction between statements of fact and statements of value. Rather, any meaningful statement of value, once it had been properly expounded, would be seen to be a particular sort of factual statement. From Bentham's perspective, the so-called naturalistic fallacy itself has no ontological basis, for it assumes that moral properties exist independently of the physical world. Since properties in general do not exist independently of the physical world, it is impossible for moral properties to do so. This same argument might be deployed against the definist fallacy, in so far as it assumes the existence of nonphysical moral properties — a nonphysical moral property cannot be confused with a physical property if there is no such thing as a nonphysical moral property. However, as I will argue below, Bentham simply did not attempt to define "good" in the way in which Moore and other critics argue that he did.

The fundamental ontological question for Bentham concerned the nature of the relationship between the human mind, and therefore human thought and communication, and the physical world. Given that the primary instrument of thought and communication was language, it was necessary to understand the nature of language, and in particular the way in which it was used to describe and indeed to misdescribe the physical world. In short, Bentham argued that language, in order to make sense, had to refer, either directly or indirectly, to physical objects. The basic unit of language was the proposition, which had to contain, whether explicitly or implicitly, at the very least the name of a subject, the name of some attribute or predicate, and the name of a copula. In other words, a single proposition always constituted a sentence, though a single sentence might contain any number of propositions.[26] Confusion arose, however, because the name of the subject, the noun substantive, sometimes represented a physical object, sometimes a property of a physical object, and sometimes an abstraction, yet the grammatical structure failed to indicate which of these classes of entities it did represent. Within the context of a proposition, it made sense to talk about a property of a physical object, such as the ripeness or sweetness of an apple, or an abstraction, such as a law or a duty, just as it did to talk about a physical object, such as a person or a stone.[27] The way in which language was used unavoidably obscured the fundamental distinction between the two former categories, which Bentham termed "names of fictitious entities," and the latter category, which he termed "names of real entities": "The only objects that really exist are substances — they are the only real entities. To convey any notion by words which are the names of any objects [other] than substances, we are obliged to attribute to such objects what in truth is attributable only to substances: in a word we are obliged to feign them to be substances. Those others in short are only fictitious entities."[28] The mind was liable to be misled by the very language which it was compelled to use in order to describe the physical world because of the tendency, as in the case of qualities such as ripeness but also in the case of abstractions such as power and obligation,[29] to associate noun substantives with real entities, with objects existing in the physical world:

Words, viz. words employed to serve as names, being the only instruments by which, in the absence of the *things,* viz. the *substances,* themselves, the ideas of them can be presented to the mind, hence, wheresoever a word is seen which to appearance is employed in the character of a *name*, a natural and abundantly extensive consequence is — a disposition and propensity to suppose the existence, the real existence, of a correspondent object — of a correspondent thing — of a thing to which it ministers in the character of a name.

Yielded to without a sufficiently attentive caution, this disposition is a frequent source of confusion: of temporary confusion and perplexity: and not only so, but even of persisting error.[30]

Despite the fact that fictitious entities had been "embodied as it were in names, and thus put upon a footing with real ones," and were "so apt to be mistaken for real ones," they could not simply be annihilated: they were "necessary fruits of the imagination without which, unreal as they are, *language* could not — scarcely could even *thought*, be carried on."[31] A proper conception of language — more particularly of the relationship between language and human perception of the physical world — was the key to distinguishing between truth and error, between physical fact and mental fancy. A real entity was a "corporeal substance" — an object which really had existence, whereas a fictitious entity was an object which "must for the purposes of discourse be spoken of as existing" — an object to which one did not intend to ascribe real existence, but still an object which it made sense to talk about *as though* it had real existence.[32] The names of fictitious entities were not capable of exposition by the traditional Aristotelian method of definition *per genus et differentiam*. Definition in this sense was applicable where the word in question represented an entity which belonged to some nest of aggregates and was not the highest object in the nest, but not where the word had no superior genus.[33] Words such as "duty," "right," "power," and "title," which "abound so much in ethics and jurisprudence," had no superior genus, and so could not be defined *per genus et differentiam*.[34] Some other method or methods had to be found.

Bentham's solution consisted in the complementary techniques of phraseoplerosis and paraphrasis, by which those noun substantives which represented fictitious entities were expounded by demonstrating their relationship to those which represented real entities, and the technique of archetypation, which revealed the way in which all language was rooted in some physical image (the word "root" being a case in point). These methods would reveal the "real source" of the fictitious entity in question.[35] If, on the other hand, such an exposition proved to be impossible, then the fictitious entity in question belonged to the class of nonentities, and the noun substantive by which it was represented was merely a sound, and any

proposition in which it occurred was nonsensical. The operation of phraseoplerosis, the filling up of the phrase, was logically prior to that of paraphrasis.[36] In other words, any ellipsis in the proposition in question needed
first of all to be removed by inserting the omitted words, as, for instance, in
the following case: "Looking at my son whose name is John — I say to him,
John. He hears me — What is it that he understands by this? The import, the
full import, belonging to one or other of these two phrases: My desire is that
you *attend* (viz. to what more I am about to say), or, My desire is that you
come, i.e. come near to the place at which I am sitting."[37] Once the sentence
had been "filled up," the operation of paraphrasis might be undertaken: "A
word may be said to be expounded by *paraphrasis,* when not that *word*
alone is translated into other *words,* but some whole *sentence* of which it
forms a part is translated into another *sentence;* the words of which latter
are expressive of such ideas as are *simple,* or are more immediately resolvable into simple ones than those of the former. . . . This, in short, is the only
method in which any abstract terms can, at the long run, be expounded to
any instructive purpose: that is in terms calculated to raise *images* either of
substances perceived, or of *emotions;* — sources, one or other of which
every idea must be drawn from, to be a clear one."[38] Bentham exemplified
the operation of paraphrasis by expounding the word "duty." A person (X)
had a political duty when someone else (Y) had a right to have him (X)
made to do it, in which case X had a duty toward Y, and Y a right against X;
what Y had a political right to have X be made to do was that for which X
was legally liable, upon a requisition made on Y's behalf, to be punished for
not doing; the notion of punishment was that of "*pain* annexed to an act,
and accruing on a certain *account,* and from a certain *source.*"[39] The definition or exposition had "resolved" the notion of duty into its simple, or more
simple, elements: namely, the prospect of suffering a pain, inflicted by the
agents of the law (a term which itself would require further exposition),
upon the forbearance to perform some action (or alternatively the performance of some action which should have been forborne) when required to
do so by the person invested with the corresponding right.

   Although the radical distinction among noun substantives was that between the names of real entities and the names of fictitious entities —
"under one or other of these denominations may be comprehended every
object that ever was or ever can be present to any faculty of the human
frame — to perception, memory, or imagination"[40] — this did not exhaust
the category of entities. Bentham referred to a variety of other entities,
including psychological entities, fabulous entities, and nonentities. These,
however, turn out to be entities which were themselves expounded by

reference to real and fictitious entities.[41] First of all, Bentham divided the category of real entities itself into two — perceptible real entities and inferential real entities. If a real entity was perceptible, then its existence was known through the senses: if it was inferential, then the senses gave no direct knowledge of its existence, but its existence was inferred through a chain of reasoning.[42] Bentham had in mind real entities which were simply incapable of being perceived, rather than real entities which the human mind would perceive were the entity in question brought before one or other of the organs of perception. For instance, a planet which was not itself observable from the Earth, but whose existence was inferred from its gravitational pull on another object which was observable, was not an inferential real entity but rather a perceptible real entity whose existence was inferred. In this case the inference might be verified by the object in question being observed from a different vantage point, but in the case of an inferential real entity it could never be verified by perception. Among the class of inferential real entities, Bentham included the human soul considered as existing in a state of separation from the body, angels, and God. If one were not convinced by the inference which purported to establish the existence of a particular inferential real entity, the noun substantive in question did not represent a real entity but a nonentity. A nonentity, therefore, was an object which never had been, nor was capable of being, "present to any faculty of the human frame." A nonentity was like an inferential real entity in that it had no perceptible existence, but different in that it could not be convincingly inferred to exist (the question of conviction being a matter of individual persuasion or belief).[43]

A fictitious entity was not a nonentity, yet had this much in common with a nonentity: it was incapable of perception by the human mind. Bentham explained the distinction between these two classes of entity by reference to the category of what on other occasions he called fabulous entities. A fabulous entity was an imaginary real entity, such as a unicorn or a golden mountain, and thus in effect a sort of nonentity but still an entity of whose existence one might be persuaded.[44] Consider an assertion which gave the address of the Devil and described his physical characteristics — "having a head, body and limbs like a man's, horns like a goat's, wings like a bat's, and a tail like a monkey's" — with the intention of producing a persuasion that the Devil did exist. If one were persuaded by the assertion, believing the Devil to be a real entity, one would expect, if one went to the address in question, to see him. However, if one were not persuaded by the assertion, believing that the Devil was not a real entity but a nonentity, then one would not expect to see him. In contrast, consider an assertion concerning the existence of a fictitious entity, such as an obligation imposed on a person. Whether one were persuaded by the truth of the assertion or not persuaded by it, one would not expect the fictitious entity in question to possess "for itself any separate, or strictly speaking any real existence."[45]

IV

Bentham's ethical standard, the principle of utility, was itself a fictitious entity and therefore, if it was to make sense, had to be expounded, like other fictitious entities, by paraphrasis. In the statement of the principle of utility which appears in the opening chapters of *An Introduction to the Principles of Morals and Legislation,* Bentham did not explicitly discuss paraphrasis or his other methods of exposition, yet he drew upon these methods, and they provide the key to understanding his whole account. In the famous opening passage he announced in effect that the perceptions of pain and pleasure constituted the "real source" both of the principle of utility and of human motivation:

> Nature has placed mankind under the governance of two sovereign masters, *pain* and *pleasure*. It is for them alone to point out what we ought to do, as well as to determine what we shall do. On the one hand the standard of right and wrong, on the other the chain of causes and effects, are fastened to their throne. They govern us in all we do, in all we say, in all we think: every effort we can make to throw off our subjection, will serve but to demonstrate and confirm it. In words a man may pretend to abjure their empire: but in reality he will remain subject to it all the while. The *principle of utility* recognises this subjection, and assumes it for the foundation of that system, the object of which is to rear the fabric of felicity by the hands of reason and of law. Systems which attempt to question it, deal in sounds instead of sense, in caprice instead of reason, in darkness instead of light.[46]

The "sovereign masters" of pain and pleasure not only accounted for human motivation, "govern[ing] us in all we do, in all we say, in all we think," but also provided "the standard of right and wrong." They constituted the foundation not only of human psychology, determining what individuals actually did, but also of morality, pointing out what individuals ought to do. The desire for pleasure and the aversion to pain lay at the root of all human action. This "subjection" was "recognised" by the principle of utility, and it was this very recognition that rendered it possible "to rear the fabric of felicity by the hands of reason and of law." Bentham concluded the passage by remarking, "But enough of metaphor and declamation: it is not by such means that moral science is to be improved."[47] Metaphor and declamation it might have been, but the passage did not misrepresent Bentham's position. In short, psychology and morality, and thus fact and value, were conceptually linked by their relation to the perceptions of pleasure and pain.

First, as far as human psychology was concerned, Bentham, writing in the 1810s, noted that everything that was known by human beings concerning the physical world was known through their perceptions. Yet the capacity to perceive the physical world would have been of no significance whatsoever except for the fact that pain and pleasure, themselves perceptions, but distinguishable from other perceptions, were almost always associated with perceptions of the physical world. Moreover, those perceptions which were not associated with pain and pleasure, which Bentham termed apathematic perceptions, were similarly of no significance and might be ignored: "Pleasure and pain being the only objects possessed of intrinsic and independent value, simple perceptions — perceptions, if any such there were, altogether unconnected with either pleasure or pain — would have no claim to attention — would not in fact engage attention — would not be comprehended within any part of the field of art and science." In general, however, pleasure and pain on the one hand and simple perceptions on the other "are experienced together — are simultaneously concomitant" — these Bentham termed pathematic perceptions. But just as perceptions might be unaccompanied by pleasure or pain, so might pain, if not pleasure, be unaccompanied by any other distinguishable perception. However, in many instances a simple perception, which "had neither pleasure nor pain for its contemporary adjunct, may, through the medium of attention, reflection, volition and transitive action, reckon feelings of both sorts in abundance among its consequences: and hence it is that, except for clearness of intellection, the distinction between pathematic and apathematic perception becomes void of practical use."[48] In practice, there was no perception which did not have some connection, immediate or remote, with pleasure or pain.

Pleasure and exemption from pain constituted both the ends of action as well as the motives to action.[49] Indeed, all psychological fictitious entities, including motives or "springs of action," desires and aversions, intentions and dispositions, and interests, were intelligible only in terms of the real entities of pain and pleasure:

Among all the several species of psychological entities . . . the two which are as it were the *roots,* the main pillars or *foundations* of all the rest, the *matter* of which all the rest are composed — or the *receptacles* of that matter, which soever may be the *physical image,* employed to give *aid,* if not *existence* to conception, will be, it is believed . . . seen to be, PLEASURES and PAINS. Of *these,* the existence is matter of universal and constant experience. Without any of the rest, *these* are susceptible of, — and as often as they come *unlooked* for, do actually come into, *existence:* without these, no one of all those others ever had, or ever could have had, existence.

Without reference to pleasure or pain, it was impossible to form a clear idea not only of a motive, but also of the related notion of interest. It was an interest which, if pleasurable, produced a desire, and if painful, an aversion, and which in turn produced a motive. Or, to put it another way, where there was a motive, there was also a corresponding desire or aversion, the idea of a corresponding pleasure or pain, and the idea and belief of the existence of a corresponding interest.[50] It might be added that, without motives, there would be no action. Bentham believed that all human beings, and indeed all sentient creatures, shared the same hedonic psychology, itself founded on the same basic physiology (or pathology, as he termed it).[51] Everyone was motivated to pursue pleasure and to avoid pain, although people had different beliefs, founded on their experience and observation, as to which activities would in the particular circumstances in question lead to the production of pleasure and the avoidance of pain.

Second, in relation to morality, in *An Introduction to the Principles of Morals and Legislation* Bentham expounded the principle of utility, like the terms "motive" and "interest," by relating it to the real entities of pain and pleasure. This exposition was achieved through a series of intermediate relationships: namely, between pain and pleasure on the one hand and happiness on the other, between happiness and utility, and between utility and the principle of utility. To say that an object possessed utility was to say that it tended "to produce benefit, advantage, pleasure, good, or happiness . . . or . . . to prevent the happening of mischief, pain, evil, or unhappiness to the party whose interest is considered," whether that of an individual or of a community, consisting of an aggregate of individuals.[52] "An action, then, may be said to be conformable to the principle of utility, or, for shortness sake, to utility, (meaning with respect to the community at large) when the tendency it has to augment the happiness of the community is greater than any it has to diminish it." The principle of utility was "that principle which approves or disapproves of every action whatsoever, according to the tendency which it appears to have to augment or diminish the happiness of the party whose interest is in question." An "adherent" of the principle of utility, therefore, would approve of any action which in his view promoted the happiness of the community and disapprove of any which in his view diminished it.[53] Again, the principle of utility "may be taken for an act of the mind; a sentiment; a sentiment of approbation; a sentiment which, when applied to an action, approves of its utility, as that quality of it by which the measure of approbation or disapprobation bestowed upon it ought to be governed."[54]

Bentham's concern in *An Introduction to the Principles of Morals and Legislation* was to explain to the legislator how the task of promoting the greatest happiness of the community subject to him might be accomplished. The key lay in having an appropriate conception both of morality and of psychology, in other words, both of the end of human action and of the nature of human motivation. In order to produce the greatest happiness, that is, the maximum of pleasure and the minimum of pain (the end), it was necessary to produce appropriate interests, which would in turn constitute motives, themselves composed of pain and pleasure, for individuals to pursue the end in question. Whatever it was that was to be done, stated Bentham, "there is nothing by which a man can ultimately be *made* to do it, but either pain or pleasure." Pain and pleasure might, therefore, be considered either "in the character of *final* causes" or "in the character of *efficient* causes or means."[55] Once the legislator recognized the "subjection" of human beings to the "two sovereign masters," he would understand not only how to produce action, but also how to produce action of the right kind: in other words, pain and pleasure operating as motives to action would direct individuals in order to bring about, as the ends of their action, the avoidance of pain and the production of pleasure.

In explaining that the avoidance of pain and the production of pleasure were not only the ends which the legislator had in view, but also the means or instruments with which he had to operate, Bentham commented that "it behoves [the legislator] . . . to understand their force, which is again, in another point of view, their value."[56] The linking of "force" with "value" is significant, for it makes explicit the conceptual link between psychology and morality: the force with which a pleasure operated was one of psychological fact; the force in question might equally be stated in terms of value; therefore a statement concerning the value of a pleasure was a statement of psychological fact. By "value" Bentham had in mind a quantitative concept: a more valuable pleasure was a pleasure of greater quantity and was therefore not only more desirable as an end, but also operated with greater force as a motive. Bentham outlined the various "circumstances," or what he also termed "elements" or "dimensions," on which "the value of a pleasure or pain considered *by itself*" to "a person considered *by himself*" depended, namely, its intensity, duration, certainty or uncertainty, and propinquity or remoteness. Two further circumstances, fecundity and purity, were not strictly properties of a pleasure or pain, but of the act by which the pleasure or pain had been produced. An act which produced pleasure had the quality of fecundity in so far as it was likely to be followed by further sensations of pleasure; it had the quality of purity in so far as it was unlikely to be followed by sensations of pain.[57] Where the value of a pleasure or pain was considered in relation to more than one person, then in addition to these six circumstances, the circumstance of extent, that is, the number of persons affected, had also to be taken into account. In order to draw up "an exact account . . . of the general tendency of any act, by which the interests of a community are affected," one calculated the balance of the value of the pleasures and pains produced in the instance of a single individual, repeated the process for each individual affected, and finally aggregated the results: "Take the *balance;* which, if on the side of *pleasure,* will give the general *good tendency* of the act, with respect to the total number of community of individuals concerned; if on the side of pain, the general *evil tendency*, with respect to the same community."[58]

This final circumstance, namely, that of extent, was crucial to Bentham's exposition of the principle of utility. In "Deontology," in a discussion in which Bentham criticized the feasibility of taking the will of God as revealed in scripture as the standard of right and wrong, and of representing the beneficence of the deity in any other terms than the promotion of human happiness, he stated, "On the occasion of any proposed act, to make application of the principle of utility is to take one account of the feelings of the two opposite kinds — of the pleasures of all sorts on the one side, of the pains of all sorts on the other side — which, in all breasts that seem likely to be in any way affected by it, seem liable and likely, in the two opposite cases of the act's being done and of its being left undone, to take place."[59] A judgment became an ethical judgment when all the pleasures and pains expected to be produced "in all breasts that seem likely to be in any way affected by [the act]" were taken into account. In short, it was the taking into account of the final circumstance by which the quantity or value of a pain or pleasure was to be measured, namely, that of extent, that superadded a statement of moral fact to a statement of psychological fact.

Bentham's position might be summarized as follows: The principle of utility was concerned with calculating the consequences of an action in terms of the pleasures and pains it produced on every individual affected by that action. An adherent of the principle of utility would approve of any action which increased the overall happiness (understood in terms of a balance of pleasure over pain) of all the individuals affected by the action in question, where more than one individual was affected. An adherent of the principle of utility would also approve of any action which increased the happiness of a particular individual where no other individual was affected by the action in question. In the former instance the extent was equal to the total number of individuals in question, and in the latter instance to one. It was only when extent was taken into account that an action could be judged to be morally right or wrong. The question as to whether an action was right or wrong, whether it would be approved of or disapproved of by an adherent of the principle of utility, was a question of fact — it would depend upon the value, understood in terms of quantity, of the pleasures and pains which would be brought into existence by the act in question. By the appearance of the second edition of *An Introduction to the Principles of Morals and Legislation* in 1823, Bentham had come to prefer the phrase "the greatest happiness principle" or "the greatest felicity principle" to "the principle of utility." The term "utility" did not sufficiently convey the idea of happiness. Moreover, the new formulation, unlike the original one, gave an indication of the number of the interests involved, for it was the number, stated Bentham, which was "the circumstance, which contributes, in the largest proportion, to the formation of the standard here in question; the *standard of right and wrong* by which alone the propriety of human conduct, in every situation, can with propriety be tried."[60]

According to Bentham's ontology, there was nothing in human experience which was not ultimately referable to some physical fact — and this was true of propositions of utility just as it was true of propositions concerning every other fictitious entity. When statements of morality were properly understood, they would be seen to be propositions about the existence, or probable existence, of pleasures and pains, which were "all of them matters of experience."[61] In Bentham's view, moral judgments were meaningful only when expounded in terms of the principle of utility: "Of an action that is conformable to the principle of utility, one may always say either that it is one that ought to be done, or at least that it is not one that ought not to be done. One may say also, that it is right it should be done; at least that it is not wrong it should be done: that it is a right action; at least that it is not a wrong action. When thus interpreted, the words *ought,* and *right* and *wrong,* and others of that stamp, have a meaning: when otherwise, they have none."[62]

Propositions which included such terms as "right" and "wrong," "ought" and "ought not," made sense only when translated into propositions concerning the utility of the action in question, while utility itself, as we have seen, was explicable only in terms of pleasure and pain.

Hence Bentham's repeated insistence that an appeal to the principle of utility constituted an appeal to matters of fact. In *A Fragment on Government,* for instance, he stated that disagreements "between the defenders of a law and the opposers of it" would be much more likely to be settled "were they but explicitly and constantly referred at once to the principle of UTIL-ITY. The footing on which this principle rests every dispute, is that of matter of fact; that is, future fact — the probability of future certain contingencies."[63] In *An Introduction to the Principles of Morals and Legislation,* he wrote, "Utility will reign sole and sovereign arbitress of all disputes. The only evidences admitted will be matters of fact: facts conjectured from facts experienced." The facts in question were the feelings of human beings or, it might be added, where appropriate, sentient creatures generally.[64] Addressing the proposal to appropriate the property of the clergy in France in the autumn of 1789, he asserted, "The question of utility is a question not of sounds but of sensations: it depends not upon your choosing to allow or to refuse to this or that class of occupants this or that name, but upon the feelings of men of all classes."[65] In "Nonsense Upon Stilts," written in 1795, he noted that regulations were to be judged "by their effect on the feelings of those whom they concern."[66] The real entities to which the principle of utility made reference, the "real source" of the principle of utility, were the perceptions of pleasure and pain experienced by sentient creatures.

It should now be apparent that Bentham did not commit the definist fallacy, and that Kelly is correct in arguing that the criticism that Bentham equated pleasure and good misses Bentham's point, which was to expound by paraphrasis the meaning of a proposition stating that a particular action ought or ought not to be done. B. Parekh, for instance, in stating that "Bentham defines pleasure as a sensation we enjoy," overlooks the point that, for Bentham, pleasure was "a simple idea" and as such could not be defined in this way.[67] Rather, the notion of enjoyment (a fictitious entity) could be expounded only by paraphrasis, in which a proposition about enjoyment would be translated into a proposition about experiencing the sensation of pleasure (a real entity).[68] Once the ontological issues had been clarified, it was possible to begin to settle the practical question of what precisely it was that ought to be done, that is, which particular action would promote the greatest happiness of the greatest number. This was a question of fact, for the answer depended upon an assessment of the pleasures and pains which would be produced by the action in question. Bentham did, therefore, place his ethical theory on a naturalistic basis, but, from his perspective, in contrast to that of Moore and those who have accepted the notion of the so-called naturalistic fallacy, there could be no other basis.[69]

V

Having considered Bentham's ontology in relation to the criticism that he committed the definist fallacy and the so-called naturalistic fallacy, I will now consider its implications in relation to a further version of the distinction between "is" and "ought" which is associated with his thought. This is his distinction between law as it is and law as it ought to be, which is commonly taken to demonstrate his commitment to the modern doctrine of legal positivism, of which the most influential exponent is Hart.[70] Yet Bentham's commitment to this distinction should not lead one to equate his general approach with that of Hart, even though Hart himself, in many respects a great admirer of Bentham, seems to encourage one to do so. In this context it is helpful to follow Stephen Perry in distinguishing between two doctrines — one of which he terms "substantive legal positivism" and the other "methodological legal positivism" — one or other or both of which might be attributed to proponents of legal positivism: "Substantive legal positivism is the view that there is no necessary connection between morality and the content of law. Methodological legal positivism is the view that legal theory can and should offer a normatively neutral description of a particular social phenomenon, namely law. Methodological positivism holds, we might say, not that there is no necessary connection between morality and law, but rather that there is no connection, necessary or otherwise, between morality and legal theory." Relying on Gerald Postema's account of Bentham's legal theory, Perry suggests that Bentham adopted substantive legal positivism but leaves open the question as to whether he adopted methodological legal positivism as well.[71] Perry's concern is with the nature of Hart's legal positivism. What is of significance here is what Hart took to be the nature of Bentham's legal positivism.

Hart identifies two main features of Bentham's legal theory: the first was his imperative theory of law; and the second was the view that the law had no necessary or conceptual connection with morality.[72] While Hart argues that the imperative theory of law is mistaken, he notes that Bentham's legal positivism — his conceptual separation of law and morality — was "a per-

manently valuable feature of his thought."[73] Moreover, Hart ascribes to
Bentham both substantive legal positivism (the distinction between law as
it is and law as it ought to be) and methodological legal positivism (the
description of a legal system in "morally neutral terms"). To be more
precise, Hart does not regard substantive legal positivism and methodological legal positivism as separate doctrines in the context of his discussion of
Bentham's legal theory. For instance, he states, "In legal theory Bentham's
sharp severance in the *Fragment [on Government]* between law as it is and
law as it ought to be and his insistence that the foundations of a legal system
are properly described in the morally neutral terms of a general habit of
obedience opened the long positivist tradition in English jurisprudence."[74]
In another passage Hart again ascribes methodological legal positivism to
Bentham, noting that Bentham insisted "on a precise and so far as possible
a morally neutral vocabulary for use in the discussion of law and politics,"
and he states that Bentham defined law in terms which were "all flatly descriptive and normatively neutral." He continues, "This calculatedly neutral approach to definition of legal and social phenomena is now familiar to
us, but when Bentham applied it to the law it was new, shocking and a tonic
for reformers."[75] Indeed, far from regarding substantive legal positivism
and methodological legal positivism as separate doctrines, Hart appears to
conflate them in his statement that Bentham "insisted on a precise, morally
neutral vocabulary for use in the discussion of law and politics as part of a
larger concern to sharpen men's awareness . . . of the distinction between
what is and what ought to be."[76] I will take each doctrine in turn and see
whether it can be ascribed to the "historical Bentham."

First, in relation to substantive legal positivism, Bentham did explicitly
distinguish between law as it is and law as it ought to be. In *A Fragment on
Government,* which took Blackstone's *Commentaries on the Laws of England* for its target, Bentham distinguished two approaches which the legal
commentator might adopt, namely, that of the expositor and that of the
censor: "To the province of the *Expositor* it belongs to explain to us what,
as he supposes, the Law *is:* to that of the *Censor,* to observe to us what he
thinks it *ought to be.* The former, therefore, is principally occupied in
stating, or in enquiring after *facts:* the latter, in discussing *reasons."* The
task of the expositor was to show what had already been done by legislators
and judges, while that of the censor was to show what they ought to do in
future.[77] In Bentham's view, Blackstone, instead of clearly distinguishing between the functions of censor and expositor, had confounded them.
Blackstone's "professed object" had been to describe the laws of England,
in other words, to perform the role of the expositor, but he had gone beyond

this and, taking on the role of the censor, had attempted to justify the laws which he had found established. It seemed to be assumed that it was inappropriate to condemn "an old-fashioned law," either on account of "a kind of *personification* . . . as if the Law were a living creature," or on account of "the mechanical veneration for antiquity," or on account of some "other delusion of the fancy." For his part, Bentham did not know "for what good reason it is that the merit of justifying a law when right should be thought greater, than that of censuring it when wrong. Under a government of Laws, what is the motto of a good citizen? *To obey punctually; to censure freely.*" Bentham's concern was not simply that Blackstone had strayed beyond the province of the expositor into that of the censor, but that he had in effect subverted the role of censor by adopting an all too complacent attitude. It was necessary not merely to approve those laws considered to be right, but also to condemn those laws considered wrong: "Thus much is certain; that a system that is never to be censured, will never be improved: that if nothing is ever to be found fault with, nothing will ever be mended: and that a resolution to justify every thing at any rate, and to disapprove of nothing, is a resolution which, pursued in future, must stand as an effectual bar to all the *additional* happiness we can ever hope for; pursued hitherto would have robbed us of that share of happiness which we enjoy already."[78] In the context of a discussion of heresy, Blackstone had remarked that, following certain legislative amendments, "Every thing is now as it should be."[79] Bentham took this phrase, which he usually rendered as "every thing is as it should be" and implying, as he saw it, that all established law was justified, to be characteristic of Blackstone's whole approach.[80]

For Bentham there was a very practical point in separating the roles of expositor and censor and in distinguishing law as it is from law as it ought to be: namely, to bring about the coincidence of law as it is with law as it ought to be. Jurisprudence, like any other science, might be organized according to either a "natural arrangement" or a "technical arrangement." A natural arrangement was one which "men in general are, by the common constitution of man's *nature,* disposed to attend to." In the case of actions in general, and hence in the case of actions regulated by the law, the feature with which men were most concerned was their utility, their tendency either to promote or to diminish happiness, to produce pleasure and to avert pain. A law was justified in so far as it produced happiness, and prevented misery or mischief. The principle of utility, therefore, should "preside over and govern, as it were, such arrangement as shall be made of the several institutions or combinations of institutions that compose the matter of this science," and, given the universality of the principle, "the same arrangement that would serve for the jurisprudence of any one country, would serve with little variation for that of any other." Those actions which diminished utility, which produced mischief, should be constituted into offences: "The *synopsis* of such an arrangement would at once be a compendium of *expository* and of *censorial* Jurisprudence. . . . Such a synopsis, in short, would be at once a map, and that an universal one, of jurisprudence as it *is,* and a slight, but comprehensive sketch of what it *ought to be*." The leading terms in a natural arrangement would therefore "belong rather to Ethics than to Jurisprudence, even than to universal Jurisprudence." Blackstone's mistake had been to attempt to justify the technical arrangement of English law, which, in contrast to the "clear" and "satisfactory" qualities associated with a natural arrangement, was "confused" and "unsatisfactory." A technical reason was one associated with an art, science, or profession — in this case the art or profession of law — and would make sense only to a person trained in the profession in question. Under a natural arrangement, the "mischievousness of a bad law would be detected, at least the utility of it would be rendered suspicious, by the difficulty of finding a place for it in such an arrangement: while, on the other hand, a *technical* arrangement is a sink that with equal facility will swallow any garbage that is thrown into it." The terminology of English law, with its "misprisions, contempts, felonies, præmunires," did not indicate any connection between the acts in question and the principle of utility.[81] In short, Bentham's fundamental criticism was that Blackstone had attempted to justify the law of England without reference to the principle of utility, the only basis for any sort of justification.

Blackstone's confusion of the roles of expositor and censor was, in Bentham's view, an inevitable consequence of his adoption of the doctrine of natural law. In *Commentaries on the Laws of England,* Blackstone had strikingly asserted the priority of the natural law over all other law: "This law of nature, being co-eval with mankind, and dictated by God himself, is of course superior in obligation to all other. It is binding over all the globe, in all countries, and at all times: no human laws are of any validity, if contrary to this; and such of them as are valid derive all their force, and all their authority, mediately or immediately from this original." The law of nature was known through "the due exertion of right reason" and through divine revelation. The role of reason was to discover what promoted happiness, since the "divine goodness" had reconciled "the laws of eternal justice with the happiness of each individual." But as man's reason was corrupt, divine providence, in order to remedy this defect, "hath been pleased, at sundry time and in divers manners, to discover and enforce its laws by an immediate and direct revelation," precepts which would again be found to

promote man's happiness. All human laws rested on "these two foundations, the law of nature and the law of revelation," derived their "force"
from them, and were pronounced invalid if they contradicted them. For
instance, the unlawfulness of murder arose from its prohibition by the
divine and natural law, and "if any human law should allow or injoin us to
commit it, we are bound to transgress that human law, or else we must
offend both the natural and the divine."[82]

Bentham condemned Blackstone's natural law doctrine for its linking of
legal validity to a particular substantive content. As John Austin was later to
express it, also in the context of a discussion which was aimed, among other
targets, at refuting Blackstone's conception of natural law: "The existence
of law is one thing; its merit or demerit another. Whether it be or be not is
one enquiry; whether it be or be not conformable to an assumed standard, is
a different enquiry. A law, which actually exists, is a law, though we happen
to dislike it, or though it vary from the text, by which we regulate our
approbation and disapprobation."[83] Moreover, not only did Bentham condemn the linking of legal validity to a particular substantive content, he also
condemned the view that the natural law provided any basis at all on which
to ground the substantive content of human law. Blackstone's view that a
human law which conflicted with the divine and natural law should be
disobeyed, argued Bentham, was a "dangerous maxim." If the law of nature was "nothing but a phrase," and if there was no really-existing standard with which the law of the state could be compared, and "if, in a word,
there be scarce any law whatever but what those who have not liked it have
found, on some account or another, to be repugnant to some text of scripture; I see no remedy but that the natural tendency of such doctrine is to
impel a man, by the force of conscience, to rise up in arms against any law
whatever he happens not to like." The nonexistence of the law of nature —
or more precisely its "non-cognoscibility," though this was a consequence
of its nonexistence — meant that any appeal to the law of nature as invali-
dating a positive law, if it was not nonsense, was a reflection of "the bare
unfounded disapprobation" on the part of the objector to the positive law in
question. No sort of government could survive in these circumstances.
Blackstone had stated that "a law always supposes some superior who is to
make it."[84] Bentham drew out the corollary: if there was no maker, then
there was no law. Paradoxically, Blackstone's position rested on a doctrine
whose ultimate tendency might as easily produce anarchy as nonresistance
and passive obedience. Only the principle of utility, "accurately apprehended and steadily applied," could provide, in theory at least and therefore

in practice as well, the means of resolving the question of when it was proper to resist government.[85] The distinction between law as it is and law as it ought to be provided the basis both for Bentham's utilitarian strategy of reform and for his attacks on the common law and on natural law. The principle of utility placed the question of the desirability of reform on a factual basis, whereas it was the mistake of the adherents of natural law, and of other nonutilitarian ethical standards, to claim that they had knowledge of right and wrong without any reference to facts.

Second, while Bentham might be categorized as an adherent of substantive legal positivism, he cannot, contrary to Hart's view, be categorized as an adherent of methodological legal positivism. According to Hart, Bentham was engaged in an enterprise which was, in respect of providing a morally neutral description of a legal system, identical with his own, albeit Bentham in his adoption of an imperative theory of law was unable to accomplish the objective with the same degree of success. Take, for instance, Hart's statement that Bentham regarded the task of universal expository jurisprudence to be the exposition of the ideas annexed to a short list of terms such as "right" and "law."[86] Hart continues, "Quite frequently and explicitly, [Bentham] departed from usage in order to construct a meaning for a term which, while generally coinciding with usage and furnishing an explanation of its main trends, would not only be clear, but would pick out and collect clusters of features frequently recurrent in the life of a legal system, to which it was important to attend for some stable theoretical and practicable purpose."[87] This may be an accurate description of Hart's own approach, but it does not capture the essence of Bentham's approach. Take again Bentham's well-known definition of a law, which appears at the beginning of Hart's edition of *Of Laws in General*.[88] Hart states that Bentham, before "choosing" this definition, "gave considerable, though . . . critical attention to common usage," but points out that his "concern" was "not 'to teach' but rather 'to fix' the meaning of terms," and that Bentham "justifies his fixing the expression 'a law' with a much wider extension than that given to it in common usage in a manner which shows that he thought along very modern lines about the criteria which should govern the selection of concepts appropriate for use in a science. Indeed what he says sounds very much like modern conceptions of analysis as a 'rational reconstruction' or refinement of concepts in ordinary use."[89] In Hart's view Bentham was here proffering a morally neutral description of "a law," just as Hart conceived himself to be proffering a morally neutral description of "a legal system." Bentham himself, however, puts forward the following account of his enterprise: "The idea of a Law has never yet been precisely settled: the conditions requisite to reduce the idea of a command so as to render it commensurate to that of a Law have never been ascertained. This task it is my purpose to attempt . . . my business therefore is not to remind the reader what *is* meant by a Law: for no one certain thing is as yet meant by a Law, but to declare what *shall* be meant by a Law."[90] Bentham's exposition by paraphrasis related the "idea of a Law" to the will of a particular individual or individuals, identified by the actions of himself or themselves and certain other individuals, directed toward specified conduct on the part of certain persons and enforced by the prospect of the experience of pains and pleasures. Bentham's concern was not to find a morally neutral language by which law might be described, still less to try to reconstruct common usage, but to relate the names of fictitious entities, which "abound so much in ethics and jurisprudence,"[91] to their "real source." Sometimes this might result in the clarification of the meaning of a term in "common usage," but sometimes it might necessitate the invention of a new term, because common usage was so vitiated as to be simply beyond repair or because the idea itself was new and no common usage existed. Bentham went so far as to argue that it was his invention of new techniques of exposition which had led to discoveries in the fields of morals, law, politics, and economics and had thereby given "a distinct and fixt meaning . . . to a numerous tribe of words of which . . . the meaning had been floating in the clouds."[92] This helps to explain why Bentham grounded his legal theory in the habit of obedience, a fictitious entity which might be explained by reference to the actions of really-existing persons, rather than something like Hart's normative conception of content independent and peremptory reasons.[93] In short, it is the different ontological theories of Bentham and Hart, a difference which Hart glosses over, which is responsible, to some extent at least, for their differing explanations of the nature of law.[94]

Moreover, according to Bentham, the very reason for undertaking an exposition of legal terms was the utility of doing so. The end to which logic and the various techniques, such as phraseoplerosis, paraphrasis, and archetypation, which Bentham subsumed under that heading, were directed was well-being or happiness — it was only to the extent that logic was conducive to "happiness . . . including every thing that for its own sake is worth having — every thing that in itself is of any value . . . that it [i.e., logic] is worth knowing — that an acquaintance with it is of any value."[95] Again, in relation to the Aristotelian view that the end of logic was knowledge, Bentham commented, "But except in so far as in some shape or other it leads to and is productive of well-being — a balance on the side of happiness — what is the value of all the knowledge in the world? — Just nothing."[96] The accurate exposition of abstract terms was in itself an exercise which had utility, and arguably greater utility than any other conceivable logical operation. When viewed in the light of Bentham's naturalistic ontology and his utilitarian project of reform, Hart's ascription to Bentham of the methodology of conceptual analysis, the purpose of which is to provide a morally neutral description of law, is misleading. If Bentham cannot be said to be offering a normatively neutral description of law, then Hart's influential reading of Bentham, while it may be said to constitute a philosophical reconstruction of his thought, misrepresents the "historical Bentham."

VI

The interpretation I have put forward is one which attempts to recover the "historical Bentham," namely, to understand what Bentham himself might have meant. I do not, as I have already said, offer this account as a criticism of the work of those scholars who reconstruct Bentham's thought in terms which they find more interesting or more plausible. However, unless the philosopher makes more explicit the nature of his enterprise, he might be accused, from the perspective of the historian, of committing his own version of the naturalistic fallacy, namely, of confusing the fact of what, as he supposes, Bentham did say, with what, as he thinks, he ought to have said.[97] Moreover, if the reconstruction of the theories of past thinkers with a view to contemporary concerns is the only approach adopted, it will be at the cost of diminishing the range of philosophical positions available to us. This gives us good reason to treat the thought of the past on its own terms, for it will then provide a "rich storehouse of materials"[98] which will form a contrast to, and thereby help to shed light on, those ideas in fashion in our own time. For instance, if my interpretation of Hart's view of Bentham's legal theory is correct, and the real issue between Hart and Bentham is not as Hart defined it, namely, Bentham's adoption of an imperative theory of law as opposed to the notion of an authoritative legal reason, but rather that their disagreement is at the level of ontology, then legal philosophers might find that there are new questions to be asked and new answers to be found in relation to Bentham's imperative theory of law and to the whole tradition of legal positivism more generally. If the study of the history of legal and political thought therefore has its use, then it is a justification of that enterprise of which Bentham himself would have approved.

NOTES

Reprinted by permission of Oxford University Press from *Current Legal Problems* 56 (2003), 1–39.

Inaugural Lecture. I would like to thank J. H. Burns and W. L. Twining for their comments on earlier drafts of this paper.

1. G. E. Moore, *Principia Ethica: Revised Edition*, ed. T. Baldwin (Cambridge, 1993; first published 1903), 91–93. Bentham, on the other hand, argued that if one abstracted all the predicates, with the exception of existence, from a physical object, the "substance" or "matter" of which that object was composed would still remain: see Bentham Papers, University College London Library cii. 74 (2 October 1814) [hereafter UC] [published in the bilingual English–French edition of *De l'ontologie*, ed. P. Schofield, J. P. Cléro, and C. Laval (Paris, 1997), 150–53].

2. Moore, *Principia Ethica*, 57–61.

3. Ibid., 62.

4. Ibid., 65–66.

5. Ibid., 69–71. Moore did not, apparently, read Bentham in the original but took his account of Bentham from a footnote in Henry Sidgwick, *The Methods of Ethics*, 6th ed. (London, 1901), 26n: "when Bentham explains (*Principles of Morals and Legislation*, chap. i. §i. note) that his fundamental principle 'states the greatest happiness of all those whose interest is in question as being the right and proper end of human action,' we cannot understand him really to *mean* by the word 'right' 'conducive to the general happiness,' though his language in other passages of the same chapter (§§ix. and x.) would seem to imply this; for the proposition that it is conducive to general happiness to take general happiness as an end of action, though not exactly a tautology, can hardly serve as the fundamental principle of a moral system." The passages to which Sidgwick refers may be found in *An Introduction to the Principles of Morals and Legislation*, ed. J. H. Burns and H. L. A. Hart (London, 1970), 11n., 13 [hereafter *IPML*] (pp. 112n. and 114 above).

6. W. K. Frankena, "The Naturalistic Fallacy," *Mind* 48 (1939), 464. Frankena argued that it was the validity of the procedure of defining ethical terms in terms of natural properties which was the point at issue between the naturalists and anti-naturalists and that to term it a fallacy was to beg the question.

7. See, for instance, B. Parekh, "Bentham's Justification of the Principle of Utility," in *Jeremy Bentham: Ten Critical Essays*, ed. B. Parekh (London, 1974), chap. 5, and J. Plamenatz, *Man and Society: Political and Social Theories from Machiavelli to Marx*, new edn, revised by M. E. Plamenatz and R. Wokler, 3 vols. (London, 1992), ii. 211–25.

8. The exception was the principle of asceticism, which did have a naturalistic foundation in that the end was the diminution of happiness, but which, Bentham

argued, could "never be consistently pursued": see *IPML*, 17–21 (pp. 117–21 above).

9. Hart's *Essays on Bentham: Studies in Jurisprudence and Political Theory* (Oxford, 1982) contains many of his most important discussions of Bentham's legal theory. Works which deal with Bentham's legal theory in detail include G. J. Postema, *Bentham and the Common Law Tradition* (Oxford, 1986); D. Lieberman, *The Province of Legislation Determined: Legal Theory in Eighteenth-Century Britain* (Cambridge, 1989); M. J. Lobban, *The Common Law and English Jurisprudence 1760–1850* (Oxford, 1991); and O. Ben Dor, *Constitutional Limits and the Public Sphere: A Critical Study of Bentham's Constitutionalism* (Oxford, 2000).

10. On different approaches to the reading of juristic texts, see W. L. Twining, "Reading Law," in *Law in Context: Enlarging a Discipline* (Oxford, 1997), chap. 11. Twining pursues the theme in relation to Bentham in "Reading Bentham," *Proceedings of the British Academy* 85 (1989), 97 (reprinted in W. Twining, *The Great Juristic Bazaar: Jurists' Texts and Lawyers' Stories* [Aldershot, 2002], chap. 7).

11. My use of the term "historical Bentham" differs from that of D. Lieberman, who by "historical Bentham" means "the figure known in the nineteenth century through the vehicles of Dumont's *Traités de législation civile et pénale* and John Stuart Mill's revisions." Rather, it is the equivalent of his "authenticity Bentham," "the figure now recovered from the manuscripts and new edition [i.e., the new edition of *The Collected Works of Jeremy Bentham*]." See D. Lieberman, "Economy and Polity in Bentham's Science of Legislation," in *Economy, Polity, and Society: British Intellectual History 1750–1950*, ed. S. Collini, R. Whatmore, and B. Young (Cambridge, 2000), chap. 5, 108.

12. See, e.g., Ben Dor, n. 9 above; Postema, n. 9 above; R. Harrison, *Bentham* (London, 1983); P. J. Kelly, *Utilitarianism and Distributive Justice: Jeremy Bentham and the Civil Law* (Oxford, 1990); D. Lyons, *In the Interest of the Governed: A Study in Bentham's Philosophy of Utility and Law*, rev. ed. (Oxford, 1991); and F. Rosen, "Individual Sacrifice and the Greatest Happiness: Bentham on Utility and Rights," *Utilitas* 10 (1998), 129.

13. A. J. Ayer, "The Principle of Utility," in G. W. Keeton and G. Schwarzenberger, eds., *Jeremy Bentham and the Law: A Symposium* (London, 1948), chap. 13, 245–48.

14. Ibid., 248–49.

15. Ibid., 250–51.

16. Ibid., 252.

17. Ibid., 252–54.

18. Ibid., 254–55.

19. Ibid., 256–57.

20. Kelly, *Utilitarianism and Distributive Justice*, 44–45.

21. Ibid., 46–48.

22. Ibid., 48–49.

23. It is my contention that while the "historical Bentham" did not treat "good" as synonymous with "pleasure," but rather, as Kelly states, argued that the term "good" was explicable only in terms of pleasure, he did ground the principle of utility on facts about the natural world.

24. It is worthy of remark that both Ayer and Kelly reject an act-utilitarian interpretation of Bentham's thought, though disagree in their subsequent reconstructions. Ayer favors a version of rule utilitarianism, while Kelly argues instead that Bentham adopts a combination of direct and indirect utilitarian strategies.

25. One of the few commentators to attempt to relate Bentham's principle of utility to his exposition of real and fictitious entities is Harrison. According to Harrison, Bentham's insistence on "the clear separation of fact and value" meant that the techniques of exposition appropriate for giving meaning to terms "in factual contexts" could not "just be carried over automatically" to "evaluative contexts." The technique of paraphrasis, when applied to moral judgments, led to the verification of statements "made in terms of utility," since such statements constituted "an absolute morality, prescribed from an absolute, or external, point of view." This did not entail "a naturalistic ethics": "the greatest happiness of the greatest number, is a genuinely moral end which . . . can be argued for, but by means of a moral argument, not by any kind of reduction of morality to psychology." See Harrison, *Bentham*, 171–72, 188–92, 274–75. By defending Bentham in this way from the charge of committing the so-called naturalistic fallacy, Harrison, like Ayer and Kelly, is engaging in philosophical reconstruction.

26. UC cii. 515 (13 November 1815) and 503–06 (22 November 1815) [printed in J. Bentham, *Chrestomathia*, ed. M. J. Smith and W. H. Burston (Oxford, 1983), 396–97, 399]. Where I give a manuscript reference, I have relied on my own transcription: if the manuscript appears in a printed source, I give a reference to that source in square brackets.

Bentham soon afterwards came to the view that a complete proposition contained four elements: "to compleat the texture of the proposition, to the sign of the subject, the sign of the *quality* and the sign of the *relation* must be added the sign of existence: the sign by which existence is brought to view: the sign by which existence is asserted to have or to have had place, viz. the existence of the relation between the subject and the attribute." See UC cii. 494 (30 January 1816) [*The Works of Jeremy Bentham*, ed. J. Bowring, 11 vols. (Edinburgh: William Tait, 1838–43) [hereafter Bowring], viii. 337].

27. UC cii. 451 (2 December 1815) [Bowring, viii. 328].

28. UC lxix. 241 (c. 1776).

29. Bentham distinguished fictitious entities themselves into physical or somatic fictitious entities (which included properties such as motion, quantity, quality, form, and relation); psychical, psychological, or noological fictitious entities (which included properties of the mind, such as desires and aversions); and ethical fictitious entities (which included abstractions such as powers and obligations): see UC ci. 323–30 (7–9 August 1814) [Bowring, viii. 263–64], and UC cii. 508 (26 November 1815) [Bentham, *Chrestonathia*, 398].

30. UC ci. 341 (7 August 1814) [Bowring, viii. 262].

31. UC ci. 95 (25 July 1814) [Bowring, viii. 219].

32. UC cii. 24 (23 September 1814) [*De l'ontologie*, 86–71]. Cf. UC cii. 16 (7 July 1821) [*De l'ontologie*, 164–65]:

"A real entity is an entity to which, on the occasion and for the purpose of discourse, existence is really meant to be ascribed.

"A fictitious entity is an entity to which, on the occasion and for the purpose of discourse employed in speaking of it existence is ascribed, yet in truth and reality existence is not meant to be ascribed."

33. UC ci. 215–16 (17 August 1814) [Bowring, viii. 245–46].

34. J. Bentham, *A Fragment on Government*, in *A Comment on the Commentaries and A Fragment on Government*, ed. J. H. Burns and H. L. A. Hart (London, 1977), 495n.

35. See UC ci. 218 (23 August 1814) [Bowring, viii. 246]: "Of any such fictitious entity or fictitious entities, the real entity with which the import of their respective appellatives is connected, and on which their import depends, may be termed the *real source*, *efficient cause*, or *connecting principle*."

36. UC ci. 219 (23 August 1814) [Bowring, viii. 247].

37. UC cii. 415 (27 December 1815) [Bowring, viii. 321–2].

38. Bentham, *A Fragment on Government*, 495n.

39. Ibid., 494–95n.

40. UC cii. 21 (23 September 1814) [*De l'ontologie*, 80–81].

41. See UC cii. 23 (23 September 1814) [*De l'ontologie*, 84–85]: "In language, the words which present themselves and are employed in the character of *names* are some of them names of real entities, others names of fictitious entities: and to one or the other of these classes may all words which are employed in the character of *names* be referred."

42. UC cii. 7 (7 July 1821) [*De l'ontologie*, 163–65]. Bentham recognized that the relationship between the human mind and the physical world was not fully captured in the view that the human mind directly perceived the physical world. His point was that what operated upon the mind were the perceptions of physical objects, and not the physical objects themselves. In strictness, if real entities were

those which were directly perceptible, the only real entities would be the perceptions themselves, while physical objects would be inferential entities. But leaving out of the account the fact that in strictness the only real entities were perceptions, and considering only the "bodies" or "substances" which were regarded as existing in the physical world, then the term "perceptible real entities" would refer to "corporeal substances," and the term "inferential real entities" to "incorporeal ones." It was entirely possible that the perceptions which the mind received did not accurately reflect, or even systematically distorted, the nature of the real entities themselves, but this was of little practical concern. See UC cii. 15 (25 September 1814) [*De l'ontologie*, 180–83]. See also Harrison, *Bentham*, 54–55.

43. UC cii. 11 (27 September 1814) [*De l'ontologie*, 176–79]. The question arises whether Bentham himself believed in the existence of any inferential real entities, and whether he might therefore be described as an atheist. For differing interpretations of Bentham's religious views, see P. Schofield, "Political and Religious Radicalism in the Thought of Jeremy Bentham," *History of Political Thought* 20 (1999), 272; and J. E. Crimmins, "Bentham's Religious Radicalism Revisited: A Response to Schofield," *History of Political Thought* 22 (2001), 494.

44. UC ci. 342, 322 (7 August 1814) [Bowring, viii. 262–63].

45. See UC cii. 23–4 (23 September 1814) [*De l'ontologie*, 84–87].

46. *IPML*, 11 (pp. 111–12 above).

47. *IPML*, 11 (p. 112 above).

48. UC ci. 406 (25 January 1816) [Bowring, viii. 279]; UC ci. 454 (19 February 1815) [Bowring, viii. 288]. Bentham elsewhere distinguished between "simple perception" and "*sensation*, i.e. perception attended with pain, pleasure or both": see UC cii. 408 (27 December 1815) [Bowring, viii. 320].

49. J. Bentham, *A Table of the Springs of Action*, in *Deontology together with A Table of the Springs of Action and Article on Utilitarianism*, ed. A. Goldworth (Oxford, 1983), 87.

50. Ibid., 87, 98–99.

51. See, for instance, Bentham, *A Table of the Springs of Action*, 87, where Bentham noted that "psychological pathology" was the foundation for "psychological dynamics," that is, the "science," or body of knowledge, which dealt with motives.

52. *IPML*, 12 (p. 113 above).

53. Ibid., 12–13 (pp. 113–14 above).

54. Ibid., 12n (pp. 112–13n. above).

55. Ibid., 34 (p. 132 above).

56. Ibid., 38 (p. 136 above).

57. Conversely, in relation to an act which produced pain, it had the quality of fecundity insofar as it was likely to be followed by further sensations of pain; it had

the quality of purity insofar as it was unlikely to be followed by sensations of pleasure.

58. *IPML*, 38–40 (pp. 137–38 above).

59. *Deontology*, in Bentham, *Deontology together with A Table of the Springs of Action and Article on Utilitarianism*, 168.

60. *IPML*, 11n (p. 112n. above). This note was written in July 1822. Throughout his career, Bentham continued to explain moral good in terms of the physical sensation of pleasure, and moral evil in terms of the physical sensation of pain. See Bentham, *A Table of the Springs of Action*, 88–89:

"*Moral good* is . . . *pathological* good, in so far as *human will* is considered as instrumental in the production of it: in so far as any thing else is made of it, either the *word* is without meaning or the thing is without *value*. And so in regard to *evil*.

"For *pathological* might here have been put the more ordinary adjunct 'physical,' were it not that, in that case, those pleasures and pains, the seat of which is not in the *body*, but only in the *mind*, might be regarded as excluded."

He made the same point in "Codification Proposal" (printed in 1822), in J. Bentham, "*Legislator of the World*": *Writings on Codification, Law, and Education*, ed. P. Schofield and J. Harris (Oxford, 1998), 256: "*Good* is pleasure or exemption from pain: or a cause or instrument of either . . . *Evil* is pain or loss of pleasure; or a cause or instrument of either . . . *Happiness* is the sum of pleasures, deduction made or not made of the sum of pains." In short, ethical judgments depended upon the physical existence of pleasure and pain. Bentham used the term "moral physiology" to describe the field within which an analysis of the factors which determined a man's sensibility to pain and pleasure would fall (*IPML*, 53n.). Here again Bentham appears to link morality with physical facts concerning human beings.

61. *Deontology*, in Bentham, n. 49 above, 169.

62. *IPML*, 13 (p. 114 above).

63. Bentham, *A Fragment on Government*, 491. According to Bentham, "The existence of any expressible state of *things*, or of persons, or of both, whether it be *quiescent* or *motional* or both, at any given point or portion of time, is what is called *a fact* — or *a matter of fact*." See UC cii. 301 (2 August 1814).

64. *IPML*, 282–83n.

65. J. Bentham, "Supply — New Species Proposed," in *Rights, Representation, and Reform: Nonsense upon Stilts and other writings on the French Revolution*, ed. P. Schofield, C. Pease-Watkin, and C. Blamires (Oxford, 2002), 216.

66. "Nonsense upon Stilts," in ibid., 375 (p. 369 above).

67. Parekh, "Bentham's Justification of the Principle of Utility," 113.

68. For Hart's defence of Bentham on this point, see "Bentham's Principle of Utility and Theory of Penal Law," in *An Introduction to the Principles of Morals*

and Legislation, ed. J. H. Burns and H. L. A. Hart, with a new introduction by F. Rosen (Oxford, 1996), lxxxviii–xci.

69. It might be left to the philosophers to determine whether Bentham's ontology, with the theory of language which accompanies it, is more or less persuasive than that of Moore. A robust defence of Bentham's linguistic theory is found in C. K. Ogden's "Introduction" to his edition of *Bentham's Theory of Fictions* (London, 1932).

70. Hart warns against confusing the is/ought distinction of legal positivism with the is/ought distinction associated with the so-called naturalistic fallacy. The latter, according to Hart, is a moral theory according to which statements of fact belong to a radically different category from value statements. He identifies such theories as fall within this definition as noncognitivist theories and points out that whether one rejects or accepts any sharp distinctions between is/ought, fact/value, means/ends, and cognitive/noncognitive, this does not undermine the legal positivist distinction between law as it is and law as it ought to be. See Hart, "Positivism and the Separation of Law and Morals," in *Essays in Jurisprudence and Philosophy* (Oxford, 1983), chap. 2, 82–84.

71. See S. R. Perry, "Hart's Methodological Positivism," in J. Coleman, ed., *Hart's Postscript: Essays on the Postscript to the Concept of Law* (Oxford, 2001), chap. 9, 311–13; and Postema, *Bentham and the Common Law Tradition*, 328–36. Postema, ibid., 256–62, undertakes a comparative evaluation of the legal theories of Bentham and Hart, but this is a philosophical rather than a historical exercise.

72. Hart, *Essays on Bentham*, 17–18. Hart adds that Bentham recognized that there were many important and often complex contingent connections between law and morality.

73. Ibid., 19.

74. Ibid., 53.

75. Ibid., 28.

76. Hart, "Bentham's Principle of Utility and Theory of Penal Law," lxxxv.

77. Bentham, *A Fragment on Government*, 397–98.

78. Ibid., 398–99.

79. William Blackstone, *Commentaries on the Laws of England*, 4 vols. (Oxford, 1765–69), iv. 49.

80. Bentham, *A Fragment on Government*, 400, 407 and n.

81. Ibid., 415–18.

82. Blackstone, *Commentaries*, i, 40–43.

83. John Austin, *The Province of Jurisprudence Determined*, ed. W. E. Rumble (Cambridge, 1995), 157.

84. Blackstone, *Commentaries*, i, 43.

85. Bentham, *A Fragment on Government*, 482–83.

86. See, for instance, *IPML*, 294–95.

87. Hart, *Essays on Bentham*, 164.

88. See J. Bentham, *Of Laws in General*, ed. H. L. A. Hart (London, 1970), 1: "A law may be defined as an assemblage of signs declarative of a volition conceived or adopted by the *sovereign* in a state, concerning the conduct to be observed in a certain *case* by a certain person or class or persons, who in the case in question are or are supposed to be subject to his power: such volition trusting for its accomplishment to the expectation of certain events which it is intended such declaration should upon occasion be a means of bringing to pass, and the prospect of which it is intended should act as a motive upon those whose conduct is in question."

89. Hart, *Essays on Bentham*, 110.

90. UC lxix. 86 (*c.* 1776).

91. See p. 434 above.

92. British Library Add. MS 33,550, fol. 5 (15 October 1814).

93. Hart, *Essays on Bentham*, 253–57.

94. In "Definition and Theory in Jurisprudence," in Hart, *Essays in Jurisprudence and Philosophy*, chap. 1, Hart identifies Bentham's method of paraphrasis with the twentieth-century notion of the "definition in use," and praises Bentham accordingly for his insight, but when one appreciates the nature of Bentham's ontological views, it is clear that this is a misidentification. Postema, *Bentham and the Common Law Tradition*, 304–36, 452, also argues that Bentham and Hart were engaged in different enterprises. Postema, however, reconstructs the legal theory of both men in terms of categories employed in contemporary philosophy, rather than interpreting Bentham in the light of Bentham's own philosophical assumptions. Having said that, Postema's account of Bentham's thought is extremely sensitive to the historical context.

95. UC ci. 156 (28 July 1813, 23 July 1814) [Bowring, viii. 232].

96. UC ci. 158 (31 July 1814) [Bowring, viii. 233]. See UC ci. 99 (29 October 1826) [Bowring, viii. 241]: "Only with reference to use — understand always to the augmentation of happiness in some shape or other — has knowledge, how consummate soever, any claim to attention — only by its subserviency to practice has knowledge any use: only by its subserviency to art is science in any shape of any use."

97. See Bentham, *A Fragment on Government*, 397, quoted at p. 445 above.

98. Despite his scathing attacks on the common law, Bentham was prepared to concede that it might be regarded as "a matchless blessing" in the sense that it formed "a rich storehouse of materials for legislation": see Bentham, *"Legislator of the World,"* 136–37.

Bentham on Codification

DAVID LIEBERMAN

In a letter of 8 October 1777, the twenty-nine-year-old Jeremy Bentham reported to his father the recent news that "The Œconomical Society of Berne in Switzerland" had offered a reward of "50 Louis for a draft of a Code of Criminal Laws." "It gave me some pleasure to see this," Bentham continued, "as it is a proof of the attention bestowed on these subjects in other countries besides our own."[1] These sentiments provide a convenient reminder that when in the 1770s Bentham embarked upon a lifetime's pursuit of systematic law reform he did so in a setting where projects of legislative codification and legal modernization enjoyed general currency. At numerous occasions in his career, Bentham hoped to exploit this situation by securing the patronage of hereditary monarchs or elected legislators who enjoyed the political capacity to transform his legislative theory into enacted codes of law. And he found it no less opportune to clarify the distinctive features of his own codification project by contrasting its merits with the distinctly less impressive examples offered in contemporary codes.[2]

By the time he learned of the Berne Society competition, Bentham was well advanced in the investigation of those principles of morals and legislation that could be applied to an envisaged "plan of a penal code *in terminis*."[3] By the mid-1780s, he had successfully identified "a complete and pretty detailed plan of a complete body of the laws," or what he described as a "*Pannomion*" — a legislative code "complete in all its branches."[4] In later decades, Bentham's conception of the Pannomion underwent further expansion and revision, particularly under the impact of his embrace of radical democratic reform. But throughout, codification remained the central and single most important institutional vehicle of his plans for the promotion of human happiness. When, as was frequently the case, he entered fields of inquiry outside the study of law — such as psychology or political economy, or language and logic — he typically did so in service to his legislative program. When, as was no less frequent, he turned his reform aspirations to institutions outside the code — such as schools and banking — he often did so as digressions from his legislative program. As late as 1830, some eighteen months before his death, Bentham buoyantly reported, "I am alive, though turned of eighty-two, still . . . codifying like any dragon."[5]

Codification as Normative Ideal

The plan for a "complete program of the laws," remarkably, never received anything like a straightforward, summary exposition at Bentham's hands in the fifty-year period following its initial formulation. *Of Laws in General*, the innovative treatise concerning "what sort of thing a law is," which set out the legal theory on the basis of which Bentham first specified the organizing logic and structure of the Pannomion, remained unpublished in his lifetime.[6] Instead, its central argument received a very compressed summary in the "Concluding Note" Bentham added to the *Introduction to the Principles of Morals and Legislation* (1789). In the period roughly from 1811 to 1823, Bentham composed several papers on codification, perceiving an opportunity to secure an invitation to produce a draft code for various states in Europe and the Americas. But these advocacy statements contained more detail concerning the benefits of the Pannomion than of its structure and content. For Bentham's contemporary admirers, as for later generations, the fullest synthetic exposition of his legislative program appeared in the form of Étienne Dumont's elegant redaction of 1802, the three-volume *Traités de Législation civile et pénale*. Bentham himself in later writings on codification frequently turned to these volumes to illustrate and clarify major elements of his legislative theory.[7] But Dumont's edition was itself a selective synthesis of Bentham's jurisprudence, produced before the changes in orientation and emphasis that accompanied Bentham's political radicalism. As a result, any discussion of Bentham's code involves a doubly interpretive exercise. There is the need both to distill a version of the Pannomion out of the several partial accounts provided by Bentham and Dumont, and to understand why, for Bentham, this specific form of law promised such powerful benefits for the happiness of humankind.

In his preface to *An Introduction to the Principles of Morals and Legislation*, Bentham laid out an ambitious program for the exposition of the principles of legislation designed "to prepare the way for the body of law itself exhibited *in terminis*." A roughly similar plan appeared in the essay "Vue générale" in Dumont's *Traités*; and central elements remain present in the nineteenth-century codification proposals.[8] What Bentham often described as the "substantive" part of the law comprised the Codes of Civil and of Penal Law. The former (also styled, "private distributive" law) distributed the legal rights and powers that preserved the property and security of the individual. The latter elaborated the body of prohibitions and sanctions that gave legal force to the body of civil rights and powers. A third Constitutional Code (also styled "public distributive" law) specified the structure of power and political offices through which law was made. A fourth Procedure Code (also styled "adjective law") set out the rules and processes for resolving disputes and remedying injuries which occurred in the operation of the substantive codes. Each of these core codes had their distinctive subsidiary goals and maxims through which the foundational goal of general happiness was advanced. (Thus the Civil Code advanced happiness by realizing and coordinating the supporting goals of security, subsistence, abundance, and equality.) These four codes were accompanied by a series of additional codes that supplemented or refined the basic system of substantive and adjective law. Bentham, for example, described a Financial Code, usually as a distinct subbranch of constitutional law, which drew especially upon the science of political economy and dealt with the management of the community's public resources. Another distinct code of law was devoted to "Judicial Establishment," which functioned similarly to the adjective law comprising the Procedure Code, but which resembled the law of the Constitutional Code in distributing and regulating government offices.

Bentham was never inclined to underestimate the value of this legislative project, or to abbreviate the number of collateral benefits that the enactment of the Pannomion would bring to human happiness.[9] The production of such a code of law endowed "in the highest degree, and operating upon the largest scale" with the leading attributes of "*Utility, Notoriety, Completeness, Manifested Reasonableness*" would constitute nothing less than a "new aera in legislation."[10] In this new era, all law would issue as the authoritative mandate of a sovereign legislator or legislative body. The body of the law would be distinguished by the comprehensiveness of its design and by the systematic unity of its goals, method, and form of presentation. The code was unified in its substantive content because all of its detailed provisions aimed at the promotion of the greatest happiness of the greatest number; it displayed "the dictates of utility in every line."[11] It was unified in its method by virtue of its consistent set of fundamental terms and organizing categories. This methodical organization and uniform terminology, in turn, served the verbal expression and presentation of the law, which formed another defining feature of the code. The Code was promulgated in a manner to facilitate ready comprehension of what the law required and of the utilitarian reasoning that lay behind its detailed provisions. The Panno-mion would furnish for the first time a complete and consistent body of law in which "there are no *terrae incognitae*, no blank spaces: nothing is at least omitted, nothing unprovided for."[12]

The Pannomion, for Bentham, was the programmatic instantiation of the general principles of morals and legislation. Law, Bentham always empha-sized, involved a distinctive set of moral challenges and institutional oppor-tunities. In the promotion of happiness, law's momentous and distinctive task was to furnish a structure of publicly articulated and maintained securi-ties, which enabled individuals to chart their futures, undertake complex cooperative ventures, and realize their plans and expectations for happi-ness.[13] But, crucially, law only produced these benefits on the basis of purposeful coercion and compulsion, which inevitably involved a sacrifice of happiness and liberty. Law created rights and promoted security by imposing duties and restraints; and law redeemed these duties and restraints by threatening and inflicting punishments for their violation. Even in those less frequent occasions when offered rewards (instead of threatened punish-ment) to secure desired lines of conduct, it still imposed burdens in terms of the resources required to maintain the system of public law itself. "To make a law," Bentham maintained, "is to do evil that good may come."[14] All theorizing about law and all practices of law needed to proceed in light of this blunt reality. "Society is held together only by the sacrifices that men can be induced to make of the gratifications they demand," Bentham insisted. "To obtain these sacrifices is the great difficulty, the great task of government."[15]

Law's necessary "evil" figured as a theoretical point of departure for much of what is most familiar in Bentham's philosophy of law and the larger legal positivist tradition with which he is associated.[16] Law was the product of human sources and human choices; and law could only secure its proper goals on the basis of an accurate understanding of its operations and social costs. This was a point Bentham pressed with greatest vehemence against the theorists of natural rights — particularly the radical rights theo-rists of American independence and especially of the French Revolution — who maintained that individuals enjoyed rights prior to the imposition of human law and that the primary purpose of human law was to secure these prior-existing fundamental rights. Such theorists, according to Bentham, correctly perceived the importance of law to the preservation of rights and property (though Bentham preferred to speak of "security" rather than "liberty" in this context), but completely confused the manner in which law functioned to achieve this critical goal. Law secured rights by imposing obligations and restraints, which necessarily involved a sacrifice of liberty. And law, when successful, maintained these obligations and restraints through the practice of punishment, which involved the threat and imposition of pain to secure the desired good of legally protected rights and security. To demand of law, as the radical rights theorists standardly maintained, that it promote liberty by preserving natural freedom was in fact to deny law just that coercive capacity upon which its critical social contribution depended. The rights arguments, taken literally, served to "annihilate all laws," much less establish a useful standard for the moral evaluation of the law.[17]

The same approach had no less profound implication for the programmatic practice of lawmaking. If law produced evil that good might come, its legitimacy required that such good actually be realized in practice — that the creation of duties and obligations through the instrument of punishment result in the social benefits these measures were designed to secure. By making evident the burdens no less than the benefits law entailed, the approach purposely put pressure on the lawmaker to demonstrate that the goals chosen for law did indeed promote the greatest happiness of the greatest number, while imposing on the community as little disutility ("evil") as the task required. For Bentham, an all-encompassing model of how to fail to meet this challenge was provided in horrific detail in the customary systems of law that formed part of every existing legal order, above all in England's system of common (or "unwritten") law. Among the important achievements of the Pannomion, for Bentham, was the anticipated eradication of this morally indefensible kind of law. Indeed, this goal loomed so large that Bentham was never able to present the case for codification without rehearsing the case against customary law.[18]

Pannomion: Leading Features

The first challenge facing the lawmaker was the decision concerning which legal rights and powers to confer on the community, which in practice meant which legal constraints and obligations to impose on the community through the instrument of punishment. In the case of customary law, these rights and obligations came to be identified over time through the course of legal practice; and for its many defenders this kind of incremental, cumulative process of legal development produced law substantively superior to that available in other forms of lawmaking.[19] Bentham's response was notoriously dismissive. The materials of historic customary law, such as England's common law, did indeed furnish the legislator with a rich body of valuable data concerning the practice of law, and no lawgiver should fail to consult this instructive legal experience. But simply to perpetuate a body of inherited legal practices was to succumb to complacent "ancestor wisdom."[20] The question of which legal rights and obligations were to be maintained in a community was, of course, to be determined by the standard of the greatest happiness principle; and historical bodies of law, when judged by this standard, were just as likely to contain records of error as of wisdom and insight. Thus, to cite an example that preoccupied Bentham throughout his career, English law maintained a host of morally illegitimate penal laws that denied religious liberty and thereby actually diminished the happiness of the community itself.[21]

In his more detailed elaboration of the principles of legislation, Bentham made plain that the normative task of determining the substantive content of the law involved a far more rigorous method of analysis than that suggested by common law's typical appeal to standards of reason and convenience. One of Bentham's more famous early publications, the *Defence of Usury* (1787), supplied, as Bentham himself suggested, a model exercise of critical legislative science. Bentham's tract advocated the repeal of laws limiting the rate of interest on monetary loans, maintaining that the same arguments for freedom of trade that applied in the case of other transactions equally applied to the case of "money bargains." Bentham invoked the economic principles of Adam Smith to demonstrate the counterproductive damage caused by laws in restraint of trade and thereby reached a conclusion concerning usury laws that Smith himself resisted in the *Wealth of Nations*. But this important economic reasoning covered only part of the critical examination of the usury prohibition. Equally significant was the argument that past treatment of this area of law had been woefully distorted by the emotive valence of the term "usury" itself, whose standard usage presupposed a pernicious practice whose social damage actually needed to be (and, for Bentham, could not be) demonstrated. The perpetuated legal restraint was as much the product of the inertial power of "prejudice" and "authority" as the result of faulty economic reasoning.[22]

The case of usury provided a classic example of a legal prohibition that required rejection because it restricted a form of conduct that actually was not harmful, and its critical evaluation typified much of Bentham's repudiation of paternalistic legal restraints in and beyond the contexts of political economy. But even in those situations where the legislator sought to proscribe lines of conduct that did harm the community's happiness, Bentham's principles of legislation demanded the further demonstration that the conduct in question could be successfully curtailed by threatened punishment or could not be more effectively discouraged through some less painful practice, such as education or moral censure.[23] The full constructive alternative to the errant methods of the past was provided in Bentham's outline for a code of penal law, which he later came to perceive as the plan for a larger body of both civil and penal codes. This was the elaborate "Division of Offences," which comprised the sixteenth chapter (and nearly one-third of the text) of *An Introduction to the Principles of Morals and Legislation*.[24]

In contrast to the methods of customary law, Bentham's legislative plan began not with inherited legal practice, but instead focused on the more abstract question of which forms of behavior "*ought* to be made offences, as the good of the community requires should be made so."[25] Beginning thus — with "the logical whole, constituted by the sum total of possible offences"[26] — Bentham organized the legal materials into principal divisions according to the manner in which the various forms of socially damaging conduct diminished the community's happiness. This could occur by damaging the happiness of an assignable individual member of the community, either the happiness of the offender himself (the basis for the category of "self-regarding private offences") or of another member of the community ("private offences"); or by damaging the happiness of the "whole community" ("public offences") or of some "lesser circle" of the entire community ("semi-public offences"). Each of these categories underwent further subdivision, again according to the particular social mischief the law sought to restrain. The class of "private offences" received the most extensive subdivision, through to the stage that Bentham's classification reached the level of specificity found in the provisions of existing bodies of law. This treatment provided the model for the other classes of offences that was to form the core of the envisaged code of penal law.[27]

Bentham's labored arrangement of offences not only correctly identified which legal burdens should be imposed on a community, but also supplied a new terminology for identifying these prohibitions and for delineating the behavior identified by the law as socially damaging. This, again, for Bentham represented a crucial alternative to the processes of customary law, where the terms for basic legal rights and obligations were themselves derived from the same processes of development and adaptation that generated the rights and duties themselves. In the case of English common law, much of this terminology was taken from foreign language (Latin and French) as well as from a purely professional vernacular (Law-French), and much of the process of legal development had been navigated through the introduction of legal fictions and the manipulation of abstruse procedural forms. The result was a set of basic legal terms — such as "misprisions, contempts, felonies, praemunires" — that remained inscrutable to all but a small number of the community's members.[28]

For Bentham, this terminological failing implicated central matters of legislative design. By relying on an arcane professional vocabulary, customary law systematically disregarded those defining goals for codification that Bentham treated under the heading of "cognoscibility": those qualities that rendered the aims and content of the law as easily understood by the community as was possible.[29] The Pannomion's anticipated achievement at the level of terminological clarity and precision formed a running point of emphasis in Bentham's case for codification — "*Clearness, correctness, and completeness,*" as Bentham explained to James Madison; "*clearness, correctness, completeness, conciseness, compactness, methodicalness, consistency,*" as he enthused in "All Nations Professing Liberal Opinions."[30] One feature of this concern with linguistic precision quickly became a notorious element of Bentham's compositions: his propensity for word invention and novel syntactical forms. As many critics observed, the neologisms and idiosyncratic prose, especially of Bentham's later years, burdened his discussion and threatened simply to replace the technical language of customary law with another (no less baffling) technical nomenclature. "He writes a language of his own that darkens knowledge," protested William Hazlitt. "His works have been translated into French — they ought to be translated into English."[31]

Crucially, for Bentham, these were not exclusively verbal issues. The linguistic precision and clarity of the Pannomion, again, directly implicated the legal order's moral legitimacy. Law ultimately depended on the practice of punishment, whose implementation could be justified only by preventing more harmful forms of conduct. To succeed, members of the community needed to have an accurate understanding of what precisely the law required of them and what legal sanctions had been established to sustain these obligations. Any failure of intelligibility weakened the efficacy of the legal order and threatened to create a situation in which punishment was imposed without securing the required social benefits. Accordingly, codification for Bentham implied a technology of communication, which the Pannomion's "cognoscibility" — its "clearness" and "correctness" — directly served.

In addition, Bentham perceived a strong connection, in law and in other fields, between linguistic precision and conceptual clarity. "In every species of knowledge," the *Traités* reported, "disorder in language is at once the effect and the cause of ignorance and error."[32] In the case of codification, the same analytical methods that eradicated legal technicality and fictions also ensured the law's "completeness" and "methodicalness." English common law, for example, adopted a system of "technical arrangement" generated by the processes of legal development. Bentham's code, in contrast, was organized according to explicit rules of classification that he referred to as "natural arrangement" and "method of bipartition."[33] "Natural arrangement" organized the materials of any science in a manner that rendered them easily understood and remembered. In the case of penal law, the natural arrangement organized legal materials according to the social mischiefs they sought to prevent; this being the "property" that most "readily" and "firmly" engaged "the attention of an observer."[34] The "method of bipartition" proceeded by "dividing each superior branch into two, and but two, immediately subordinate ones; beginning with the logical whole, dividing that into two parts, then each of those parts into two others; and so on."[35] By starting with "the logical whole" of all offences required to promote the community's happiness and by proceeding by bipartition, Bentham ensured that the Division of Offences was systematic and comprehensive. The same aspiration was retained as a distinguishing goal for the Pannomion as a whole: "From beginning to end, one object kept in view and aimed at, is — that the whole field of legislation being surveyed . . . — no case that can present itself shall find itself unnoticed or unprovided for."[36]

A code that comprehended "the whole field of legislation" entailed a no less fundamental transformation in the manner in which legal knowledge was conveyed to the community whose conduct it guided. In the processes of England's customary law, this information was conveyed principally through the practices of the courts; the common law judges, in William Blackstone's influential formulation, serving as "the living oracles" of England's unwritten law.[37] Bentham, for whom Blackstone served as an irresistible target, found much to repudiate and condemn in this approach of lawmaking. Common law, for Bentham, stood condemned as a species of "*ex post facto* laws."[38] In deciding cases courts vindicated legal rights or clarified legal obligations only on the initiative of private litigants, after the injury which occasioned a legal dispute had already occurred. The retrospective character of adjudication entailed an unnecessary and therefore unjustifiable squandering of legal force. Until a legal rule was settled through the repeated pattern of adjudication, forms of misconduct might continue, and individuals would receive punishment without the members of the community knowing confidently the precise benefits and burdens the law specified. As Bentham famously put the point in a polemic composed in

1792, common law judges made law for the community "just as a man makes laws for his dog."[39] First appeared the social mischief; then came the blow; and then the animal (or community) was left to work out the relationship between penalty and violated rule.

Even more cripplingly, the processes of common law in themselves never generated those authoritative general rules that best served to guide the conduct of the community and thereby secure the felicific benefits the law intended. According to the orthodox legal theory of his era, common law judges did not make law. Rather, their decisions provided evidence as to which customs and norms had been received as common law. Bentham recognized that common law was the product of courts; and in his radical political writings he denounced the opaque nomenclature and costly procedures that, he charged, directly served the power and wealth of "judge and company."[40] But he took care to emphasize that adjudication created merely a "spurious and fictitious substitute to really-existing law," not authentic law itself.[41] What was authoritative in the practice of the common law was the particular decisions of right determined in individual cases. But what was conventionally understood to comprise the common law was not these discrete authoritative acts, but a set of ideas concerning a presumed set of general rules that were applied in these individual cases. Professional practice generated a fund of literary materials — practitioners' manuals, pedagogic guides, privately assembled reports of cases, antiquarian treatises — that supplied sources for the inference of these general rules. Yet such inferences were not the work of legal authority, but the "fictitious offspring of each man's imagination."[42] Common law never received definitive formulation as a system of general rules and thus never attained the certainty and stability available in legislation.

In the place of customary law's individual ex post facto acts of judicial force, codification furnished a complete and methodically ordered body of general rules. Instead of "dark chaos" and "glorious uncertainty,"[43] it offered authoritative pronouncements, purposely formulated to achieve maximum "cognoscibility." One major benefit of this form of law was that it provided clear, prospective guidance to judges and other legal officials as well as to the general community. The Pannomion would both replace existing customary law and provide a prophylactic against its reemergence through the practice of adjudication. "The legislator might need a censor," Bentham explained, "but he would need no interpreter. He would be himself his own and sole interpreter."[44]

A final task of the lawgiver was to ensure that the content of the legal order was effectively conveyed to the members of the community, whose legally guided conduct would then produce the social benefits realizing the law's moral promise. Here the Pannomion, for Bentham, revealed another distinguishing strength that, in effect, extended the technology of communication initially built on the code's linguistic precision and clarity. Under the general heading "Promulgation," Bentham considered the variety of previously neglected methods by which a lawgiver could advance the legal subject's comprehension of the content of his rights and duties.[45] One such technique was the promulgation of "particular codes," in which relevant provisions of the Pannomion were reorganized for presentation to specific subgroups within the community (for example, masters and servants, husbands and wives, individual trades, and so on) or to facilitate the private exercise of legal rights and powers (for example, a separate "Promulgation-paper" containing standard form conveyances, agreements, instruments of legal process, and so on).[46] The Pannomion's notoriety was advanced by other techniques attending its composition and presentation. Thus, in the case of the *Constitutional Code*, the code's separate provisions were systematically equipped with identifying headings — enactive, ratiocinative, expositive, instructional, exemplificational — that made explicit the nature and purpose of each and every paragraph of legislative text.

Most important for Bentham was the requirement that the Pannomion be promulgated with what he termed a "perpetual commentary of reasons," through which the code was furnished with a comprehensive rationale explaining how the law's specific mandates contributed to the "all governing" goal of promoting the community's happiness.[47] The provision of such reasons furthered the individual's understanding of the law, thus enhancing the knowledge and (in turn) the efficacy of the law's provisions. A body of law "how complete soever, would be comparatively useless and uninstructive, unless explained and justified . . . [by] a perpetual commentary of *reasons*."[48]

Codification and Democracy

Bentham's conception and defense of the Pannomion showed striking continuity over the fifty-year period of its advocacy. However, with his embrace of radical democratic reform in the first decade of the nineteenth century, notable changes of emphasis occurred. Bentham had always thought of the Pannomion in expressly cosmopolitan terms. Its methods of legal classification, its organizing structures, and its analysis of basic legal terms formed part of a system of "universal jurisprudence." The detailed content of its specific provisions would vary according to the situation in any given community. But these adaptations could be treated as modifications within a basic structure of wide application.[49] In his democratic period, Bentham continued to see applications for the Pannomion on an international scale. However, the program was now given a specific political and politically radical cast. Thus in the *Codification Proposal* ("Addressed . . . to All Nations Professing Liberal Opinions") (1822), Bentham for the first time began the rehearsal of the case for codification by considering the several political obstacles facing the Pannomion.[50] Previously, he had often attributed the carefully enumerated failures of existing legislation and customary law to the forces of indolence and ignorance. Now these failings were seen as the products of political corruption, which served the power and profit of judges, lawyers, and other elites at the expense of the subject many. Codification now figured as one of several institutional devices, like the democratic franchise, which would function as a security against such abuse and misrule. Accordingly, its enactment directly threatened the "sinister purposes" of lawyers and "party men" who had the most to lose from comprehensive codification.[51]

One measure of this new perspective is the altered priorities Bentham gave to the component parts of the Pannomion. Given his reading of the political obstacles facing codification, the constitutional branch of the code became the linchpin of the legislative project. A community first needed a constitutional order committed to the greatest happiness, which for Bentham had come to mean representative democracy, before it could secure an entire legal order dedicated to the same moral goal.

Perhaps most revealing was the new weight Bentham gave to the Pannomion's rationale and the purposes served by the code's "perpetual commentary of reasons." From the start, Bentham had identified two distinct and complementary ways in which the rationale advanced general utility. In the first place, the "commentary of reasons" advanced the community's understanding and knowledge of the law, which on this basis furthered the effectiveness of the threatened sanctions imposed by the law. All this, in turn, advanced the legitimacy of the law by helping to ensure that the deployment of legal force achieved its intended social purposes. The rationale thus promoted the power of law and what the legislator thereby might legitimately achieve through the instrument of law. But, second, the rationale simultaneously served a regulative function against the abuse of legislative power. By requiring the lawgiver to assign "a sufficient reason for every law," the rationale provided a "preservative" against "blind routine" and a "restraint to every thing arbitrary."[52]

In his democratic defense of codification, both these functions of the code's rationale remained. For the members of the community, the rationale continued to perform as "an anchor" (imposing legal restraints) and as "a compass" (orientating legally guided social conduct).[53] But far more emphatically, in this presentation, the perpetual commentary of reasons served as a "bridle" on the "power of the constituted authorities."[54] For the legislator, the code's rationale meant that the work of imposing legal burdens never occurred in the absence of an official explanation of public purpose, whose merits could then receive full scrutiny "at the hands of public opinion." The rigorous utilitarian reasoning of the rationale supplied a valuable corrective to the dense fabric of "interest begotten prejudice," "authority begotten prejudice," and "habit begotten prejudice" which currently cloaked prevailing political corruption and lawmaking.[55] For the judge, the rationale operated as a bridle against the abuse of office, by rendering more obvious to other observers any judicial lapses in the implementation of the law. For the "subject citizen," the "perpetual commentary of reasons" served as a vehicle of democratic empowerment. The readiness of the lawmaker to furnish the explanatory rationale and the quality of its utilitarian reasoning provided the democratic public with a reliable measure of the elected legislators' moral commitment. "Conceive now the advantage," Bentham wrote enthusiastically, "with which, in his capacity of censor, every citizen will be enabled to act, while calling to account this or that member of the legislative body, in respect of the Code, or any part of the Code, to which his concurrence has been given."[56]

In so characterizing the Pannomion's "*indispensable*" rationale,[57] Bentham brought codification into alignment with his more general plan for democratic statecraft. In the *Constitutional Code*, Bentham explored a wide range of institutional arrangements to prevent the abuse of political power and secure a government that pursued the greatest happiness. Most important among these devices was the institution he described as the Public Opinion Tribunal, which functioned to keep all of the activities of the state "under the surveillance of the public."[58] To fulfill its task, Bentham required that government officials maintain comprehensive documentation of their decisions and actions, that this information be recorded according to a uniform system of official registration, and that this carefully assembled material routinely be made available to the public for critical and uncensored evaluation. "Publicity will at all times be maximized" ran the standard formula of the *Constitutional Code*; and the democratic legislator pledged to conduct himself with "the greatest degree of *transparency*" possible.[59]

In making law according to the elaborate specifications of the Pannomion, the legislator fulfilled the political demands of democratic accountability. Not only did the law advance the greatest happiness of the entire
community, but the mechanisms by which the law achieved this unifying
goal were made fully public to the community. In this democratic formulation, Pannomion's "new aera" in lawmaking gained its fullest expression.
As Bentham frequently observed, lawmaking could be, and in the past
routinely had been, chiefly a function of power: the exercise of political will
over a subservient people. But a code which made explicit the terms of its
own legitimacy constituted a form of lawmaking that relied on understanding as much as on will and that invited the critical scrutiny of its own claims
to moral authority. "The easiest of all literary works," Bentham maintained,
was "a code of law stark naked." Only slightly more demanding was a code
equipped with occasional justifications or "vague and common place generalities." In contrast, an "all-comprehensive code of law, accompanied
with a perpetually interwoven rationale, drawn from the *greatest happiness
principle*" could be "safely pronounced" "not only the most important but
the most difficult of all human works."[60]

NOTES

1. *Correspondence of Jeremy Bentham*, vol. ii, ed. Timothy L. S. Sprigge
(London, 1968), 68–69.

2. Bentham's efforts to secure a political patron for his codification program are
surveyed in Philip Schofield, "Jeremy Bentham: Legislator of the World," *Current
Legal Problems* 51 (1998), 115–47. Bentham's criticisms of contemporary codes
appear in *General View of a Complete Code of Laws*, in *The Works of Jeremy
Bentham*, ed. John Bowring, 11 vols. (Edinburgh, 1838–43), iii. 206 [hereafter
Bowring], and *Papers Relative to Codification and Public Instruction*, in Jeremy
Bentham, *"Legislator of the World": Writings on Codification, Law, and Educa-
tion*, ed. Philip Schofield and Jonathan Harris (Oxford, 1998), 11–12.

3. Jeremy Bentham, *An Introduction to the Principles of Morals and Legislation*, ed. J. H. Burns and H. L. A. Hart (London, 1970), 1 [hereafter *IPML*] (p. 103
above).

4. Jeremy Bentham, *Of Laws in General*, ed. H. L. A. Hart (London, 1970);
IPML, 6 (p. 108 above), 305.

5. *Memoirs of Bentham*, in Bowring, xi. 33.

6. An earlier and faulty edition of the work published in 1970 as *Of Laws in
General* appeared in 1945 under the editorship of Charles Everett and with the
title, *The Limits of Jurisprudence Defined*. The composition of the work and its

relationship to *An Introduction to the Principles of Morals and Legislation* are discussed by H. L. A. Hart in the introduction to *Of Laws in General*, xxxi–xxxvi. See also the new introduction to *Of the Limits of the Penal Branch of Jurisprudence*, ed. Philip Schofield (Oxford, 2010), which replaces *Of Laws in General*.

7. See, for example, Bentham's discussion in *Codification and Public Instruction*, 138, 171.

8. *IPML*, 6 (p. 108 above), and Jeremy Bentham, *General View of a Complete Code of Laws*, Bowring, iii. 155–210, esp. 155–62. *General View of a Complete Code of Laws* was an English translation of material that originally appeared in Dumont's *Traités de Législation civile et pénale*, 3 vols. (Paris, 1802), iii. 195–434.

9. See, for example, the discussion in *Of Laws in General*, 232–46.

10. *Codification and Public Instruction*, 168.

11. *An Introduction to the Principles of Morals and Legislation*, 7 (p. 109 above).

12. *Of Laws in General*, 246.

13. Jeremy Bentham, *Principles of the Civil Code*, Bowring, i. 307–08.

14. *Of Laws in General*, 54.

15. *Nonsense Upon Stilts*, in Jeremy Bentham, *Rights, Representation, and Reform: Nonsense Upon Stilts and Other Writings on the French Revolution*, eds. Philip Schofield, Catherine Pease-Watkin, and Cyprian Blamires (Oxford, 2002), 321 (p. 321 above). (*Nonsense Upon Stilts*, Bentham's attack on the "Declaration of the Rights of Man and the Citizen" [1789] is perhaps still better known under the earlier title of *Anarchical Fallacies*.) For later renderings of this central idea, see *Codification and Public Instruction*, 77; *Codification Proposal, Addressed by Jeremy Bentham to All Nations Professing Liberal Opinions* and *First Lines of a Proposed Code of Law for Any Nation Compleat and Rationalized*, in *"Legislator of the World": Writings on Codification, Law, and Education*, 191, 213, 256.

16. See, in addition to Schofield's essay in this volume, the classic treatments of Bentham's jurisprudence in H. L. A. Hart, *Essays on Bentham* (Oxford, 1982), and Gerald J. Postema, *Bentham and the Common Law Tradition* (Oxford, 1986).

17. *General View of a Complete Code of Laws*, Bowring, iii. 185n; and also see *Nonsense Upon Stilts*, 322–28 (pp. 322–27 above).

18. For characteristic examples, see *Of Laws in General*, 184–95, 239–41; *General View of a Complete Code of Laws*, 206; *Codification and Public Instruction*, 123–39.

19. See A. W. B. Simpson, "The Common Law and Legal Theory," in A. W. B. Simpson, ed., *Oxford Essays in Jurisprudence*, 2d series (Oxford, 1973), and Martin Krygier, "Law as Tradition," *Law and Philosophy* 5 (1986), 237–62.

20. On the value of common law as a "stock of materials" for the drafter of a

code, see *Codification and Public Instruction*, 22, and *First Lines of a Proposed Code*, 226–27. Bentham described his own *Fragment on Government* (1776) as "the very first publication" that invited the public "to break loose from the trammels of authority and ancestor-wisdom on the field of law"; see Jeremy Bentham, *A Comment on the Commentaries and A Fragment on Government*, ed. J. H. Burns and H. L. A. Hart (London, 1977), 424n.

21. See *A Fragment on Government*, 407 and n., and *IPML*, 291.

22. *Defence of Usury*, in *Jeremy Bentham's Economic Writings*, ed. W. Stark, 3 vols. (London, 1952–54), i. 130, 153–56, 157, 158–59; and see *IPML*, 4–5 (p. 107 above), for Bentham's later characterization of the work as an application of his general principles of critical legal classification.

23. See *IPML*, 160–64, 286–93.

24. See ibid., 187–292. The relationship between Bentham's initial plan for a code of penal law and the subsequent program for the Pannomion is discussed in my *Province of Legislation Determined: Legal Theory in Eighteenth-Century Britain* (Cambridge, 1989), chap. 13.

25. *IPML*, 188.

26. Ibid., 271.

27. Ibid., 222.

28. *A Fragment on Government*, 418.

29. See *Codification and Public Instruction*, 8–12, for a summary discussion. For Bentham's earlier treatments of this goal, see *Province of Legislation Determined*, 246–51.

30. *Codification and Public Instruction*, 180; *Codification Proposal*, 268.

31. William Hazlitt, "Jeremy Bentham," in *The Spirit of the Age* (Oxford, 1904), 16. Bentham himself acknowledged the difficulties produced by the new terms he introduced for the sake of linguistic precision; see *IPML*, 271–72.

32. *General View of a Complete Code of Laws*, Bowring, iii. 171.

33. See *A Fragment on Government*, 415–18, and *IPML*, 272–74. A slightly different version appears in Dumont's *Traités*; see *General View of a Complete Code of Laws*, Bowring, iii. 171–74.

34. *Fragment*, 415–16. Because the "natural arrangement" of law organized legal materials in terms of their utilitarian purposes, the system of classification served critical as well as expository purposes. The natural arrangement would expose the impropriety of a "bad law" because of the difficulty that would occur in "finding a place for it in such an arrangement." In the case of a good law, the natural arrangement "points out the reason of the law" by disclosing its contribution to general utility.

35. *IPML*, 187–88n. Bentham, in practice, found this method difficult to sustain, see *Province of Legislation Determined*, 265–66.

36. *Codification and Public Instruction*, 10.

37. William Blackstone, *Commentaries on the Laws of England*, 11th ed., 4 vols. (Dublin, 1788), i. 68.

38. See *Comment on the Commentaries*, 49–51n, for an early rehearsal of this argument.

39. *Truth versus Ashhurst*, Bowring, v. 235.

40. See *General View of a Complete Code of Laws*, Bowring, iii. 306, and *Scotch Reform*, Bowring, v. 5–7; and the important discussion by Philip Schofield, *Utility and Democracy: The Political Thought of Jeremy Bentham* (Oxford, 2006), 109–23.

41. *Codification Proposal*, 271.

42. Ibid., 271, and see *Codification and Public Instruction*, 123–31. For Bentham's initial elaboration of this theme in his early jurisprudence, see the discussion in *Province of Legislation Determined*, 222–40.

43. See *Comment on the Commentaries*, 198, 251n.

44. *Of Laws in General*, 232.

45. Dumont's *Traités* contained a discussion of "promulgation" to which Bentham continued to refer in his later codification proposals. A modified version of this material appeared in the Bowring edition as *Essay on the Promulgation of Laws . . . with Specimen of a Penal Code*, Bowring, i. 155–68.

46. See, for example, *Codification and Public Instruction*, 9–10. For earlier rehearsals, see *Of Laws in General*, 239, and *Promulgation of Laws*, Bowring, i. 158.

47. *Codification and Public Instruction*, 7.

48. *IPML*, 9 (p. 111 above).

49. The relationship between the structure of the Pannomion and what Bentham termed "universal jurisprudence" is presented in *IPML*, 6 (p. 108 above), and *Of Laws in General*, 242–45. For Bentham's approach to the challenge of adjusting the content of the code to the particular conditions of a given state, see *Codification Proposal*, 291–93.

50. See *Codification Proposal*, 245–48.

51. Ibid., 245. In a new preface Bentham intended for the 1823 reprinting of the *Fragment on Government* (1776), he explained that in the earlier period he attributed the defects of law and government to "inattention and prejudice" and only later came to recognize these failings as "the elaborately organized, and anxiously cherished and guarded products of sinister interest and artifice." See *Fragment on Government*, 508.

52. *Essay on the Promulgation of Laws*, Bowring, i. 161.

53. *Codification and Public Instruction*, 141, and see *Codification Proposal*, 248–49.

54. *Codification Proposal*, 269.

55. Ibid., 259–60.

56. Ibid., 270.

57. Ibid., 248.

58. Bentham, *Constitutional Code: Volume 1*, F. Rosen and J. H. Burns, eds. (Oxford, 1983), IX.25.A30–31, pp. 427–28. Also see *Constitutional Code: Volume 1*, VI.31.A32, p. 125: "Of the aggregate mass of securities against abuse of power in functionaries, the greatest part . . . unavoidably depends upon the power of the Public Opinion Tribunal." For further explanation of the function and nature of the Public Opinion Tribunal, see Schofield, *Utility and Democracy*, 259–63, and my "Economy and Polity in Bentham's Science of Legislation," in Stefan Collini, Richard Whatmore and Brian Young, eds., *Economy, Polity, and Society* (Cambridge 2000), 124–34.

59. *Constitutional Code: Volume 1*, VIII.11.A2, p. 162, and VII.13, p. 146.

60. *Codification Proposal*, 260.

"Great and Distant Crimes"
Empire in Bentham's Thought

JENNIFER PITTS

From the time of his earliest followers — John Bowring, James Mill, and John Stuart Mill — both friends and enemies of utilitarianism have contributed to an image of Jeremy Bentham as a thinker of stunted imagination, authoritarian tendencies, and boundless hubris. John Stuart Mill's efforts to distance his philosophy from what he saw as Bentham's crude understanding of human nature were so successful that his own critical portrayal of Benthamite utilitarianism has survived as probably the dominant picture of Bentham's thought.[1] In the popular and even the scholarly imagination, Bentham and Mill are lumped together, and Bentham is the crude Mill. Lost in Mill's portrait and to a great degree in Mill's own work was Bentham's lively sense of irony and self-mockery, his healthy disgust for existing political and legal systems, and his suspicion of those who presume the superiority of their own tastes and judgments.[2]

Bentham's sense of restraint and salutary self-doubt, a corollary of his belief in human fallibility, is particularly striking in his thought on empire and international politics.[3] It is evident in his contempt for British and European pretensions to cultural superiority, in his lack of interest in triumphant narratives of progress and in ranking societies as barbarous or civilized, and in his resistance to the languages of character and national character that came to dominate Victorian political debate. He was alert to the dangers of hubris and complacency in the thought that people's interests could best be ascertained by others of supposedly more cultivated or more advanced judgment. Bentham also had a sense of political possibilities outside Europe that was distinctly more expansive than that of his followers, who saw Europeans as uniquely capable of self-government and as morally authorized to rule over other societies in the name of their improvement.

At the same time, with his outrageously (and self-consciously) ambitious schemes for social reform, with his confidence that the philosopher in his study could construct a complete apparatus of legislation, Bentham bequeathed to his followers — theorists and government officials alike — a certain arrogance. When divorced from Bentham's ironic, self-critical disposition, this overconfidence contributed to utilitarianism's tendency toward and reputation for imperial insensitivity. Bentham's own international thought, however, may help us see in Bentham's philosophy of reform a way around or beyond an antinomy that continues to haunt liberal thought, in which liberalism's aspiration to emancipate or to liberate people is conceived as at once a matter of releasing them from domination and also improving them. Bentham offers something of an antidote to liberal imperialism and to the interventionist universalism that is its heir: to the view that Europeans or the West or liberals have reached the truth about subjects on which other peoples remain mired in ignorance and that "we" have a right or even a duty to impose freedom or democracy or good governance on them.

Before Benthamite principles came to have resonance in domestic politics in Britain, utilitarianism had already become associated closely with colonial governance, especially in India. This was not because Bentham himself was enthusiastic about the British empire as a vehicle of reform. Rather, Bentham's schemes of codification, though they were initially envisioned with Britain foremost in mind, involved too extreme an overhaul of domestic politics to be palatable to any but a radical few within Britain, where the gradual evolution of the common law was seen as one of the nation's greatest political strengths.[4] By contrast, such codes were seen by many in the British political and colonial establishment as precisely what was needed in India. Although the philosophic radicals who saw themselves as his disciples shared to some extent Bentham's sense of the rottenness of Europe's domestic institutions, their faith in the superiority of European civilization left them largely complacent about the use of British power and institutions to impose laws and progress as they saw it on backward peoples. Thanks in part to the theories of progress that came to dominate British liberalism, Bentham's ideas were commandeered by men far less critical than he was of the moral and political perils of colonial rule, and his views were adapted to become the foundation of one of the most self-confident and interventionist strands of British imperial governance.[5]

Bentham's liberal and utilitarian successors lacked his own profound understanding of the ruinous costs of empire for both metropole and colony. European colonial expansion was among Bentham's most long-standing, if intermittent, concerns. Indeed, he was already writing critically of colonial greed and aggression at the age of fifteen, in a Latin verse he wrote while at Oxford, at the end of the Seven Years' War in 1763.[6] By the 1780s, when he first wrote extensively on international politics, Bentham's sense of the dangers of empire rivaled that of better-known contemporaries like the

Abbé Raynal, Denis Diderot, Adam Smith, and Edmund Burke.[7] He depicted the international politics of his era as dominated, and poisoned, by the effects of colonial expansion. Colonization was, in Bentham's words, the "race of vulgar ambition" and a "war against mankind."[8] Above all, he saw colonies as the chief cause of war in the modern world. He cited as recent examples the war against Spain in the 1740s (the War of Jenkins' Ear), and the Seven Years' War, whose violence, he said, stretched from "North America to the East Indies" and which, in the needless destruction it caused Britain, demonstrated "the extreme folly, the madness of war."[9] Colonies provoked wars not only by multiplying the possible sources of conflict but also because in their newness and their distance from Europe they were fraught with uncertainty, which Bentham saw as a principal source of instability and violence. When he set out to envisage a new code of international law — and it was Bentham who coined the term "international" — one of his central aims was to reduce conflict by reducing uncertainty.[10] A code would do so, he thought, in part by minimizing the many offenses against international peace that were committed by sovereigns either unsure of or in good-faith disagreement about what constituted their obligations toward one another. Together with the emancipation of all colonial holdings, such a code would serve as the basis for a new era of peaceful commerce and cooperation.[11]

Bentham was also much less confident than later nineteenth-century liberals would be that European government constituted a benefit — a "blessing of *unspeakable magnitude*," in James Mill's words — for colonized societies like India.[12] To John Stuart Mill's claim that "despotism is a legitimate mode of government in dealing with barbarians, provided the end be their improvement, and the means justified by actually effecting that end,"[13] Bentham's likely response would have been, "Reform the world by example, you act generously and wisely: reform the world by force, you might as well reform the moon, and the design is fit only for lunatics."[14] Mill's claim indicates the very great distance that he and so many liberals of his day had traveled from Bentham. It reveals his easy division of the world into civilized and barbarian and his faith in the superior wisdom of Europeans, his confidence that well-intentioned Europeans could and would rule for the benefit of their colonial subjects, and his belief that despotic power need only be justified before a suitably impartial and knowledgeable European judge, rather than to the subjects of that power.

It might be said that Bentham had imperial projects of his own: indeed, he himself said so with his characteristic marriage of zeal and self-mockery:

"J.B. the most ambitious of the ambitious. His empire — the empire he aspires to — extending to and comprehending the whole human race, in all places. — in all habitable places of the earth, at all future time. . . . Limits it has no other than those of the earth."[15] One of his many global correspondents, a Guatemalan politician named José del Valle who was seeking Bentham's help in creating a civil code for his newly independent country, admiringly called him "legislador del mundo" (legislator to the world).[16] Bentham did indeed aspire to assist in the writing of laws for countries from Greece and Portugal to Tripoli to Peru, and he was inexhaustible in his correspondence with and cultivation of those he thought might be kindred spirits in reform: Simón Bolívar; John Quincy Adams; Rammohun Roy in Bengal; Mohammed Ali, the Egyptian leader; Jean Pierre Boyer, president of Haiti; and many others.[17] But he saw empires, whether British, French, or Spanish, as quite ill-suited for the work of reform. When he did propose legal reforms through the vehicle of the British empire, it was not in the spirit of a superior assisting those too backward to govern themselves, but with the thought that existing imperial governance was so corrupt and abusive that any improvement would be a boon.

Bentham also sought to develop an international politics from the perspective of the "citizen of the world," a politics with the cosmopolitan purpose of serving the "common and equal utility of all nations."[18] This too was an imperial project of a kind, as Bentham once again acknowledged: "The globe is the field of dominion to which the author aspires, — the press the engine, and the only one he employs, — the cabinet of mankind the theatre of his intrigue."[19] But one of the pillars of this project was precisely the "emancipation of the distant dependencies of each state," for he judged the pursuit and defense of imperial territory the greatest threat to peace among European states.

The concerns Bentham brought to bear in considering colonial rule, particularly his belief that colonial rulers and administrators could never be trusted to rule well, and his hostility to the notion of civilizing non-Europeans stand in sharp contrast to the technocratic and cultural confidence of his successors. Bentham had a keen grasp of the social psychology of empire. Colonies, he believed, exacerbated the pathologies of European power politics. And they produced an exaggerated form of a more general danger in international politics: that although ordinary people could be trusted to defend themselves against "sinister interests" at home, the same public could not be counted on to rein in abusive colonial rulers because people are complacent about violence and injustice carried out at a distance.

In one fragment, he wrote, "Petty crimes committed under our eyes awaken our resentment. Great and distant crimes though of a million times deeper die call forth no other sentiment than admiration."[20]

Bentham's pungent and forcefully argued anticolonial writings span the length of his career. His appeal to the revolutionary French National Assembly "Emancipate Your Colonies!," based in part on the manuscripts of 1786–89, was first printed in 1793, and his views apparently remained so substantially the same that he could republish the essay nearly verbatim in 1830, adding a complicating postscript (see below), two years before his death at the age of eighty-four. And in his Spanish anticolonial writings of the 1820s Bentham repeatedly claimed that his views on colonies had not changed in thirty years.

Yet Bentham's views on conquest, expansion, and colonial rule were not entirely consistent, as is to be expected given his remarkably long career, his voluminous and often unedited output, and his diverse audiences. A wide range of related considerations caused his views on colonies to vary, including his fitful pacifism, his periodically expressed hopes that emigration might aid Europe's poor, and the differences between settler colonies such as Latin America and colonies such as British India that primarily involved the domination of a large indigenous population.[21] His lifelong anticolonial claims are interspersed with periodic statements in support of empire, particularly during the first years of the nineteenth century, in which, it has been said, "Bentham's Toryism seems to have reasserted itself."[22] He proposed, for instance, that both Egypt and America (the latter an "unvaried scene of sordid selfishness, of political altercation, of discomfort, of ignorance, of drunkenness") would have profited from the stability and moral guidance of British governance.[23] Bentham later repudiated many of his views of this period, and his later insistence that he had consistently held to the anticolonial views he expressed in "Emancipate!" suggests such a rejection, or even a willful forgetting, of some of the imperialist arguments of the texts from 1801–04.[24] Finally, in the short postscript for the republished "Emancipate Your Colonies!" he noted that while as a citizen of Great Britain and Ireland he was confirmed in his views, as a citizen of the British empire, including the one hundred million Indians already or likely to be under its government, his "opinions and consequent wishes are the reverse."[25] The postscript would seem to suggest that for all his earlier insistence on the evils of British rule in India as elsewhere, he had come to accept the claims of disciples like James Mill that British government, if imperfect, was in India's best interest. Bentham's readers have often concluded that, in Donald Winch's words, Bentham's ambivalence "epitomizes the ambivalence towards the empire felt by philosophic radicals as a group."[26] For much of his career, however, and despite these moments of ambivalence, Bentham should be read *not* as a participant in the imperial liberalism of the nineteenth century but as a counterpoint to it.

To the new governments of revolutionary France and, later, liberal Spain, Bentham insisted that empires imperiled constitutional government and turned liberals into hypocrites. In "Emancipate Your Colonies!" he declared that revolutionary principles were inherently anti-imperial, in effect telling the French they had already "given judgment against [them]selves." Though himself hostile to the language of natural rights as "rhetorical nonsense" and "terrorist language," Bentham insisted on the hypocrisy involved in colonial conquest by a nation supposedly committed to the rights of man.[27] He later pointed similarly to the new Spanish constitution and insisted that to keep the colonies in subjection was to fly "in the teeth of [its] precepts of equality."[28] Liberal imperialism was not only a moral self-contradiction but also bad policy: by pursuing the "insane graspings" of a colonial agenda, Bentham argued, the new liberal Spanish government was merely playing into the hands of reactionaries and royalists.[29] Conscious of the great respect in which he was held by republicans in both countries, Bentham appears to have nourished hopes that he could persuade these new regimes to give up their colonies, given that they were establishing themselves through highly self-conscious national debates about justice and equality.

Bentham never wrote such an "Emancipation" pamphlet to the British, perhaps from a sense that such a gesture would be useless. He knew only too well of his limited influence in Britain, having failed, disastrously and famously, to persuade the British government to institute his panopticon prison-workhouse in the 1790s.[30] He found the British public too "dazzled and fascinated by that *phantasmagoria* of power, which their oppressors, corruptors, and deluders have never ceased to ply them with."[31] He lamented that the British public, duped by an illusory national glory that had already sunk deep roots in the national psyche, saw the empire as a source of opulence rather than as a burden, and they failed to recognize that their true interests were exactly those of the subject peoples of distant dependencies: emancipation, equality, and free trade.

Although Bentham tended to avoid using narratives of progress or the language of civilization to justify political arguments, he appealed to just such rhetoric to depict imperial expansion as a throwback to earlier ages, when tyrants exercised despotic power with no accountability to the governed. As long as the British continued to acquire new colonies with such "disastrous success," as he put it, they were little better than "the primaeval Persian tyranny."[32] He acknowledged that a program of colonial emancipation might have been premature in earlier ages, when nations, in the grip of "barbarous ambition," had not yet come to understand the true end of government — the greatest happiness of the greatest number — and mistook conquest itself as the end.[33] But he insisted that empire had become anachronistic, that conquests by the modern British nation were "bungling imitations of miserable originals," for there no longer existed even the motive of interest that had explained, if not justified, conquests by ancient Greeks and Romans and by more recent absolute monarchs. If the major powers, France and Britain, were to give up their colonies, the ground would be laid for a stable peace among all the European powers. And he held that Britain, whose economic preeminence meant it had little to fear from any other power, could well afford a unilateral colonial emancipation that might launch this larger process. Bentham vacillated on the question of whether his proposals — especially the anticolonial arguments — were visionary and utopian or so reasonable as to be all but inevitable.[34]

The major anticolonial essays Bentham directed at France and Spain primarily concerned New World colonies with substantial European populations, and there has been some question whether he meant his arguments for independence to apply only to such settler colonies or also to territories like British India with large non-European populations.[35] While some scholars have insisted that Bentham always believed British despotism was necessary for a backward India and that his anticolonial arguments were never intended to apply in the case of India, he repeatedly argued in both published and unpublished texts that all colonial relationships, including Britain's with India, should be severed for the sake of both metropoles and colonies. One of his central objections to colonial rule rested on the inherent problems of governing at a distance: Europeans, he argued, could not possibly imagine the lives, desires, and problems of subjects, whether of European descent or not, thousands of miles away.[36] Bentham regularly listed India among the colonies that suffered from misgovernment as a result of such inevitable failings, and he was graphic and insistent about the varieties of oppression that beset British India. To the Spanish in the 1820s, he described the evils of the British empire as follows: "Uncertainty, inconsistency, complication, delay, vexation and expense . . . denial of justice, oppression, extortion, corruptive influence, despotism"; and he said these conditions were to be found in "East, West, [and] South," naming "Hindostan" along with the West Indies, South Africa, Canada, and other colonies.[37] In a manuscript headed "International Principles and Measures,"

Bentham's list of "Measures final" includes "Give up the E[ast] Indies," along with North America, the West Indies, and Gibraltar.[38] Bentham did express ambivalence about whether India, if independent, would develop free or representative government, most emphatically in the postscript to "Emancipate Your Colonies."[39] And yet there are good reasons to reject the idea that Bentham embraced the British empire as an opportunity to legislate for and civilize India or that James Mill's characterization of a barbarous India at the bottom of the scale of progress reflected Bentham's views, as some have argued.[40]

Ironically, a text that has been often cited as evidence of Bentham's desire to use the British empire to impose reforms on a backward India, "On the Influence of Place and Time in Matters of Legislation," offers one of his most extensive and detailed critiques of British imperial practice in India.[41] In the essay, Bentham harshly criticizes British law; he warns against the presumptions of legislators, particularly those who seek to transplant laws to distant and unfamiliar societies; and he registers profound skepticism toward the motives and bona fides of colonial governors. Bentham's horror at the complications and the dangerous vagueness of English common law is well known; it was his frustration with the absurdities and corruptions of the British legal system that had driven him from a legal career as a young man. In "Place and Time," he argued that these imperfections were compounded by the inappropriateness of British laws to Bengali society, by the British failure to see the problems with their laws, and by the incapacity of metropolitan laws to deal with colonial circumstances, especially the rampant greed and corruption that despotic rule breeds. The laws were poisonous not only in their direct effects, but also because they were sure to undermine any sense of trust or goodwill that managed to emerge on the part of Indians toward their British governors. Fragments not included in the Bowring edition of the essay contain some of Bentham's severest criticisms of British imperial practice. Here he excoriates as a form of "persecution" the common law doctrine that a Christian conquest of an "infidel country" makes void any laws that Europeans believe are in violation of divine law.[42] And he vividly depicts the sense of insecurity felt by Britain's Indian subjects — for Bentham the cardinal sin of any government.[43]

"Place and Time," in that it proposes to examine how British laws might be made suitable for Bengal, clearly bears some resemblance to nineteenth-century liberal arguments for importing superior European laws to improve colonized societies. Indeed, Bentham may have chosen to address the question of comparative legislation by proposing to adapt English laws to fit a British colony because he sought to write in a vein that would be recognizable to, and even regarded as useful by, his readers in imperial Britain. But his exasperation at the cruel incompetence and outright oppression of existing British legislation in India is apparent throughout. And the spirit of the work as well as its irreverent tone differ markedly from that of later liberal and utilitarian efforts to legislate for India. He whimsically affects a certain arbitrariness about the choices of England and Bengal, choosing England, he says, not because its legal system is in fact excellent, but because he knows it best and "because to that country, if to any, I owe a preference." He calls his working hypothesis that the laws governing Britain itself are "the best that can be devised" a "magnificent and presumptuous dream."[44] And he draws two conclusions from his sometimes comically detailed examples of the relevant differences among nations. First, would-be legislators must be chastened, hesitant, and self-doubting in their efforts to use new legislation to remedy apparent evils in a society. Second, when it comes to much of the diversity among societies — in religion, manners, political institutions — it is simply inappropriate to rank certain practices as better or worse than others.[45] Bentham almost ostentatiously declines to typecast societies as savage or civilized, writing more precisely and impartially of nations that are "unletter'd, however civilized in other respects."[46] This caution, ecumenism, and nonjudgmental posture distinguish Bentham sharply from the earnest, improving liberalisms that followed, whether in the form of Victorian imperial liberalism or more recent liberals' desire to impose narrowly and self-interestedly conceived standards of "good governance" on developing countries.[47]

The critical conversation with Montesquieu that runs through "Place and Time" shows Bentham to be far more suspicious than Montesquieu had been of European pretensions to superiority over, and even reliable knowledge of, non-European societies.[48] The essay includes a number of subtle efforts to de-exoticize non-European societies and to turn a critical eye on European practices whose familiarity left them widely unscrutinized. Many of these were purged from the Bowring edition and are only now recovered from the manuscripts for publication. Bentham chides Montesquieu for describing certain unpalatable practices such as infanticide and the selling of daughters as distinctively Asian, without mentioning the existence of the same practices in ancient Greece and Rome, and indeed (in the case of selling daughters) in attenuated form in modern Europe.[49] He rejects Montesquieu's credulous references to reports of outlandish customs among foreign peoples, such as a supposed Formosan abortion practice that he calls "too foolish and too atrocious to have the force of law in any country under the sun."[50]

Contrary to his reputation as a radical innovator indifferent to or contemptuous of custom and lived experience, Bentham insists that would-be legislators exercise great caution before presuming to interfere with existing practices. They must never imagine that "repugnancy" to their "own manners and sentiments" should count as a reason to change a law or forbid a practice; and they should never abolish a "prevailing usage . . . without some specific assignable benefit" that can be shown to be a likely result of the change.[51] There is a calm, deflationary tone to Bentham's discussions of such practices as *sati* in India that contrasts sharply with the hysterical references to such practices as evidence of the Indian people's depraved character, utter barbarity, and unfitness for self-government that were typical of later British views. While some of these passages appear in the Bowring text, a number of Bentham's most caustic remarks about European and Christian practices and scruples were purged or altered for the Bowring edition, so that the Bentham received by nineteenth-century and later publics was more conventionally smug about European superiority than Bentham himself had been.[52]

The idea of character — both individual and national — was to become a central preoccupation of Victorian political thinkers.[53] For John Stuart Mill, a society's fitness for self-government and independence was a matter of national character, of inclinations, passions, and tendencies shared throughout that society.[54] Most important for Mill was the distinction between nations characterized by dynamism and progressiveness and stagnant societies mired in custom. Mill generally treated national characters as the product of environments and circumstances that over time could be altered; as he wrote in 1848, "Of all the vulgar modes of escaping from the consideration of the effect of social and moral influences on the mind, the most vulgar is that of attributing the diversities of conduct and character to natural differences."[55] At the same time, he homogenized "Oriental" and "barbarous" peoples and ascribed to them very deeply rooted disabilities of mind and character.[56] Although he saw these vices as cultural and in principle changeable, he tended to give great weight to such cultural disabilities in explanations of Asians' behavior, whereas in comparable cases regarding Europeans, such as impoverished and backward Irish peasants, he looked for the perverse incentive structures that produced "unimproving" behavior and assumed individuals to be capable of responding quickly and rationally to a changed environment.[57]

Bentham was largely immune to such cultural or national typecasting, in part because his project was quite different from Mill's in ways that Mill himself failed fully to recognize.[58] Bentham regarded legislation and other forms of social sanction as means of shaping people's motives by adjusting their expectations of pleasure and pain, not as means of shaping individuals' character. Indeed, it was Bentham's indifference to character that was the source of some of Mill's most severe criticisms of his thought. In Bentham's work, according to Mill, "it is not considered (at least, not habitually considered,) whether the act or habit in question, though not in itself necessarily pernicious, may not form part of a character essentially pernicious. . . . To apply such a standard as this, would indeed, often require a much deeper insight into the formation of character, and knowledge of the internal workings of human nature, than Mr. Bentham possessed."[59] Mill attributed these lacunae in Bentham's thought to his limited experience of life and restricted sympathies, and he concluded that Bentham's failure to consider individual character also strictly limited the applicability of his philosophy to questions of social organization. For Mill, "a philosophy of laws and institutions, not founded on a philosophy of national character, is an absurdity."[60] Lacking a conception of national character, Mill concluded, Bentham was unable "to regard political institutions in a higher light, as the principal means of the social education of a people."[61]

Mill insisted that the study of character must be at the center of moral and political philosophy and that a person's actions and indeed his or her "likings and dislikings" were "full of the most important inferences as to every point of their character."[62] The aim of both social and legal sanctions is to shape that character, with the ultimate (twinned) end being the creation of autonomous, self-directed individuals and progressive nations.[63] Bentham, in contrast, believed that the relevant aspects of identity are largely determined by interest, which is for the most part circumstantial. Thus when discussing the reliability of testimony in legal trials, Bentham points not to the character or habits of individuals or nations but to their expectations of pleasure or pain, which "exist[] in the mind in the shape of interests."[64] The aim of sanctions, whether legal, social, or religious, is to adjust the balance of motives operating on a person (such as their shame at being caught perjuring themselves versus their shame at confessing themselves guilty of a crime), so as to try to induce the most correct and complete testimony.

As "Place and Time" makes clear, for Bentham societies were distinguished not by their different characters but by what he called circumstances. He described these differing circumstances dispassionately and often with a sardonic aside about European practices, as when he favorably compares the phenomenon of harem eunuchs to that of *castrati*. Religious beliefs, traditions, and customs were seen by Bentham not as the basis for judgments about the character of a people as a whole but as parameters within which individuals make choices and as features of a society that must and can "with perfect propriety" be acknowledged by any legislator. In penal law, for instance, what constitutes a crime or extenuating and aggravating circumstances will have to vary according to the beliefs prevailing in a society, as will appropriate punishments. He treats such customs as analogous to physical circumstances, such as the frequency of avalanches versus floods or famines, that should properly affect legislation. So he describes Hindu customs of caste forfeiture, for instance, not as evidence of superstition and barbarism, but simply as a constraint on appropriate penalties.

I have suggested that Bentham's global legislative ambitions might be seen as his own imperial project, though one very different in spirit from later liberal aspirations to use British despotism to civilize the backward. Bentham spent much of the last decade of his life at work on his *Pannomion,* his complete code of law, meant to be usable by, as he put it, "All Nations Professing Liberal Opinions" (for a discussion of the Pannomion, see David Lieberman's essay in this volume). As he acknowledged in a draft of a letter to the president of Haiti offering his legislative guidance, "From so perfect a stranger as myself. . . . advice will naturally enough wear the aspect of impertinence." At the same time, he was drafting extensive constitutional writings for Tripoli and expressing to a French correspondent his "hope of being more or less of use to the Persian empire."[65] His ambition to produce complete legislative codes for distant societies was undoubtedly presumptuous, but he was at least partly aware of its perils.

Bentham was not entirely immune to the thought that European governments, for all their flaws, might be able to provide security and decent government to Arab and Asian countries laboring under despotism. But he largely resisted the tendency of later nineteenth-century thinkers to draw a stark divide between Europe (and European settler colonies) and the rest of the world. Far from assuming that European imperial rule was the only means, or indeed even a desirable means, by which non-Europeans might achieve constitutional government, he believed these societies could and would initiate such reforms and participate in their own governance. And in contrast to the standard portraits in his day of Muslim fanaticism, Bentham often approached Islam with respect and went to some lengths to understand and accommodate Islam's social and institutional role in countries like Tripoli, though here, as on many subjects, he was not entirely consistent.[66]

Bentham devoted substantial time and energy during the *pannomion* period to the project of drafting legal codes for a constitutional regime that he hoped might replace the Pashalik that ruled the regency of Tripoli, a former dependency of the Ottoman empire.[67] His writings and letters surrounding this episode are striking for their detailed consideration of the questions Bentham believed might be involved in attempting such a project in a Muslim country. Typically, some of Bentham's proposals are comical in their detail; here as elsewhere he seems to mistake attention to detail for realism. He drafted addresses and proclamations in which the Pasha would explain and defend the reforms to his people in a suitable language and moral register, by describing a dream in which Mohammed appears to him and proclaims the injustice of despotism, the advantages of constitutional government, and even the need to accept a certain degree of inequality in the society for the common good. And if the Pasha refused to cooperate, Bentham imagined local reformers marching into the city under a banner proclaiming "the greatest happiness of the greatest number" in Arabic, under a suitable Koranic verse.[68] Such details seem to confirm the image of the eccentric spinning fantasies in his hermitage. But the respect with which Bentham approached the prospect of the nonimposed, indigenously crafted emergence of a constitutional, representative government in a non-European and Muslim society is unusual and noteworthy.

Just as, a few years later, Bentham would see a newly independent Greece as a promising field for democratic government and would congratulate the Greeks on their freedom from the burden of colonies that beset the older European powers, here he suggests that Tripoli offers at least the possibility of a democratic renewal that could in some respects surpass Europe's example.[69] He writes of the Pasha, "Supposing the system established, his nation, and above all he as the head of it, will be illustrious among, and even above, all the Sovereigns of Europe and the other parts of the Christian world. In every one of these instances without exception, whatever portion of power has been given up — whatever change has been made for the better in the condition of the people in the character of subjects, it has been the work of necessity, not of free will on the part of the Monarch."[70] Bentham's awareness of the widespread hostility to reform among the ruling classes of Europe contributed to what seems to be his almost gleeful sense of the political possibility latent in the peripheries.[71] In many of his letters to non-European correspondents, whether in India, Muslim countries, or the new states of South America, he conveys his sense that real innovation may come from such newer polities.

Bentham also seems to envision, in these writings, an integration of the countries of North Africa into the European system. In a late letter draft to Mohammed Ali, Bentham urges the Egyptian ruler to declare independence from the Ottoman empire: "Declare yourself *independent,*" he writes, "there are no foreign powers with whom you could not right away make whatever treaties you liked. . . . You would then take your place among the Sovereigns of Europe. And why not? Look at them in population and in revenue — if you find some that are your superiors — you find more that are your inferiors."[72] His insistence on the similarities between European and other states and on circumstances like population and revenue, rather than character or culture, once again sets him apart from his liberal heirs.

Around this time, Bentham was drafting a new set of notes for a code of international law, notes which indicate that the international community he envisioned was for the moment limited to what he called "all civilized Nations," which "at present is as much as to say, all Nations professing the Christian Religion."[73] And in contrast to the earlier writings on international law, which saw the emancipation of colonies as the necessary means to peace among European states, these late notes propose a rather different solution: an agreement not to interfere in one another's colonies. The fundamental axiom of this late code is equality among states: each participating state is to recognize the equality of every other and to respect the others' form of government, religious arrangements, and customs. Bentham now argues that this principle of equality also entails that the states must not "pretend to any authority over any other State (a) on sea, (b) on land in the territory of a barbarous nation not being a member of the Congress."[74] This would seem to indicate a new acceptance of colonies as part of the European system. The international code and the postscript on India, then, indicate a new willingness by Bentham in his final years to conceive an international system divided into the civilized and barbarous and to accept colonial status as appropriate for the barbarous. At the same time, the writings on Tripoli and Egypt suggest that the boundary between these worlds remained more permeable for Bentham, even at the end of his life, than for many who followed.

Although Bentham may have come by the end of his life to accept Britain's colonial vocation in India and to endorse an international hierarchy of metropoles and colonies, his lifelong engagement with colonial and international questions offers an instructive counterpoint to the imperial liberalism that regarded itself as an heir to and a refinement of his thought. For that Millian liberalism, which oversaw the entrenchment of British power in India in the mid-nineteenth century, freedom and self-government were capacities that had to be developed in the characters of individuals and nations. The aim of political and social analysis, for Mill, was to grasp the natural tendency, or the character, of each society;

understanding the diversity of national characters meant, in the end, being able to identify each society's "degree of civilization," so as to exercise the "social influence necessary for carrying the community forward to the next stage of its progress."[75] If people today have shed the language of barbarity and civilization, legacies of that nineteenth-century liberalism remain. The spirit of improving rule did not die out with the mandates of the interwar period, or with the now largely discredited modernization theory of the 1950s and 1960s; it persists today, for instance, in projects to instill good governance in so-called developing nations seen as suffering from a culture of corruption or as lacking the cultural capital necessary to sustain democracy. Bentham's own approach to reform, with its attention to circumstances rather than to character, culture, or some similar terrain to be improved, avoids framing dilemmas of difference in such terms. The "norm of democracy" is now celebrated by many international lawyers as a new principle of international law, one that should guide various forms of intervention in undemocratic states by states and international financial institutions.[76] But such a norm threatens to serve simply as a "call for contextual management of far-away societies in reference to Western-liberal practices," a means by which powerful states can intervene to mold weaker and poorer states in their own image or in line with their own interests.[77] Bentham's perhaps surprising humility, and his insistence on both the reasonableness of diverse customs and the illegitimacy of imposing one's judgments on others, may serve as a helpful corrective to the persistent liberal temptation to liberate others by "improving" them so that they are more like ourselves.

NOTES

1. See J. S. Mill, "Remarks on Bentham's Philosophy" (1833), *Collected Works of John Stuart Mill*, ed. John M. Robson (Toronto: University of Toronto Press, 1963–1991), 33 vols., x. 3–18 and "Bentham" (1838), x. 75–115. For recent scholarship that largely adopts Mill's account of Bentham's limitations, see Brian A. Anderson, "Mill on Bentham: From Ideology to Humanized Utilitarianism," *History of Political Thought* 4.2 (1983), 341–56; and Martha C. Nussbaum, "Mill Between Aristotle and Bentham," *Daedalus* 133.2 (2004), 60–68. I am grateful to Princeton University Press for permission to draw here on material in chapters 4 and 5 of my *A Turn to Empire: The Rise of Imperial Liberalism in Britain and France* (Princeton: Princeton University Press, 2005).

2. He scorned as "ipsedixitism" the presumption that one's own judgments should be authoritative for others.

3. Melissa Schwartzberg suggests that Bentham's belief in the fallibility of human knowledge and judgment, especially that of political and religious authorities, was central to his radicalism; "Jeremy Bentham on Falliblity and Infallibility," *Journal of the History of Ideas* 68.4 (2007), 563–85.

4. A typical response was that of Sir James Mackintosh, who wrote that "the sudden establishment of new codes can seldom be practicable or effectual for their purpose," *Dissertation on the Progress of Ethical Philosophy* (Edinburgh: A. and C. Black, 1836), 290; see Dinwiddy, "Early Nineteenth-Century Reactions to Benthamism," *Transactions of the Royal Historical Society* 34 (5th series), 47–69, at 60–61.

5. See Eric Stokes, *The English Utilitarians and India* (Oxford: Oxford University Press, 1959), esp. 184–233.

6. See *The Correspondence of Jeremy Bentham*, vol. i, ed. Timothy L. S. Sprigge (London: Athlone Press, 1968), 78. David Armitage has observed that Bentham belonged to a "war-time generation, raised and schooled during the Seven Years War and come of age in the immediate aftermath of that titanic struggle for imperial dominance," and he notes the relevance of Britain's struggle with its American colonies for Bentham's thinking about liberty and sovereignty in his first, anonymous, major publication, the *Fragment on Government* of 1776. See David Armitage, "A New Vattel: Bentham on Liberty, Sovereignty and the Law of Nations," conference paper presented at the workshop "Bentham in the World," Center for European Studies, Harvard University, 6 June 2006.

7. Some of Bentham's substantial manuscripts of 1786–89 on international politics were radically reorganized and revised to produce the *Principles of International Law*, in *The Works of Jeremy Bentham*, ed. J. Bowring, 11 vols. (Edinburgh: William Tait, 1838–43), vol. ii [hereafter Bowring] (the editor credited for the work on this text is not Bowring himself but Richard Smith). Other portions of the manuscripts appear in Werner Stark's edition of *Jeremy Bentham's Economic Writings* (London: Allen and Unwin, 1952–54), i. 209–18 ("Colonies and Navy"). On the Bowring edition's changes to these texts, see Stark's introduction, 46–47, and Gunhild Hoogensen, *Jeremy Bentham and International Relations* (London: Routledge, 2005), 40–54.

8. "Emancipate your colonies!," *Rights, Representation, and Reform*, ed. Philip Schofield, Catherine Pease-Watkin, and Cyprian Blamires (Oxford: Oxford University Press, 2002), 291, 308.

9. "Colonies and Navy," *Jeremy Bentham's Economic Writings*, i. 211 (where he also mentions the War of Jenkins' Ear); "Pacification and Emancipation," Bentham Papers, University College London Library, xxv. 26 [hereafter UC]. I am grateful to the Bentham Project for very generously making available transcripts of the entire contents of box 25, which includes much of the international law

material. Bentham was preoccupied at this period with what he saw as the dangerous machinations of the Pitt government in European politics, a concern that led him to publish his "Letters of Anti-Machiavel," in which he attacked what he saw as Pitt's efforts to drive Sweden into war with Russia. Bowring, x. 201–12; Stephen Conway, "Bentham versus Pitt: Jeremy Bentham and British Foreign Policy 1789," *Historical Journal* 30.4 (1987), 791–809.

10. Bentham, *An Introduction to the Principles of Morals and Legislation* [1789], ed. J. H. Burns and H. L. A. Hart, introd. F. Rosen (Oxford: Oxford University Press, 1996), 6 (p. 108 above), 296. As Bentham noted, his new term was meant to replace the standard but confusing "law of nations," which seemed to refer to "internal jurisprudence"; Bentham's new word was meant to translate the phrase "droit entre les gens" used by Louis XIV's Chancellor D'Aguesseau (see 296). See Mark Janis, "Jeremy Bentham and the Fashioning of 'International Law,'" *American Journal of International Law* 78 (1984), 405–18.

11. See "Principles of International Law," Bowring, ii. 540, and "A Plan for an Universal and Perpetual Peace," Bowring, ii. 546–60.

12. James Mill, "Review of *Voyage aux Indes Orientales* by Le P. Paulin De S. Barthélemy, Missionary," *Edinburgh Review* 15 (1810), 371.

13. *On Liberty* (1859), in *Collected Works of John Stuart Mill*, xviii. 224.

14. Bowring, iv. 416. The moon was Bentham's usual analogy for distant dependencies. In a passage typical of Bentham's quirky and biting wit on the subject of colonies, he wrote of the Spanish imperialists, "Spain is *one!* such will be their *arithmetic*. It has its *Peninsular* part and its *Ultramarian* part! such will be their *geography*. As well might it be said — Spain and the Moon are *one!* it has its *earthly* part: it has its *lunar* part. Such, it is but too true, is the language of your *Constitutional Code*. But, a body of human law, how well soever arranged in other respects, does not suffice for converting *impossibilities* into *facts*"; "Rid Yourselves of Ultramaria!," in *Colonies, Commerce, and Constitutional Law*, ed. Philip Schofield (Oxford: Oxford University Press, 1996), 52.

15. Bowring, xi. 72; cited in Armitage, "A New Vattel."

16. See *Legislator of the World*, ed. Philip Schofield and Jonathan Harris (Oxford: Oxford University Press, 1998), xi, xxxiv.

17. Simón Bolívar called him the "preceptor of Legislators"; letter of 27 September 1822, in *Correspondence of Jeremy Bentham*, vol. xi, ed. Catherine Fuller (Oxford: Oxford University Press, 2000), 155. Bentham was not only an enthusiastic participant but also perhaps the crucial connective figure in the "liberal constitutional moment" that C. A. Bayly has argued constituted a global phenomenon in the 1820s; "Rammohan Roy and the Advent of Constitutional Liberalism in India, 1800–1830," *Modern Intellectual History* 4.1 (2007), 25–41.

18. See "Principles of International Law," Bowring, ii. 537.

19. Bowring, ii. 546.

20. UC xxv. 106, "Inter-nat. Protest" (rudiments sheet, no date). A related fragment added: "Hanover corrupts only the King of England. Our colonists and conquests [in America and the East Indies] corrupt King and Parliament: all are victims to the corruption they infuse" (UC xxv. 107).

21. Stephen Conway has discussed Bentham's ambivalent pacifism in "Bentham on Peace and War" (*Utilitas* 1.1 [1989], 82–101) and "Bentham, the Benthamites, and the Nineteenth-Century British Peace Movement" (*Utilitas* 2.2 [1990], 221–43). Some of Bentham's economic objections to settler colonies were overcome at the very end of his life, when he was persuaded by the arguments of Edward Gibbon Wakefield for "systematic colonization" of Australia: see Bernard Semmel, "The Philosophic Radicals and Colonialism," *Journal of Economic History* 21.4 (1961), 518–19. But Semmel, by discussing the "Benthamite Radicals" as a group, too readily assimilates Bentham's views and doubts about colonialism to the more consistently enthusiastic views of his followers. It is also important to note the great extent to which Bentham left the writing of his later works to his disciples; see John M. Robson, "John Stuart Mill and Jeremy Bentham, with Some Observations on James Mill," in *Essays in English Literature Presented to A. S. P. Woodhouse*, ed. M. MacLure and F. W. Watt (Toronto: University of Toronto Press, 1964), 257.

22. Donald Winch, *Classical Political Economy and Colonies* (Cambridge: Harvard University Press, 1965), 34.

23. "Institute of Political Economy," in Bentham, *Jeremy Bentham's Economic Writings*, iii. 356–57.

24. John Dinwiddy's classic account suggests that Bentham's early commitment to democracy was brief and considers James Mill a major influence on Bentham's later radicalism; see "Bentham's Transition to Political Radicalism," *Journal of the History of Ideas* 35 (1975), 683–700. But see Philip Schofield, *Utility and Democracy: The Political Thought of Jeremy Bentham* (Oxford: Oxford University Press, 2006), 78–108, 137–40, arguing for an earlier date for Bentham's return to radicalism and suggesting that it may rather have been Bentham who influenced Mill.

25. *Rights, Representation, and Reform*, 314–15.

26. Winch, *Classical Political Economy and Colonies*, 26. Also see Stokes, *The English Utilitarians and India*; Lea Campos Boralevi, *Bentham and the Oppressed* (New York: Walter de Gruyter, 1984); Uday Mehta, *Liberalism and Empire* (Chicago: University of Chicago Press, 1999). For a powerful counterargument, see Allison Dube, "The Tree of Utility in India: *Panace* or Weed?" in *J. S. Mill's Encounter with India*, ed. Martin I. Moir, Douglas M. Peers, and Lynn Zastoupil (Toronto: University of Toronto Press, 1999).

27. See *Rights, Representation, and Reform*, 291–92, 330 ("Nonsense Upon Stilts," p. 328 above).

28. *Colonies, Commerce, and Constitutional Law*, 110.

29. Ibid., 29. The liberal government in Spain fell in 1823. Philip Schofield discusses Bentham's worry that colonies increase patronage and corrupt metropolitan politics in *Utility and Democracy*, 199–220.

30. William Hazlitt quipped that Bentham's influence increased in proportion to the distance from his house in Westminster; Hazlitt, *The Spirit of the Age* (London: Henry Colburn, 1825), 3–4.

31. *Colonies, Commerce, and Constitutional Law*, 52.

32. "Rid yourselves of Ultramaria," in ibid., 137. In his pamphlet "The Spirit of Conquest and Usurpation and Their Relation to European Civilization" (1814), Benjamin Constant developed, to great effect, just such an argument that conquest is an anachronism in the modern world. See Constant, *Political Writings*, ed. Biancamaria Fontana (Cambridge: Cambridge University Press, 1988), 43–167, esp. 51–56.

33. UC xxv. 121.

34. See, for instance, UC xxv. 32: "Of this visionary project, the most visionary part is without question that for the emancipation of distant dependencies." But in a letter of 1789, after noting that the project of reciprocal disarmament that he advocated had been attempted on a "small and temporary scale" in a convention of 1787 between Britain and France, he asked, "What has been practiced so lately, can it be justly looked upon as visionary and impracticable?"; letter to André Morellet, 18 June 1789, *Correspondence of Jeremy Bentham*, vol. iv, ed. Alexander Taylor Milne (London: Athlone Press, 1981), 76.

35. See, e.g., Hoogensen, *International Relations, Security, and Jeremy Bentham*, 152; Boralevi, *Bentham and the Oppressed*, 127 ff.

36. See UC xxv. 134, headed "International Principles and Measures" (undated, but written 1787 or later and probably by 1789).

37. From "Emancipation Spanish. From Philo-Hispanus to the people of Spain," in *Colonies, Commerce, and Constitutional Law*, 153.

38. See UC xxv. 134.

39. *Rights, Representation, and Reform*, 314–15. Also see the doubts expressed in the main text about whether the "tree of liberty" would grow in India (310–11).

40. See Boralevi, *Bentham and the Oppressed*; Mehta, *Liberalism and Empire*, 20.

41. See, e.g., Stokes, *The English Utilitarians and India*, 51; Boralevi, *Bentham and the Oppressed*, 131. Mehta draws the connection somewhat more obliquely, at *Liberalism and Empire* 2, 92.

42. "Place and Time," p. 213n.37 above. For a discussion of that doctrine, most

famously articulated by Lord Coke in Calvin's Case of 1608, see Richard Tuck, "Alliances with Infidels in the European Imperial Expansion," in *Modern Political Thought and Empire*, ed. Sankar Muthu (Cambridge: Cambridge University Press, forthcoming).

43. He asks rhetorically whether Hindus can hope for any security when they "suffer" under an "endless heap of laws which it is impossible to know" ("Place and Time," p. 214n.37 above).

44. Ibid., p. 153 above.

45. He writes that with regard to manners, forms of government, religion, and indeed "every thing that concerns the temporal interests of society," there are "many points that are indifferent" (ibid., p. 169 above).

46. This qualifies comments about Tahitians and various "African tribes"; Bowring, i. 176; cf. "Place and Time," pp. 164–65 above.

47. For a trenchant critique of the "good governance" ideology within such institutions as the World Bank and International Monetary Fund, see Susan Marks, *The Riddle of all Constitutions: International Law, Democracy, and the Critique of Ideology* (Oxford: Oxford University Press, 2000).

48. He credits Montesquieu with having transformed the business of legislating for distant societies ("Place and Time," p. 156n. above).

49. Ibid., pp. 172–73 above. The Bowring edition removes the reference to Greek, Roman, and modern European practices, and the criticism of Montesquieu in this edition appears to be merely that he puts customs on a par with principles; see Bowring, i. 180.

50. "Place and Time," p. 173 above. Bowring removes this remark and another casting doubt on the account; Bowring, i. 180.

51. "Place and Time," pp. 173–74 above.

52. To give some examples: Bentham's manuscript, in speaking of the "dread of invisible agents" felt by most people in various cultures, compares the fears of a "Gentoo nurse or her nurseling" with those of "a Christian" (ibid., p. 159 above). The Bowring edition compares the fears of "a Gentoo" with those of "an ignorant Christian," insinuating that all Hindus suffer under illusions that only the most backward Europeans do (Bowring, i. 174). Or compare the passages on marriage and polygamy: the manuscript notes the basic similarities between Christian and Muslim norms, writing that most of the offenses regarding marriage in Christian countries will have counterparts in Muslim ones (see "Place and Time," pp. 165–66 above); Bowring instead insists on the differences ("The matrimonial condition is not the same in reality in Mahometan and Christian countries") [Bowring, i. 177]. The Bowring edition also removes the remark that in "certain Christian countries, polygamy on both sides, for want of a proper police in this behalf, happens but too often"; see Bowring, i. 176.

53. See Stefan Collini, "The Idea of 'Character' in Victorian Political Thought," *Transactions of the Royal Historical Society* (5th series) 35 (1985), 29–50, and Georgios Varouxakis, "National Character in John Stuart Mill's Thought," *History of European Ideas* 24.6 (1998), 375–91.

54. See *Considerations on Representative Government, Collected Works of John Stuart Mill* xix. 418–21. The British people's lack of interest in exercising power, along with their suspicion of those who sought power, was the "point of character which beyond any other, fits the people of this country for representative government" (421). Also see John M. Robson, "Civilization and Culture as Moral Concepts," in *Cambridge Companion to Mill*, ed. John Skorupski (Cambridge: Cambridge University Press, 1998), 338–71, and Georgios Varouxakis, *Mill on Nationality* (London: Routledge, 2002).

55. *Principles of Political Economy, Collected Works of John Stuart Mill*, ii. 319. See his similar remarks in *On the Subjection of Women* of 1869, in *Collected Works of John Stuart Mill*, xxi. 277. Also see Georgios Varouxakis, "John Stuart Mill on Race," *Utilitas* 10.1 (1998), 17–32; and "Empire, Race, Euro-centrism: John Stuart Mill and His Critics," in *Utilitarianism and Empire*, ed. Bart Schultz and Georgios Varouxakis (Lanham, Md.: Lexington Books, 2005), 137–53.

56. For instance, "The most envious of all mankind are the Oriental," *Considerations on Representative Government, Collected Works of John Stuart Mill*, xix. 408. Also: "barbarians will not reciprocate. They cannot be depended upon for observing any rules. Their minds are not capable of so great an effort." "A Few Words on Non-Intervention," *Collected Work of John Stuart Mill*, xxi. 118.

57. See, e.g., Mill, "The Condition of Ireland (3)" (*Morning Chronicle*, 10 October 1846), *Collected Works of John Stuart Mill*, xxiv. 889–92.

58. See Stephen G. Engelmann, "Mill, Bentham, and the Art and Science of Government," *Revue d'études benthamiennes* 4 (February 2008), 7–17.

59. Mill, "Remarks on Bentham's Philosophy," 8.

60. Mill, "Bentham," 99.

61. Mill, "Remarks on Bentham's Philosophy," 16.

62. Mill, "Bentham," 113.

63. As Engelmann notes, while in *On Liberty*, Mill insists precisely that we not consider the effects of people's actions on their own character but only on the interests of others, the ultimate purpose of such a policy of noninterference is to cultivate character. See "Mill, Bentham, and the Art and Science of Government," 16.

64. See, for instance, *Rationale of Judicial Evidence*, in Bowring, vii. 17–20.

65. Letter to Jean Pierre Boyer of 29 December 1822, *Correspondence of Jeremy Bentham*, xi. 180; letter to Marc René Argenson, 2 January 1823, ibid.

66. In keeping with a common pattern, Bentham's most pointed expressions of intolerance occur during the so-called Tory period of 1801–04: see, for instance,

his description of Islam as "a religion of which incurable barbarity and ignorance seem to be inseparable features" ("Institute of Political Economy," in Bentham, *Economic Writings*, iii. 356). "Place and Time" largely treats Muslim practices dispassionately, though it also speaks of the "mischievous effects of that barbarous religion" ("Place and Time," p. 162 above).

67. Bentham's main collaborator was Hassuna D'Ghies, an adviser to the Pasha who spent much of the 1820s in England. Although Bentham introduced him as an ambassador from Tripoli, D'Ghies's diplomatic credentials were never recognized by the British government. See Philip Schofield's editorial introduction to *Securities Against Misrule* (Oxford: Oxford University Press, 1990), xv–xxxvi; and Bentham's correspondence with and about D'Ghies, in *Correspondence of Jeremy Bentham*, vols. xi, xii. Also see L. J. Hume, "Preparations for Civil War in Tripoli in the 1820s: Ali Karamanli, Hassuna D'Ghies and Jeremy Bentham," *Journal of African History* 21 (1980), 311–22.

68. D'Ghies to John Quincy Adams (drafted by Bentham), *Securities Against Misrule*, 165–66.

69. For his congratulations to the Greeks, see *Securities Against Misrule*, 195.

70. Ibid., 111.

71. Bentham's sense of the possibilities for innovation generated outside Europe stands in strong contrast to the more common European use of colonies as laboratories for governing and disciplinary techniques that were then imported back into the metropole; see, for instance, Timothy Mitchell, *Rule of Experts: Egypt, Techno-Politics, Modernity* (Berkeley: University of California Press, 2002).

72. *Correspondence of Jeremy Bentham*, vol. xii, ed. Luke O'Sullivan and Catherine Fuller (Oxford: Oxford University Press, 2006), 471–72.

73. Bentham, "International Law" (11 June 1827), British Library Add. MS 30151, fol 12b ff.; also see Ernest Nys, "Notes inédites de Bentham sur le droit international," *Law Quarterly Review* 1 (1885), 225–31 at 229.

74. Bentham, "International Law" (11 June 1827), British Library Add. MS 30151, fol 12b ff.; quoted in Nys, "Notes inédites," 230.

75. Mill, "Remarks on Bentham's Philosophy," 16.

76. Thomas Franck celebrated "the emerging right to democratic governance," in an article of that name, *American Journal of International Law* 86.1 (1992), 46–91; also see Anne-Marie Slaughter [Burley], "Toward an Age of Liberal Nations," *Harvard International Law Journal* 33 (1992), 393–405.

77. See Martti Koskenniemi, " 'Intolerant Democracies': A Reaction," *Harvard International Law Journal* 37 (1996), 234. Also see Susan Marks, *The Riddle of all Constitutions*.

Bentham, Utility, and
the Romantic Imagination

MARK CANUEL

Was Jeremy Bentham a Romantic writer? The very thought of including the notorious system builder in the company of the exalted English poets of the late eighteenth and early nineteenth centuries would seem to be flatly contradicted by the likes of William Hazlitt, whose *Spirit of the Age* accuses him of reducing the "theory of human life" to a "*caput mortuum* of reason, and dull, plodding, technical calculation."[1] Even Hazlitt himself, though, is far from settled in his judgments. Surely the fact that the essay on Bentham occupies the leading position in Hazlitt's brilliant series of portraits of notable public figures of the day suggests that something more is at stake than merely dismissing him as a plodding rationalist. And the full range of Hazlitt's comments on his subject is hardly decisive; it makes the philosopher's impact seem both small and large, inspiring alternating doses of ridicule and awe. The first page of the essay is consistent with the negative assessment I have already mentioned, dismissing Bentham's influence as purely intellectual, devoted only to abstract thinking (3). He has not discovered any new "parent truth," Hazlitt goes on to say; what he has written is not frequently read and will not endure. And this can only lead to the provisional claim that "Mr. Bentham, perhaps, over-rates the importance of his own theories" (7).

But Hazlitt, the greatest essay writer of his day, is always at his most brilliant when he steps back from a point, modifies it, or contradicts it; here is no exception. For it turns out that the abstraction of Bentham's "logical machinery" is precisely what allows it to have a broad influence in nations beyond Great Britain (6): "His reputation lies at the circumference; and the lights of his understanding are reflected, with increasing lustre, on the other side of the globe" (3). The principle of utility, which the essay attacks at length, is to be opposed because it is so capacious that it includes everything in it: it has simply gone "too far" (8). And suddenly we find that Bentham stands perhaps less in opposition to the essayist than in competition with him: Bentham is a thinker brazenly "aiming at too much," with a soul "extending itself to the farthest verge of the conceivable and possible" (9).

It's not that he plods, it's that he soars too high. If this sounds like inadvertent praise, it agrees with Percy Bysshe Shelley's linking of Bentham with William Godwin, Hazlitt, and Leigh Hunt, all writers who, Shelley claims, hold a powerful public influence and are capable of encouraging beneficial political change.[2]

In this essay, I want at first to emphasize precisely this line of influence and affinity between Bentham and the Romantics — I concentrate mostly on English writers of the late eighteenth and early nineteenth centuries — that I have just hinted at. Second, though, I want to get to the heart of Hazlitt's interesting and revealing ambivalence. Far from dismissing the tension between Bentham and writers from William Wordsworth to Lord Byron, I want to emphasize how crucial it was for a particularly powerful antipathy to build up around the issue of utility and its supposed opposition to imagination and individual volition.[3] While I want to emphasize the importance of that antipathy to the constitution of Romantic thought — both by the writers of this era and by generations of their interpreters — I eventually want to argue that the opposition between imagination and utility is a false one. Following this line of discussion, I think, will encourage us not only to view Bentham's influence on and affiliation with his contemporaries in a new light. It will encourage us to redefine the very meaning of "Romanticism" itself.

The initial drift of my argument, then, runs counter to the frequently voiced claim that the relationship between Bentham and writers of the Romantic period is conditioned by dramatically antithetical values: communal versus individual, empirical versus ideal, mechanical versus spiritual. Guided by this assumption, scholarly work on Romantic literature has usually claimed that late eighteenth- and early nineteenth-century writers of imaginative literature in poetry and prose were opposed to everything — the legal reforms, the sweeping institutional designs — that Bentham and his followers stood for.[4] Political theorists, furthermore, have had little reason to suggest that Bentham had any interest in the picturesque landscapes and rural cottagers so endearing to the writers most commonly known as Romantic.

To adjust this picture, we might first reexamine Hazlitt's suggestion that Bentham's reputation was more lustrous beyond the shores of his native country, since such a statement obviously questions the specific influence Bentham may have had on the work of other Romantic-era writers. True, Bentham's work was well known on the continent. But even if Bentham never approached the fame of William Godwin in the three or four decades following the French Revolution, his writing was still well known to and widely publicized among an English audience, despite Hazlitt's claim that "his name is little known in England" (3). That audience would have read works like *An Introduction to the Principles of Morals and Legislation*, *Church of Englandism and its Catechism Examined*, and the *Defence of Usury* (Hazlitt's favorite) in English. A significant amount of material was available only in French through Étienne Dumont's translation of it in the *Traités de Législation*. Yet even the *Traités* attracted enough attention to receive an extended commentary by Francis Jeffrey in the *Edinburgh Review*. Henry Brougham also wrote in the *Edinburgh Review* on Dumont's translation of the *Théorie des Peines et des Recompenses*.[5]

The mere fact of wide dissemination cannot in itself make an argument for the work's importance or influence. Still, the estimations of both Jeffrey and Brougham were quite different from Hazlitt's in their impressions of the work's innovation and influence. Jeffrey was hardly lavish in praise, but he still admitted the "sagacity and independence which distinguish all his speculations";[6] Brougham remarked upon the "repeated allusions" to Bentham's work in legislative measures both at home and "in different parts of Europe."[7] John and Leigh Hunt published excerpts from Bentham and praised his work in the columns of their newspaper the *Examiner*. In accounts of English Romanticism, then, it is surprising that Bentham often goes unmentioned, even though scholars have carefully researched the work of radical thinkers from William Cobbett to Thomas Paine, whose support for democratic politics at home and for the revolution of 1789 in France is said to have made them congenial to many poets and novelists of the day.[8]

Bentham was in fact a friend and supporter of these influential radicals.[9] For instance, through Thomas Wooler, the manager of the *Black Dwarf* and publisher of Bentham's *Plan of Parliamentary Reform, in the Form of a Catechism*, he met the publisher Richard Carlile and later enlisted his friends in Carlile's treason trial. Carlile also published Bentham's *Influence of Natural Religion on the Temporal Happiness of Mankind* in 1822. Bentham was an avid admirer of Paine and collaborated with William Hone on his *Reformists' Register*.[10] Other correspondents and collaborators included Francis Place, radical writer and member of the London Corresponding Society, and Daniel O'Connell, most famous for his campaign for Catholic Emancipation in the 1820s.

Bentham's proximity to these contemporaries wasn't merely a matter of biographical fact, though. His writings in fact reveal many intertwined political and aesthetic affinities with their politically radical orientation. Consider Bentham's early *Fragment on Government* (1776) as a first instance—

a bold and creative work that attacks a whole range of obfuscations in William Blackstone's defense of common law in *Commentaries on the Laws of England*. One of Bentham's opening gestures in the *Fragment* is to identify his own work as that of a "censor" of law rather than as a mere "expositor": the censor examines the work of traditional judgments and evaluates them, while the expositor simply submits to them.[11] And that opening move leads the way to a complex generic mixture of political theory and Juvenalian satire in which the legislative expositor is described as an obtuse, effeminate idol worshiper.[12] He attributes Blackstone's defense of the common law to a habit of "*personification*" in which the law is treated as a "living creature" with inviolable authority (10). We must treat Bentham's precision about personification — the attribution of human qualities to objects or ideas — seriously here. For the problem with the legal expositor or "Apologist" is not simply that he is superstitious — not simply that he believes in higher powers that move or influence things or relations in the material world. The real problem is that he is fundamentally and visibly confused about the very thing he worships. As Blackstone brings out "the toilette of classic erudition" (24) with which to "deck" the laws that he so idolizes, he ends up worshiping the common law's awesome authority without realizing that he is simply worshiping a fiction of his own making. He mistakes his own human agency for the work of a higher power.

Laws cannot be defended because of the respect that is supposedly owed to them, Bentham says; they can be defended only because they are beneficial to those who live by their rules. In one very important sense, Bentham's practical appeal to human needs and desires ranks him among the leading political and literary figures of his day who devoted themselves to clearing the cobwebs of myth and tradition from laws and institutions. The intent of the *Fragment* is to "overthrow" an old way of thinking (31) and likewise to encourage the utilitarian legislator to tear "the Mask of Mystery from the face of Jurisprudence" (21). This aspect of the *Fragment* is logically and rhetorically reminiscent of Voltaire, whom Bentham admired and even translated into English; it also looks forward to a whole range of Romantic political and aesthetic iconoclasts: to Paine's *Rights of Man*, for instance, with its critique of Edmund Burke's worship of principles rather than persons ("he pities the plumage, but forgets the dying bird"), or even to William Wordsworth's desire to fashion a poetic "language of men" in the landmark collection of poems *Lyrical Ballads*, coauthored with Samuel Taylor Coleridge.[13]

The specific image of the effeminate Blackstone at his toilette elaborates on this position. It is most likely a clever allusion to Alexander Pope's

Belinda (in his mock epic poem *The Rape of the Lock*), who similarly decks herself out with a host of "Cosmetic powers" in the form of combs, gems, and powders.[14] But Bentham is less generous in his critique of Blackstone than Pope is toward his Belinda. This ridicule of Blackstone's love of ornate classical erudition — analogized to a woman's attention to gorgeous, seductive ornament — joins forces with Wordsworth's Romantic critique of the early eighteenth century's "falsehood of description" (exemplified in the frequent use of personifications) so often considered to be "the common inheritance of Poets."[15] Both attempt to found a newer, truer politics and aesthetics founded on the rejection of a long-venerated but highly artificial inheritance. At the same time, Bentham's point in satirizing Blackstone in this manner is not simply to fault the jurist's vain desire to cover up nature with the trappings of culture. His real point is that Blackstone doesn't admit the extent to which his personifications are a game of dress-up; he doesn't acknowledge the level of artifice that is required in order to honor a legal tradition. The *Fragment* thus defends neither nature nor tradition, since "the state of nature" is simply another way of saying "society," and "society" ends up being some form of "government" (38). Bentham's aim here, as in his later response to the French Declaration of the Rights of Man (in *Nonsense Upon Stilts*), is not to get beyond society to nature but to realize that comparisons of social relationships are comparisons between ways of governing. The errors in any given set of relations can be corrected in order to achieve a desirable modification or improvement.[16]

I will have more to add about the importance of this particular strain of Bentham's thinking in relation to English Romantic writers, but it is worth noting and emphasizing just for the present moment that his more general commitment to breaking free from the weight of traditional and oppressive systems was continually connected to rhetorical analysis: to an awareness of language's power to deceive and promote unnecessary injuries. The *Fragment*, for instance, is first and foremost a critique of Blackstone's linguistic imprecision and circumlocution; Bentham wrote an entire book called *The Book of Fallacies*, specifically aimed at demystifying political rhetoric that was not merely artificial but dangerously deceptive, causing "a pernicious course of action to be engaged in or persevered in." Among these fallacies, the "wisdom of ancestors" was the one that Bentham subjected to his most sustained scrutiny, opposing a whole range of laws and institutions that had achieved authority primarily because they had the honor of being old.[17] In the *Defence of Usury*, for instance, he urged the withdrawal of penalties that were based on ancient and thoroughly irrelevant prejudices. And as Louis Crompton notes in his groundbreaking *Byron and Greek Love*, Bentham wrote unpublished papers and fragments and one complete paper on the damage caused by equally prejudicial sodomy laws (not published until 1978): "death to a human creature, confusion, reproach, and anguish to an innocent family" were the inevitable results.[18] Although the dashing and adventurous Lord Byron would seem to have little in common with Bentham, then, their attitudes toward the stifling sexual morality of English Regency culture are actually surprisingly similar. The eponymous hero of Byron's *Don Juan*, who travels the world freeing daughters from oppressive fathers, wives from husbands, and the oppressed from their tyrants, is in many respects the embodiment of Benthamite liberalism.[19]

Of all repressive and injurious institutions, it was the Church of England that received Bentham's most sustained criticism. One of the most prominent themes that resonates throughout the poet and graphic artist William Blake's *Songs of Experience* is that of the Anglican church's hypocrisy — its claims to holiness matched by violence and exclusion. In the poem "Little Boy Lost," the child who questions the doctrines of his priestly "Father" is admonished with "Priestly care"; he is finally bound in chains and burned in a "holy place."[20] Blake later wrote an entire epic poem, *Milton*, a fictional account of how the great English poet John Milton needed to free himself from the chains of his own repressive religious beliefs. Bentham is entirely sympathetic with that view in his important and voluminous writings on the Church of England, in which he argues against the primacy of belief — the "all-sufficiency of faith" — in the formation of political community.[21] Such a system resembled the logic of the "Inquisition," he writes in *Church of Englandism*, the mode of government "employed for clearing the country of persons guilty of thinking differently from what was professed to be thought by the Church of Rome." The problem with the church is with its combination of falsehood and oppression. Dissenters in England are treated as criminals under the law, but the crime is entirely invented by judges since it is not clear that anyone is truly hurt by it: as in the Inquisition, "the judges [make] the crime; those same judges [punish] it."[22] The church thus amounts to an "*exclusionary* system" that is nothing more than "a tissue of *imposture*: of imposture, and if not of direct *forgery*, something extremely like it."[23]

It is this secular opposition to the logic of the confessional state that brings Bentham particularly close to many other thinkers of his day besides Blake, including Joseph Priestley, Anna Laetitia Barbauld, Coleridge, Wordsworth, Byron, and Shelley. John Keats's extraordinary verse fragment *The Fall of Hyperion* deliberately and self-consciously frames the poet-figure as a failed religious votary — one who has come to the altar of great poetry too late to partake in a sacred rite that will signify his ascendancy into the sphere of great epic writers; Manfred, Byron's greatest hero (frequently identified by critics with the poet himself), defines himself in opposition to the pompous strictures of the established church.

Still, even while we note some of these basic affinities between Bentham and those contemporaries most often considered Romantic writers, we should not be distracted from a source of apparent disagreement between most Romantic writers and Bentham — a rift between the Romantic celebration of imagination and what Hazlitt called Bentham's technical account of reason and utility (8). Pleasure and pain are the primary motivations for human action, Bentham repeatedly insists (he gleaned this view from predecessors from David Hume to Claude Adrien Helvétius), and thus they are the only true object of the utilitarian legislator's efforts to secure the greatest good for the greatest number.[24]

In the work of Bentham's contemporaries, arguments against this view are as numerous as they are vociferous. They are not all aimed at Bentham, but against some aspect of utility that was also embraced by writers who influenced Bentham or were influenced by him.[25] It is nevertheless important to capture the drift of this opposition in order to assess the scope of Bentham's connection to other thinkers of his day. Coleridge rails against the "prudential motive" of utility that characterizes "political Empirics" of his time who reduce all axioms of virtue into a theory of "prudential obligation" based upon the political subject's desire to attain pleasure and avoid pain.[26] Wordsworth's monumental poem *The Excursion* is no less vehement in its assault on the principle of "Gain, the master idol of the realm," which sacrifices "The old domestic morals of the land" to "unceasing toil."[27] Similarly, in a host of shorter lyric poems, like "The Old Cumberland Beggar," the significance of the rural poor as an incitement to love, which in turn reminds us "that we have of us one human heart," might easily be taken as an argument against the emphasis on increasing the profitability of the poor in Bentham's *Tracts on Poor Laws and Pauper Management*.[28]

The list of utilitarianism's detractors could go on for some time, and their opinions echo in John Stuart Mill's *Autobiography*, with its account of how reading Wordsworth's poetry helped to regenerate that power of feeling which had been worn away by the mechanical analysis of pleasures and pains.[29] This list would conform loosely to the basic parameters of Coleridge's and Wordsworth's responses, even though those responses are not saying quite the same thing. For if the problem with utilitarianism in Coleridge's view is that individuals dominate the world with their reason, the problem with it in Wordsworth's view is that "Gain" dominates all human faculties. In one view, the individual's powers loom too large over all of humanity, and in the other view there is no individuality at all. The apparent contradiction condenses within a few lines in Wordsworth's late poem "To the Utilitarians," in which utility falsely "elevate[s]" human "Knowledge" above the appropriate purview of "internal seeing," while it simultaneously submits "imagination" to "Fact."[30]

But what lies behind this apparent tension is the profound way in which the Romantic antipathy toward utilitarianism is frequently directed not merely toward its epistemological claims to rationality but toward its linking of enlightened epistemology and enlightened politics. In other words, utilitarianism is at fault not merely for imposing mechanistic reason on imagination but for dissolving individuals into groups and groups into individuals. There is no difference between the individual and the group, or rather one is always swallowed up into a version of the other. If this is the problem with utilitarianism, however, it appears that the critique depends upon a very narrow reading of utility, which is interpreted as an imposition of one rational standard or rule for the useful upon a social group, and thus it represents the failure of a social group to make enough room for the individuals governed by and within it. This dimension of the Romantic response to Bentham's utilitarianism has been so powerfully reinforced that it is repeated in John Rawls's liberal critique of utilitarianism's tendency to require a comprehensive set of desires and preferences that political agents must share in order to achieve social unity and cooperation.[31]

Now in one sense, the Romantic critique of utility is justified because of the way that Bentham occasionally describes utility as an attitude or disposition held by individuals that live in a utilitarian society. "Under a well-constituted, or even under a well-administered though ill-constituted government," he writes in *An Introduction to the Principles of Morals and Legislation*, "men's moral sensibility is commonly stronger, and their moral biases more conformable to the dictates of utility."[32] This reasoning, perhaps actually a form of wishful thinking, informs the many instances in which Bentham easily shifts from talking about "the happiness of the community" to "the happiness of [the] individual."[33] Bentham, in these instances, makes it appear as if the object of the entire notion of utility is to strengthen agreement between individuals on the principles or standards that would guide their actions. To ensure the greatest good for the greatest number would involve determining which principles were accepted as good by most people — counting up the number of persons to benefit from specific actions in order to determine the good or bad tendency of those actions — and establishing those principles as legal rules to be followed by everyone.[34] Obviously this logic is connected to the way Bentham occasionally makes it seem (in the *Tracts on the Poor Laws*, for instance) as if the purpose of all institutions is to measure the value of all people according to a single standard of economic measurement. From this vantage point, Wordsworth's poem "To the Utilitarians" might seem entirely accurate, since utilitarianism, according to the poet, is devoted to extracting a certain specific knowledge of utility which it then universalizes as fact. That logic, which Mary Poovey investigates in her *History of the Modern Fact,* makes any particular individual's account of fact increasingly irrelevant in the quest for a utilitarian system.[35]

But the apparent demotion of "internal seeing" that Wordsworth laments seems less pervasive in Bentham's thought than Wordsworth's critique of utility, like other Romantic critiques of utility, might make us think. In fact, Bentham's version of utility had, paradoxically, much in common with Romantic critics of utility and utilitarians. First of all, even as Bentham seems to make utility into an attitude that could or should be adopted by all people, he also indicates that policies need to acknowledge the actual disparities among individuals. For instance, Bentham's grand attempt to identify sources of pleasure and pain for the purposes of effective legislation is accompanied in his *Table of the Springs of Action* by clarifying statements about the fact that people's interests and desires are frequently opposed and even inconsistent in one person.[36] Penal sanctions, he argues in the *Introduction*, would not simply produce uniform and predictable effects but could conceivably be applied to individuals with "perhaps an indefinite variety of degrees" of variation, as if to underline the legislator's work not as an attempt to enforce uniformity but to assemble an orderly community as a "fictitious body" that could not be said to resemble any particular person's moral outlook at all.[37]

Second, the "fictitious body" of the community not only permits recognition of the "indefinite variety" among subject persons; it in fact enables the constitution of such persons as various and facilitates their transactions within secular social environments.[38] That is to say, the sympathy with the causes of personal liberty that I mentioned earlier in this essay — political, religious, and sexual — is not simply the result of a grudging admission that different orientations and beliefs among persons privately exist. Personal liberty was in fact enabled and produced by a commitment to the artifices of secular government that Bentham so vigorously defended in his institutional schemes for schools, prisons, and workhouses. We are thus brought back now to a logic that was at work in the *Fragment on Government*: the utilitarian legislator departs from the poetic fantasies of Blackstone or the logic of natural rights because he avoids the folly of either worshiping the collective judgments of the past or stripping them away to find an impossibly receding law of nature. He evaluates, removes, or replaces laws with the knowledge that they are functional artifices capable of adjustment. By stating the matter in these terms, I mean to be saying that Bentham's commitment to utility was primarily an interest not in enhancing social agreement but in orchestrating the movements of persons with divergent interests and goals, and thus the notion of utility not only acknowledged utility as plural but helped to articulate and organize disparate utilities within felicitous schemes of legal and institutional cooperation. To state the matter in these terms is to say that Bentham's notion of utility contributed to a notion of community beyond communion: a community protecting and fortified by disagreement.

This aspect of Bentham's way of thinking encourages us to evaluate a profound series of logical connections between his work and Romantic cultural productions that investigate the lineaments of secular institutions and legal arrangements.[39] The issue of religious toleration I discussed earlier, it turns out, is central to Bentham's thought not merely because he opposes religious hypocrisy but because he embraces the possibilities of inclusion within ecumenical legal and institutional frameworks. The entire possibility of the secular, that is, depends upon a commitment to legal and institutional construction rather than to any collective change in belief. Wordsworth's *Excursion* represents the church itself as a structure that is accommodating in many of the same ways that Bentham imagines utilitarian governments to be. John Constable's many paintings of Salisbury Cathedral are a pictorial equivalent of this attempt to make the church into a source of unity that does not require uniformity; surrounded by trees, grass, and fair skies, the church looks as nondenominational as nature itself. And it turns out that Shelley is entirely on Bentham's side in his "Letter to Lord Ellenborough," a short composition appearing in only twenty-five copies, when he claims that Jesus embraced regulations that were "more moral and more humane"; the logic is identical to Bentham's *Not Paul but Jesus* in its rejection of religious doctrine as the foundation for government and as the justification for persecuting Daniel Isaac Eaton and others accused of blasphemous libel by the lord chancellor.[40] Shelley's alternative account agrees with Bentham, moreover, in its way of describing the legislator's role as the organization of actions rather than beliefs: "It is admitted that a virtuous or moral action is that action which, when considered in all its accessories and consequences, is fitted to produce the highest pleasure of the greatest number of sensitive beings."[41]

It is crucial, then, to contrast Bentham's opposition to the church establishment with that of Paine and other more typical followers of the enlightenment philosophes, who were more susceptible than Bentham to Wordsworth's charge of sacrificing imagination to fact. While Bentham could be entirely sympathetic with some of their goals, as I mentioned earlier, his reasoning was actually somewhat different. To Bentham's mind, the problem with the church was not strictly with its religion — that it made up stories about miracles and other events that did not correspond to the world of fact and reason. This was Paine's line of attack in *The Age of Reason*, but it was not Bentham's. The problem was strictly with its establishment: the fact that religion had been made a part of the state and that it therefore made such doctrines into the basis for distributing rewards and punishments within that community. The value of toleration thus consisted not in persuading people to disbelieve their prior beliefs but in providing a model for community that might be extended to members with distinct and even opposing backgrounds and predispositions.

One of the most revealing outcomes of this commitment was Bentham's plan for a school, *Chrestomathia*. Much has been written about the ongoing debate over monitorial schools during Bentham's day. Joseph Lancaster became the most prominent supporter of a national secular system of education, while Andrew Bell supported a system of education requiring religious instruction. Bentham in fact sought to minimize the differences in these educational schemes, stressing that the school provided a system of "social co-operation." With its elaborate routing of individual students through collective exercises, the regime of the school coaxed students with varying dispositions into unified patterns of action; the system of the school emphasized coordinated trajectories for individual advancement while simultaneously avoiding "controverted points of *Divinity*." Similar sentiments about what schools should be echo throughout Romantic writing. Maria Edgeworth's *The Absentee* speaks of Anglo-Irish schools as ideally tolerant institutions, and she joined her father in composing a popular book on nondenominational instruction. Byron's parliamentary speech on Catholic emancipation similarly critiques the adherents of Protestant ascendancy in Ireland, likening their schools to "dunghills" that violate the aim of secular education to include "men of different religious persuasion" who can "sit on the same bench" and discuss any topic of "natural history, philosophy, or ethics."[42]

The educational scheme was connected to a range of other projects for reimagining institutions and legal procedures, which combined to acknowledge varieties of belief and custom while organizing that variety within new frameworks of obligation. We thus find that, even when Bentham echoes Montesquieu's concern with the locality of belief and custom in matters of legislation (in *Of the Influence of Time and Place in Matters of Legislation*), he nevertheless views legislators as those who "have learnt to soar above the mists of prejudice" through the felicitous art of legislative "management."[43] In the *Pannomial Fragments*, the very notion of utility itself gets to be understood less as a uniform sense of agreement than as a formal impulse according to which political subjects could look to law as a source of juridical command, and thus as an impulse toward "fixation of the text of the laws."[44] By these means, Bentham claims to be correcting the errors of both the common law tradition and the natural law tradition, espoused by the dueling proponents of tradition and revolution. For if common law idolizes a concrete series of decisions without rules, and natural law idolizes rules without reference to concrete acts of government, Bentham's emphasis on statutory stipulation gave shape to individual actions with reference to a map of interwoven obligations.

The desire to make the law more accessible and consistent is certainly one of those elements of Bentham's thought that were culled from the writings of other thinkers before him, to be sure. But that wish is so pervasive among Romantic writers that it still deserves mention. The Gothic novels of Ann Radcliffe are all preoccupied with the intervention of a secular realm of judicial procedure within the horrors of aristocratic and monastic secrecy. Mary Wollstonecraft's novel *Maria or The Wrongs of Woman* criticizes English laws as "partial laws": laws that are written by and for men, in which women are either ignored or are made into "outlaws." The fact that marriage defeats a woman's utility, Wollstonecraft suggests, is not her own fault but the result of woman's condition as a legally invisible being.[45] Shelley not only calls poets legislators but likens the working of penal law to creative authorship.[46] The conflict in Shelley's brilliant drama *The Cenci* arises almost entirely out of the fact that the law serves only those tyrants in power; a consistent form of retributive justice is unavailable and exists only in the imaginative renderings of the tragic heroine and those who support her.

Wollstonecraft's *Maria* brings us to one more question about the power of utilitarian thinking. We have seen now that utility in Bentham's writing does not require the kind of strenuous adherence to a "technical calculation" the way Hazlitt claims. And we have seen that Bentham's more generous approach to institutional and legal structures actually was shared by a good number of writers who had objections to other aspects of his thinking. But what about the place of imagination in his work?[47] Is Hazlitt correct in assuming that Bentham ignores it? Certainly this view, sustained by Mill's account of Bentham's "contempt for the pleasures of imagination," has convinced interpreters of Bentham even up to the present day.[48] Virtually any recent history of Romantic poetry or fiction that includes Bentham's name dismisses his relevance with one of the author's many quotations that questions the value of poetry: "It can apply itself to no subject but at the expense of utility and truth," he writes, leading Tim Milnes to conclude that Bentham countered Romantic philosophies of mind and imagination with a "utility-based reduction of art."[49] Perhaps a hostility to art in general or poetry in particular may seem to be implied by Bentham's objection to *Blackstone's* poetic personifications. But, as I explained earlier, the problem with Blackstone (Bentham says) is not with poetry but with the fact that poetic erudition is being used to naturalize something that is artificial. It is thus poetry that is unpoetic; it attempts to deny its status as poetry and thereby escape any evaluation based upon its merits as an artifice.

Any sweeping claims about the complete exclusion of imagination in Bentham's thought should be submitted to further examination in order to get a better sense of the author's actual relationship to the well-known poets and other artists of his time. If we return to Wollstonecraft's *Maria*, Maria's inability to achieve utility in her marriage — a concern so vital that it occupies a central position much later in the novels of Anthony Trollope, whose heroines are always mistaken precisely insofar as they wish to be useful rather than ornamental — is repeatedly connected to her limited access to the world of letters. Meanwhile, her writing and reading demonstrate the power of her "improving mind" and her will to participate in a conversation and discussion from which women are excluded (49). The "animated imagination" that Maria admires and aspires to cultivate in herself is an imagination that wishes to make itself public (19). The imagination connects the internal state of the individual to the actions and projects of others and is thus distinct from the mere cultivation of private, domestic sensibility that Wollstonecraft criticizes in her *Vindication of the Rights of Woman*.[50] Imagination is therefore not lost or suppressed in the connection to community, but rather found through such an act of speculative extension. As if to strengthen the connection that Wollstonecraft makes, the novel's advertisement, most likely written by Godwin, laments the author's death that cut short the work of a genius devoted to "schemes of usefulness, and projects of public interest" (120).

These few statements alone begin to suggest that something more complicated is at work than a mere opposition between imagination and utility. They begin to lead us to something that has perhaps been implicit all along in my discussion of Bentham's work: his account of inclusive and articulate legal and institutional structures in fact heightens rather than diminishes the importance of the imagination because those structures involve and engage imaginative acts and productions. This is because they extend the mind beyond the local precincts of individual custom and belief into a cooperative scheme of relations that more widely encompasses thoughts of the good of others. At the same time, this scheme of relations allows basic components of a person's belief system to remain intact (unlike sympathy, which in Adam Smith's view allows people to share dispositions like resentment toward a criminal). It is interesting and not at all coincidental that this predicament — in which persons attach their beliefs to new verbal structures — is analogous to that which Richard Moran describes as the operation of literary metaphor.[51] And thus we can hardly wonder at Bentham's suggestion that the very contemplation of regular and consistent laws is itself an aid to imagining: "In a system thus constructed . . . a man need but open the book in order to inform himself what the aspect borne by the law bears to every imaginable act that can come within the possible sphere of human agency." The law is a map that leads the eye in "all imaginable directions."[52] If utilitarian structures work as aids to the imagination, the reverse is also true: imagination or invention is to be most highly prized according to the amount of good that that the invention can effect.[53]

Wollstonecraft and Godwin help to bring us closer to the real connection that can be made between Benthamite utility and the powers of the imagination as they were understood by the Romantics. Although it would be impossible to do a wide investigation of the connection here, a brief look at one of the most often quoted early nineteenth-century texts on the nature of poetry can point us in the right direction. Shelley somewhat circuitously registers an agreement with Bentham in his *Defence of Poetry*, particularly when he makes an important distinction between two kinds of utility. One kind of utility is only "transitory and particular," Shelley writes, while the other is "durable, universal, and permanent" (528). While admitting that utilitarians of the first kind have "their appointed office in society," he warns that they may use their "calculating faculty" only to enrich a particular group rather than extending their views to the good of society more generally (529). Such utilitarians are opposed to poetry and to the poetic imagination. Those who concentrate on the second form of utility, however, are aware of the complexities and "paradoxes" that arise in the contemplation of pleasure; alive to the difficulties of defining pleasure in its "highest sense," they realize that utility cannot be defined according to one single standard and imposed on a group (529). The second form of utility is universal not because it is uniform but because it allows for variation.

Shelley's distinctions between transitory and durable utility are probably adapted from the pages of Helvétius, but what's interesting is that he makes precisely the same distinction that Helvétius uses in order to describe the proper object of the utilitarian legislator's attention: the "durable," "unalterable" public good.[54] The ruler following the first "fleeting" form of utility is a despot, while the one following the latter form is an "intelligent prince."[55] The common ground with Helvétius — besides reinforcing Shelley's connection to Bentham — emphasizes the political valences of Shelley's aesthetic pronouncements. When Shelley refers to pleasure "in its highest sense," he is not simply restricting or rarifying the idea of pleasure and thus utility; he is making pleasure "in its highest sense" into an awareness of pleasure's complexity. The poet is not the one who attempts to restrict pleasure but one who sees that pleasure comes from many sources. "Those who produce and preserve this pleasure are Poets or poetical philosophers," he declares (529). "Poetical philosophers" needs to be read quite broadly here: the purpose of opposing a "transitory" utility is not to oppose politics with poetry but to suggest that any overparticularized notion of utility should be revised to become more poetic: that is, that it should open itself to a wider view of what pleasure is and how it is obtained (this is why Shelley thinks that tragedy is a demonstration of a complex pleasure to which poets and poetical philosophers might attend, since its pleasures arise from a feeling of pain — even while some poetic pleasures are wholly "unalloyed" [529]).

What I have been arguing thus far should make it clear that Bentham cannot be included among those enemies of the "creative faculty" that Shelley finds in the philosophers dedicated to the "accumulation of facts and calculating processes": namely, "Locke, Hume, Gibbon, Voltaire, Rousseau" (530). Shelley sees these philosophers not merely as rationalists, but as political rationalists — that is, those who use rationality for the sake of "personal advantage" by controlling others (529). The inclusion of Rousseau is striking here. Although he was celebrated as the creative genius of his age, Shelley sees him here primarily as small, calculating, and self-interested — not far from the way he would portray him in his unfinished poem *The Triumph of Life*. No less crucial is the exclusion of Bentham from those whom Shelley accuses of bringing "facts and calculating processes" to bear against the "creative faculty." Philip Connell's sense that Shelley opposes Bentham in the *Defence* seems entirely inaccurate because of this exclusion.[56] Although there would be no point in denying, as I have already argued, that Bentham occasionally demonstrates sympathies with the enlightened philosophes, it is equally important for us to analyze what has been denied by generations of readers who have taken those occasional sympathies to represent an entire body of work.

Bentham is committed to the imagination and its powers, making it into the means through which disparate utilities can be combined into larger orchestrations of social movement. Still more, though, he calls upon the work of poet-legislators to do the work of legal reform. As he looks back to a golden age when "poetry was invited to the aid of law," he calls upon poets in his own day to correct "the barbarous language that disgraces our statute book."[57] Poets, in their mastery of form and embrace of innovation and imagination, are the exact opposite of the adherents of the fallacies criticized in the *Handbook*, which obscure acts of creation and stall inquiry. Perhaps Bentham, in his praise for poets, is not really asking for poets to write laws but is simply asking legislators to be more clear and logically elegant in their legal formulations. Maybe so, but even this qualification cannot detract from the fact that poetry (above any science, social or natural) is being invoked to help cure or revise the law and therefore accrues an undeniably positive value. Bentham was more of a "poetical philosopher" than most scholars have previously thought.

NOTES

1. William Hazlitt, *The Spirit of the Age, or, Contemporary Portraits*, ed. Harold Bloom (New York: Chelsea House, 1983), 8. Further references to this work are noted by page number in parentheses.

2. *Shelley's Prose, or The Trumpet of a Prophecy*, ed. David Lee Clark (London: Fourth Estate, 1988), 254, 259. William Godwin, the author of *Enquiry Concerning Political Justice*, was one of the foremost political theorists of his day; Percy Shelley and Leigh Hunt were both poets.

3. William Wordsworth — the author of *The Prelude* and coauthor (with Samuel Taylor Coleridge) of *Lyrical Ballads* — and Lord Byron — the author of *Don Juan* — were poets.

4. See, for instance, David Simpson's account of Wordsworth's objections to Bentham's pauper management schemes in *Wordsworth's Historical Imagination: The Poetry of Displacement* (New York: Methuen, 1987), 160–84.

5. Francis Jeffrey was editor of the *Edinburgh Review*; Henry Brougham was a prominent Whig reformer and helped found the *Edinburgh Review*.

6. Francis Jeffrey, review of Bentham, *Traités de Legislation Civile et Penale*, *Edinburgh Review* 7 (1804), 26.

7. Henry Brougham, review of *Théorie des Peines et des Recompenses, Edinburgh Review* 43 (1813), 3.

8. See, for instance, Kevin Gilmartin, *Print Politics: The Press and Radical Opposition in Early Nineteenth-Century England* (Cambridge: Cambridge University Press, 1996), and Steven Goldsmith, *Unbuilding Jerusalem: Apocalypse and Representation* (Ithaca: Cornell University Press, 1993).

9. For an account of Bentham's utilitarianism in connection with English radicalism, see F. Rosen, "Jeremy Bentham's Radicalism," Glenn Burgess and Matthew Festenstein, eds., *English Radicalism, 1550–1850* (Cambridge: Cambridge University Press, 2007), 217–40.

10. Élie Halévy, *The Growth of Philosophic Radicalism* (Boston: Beacon Press, 1955), 295.

11. Jeremy Bentham, *A Fragment on Government*, ed. Ross Harrison (Cambridge: Cambridge University Press, 1988), 7. Further references to this work are noted by page number in parentheses.

12. Juvenal was a Roman poet active in the first and second centuries AD and the author of *Satires*. His satiric mode is best known for its humor as well as its biting criticism.

13. Thomas Paine, *Rights of Man* (Harmondsworth: Penguin, 1984), 51; William Wordsworth, *The Oxford Authors William Wordsworth*, ed. Stephen Gill (Oxford: Oxford University Press, 1984), 600.

14. Alexander Pope, *The Poems of Alexander Pope*, ed. John Butt (Yale: Yale University Press, 1963), 222.

15. Wordsworth, *Oxford Authors*, 600.

16. On Bentham's place within a legal tradition in which the improvement of laws combines usage with the restraint of reasoned commands, see David Lieberman, *The Province of Legislation Determined: Legal Theory in Eighteenth-Century Britain* (Cambridge: Cambridge University Press, 1989), 119–90.

17. See Bentham, *Handbook of Political Fallacies*, ed. Harold A. Larrabee (New York: Harper, 1952).

18. Louis Crompton, *Byron and Greek Love: Homophobia in 19th-Century England* (Berkeley: University of California Press, 1985), 29.

19. See F. Rosen, *Bentham, Byron, and Greece: Constitutionalism, Nationalism, and Early Liberal Political Thought* (Oxford: Clarendon Press, 1992).

20. William Blake, *Complete Poems*, ed. Alicia Ostriker (Harmondsworth: Penguin, 1977), 130.

21. Bentham, *Not Paul, But Jesus* (London: John Hunt, 1823), 287.

22. Bentham, *Church-of-Englandism and its Catechism Examined* (London: Effingham Wilson, 1818), 62, xvi.

23. Ibid., 75.

24. David Hume was the author of *A Treatise of Human Nature* (1739–40); in 1758 Claude Adrien Helvétius published *De L'Esprit*, or *Essays on the Mind and its Several Faculties*. Both of these works had a profound influence on Bentham's thought.

25. Philip Connell investigates the role of Malthus in Romantic writing in *Romanticism, Economics, and the Question of 'Culture'* (Oxford: Oxford University Press, 2001), 13–62. Connell, however, is primarily interested in rationalism rather than the theory of utility and simply accepts the opposition between Romantics and utilitarian philosophy.

26. Samuel Taylor Coleridge, *The Collected Works of Samuel Taylor Coleridge*, ed. Kathleen Coburn (London: Tourledge. 1972), vi. 186–vii. 150.

27. William Wordsworth, *The Poems*, ed. John O. Hayden, 2 vols. (Harmondsworth: Penguin, 1977), ii. 255–57.

28. Wordsworth, *Poems*, i. 267.

29. John Stuart Mill, *Autobiography, Essay on Liberty* (New York: P. F. Collier, 1909), 96–97.

30. Wordsworth, *Poems*, ii. 744.

31. This argument is central to all of John Rawls's work. See, for instance, "Social Unity and Primary Goods," in *Collected Papers*, ed. Samuel Freeman (Cambridge: Harvard University Press, 1999), 359–87.

32. Bentham, *An Introduction to the Principles of Morals and Legislation*, ed. J. H. Burns and H. L. A. Hart (London: Athlone Press, 1970), 68.

33. Ibid., 12 (p. 113 above).

34. Ibid., 40 (pp. 137–38 above).

35. Mary Poovey, *A History of the Modern Fact: Problems of Knowledge in the Sciences of Wealth and Society* (Chicago: University of Chicago Press, 1998), 214–63.

36. Bentham, *A Table of the Springs of Action, Deontology together with A Table of the Springs of Action and The Article on Utilitarianism*, ed. Amnon Goldworth (Oxford: Oxford University Press, 1983), 112–13 ("Observations").

37. Bentham, *Introduction*, 69, 12 (p. 113 above).

38. I am thus downplaying the role of rationalism in Bentham's account of the secular, in contrast to James E. Crimmins in *Secular Utilitarianism: Social Science and the Critique of Religion in the Thought of Jeremy Bentham* (Oxford: Oxford University Press, 1990).

39. In this paragraph and the two that follow I summarize some arguments I make in my *Religion, Toleration, and British Writing, 1790–1830* (Cambridge: Cambridge University Press, 2002).

40. *Shelley's Prose*, 77, 182.

41. Bentham, *Chrestomathia*, ed. M. J. Smith and W. H. Burston (Oxford: Oxford University Press, 1983), 31, 89.

42. George Gordon, Lord Byron, *The Complete Miscellaneous Prose*, ed. Andrew Nicholson (Oxford: Clarendon Press, 1991), 37–38.

43. Bentham, *Of the Influence of Time and Place in Matters of Legislation*, in *The Works of Jeremy Bentham*, ed. J. Bowring, 11 vols. (Edinburgh: William Tait, 1838–43), i. 180, 182 [hereafter Bowring]; cf. the discussion in "Place and Time," pp. 173–75 above.

44. Bentham, *Pannomial Fragments*, Bowring, iii. 215, 227 (pp. 248–49 and 271 above).

45. Mary Wollstonecraft, *Maria or The Wrongs of Woman*, intr. Anne K. Mellor (New York: Norton, 1994), 87, 88.

46. Percy Bysshe Shelley, *A Defence of Poetry*, in *Shelley's Poetry and Prose*, ed. Donald Reiman and Neil Fraistat (New York: Norton, 2002), 514. Further references to this work are noted by page number in parentheses.

47. Hazlitt, *Spirit*, 9, 8.

48. John Stuart Mill, *Mill on Bentham and Coleridge*, intr. F. R. Leavis (London: Chatto and Windus, 1950), 95.

49. Tim Milnes, *Knowledge and Indifference in English Romantic Prose* (Cambridge: Cambridge University Press, 2003), 26.

50. Wollstonecraft, *Vindication of the Rights of Woman*, ed. and intr. Miriam Brody (Harmondsworth: Penguin, 1975), 152. Wollstonecraft's notion of reason is located in this place where imagination seeks out a place for the individual in public discourse.

51. Richard Moran, "Seeing and Believing: Metaphor, Image, and Force," *Critical Inquiry* 16 (autumn, 1989), 87–112.

52. Bentham, *The Limits of Jurisprudence Defined*, in *A Bentham Reader*, ed. Mary Mack (New York: Pegasus, 1969), 166, 167. For a full discussion of the role of imagination in the conception of interest in Bentham's thought, see Stephen G. Engelmann, *Imagining Interest in Political Thought: Origins of Economic Rationality* (Durham: Duke University Press, 2003), 48–76.

53. Bentham, *Logic*, Bowring, ix. 276.

54. C. A. Helvétius, *De l'Esprit, or, Essays on the Mind and its Several Faculties* (London: J. M. Richardson, 1809), 148.

55. Ibid., 299.

56. Connell, *Romanticism, Economics, and the Question of 'Culture,'* 227.

57. Bentham, *The Rationale of Punishment* (London: Robert Heward, 1830), 244–45.

Index

Page citations ending with *n* indicate Bentham's footnotes. Page citations ending with *n* followed by a number indicate endnotes.

God: ascetic self-mortification and, 117–18n; fear of, 69–70; immutable laws and, 206–7, 213n.37; judgment of, 134–35n; natural law and, 447–48; nature of, 68; sacrifice and, 43–44, 45; will of, 130–31, 441, 485

Godwin, William, 501, 512, 513

good: Bentham conception of, 246, 426, 427–31, 433, 443, 457n.60; as indefinable, 425, 426; legally protected rights as, 245, 250, 251, 259, 463, 464; naturalistic fallacy and, 426–27; as object of desire, 428; positive vs. negative, 246; utilitarian, 1, 2, 40, 247

"good governance" ideology, 485, 492, 497n.47

good-will, 140, 141, 144n, 228n, 236; pains of, 145; pleasures of, 141. *See also* sympathy

Gordian knot, 175, 283

Gordon riots, 295n

Gospels. *See* Bible

government: asceticism and, 119; Bentham ideas on, 4–5, 6, 7, 8, 9, 11, 12, 16–17, 395, 410–17, 428, 504; changing of local customs by, 177–78, 480, 486; collective greatest happiness as proper end of, 112n, 115–16n, 228–30; deputation and, 234; distant colonies and, 484–85; economic intervention by, 16–17, 315–17; four sanctions and, 11–16; French Declaration of Rights on, 335–36; insurrection incitement against, 338–39, 350, 351, 354; junction-of-interests principle and, 233–

38; law as basis of, 249, 256; legal system and form of, 167–71, 180–81, 186–87; legislative vs. judicial power and, 193; national character concept and, 478, 487, 488; obedience to, 335; obligations to, 259; origin of, 327, 330; political tactics and, 108; real rights vs. natural rights and, 256–59, 261, 322–23, 327–28; religion and (*see* disestablishment); representation and, 5, 301–2, 342, 471; rights and services and, 260–61, 321; role of, 16–17, 310, 315–17; secularism and, 508; sinister interest and, 17, 231–38; societal sacrifices and, 463; supreme operative power and, 235–36; transparency in, 291–306, 472, 473; treason and, 191, 378; utility principle and, 113–14; vested interest and, 411, 414. *See also* democracy; monarchy

greatest happiness principle, 112–13n, 115–16n, 247, 426–31, 441–44; Bentham's terminology shift from principle of utility to, 2, 241, 442; competing interests and, 243; components of, 227–33; contract fulfillment and, 400–403; as desired end, 112n, 426, 428–29, 440; determining factors for, 507–8; disappointment-prevention principle and, 395–97, 400, 412; for greatest number, 241, 243, 404–5, 429, 441, 442, 506; imperial conquest vs., 484; legal codification and, 241–45, 462–65, 471–73; legal perfection and,